Yoruba Traditions and African American Religious Nationalism

Editors: David Carrasco and Charles H. Long

First Rite of Passage '72.   where?

head:
Goddess is
oya
Goddess of the
Niger River,
warrior queen
wife of Shango

Set up an
altar for you
ancestors: say
Mojuba gbogbo
ariku
oluwa
say names

FRONTISPIECE: Handwritten spiritual prescriptions by Oseijeman
Adefunmi following a divination reading for a supplicant in 1972.
Photograph courtesy of Djisovi Ikukomi Eason and Lillian Ashcraft-Eason.

Yoruba Traditions & African American Religious Nationalism

TRACEY E. HUCKS

Foreword by Charles H. Long

University of New Mexico Press | Albuquerque

Library of Congress Cataloging-in-Publication Data

Hucks, Tracey E., 1965–

Yoruba traditions and African American religious nationalism /

Tracey E. Hucks; foreword by Charles H. Long.

pages cm. — (Religions of the Americas)

Includes bibliographical references and index.

ISBN 978-0-8263-5075-6 (cloth : alk. paper) — ISBN 978-0-8263-5077-0 (electronic)

1. Orisha religion—United States—History.

2. African Americans—Religion—History.

3. Black nationalism—United States—History.

4. Adefunmi, Oseijeman, 1928–2005.

5. Oyotunji African Village (S.C.)—History.

I. Title.

BL2532.S5H83 2012

299.6ʹ83330973—dc23

2011047655

DESIGN AND LAYOUT: MELISSA TANDYSH

Composed in 10.5/14 Minion Pro

Display type is Italian Old Style MT Std

To my parents
My mother, Doretha Leary Hucks (1936–1984),
my first teacher in life
My father, Joseph Richard Hucks,
the "High Priest" in my life
As co-creators, you will forever remain
"the strongest leaves of my tree"

Pray to the Gods who are not White, who are not Western, for your Life, for your Brother's Life.

—James Baldwin

CONTENTS

ILLUSTRATIONS

FOREWORD

T HIS TEXT CONTAINS two interrelated and overlapping travel narratives. One of the narratives is in the form of a travel in time—the history of ideas, meanings, symbols, and images of Africa in African American culture; this narrative contextualizes the second one. The second narrative tells the story of a young African American male from Detroit, Walter Eugene King, and his journey from Detroit through a variety of times, spaces, and imaginations to his emergence as Oba Efuntola Oseijeman Adefumi I in the new space of the Oyotunji Yoruba Village in South Carolina. It is in fact this story that evoked the necessity for the larger historical narrative that encompasses it.

Both narratives are concerned with the image and symbol of Africa as a religious orientation. The first narrative traverses historical time, describing and explaining the meaning of Africa in the life and culture of black folk and especially in African American nationalist ideology. Because the narratives are concerned with religious quests, we are immediately reminded of the religious rite of pilgrimage. The encompassing historical narrative takes us through the passages of time, space, actions, and thought of persons and communities of African Americans from their initial enslavement in North America to the present. Within this fulsome narrative we are made aware of the significance, power, and necessity of a "place to be called home" for millions of persons of African descent who were separated from their original homeland and denied authenticity as human beings in

North America. The continent of Africa, their place of origin, was remembered, invented, symbolized, and remade within the new spaces and times of North America as a foundation for their humanness as well as a vision for a viable human future.

The prominence of religious journeys in this study brings to mind the religious rite of pilgrimage, especially in the research of Victor Turner.[1] The quest of the young Walter Eugene King, which takes him from Detroit to New York, Haiti, Europe, Africa, and Cuba, corresponds to the *liminal* phase of the pilgrimage phenomenon as described by Turner. The liminal phase of the pilgrimage is that period between the pilgrim's departure from home and familiar circumstances until the arrival at the sacred site that is the goal of the pilgrimage. Turner analyses the new social relations and identities that are formed during this phase and time. In addition, during the liminal period tensions, contrasts, and critique of the reigning social order come to the fore. Victor Turner's other pertinent term of analysis, the notion of *communitas*, fits well with the kind of knowledges of Africa and the various practioners of African-derived religions King met and consulted with during his pilgrimage and the founding of Oyotunji Village in South Carolina as what Turner might have referred to as a "normative mode of communitas."

Now while this text is a biography of Walter Eugene King's bildungsroman as a religious pilgrimage, it is much more than this. It is at the same time a descriptive and critical history of African American nationalism as a religious phenomenon. It shows how the image and symbol of Africa became the basis for an alternate authenticity for the communities of African Americans in North America. From this discussion we are confronted with the broader issue of the meaning of religion in the contemporary world. The text employs a variety of methods ranging from ethnohistory, history, history of religions, and political science. In so doing, the issue of theory and method in the disciplines of religious studies is raised. Tracey Hucks as the narrator and author of the biography of Walter Eugene King/ Oseijeman Adefumi I and the interwoven narratives of African American nationalism suggests a hermeneutical position that parallels the role of a novelist. This novelistic tonality refers us back again to the thematic and stylistics of religious pilgrimage—pilgrimage as the sources of knowledge that combines both the larger context of the history of African American nationalism and the biography of Walter Eugene King. Such a procedure in method is reminiscent of an older meaning of pilgrimage as not only the visit to sacred sites, but equally pilgrimage as the mode for the acquisition of knowledge—pilgrimage as *theoria*.

It is at this juncture that we should remember that our word "theory" is from a Greek term that means "spectacle"—seeing, sight. Seeing here refers to knowledge and knowing. Echoes of this older meaning were revived by Michel Foucault when he introduced the term "gaze" as a mode of knowing. Theory as sight refers to a meaning it had in the fourth century BCE in Greece. It did not, however, imply the abstracting domineering "gaze" of scientific technology made popular by Foucault, but it is rather more closely related to what Clifford Geertz, the anthropologist, has called "thick description."

Andrea Wilson Nightingale has recently explored the hermeneutical, religious, and philosophical meaning of theoria in Greek thought and culture.[2] At one place she describes the pilgrimage structure of theory: "When directed towards a religious sanctuary or festival, theoria took the form of a pilgrimage in which the theoros departed from his city or hometown, journeyed to a religious sanctuary, witnessed spectacles and events, participated in rituals, and returned home to ordinary civic life."[3] This description fits the pilgrimage of the young Walter Eugene King almost perfectly. There is an added dimension when we understand the context of the body of knowledge that evoked his pilgrimage, on the one hand, and how the *theoros* (pilgrim) journey enhanced the meaning of this body of knowledge.

In the same book, Nightingale notes that scholars of Greek thought have debated the meaning of theoria, some emphasizing *theos*, thus interpreting theoria as having to do with sacred things, while others have insisted on *thea*, spectacle and sight. Nightingale wisely suggests that both meanings are and can be incorporated into the meaning of theoria. In this book, Tracey Hucks has presented to us in a masterful way the rich complexity and seriousness of those religious forms, modes, and styles of a neglected modernity. She has shown why any adequate study of African American religions must undergo a kind of metaphorical pilgrimage that traverses many of the passages, rims, and borders of modern time, space, and imagination. Through her undertaking she has added immeasurably to the theory and method of the study of religion.

—Charles H. Long, coeditor, Religions of the Americas series

PREFACE

IN OYOTUNJI AFRICAN VILLAGE, nestled off the coast of South Carolina's Lowcountry, Her Royal Grace Iyashanla beckoned me to wait as she performed a ritual divination in search of a "new name." Revealed for me was the Yoruba name Ifasanu—"Ifa Has Mercy."[1] After more than a decade of archival and ethnographic research (1994–2009); thousands of miles of travel throughout the United States, Nigeria, and Cuba; steadfast attendance at Yoruba-related ritual ceremonies and national and international conferences, along with hours of richly textured interviews with African American and Latino/a Yoruba practitioners, *Yoruba Traditions and African American Religious Nationalism* has indeed culminated in a gift of Ifa's mercy. This work is not simply a compilation of research. It represents an "experience of research" and an exercise in lived history gathered among communities of African descent in North America whose religious identities, inimitable practices, and shifting social realities form the center of my scholarly investigations.[2] Similar to Brazilian Candomblé practitioners' "struggles for cultural freedoms" in the early twentieth century, black North Americans in the 1950s and 1960s "pioneered the *politicization* of African-based cultures as an important aspect of their struggle for self-determination."[3] Practitioners, as historian Kim Butler suggests, created a transformative discursive space where "African identity became an articulation of personal choice, rather than an indicator of birthplace."[4]

At its core, this book undertakes the study of a religious symbol—
Africa—as historian of religions Charles H. Long critically theorized it
close to forty years ago and examines it within the historical context of
an *extrachurch* black-nationalist tradition that chose to revitalize this religious symbol as an effective strategy for mobilization in the second half
of the twentieth century.[5] As a study in dynamic symbolism, it "allows
multiple, often competing, interpretations" of Africa to emerge rather
than seeking one definitive historical truth.[6] It chronicles the voices of
African Americans and their journeys to and through the complex alternative meanings of Yoruba in the United States as its production includes,
but remains unbounded by, religious practice, cultural appropriations,
and distinct diasporic racial ontologies. It also encourages new theorization on the complex relationship between religion and geo-symbolism,
examining the ways physicality and land (i.e., Africa, Jerusalem, Mecca,
Rome, and so forth) are infused with "geo-theological" meaning and geo-
sacrality. By negotiating a complicated association with distant origins,
blurred genealogies, reconstituted identities, and subaltern yearnings,
Yoruba Americans framed new discourses on how Africa could be seen
as what Ernst Cassirer calls an "index symbol."[7] Africa as index symbol ultimately became envisaged as the transubjective center of a religio-
nationalist movement in the New World. Through African reflections of
God, they entered into a new religious correspondence that brought new
names and new experiences to the history of Yoruba religious studies,
thus expanding the geographical, ideological, and theological landscape
of Yoruba locales across the globe.

Yoruba Traditions is a study that examines the performativity of Africa
as enacted within a wider "theatricality of nationalism."[8] It seeks to understand the "Pan-Yoruba Diaspora" and its multiple articulations (Ifa, Ocha,
Santería, Lucumi, Orisa, Orisha) not as a single fixed religious tradition
but as a global religious complex developed within varying "socioreligious
locations."[9] Within these various geographical "embodiments of Yoruba
religious culture," innovation, dynamism, and fluidity in practice are all
diversely expressed.[10] What have come to be known as Yoruba religious
cultures in North America, Africa, South America, the Caribbean, and
parts of Europe can best be understood not as one rigidly bounded religion but as "a decentralized network of lineages, cults, and disparate public and private ritual practices that readily intermingle across definitional

boundaries with other religions."[11] Because of the "emergence of Yoruba as the emblem of the Africanization of the Americas,"[12] we must, as anthropologist J. Lorand Matory advises, understand Yoruba worship not as a permanent or predetermined tradition but "instead amid its modern political, economic, and ideological conditions."[13] The orisa acquire significance less in fixed historical domains than in their meaning as living entities across the globe. Thus, orisa worship in the twenty-first century cannot be easily relegated to a single geographical region but exists instead in what Eugenio Matibag identifies as the domain of the "extraterritorial"[14] and comprises "multicultural, multilingual, multilayered traditions and expressions" that span across the globe.[15] However, as Olabiyi Babalolo Yai discerns, "One of the paradoxes of globalization is that it encourages or produces standardization as it creates multipolarity."[16] These dynamic tensions between standardization and multipolarity are explored throughout the book. A primary assertion is that it is through Yoruba's myriad of global religious, cultural, and linguistic expressions that we might come to ultimately value the elastic and innovative points of view derived from what Christopher Antonio Brooks labels "localized Yoruba practices."[17] For the descendants of enslaved African communities in North America, what W. E. B. Dubois calls their "foster land,"[18] Yoruba religion invokes a meaningful connection to Africa as "originary space" that substantiates human value and provides restorative ontological, historical, and spiritual integrity.[19]

In this book, Yoruba religious culture speaks in vernacular—*African (North) American* vernacular. This vernacular discourse celebrates the dynamic endurance of African religious expressions not as they remained in static and bounded spaces on the continent but as they were creatively embraced and adapted to fit the socially and spiritually tortuous climate of the Atlantic diaspora. Within this geohistorical context, the book explores a distinct path of those Jennifer Morgan identifies as a network of diasporic racialized subjects who use "vernacular creativity" to express their own unique ritual grammar, "distinctive vocabulary or languages," and social systems of meaning.[20] Meaning within this diaspora configuration is never resolutely fixed but is "constant (not given), multiple (not univocal), contested (not shared), and fluid (not static)."[21] North America is an emerging site where African, Latin American, African American, and Euro-American Yoruba traditions have created a plethora of interactive and integrative meanings.

This text is not a history of linear approaches to cultural and religious retentions in the African diaspora.[22] *Yoruba Traditions* instead is a historical analysis of the processes of religious transliteration. Figuratively, I engage in an exercise of religious phonetics determined to reveal representations of how Yoruba religion is articulated and exercised in North American expressions and the ways its subjects choose to be *purposefully African* in this context.[23] Africa as such is embraced not so much as concrete materiality but as "shared, public fact" whose symbolism "can be analyzed . . . regardless of its source or objective truth value."[24] Increasingly indebted to the works of George Brandon and Steven Gregory for their North American studies, I concur that a Herskovitsian model of retentions is not the exhaustive analytical measure of Yoruba religious cultures in the diaspora and that alongside this model, diasporic religious cultures can also be viewed theoretically as "a sociohistorical site or 'space of resistance' . . . to racially and ethnically-based forms of social domination."[25] Moreover, George Brandon's trispatial understanding of Yoruba religion as *"global, New World, and local-national"* provides an important lens for contextualizing this North American study. It allows for an analysis of Yoruba religion in North America whose primary focus is not on "the retention of African tradition but rather the convergence of the reintroduction of African tradition by immigrants from areas where African religions have been retained with greater influence and greater fidelity, with the purposeful revitalization of that tradition by U.S. blacks and Puerto Ricans."[26] Thus, Brandon asserts that "the issue of Africanisms in the United States becomes not only an historical one but contemporary as well and concerns processes of culture change that can be observed in the present and over the very recent past."[27]

Yoruba Traditions is a study of "the very recent past" and a reflection of my intellectual interests in the cross-fertilization of religion and nationalism; the fluidity of black religious practice; and the historical ambiguity of home, place, and national identity for African Americans. I am fascinated by the religious power of African Americans to rename, rehistoricize, ritually produce, culturally express, and textualize in the midst of this ambiguity. It is this power of intentional agency and self-established authority that weaves throughout the pages of this text, seeking to understand what bell hooks names "the authority of experience" in the "lived conditions" of African American religious life in the United States.[28]

Above all, *Yoruba Traditions* is a story of diaspora and an *Atlanticized* Africa.[29] Amidst a growing trend of specialization within Diaspora Studies that often draws an invisible circumference around the Caribbean and South America, my efforts are to maintain the geographical suppleness of *diaspora* by adding this study to others such as Carol Duncan's outstanding Canadian study *This Spot of Ground: Spiritual Baptists in Toronto*, which describe important components of Africa's *North American* diaspora and *re-*diasporaed communities. Because "each diaspora has unique historical circumstances" and "choices of identity and integration vary within diasporan groups," a dynamic understanding of diasporan identities, particularly in North America, can readily be accommodated to include the "ethnonationalism of communities" like African American Yoruba "whose territories have little to do with physical space."[30] If the black Atlantic can be defined as a "geographical focus, an identity option, and a context of meaning-making, rather than a uniquely bounded, impenetrable, or overdetermining thing," then black North America is clearly a key contributor to its development.[31] Thus, this story begins in the same North American social setting of racialized subjectivity where James Baldwin once aptly acknowledged that "the auction block is the platform on which I entered the Civilized World," and therefore, "my diaspora continues, the end is not in sight."[32]

Researching a religious tradition that values modes of African sacred knowledge and authority has not been without its challenges. Quite often, combinations of Western Christian hegemony and maligning anti-Africanness both on the African continent and in the African Atlantic diaspora have questioned the legitimacy of Yoruba religious cultures and their merits for scholarly inquiry.[33] For example, while I was conducting research in Nigeria, an ethnically born Yoruba and religiously affiliated Deeper Life Church member asked me why I was spending my time studying *witchcraft* among Nigeria's Yoruba *babalawos*, specialists, healers, and practitioners. During my time in Nigeria, I also listened intently as Yoruba Christian ministers on the campus of Abafemi Owolowo University in Ile-Ife definitively pronounced from the pulpit those who were "going to hell," positioning all Yoruba traditional practitioners and participants in Ogboni and Mami Wata at the head of the hellward bound processional. Yoruba traditional priests such as Oyebanji Awodinni Marawo (Baale Marawo) who perform Ifa divination in Nigeria speak candidly of these pejorative trends in Nigeria when remarking that "today, many people hate Ifa, it is like a filth to them, they call us eaters of sacrifice."[34] Along similar lines, several Oyotunji African Village residents in North America revealed the deep sadness they faced as family members vilified their choice to revere the gods and ancestors of Africa and often chose to distance themselves over time. Thus, I have discovered that to write about the unique Yoruba religious cultures of black North America has meant I must challenge what E. U. Essien-Udom calls "anti-African feelings" and the stereotypical mis-readings of "voodooism."[35]

This study spans the period from the earliest decades of the twentieth century through the 1960s, to the subsequent creation of Oyotunji African Village in Sheldon, South Carolina, in 1970, to Yoruba religion's urban proliferation, and concludes with new trends in the twenty-first century. Published three years after the fiftieth anniversary of Oba Osei-jeman Adefunmi's (formerly Walter Eugene King) 1959 initiation into Cuban Santería, Oseijeman Adefunmi is considered to be among the first known non-Hispanic African American males born in the United States to undergo full initiation in Cuba into the diasporic Yoruba tradition of Santería/Lucumi/Ocha. His initiation solidified a new, pioneering, non-Hispanic American Yoruba lineage during the 1950s and 1960s in the United States, joining a small community of initiated priests and priest-esses in the United States, such as Pancho Mora (1944), Juana Manrique Claudio (1952), Mercedes Nobles (1958), Asunta Serrano (1958), Cristobal Oliana (1959), José Manuel Ginart (1959), Julia Franco (1961), and Marjorie Baynes Quiñones (1969), the latter initiated by Leonore Dolme (1957) and the first U.S.-born African American woman to receive full initiation.[36] This new African American lineage was created not by giving preference to the traditional priestly "seniority" of other "Second Diaspora" Caribbean or South American orisa communities already in the United States but by appealing to new standards of purity and authenticity based somewhat paradoxically on hybridized models of African restoration, recovery, and re-ownership.[37]

Although this study foregrounds the life of Oseijeman Adefunmi I, he cannot be isolated from numerous other African American practitioners in the United States who have brought and continue to bring texture to the broader African American Yoruba chronicle. Some among those who have sustained and continue to sustain this religious and cultural community were or are North American–born practitioners and their Caribbean-born supporters like Mama Keke; Cristobal Oliana; Pancho Mora; Queen Mother Moore; Katherine Dunham; Marjorie Baynes Quiñones; Clarence Robins; José Sardinas-Alabumi; John and Valerie Mason; Orisa Mola Akinyele Owolowo; Baba Medahochi Kofi Omowale Sangodele Zannu; Akanke Omilade Owolowo; Oya Dina; Larry Neal; Djisovi Ikukomi Eason; Lionel Scott; Teddy Holliday; Baba Alfred Davis; Edward James; James Hawthorne (Chief Bey); Barbara Kenyatta Bey; Baba Bernard; C. Daniel Dawson; Ted Wilson; Oba Lumi; John Turpin; Osa Unko; Manuel Vega; Oreste Blanco; Olobunmi Adesoji; Majile Osunbunmi Olafemi; Yeyefini Efunbolade; Osun Meka; Cynthia Turner; Lloyd and Stephanie Weaver; Oseye Mchawi-Orisa Aiye; Irene Blackwell; Tejuola Turner; Adekola Adedapa; Baba Ifatunji; Omowunmi Ogundaisi; Obalumi Ogunseye; Ayobunmi Sangode; chiefs Ajamu, Olaitan, Akintobe, Eleshin, and the entire chieftancy and male and female priesthood of Oyotunji African Village; Oba Adejuyibe Adefunmi II; Oba Sekou Olayinka; Iyanla Vanzant; Luisah Teish; Marta Moreno Vega; Angela Jorge; Awo Fasina Falade; Mary Cuthrell Curry; Baba Ifa Karade; and a host of many others too numerous to name who first encountered the deities of Africa on diaspora soil.[38]

This study is not one of a single movement but an exploration of a series of Yoruba "religious networks" that African Americans have formed throughout and beyond North America.[39] Studies of these religious networks are in progress, and I encourage and especially look forward to the future publication of those women scholars whose doctoral research has made outstanding contributions to expanding North American Yoruba scholarship: Marta Moreno Vega's "Yoruba Philosophy: Multiple Levels of Transformation and Understanding," which provides an important regional study of the Yoruba community in New York City; Velma Love's "Odu Outcomes: Yoruba Scriptures in African American Constructions of Self and World," which examines the role and meaning of the Ifa sacred oracle among African American Yoruba practitioners in New York City and in Oyotunji African Village; Velana Huntington's "Bodies in Contexts: Holistic Ideals of Health, Healing, and Wellness in an America Orisha Community," which explores wellness practices among American orisa practitioners in the Midwest; Elizabeth Pérez's "Returning to the Drum: Healing and Conversion in an African American Santeria Community," whose work, like Huntington's, documents the regional breadth and expansiveness of orisa religious networks as she explores its practice on Chicago's South Side; Patricia Williams Lessane's "Tell My Feet I've Made It Home: African-American Imaginings of Home and to Find the Orixas," whose work as an anthropologist continues in building an important corpus of work on Candomblé in Salvador de Bahia, Brazil, and looks specifically at African Americans who opt to perform initiation rites there; Suzanne Henderson's "The African American Experience of Orisha Worship," which brings an interesting view to the discourse on African American Yoruba through the discipline of psychology; and Amanda Holmes's "Spirits in the Forest: Yoruba Religion and Ecology in Cuba," whose work in ecological and visual anthropology brings a unique disciplinary gaze to African diasporic traditions.

Although the narrative aspects of this study begin in Detroit, Michigan, it is my home of Harlem, New York, that historically surfaces as one of the formative centers of Yoruba religious practice among African Americans in the United States. For the emically trained specialist in Harlem geography, I grew up in El Barrio—a short distance from La Marqueta—amidst a Cuban, Puerto Rican, Dominican, Honduran, and Panamanian world of rich cultural sounds, tastes, and aromas from Cuchifritos restaurants, coquito icys, *ganipas* in brown paper bags, green and yellow platanos, Chuck-a-Lug, street-corner dominoes, three-card monte, corner bodegas, Puerto Rican Day parades, Valencia's cakes, and congas in the summer night air. For an African American, El Barrio coalesced with Harlem creating a parallel African American landscape consisting of architectural icons like the Nation of Islam's Mosque #7, centrally located on 116th Street, the Nation of Islam's Steak-in-Take restaurants featuring Hunger Stoppers and bean pies, the black-owned 125th Street Carver Savings Bank, Sylvia's Soul Food, the world-famous Apollo Theatre, fish 'n' chips joints, record shops, Olaf's sporting goods store and basketball tournaments, the Lenox Lounge, lodies game boxes painted on the ground, Sherman's Ribs, the men and women on tenant patrol at the James Weldon Johnson Houses, the sounds of hip-hop and "scratchin'" blanketing crowds five hundred strong in New York City's public parks, Well's Chicken and Waffles, Better Pie Crust, Harlem Week, Mr. Softee with the scratched record, opening the "pump" on a hot summer day, Adam Clayton Powell's Abyssinian Baptist Church, and community center or "down the ramp" wedding receptions and blue-light parties.

This African American/Latino community was physically bordered and spiritually resourced by four botanicas—El Congo Real at 1789 Lexington Avenue, Otto Chicas Rendón at 60 East 116th Street, Botanica Almacenes Shango at 1661 Madison Avenue, and Paco's Botanica at 1864 Lexington Avenue. Paco's Botanica on Lexington Avenue was where my mother purchased her white, red, green, blue, and 7 African Powers candles that prominently burned on a faux gold ornate mirrored shelf in our home. Paco's Botanica also supplied the fresh herbal leaves she boiled for cleansing as well as her Murray and Lanman's Florida Water that perfumed away all bad luck. In Harlem, a mysterious spiritual and folkloric world of Africa was revealed to me most intimately through African American migrants from the South like my mother. My mother, of Cherokee and African American parentage, undoubtedly knew little or nothing about the spiritual world of Santería that the descendants of my Latino neighbors practiced long before their various migrations to the United States. In sharing religious pharmacopeia and botanicas, however, these two sacred worlds comingled, enabling each, like my mother, to draw on spiritual reservoirs from distant places. Thus, Harlem's community of mestizo and black Latino/as, Caribbean immigrants, and African Americans form the backdrop to this study. It represents a moment in American religious history when Latino/a, Caribbean, and African American cooperation in the persons of Oseisjeman Adefunmi (Walter King), Cristobal Oliana, Asunción "Sunta" Serrano, and Mama Keke helped bring to life in 1960 the African Theological Archministry Inc., giving birth to a new North American trajectory in the wider Yoruba cultural and religious geography.

I come to this text, therefore, blending two worlds, the world of Harlem, which bequeathed to me spiritual and cultural sustenance, and the world of the academy, which affords me the freedom of public scholarly and literary expression. I embody both worlds and continually translate the hieroglyphics of one world into useable fodder for the other. When these worlds collide (as they often do), I am never ambiguous about my location. Like womanist scholar Barbara Omolade, I understand that you must always choose the integrity of your ancestors. For me, however, the ancestors are not a homogenous spiritual entity lacking distinguishable histories and identities but scholarly motivation for perfecting my craft as a religious historian seeking to uncover the multifarious ways in which people of African descent have been religious in the Americas. Thus, this story seeks to broaden our understanding of religions of the Americas and the lived experiences of religiosity that African Americans have contributed to its development. It examines the descendants of "those who were denigrated to the point of invisibility, inaudibility, and inconsequentiality" and their attempts to "create a discourse through which they could be seen, heard, and respected as part of the American family."[40] Therefore, although its historical actors speak "in the name of *Africa* and *African* identity," it is in actuality a complex negotiation of what pastoral theologian Lee H. Butler Jr. calls "an African past that is coordinated with an American past."[41] Thus, it is ultimately a narrative that is "fostered in America and is an integral part of American history and life."[42]

African American and *Yoruba* are experienced as a complex composite within North America. Throughout my research, I have found that African American practitioners do not readily make historical claims of an uninterrupted or continuous Yoruba cultural heritage (as tacitly assumed in many postslavery South American and Caribbean contexts), nor do they claim a geographically natal and linguistic specificity equivalent to Nigerian Yoruba. The complex pronouncement of Yoruba Americans, however, is this: while positioned in North America, they embody a "self-identification as ritually reborn Yoruba" as Stephan Palmié asserts, yet they also invoke what Fran Markowitz calls an "anterior authenticity" in order to "confront and transcend diasporic displacement."[43] As a component of this anterior authenticity, they posit an undeniable and historically factual ancestored authority that enables them to reclaim the religions and cultures of Africa, recover and re-own Africa as a "continental entity" of primordial origin, and use Africa in religious and cultural strategies of rehumanizing and rehistoricizing their despised identities as located within "the most brutal . . . and prolonged of human dispersals or diasporas."[44] More important, as Palmié fittingly suggests, because of complex notions of "racially emancipatory—diasporic *connaissance*," they do not consider themselves *converts* but instead *reverts* to traditional African ancestored epistemologies.[45] Thus, Yoruba religion becomes a complex vehicle that "historicizes the African-American within the traditional African context."[46] Yoruba functions as a spiritually pragmatic gateway for ethnicizing ancestral connections broadly understood as African. Its African American expressions reflect the ways the "Africas" produced in the diaspora and the religious traditions they have inspired have been important responses to what James

Baldwin calls a wider "terrified dialogue" within the imperializing presence of white supremacy and its subsequent alienation of blackness.[47] Yet, as these African Americans navigate a "shipwrecked" identity in the New World, they make no pretense of a possible return to a preslavery "original Africa," for as Stuart Hall reminds us, "it is no longer there. It too has been transformed."[48] In the end, therefore, Yoruba religious expression among African Americans is not a classical journey of return to a recoverable "original Africa" but instead the undertaking of a new journey—one that has been ultimately transformed into *what Africa has become in the New World.*"[49]

Paris, France

ACKNOWLEDGMENTS

We acknowledge that we are here today because of something someone did before we came.

—Sweet Honey in the Rock

I BEGIN BY ACKNOWLEDGING my paternal great-grandparents, Jacob Octavius Dozier and Lelia Dozier, and my maternal grandparents, Bertha Bond and John Henry Leary. Jacob Octavius Dozier was born in 1852 in Virginia among the community of the enslaved. Following emancipation, he learned to read and write and dedicated his life to the education of Virginia's African American population. After the Ku Klux Klan twice tried unsuccessfully to end his life in Virginia, he fled to Bertie County, North Carolina, where he continued his educational mission, opened a general store, purchased three hundred acres of land, and built an eight-bedroom house on a lake that became the site for social activities for African Americans in a segregated South. He met and married his wife, Lelia, who became a renowned midwife, skilled herbalist, and known healer to the Bertie County, North Carolina, community and who eventually gave birth to my grandmother, Margaret Dozier Hucks. Together my paternal great-grandparents bequeathed to me the interconnected roles of educator and healer. My maternal great-grandparents, Metta and John Bond, gave birth to my maternal grandmother, Bertha Bond, born in 1914 in North Carolina as a member of the Snowbird people of the Cherokee Nation. She and my African American grandfather, John Henry Leary (named after the famed folkloric figure of power and strength) were among the vast southern migrants to New York City in search of a better life. It is through this maternal lineage that I eventually came to be born in the rich cultural nexus of Harlem, New York, where this study flourishes. These ancestors are among my family's divinized dead and are the sources of my inspiration and sacred reverence.

Other sources of inspiration have been extended family members from the Dozier, Bond, Leary, Speller, Sutton, Catten, and Hucks lineages. I especially give thanks to Joseph and Doretha Hucks, whom I would choose forever and again as parents in every lifetime. I thank my sister, Terri, who embodies love and protection for me. It is she who gave birth to two of the greatest gifts in my life, my niece, Kareemah Shaeton Mims, and my nephew, Omar Kasim Mims. My grandnieces, Sanai and Kareemah Mims, begin a new generation for those of us "who gone up North." To Dr. Darrell Cleveland Hucks, you fill me with immense pride, love, and laughter. Charlene Hucks Richardson—you are the light of God in my life, God's divine favor in this world. In 1999, my family expanded with the marriage of my father to Joan Dalton Hucks, bringing a new family of brothers, sisters, nephews, and nieces. I thank my siblings Dawn, Dondi, and his wife we affectionately call Lu, my nephews Kevin, Drew, Dee, and Julian, and especially my niece, Cheyenne, who is one of my greatest and most endearing fans. Life has also encircled me with a compassionate circle of friends: Cynthia Alvarez, Marcella Hyde Roulhac, Amira Delle, Sunni and Juhudi Tolbert, Evelyne and Ronel Laurent-Perrault, Lamine Diaby, Stephanie Sears, Tracy Rone, Ian Straker, and James Noel.

To the "teachers of my sound," I thank you. I give particular thanks to the late Manning Marable, Josiah Young, Harvey Sindima (who taught me to write from my center), Lewis Baldwin, Perla Holder, Kwame Anthony Appiah, Christopher Vecsey, Marilyn Thie, Don and Wanda Berry, Coleman Brown, Anne Ashbaugh, Margaret Darby, John Ross Carter, and Peter Ochs. I also give thanks to Nell Painter, Albert Raboteau, and Cornel West, whose mentorship and teaching were invaluable to me while on graduate exchange at Princeton University. I extend special thanks to David D. Hall, who devotedly taught his doctoral students "the instincts of the historian" and "the commitments of an interested fieldworker." An added debt of gratitude goes to Evelyn Brooks Higginbotham and J. Lorand Matory, who modeled and expected nothing short of quality and excellence; I thank them immensely for their high standards. While under their collective tutelage at Harvard University, Hall, Higginbotham, and Matory subsequently taught me deeply meaningful and enduring lessons in loving partnerships as they engaged their beloved Betsy, Leon, and Bunmi. Even in the midst of losing Betsy and the Judge, I never lost their commitment and support as their student.

I am indebted to the works of the late Carl Hunt and the late Djisovi Ikukomi Eason, along with Mary Cuthrell Curry, George Brandon, Steven Gregory, Marta Vega, and Kamari Clarke, for forging intellectual pathways for African American Yoruba studies in the academy. I am exceedingly grateful to Mikelle Smith Omari-Tunkara, who helped to provide my first entry to Oyotunji African Village over a decade ago. I also give special thanks to Gina Bonilla. Our travels to Ocha and Palo communities throughout Cuba and New York City were deeply invaluable for me and for this book.

I thank the Fund for Theological Education for supporting this research, along with Haverford College's Faculty Research Support Fund. I also thank my colleagues, past and present, in the Department of Religion at Haverford College—Michael Sells, Anne McGuire, David Dawson, Ken and Naomi Koltun-Fromm, Travis Zadeh, and Terrence Johnson—for embracing collegiality, cooperation, and collaboration as its highest departmental ideals. Our departmental reputation for running like a "fine Swiss watch" is well deserved. I also want to thank Kathy McGee, Andrea Pergolese, and Julie Coy for their administrative and digital support. Numerous Haverford colleagues and students have assisted and supported me in my work over the years and include Lucius Outlaw, Kimberly Benston, Mark Gould, Raji Mohan, William Williams, Wyatt McGaffey, Sunni Green Tolbert, Evelyne Laurent Perrault, Yolande Thompson, Dalila Zachary, Princess Toussaint, Joslyn Carpenter, Shani Meacham, Nicole Myers Turner, Benesha Bobo, Abayomi Walker, Erika Powell, Nicholas Jones, Carri Devito, Elana Bloomfield, Drew Steinberg, and Cathy Norise, along with some of my greatest student cheerleaders of past years Amina DeBurst, Brady McCartney, Amanda T. Brody, Sam Edmundson, Tamia Harris, Neil and Ali Kronley, Dorcas Davis, Craig Dorfman, Raymond McLeish, Jeremy Kanthor, Ned Tompsett, Anna Mudd, Barbara Breckinridge, and Jasmine Harrington. Finally, I give special thanks to Haverford College reference librarian and bibliographer James Gulick who has demonstrated through-out the years the true meaning of professional support and generous giving.

To those colleagues in the discipline who inquired about the book for their courses and awaiting students, I thank you—Lillian Ashcraft Eason, Judith Weisenfeld, Shawn Copeland, Wallace Best, Barbara Savage, Monica Coleman—and chiefly to Michael Sells, Yvonne Chireau, and Eddie Glaude Jr., who offered good counsel on earlier drafts of the manuscript. A special thanks to Joyce Flueckiger at Emory University whose wise words from Amma in her healing room made it okay for me to cease writing and live with the fact that if I had another hundred years, I could never finish this story. As women ethnographers, Joyce Flueckiger and Karen McCarthy Brown were inspirations to me and made it permissible for me to work within my own scholarly time frame. If this book proves as meaningful to its readership as *In Amma's Healing Room*, which represented fourteen years of research, and *Mama Lola*, which represented twelve years of research, then I know I fall within good scholarly gendered company. I also thank Severine Menetrey for her flat in Paris's Montparnasse area, Paris's Jazz station FM 89.9, and *My Suites* flat with a view of the Swiss mountains for providing me beautiful spaces to revise and complete my writing.

To the University of New Mexico Press—I thank you and your staff for a supportive journey to publication. I especially thank Elizabeth Ann Albright, Felicia Andrea Cedillos, Elise M. McHugh, and Meredith D. Dodge for the professional graciousness, expertise, and care given to this manuscript. Davíd Carrasco worked tirelessly to make this intellectual union happen, and I thank him with a profound indebtedness and appreciation.

I thank Wande Abimbola, Kola Abimbola, and Jacob Olupona for their intellectual respect for the study of Yoruba religious cultures in the Americas and the Caribbean. I wholeheartedly thank Jacob Olupona for following his *ori* into the Peabody Museum at Harvard University where we met and from that day allowing me to experience a level of selflessness, support, and generosity I will forever honor. I also want to extend deep appreciation for Rachel Harding and her generous expressions of support, spirit, and friendship.

I reserve the deepest love, affection, and intellectual reverence for Dr. Charles H. Long. In you I have known unconditional, steadfast, and unwavering support. You dared to challenge and disrupt sacred Western epistemologies in the humanities and the social sciences, dared to think that the study of black religion deserved sophisticated and complex analysis and theorization, and I dared to believe you. Your prophetic presence in the field has transformed my life forever. I owe you a debt only the ancestors can repay.

My gratitude extends to the members of the Society for the Study of Black Religion for their warm encouragement and reception of my work at the 2008 annual meeting; Marcia Riggs, Shawn Copeland, Larry Murphy, Art Priestley, and Stephen Ray especially come to mind. Special thanks go to its former executive director, Anthony Pinn, for extending this warm invitation. I also thank the president, Lee H. Butler Jr., who continues to lead the society in the dignity, honor, and grace of Africa and whose proverbial wisdom will forever resound, "God is the First Ancestor with whom we are to be connected."

I create a special place of acknowledgment for Dianne Stewart Diakité: like Rebecca Jackson and Rebecca Perot, the womanists before us, our intellectual destinies and legacies have been inextricably bound. At the end of our life journeys as friends, colleagues, and sisters, I hope to say that we were compliant to the same inner voice of the divine that commanded Mother Rebecca Jackson in 1830 "to travel some and speak to the people." As you gaze in the mirror of Oshun, may you always see a reflection of your own giftedness, beauty, and power.

Moreover, I give thanks to Esu-Elegba, my orisa Osossi, and to those who reside in the "Room of Spirits" in my home. Among those, I honor the spirits of my great-grandparents, grandparents, my mother, Doretha Hucks, S. P. Tatum, and my blessed Angel spirit. You teach me to be a loving healer on this earth by loving me daily into the fullness of life. Together we commune, and I am able to glimpse the face of God.

Finally, a nineteenth-century writer once wrote, "The truest [eulogy] that one can make of [a] book is to love its very faults." I, therefore, encourage readers to love the book's strengths and as well as "its very faults." Know that as a dynamic story forever unfolding and in the making, my humble words could never exhaust the wealth of history, memories, experiences, and spiritual resources of North America's Yoruba. And lastly, to HRH Adejuyigbe Adefunmi II, the residents of Oyotunji African Village, and all of the practitioners of the orisa in North America who granted me access to your spiritual lives, your orisa, your shrines, your iles, your bembes, your homes, and your hearts, I thank you. This text is deeply enriched because of your narrative presence. It was an honor to work with such vibrant living data. I grieve that HRH Oseijeman Adefunmi I, Baba Medahochi, Chief Ajamu, Djisovi Ikukomi Eason, and Edwina Wright did not see this book come to completion. May they read it in spirit with ancestral eyes.

Modupe.

The Harlem Window

An Introduction

ᏄᎯᏛᎬᎯ

O N A COLD WINTER evening in the early 1970s, my uncle Johnny "Spip" Speller accompanied my cousin Debbie, my sister Terri, and me to the place where the sacred had allegedly manifested itself to the people of Harlem through a cross of light.[1] We arrived at an old Harlem brownstone and proceeded on our journey up several flights of stairs. As we reached the final landing, we entered a crowded apartment filled with numerous African Americans forming a single queue leading to a room at the end of the corridor. Murmurs and chatter filled the apartment as each person exited the tiny room and voluntarily left a small monetary offering in the adjacent shoebox. When my turn came to enter the room and look through the window, I remember not being tall enough to reach the sill and being lifted onto a wooden stool in order to see the great mystery. Filled with the anticipation of a young child, I could hardly wait to see what lay beyond the frosted window: three glowing white crosses. A single large cross loomed in the center of two encircled crosses, all three arising from a smoky haze. The affirmations of those who preceded me confirmed that what I beheld was indeed "real." Images of the firmament of heaven and God filled my young mind as I was quickly whisked from the stool to accommodate the long processional behind me, a community of witnesses who peered through a window above the streets of Harlem and believed in the power of divinity. Although I was but a child, I understood that this was no ordinary manifestation. I, along with a community of others in Harlem, believed that something transcendent was orchestrating this supernatural moment. In a sense, this event defined one of my earliest formulations of religious meaning and experiences of how communities interpret notions of the sacred.

The black southern migrants who populated Harlem in the 1960s and 1970s were no strangers to spiritual signs and wonders. My uncle, like so many other Harlem residents, had "gone North" carrying old southern religious orientations to new northern spaces. In the American South of the descendants of Africa, encounters and visitations from the supernatural were not uncommon. Believing in the Harlem window was not unlike believing in the stories my mother told me of people who could see spirits, death being able to knock on the door, or dreams that served as premonitions. In Harlem, these beliefs persisted through northern and southern transmigration lores: Dad's Harlem barber traveled to consult with one of the succession of Dr. Buzzards in South Carolina whenever in serious crisis; spiritual closure was still sought by driving the bodily remains "back past the house" before interment; and a 7-day African Powers votive candle burned in the home could clear away negative spiritual energy as well as help you hit an occasional bolita in the illegal numbers system.

At the core of these North/South transmigration dialogues regarding the supernatural was a sustained allegiance to African diasporic folk cosmologies, an allegiance constantly reinforced through the print media of Harlem. Northern newspapers such as the *New York Amsterdam News*, which South Carolinian James Henry Anderson established in 1909, regularly featured advertisements for spiritual consultations and healers as a service to its southern migrant readership. Scholars such as Yvonne P. Chireau in her book *Black Magic: Religion and the African American Conjuring Tradition* examine the multiple strategies of self-authentication used in these advertisements to establish spiritual expertise and African authority.[2] Maintaining spiritual ties to the African diasporic heritage of America's black South was an important part of a larger negotiation of identity politics in Harlem. Regarding the Harlem window, the reader might think it absurd for an African American community to believe that God sent a sign through a window in Harlem. Yet the real value in the story lies not in the implausibility of such an event but in the assertion of a community's agency in the realm of religiosity.

For scholars of religion, emphasis is placed less on the authenticity or provable empiricism of events deemed sacred and more on the processes or "authenticity of intent" involved in constructing these events as religiously meaningful.[3] Similar to the African Americans who found religious meaning in a Harlem brownstone in the 1970s, African American Yorubas found meaning in the new gods of Africa that appeared to them in the late 1950s. Nearly two decades after viewing the Harlem window, I found myself in the royal compound of Oba Oseijeman Efuntola Adelabu Adefunmi I at Oyotunji African Village in South Carolina. Like my uncle, Adefunmi also came to Harlem in the 1950s. Arriving from Detroit, Adefunmi (formerly Walter Eugene King) represented a generation of young migrants attracted to the bohemian life-style of New York City and the black-nationalist fervor of Harlem. Cofounding Shango Temple in 1959 and Yoruba Temple in 1960, Adefunmi and other African Americans in that period renamed themselves Yorubas and engaged in the task of transforming Cuban Santería into a new religious expression that satisfied African Americans' racial and nationalist leanings and eventually helped to place them on a global religious schema alongside other Yoruba practitioners in Africa and the diaspora.

Depending on the source of one's statistics, the number of practitioners of Yoruba religion worldwide can range from Sandra Barnes's 70 million to Kola Abimbola's "close to 100 million 'black,' 'white,' and multi-racial peoples in Argentina, Australia, Brazil, Columbia, Cuba, France, Haiti, Italy, Jamaica, Japan, Mexico, Spain, Trinidad and Tobago, UK, USA, and Venezuela."[4] African Americans in the United States form a small subset of this number and are now approximately three generations or more in the making. Some scholars estimate a combined figure of African American and Latino-American practitioners in the United States at half a million.[5]

Many within this number enter Yoruba religious traditions through paths of nationalism and identity politics; from affiliations with other African spiritual traditions; as a way of alleviating malady and misfortune; as a "rejection of a racist and oppressively political, cultural and economic system"; to fill "a religious or spiritual void created by a secularized world"; in search of a "more corporeal, earth-centered spirituality" or "feminine empowerment"; and desirous of spiritual grounding, clarity, healing and guidance.[6] These devotees include a broad class range of professionals such entrepreneurs, health practitioners, state senators, social workers, educators and professors, Christian pastors, full-time diviners, scholar-practitioners, musicians, artists, journalists, masons, life coaches, actors, and dancers. Collectively, they form a network of adherents with varying degrees of "religious insidership" ranging from those with full *orisa* initiation to those with *elekes* or beaded necklaces; with spiritual pots of the warriors (Esu-Elegba, Ogun, Oshosi, Osun); with one hand of Ifa-Orunmila (the deity of destiny and divination); the uninitiated participants who attend *bembe* drum ceremonies as well as the clients who seek spiritual counsel from divining priests.[7]

African American Yoruba in the 1950s and 1960s engaged in complex identity building that cemented ties not just to the black folk culture of the South but to the spiritual traditions of Africa as well. As an emerging northern generation in the 1960s, cultural revolutionaries and political nationalists helped to extend the scope of black cultural dialogue from transmigratory to transatlantic. Throughout the 1960s the politics of black identity in Harlem gained new potency by engaging in forms of religious nationalism that mobilized around hermeneutical conceptions of Africa that affected religion, history, culture, style, language, and ideology. The history of African Americans in the Yoruba movement in Harlem emerged in large part from these religio-nationalist conceptions of Africa. This book is devoted to the formation of this movement.

Overall, this text is less concerned with measuring the orthodoxy or authenticity of African American Yoruba religiosity than with examining it as one of many locally expressive Yoruba cultural sites across the globe.[8] Stephan Palmié raises for religionists and social scientists of Afro-Atlantic religions the crucial question as to whether or not "New World conceptions of 'Africanity' can—or even ought to—be subjected to anthropological or historiographical authentification."[9] The ways African Americans in North America and other global practitioners of Afro-Atlantic Yoruba religions create meaning is extremely diverse. Therefore, studies of the various groups (even intragroups) must always be historicized, contextualized, and localized. It is perhaps more useful to think of Yoruba religion as a dynamic tradition possessing various historical and social moments that are lived out concurrently between Africa and its diaspora. These moments,

however, are constantly shifting, evolving, creating new images and iconography, and generating new systems of meaning within their localized
contexts. The richness of these plural contexts lies in the fact that over
space and time they have created distinct and important interpretations
of Yoruba religion that must be viewed as a compilation of multiple spatial African and diasporic trajectories. Understanding Yoruba religion as
a mélange of many local interpretations minimizes the need for substantiating notions of authenticity, orthodoxy, legitimacy, or purity. Between
Africa and the Americas there are a vast array of sacred Yorubalands in
which the orisa reside and engage in meaning making.

In an area of study where social scientists have made some of the rich-
est scholarly contributions to the study of African diasporic traditions, this
text provides a forum for the discipline of religion to offer its unique analysis of the systems of meaning that define African American Yoruba in the
United States. As a religious historian, I am most interested in exploring
particular historical moments in the United States where African American
Yoruba represented and expressed themselves religiously, reformulated the
boundaries of their religious identity, and generated their own forms of
African-Atlantic religious expression. Albert Raboteau's assertion in *Slave
Religion* that African Americans made Christianity "their own" is similar
to my belief that African Americans made Yoruba religion "their own" and
like other diaspora communities "played a critical role in the making of its
own alleged African 'base line' . . ."[10]

This study explores religion as a multilayered site of "conventional-
izing signification, of reducing ambiguity, . . . [of] checking slippage"
that "encodes" a subjective "version of the real."[11] It provides a disciplinary analysis of the lived religious space that Charles H. Long calls *extrachurch* and David D. Hall calls *extra-ecclesial*.[12] In this space, I argue that
African Americans ultimately created new ways of traditionalizing Yoruba
religious cultures in North America. From the standpoint of a religious
historian, I use the categorical designator—*African diasporic* religious traditions—that speaks with greater precision to the historical processes of
dispersed African communities and the diversity of innovative practices
they attempted to localize and traditionalize throughout North America,
South America, and the Caribbean without having to engage the laby-
rinthic conundrum of quantifying Africanity. *African diasporic* religions
make the category of *African* much more fluid and receptive to flexible

interpretations and point the reader to historical processes without the weighty conclusions and assertions of African-*derived*, African-*inspired*, and African-*based*.

As I keep in mind J. Lorand Matory's contention that we live amidst "historically changing realities of what we call 'Yoruba religion,'" I attempt to engage four theoretical rubrics in shaping the structure and content of this book.[13] First, I am interested in narrative and, more pointedly, ethnographic approaches to history. For me, these probe metaquestions of how communities encode themselves in history, narrativize meaning, and engage in active modes of self-representation and traditionalizing. Because "narrations of the self are always in flux and subject to revision with each new telling," I am aware that they are neither synonymous with history nor a justification for strict methodological teleology but are nonetheless "life histories" whose value lies in the "ways in which people make sense of the events around them" and the ways their "lives are embroiled in larger social, cultural, economic and political processes."[14] Related to this, I am deeply fascinated by the multiple "systems of narration" (texts, autobiographical narratives, cultural expressions and the body, ritualization, and religious practice) that govern the ways that African American Yoruba approach history and divinity.[15] I also value insiders' texts as insightful resources for how African American Yoruba ascribe meaning to history and politics, theology and culture. Throughout the book I employ an "ethnohermeneutic approach" that "pays attention to theories and models" of both scholars and members of the Yoruba priesthood as important epistemological and typological resources for interpreting community identity, texts, and social meaning.[16] Finally, as a religious historian I discovered that ethnography proved in the end to be more than just a scholarly method of gathering data; it is what James Spickard calls "a path of knowledge that seeks to understand people rather than explain them."[17] Karen McCarthy Brown rightly asserts that "ethnography is written by making meaning out of others' processes of meaning making."[18] Ethnography, history, and religion collectively brought me to an understanding of the multiple layers of meaning embedded within this complex tradition.

For me, engaging in the ethnographic process among insiders in deeply honest ways has meant accepting that narratization is often ambiguous and, at times, a forum for internal community critique.[19] Within the multivoiced narratives I have gathered over fifteen years, I have found that

African American Yoruba are not univocal and that voices of difference and contestation inevitably arise. The ability to include the diversity and range of these voices, however, has made this study that much richer.[20] In an effort to preserve this candid richness as well as to minimize the effects that a scholarly text might have on the internal dynamics of living religious communities, I identify some of my interviewees, often at their distinct request, using pseudonyms or as anonymous informants in order to protect them from reproach within their tightly woven communities.

My second theoretical rubric rests with my interest in the ways religious communities become active agents in history and manipulate historical production as a way of reclaiming subjectivity. Considering Victor Anderson's important assertion that "race constructs not only social ontology," how might race also express "religious intentions" as it relates to a community's "historical self-understanding?"[21] One answer lies in textuality. Written texts functioned within the African American Yoruba movement as sources of empowerment, purpose, identity, and as meaning inscribers. Religiously negotiating *Africa* in the early days of the Yoruba movement involved texts and the creation of a literary ontology. My use of textuality here is more than the reading and writing of books; it is the use of texts as a portal to Africa that could be accessed, embodied, and re-owned. In important ways, texts provided a literary link that African Americans needed to establish with Africa. They were more than just reference and resource; they were history and memory that provided possibilities for recovery.

Connected to this is my third theoretical rubric, which speaks to the ways African Americans sought to re-own or repossess Africa through textual reflections and religio-cultural expressions that centered Africa as the progenitor of a reestablished history. They saw in history what Stephen Palmié ultimately defined as "an assemblage of collective representations" that offered not only a linear subjectivity but ways of re-envisioning their African identity and reconstituting their religious validity.[22]

Finally, my broader theoretical query focuses on the shifting social contours of contextual North America and the fertilization, formulation, and articulation of religious identities therein. In examining African Americans in particular, this necessarily involves analyzing complicated negotiations of American national identity; encounters with race (often the "unnamed" and "unmarked category") as both social constriction and as cultural capital; as well as complex connections to Africa as land, image, and symbol.[23]

I found it difficult to conceive of the complicated ways black communities historically negotiated this very concrete amalgam of American social location, racialization, and identification with Africa, and have it conceptually annexed to the *imagined* or the *imaginary* in contemporary scholarship. Since the revised edition of *Imagined Communities* in the early 1990s, Benedict Anderson's category of the *imagined* has surfaced as a central paradigmatic and theoretical framework for examining the articulation of black diasporan identities and nationalisms.[24] *Imagined* can often be applied to the Atlantic world myopically as though Africans were exclusively imagining their cultural identities in some way detached from a wider imagined consciousness on the part of European creoles and colonists. As I write in the post-Katrina era, where black humanity in New Orleans was in a very real, *unimagined*, and pernicious way collectively abandoned and discarded as wasted refuse in floodwaters (reminiscent of the waters of the Atlantic Ocean three centuries earlier), I am compelled to be more attentive to the ways categories are haphazardly applied to the historically lived experiences of African Americans. If religious scholar Cornel West is correct when he concludes that "from slave ships to the [New Orleans] Superdome was not that big a journey," then as academicians we tread perilous ground when we relegate to the realm of the imagination the historically complex modes in which people of African descent in the New World have reformulated their subjective identity and rehumanized personhood in response to this tragic journey.[25] In so doing, we run the risk of overlooking the ways the newfound scholarly terminology of the "imagined" and the "imagination" can be subtly juxtaposed with earlier scholarly discourses that denied people of African descent in the New World an assumed natural capacity for intelligence. Curtis J. Evans cites developmental psychologist G. Stanley Hall on this point as Hall identifies the "tropical imagination" of African Americans which has "given birth and currency to the rankest growth of superstition to be found among any race...."[26] Thus, these potent discourses placed the inferior faculties of African peoples with their childlike *imaginations* center stage in centuries of pseudoscientific debates on brain size and capacity; pseudophilosophical debates on undeveloped reason and intellect; pseudoreligious debates on soul depravity and moral primitivism; pseudosociological debates on social deviance and inherent pathology; and pseudo-psychobehavioral debates on natural childlikeness and innate emotionalism.

This is not to say that I am wholly dissuaded by scholarly arguments that attempt to parallel African peoples' conceptions of nationalism and nationhood to Anderson's focused reading of Europeans, New World white creoles, and Southeast Asians with hopes of broadening his conceptual applications of the imagined. If mediating African American religious, cultural, and sociopolitical discourses of identity through theoretical lenses of the "imagined" means subtly limiting or undermining the legitimacy of the distinctive psychosocial and religio-cultural ways that African diasporic people have attempted to transform and resist their origins as chattel in the New World, however, my sympathy will inevitably wane. I wholeheartedly agree that "cultural identity," as Stuart Hall argues, "is not a fixed essence at all, lying unchanged outside history and culture" where one can "make some final and absolute Return."[27] As he exclaims, though, "It is not a mere phantasm either. It is *something*—not a mere trick of the *imagination*."[28] J. Lorand Matory is insightful in pointing out that historically Africans on the continent and their descendants in the diaspora held complex conceptions of "nation" and nationhood "of a sort *un*imagined by Benedict Anderson."[29] Moreover, a theoretical primacy of the "imagined" as a fixed and stable category in understanding black communities in the Atlantic world can inadvertently realize a threefold analytically limiting effect: First, it homogenizes difference and competing notions of identity both social and religious that undoubtedly exist *within* the presumed "imagined" community. Second, it obfuscates and obscures religious practice and the complex modes of religious meaning that are played out in the daily lives of religious practitioners in conflicting and ambiguous ways. Finally, and most important to me, the black "imagined" paradigm often circumvents historical connections with the extremely violent (grotesque) and very real implications of the larger, New World metaimagined narrative of "racial alterity,"[30] where blackness was legally and socially constituted as "social and geographical misplacement"[31] and inherently designated as "transgressive."[32] Because I, like Jonathan Z. Smith, "accept willingly the designation 'historian of religion'" knowing that this obligates me "to submit to a lifelong sentence of ambiguity," I am far less interested in the heuristic category of the *imagined* than I am in examining the *lived* aspects of African American religiosity as it imports and neutralizes boundaries, mollifies and generates both meaning and ambiguity.[33] For my purposes, imagined may only be a useful lens of analysis if invoked in the ways Charles H. Long deploys *imagination of matter* or the ways in which James A. Noel in his *Black Religion and the Imagination of Matter in the Atlantic World* richly uncovers the "new modes of imagining materiality" through epistemologies of race, religion, and commodification in the Atlantic world, where "black folks were *imagined* as objects through the discursive practices of their oppressors."[34]

There is, of course, theoretical utility in Anderson's *Imagined Communities* for the study of African-descended communities, and for me it lies in an often-overlooked chapter Anderson entitles "Patriotism and Racism." In this chapter he engages in useful discussions on the role of *subnationalisms* or *popular vernacular nationalisms* within dominant societies, their formulation of transnational cross-fertilizations, and their creation of *countervocabularies* within racialized national contexts.[35] Especially persuasive are Anderson's discourses on religion, history, and race and his insightful articulation on how racialized adversaries are reduced to "biological physiognomy" and how "racism dreams of eternal contaminations, transmitted from the origins of time through an endless sequence of loathsome copulations: outside history."[36] Furthermore, analytical parallels can be made specifically to Yoruba Americans and their use of what Anderson understands as an intentional *historiographical consciousness* in order to recast history in written form and create a self-defined narrative of the past.[37] Taken collectively, the resources of history, along with race and religion, helped to provide important silage for the creative indigenization of Yoruba religion in the United States. Thus, Yoruba's American-born practitioners innovatively used history, race, and religion as sacred currency for ritual, culture, and textual articulations of Africa.

History and Textuality in the Shaping of Religious Identity

The fictional characters Red and Brooks in the Hollywood film *The Shawshank Redemption* represent the human desire to affect history by inscribing themselves into a particular space and time. At certain points throughout the film, each character etches his name into the wall's plaster as a reminder to an unknown future viewer that they "were here." As historians of religion, we are undoubtedly aware that persons and communities "were here," but we face the daunting challenge of producing convincing histories conveying the complexity and integrity of their existence. According to John

Ernest, "African American historical representation is both a reading and an unreading" and requires "a juxtapositioning of documents, ideology, and individual lives...."[38] In this study of African American Yoruba, I incorporate narrative voices as important informational resources. As a historian, however, it is also my task to present a historical reality that unearths moments of tension, conflict, and ambiguity as lived out by religious practitioners and also identify those moments where practitioners may not have yet fully worked out all the layers of ambiguity.[39]

Currently, the academic field of Yoruba studies comprises an array of works on culture, language, antiquity, politics, geography, ritual, art, and religion. Its current religious historiography ranges from its traditional practice in Nigeria to its African diasporic expressions in the Americas and the Caribbean. Within Yoruba studies, transatlantic interpretations of the tradition have emerged as important foci for understanding the Yoruba continuum from Africa to the New World. Still needed are comparative studies that uncover the ways many of these diasporic histories intersect and overlap. For example, a story not chronicled to any great degree in this study is that of Yoruba Latinos in New York City since the 1940s, a history Marta Vega richly documents in her "Yoruba Philosophy: Multiple Levels of Transformation and Understanding."[40] Although this book does not engage in this ethno-comparative work, it does offer brief insight into the moments of cooperation and conflict shared between African American and Latino communities that were vital to the development of the tradition in North America.

Historians of religion like Jacob Olupona recognize that "something *different* is happening" in the United States when examining the African American expression of Yoruba religion.[41] A significant part of this difference lies in the ways texts, race, and nationalism functioned as important variables in the formation of Yoruba religion among African Americans in North America. As James A. Noel stresses, "The *conditions* within which the gods made their hierophany or appearance in Africa and the Americas" is crucial.[42] For this reason, Olupona poses an analytical challenge to scholars of Yoruba traditions to move beyond dichotomous categories of "Africa" and "diaspora" and into more nuanced inquiries that closely examine local communities both in Nigeria and in the New World and the ways these localized geographies contribute distinct sets of meanings to what it means to be "Yoruba" in a global context. I am also indebted to J. Lorand Matory for challenging me to find an alternative discourse that moved beyond traditional discussions of syncretism and survivals that would ultimately have proven analytical misnomers in this study. A new African American Yoruba tradition arose in the United States in the late 1950s and 1960s, initially in the absence of any real immediate physical contact with Africa. As a consequence, African Americans actively began to generate their own religious meaning, produce their own cultural institutions, and historically remake themselves according to their collective understandings of Africa. Within these boundaries of deliberate choice and conscious agency, African Americans determined what would be defined for them as *African* and *Yoruba* in North American society.

The continuity of religious and cultural traditions in Africa is most often attributed to the power of the "oral" and "orature" in history, memory, and expression.[43] North American Yoruba transformed this notion of historical transmission in the 1960s by installing written texts as important disseminators of African religion and culture, a practice that continues until today. Texts possessed the transformative power of creating a national sense of community and providing this community with access to a new African world. Many narrative accounts in this study name a pivotal text or set of texts that assisted in the quest toward a more positive relationship with Africa. This was undoubtedly the case with Oseijeman Adefunmi in his formative years. Moreover, equally important to the reading of texts was the production and distribution of texts in the early 1960s. These texts helped to canonize new African American interpretations of and points of view on Yoruba religion, and from this literary agency emerged a distinct written corpus by black North American Yoruba of both non-Hispanic and Hispanic descent. These new "indigenous literacies" were important to understanding the multiple mediums through which reflections on Africa were disseminated.[44] The positive depictions of Africa these works represented functioned as emblems of countertextual resistance against a racist literary corpus.

For many centuries, the portrayal of Africa in pseudohistorical and ethnographic texts conveyed to an American readership negative images of cultural dearth, heathenism, and backwardness. Because "knowledge about Africa was, as a rule, not acquired by direct experience, but was transmitted via the dominant white culture," many African Americans consumed these distorted depictions as uncritically as their white counterparts.[45] This relationship with what Marion Berghahn calls a "textbook-Africa" laid the foundation for much ambivalence on the part of African Americans.[46] According to Berghahn, African Americans "were confronted with this negative image in reports by travellers and missionaries, in the mass media, in theatre, literature and school text-books."[47] She painfully concluded that "there existed . . . a general belief that their dark skin, their curly hair, their physiognomy were direct manifestations of the 'backwardness' and of the 'wildness' of their African ancestors."[48] African Americans who advocated early emigration movements in the nineteenth century were of little exception and upheld images of Africa equally conflicted. The cultural and political nationalism of the 1960s, however, paved the way for a renewed literary engagement with Africa. A close reading of African American texts on Yoruba religion and culture, particularly those written during the black-nationalist years of the 1960s, reveal several overarching themes. First, they sought to rescue Africa from the grips of "primitivism" and reestablish it within the context of ancient civilizations such as Egypt, Ethiopia, Mali, and Oyo. Second, these texts quite intentionally shifted the history of African American ancestral origins from North America to the continent of Africa. Finally, they endeavored to unify their black literary audience into a common racial nation of African descendants whose humanity was not totally subsumed in Atlantic slavery. Designs of "pastfulness" and "pastness" were richly at play here as Stephan Palmié has aptly suggested. Histories of Africa could conspire with distance by mitigating the distance between a "transcendent 'Africa-past'" and a "tumultuous 'New World present'" while at the same time creating ontological distance from the totalized identity of American slave.[49]

Although the 1960s can be seen as a moment of heightened racialization, many African Americans at times chose to eschew these racialized notions when it came to acquiring careful textual representations of Africa. Noted scholars such as Melville Herskovits, William Bascom, Ulli Beier, Robert Farris Thompson, and later Wyatt McGaffey were among the "acceptable" white researchers whose textual Africa was not solely rooted in primitivism and thus received more favorably by an African American readership. Both the texts that African Americans chose to read and the texts they chose to produce during the 1960s formed counterimages to the distorted Africa of the American textual past. In the absence of a physical relationship with Africa, African Americans creatively used texts to assuage this spatial cleft. This territorial distance made Africa no less meaningful or useful for the building of a new African diasporic consciousness and for the spiritual re-owning of their former homeland.

Yoruba Religion and the Reclamation of Africa

During the academic year 2002–2003 at a conference Dr. Daphne Brooks hosted at Princeton University entitled "Elvis is Dead," African American rock guitarist Vernon Reid pondered the lack of contemporary black response and outrage at the recent genocidal decimation of Rwandans. He concluded that the dilemma was the result of the fact that for the most part African Americans in the United States possessed a "disembodied idea of Mother Africa," that African American connections to Africa did not readily translate into the concrete physicality of the continent and the challenges of materiality facing its contemporary inhabitants. For African Americans, exile and diasporicity often created an Africa that primarily fulfilled a yearning for recovery and reconnection. Thus, according to Nicholas D. U. Onyewu, African Americans' "interest in the welfare and development of Africa stemmed from painful dilemmas within their *own* country. At the earliest stages they were not particularly concerned with the political aspects of African problems . . . Their concerns were more racial or cultural in nature. . . ."[50] Reid's comments on African disembodiment quite vividly expose the complex and paradoxical nature of African Americans' relationship with Africa and its historical focus more often on *Africa* than on *Africans*. From Ethiopia stretching out her hands, princes coming forth from Egypt, the civilizations of the Nile Valley, and the West and Central African connections to the transatlantic slave trade, these "disembodied Africas remain the primary means by which peoples whose ancestors were forcibly spread across the world—from Brazil to the Caribbean to North America and Europe—look to find some speculative origins of their own."[51] Thus, in understanding diasporicity both as a historical event and as a subsequent set of conditions and ongoing processes, the Africa most sought after in the New World was the Africa of symbol that could assuage the alienation of exilic ontology. According to Stephan Palmié, Africa "is not just a 'place' but a trope that encodes and evokes complex, historically sedimented, and contextually variable bodies of knowledge pertaining to the nature of human beings, social arrangements, and cultural forms that have variously entered into its semantic purview."[52]

It is in the ancient, not modern, Africa where this great ontological currency is held. Contemporary Africa is potently charged in that it heightens historical chasm and distance and situates identity politics beyond "biogenetic meanings,"[53] thus making it duly complicated for a relational Africa beyond an ancestral symbol. Contemporary Africa and its migrants to the diaspora hold the voices that often assertively delegitimize "Africans" of the Atlantic world. This delegitimization is authoritatively ventriloquized in voices like the Ghanaian taxi driver in New York City who admonished that I should not self-reference as *African* American because I am *not* an *African* or the Nigerian man at the Mobil station in Harlem who, in the midst of a dispute with one of my former students, sought to publically humiliate her by shouting, "You Slave! You Slave! You don't even know where you're from? You Slave!" Present-day Africa possesses these condemnatory voices and disparaging gazes for African Americans, whereas ancient Africa holds their undisputed "originating ancestors" and an epistemology of ancestral connection and primordialism.[54]

Although the transatlantic slave trade was a lethal enterprise in African "bodies," scholars of the slave period are often primarily concerned with how many "bodies" were transported, how many "bodies" survived, how much labor these "bodies" performed, how much violence these "bodies" endured, and how much culture and historical memory was retained within these "bodies." Reid's comments on Rwanda, however, force reflection upon the "disembodied Africa" and this paradoxical disembodiment in African American consciousness. While for centuries North America forced African Americans to undergo a physical detachment from the continent of Africa through slavery, black-nationalist movements and ideologies as early as the eighteenth century helped to foster a subsequent re-ownership of this distant land and a belief in an earlier moment when Africa was "their own."[55] These nationalist projects were also a re-ownership of the black body where the exogenously owned chattled slave could be restored to rehumanized subjectivity.

Africa in the eighteenth century as well as today continues to be an important hermeneutical resource for theorizing on African American identity. Throughout history, African Americans have formed ambiguous relationships that recoiled and rejected as well as remembered and re-owned the continent of Africa. Ultimately, what these relationships revealed, and what Yoruba movements in North America most clearly exhibited, was that re-owning Africa for African Americans was less about repatriating physical bodies back to Africa than about recouping a spirit of Africa in North American materiality.

Organization of the Study

A mentor once remarked to me that my job as the scholar-historian-ethnographer was not to defend, consent to, denigrate, or uncritically mirror the emic claims of religious communities but instead to "add breadth and depth to our *understanding* of them." He informed me that this unique study of North American blacks and Yoruba religion "deserves a reconsideration from a new point of view." His advice fell on fertile ears, for older analytical models of survivals, syncretism, reconstructionism, purification, revitalization, and retentions proved much too static to capture the dynamic fortitude, resolute agency, and determined innovation that characterize African American Yoruba.

Situating this study within the larger social context of black nationalism and specifically black religious nationalism instead allows the reader to examine the African American Yoruba movement within important articulations of racial solidarity, productions of new histories, creations of cultural countervocabularies, and declarations of nationhood. Thus, the practice of Yoruba religion emerged as a "site of counter-discourse" for African Americans.[56] Reminiscent of other African Americans in the 1960s, those involved in the Yoruba movement were not exempt from the black-nationalist impulse either to physically form or ideologically conceive of themselves as a "nation" based on their race as "Africans." This racialized conception of community, nationhood, and history was linked to an understanding of a shared narrative that predated America and found its roots in Africa. Within the Yoruba movement, Adefunmi, along with other African Americans, promoted a unique expression of Africa, based less on physical encounters with it than on historical and symbolic interpretations of it. They appropriated the symbols of *Africa* and *Yoruba* and applied them to "some remarkably different political, economic, and cultural circumstances" creating a "variety of new life ways" within their existing American context.[57] These "life ways" emerged as a conglomeration of newly inspired religious practices that possessed their own distinct innovations, variations, and interpretations. Although early pioneers like

Adefunmi were determined to restore Cuban Santería to a more authentic and less amalgamated fusion of iconography and practice, paradoxically what eventually emerged were new forms of ritual and theological hybridizations and improvisations.

The book is divided into two parts: "The Harlem Years" and "African American Yoruba Since 1970." Collectively, they examine the historical emergence of Yoruba religion among African Americans in Harlem; the relationship between early African American and Cuban practitioners; the importance of Yoruba religion as a source for black identity formation; and the localization, institutionalization, textualization, and racialization of Yoruba religion by black North Americans since 1970. Chapter 1 provides the reader with a broader theoretical contextualization of the intersection between black nationalism and religious meaning. In this initial chapter, I highlight early nineteenth-century moments of African American religious nationalism and their revolutionary efforts to racialize the divinity of God and sacralize black humanity in the midst of American social demonization and violence. In response to the lived contexts of entrenched Anglo anti-blackness, I explore how religious nationalist formulations provided counternarrations and countertheologies to deprecating images of blackness, black humanity, and divinity. Chapter 2 begins with history and biographical narrative as it situates Walter Eugene King, later known as Oseijeman Adefunmi I, as an emerging leader, in both the institutional and figural sense, among African American Yoruba in Harlem, New York. Adefunmi's narrative functions as one important trajectory into the broader contours of the Yoruba movement as it relates to issues of race, identity, textuality, nationalism, and burgeoning notions of Africa. African American conceptualizations of Africa in the early twentieth century were to a large degree shaped by available historical, periodical, and anthropological resources. These print media on Africa took on new meaning as they fused with black-nationalist ideologies such as Garveyism and pan-Africanism in urban America. Following this, chapter 3 recounts the detailed institutionalization and localization of Yoruba religion among African Americans in New York City's Harlem. Intricately linked to the larger social nuances of African decolonization, Cuban immigration, and black-nationalist consciousness, Yoruba religion functioned within African American communities as an important medium for locating and localizing a new Africanity as a pre-American and pre–Middle Passage frame of reference. Yoruba Temple was at the heart of cultivating this new frame of reference in Harlem's urban arena. Chapters 4 and 5 expand upon this and document the challenges in seeking to establish African American legitimacy and authority within the Yoruba tradition. Chapter 4 provides a close examination of the insider literature and literary texts Oseijeman Adefunmi as Temple leader primarily produced in the formative years of the Yoruba movement, examining the ways literary texts strategically mediated the historical, cultural, and restorative recovery of African identity for African Americans. Chapter 5 examines the orthopraxic philosophical tensions that developed between African American and Cuban immigrants over the issue of religious practice, exploring the multiple ways that orthodoxy and orthopraxy were subverted, contested, and negotiated within the two communities. The chapter concludes in the year 1970 with the formation of Oyotunji African Village as an alternative institutional and structural mechanism for advancing African American Yoruba authority, legitimacy, and autonomy. Chapter 6, the first in part 2, "African American Yoruba Since 1970," explores the internal life of Oyotunji African Village in Sheldon, South Carolina. More important, it examines the ways Oyotunji African Village represents an African American attempt to localize the religious and cultural symbol of Africa within a philosophical context of black nationhood. Chapter 7 explores the lived intersections between African American Yoruba and African American Protestantism and the complex ways a rich "theological openness" informs this unique religious orientation. It broadens the scope of religious practice, complicates issues of religious self-identity, and examines the coexistence of multiple religious affiliations among African American Yoruba. In Chapter 8 the reader is presented with a close analysis of the distinct theological, racial, and ritual interpretations of African American Yoruba and their unique North American diasporic contributions to the global Yoruba tradition. Finally, in the conclusion, I offer reflections on the future challenges and demands facing Yoruba communities in North America relating to globalization, institutionalization, gender, ecology, sexual orientation, and religious authority.

Yoruba religion has become a valuable passageway for African Americans on a quest for an African sacred source. In this study, I ultimately seek to bracket North America as an important diaspora site and resource for contemporary Yoruba religious articulation. Since the late 1950s, African Americans in the United States have supplied new religious institutions, new theological and ritual vocabularies, and tens of thousands of adherents to the religious and cultural complex known as Yoruba. No longer solely content with the southern religious traditions of their forebears, African Americans in the 1950s and 1960s reshaped the boundaries of Cuban Santería and as "New World traditionalists," to use John Mason's words, refashioned it into what was for them an African religion that met their immediate social needs as black North Americans.[58] Oseijeman Adefunmi captured the sentiment of this time: "Armed with a growing sense of cultural awareness [and] racial polarities, we no longer attempted to find religions outside of Africa but made a pretense, as it were, admittedly . . . to begin to organize or *devise our own methods of approaching the African God.*" This is the story of that approach.

PART ONE

The Harlem Years

CHAPTER ONE

"We Have as Much Right . . . to Believe that God Is a Negro"

Religious Nationalism and the Rehumanization of Blackness

ⱺ৩৩

D ESCRIBED AS THE "vociferous and controversial bishop" of the African Methodist Episcopal Church, Henry McNeal Turner asked on February 1, 1898, "Why should not the Negro believe that he resembles God as much as other people?"[1] In the late nineteenth century, Turner believed that African Americans had "as much right . . . to believe that God is a Negro" as "buckra or white people have to believe that God is a fine looking, . . . ornamented white man."[2] Severely criticizing "all the fool Negroes" who believed that God was a "white-skinned, blue-eyed, straight-haired" and "finely robed white gentlemen," Turner thought it debilitating to the psyche of African Americans not to believe that the image of God was in fact "symbolized in themselves."[3] He was decisive in his position: "We certainly protest against God being white *at all*."[4] Turner argued for an implicit ontological and anthropological correspondence between the image of God and the humanity of black people. This correspondence subversively undermined Western legacies of racial cosmogony that for centuries had considered black people aberrations and negations of the divine Godhead.

For Turner, bridging the inherited dichotomy between black materiality and divine essence was as much about religious identification as it was
about geographical location. He believed America to be a country where
"white represents God, and black the devil"; thus African Americans inevitably inherited a socialized ontological deficiency and would remain "obse-
quious believers in their own inferiority."[5] He reasoned that as long as the
Negro remained among whites in America, "the Negro will believe that the
devil is black and that he (the Negro) favors the devil, and that God is white
and that he (the Negro) bears no resemblance to Him."[6] As a consequence,
Turner staunchly advocated voluntary emigrations to Africa, viewing the
"home" continent as "the one place that offers . . . manhood and freedom"
for African Americans.[7]

At the dawn of the twentieth century, Turner believed that African
Americans harbored a collective need to "find a domain" that rejected the
demonization of blackness and precluded its "contemptuous and degrad-
ing" effects upon the black soul.[8] Black liberation theologian James H. Cone
supportively argues that "in a society where blacks have been enslaved and
segregated for nearly four centuries by whites because of their color and
where evil has been portrayed as 'black' and good as 'white' in religious
and cultural values, the idea that 'God is black' is not only theologically
defensible, but is a necessary corrective against the power of domination."[9]
This sentiment would carry over into African American Yoruba theology
when more than one hundred years after Turner, Baba Akinkugbe Karade
would similarly declare, "We Africans must see the Creator and the angelic
forces in our image just like any other culture."[10] For African Americans
like Karade, Yoruba expression not only provides a reifying of blackness
within the realm of the sacred but also what he calls a "deifying" of African
American experience in light of its slave past.[11]

More than a century preceding African American Yoruba, Turner
helped to lay the groundwork for a tridimensional nationalism that solidly placed religious reflection alongside the dual traditional nationalist
goals of sociopolitical autonomy and sovereign nationhood. Therefore,
while black-nationalist advocates like Turner were more commonly political in their agenda, scope, and orientation, they also readily employed religious and theological approaches as necessary strategies for rehumanizing
pejorative impressions of blackness. Within the early nationalist context
of Bishop Turner and later within the twentieth-century context of the

African American Yoruba movement, religion functioned as an important stratum for confronting the historical ways that blackness figuratively presaged evil and human negation. With religious appeals to an African God, the Yoruba movement six decades after Turner similarly countered and encountered challenges of the sociopolitical invisibility of African Americans, the internalization of black inferiority, and, most acutely, the heathenization, pathologization, and demonization of blackness.

Within nineteenth- and twentieth-century North America, black-nationalist discourses circuitously responded to religious debates several centuries old that equated the blackness of Africans to evil and to incarnations in Satan or the devil. Within these debates religion was almost always the source of these perverse racial ruminations. Even more striking is that this early conundrum of religion and insidious racialization was so enduring that it required African Americans to defend the beauty of blackness and protect the integrity of Africa well into the 1960s. In general, Yoruba Americans, like their nationalist predecessors and other black social movement groups, used religious symbolism and language in their struggle "to escape the biologization of their socially and politically constructed subordination" as determined through their designated and marked blackness.[12]

Scholars such as Winthrop Jordan, Joseph Washington, Robert Hood, David Goldberg, and Sylvester Johnson document the prevailing association of blackness with evil, the sinister, the fearful, the diabolic, the licentious, and the morally degenerate within English and English-American religious lore.[13] If traced along an exegetical biblical trajectory, scholars such as David M. Goldenberg in his *The Curse of Ham: Race and Slavery in Early Judaism, Christianity, and Islam* and Sylvester A. Johnson in *The Myth of Ham in Nineteenth-Century American Christianity: Race, Heathens, and the People of God* periodize this blackness-as-evil paradigm beginning in early antiquity and extending well into the modern periods in Europe and America. According to Johnson, Europeans and their descendants in America designated the descendants of Africa "as (questionably) human beings of a different *kind*."[14] European and European Americans developed a complex relationship of "negrophilia" that "primitivized," subhumanized, and imprisoned African subjectivity in a "complex semiology" of racial and religious signs and symbols.[15] As James W. Perkinson argues, Europeans were able to "conjure" demons, terror, and evil by mapping these on to a racial blackness while at the same time shielding whiteness from all inflections of deviance.[16]

A Western portfolio of anti-blackness emerged throughout Europe and America that historian of religion Joseph R. Washington persuasively argues "can only be understood as a *religion*."[17] According to Washington, "When the Devil and black people are equated or related and thus condemned, anti-blackness is anti-Blackness personified. I define anti-Blackness as a religion because that is what [it] is; religion is the greatest power of humankind for evil and/or good, but, it is not, like the religion of anti-Blackness, an unmitigated evil."[18] Washington maintains that the intense "spirit of malevolence" with which blackness was brutally negated in the Western world can best be equated to the passion of religious fervor. For Washington, "anti-Blackness" as it relates to African-descended people became "a learned response embellished with religion" that would then "recede into the permanent condition of anti-blackness [an ancient, historical primordial frame of reference], correspondent with the laws of nature, only through the process of unlearning combined with dereligionization."[19] As such, "anti-Blackness" results in "an anti-people religious spirit, or a spirited religion, antiblackness," where it can become "most dehumanizing."[20] In other words, this occurs when historical signifiers of blackness as evil (anti-Blackness) evolve into direct human associations with a particular racial or ethnic group.

Some twenty years after Washington, Sylvester A. Johnson's work would revisit this religio-racial analysis with even more precision. According to Johnson, "nineteenth-century American race discourse, whether religious or scientific, was persistently *theological*. Race ideas bore immediate implications for claims about the deity and about human access to divine knowledge and divine identity" and "the most enduring renditions of these claims identified the white race as first peoples who had first knowledge of the one true God."[21] Johnson concluded what was at stake *theologically* "was not a mere association between white identity and the Christian religion." At stake was something more profoundly significant, what Johnson insightfully calls "the race-ing of divinity."[22]

African American nationalists like Henry McNeal Turner, Marcus Garvey, and decades later, African American Yoruba leader Oseijeman Adefunmi felt compelled, as a consequence, to *counter-race* the divinity making God *Negro* in the nineteenth century, *Black* in the early twentieth century, and *African* in the mid-twentieth century. This need to counter-race the divinity, I argue, emerged in direct response to the demonic and pejorative "race-ing" of black existence by many Europeans and Euro-Americans who categorically severed black humanity and personhood from ultimate Divinity.[23] Within this quasi-*theological* world view, negative tropes of blackness were mutable within early Christianity and later became easily equated with raced black corporeal beings by large populations of European Christians, a trend intensified with the onset of the transatlantic slave trade. Johnson argues, more specifically, that Anglo religious identity in early America cannot be distinguished from the "confluence between the religious and the racial" and that "ultimately, it confounded attempts to image/perceive the humanity of the Negro, and it bred incredible mythologies of ontological whiteness." The confluence of race and biblical narrative, in other words, is rightly viewed as an anthropological concern because it principally regards the question of which people are treated as human beings and which are not.[24] Collectively, Washington's notion of the "religious" and Johnson's notion of the "theological" capture the religio-racial complexities that were quick to correlate "dark bodies with ontological evil, human depravity, and existential abasement."[25]

As scholars of religion and black nationalism in the North American historical context address the ever-persistent quandary of black "ontological evil" and "existential abasement," it will become clear that although, as Eddie Glaude Jr.'s work points out, "most traditional histories of black nationalisms tend to focus only on the politics as they related to the state," black nationalism was never exclusively about seeking self-determination and territorial autonomy.[26] Eclipsed in many understandings of black nationalism, I argue, is the inherent resistance to social definitions of blackness as a "negatively marked reference" and the accompanying counterforms of religious nationalism adopted in order to reclaim ultimate human worth, meaning, and transubstantiality with the divine.[27] Therefore, a call for religious analysis and reflection within the discourse of black nationalism should begin not at its goals of racial unity and national sovereignty but at its root as it attempts to respond to racial alterity, the systematic devaluing of black humanity, and the disciplined efforts "in pathologizing the religious experiences of blacks."[28]

Religious nationalism presumes as its starting point the normalcy, and not the aberration, of blackness and argues for its theological integrity and sacredness. What I am calling religious nationalism in many ways

metaphorically begins with Toni Morrison's literary character Shadrack—
who fought in WWII and saw a man's head blown off and body run head-
less—the character who occupies the space where Western trauma and
black humanity coalesce. To begin African American historical narration
any other way, echoing Morrison, would be to "squeeze the specificity and
the *difference*; . . . the violence done to it and the consequences of that violence."[29] It is a specific sociopolitical and religio-cultural grammar those
Morrison calls the "new world black" speak, those she says have been able
to extract "choice from choicelessness, responding inventively to found
things."[30] Thus, to begin with Shadrack in the dialogical encounter between
religion and black nationalism is to come "into immediate confrontation
with his wound and his scar" and to call "greater attention to the traumatic
displacement this most wasteful capitalist war had on black people in particular, and throwing into relief the creative . . . determination to survive
it whole."[31]

Reconciling black humanity with the essence of divinity has been part
of a history of black-nationalist responses of resistance from which African
American Yoruba proceed. Black nationalism sought to combat the "traumatic displacement" of black social definition and personhood that so often
found political and religious refuge in constructed scientific eugenics and
Christian doctrinal and theological thought. Within Christianity, "images
of blackness" were readily characterized as "a dialectic between evil and
sin, eroticism and carnality, sanctity and magic."[32]According to Robert E.
Hood, "The Christian tradition provided the moral and metaphysical category of the inferiority of blackness via its doctrines of struggle between
darkness and light and its reinterpretation of the devil as a creature of evil
and sin."[33] Moreover, he asserts that "blackness symbolized the way of death
and eternal punishment, superstition, and transgression. . . . Later in medieval Europe, this inferiority of being was transformed into inferiority of
intellect and religion with regard to black Africans and slaves."[34] Hood concludes that the transatlantic slave trade in African peoples necessarily reinforced the belief in blackness as theologically representing "cosmic chaos
and disorder" and culturally representing "bestiality and paganism."[35] The
meaning of blackness crystallized as a "fixed negative boundary."[36]

We are left to probe the depths of the religious and theological implications for Africa and its people where negative interpretations of blackness served not simply as physical indicators of difference but as the very

core of "African essence."[37] Within this discourse, the color of blackness became translatable into other infected vocabularies. According to Colette Guillaumin, "Taxonomies were transformed into classification systems based on a morphological mark, in which the latter is *presumed to precede* the classification" and through concrete "social relationships" creates how the marked group will be "seen" and "attached."[38] Therefore, what is the effect on Africans and their descendants as a result of the definitional power exercised in the modern world to relegate Africans to bounded and marked prisons of culture (primitive); science and intellect (inferior); physiology (infectious and diseased); religion and morality (heathen, depraved); and ontology and theology (evil, devil)? How are we to fully understand the cataclysmic impact upon Africa and its fixed meaning in the European imagination "if Africa functions largely as an *epistemic gap?*"[39]

What appeared over time under the rubric of anti-blackness was, in essence, a litany of associations between blackness and the humanity of Africans that expanded to include the moral fiber of Africans and their indigenous religions; African physiology and the black body as a locus for religious and social ideology; dark skin color and hue as a site of infection; and the black soul as depraved spiritual entity. Each rubric merits a brief discussion as a way of connecting the complex inherited legacies of blackness that became an inevitable target of future black religious nationalist counternarratives, countervocabularies, and counter-"race-ings."[40]

Blackness and the Continent of Africa

By the mid-1560s, the symbol of blackness and the continent of Africa became wedded in the European psyche.[41] Africa was perceived as a continent of void and dearth marked by intellectual, religious, and cultural deficiencies and as savage, beastly, heathen, and idolatrous. Geopsychically, Africa became the ultimate "*symbol* of difference" whereby an objectified and reductionist meaning of its humanity and civilization functioned as its primary global representation.[42] As Lee H. Butler Jr. typologized it, this "conjured legacy" served to codify Africa in savagery, primitivism, and debasement, successfully removing it "from the center of any discussion of human equality."[43]

Using the binary lenses of Christendom with which to interpret African traditions, Europeans found it natural to mark the blackness they

encountered on the continent as physically and morally evil and degenerate. Winthrop Jordan argues that "steeped in the legacy and trappings of
their own religion, Englishmen were ill prepared to see any legitimacy in
African religious practices."[44] They used a distorted "Christian cosmology" with which to judge African people that decisively relegated them
to "a separate category of men."[45] Hood reinforces this by observing that
"Christian exegesis and popular prejudice put together a stable image in
which blackness was a sign of evil. Although this was not a matter of conscious hostility to black people, the picture impressed upon the Western
European mind was added to the ancient tradition, with the result that *the
black and his land* were thought of as abnormal elements in creation."[46]
Thus, European encounters with the land of Africa and its inhabitants were
not merely physical but must also be seen as religious. Primary sources
observe, for example, that Africans "seeme at certaine times to live as it
were in Furnaces, and in manner already halfe way in Purgatorie or Hell."[47]

In many ways, some of the Europeans' harshest characterizations of
the continent of Africa directly targeted the religious identity of Africans
and their traditional religious practices. Substantiating this claim was a
series of disparaging accounts of Africa and its religions found in English
writings from 1553 to 1689. As early as 1553, Richard Eden wrote that the
Africans of Guinea were "pure Gentiles, and idolaters, without profession
of any religion, or other knowledge of God, than by the law of nature."[48] The
following year, in Hakluyt's "*The Second Voyage of Guinea*," Africans are
characterized as "a people of beastly living, without a God, lawe, religion,
or common wealth."[49] A decade later, during his 1564 voyage to Africa,
English Puritan and slave trader John Hawkins remarked of its traditional
religions: "For their beleefe, I can heare of none that they have, but in such
as they themselves imagine to see in their dreames, and so worshippe the
pictures, whereof we sawe some like unto Divels."[50] In 1625, Samuel Purchas
published *Hakluyt Posthumus or Purchas his Pilgrimes* in which he said of
Africans, "No Christians among the Negroes. Wee may hold it a punishment of God for their many giddie heresies."[51] Finally, in 1689, echoing
this same sentiment was English minister John Ovington, who represented
Africans as having a "magical and diabolical" belief system operating in
"compact with Evil Spirits."[52] The European imagination perceived Africa
primarily as "a land of men radically defective in religion,"[53] thus according
"moral characteristics to biological difference."[54]

European textual sources ultimately reveal that Africa and its religious mores signified "aberrations in the divine order of creation."[55] Although "heathenism" was universally employed within early Western Christian vocabulary, when applied to Africans it became imbued with anti-black ideology suggesting an "inherent characteristic," a "natural condition," and a "fundamental defect."[56] Europeans envisaged that Africans "lacked a universal religion"; that "indigenous African beliefs were idolatrous"; that Africans were "basically polygamous, libidinous, heathen, savage, idolatrous, barbaric, and promiscuous" and were therefore "defective in race, culture, and religion."[57] Their heathenism functioned as a "counterimage" to Euro-Christianity. Taken to metaphorical extremes, these early documents suggest that "blacks were bastard children of religions' mother whore, Africa."[58]

European and Euro-American texts were crucial in mounting a figurative transformation of the image of Africa and Africans. The ethnic particularities and the cultural and religious complexities through which Africans understood themselves were folded into a wider, sacred European cosmology that now relegated Africans to the realm of the primitive and contra-divine.[59] In the end, Europeans believed that Africa and its indigenous traditions possessed no religious capital worthy of divine merit. With the onslaught of the transatlantic slave trade, Africans were systematically robbed (with the exception of their bodies) of "their relative worth in the world economy."[60] As such, they functioned as what Charles H. Long labels "a *negative structure of concreteness* that allows civilization to define itself as a structure superior to this ill-defined and inferior other."[61]

Blackness: The Veil of Skin and the Sexualized Body

According to Winthrop Jordan, documentary evidence revealed that for Europeans "the most arresting characteristic of the newly discovered African was his color."[62] Although African skin hues would have ranged from the color of sand to the color of deep molasses, "black" became the primary undifferentiated signifier for demarcating skin color from that of Europeans. The origins of blackness preoccupied the European imagination and readily crept into scientific and religious discourses over the course of several centuries. According to Matthew Frye Jacobson, "Science provided an alternative vocabulary to the polarities of 'heathendom' and

'Christianity.'"[63] The European fascination with blackness led to theories of polygenesis, environmental and biological abnormalities, climatophysiology, as well as divine curses and sexual deviancy. Sixteenth-century European travelers to the continent of Africa expressed a general preoccupation with the origins of black physicality. Many speculated that the origin of blackness derived from the scorching of the sun or a liver disorder involving the secretion of bile and the blackening of the blood or that blackness "proceedeth of some naturall infection."[64] Thus, through the transmission of sperm, the descendants of Africa were repeatedly "polluted with the same blot of infection."[65]

Early travel logs, dairies, journals, and letters provide evidence of the multifarious assumptions Europeans held on the question of blackness. In 1695, in a document entitled *Two Essays, Sent in a Letter from Oxford, to a Nobleman in London*, the author remarked, "This colour (which appears to be as ingenite, and as original, as that in whites) could not proceed from any accident; because, when animals are accidentally black, they do not procreate constantly black ones, (as the negroes do)." The author thus concluded that "a negroe will always be a negroe . . ."[66] In 1732, it was argued that perhaps the blackness of Africans was attributable to their living "betwixt the tropicks in the torrid zones, where the perpetual scorching heat of the sun blackens them."[67] The speculator was perplexed that theories related to hot climates were not always reliable, however, and that "Europeans living within the tropicks, tho' ever so long, will never turn black and sooty" while curiously enough "Blacks living many years in Europe, will always breed black or sooty children."[68]

Some of the most deep-seated explanations of the blackness of Africans were tied to religious and Western Christian biblical inference. In 1703, prominent Anglicans speculated as to whether the black skin hue would be admissible in the final Christian resurrection. It was concluded, "Black is the Colour of the Night, Frightful Dark and Horrid; but White of the Day and Light, refreshing lovely. Taken then this Blackness of the Negro to be an accidental imperfection . . . I conclude thence, that he shall not arise with that Complexion, but leave it behind him the Darkness of the Grave, exchanging it for a brighter and a better [one]. . ."[69] In catechism instruction, this Anglican query was asked even more pointedly: "Q. Whether, think you at the Resurrection, there will be any difference in the Colour of the Ethiopians and other Men?" The printed acceptable response stated,

"A. If their Black *Colour* be a Deformity now, they will doubtless then be cured of it, rising perfect Man, as they would, if lame or monstrous."[70]

The associations between blackness and the devil and blackness and cursedness were powerfully persuasive. As early as the eighth century, "the devil is portrayed as *black* and naked."[71] In some medieval Western Christian iconography, the devil appears black with hair, horns, hooves, and a large penis, reinforcing in later centuries "an interplay between blacks and carnality."[72] According to Hood, "the moral and social values attached to black skin emerged early in the formation of the Christian tradition. The interplay between curiosity, ambiguity and ambivalence, and the sensual were joined with the devil as the symbol of evil and sin to confirm traditional myths and establish new myths about blackness and black skin."[73] When constructed as "blackness," something seemingly as random and arbitrary as skin color became powerfully conflated with "moral significance" and came to permeate both early Western Christian religious discourse as well as future modern intellectual thought in America and Europe.[74] Hood states, "In England perhaps more than in southern Europe, the concept of blackness was loaded with intense meaning. . . . Black was an emotionally partisan color, the handmaid and symbol of baseness and evil, a sign of danger and repulsion. Embedded in the concept of blackness was its direct opposite—whiteness. . . . White and black connoted purity and filthiness, virginity and sin, virtue and baseness, beauty and ugliness, beneficence and evil, God and the devil."[75] In the most severe interpretations, "blackness not only had a distinctive negative connotation, but also was personalized as the devil."[76] One early European source said of Africans that "in colour so in condition are little other than Devils incarnate," and "the Devil . . . has infused prodigious Idolatry into their hearts, enough to relish his pallat and aggrandize their tortures when he gets power to fry their souls, as the raging Sun has already scorcht their cole-black carcasses."[77] Thus, as Europeans physically encountered Africans on the continent, handled and mishandled their black bodies, and sought to find meaning in it all through Christianity, the racial distinctions designating good and evil intensified and sought to justify inhumanity through the creation of supportive Christian exegesis.

In addition to comparing Africans to the devil, European religious discourses also depicted blackness as the result of a divine curse: the curse of Ham. "The original story in Genesis 9 and 10 was that after the Flood,

Ham had looked upon his father's nakedness as Noah lay drunk in his tent, but the other two sons, Shem and Japheth, had covered their father without looking upon him; when Noah awoke he cursed Canaan, son of Ham, saying that he would be a 'servant of servants; unto his brothers.'"[78] Although the biblical text made no specific reference to race, a racial association was, nonetheless, theologically conferred as a justification of inferiority and enslavement. Moreover, contemporaneous Talmudic and Midrashic sources contained such suggestions that "Ham was smitten in his skin," that Noah told Ham "your seed will be ugly and dark-skinned," and that Ham was father "of Canaan who brought curses into the world, of Canaan who was cursed, of Canaan who darkened the faces of mankind," of Canaan "the notorious world-darkener."[79]

A resurgence of these early interpretations became most pronounced as European and African encounters converged within the institution of slavery. What became more commonly held was that the skin color of Africans was "a perpetual memento of their servile origin" and a mirror of divine sanction.[80] Dexter B. Gordon interprets this theological racialization of the Genesis text: "In the biblical version of the proslavery story, the black subject is aligned with the action of Ham. This action meets with condemnation and results in a curse from God. In contradistinction, the white subject is aligned with Abraham, whom God delights to honor. While whites are embraced in the center of the universe by God through the blessing and honoring of Abraham, blacks are cast as the troubling other who must be constrained by being made subjects to white governance."[81] The real potency of the mythologized curse of Ham lies in its ability to symbolically equate a membrane of human skin not only with divine disfavor and servitude but also with sexual abnormality. Blackness, evil, and sexual perversion coalesced in the Euro-Christian imagination and sought to concretely "establish black otherness and exteriority."[82]

Within European popular opinion, the blackness of the African body was most readily associated with licentiousness, perversion, and sexual deviance resulting in what Lee H. Butler Jr. theoretically designates as the "racialization of sexuality."[83] Over time, the carnality of the black body resulted in new discourses of theoretical animalization that equated Africans and their bodies to apes and orangutans. African sexuality was normalized along a narrow spectrum between deviant at best and bestial at worst. Further complicating this lore was a deep-rooted European hermeneutic of nakedness. In 1600, one account of Africans in Guinea described them as "given to Lust and uncleannesse, for a great while they goe with their private members uncovered," thus concluding that they were indeed "lecherous."[84] Moreover, Europeans easily imagined the genitalia of the African body as biblically cursed, echoing the sentiments of English slave trader, Richard Jobson when he stated that "the enormous size of the virile member among the Negroes as an infallible proof, that they are sprung from *Canaan* [*sic*] for uncovering his father's nakedness, and had . . . a curse laid upon that part."[85] This alleged divine curse of blackness was often linked to discourses of innate carnality, physical grotesqueness, and hypersexuality. Hints of this connection can also be found in early rabbinical texts on the Hamidic curse his father Noah pronounced: "Since you have disabled me from doing ugly things in the blackness of night, Canaan's children shall be born black and ugly. Moreover, because you twisted your head around to see my nakedness, your grandchildren's hair shall be twisted into kinks, and their eyes red; again, because your lips jested at misfortune, they shall swell; and because you neglected my nakedness, they shall go naked, and their male members shall be shamefully elongated."[86] Again, embedded within this early religious discourse were the seeds that would come to strengthen the perceived "interplay between blacks and carnality."[87]

Before the fifteenth century, these associations were mainly somatically debasing. With the authority of the slave trade, however, these associations between evil and blackness materialized into ontological representations of entire African peoples. Specifically examining British encounters with Africans, Washington writes, "Everything cherished in the English bifurcated reality appeared to be seduced and prostituted by blackness. . . . Black and African and Lecherous symbolized one gigantic threat to the body and soul of beloved purity."[88] The slave trade ultimately viewed Africans as "equivalent to a usable, marketable 'body.'"[89] Africa became a symbol of black subhumanity and the captured African body the site for mapping subhuman meanings. Slavery's real offense and "primordial disaster," however, rested in the reduction of Africans, their skin, and their bodies to a "perverse negation" of sacred and divine essence and to codified symbols of evil and carnality.[90] Thus, chattel enslavement "de-souled" African people and created what religious scholar Riggins R. Earl labels a "flagrant disregard for the natural sacredness" of black bodies.[91]

Blackness and the Souls of Africans

The constitutive moral essence of black people was highly contested through-out the eighteenth and nineteenth centuries in Europe and America. Beliefs in polygenesis and the probability of different genetic origins were not uncommon within European and American intellectual circles. For example, British naval surgeon John Atkins, in his 1735 *A Voyage to Guinea, Brasil, and the West-Indies: In His Majesty's Ships, the Swallow and Weymouth*, concluded the following: "I am persuaded the black and white Race have, *ab origine*, sprung from different-coloured first Parents."[92] Thirteen years later in his *The Spirit of the Laws*, Charles-Louis Montesquieu engaged similar suspicions regarding the nature of the African soul. He argued, "It is hardly to be believed that God, who is a wise Being, should place a soul, especially a good soul, in such a black ugly body. . . . It is impossible for us to suppose these creatures to be men. . . ."[93] Montesquieu's conclusions called into question both the humanity of Africans as well as their divine being.

Despite the entrenched depravity of black souls, some New England Puritans, like Cotton Mather, were hopeful that Christianity would improve the spiritual lot of the "Wretched Negroes." In his 1706 publica-tion *The Negro Christianized*, Mather said of enslaved Africans, "very many of them do with Devillish Rites actually worship Devils, or maintain a magical conversation with Devils. And all of them are more slaves to Satan than they are to You. . . ."[94] Decades later, prominent nineteenth-century naturalist Louis Agassiz revived the alternative creation theory of previ-ous generations for people of African descent. He confessed, "Nonetheless it is impossible for me to repress the feeling that they are not of the same blood as us."[95] The mere physicality of African people caused Agassiz deep revulsion, and when he encountered a black person for the first time, he could not help but comment on their "black faces with their thick lips and grimacing teeth" and "wool on their head."[96] The beliefs on race and black-ness Agassiz and other major European and American intellectuals held reinforced a dismal picture of the fundamental spiritual nature of African peoples. Although Agassiz and his contemporaries would have contested multiple taxonomies of "European races" and American whiteness, they were nonetheless unified in their totalizing definitions of blackness.[97] According to historian Nell Irvin Painter, even with "the change from white races to one white race," which "occurred in the mid-twentieth cen-tury," what remained eternally captive and imprisoned were "the roles of power and privilege in defining . . . blackness."[98] Like Painter, Susan Nance argues that the processes involved in Anglo "subjectification" highly valued "the concept of race" in both "its verbal and extraverbal dimension." The injurious brilliance of the marking of race lies in its ability to racialize others while safeguarding "white" as the normalized "unraced race."[99] Hence, race as "the representation as well as self-representation of individuals in American society" inherently resulted in meaningful forms and language that would forever defy neutrality.

Finally, a crucial question raised in the scholarly works of Winthrop Jordan, Robert E. Hood, Joseph R. Washington, and Sylvester A. Johnson still remains: what are the historical, social, and religious implications that have evolved over time as "diabolical blackness" and "congenital sin" became theologically equated with black people?[100] In other words, what does it mean to conflate racial and religious essence in such a way as to render African peoples morally disadvantaged, inferior to Europeans "in the endowment, both of body and mind," as well as depraved, heathen, and wretched in their "inherent" spiritual constitution?[101] Victor Anderson astutely identifies one plausible answer in that the Anglo "racial aesthetic" rendered "the other (non-Europeans) a false species, lacking in essential properties which make European genius representative of universal human genius."[102] Thus, the true power in anti-blackness imagery, discursive symbols, and metaphors rests in its ability to equate "an African people's total ethnic and cultural complexity" with their "complete debasement."[103] It is this distorted, sacred power that black religious nationalism has continually sought to resist, dismantle, and recast.

Toward a Discourse on Black Religious Nationalism

"Religious nationalism is about home," according to Roger Friedland.[104] My own interest in African American Yoruba as an expression of religious nationalism is related to the ways Africa as a religious symbol has been rescued from an inherited legacy of maligned blackness and moral depravation and recast in the twentieth and twenty-first centuries as a powerful sociocultural and religious metaphor of self-designation, legitimacy, and ancestral homeland and territoriality. More specifically, I am concerned with how religious nationalist discourses fortify a sacred reclamation of Africa. Through this reclamation tensions regarding identity are allayed as African Americans in North America make Africa and its indigenous, pre-Christian religious traditions the basis for a diasporic recovery movement while transmuting their current geohistorical site of enslavement and social bondage.

For black diasporic communities in North America, black nationalism helped in the navigation of what Lena Delgado de Torres calls "multiple citizenships—one in the nation-state, which is a tenuous and often incomplete citizenship," and the other "in their African identities."[105] Throughout much of African American history in the United States, traditional black-nationalist discourse included corresponding ideologies as a social strategy for addressing the instability of multiple citizenship. These ideologies were largely focused on the politics of religion, race, national identity, and prospects of territorial return (whether physical or symbolic) and were often positioned within a larger African American "narrative of counter-citizenship."[106] According to Jeffrey Stout, black nationalism was "not only a vehicle for expressing piety, directed toward the past, but also a vehicle for expressing aspirations, directed toward the future."[107] The inner crux of most black-nationalist discourse lay in interrogating the complex ways African Americans reconciled issues of origins, humanity, and national belonging while challenging a system that diminished their social status and questioned their human worth. As Stout indicated, its goal was not to "denigrate whiteness per se" but to treat "blackness as emblematic of something worthy of respect or admiration."[108]

A genealogy of black nationalism in the United States can be easily accessed through the scholarly studies of E. U. Essien-Udom, Wilson Jeremiah Moses, Manning Marable, William L. Van Deburg, and others. Requiring only the briefest of summaries for the purposes of this study, the authors mentioned provide important in-depth analysis of the various tenets and formulations black-nationalist leaders assumed amidst a vastly changing social landscape and consistent racial philosophy in America. Most scholarly works on the historical evolution of black nationalism within the United States emphasize the efforts on the part of African Americans to create spaces of autonomy and self-sufficiency based on territorialism, race, a shared cultural identity, and alternative forms of citizenship. Black nationalism, however, was largely about transcendence and the ability to formulate ideological strategies that rose above deeply entrenched American definitions of race, human value, and national rootedness.

Manning Marable characterizes the multiple components of black nationalism as "a rejection of racial integration; a desire to develop all-black socio-economic institutions; a commitment to create all-black political structures to fight against white racism; a deep reluctance to participate in coalitions which involved a white majority; an ethos and spirituality which consciously rejected the imposition of white western dogma; and an affinity for the cultural and political heritage of black Africa."[109] Moreover, Wilson Jeremiah Moses's study of classical black nationalism describes one of its primary goals as creating a "national homeland" or a black nation-state where African Americans would retain sovereignty.[110] No longer would African Americans operate as an "internal colony of the United States."[111] In their independent territory, national citizenship would be based on a transformed understanding of race. According to Moses, "Black nationalism differs from most other nationalisms in that its adherents are united neither by a common geography nor by a common language, but by the nebulous concept of racial unity. . . . It attempts to unify politically all of these people whether they are residents of African territories or descendants of those Africans who were dispersed by the slave trade. It is essentially a trans-Atlantic phenomenon . . . It seeks to unite the entire black racial family, assuming that the entire race has a collective destiny. . . ."[112] For most black nationalists, commonality in race constituted the basis of national citizenship. Racial identity functioned as the primary catalyst of a renegotiated kinship and connected disparate people of African descent throughout the world. For Moses, implicit within black-nationalist thinking was "the assumption that membership in a race could function as a basis of national identity."[113] The definition of national identity, however, was consistently fraught with uncertainty as it oscillated among the unfixed boundaries of American citizenry, national black racial citizenry, global African citizenry, and universal human citizenry.

Finally, in addition to territorial and racial nationalism, William L. Van Deburg in his important text, *New Day in Babylon*, underscores the added dimension of cultural nationalism within the schema of black nationalism. Cultural nationalism distinguished people of African descent through distinct idioms of art, music, literature, customs, and practices. According to Van Deburg, "For cultural nationalists, black culture was Black Power. By asserting their cultural distinctives via clothing, language, and hairstyle and by recounting their unique historical experiences through literary and performing arts, cultural nationalists sought to encourage self-actualization and psychological empowerment."[114] Although Van Deburg does not specifically generate a category of *religious nationalism*, the Yoruba communities of North America occupy a fluid categorical space between cultural to religious nationalism.

As a scholar examining the African American Yoruba movement within the rubric of black nationalism, I find the definitions and categories of Moses, Marable, Van Deburg, and other scholars insightful and useful. The challenge becomes locating where early Yoruba Americans should be placed along this nationalist spectrum. More recent black-nationalist scholarship helps to directly engage this challenge. Patricia Hill Collins, in "Black Nationalism and African American Ethnicity," argues for the "flexibility" and "resiliency" of black nationalism and its ability to provide fluid and continuous responses "to the specific political challenges raised by slavery, Jim Crow segregation, industrialization, and urbanization."[115] Rather than defining black nationalism within rigid principles and precepts, she analyzes its "potential functionality" and "utility" as an African American response to social and racial subjugation.[116] What is especially insightful in Collins's work is her analysis of "the diverse ways in which African Americans deploy Black Nationalism as a system of meaning" and as a reflection of "ethnic politics."[117] For Collins, often wedded within this system of meaning are ethnicity and religion. According to Collins, "Black ethnic identifications that take religious and/or spiritual forms may be more readily recognizable to far greater numbers of African Americans because they invoke preexisting religious, spiritual, and cultural traditions."[118]

Religious nationalism, in particular, redresses these historical problems of black moral essence, ontological heathenism, and spiritual pathology. Thomas Hylland Eriksen cites scholars such as Bruce Kapferer who challenge us to see nationalism itself as "an *ontology*; a doctrine about the essence of reality" that "frequently draws on religion and myth for its symbolism."[119] In general, scholars who theorize on religious nationalism or religio-nationalist subcultures make several suggestions, namely that these movements "commonly emphasize periods of political autonomy or independence prior to the current regime," create "metaphoric kinships," revive "forbidden histories," and provide "alternative systems of belief that can be deeply associated with self-concept" and a "form of collective representation."[120] Religious nationalism allows for the exercising of racial and religious agency and focuses its energies, efforts, and strategies on "the inner side of the color line."[121] More important, religious nationalism is concerned with formulating a "new collective subjectivity" and a space where an "alternative vision of the social can be . . . prefigured."[122] For the Yoruba movement, the efficacy of religious nationalism, as with other forms of nationalism, is that it "reinforces the inspirational, identity, and integrative elements of every culture and can be productive as a [social] conflict resolver."[123]

John H. Bracey, August Meier, and Elliott Rudwick, in their 1970 groundbreaking text *Black Nationalism in America*, were among the first scholars to make an analytical connection between the category of religious nationalism and Harlem's Yoruba Temple. In their brief reference, Yoruba Temple was grouped with the Moorish Science Temple, the Nation of Islam, and black Jews as "non-Christian forms" of *religious nationalism* generally espousing a black God, reconfiguring the theological boundaries of Christianity and, at times, declaring divine chosen-ness.[124] The following year in 1971, J. Deotis Roberts, in his article "Afro-Arab Islam and the Black Revolution," also used the category of black religious nationalism to describe religious movements such as the Moorish Science Temple, Garvey's UNIA, and the Nation of Islam.[125] Discourses of religious nationalism and the formation of sacred vocabularies to counter definitional maladies of blackness are not new; the Yoruba movement steps into a history that includes such nationalist forerunners as Frederick Douglass, Martin Delany, Henry McNeal Turner, Marcus Garvey, the Honorable Elijah Muhammad, and others who responded to a Anglo-Atlantic demonization of blackness that permeated American psychic, social, and religious culture and vocabulary.

Through an extensive examination of Harlem's Yoruba Temple and African American Yoruba, we can explore the ways that black religious nationalism was able to create "ensembles of practices . . . and of knowledges" that recast black sacred and historical identity.[126] In many ways, Oseijeman Adefunmi and others created a new "symbolic vocabulary" that authenticated African American subjectivity within a wider world of Africa, ancient deities, and ancestors.[127] An important nuance to keep in mind is that participants of the movement internally understood this new authentication not so much as a newly created or invented identity but as a *re*-authentication of a past African identity, which would eventually provide a countercorrective to America's "social falsehoods" on black-ness.[128] Similarly, James H. Cone argues that religious nationalists like members of the Nation of Islam, and I would also include Harlem Yorubas, "needed a philosophy that could speak to their existence as black people, living in a white society that did not recognize their humanity." Thus "in place of an American dream," Cone continues, nationalists ultimately offered "an African dream."[129]

This dream provided a space of "transcendence" for African Americans in the United States. R. Drew Smith, in "Black Religious Nationalism and the Politics of Transcendence," argues that this notion of transcendence is rooted in exacting radical resistance and "objections to who has defined social reality and how black life has been specifically defined within that framework."[130] Smith contends that religious nationalism is concerned with "overcoming American distortions and denigrations of the humanity and self-worth of black people," taking into account the analysis of Cornel West that "Black people will never value themselves as long as they subscribe to a standard of valuation that devalues them."[131] Therefore, the task of religious nationalists has been to create a space of transcendence and provide "new categories of religious and cultural definition for blacks to draw upon in their search for affirmation."[132] Most often, this transcendence involved the search for a trans-American identity that equipped African Americans to navigate their very real social location within North America.

"Bear the Image of God Naturally": Religious Nationalism and the Historical Rehumanization of Blackness

Within nineteenth- and twentieth-century African America nationalist contexts, rehumanizing processes of blackness were largely connected to resacralizing black bodies, reinstating full humanity, realigning blackness with divinity, reclaiming and recasting black history and experience, and redeeming and revaluing the continent of Africa. The power of religious nationalism was in its ability to refute the commonly held premises many white clergy, missionaries, slavers and slaveholders, citizens, and intellec-tuals historically espoused. These were that African-descended peoples were synonymous with evil and the devil; blacks were naturally deficient in intellect, religion, and culture; Africa and its traditions are inherently primitive, dark, and savage; black subjectivity can be understood by its reductionist equivalent as *slave*; blacks are morally deprived and ontologically aberrant; black skin is representative of a divine curse; and blacks are naturally deviant in social and sexual behavior.

Within a racially and religiously defined social strata in late nineteenth-century America, African Americans found little existential evidence that "they bear the image of God naturally" as black nationalist Edward Blyden so desperately hoped they could.[133] Blyden emphatically declared to black people: "You need to be told constantly that you are Africans, not Europeans—black men not white men—that you were created with the physical qualities which distinguish you for the glory of the Creator, . . . and that in your endeavors to make yourselves into something else, you are not only spoiling your nature and turning aside from your destiny, but you are robbing humanity of the part you ought to contribute to its complete development and welfare. . . ."[134]

Blyden did not see the need to sacrifice the specificity of African-ness in favor of a universal concept of humanity. In this he differed radically from black Christian nationalists in the nineteenth century, who were reluctant to speak of the godhead in racialized terms. Instead, Christian nationalists preferred the safer theological stance of a universal Christian divinity and a universal human race, thus ultimately creating a "universalist subject that transcended race."[135] In other words, early black Christian nationalists posited less radical theological conceptions and chose to equalize the humanity of blacks and whites under Christendom, strategically avoiding the need for a resacralized, divinized, or revaluated black or African subjectivity. Robert E. Hood accounts for this possible theological avoidance on the part of early black Christian nationalists as being because "the relationship between American blacks and Africa has been complex and tortuous, complicated by blacks internalizing religious and popular views about the color black and Africa."[136] Among nineteenth-century black nationalists, this ambiguous relationship would have inherently complicated theological efforts to have African-ness or "their blackness . . . taken into the godhead."[137] Promoting universality in many ways eclipsed the particularity of created blackness. Thus, religious nationalists such as Henry McNeal Turner, who believed in the Negro-ness of God, or Edward Blyden, who proclaimed that "Africa's lot resembles Him," were not in the majority.[138] Although perhaps problematically traditional and conservative in other areas, both Turner and Blyden nonetheless constructed God as coterminous with blackness and

African-ness, thus radically pushing their peers' scope of ontological universality and homogeneity. They blazed a trail for religious nationalists who, like African American Yoruba, would in the next two centuries continue to engage the sacred in such a way that it reflects, validates, and affirms black humanity and physiological and phenotypical embodiment.

Understanding the African American Yoruba movement within a conceptual framework of religious nationalism invites scholars to be creative in retheorizing black nationalism beyond the analytical categories of politics, economics, and nationhood. The category of religious nationalism is useful as a means of engaging the complex impact of religious reflection on the scholarly interrogation of black nationalism's social and historical expressions in the United States. With the category of religious nationalism, an analytical space can be demarcated within black-nationalist discourse for religious analysis and diverse modes of sacred meaning, thought, representation, and iconography.

Finally, the discipline of religious studies offers important analytical frameworks from which to broaden our understanding of North American black nationalism. For scholars interested in further pursuing the interconnections between religion and nationalism, these seven identifying characteristics help delineate a critical scope of analysis:

1. Black religious nationalism subverts the association of blackness with deified evil and makes a deliberate attempt to theologically realign blackness with divine essence.

2. A primary motivation is the need to *de-slave* or deobjectify (thus rehumanize) the *historical corporality* of black Atlantic people in the aftermath of traumatic enslavement, with the goal of redesignating as sacrosanct the spiritual body and essence of postslavery African people.

3. Race becomes a central hermeneutical prism for conceptualizing sacred community and determining religious membership. In this collective community, individual differences are transcended, and direct continuities and links to ancient black communities are envisaged.[139]

4. Religious practices reflect strict moral and ethical codes of behavior and religious expression is often patterned on ancient or traditional interpretations of culture.

5. New modes of creation and primordialism are mythologized and often textualized. History is also used as a "system of narration" in the quest "not only for identification and inspiration" but also for collective "legitimacy."[140]
6. Iconic renderings of the sacred and the divine are racially recast and rearticulated as affirming of black physicality while subverting the supremacy of an Anglo *imago dei*. New theologies are espoused that emphasize the inherent divinity or primordial universality of blackness.
7. Africa is often revalued and historically honored as a sacred source of ancient philosophies and traditions. The image of Africa and African humanity are deprimitivized and rescued from pejorative European typologies.

More broadly, within this constructive framework black religious nationalism in the Atlantic world seeks to find sacred meaning within the dismembering hermeneutics of the West. Its quest is often for a place of shelter from the political disenfranchisement, bodily invasion and assault, and socioeconomic and identity trauma visited upon people of African descent. It posits an alternative moral discourse of sin and relocates sin within the evils of slavery, racism, and white supremacy as well as in black passivity, submission, and internalized inferiority in the face of these evils. Henry Highland Garnet understood internalized inferiority as black compliance, duplicity, the "highest crime against God," and "sinful in the extreme."[141] The diasporic spatiality that religious nationalists envision must be imbued with affirming signifiers of black bodies, minds, and spirits.

Early Yoruba nationalists in the United States did not differ in this desire for self-actualization within unfettered and unbounded spatiality. Throughout the book, I examine the African American Yoruba movement as an expression of what theologian Dianne Stewart identifies as "an alternative resource for rethinking the meaning of being human in the African experience."[142] Similar to their nineteenth- and twentieth-century predecessors, African American Yoruba endeavored to respond to America's covert negations of blackness against its black citizenry. They did so, however, by attempting to reject the previous generation's Christian elitism, "civilizing mission," "imperialist ramifications," and what Tunde Adeleke calls their "*Un*-African" American attitudes toward the continent.[143]

Therefore, for African American Yoruba in the 1960s, no longer privileged were the anti-conjure discourses of Martin Delany; the anti-Voodooism campaigns of Daniel Payne; the primitivization of African traditional culture of Alexander Crummell; or the Arabization philosophy of the Nation of Islam. No longer did Western Christian or even Islamic religious traditions hold positions of sacred esteem for African American Yoruba but instead the sacred sciences, divinatory systems, gods, spirits, and ancestral powers of Africa did. Africa (and not America) would become the sacred source of religious expression and ultimate authenticator of black humanity. The religious nationalism of African American Yoruba would proclaim a new epistemology of the sacred and provide an important reflection upon the past. The past would always be twofold, though—one in Africa and one in America—and a symbiotic relationship between the two would forever inform this new nationalist formation as it sought a generative future.

"A Highway Made Across the Atlantic": Recovering Africa in the Twenty-first Century

Nineteenth-century American black nationalists like Henry McNeal Turner searched earnestly for the one true place where the essence of "Negro naturalization" could be found. Turner believed that African Americans in the United States should establish a reconnection to the continent of Africa, building "a highway made across the Atlantic."[144] Traversing this highway, American Negroes could envision resettlement in Africa. For U.S.-born Yoruba in the twentieth and twenty-first centuries, traversing this highway meant invoking the African orisa spirits to resettle in America. Despite differing approaches across the centuries, both groups of nationalists in their own ways "acknowledged and sought to mobilize the revolutionary potentialities of indigenous Africa."[145] North American Yoruba, however, were less concerned at the inception of their movement with developing a separate nation-state on the continent of Africa than with demarcating diaspora spatiality in North America where Africa could be lived as a sacrosanct "cultural object" that possessed religious meaning and provided "subjective relief" from "race and racialism" and its social consequences in America.[146]

As a result of enslavement and racial dehumanization, Africans in the Atlantic world were forced to negotiate an identity that oscillated between objectified chattel and dispossessed racialized being. For Europeans and their creole descendants as well as displaced Africans in the New World, Africa and blackness posed what Sylvester Johnson calls "an ontological fissure or disjuncture between (legitimate) divine identity and racialized, heathen existence."[147] New World Europeans embraced and upheld the debilitating aspects of racialization and heathenization while New World Africans remained on the other side of the fissure struggling to maintain their "legitimate divine identity."

The symbol of Africa helped diasporic Africans to normalize blackness and their disparate New World identities. In need of recovery was a "counterimage of Africa that seemed to directly contradict the one in European thought."[148] According to religious scholar Lewis R. Gordon, blackness had to be transformed "from the negative blackness signified by 'Dark Continent' to a treasured blackness."[149] Severed by Europeans from the physical and existential source of their identity, Adeleke argues, New World blacks deemed a *repossession* of Africa as their "rightful inheritance."[150]

For diasporic communities in the New World, Africa was never simply a geographical locator but functioned simultaneously as a "theological category."[151] In the nineteenth century, Benjamin Tanner declared that "the doctrine of the Negro's humanity is [Africa's] primary significance."[152] In Africa, Tanner says, Africans were constituently human and "not slaves," "equals" and not "inferiors." Contained within Africa, therefore, was the image of religious reflection where the doctrine of black humanity could ultimately find what Charles H. Long theorizes as legitimization, validation, and authentication.[153]

Moreover, Africa has consistently had meaning as the "ethnic homeland" of African Americans.[154] Throughout the Americas and the Caribbean, Africa would come to function not just as "an anthropological-physiogenetic concept" but as an "ontological and historical construct."[155] It served as a symbolic answer to questions about their unknown ethnic origins and as a potent emblem for what Baba Medahochi calls African American "re-tribalization." For African-descended people in the Americas and the Caribbean who found themselves geographically displaced from the continent, the notion of race became a valid unifying concept over time and a legitimate substitute for African ethnospecificity.

As scholars seeking to engage these new meanings of Africa among black Atlantic diasporic communities, we must, as Stewart suggests, "be willing to surrender, or at least suspend, postmodern critiques that render

diasporic ethnocultural and racial identifications with Africa essentialist, romantic, and therefore inauthentic and contrived."[156] Like Stewart,
Michael J. C. Echeruo is extremely alarmed that within the context of the
historical diaspora of Africa "we call any notion that we might have remained
African through these experiences a form of 'essentialism' and are only too
glad to choose to be nothing."[157] By suspending these analytical predisposi-
tions and overdeterminisms of essentialism, romanticism, inauthenticity,
and Frazierian cultural "nothingness," scholars might be able to interrogate the complex meanings of how being *African* was always dynamic
within diaspora cosmology and functioned as an important act of *counter-
essentialism* against the Western essentialism of demonized blackness. We
might more carefully investigate the impact of how the diasporic notion of
being *African* is often theorized on the premise that Afro-diasporans were
ancestored centuries ago to a specific regional and cultural-ethnic group
in Africa, these ties being disrupted by European economic expansionism
and the transatlantic slave trade. As a consequence, new meaning emerged
as the existence of an African in New World Atlantic locales became that
of a "nationless nomad" or what James Baldwin calls a "transatlantic com-
muter . . . a stranger everywhere."[158]

Within this complex paradigm, Africa as a sacred religious symbol
emerges as a result of "diasporization" and has consistently functioned as
what Kim D. Butler calls a "reference and authenticator for new identities."[159] These new identities are "anchored in past time, but always looking to a future time"; "rooted in a particular place" but with "dreams of an
'elsewhere.'"[160] For African American Yoruba in the United States, Africa
ultimately became, as Melani McAlister states, "A way of mapping themselves in relationship to the world" that was fundamentally "different from
dominant constructions of 'America.'"[161]

In the end, a foreboding question remains ever haunting black-
nationalist discourse: "Just where is 'home' for those of us in the West"
who were "enslaved and sold into bondage on this side of the Atlantic?"[162]
The nationalist response remains suspended somewhere between an elusive Africa and a harrowing diaspora, between ideological yearning and
geographical reality. One navigates this geography with a deep wrestling
that is never fully resolved either in Africa's mournful loss or in its hopeful
recovery. Instead, "Africa stands primarily as a principle of narrative and
historical uncertainty."[163]

Thus, the reality of "diasporan living has meant a constant rethinking of one's outlook on . . . one's identity and ideals about 'home.'"[164] This "New World soul," as Charles H. Long names it, remains ensconced in an "orientational meditation" upon itself as it navigates this New World locus and its subsequent "terror of time."[165] This New World soul finds itself in constant search of "a world equal to the terrain of its reality" where it "can reveal itself as well as endure and be creative for the future of human civilization and meaning in this world."[166] W. E. B. Dubois recognized this in 1903 in that the challenge for African Americans was how to maintain endurance and creativity after having lost what he called "ancient African chastity," intimating a rape and violation of African peoples through the institutions of slavery and colonialism.[167]

Yoruba Traditions and African American Religious Nationalism, as stated in the preface, is not an exposition of African survivals in the classical sense but on the ways that Africa was positioned as a reontologizing device and revalued as a sacred, philosophical, cultural, and religious resource for African American Yoruba in the United States. Oseijeman Adefunmi, one of the Yoruba movement's early leaders, matures in the urban center of Detroit, Michigan, in the 1930s and '40s and observes the impact of Garveyism and Noble Drew Ali's Moorish Science Temple upon African Americans. Yet he inevitably comes to locate his religious inspiration in the traditions of West Africa in pursuit of an "African God" and eventually finding spiritual sustenance first in Dahomean-Vodun and later through his own indigenized version of Santería known as Orisha-Vodu. Through narrative biography, ethnographic reflection, and religious social history, the chapters that follow seek to engage deeper questions of authentication and belongingness[168] and ultimately theorize more broadly on the ultimate question of *ile*—of home—and of the African America Yoruba journey to find its meaning and the spiritual and cultural validation associated with it.[169]

CHAPTER TWO

"Here I Is Where I Has Longed to Be"

Racial Agency, Urban Religion,
and the Early Years of Walter Eugene King

ɢɔɔɛʚɢ

"WHO IS THE AFRICAN GOD? That's what I want to know," inquired Walter King of his mother at the young age of fifteen in Detroit, Michigan, in 1943.[1] With Africa at the center of his query, King's mother was unaware that decades later this question would be the raison d'être for her son's renaming himself Efuntola Oseijeman Adelabu Adefunmi I, situating himself at a pivotal intersection between religion and black nationalism in Harlem and South Carolina, and fashioning himself among the leadership of a Yoruba movement of African Americans in the United States.

King's bio-narrative and his reflective question, "Who is the African God?" invite new ways of thinking about the meaning of an *African* God in North America. King steps into an urban tradition of religious nationalism where Africa became a centripetal metaphor for social mobilization, cultural reformulation, and religious transformation, encouraging new diaspora conversations. This new conversation takes seriously the challenge Sidney Lemelle and Robin D. G. Kelley posed to "move beyond the diaspora studies' focus on cultural survivals from Africa and explore how diasporic identities are constituted, reconstituted and reproduced."[2] The study of black North American Yoruba as a religio-nationalist movement offers a new discourse on the ways Africa is envisaged in the diaspora religious consciousness. My goal in this chapter and those that follow resonates with that of Robert Anthony Orsi: to write "a social history of a religious symbol" and in writing a social history of the meaning of Africa "to understand as intimately as possible why a particular religious symbol meant what it did and how it came to acquire this meaning" within a specific lived context.[3] In doing so, the challenge, as David D. Hall reminds us, lies in "explicating the multiple, overlapping, even contradictory meanings embodied" within this religious symbol.[4] For Robert Anthony Orsi's Italian Roman Catholics of Harlem, the religious symbol of devotion was the Madonna. For African Americans in Harlem in the 1960s, the symbol was Africa. In revering the symbol of Africa, African Americans, like no other group of North Americans, imbued the continent of Africa with religious meaning and expressed this meaning through incarnations of race philosophies and nationhood and through sacred canonizations in texts. Walter King would eventually find himself at the forefront of these efforts as African consciousness expressed as Yoruba gradually emerged in the late 1950s and early 1960s.

Although King poses his question regarding the African God some sixteen years before both his formal initiation into Cuban Santería and the formation of Shango and Yoruba Temples in Harlem, what becomes evident is the ways his exposure to neo-Garvey and post-Moorish Science Temple philosophies in his formative years in Detroit helped to influence the tenor of these later institutions. The Detroit of King's youth in the first half of the twentieth century reflected a period of intense "racial agency where religious and secular organizations within black society worked to build solidarity and community power among blacks."[5] As we will see throughout this chapter, it was within this complex urban environment of race and religion and later in Harlem, New York, that King came to value the Africa of nationalist ideology. Although an Africa fertilized primarily by written texts, it nonetheless possessed the ability to "maintain transatlantic connections" while destabilizing normative understandings of black subjectivity in America.[6]

Biographically, Walter Eugene King was born in Detroit, Michigan, on October 5, 1928, on the eve of major economic and social depression in America. As with most emerging urban centers at that time, Detroit's

African American population largely comprised recent southern migrants seeking economic opportunities and political empowerment.[7] Walter King's parents were members of this demographic profile. His mother was born in Anderson County, South Carolina, and like many African Americans, she worked for the Works Projects Administration (WPA) under the Franklin D. Roosevelt administration.[8] King's father was born in Rome, Georgia, and migrated to Detroit, Michigan, in 1912 with the hope of securing employment.[9] He eventually founded King and Sons Light Moving and Hauling, specializing in furniture re-upholstery and moving.

King's parents met at what later became the Hartford Avenue Baptist Church in Detroit. In urban settings such as Detroit, African American denominational history generally paralleled social migration history. According to historians Franklin and Moss, "As many African Americans went to the city in ever-increasing numbers, they took with them their habits of church affiliation, churchgoing, and a general loyalty to religious institutions."[10] Detroit had increased its African American population to more than forty thousand by 1920. Paralleling this was an increase in African American churches from six in 1916 to more than forty in 1926. The Hartford Avenue Baptist Church was founded during this period, and it was here that Walter King would acquire his early Christian teachings. King remembers that his mother's strong allegiance to the Baptist Church ensured that as a youngster "he was exposed to Christian thought and preachings,"[11] while at the same time she subsequently told him stories that his "great, great, great grandmother [had been] African."[12] As King's attentiveness to Africa and racial awareness increased, the Christian teachings he learned from the church were eventually brought under deep scrutiny.

As a young student around the age of twelve attending a Detroit public school, King recalled that he began to develop a rudimentary awareness of racial and ethnic distinctions and the celebration of these distinctions within American society. He recounts, "Naturally being a colored child (as we were all called then) in public school and . . . seeing Jewish kids have holidays and to also notice that Polish people had special holidays that they took off from school and the rest of us [blacks] were always there in classes, I began to wonder why it is that we didn't have holidays and festivals."[13] King's mother explained to him "that Blacks didn't really have any knowledge of their history and culture before slavery and so . . . didn't have any history of our holidays we had preserved as a people."[14] This experience made an indelible impression upon King, framing the "beginning of [his] consciousness of race and culture."[15] As a young man, King began reading black history, first in newspapers and magazines and later in more scholarly black American and African history texts. He began to see at a very early age the value literary depictions of Africa proffered black descendants of Africa in America.

Africa of the Literary World

Before his first visit to North Africa as an adult in 1957, the Africa King experienced most intimately was literary. It was this textual world that came to shape his early formulations of the continent of Africa and the cultural resources it had to offer. In the mid-1940s, while attending Cass Technical High School in Detroit, King and his childhood friend Crandall Eaton first experienced "Africa" by exploring the pages of the *National Geographic Magazine*. According to King, "We'd go to the library and look at National Geographic and see these Africans there and we would just eulogize and use all kinds of euphemisms and descriptions about how great Africans are and were."[16] As a result, King and Eaton decided to take new names from a Zulu naming book. In this first renaming in his teenage years, King took the name he pronounced as Nhomanzundela, which meant, he said, "brother of lions."[17] Exploring the pages of *National Geographic*, King was introduced to the cultural and ethnic diversity of Africa and the Yoruba of West Africa. He recalls Crandall's initial response: "We had seen a picture of a Yoruba man and he was sitting with his legs akimbo and he was carving something. . . . He had a floppy hat on and he was in his robe. And [Crandall] said, 'You're probably Yoruba.' And we both laughed and the joke was really on me because this picture of this Yoruba man was not one in which as people you could see anything . . . glorious about them like you could the Zulus. . . . That was really the first time I heard the term *Yoruba* . . ."[18]

The collective literary resources of the *National Geographic*, the articles and drawings of historian Joel Augustus (J. A.) Rogers in the African American newspaper, the *Pittsburgh Courier*, and the writings of George Washington Williams and Mbonu Ojike and others like Somerset Maugham had a profound effect upon King's racial thinking and conceptions of Africa. Most noted among these authors was self-trained and self-published J. A. Rogers, a native of Jamaica, who spent most of his life in

Harlem, New York, where he died at the age of eighty-three in 1966, having written sixteen books and countless pamphlets and newspaper articles based on his research in libraries and museums throughout the United States, Europe, and Africa.[19] Rogers's writings had a tremendous impact on readers of the black popular press of his day and were read widely by his national and international contemporaries including W. E. B. Dubois, Marcus Garvey, John G. Jackson, St. Clair Drake, Haile Selassie I, and John Hendrick Clarke.[20] As a young teenager in Detroit, King was deeply influenced by Rogers and his graphic artistry. "We subscribed also to an Afro-American newspaper, the *Pittsburgh Courier*, the Detroit edition, and J. A. Rogers had a cartoon section in there. He drew large cartoons. They were explained in his own words by descriptions of what the illustration was all about. He pointed out that the various Pharaohs in Egypt were Africans; they were Black people. . . . So his column fired me."[21]

Between 1941 and 1944, Rogers published a three-volume work entitled *Sex and Race: Negro-Caucasian Mixing in all Ages and all Lands*, countering traditionally held notions of white racial purity and superiority by chronicling contributions of Africans in ancient societies, the phenomenon of race mixture in the New World, and the nebulousness of Western racial categories.[22] Inspired by the brief mentions of Rogers in the Detroit newspaper, King secured personal copies of his longer works. As King recalls, "I sent off for [three] of his books, *Sex and Race*, and looking through those things [I] discovered a number of things: Beethoven was a colored man, discovered also that the English royal family had a colored woman who was a consort of whichever George it was that was on the throne at the time of the American Revolution. All of these things of course were new. It was something we were not being taught in school. It was something the church *certainly* did not teach us. So I realized there are institutions which serve different purposes."[23] It was in response to the writings of J. A. Rogers on African and African American history that King set about the task of "find[ing] a holiday that would be ours" alongside other school holidays. In pursuit of this mission, which in his teenage years appeared grand and meaningful, King voraciously thumbed through books, magazines, and any other sources for the hidden contributions of Africans and African Americans. During one of his literary investigations, King came across a mail-order form for purchasing an African mask. King ordered the mask and recalls the meaning it instilled in him. "So I sent away for that mask, received it, and put it on my wall. I was enormously proud of it and showed it to all my friends. Their response was nonchalance. They didn't seem to be aroused or awakened by it, by any exposure to it. But my brother, my older brother . . . he was intrigued by it and by a lot of the things I was talking about. . . ."[24]

For King, the writings of J. A. Rogers and the impression of the African mask were part of a much larger sphere of influence that would eventually include religion. Shortly after World War II, King's father died, and a grief-stricken King experienced for the first time in his life what he called a "spiritual conflict."[25] The conflict centered largely on King's inability to reconcile the teachings of the local Baptist church he attended with his mother with the knowledge of Africa he acquired from written texts. King had grown uneasy with the disconnect between his church and his texts, leaving him unable to articulate why the church discussed *God* and *not Africa* and why his readings discussed *Africa* and *not God*. A similar conflict with the church occurred for King's older brother, who was then closer to eighteen. He recalls a conversation he had with his brother at that time concerning this "spiritual conflict." According to King, "I do remember at one point I said to [my brother], 'Aren't you going to church with Mom and me?' And he said, 'No, I'm not interested in going to church. When they find a *Black God*, then I'll go!' And I was pretty shocked by that. . . . But that was a real turning point in my thinking in that he said something about a *Black God*. . . ."[26] This reflection on the plausibility of a *Black God*, coupled with his reading of George Washington Williams's *History of the Negro Race in America from 1619 to 1880* and Mbonu Ojike's *My Africa*, helped to reconcile history and religion in a way that would give meaning to Africa.

Originally published in New York by Putnam's Sons in 1883, George Washington Williams's two-volume text was one of the earliest comprehensive studies of African Americans and their historical antecedents in Africa. Extensively documented and written in the classic tone of a nineteenth-century black nationalist, Williams's text spanned some one thousand pages and reflected his training in theology and law as well as his political experience as the first African American elected to the Ohio legislature from 1880 to 1881. Williams's interest in Africa was twofold. First, he wanted to dispel any claims that African society in antiquity lacked powerful empires, organized culture, and structured governance. He argued that it was "unnecessary to multiply evidence in proof of the antiquity of the Negro. His presence in this world was coetaneous with the other families of

mankind: here he has toiled with a varied fortune; and here under God—
his God—he will, in the process of time, work out all the sublime problems
connected with his future as a man and a brother."[27] Implicit in his discussion of ancient African civilizations was a critique of commonly held beliefs
that Africans were racially inferior based on physiological or biblical evidence. Instead, Williams counteracted that there was a surplus of evidence
supporting the prominence of African civilizations, citing the kingdoms
and cultures of Benin, Dahomey, and Yoruba as ancient examples. Second,
Williams's expressed literary motivations echoed a familiar philosophy of
racial uplift and civic responsibility regarding Africa in postemancipation
America. Williams asked, "If the Negro slave desired his native land before
the Rebellion, will not the free, intelligent, and reflective American Negro
turn to Africa with its problems of geography and missions, now that he can
contribute something towards the improvement of the condition of humanity?"[28] His response was a resounding prophecy or "prospection" on the
future of the "American Negro" and Africa where "race prejudice" would
"give way before the potent influences of character, education, and wealth."[29]
These would be "necessary" indicators of "the growth of the race."[30] Using
these resources, the African American would bring about "improvement
here in America" and eventually "turn his attention to the civilization of
Africa."[31] Williams impressed upon his targeted black readership that "the
Lord is going to save that Dark Continent, and it behooves his servants
here to honor themselves in doing something to hasten the completion of
this inevitable work! Africa is to be redeemed by the African, and the white
Christians of this country can aid the work by munificent contributions."[32]
Williams's nineteenth-century text, however, was wrought with complicated images of Africa as both historically civilized, yet in need of civilization; culturally and politically sophisticated, yet scientifically lacking;
possessing its own religious history, yet "dark" and ripe for Christian missions.[33] Therefore, whereas Williams offered readers like King a depiction
of Africa that was useful yet inconsistent and ambiguous, Mbonu Ojike's
twentieth-century text offered King a view of Africa less so.

Nigerian-born Mbonu Ojike published *My Africa* in the United States
in 1946, the year King celebrated his eighteenth birthday. Ojike chronicled
his life from his early days in Nigeria, including elaborate descriptions of
local Ibo polity, culture, and religion; his sojourn to America to the historically black Lincoln University in the state of Pennsylvania; and an analysis

of his status as a naturalized U.S. citizen. He juxtaposes this narrative with a strong critique of slavery, European domination, colonization, and missionary activity, which in his opinion left the continent of Africa "often misrepresented, traditionally neglected, generally exploited."[34]

Ojike's text argued for an Africa that possessed a "respectable culture" with intricate kinship ties, fixed political and social codes, and sophisticated understandings of religion and ritual.[35] In the appendix, he included "Important Dates in African History" in which he traced the beginning of West African culture to 28,000 BC, preceding "the age of the Hebrews, the classical period of the Greeks, the commercial epoch of the Phoenicians, the expansion of the Roman Empire, the military and religious crusade of the Arabs, and the all-out European scramble for Africa . . ."[36] In comparing the texts of Williams and Ojike, King might have discovered that Williams's earlier text drew heavily from older European bibliographical sources such as David Livingstone's *Livingstone's Africa*, Henry Morton Stanley's *Through the Dark Continent*, John George Woods's *The Uncivilized Races of Man*, and William Winwood Reade's *Savage Africa*.[37] Ojike's bibliography, in stark contrast, cited numerous authors of African descent from West Africa, North America, and the Caribbean. Therefore, alongside noted white scholars such as Leo Frobenius, George Ellis, and Melville Herskovits were prominent Afro-scholars such as W. E. B. Dubois, James Weldon Johnson, Prince Nyabongo of Uganda, Trinidad's George Padmore, W. Tete-Ansa, Prince Orizu of Nigeria, Yoruba scholar Samuel Johnson, Alain Locke, African American ethnographer Eslanda Robeson, William Hansberry, and Howard University historian Carter G. Woodson.[38] Ojike annotated each source, indicating its utility to serious readers of African history.

Moreover, Ojike's treatise on religion argued for the integrity and legitimacy of African religions before the arrival of European missionaries and Christianity. In his chapter "Religious Life," Ojike provided a detailed account of traditional African religions, giving a systematic examination of its use of symbols, shrines, prayers, offerings, oracles, moral codes, and priesthoods. He refuted Western perceptions of African religions as "superstitious and confused"[39] and posited that "different faiths express and serve different peoples" and declared that "the African's is valid and effective for him . . ."[40] Ojike ended his discussion on religion with a strong critique of the presence of Western missionary Christianity in Africa. He accused the West and its missionary agents of "religious imperialism" that ultimately brought forth a "massacre of African religion."[41] He concluded that "this superimposed religion has not touched, and can never permeate the depth of the African mind because its practice and theories do not square with the fundamentals of African society. Yet it renders the African impotent because it imprisons his deeper culture."[42] King felt an affinity for Ojike's text and embraced the understanding that Christianity imprisoned the "deeper culture" of North American blacks with regard to Africa. In a rather lengthy quote, King revealed these impressions:

> Somehow I ran across a book called, *My Africa*, by a Nigerian Ibo named Mbonu Ojike. . . . He described Africa and then he came to the point on African religion and his writing suddenly became very emotional and he began to almost sermonize. He said that . . . religion . . . was the one area in which it was dangerous . . . to tamper with the African because the African was religious in all things. And then he went on to describe aspects of African religion. . . . One phrase which really struck me, which caused me to really go into deep thinking. He said, "Whether God created Man or Man created God is not yet clear or is still uncertain." And I said, "Wow, Man created God." And that really said to me at that age . . . that Africans had their own religion. And so gradually I became . . . disillusioned . . . with Christianity so that by the time I was eighteen I had reached the same kind of thinking that my brother had: "I'm not going to church anymore because that's not really African religion, they're not talking about an *African God* . . . "[43]

Reading Rogers, Williams, and Ojike had a tremendous impact on King in his early years as he began to reconcile notions of Africa and an African divinity. Years later he would employ similar textual strategies as a way of connecting a wider African American readership and audience to Africa and its divine expressions.

Africa as Sacred Symbol in Two Early Twentieth-Century Urban Nationalist Movements

Africa as both the seat of black American origin and the projected object of redemption and recovery has repeatedly found its way into African

American nationalist movements. Both nineteenth- and twentieth-century black nationalists looked to Africa as a means of healing the social, economic, and racial wounds of a community lacking concrete territoriality in America. Anchoring this text is historian of religion Charles H. Long's compelling argument that the image of Africa has been a complex and enduring symbol within African American religiosity. The next chapter examines this symbol in greater detail within the context of Harlem, New York. However, to begin this discussion Africa as a figurative trope has historically invoked the prospects of the continent, resolved questions of origin and descent, and emphasized the interconnections between power and land for African Americans.[44] Throughout their continuous presence in North America, it functioned as a potent source of racial validation and affirmation, territorial authority, and religious inspiration. For African Americans, both Africa and America emerged as "hermeneutical situations" out of which African Americans interpreted knotty issues of identity, ancestry, and human meaning.[45] Contemporary urban nationalisms attempted to address these issues in multiple forms.

At the dawn of the twentieth century, the Moorish Science Temple of America (MSTA) and the United Negro Improvement Association (UNIA) professed nationalist philosophies that viewed the continent of Africa as civilized antiquity, ancestral origin, and future redemptive host. Walter King was very much influenced by his parents' affiliations with these leading black-nationalist organizations, which saw Africa both northern and sub-Saharan as possible sites of recovery and repatriation.

In the early 1900s, North Carolinian Noble Drew Ali (then Timothy Drew) returned from Morocco urging African Americans to relinquish their "Negro" identity and embrace the Islamic religion of their Moorish heritage. By 1913, Noble Drew Ali, supported by his wife Pearl Ali, had founded the initial Moorish Science Temple in Newark, New Jersey, and from this temple emerged in rapid succession temples in Chicago, Pittsburgh, Philadelphia, and also Detroit, where Walter's father Roy King became one of its ardent followers.[46] By the onset of the Great Depression and Ali's death in 1929, it was estimated that some thirty thousand African Americans joined the MSTA.[47]

At the height of the movement, Noble Drew Ali authored *The Holy Koran of the Moorish Holy Temple of Science 7 Divinely Prepared by the Noble Prophet Drew Ali*. This "secret" text, with circulation only among its formal members, appropriated the image of the seven seals in the biblical book of Revelation and became a primary text for the newly proclaimed "Moors" of North America. Its intentional use of "science" in its name "clearly linked it to all the students of New Thought and Christian Science, the Gnostic Freemason and African American Spiritualist" of the nineteenth and twentieth centuries that collectively emphasized "the divine essence within" and that the notion of "power for divine transformation from a fall state is derived, not from God or Jesus, but from within each person."[48] In addition, some African Americans were heavily attracted to its notions of "mystical self-help" and its esoteric knowledge gained through spiritual readings and consultations, as well as to a pharmacopeia of healing oils and medicines.[49] Ali declared that North American blacks were no longer "Negroes, Colored Folks, Black People, or Ethiopians, because these names were given by slaveholders . . ."[50] They were now "Moors" and "must proclaim their free national name to be recognized by the government in which they live and the nations of the earth, this is the reason why Allah, the Great God of the Universe, ordained Noble Drew Ali, the prophet, to redeem the people from their sinful ways."[51]

The Moorish Science Temple is understood as "the first American black Muslim movement." It advocated a "religious nationalism that viewed Christianity as irrevocably white and held Islam to be the black man's true religion."[52] Christianity, maintained Ali, was used "to justify racism, discrimination, and slavery"; thus African Americans as a chosen people, "must maintain spiritual autonomy from whites."[53] The mythological world Noble Drew Ali espoused stated that black Americans were descendants of the "ancient Moabites" from north and southwestern Africa. These Moabites, or Moors, although possessing a history of New World enslavement, also possessed a "royal history" and a "glorious future." With an air of apocalyptical prophecy, Ali preached that "following the coming destruction of white people, the Moors will establish a world in which love, truth, peace, freedom, and justice will flourish."[54] According to Hans Baer and Merrill Singer, this philosophy was supported materially by an "array of national symbols, including a national flag, . . . a distinctive garb (red fezzes and long beards), a sacred book (a self-composed 'Koran'), and membership cards (which identified holders as Muslims 'under the Divine Laws of the Holy Koran of Mecca, Love, Truth, Peace, Freedom, and Justice.')"[55]

Ali structured an emic approach to African American self-knowledge that decentered birth origin and transformed geonationality. Conducting fieldwork less than fifteen years after the death of Ali, anthropologist Arthur Fauset began chronicling the origin, beliefs, and practices of the MSTA for his *Black Gods of the Metropolis.* In reading MSTA's sacred literature and conducting interviews with former followers, Fauset concluded in his 1944 study that religion and nationality were inextricably tied for Ali. In the formal charter of MSTA, Ali argued that "before you can have a God, you must have a nationality."[56] Subverting American allegiance, Ali declared that Morocco, and not Ethiopia, would be the African national self-reference for African Americans and that Islam would replace Christianity as their new religion. According to Fauset, Ali believed that Negro or black signified negative images of death and that "Colored" signified "something that is painted."[57] In defense of their new identity, Moorish Americans publicly flaunted their new identity and challenged civil officials in King's hometown of Detroit, where disturbances were reported with Moors who, "made conspicuous by their fezzes, walked the streets, treating white folks with open contempt."[58]

Thus, for a membership fee of one dollar, Roy King, Walter's father, entered into Ali's dissenting world of Moorish identity.[59] Members were given an ID card that read as follows: "This is your Nationality and Identification Card for the Moorish Science Temple of America, and Birthrights for the Moorish Americans, etc. We honor all the Divine Prophets, Jesus, Mohammed, Buddha and Confucius. May the blessings of the God of our Father Allah, be upon you that carry this card. I do hereby declare that you are a Moslem under the Divine Laws of the Holy Koran of Mecca, Love, Truth, Peace, Freedom, and Justice. 'I AM A CITIZEN OF THE U.S.A.'"[60] For many black-nationalist organizations like the MSTA, citizenship and nationhood were analogous. Moorish Americans existed within the political interstices of Moroccan allegiance while maintaining American citizenship. They eschewed interracial marriage. As Ali stated, "We, as a clean and pure nation descended from the inhabitants of Africa, do not desire to amalgamate or marry into the families of the pale skin nations of Europe."[61] Although African Americans would have consisted of a racial amalgam, Ali declared that the posterity of African descendants rested primarily on their future ethnic integrity.

External recognition was not an essential requirement for legitimating their new cultural and national status as Moors or North Africans. Therefore, it did not matter whether the Moroccan government officially recognized their newfound status, for like most black-nationalist groups, the MSTA sustained itself by its ability to maintain new identities through organized internal structures such as texts, beliefs, rituals, iconography, material artifacts, and designated bodily apparel. Ali's Moors used elaborate dress codes, attire, and accessories to fortify their Moorish identity. As indicators of "royal descent," they "donned fezzes, colorful gowns, and turbans and identified themselves as 'Moslem' in order to divorce black identity from black southern culture and the ostensible lawlessness, laziness, and immorality typically associated with it."[62] What was most paramount was that North African Moorish identity "provided a noble black heritage divorced from stereotyped images of the African savage."[63]

Because Walter King was never directly informed about his father's nationalist affiliation, two key pieces of material culture Walter accidentally discovered confirmed the connection between his then late father and the MSTA. According to King, while he was "rummaging around in [his parents'] dresser drawers" after his father's death he found "a tarbush in that collection of things. The tarbush, of course, had a tassel on it and that was based on the Turkish idea of what a tarbush was. I guess in more [recent] terms they refer to it as a fezz but at that time it was called a tarbush."[64]

The more meaningful discovery that King made attesting to his father's Moorish affiliation was the discovery of a picture postcard inscribed with words that Walter King later confirmed left an indelible and profound mark on his consciousness regarding Africa. The sender of the postcard was a friend of Roy King who had traveled to North Africa as a follower of Noble Drew Ali in pursuit of his Moorish roots. Upon arrival, he sent a postcard to King's father in Detroit. The postcard was addressed to Brother Roy King Bey and was adorned with a self-portrait of an African American man mounted on a camel in the midst of the Egyptian pyramids.[65] Summarizing his reflections on Africa and its effects on his psychoexistential identity, the friend wrote with profound vernacular simplicity, *"Here I is where I has longed to be."*[66]

Physical connections to Africa as a source of ancestral derivation and empowerment were foundational to Noble Drew Ali's movement, as well as to black-nationalist leader Marcus Garvey's thought. Although the national and international appeal of Garvey's movement by far exceeded that of Ali's, they each made similar appeals to a symbolic Africa of origin that could be recovered through expatriation. According to King, Ali and Garvey's movements had an overwhelming effect upon his parents. The history of these movements was contemporaneous with overlapping membership, as in the case of King's father. Moreover, if we assume that as a member of the MSTA Roy King had access to its *Holy Koran*, he would have read in chapter 48 Ali's prophecy that "in the modern days there came a forerunner who was divinely prepared by the great God-Allah and his name is Marcus Garvey, who did teach and warn the nations of the earth to prepare to meet the Prophet."[67] Walter King in later years speculated that in the end it was Garvey's movement that had the greatest impact on his parents, concurrent members of both the MSTA and the UNIA.

On August 1, 1914, the eighty-first anniversary of the emancipation of slaves in the West Indies, Marcus Garvey founded the Universal Negro Improvement and Conservation Association and African Communities League in Jamaica and called for African self-reliance and emigration.[68] Scholars see Marcus Garvey as among "the first to create a 'New Vision,' based on a revaluation of the African cultural heritage, as a source of inspiration to the blacks in America and in the world."[69] Born Marcus Mosiah Garvey in St. Ann's Bay, Jamaica, and a direct descendant of the Maroons, Garvey began his early life as a printer and a journalist.[70] Throughout the course of Garvey's career, his travels took him to places such as Costa Rica, Panama, Ecuador, Nicaragua, Honduras, Colombia, Venezuela, the United States, and London. In forming the UNIA, Garvey conveyed a vast pan-African vision and "an emerging self-awareness as an historically interconnected Afro-Atlantic people." According to historian Kim D. Butler, "Marcus Garvey was the first to address this new diasporan consciousness with the Universal Negro Improvement Association."[71] "Through the development of self-image, education, and cooperative economic activity," the UNIA would usher in the "redemption of Africa" and gather all its dispersed black citizens.[72] It revived many of the former black-nationalist sentiments of Garvey's nineteenth-century predecessors, particularly as it exalted Africa as the seat of black civilization and redemption.

By 1919, Garvey had moved his Caribbean headquarters from Jamaica to New York's Liberty Hall on 138th Street in Harlem. A year later, more than a hundred convention delegates officially signed the "Declaration of

Rights of the Negro People of the World."[73] Within five years of the UNIA's relocation to Harlem, local divisions and chapters began to develop in more than thirty-eight states.[74] According to Randall Burkett, Garveyism was "the largest mass-based protest movement in black American history."[75] Although the strongest of the UNIA's local U.S. chapters were located in New York, Chicago, Philadelphia, Cincinnati, Pittsburgh, Boston, and Cleveland, King's parents became members in one of its smaller chapters in Detroit.[76]

According to King, what interested his parents most about the philosophy and vision of Marcus Garvey was the possibility of leaving the United States and emigrating to Africa. Thus, King's parents were among the tens of thousands of African American investors who contributed to Garvey's vision of the "Empire of Africa" he hoped to establish near Liberia.[77]

Garveyism and Textuality

Garvey's interpretations of Africa and the foundations of his black nationhood were intricately connected to textual influences. Three literary sources that profoundly affected Garvey's nationalist thought were the Christian Bible, the writings of Duse Mohammed Ali, and the monthly London periodical *African Times and Orient Review*.

The Old Testament prophecy in the Book of Psalms, "Princes shall come out of Egypt; Ethiopia shall soon stretch out her hands unto God," became the biblical basis by which Africa was made sacred for Garvey. According to Burkett, "The concern for Africa that was so central to the UNIA, and the conviction that God was working in history through the instrumentality of the UNIA to create a nation, Africa, as a part of His larger purposes, rendered this verse from the Psalms uniquely appropriate to the Garvey movement."[78] Because of its prophetic centrality to the movement, Psalms 68:31 was emphatically reconstituted in UNIA liturgy, ritual, and catechism.

> Q. What prediction made in the 68th Psalm and the 31st verse is now being fulfilled?
> A. Princes shall come out of Egypt, Ethiopia shall soon stretch forth her hands unto God.
> Q. What does this verse prove?

A. That Negroes will set up their own government in Africa, with rulers of their own race.[79]

Although Garvey never wrote a formal theological treatise for the UNIA, he did make use of religious imagery and language within his own nationalist reflections. Religiously, Garvey "boldly posited a coherent theological system complete with a doctrine of God—a Black God, the express designation of which was to shatter old patterns of belief and to demonstrate the fact that all men, all Black men, are created in His image."[80] Garvey believed that for African Americans "participation in White religion and worshipping a White God was counterproductive."[81] With regard to religion, some scholars would argue that "the power of the Garvey movement was that it worked on many levels, and religion was a very important factor. He came to the poor Blacks of America as a Moses ready to lead them to the promised land. He argued that possession of a homeland for Blacks was inseparable from redemption."[82] On a broader level, Garvey appropriated the biblical themes of chosen-ness, divine providence, and promised land. Inserted within each biblical appropriation was Garvey's vision of a chosen African people who would be divinely guided by a black God and eventually repatriated to an African sacred homeland.

Supplementing Garvey's biblical extractions was the literature of African Sudanese writer Duse Mohammed Ali, author of *In the Land of the Pharaohs: A Short History of Egypt* and editor of the journal *African Times and Orient Review*. According to one historian, Garvey's "close association with Duse Mohammed Ali, Egyptian scholar and nationalist of Sudanese descent, helped to sharpen his ideas about African redemption."[83] Garvey's association with Duse Mohammed Ali began in 1912 in London, where Garvey began "meeting with African and West Indian students, African nationalists, sailors, and dock workers," delving "deeply into the condition of Africans under colonial rule."[84] The relationship between Garvey and Mohammed continued over the course of a year as they worked on the monthly British journal, *African Times and Orient Review*. Their working relationship briefly rekindled years later when Garvey sought Mohammed's literary advice on the *Negro World*, the official paper of the UNIA, which mirrored the original format of Mohammed's earlier journal.[85]

In 1911, Duse Mohammed published *In the Land of the Pharaohs* and as a result of Mohammed's participation in the First Universal Races Congress at the University of London the previous year, founded the monthly periodical *African Times and Orient Review.*[86] Influence from both documents can be found in Garvey's later work. Mohammed's full-length book was largely a commentary on anticolonialism and African nationalism. Mohammed's texts posited a global understanding of African nationalism that included the descendants of Africa in the Western Hemisphere. In his writings, he directly addressed African Americans in the United States and encouraged them to invest in the development of Africa. He also critiqued the United States for the treatment of its African citizenry, vehemently denouncing the country's practices of "color prejudice" and lynching.[87] According to Mohammed, "Lynching and burning of defenceless Negroes, who, in the sweat of their faces, have helped to make the power of the United States which is unable to protect them, convicts that Government of being 'incapable of guaranteeing even primary justice,' and exposes its Government before the civilised world as 'an empty and noxious farce.'"[88] Mohammed's *African Times and Orient Review* appealed to a black "trans-oceanic" readership that helped to foster a sense of global solidarity and nationhood among black people.[89] The journal's staunch critique of European colonialism in Africa helped to create a mood among its black readership regarding a presumed "solidarity among whites, which linked colonial rulers from different metropoles, whatever their rivalries and conflicts."[90] The stamp of Garvey's affiliation with the *African Times and Orient Review* was permanently etched on his later movement.

In 1917, the journal also included mention of one of Garvey's strongest inspirational figures in his early years, Booker T. Washington. The journal's endorsement for the *Negro Year Book*, published by Booker T. Washington's Tuskegee Institute, reads as follows: "One of the signs that the Negro is making progress is the fact that he is evolving a *literature*. When a race expresses its thoughts, emotions, longings, and aspirations in written words, it is immortalising itself."[91] Garvey was very forthcoming in revealing that the philosophies of North American Booker T. Washington stimulated his budding nationalist thought. "I started to take an interest in the politics of my country, and then I saw the injustice done to my race because it was black, and I became dissatisfied on that account. I went traveling to South and Central America and parts of the West Indies to find out if it was so elsewhere, and I found the same situation. I set sail for Europe to find out if it was different there, and again I found the same stumbling-block—'You are black.' I read of the conditions in America. I read *Up From Slavery*, by Booker T. Washington, and then my doom—if I may so call it—of being a race leader dawned upon me in London . . ."[92] In fact, Garvey and Washington corresponded with one another while Garvey was solidifying his early formulations of the UNIA in Jamaica. Garvey wrote a letter dated April 12, 1915, to Washington at the Tuskegee Institute notifying him of his impending arrival in America as a promotional tour for the UNIA. Garvey informed Washington: "I am expecting to leave for America between May and June and I shall be calling on you. I intend to do most of my public speaking in the South among the people of our race. I enclose . . . a manifesto of our Association which will give you an idea of the objects we have in view. I am now asking you to do your best to assist me during my stay in America; as I shall be coming there a stranger to those people. I need not acquaint you of the horrible conditions prevailing among our people in the West Indies as you are so well informed of our happenings all over Negrodom."[93] On April 27, 1915, Washington responded to Garvey's request: "I have yours of April 12th advising of your proposed tour of this country and of your plan to visit Tuskegee Institute while in the South. I am very glad indeed that you have decided to come here and it will give us all very great pleasure to make your stay as pleasant and as profitable as we can. Certainly I shall do what I can to help you while in this country. I thank you for sending me the statement outlining the aim and purpose of the Negro Improvement Association."[94]

In laying the groundwork for the UNIA, Garvey experienced the ideological influence of important figures such as Washington and Duse Mohammad as well as the transformative power of written texts. Texts were crucial in promoting Garvey's thoughts on African redemption as well as in concretizing his concepts of black nationhood. Milton Sernett asserts that the intensity of the readership of the *Negro World* became the key mobilizing agent in launching Garvey's mass campaign. In sum, he states that Garvey arrived in the United States in 1916 "unknown to anyone" and "did not capture much public attention until two years later when he began publishing *Negro World* and promoting his vision of black pride and unity."[95] Garvey's periodical attracted a global readership of some two hundred thousand throughout North America, South America, the Caribbean, Europe, and Africa. Its perceived subversive and controversial content sparked the attention of European colonial governments who banned its distribution in parts of Africa and the Caribbean.

Referencing Garvey's impact upon his parents, King remembers the cynicism with which his father spoke of racial issues and connects this cynicism in later years with his father's ideological affiliation with Garveyism:

> Well, now his conversation did reflect a lot of racism. I remember while we were up in the country, up at Kohopta, Michigan, that I came home one day and there was some phrase in one of my textbooks, "When the white man first came to America..." And I came back and my little brother and I kept repeating that phrase, "When the white man first came to America, when the white man first came to America, when the white man first came to America." And my father said, "What did he do? Raise the devil and still is!" And so right then and there was some type of reservation my father had about white people. And from time to time, I didn't know where it was coming from, didn't know the motivation behind his thinking.[96]

Historian Carl Hunt, writing in the 1970s in the early years of the American Yoruba movement, argued that King received an "early orientation into the Nationalist Movement because his father and his associates often took him to rallies and lectured to him on the condition of Blacks in America and their relationship to Whites."[97] Through his association with his father and his father's nationalist circle, King observed the deep disdain this elder group collectively felt for America. In one instance, a young Walter King asked one of his father's friends whether he was going to join the army and fight in World War II, to which his father's friend responded, "To fight for *this* country?" He then conveyed the sentiment to the young King that he should not be a "fool" and that ultimately "this country is not yours or mine."[98] It was this sense of landlessness and civil disconnect that made Marcus Garvey's philosophy attractive to King's parents and to countless other African Americans who sought meaning in the recovery of Africa. He recalls his mother referring to Garvey as a "very silver-tongued orator" who "could just rouse you to all kinds of emotions and consciousness..."[99] King's parents and intimate associates fervently believed in Garvey's vision of redemption and an African homeland. His parents were committed to the dream of eventually leaving Detroit and relocating to Garvey's new African republic. With the dismantling of Garvey's movement, the dream of King's parents to relocate to Africa never materialized. The legacy of Garvey extended beyond the life of the UNIA, however, and evidence of neo-Garvey movements would be found for decades to come. For Walter King, hearing stories about Garvey and other nationalist movements helped to raise his young racial awareness and positive curiosity about Africa. In his own reflection, he concluded, it fed "a kind of race consciousness that I was developing and increasingly I began to think in terms of Africa and wanted to know more about Africa."[100]

Africa, Dunham, and Black Arts

After graduating from Cass Technical High School in Detroit in the late 1940s, King and his classmate Crandall Eaton channeled their shared interest in Africa toward black arts. They joined a black-arts organization called the Pen and Palette Club the Detroit branch of the Urban League formed in 1928. There they focused their attention on the performing arts and according to King "became interested in relating our African awareness to African dance."[101] King and Eaton earned reputations for their interests in Africa. King recalls, "Since we were always trying to talk about Africa, Africa, Africa . . . we became known as the 'Voodoo Twins.'"[102]

Through the African arts of dance and music, King's love for Africa intensified. African dance especially allowed him to develop an orientation he called "Africanism." He studied dance more formally at dance schools throughout Chicago and Los Angeles and auditioned for the Katherine Dunham Dance Company. He was accepted and went to New York to the Katherine Dunham School.[103] Dunham's Dance Company, founded in 1931, offered an interpretation of Africa to black North Americans that challenged their pejorative images of the continent. Trained as a cultural anthropologist and mentored by leading scholars of her day such as Bronislaw Malinowski, Franz Boas, Margaret Mead, A. R. Radcliffe-Brown, and Robert Redfield, Dunham developed her interpretation of Africa based on her fieldwork in Jamaica, Haiti, Cuba, Trinidad, Martinique, and West Africa.[104] Claude Levi-Strauss once said of Dunham that she had managed to distinguish herself "not only as a dancer and choreographer but also as a solidly trained specialist . . ."[105] Dunham, moreover, was initiated as a Vodou priestess, or a *mambo-asegue*, what she understood as "the highest degree of the Rada-Dahomey cult."[106] Dunham was a student of noted anthropologist Melville J. Herskovits at Northwestern University, and her artistic work evidenced a close theoretical connection to Herkovits's interpretive philosophy on "origins" and the belief that "Africa" could indeed be found in its Atlantic diaspora. From Dunham's unpublished autobiography, Marta Vega cites one clear example of her inclusive notion of the New World's religious antecedents resting in Africa: "I am definitely *Yemanja*. She is my guide and my mother . . . Fortunately, there is no conflict between *Yemanja* sent out to sea in her gift-laden barque on the shores of Corcavado in Brazil, or a river whose name I do not know in Ibadan, Nigeria, or a leaky, Haitian boat sent out to sea, hardly seaworthy, with a time-worn *Yemanja* bedspread, or on my balcony at Leclerc in Haiti, or right here on my small altar in East St. Louis, Illinois . . ."[107]

Within this vein, Walter King attributes to Dunham his "first exposure to something genuinely African . . . She had some Cubans in the company; she had some Brazilians in the company; and she had some Haitians and these were all dark-complexioned people. . . . Each of them was showing what they knew or doing what they knew well . . ."[108] Within Dunham's company, King encountered priests of Cuban Santería, Brazilian Candomblé, and Haitian Vodou. Performances often included songs to the *orichas* and *orixas*, and King remembered that most strikingly they frequently concluded "with a dance to Damballah Hwedo in which a man got possessed, and he crawled all along the floor, and finally they gathered him up and on their shoulders, and he was still doing all these gyrations and sensuous like a snake and it ended on that."[109] Trance possessions were seemingly common at Dunham's performances, and according to Nigerian drummer, Babatunde Olatunji, "It happened one time to a whole dance company from Jamaica that came to perform with us . . . The entire dance company got possessed on me, right on stage, one right after the other. We had to stop the show . . . I had to stop my drumming and call for an intermission . . . When this happens I stop playing . . . I sprinkle water on them, read some incantations."[110]

In 1950, King left the Dunham Company and introduced the art of European ballet into his dance repertoire. During this period, he found the world of New York City's Greenwich Village quite exciting with its flavor of European art and literature and its bohemian culture, beginning what he called "a deep European period." An old acquaintance he knew from

Detroit introduced him to a young Dutch woman, Jennie DeVries, who made a career as a dancer, actress, and model in New York. In 1951, at the age of twenty-four, Walter King married Jennie DeVries. From this union was born a daughter, Tejla.

Ironically, it was within the context of an interracial marriage that King began to renew his interest in Africa. Africa functioned for King as an infusion of solid origins and a concrete source of inspiration for formulating self-awareness. Witnessing his wife's strong national and cultural self-understanding as "Dutch" gave King a desire for a more grounded identity. According to King:

> Somehow after I married the white girl, . . . it renewed my inspiration to be African again. I guess because she was Dutch and she *knew* she was Dutch. She used to use a lot of Dutch words in conversation. Her father, interestingly enough . . . was from South Africa . . . , but she *knew* what Dutch was. She would always be mentioning different things about Dutch people and the club they used to go to . . . in Detroit, and there they would celebrate their days and festivals. And so once again, that fire, that urge, that had vanished now made me want to know more about Africa and second of all to know as much about Africa and my nationality as she knew about hers.[111]

In King's own analysis of his marriage, he concluded that they "got along beautifully, she and I did, except that she had a nationality and I didn't have one."[112] The politics of race and color were to a certain degree downplayed in the marriage as King emphasized ethnicity and nationhood as concrete forms of identity. The scattered pieces of "Africa" King unearthed from his previous readings did not fully suffice in the face of his wife's solid sense of self. As a result, King looked to other sources and through his wife met an acquaintance named Harvey, who helped King to assuage the distance between the ambivalence in which he found himself and the identity world of Africa he desired. King noted that his journey toward Africa resumed after meeting Harvey, a member of the black-nationalist scene in Harlem. His exposure to the diverse nationalist landscape in Harlem marked a return to what King called the "Africa thing."[113]

Harlem, New York, and the "Africa Thing"

In the early years of the 1950s, King oscillated between attending various European bohemian activities in New York's Greenwich Village with his Dutch wife and participating in all-black-nationalist events in Harlem with Harvey. Over time, King began to spend more time in Harlem and attempted to fulfill his newly defined interests in African culture and religion by joining two neo-Garveyite organizations: the Afro-American Rotary Club and the Afro Arts Theatre Group. Dissatisfied with the former organization because of its lack of cultural intentionality, King left the organization and joined the Afro Arts Theatre Group. Again, King found the organization concentrated its efforts on a double-edged support of Garvey and the UNIA, on the one hand, and a political denigration of W. E. B. Dubois and the National Association for the Advancement of Colored People (NAACP), on the other. According to King, "I learned that their doctrine of course was that we shouldn't be in this country. We should be in Africa. . . ."[114] Unlike his parents, King found himself both a supporter and a critic of Garvey's philosophies. He "concluded that Garvey and most of the other Black leaders had failed because they had not given the people enough cultural background to draw from."[115] In King's point of view "Their understanding was simply economic. Garvey's was an economic plan. [The UNIA] had organized an Ethiopian Orthodox Church. That was nothing but just Baptist all over again. Nothing was changed, and they made no real cultural program."[116] Although Garvey's nationalist movement did not create an African cultural and religious transformation in the ways in which King imagined, it did pave the way for new interpretations of Africa and a useful category of a "black God." Remarking on this impact, historian Milton Sernett contends, "Garvey's deportation and the dissolution of the U.N.I.A. left a spiritual vacuum that groups filled in part with non-Christian teachings and practices."[117] Thus, decades after Garvey, the Yoruba movement in Harlem and the religious teachings of King (later Adefunmi) would broaden this "non-Christian" trajectory and incite a new blend of religion and nationalism.

Finding Africa in the Diaspora

International travel in the African diaspora was another way for King to understand Africa. Finding what he felt was some sense of Africa in Haiti in

1957 strengthened his connection to Africa as a religious and cultural idiom for African Americans. A year before his trip to Haiti, King and his wife had traveled to Europe and then on to North Africa. In earlier years, Egypt had been a symbolic center of his father's Moorish activity and was also the place where his father's friend had "longed to be." According to Hunt, although King's "experience with the Egyptian antiquities rekindled his desire to gain knowledge of African culture," it lacked the religio-cultural dynamism and concrete African spiritualities he thought characterized Haitian and sub-Saharan traditions.[118]

The African roots of Haiti, by contrast, offered a vibrantly religious and cultural alternative equipped with an established Vodou priesthood. Traveling to Haiti inspired King's "desire to become an African priest" and in his own words was "more popularly known as a place for the preservation of the African religion."[119] His textual encounters had introduced him to the religion of Vodun in West Africa, and as a result King saw Haiti as a viable option for exploring this West African transplantation. Though King's time in Haiti was limited, the power of its effect appeared limitless. Exposure to what he understood as the religions of Africa in Haiti made his textual readings come alive. His experiences in Haiti, along with his trip to Egypt, added texture and dimension to the Africa of his books. Upon his return to New York, King's collective experiences of reading, activism, the arts, and travel culminated in the formation of a new black religious organization, reflecting the diversity and eclecticism of King's Africa.

The Order of Damballah Hwedo Ancestor Priests

In 1956, the Order of Damballah Hwedo Ancestor Priests was established and became King's first effort in North America at harnessing an institutional approach to an African God.[120] Following his trip to Haiti, King became enthralled with the spiritual figure of Damballah, the Haitian snake god who represents a primordial returning to the ancestors. In the Haitian pantheon, Damballah's role is multiple. He is the oldest ancestral spirit and symbolizes those ancestral spirits whose specific ancestral lineage is transcended and no longer remembered.[121] When ritualized in Haiti, Damballah's invocation brings protection and venerates the spirits of enslaved Africans whose direct lineage from Africa was severed. Damballah as metaphor helps in understanding King's complicated relationship to Africa and to his American enslaved past. Its sinuous nature offered possibilities for shedding and renewal as well as death of one identity and the restoration and recovery of another. King transformed a small café he owned with his wife on East Sixth Street in Greenwich Village into a meeting place for the Order of Damballah Hwedo. The café, Port Afrique, became the residential host for the veneration of Damballah and the spirits of Africa and its diaspora.

The Order of Damballah Hwedo Ancestor Priests became an important forum for channeling King's textual readings, particularly his readings of Herskovits, into ritual practice. In two sections of Herskovits's *Dahomey* entitled "The Ancestral Cult: Deification of the Ancestors" and "The Ancestral Cult: Worship of the Ancestors," he describes the snake deity as representing "those ancestors who lived so long ago that not even their names are known . . . The Dahomean believes that it is impossible for any group of human beings to know all their relatives. As will be seen, he is fully aware of the fact of the slave-trade, and understands perfectly that many men, women, and children related to him were carried away to die in places unknown."[122] King and his organization of ancestor priests neatly situated themselves within this historical drama as the descendants of those Africans who had been "carried away" to "places unknown" during the transatlantic slave trade and developed crude ritual means with which to honor them.

The Order of Damballah Hwedo meshed patches of African culture and knowledge together into a spiritual tapestry. Sunday evening meetings were attended by fewer than a dozen people who shared an interest in the culture of Africa. Ritual space was centered around a Ghanaian stool mounted on a table and a displayed replica of a Haitian Vodou flag with an image of Damballah, the serpent. Ritual activity assumed the form of oral readings on various African cultures. Collectively, the group attempted to learn the Ghanaian language, Twi, and sought to learn cultural practices from the Ghanaian Akan and Fon-Yoruba traditions.[123] In the absence of African songs, group members recited poetry.

Race was an intentional element in the organization's membership. Because the members wanted to forge an exclusive religious space predicated on Africa, the order excluded all whites from attendance. A mutual agreement was reached among the membership that this exclusion would include King's wife. According to King, "No whites came. They weren't welcome at all. You could see already the problem there so my wife didn't even come. I never invited her because we were talking nationalistic things: racist, racist, racism, black, black, black."[124]

A major turning point in the organization occurred when King met Fritz Vincent, a Haitian actor performing with the National Negro Opera Company, who professed firsthand knowledge of Haitian religion and culture. The following year, Vincent became one of the organizational heads and concentrated the order's ritual practices on Haitian Vodou. By King's account, "because he was Haitian, he was much more African in appearance . . . and he said his grandmother was a mambo and had three worshipping houses in Haiti, and so assuming that he was much more familiar with the religion than I was, I made him the head of it."[125] Describing this period, Hunt stated that "the society flourished for a time. A number of shrines, altars, and statues from Haiti were built, and though attendance was small, the interest of the members was strong."[126] As a way of attracting a new constituency of African sympathizers, the group collectively decided in 1957 to relocate the Order of Damballah Hwedo to Harlem on the fourth floor of 303 West 125th Street.

The year 1957 was also an important transitional year for King, not simply because of the order's relocation to Harlem, but also because it was a year of both personal and international symbolic renaming. During this year, King rejected his birth name and adopted a new self-designated African one. Also, the first African nation, the Gold Coast, gained its independence and renamed itself Ghana, sending reverberations of independence and nationhood throughout African American communities in the United States. George Brandon summarizes this moment in King's life as "a period marked by much study of anthropological and political literature, attempts at liaisons with Haitian Vodou practitioners and the remains of the old Harlem Garveyite movement, and cultivation of personal relationships with Africans and people knowledgeable about African culture."[127]

For King, Africa was a continental resource that offered its distant siblings in America various ways of being authentically reconnected. Therefore, implicit in King's act of renaming himself was an understanding of the utility of ethnic pluralism in amassing an African identity. King's blend of ethnic languages to reinscribe his identity spoke to the disparate ethnic roots that comprised African American communities. Thus, Walter King would now be known to others and to himself as Nana Oseijeman

Adefunmi I. Nana he translated as "honorable chief"; Oseijeman, an Akan name he understood as "savior of the people"; Adefunmi, a Yoruba name that asserted royal lineage meaning "a crown for me"; and "I," which designated "the first" in this new African lineage in America.[128]

With a new name and a new location in the core of New York's black metropolis, Adefunmi began to use the streets of Harlem as a venue for advocating a revived African culture and religion. Encouraged by one of the order's members, Mama Keke, Adefunmi joined the public oratory platform in front of Micheaux's famous bookstore in Harlem. Like his counterparts, Adefunmi made "all kinds of nationalist speeches," increasing the visibility of the Order of Damballah Hwedo.[129] According to Adefunmi, exposure of the order in Harlem increased and even included a visit from Nation of Islam's Louis Farrakhan, then Louis X.[130]

During these early years, Harlem became an urban forum for an upsurge of the religious nationalism of both the Muslim and Yoruba movements. More broadly, religion and nationalism were played out in larger social arenas. Blacks in the United States as well as Africans worldwide redefined themselves using nationalist vocabularies, hoping to fashion new worlds and build new nations inspired by the independence of Ghana and later Nigeria, the Congo, Tanzania, Kenya, Senegal, and other African nations. The independence of Ghana in particular made a strong impression on Adefunmi. He recalls, "I just nearly went insane when it came out that Ghana was to become independent . . . I had read something about the Gold Coast in the *National Geographic* magazines, and so I had a special interest in the Gold Coast . . . the Gold Coast was going to become Ghana."[131]

In the wake of Ghana's independence, Adefumni played a larger public role on the stage of black nationalism in Harlem. He wanted to etch the moment of Ghana's independence into history through celebration. Along with Afro-American Rotary Club leader Simon Blye, Adefunmi helped to organize Afro-American Day, which later became African Freedom Day. In May 1957, Harlem celebrated its first Afro-American Day, featuring a parade, African garments Adefunmi personally made, and black nationalists on horseback—a tradition that continued annually in ensuing decades:

> I rented ten horses with my own money, cost me a hundred
> dollars, but I was determined to do something really big in

Harlem . . . Parades in Harlem were a pretty common thing and so I wanted a parade . . . I rented the horses, dressed the men up in turbans and robes, and they rode the horses through Harlem. Everybody thought it was a beautiful sight . . . We established the fact that blacks could ride horses, and they had other types of outfits . . . I remember some little boy asking me, "Are you all Bengali dancers?" And I said, "No, we're from Africa; we're Africans. . . ." And then the big deal happened, Kwame Nkrumah was coming to America . . . and he wanted to go to Harlem because he said he learned his philosophy of nationalism and freedom from the Street Speakers . . .[132]

According to Hunt, "The parade launched [Adefunmi] as a cultural leader, and from that point on, he was called upon to speak and plan various activities."[133]

African Americans like Adefunmi began to reframe their struggles against racial, social, and political discrimination in North America using borrowed global categories of colonialism and independence.[134] In his book, *Ebony Kingship*, Weisbord asserts that African Americans "were beginning to feel that they were involved in a larger battle. The partial freedom of Africa had augmented the black American's frustration and caused him to fuse his own struggle to that taking place in Africa. . . . Prodded and emotionally buttressed by political ferment in Africa, black Americans initiated and quickly escalated the process of redefining themselves within the American context and reassessing the relationships of Africa and its inhabitants."[135] Many African Americans in Harlem began to focus their attention on the global African world, resulting in the manifestation of African cultural and religious styles. Reporter Roi Ottley said of Harlem that "perhaps nowhere in America . . . is religion so extensively and so variously expressed. Cults of every description abound. Closed picture houses, dance halls, empty stores, and lodge halls are converted into places of worship."[136] Mary Cuthrell Curry in her book on the American Yoruba movement concurs: "African nations were gaining independence. New religious groups appeared on the scene that positively valued African origin and completely identified Blacks as of African origin. Blacks were Africans and this was something to be proud of. The two most prominent of these were the Yoruba Religion and the Akan Religion."[137]

Cristobal Oliana, the Emergence
of Santería, and Harlem's New Vision

Despite his rising public reputation, by 1959 Adefunmi found himself in intense conflict with the Order of Damballah Hwedo. Adefunmi's newfound commitment was to the restoration of African culture. He vehemently contested the organization's belief "that Black Americans could not understand and would not accept more than one god," retorting that "Blacks understood and accepted Christian emphasis on the Father, Son, and the Holy Ghost, as well as the Saints who numbered in the hundreds."[138] Before severing ties with the order in mid-1959, Adefunmi's religious and nationalist journey was drastically altered by an encounter with Cristobal (Christopher) Oliana, who was of Cuban and Curaçaoan ancestry.[139] According to Adefunmi, Oliana "sympathized with our aspirations, but at the same time being more familiar, as a Cuban, with a more purely African approach. He criticized us as well as encouraged me that if I really

FIGURE 1.
Cristobal Oliana (1924–1994), initiated in Cuba August, 1959. Courtesy of John Mason, *Who's Knocking on My Floor?: Esu Arts in the Americas* (Brooklyn: Yoruba Theological Archministry, 2003).

wanted an authentic African religion, I should go to Cuba."[140] Oliana introduced Adefunmi to a complex religious tradition that had undergone continuous change over time and had been a part of Cuba's cultural legacy for
centuries. Adefunmi's introduction to the religion commonly referred to
as Santo, La Regla de Ocha, Lukumi/Lucumi, or Santería, would radically
change the nature of Adefunmi's religious orientation of Africa in the aftermath of the Order of Damballah Hwedo.

Adefunmi's first ritual introduction to the tradition of Santería
was through Oliana and the ritual of divination. Divination in Yoruba-
structured traditions such as Santería uses natural elements such as palm
nuts, shells, coconut pieces, or metal as a way of accessing spiritual knowledge. It is not clear from Adefunmi's account what method of divination
was used to perform the rite, but it is clear that its impact upon him was life
altering. When Adefunmi met Oliana, he was someone "deeply involved
in Santo, the Cuban form of Yoruba worship which the slaves had brought
with them from Western Nigeria."[141] Oliana had traveled to Cuba on several occasions, "had an Elegba, which is an actual God, and had learned
to divine."[142]

Oliana exposed Adefunmi to an interpretation of Santería that he
understood from his immediate Cuban cultural context. For Oliana, this
included Roman Catholic iconography and saints; Adefunmi, however, who
wanted to emphasize the African in the religion, challenged the Roman
Catholic presence as a European colonial imposition upon the religion.
When Oliana revealed during the course of the reading that Adefunmi
needed to construct an altar for Shango, the Yoruba deity of thunder and
fire, Oliana assured him that the Roman Catholic image of Santa Barbara
would suffice as a valid representation for Shango.[143] Adefunmi recalls his
strong reaction to Oliana's counsel:

> Chris Oliana knew about *Santo*. He told me I should get a statue
> of St. Barbara. But, of course, at that time I was deeply involved in
> the Nationalist Movement of the 60's. So the mention of a thing
> called *Santo* which, of course, translated into English means saint,
> [and for us] who are raised in the Protestant religion and have no
> knowledge of Catholicism, to tell you that you must get a statue of
> St. Barbara, a saint, means that you are going to become a Catholic.
> So quite naturally I objected to this and refused to get involved with

it and told him: "No, I'm interested in *African* [religion]." But he
says: well, it is *African*! I say: "How can it be African and you want
me to get a statue of St. Barbara? This is not an African name. This
is not an African saint. And from the picture you showed me, this
certainly is not an African lady. This is not an African god. This is
a white woman!" And I refused to get involved with it. Finally, he
explained to me: This is just called *Santo*. This is a Spanish name.
It's got an African name. The African name is *Ocha*, he explained.
And all of the ceremony in it is all purely African.[144]

Nevertheless, Adefunmi's approach was antisyncretic and he refused to
display the Roman Catholic saint. He stated that "it would have been em-
barrassing if some of the people of my society and organization came to my
house and found I had an altar for Santa Barbara. They wouldn't have been
able to understand it. It took me a year before Oliana clearly described to
me that Santería had only a veneer of Christianity and that underneath it
everything else was purely African."[145]

For Adefunmi and Oliana, as for many African American practitioners,
purity and authenticity were not formally assigned, measurable standards.
They would shift and fluctuate along a spectrum of five major domains:
social and geographical contexts; competing ethnic orthodoxies; inherited
historical knowledge and local modes of authority; multiple claims of legitimacy; and exclusive citizenries.[146] As we will come to see in the chapters
that follow, purity and authenticity for African Americans like Adefunmi
would largely come to mean that which was more seemingly void of visible European influences and visual representation. More important, purity
and authenticity could foreseeably take on expanded meanings to include a
myriad of hybridized cultural elements across all African ethnic traditions,
not just Yoruba.

Over time Adefunmi became more and more convinced that Oliana's
Afro-Cuban religion appeared much more African than the diffuse elements and representations of Africa formerly used in the Order of Damballah Hwedo. Adefunmi saw a glimpse of Africa in Oliana's teachings
of Santería and understood the religion as possessing Yoruba provenance. The new religion held great potential and would become a workable resource for fertilizing Adefunmi's local adaptations of Africa among
African Americans. Therefore, despite the knowledge that the religion's

practice remained largely concealed and clandestine in the United States, Adefunmi began to envision Harlem as a viable setting where Africa could be publicly displayed. Harlem's ethnic populations, however, were in constant flux throughout the twentieth century, and not all would be in consensus with Adefunmi's tightly defined notions of race and Africa. Harlem was also home to a plethora of cultures and religions from various European and Caribbean locales. By the 1950s and 1960s, the ethnic communities in Harlem consisted of African American migrants from the southern United States; West Indian immigrants from various Caribbean islands; an increasing number of Africans from the continent; and residual pockets of European Italians. Into this multiethnic populace entered Cuban nationals.

The 1959 Cuban Revolution was the immediate occasion for the influx of countless immigrants into the United States.[147] Large numbers of Cuban immigrants resettled throughout major cities in the United States, with heavy concentrations in Miami, New York, New Jersey, California, and Puerto Rico.[148] According to American immigration statistics, Cuban immigrants who were upwardly mobile were more readily selected to enter in the United States.[149] Given the complicated history and social politics of prerevolutionary Cuba, occupational and class designations often corresponded directly with race and color distinctions. Sociologists Nancy A. Denton and Douglas S. Massey argue that in Cuba "racial identity forms a multicategory continuum" and that in general "race in the Caribbean is perceived as a spectrum running from white to black, with many falling in between."[150] In a rather shocking disclosure, anthropologist Sidney Mintz once called prerevolutionary Cuba "the most prejudiced country in the Hispanic-speaking Caribbean."[151] This highlighted the fact that Cuba was "dominated by a wealthy white elite"; where "social clubs, beaches, beauty contests, casinos and some sporting events were racially exclusive"; where "stores, restaurants and banks hired blacks only as cleaning help"; and where nearly 70 percent of the black population was not literate.[152]

Unlike the United States, the racial designation of "white" was quite complicated in Cuban society. Existing within this heteroprivileged racial category was an "intra-ethnic stratification" that accommodated rigid distinctions between "creole Cubans (white, Cuban born) and Spanish-born *peninsulares*, and *guajiros* (white small farmers)." These racial and social distinctions of whiteness (against a relatively fixed social blackness with respect to economic class) Lena Delgado De Torres ultimately roots in "the reproduction of colonial relationships" and the "coloniality of power."[153]

Describing an island whose population is 27 to 30 percent (and some scholars would argue as high as 50 percent) of African descent, Fidel Castro once remarked: "We are not only a Latin nation; we are also a Latin-*African* nation."[154] This understanding to some degree undergirded much of Cuba's foreign aid to African nations and the revolution's efforts to address "racial discrimination in Cuba" and "help to eliminate those prejudices and injustices that remain latent."[155] Before the revolution, Cuba's historical black population was quite diversified, when between 1921 and 1925 approximately 90,276 Haitian and Jamaican immigrants entered the island as laborers.[156] This figure rose to nearly 200,000 in 1931 as Jamaican, Haitian, Barbadian, and other Antillean blacks came largely as *macheteros* to harvest sugar cane.[157] By 1943, however, this number significantly declined because as labor needs decreased, Cuba instituted a "forced repatriation" of black immigrants to their former islands, barring attempts at permanent residency.[158]

Official census records for the island from 1899 to 1953 put the black Cuban population at 32.1 percent, or 505,443, in 1899. By 1953, however, this number is disaggregated into "Negro" and "mulatto" with a total representation of 27.2 percent of the Cuban population, or 1,568,416, persons.[159] According to Marianne Masferrer and Carmelo Mesa-Lago, Cuban's black population was "consistently overrepresented in menial, unskilled, low-paying occupations and underrepresented in better-paying, skilled, and professional occupations."[160] Heriberto Dixon characterized pre-1959 social relations as a "caste-like system" consisting "of occupational discrimination and segregation that had isolated [Afro-Cubans] from full participation in Cuban society."[161] Vices such as "prostitution, laziness, superstition, and criminality were said to have originated with Cuban blacks," and their religious associations were seen as "syncretistic and superstitious, if not demonic."[162]

Cuba's racial history was not without its violent uprisings and political upheavals. Black assertions of political and civil equality were met with violent civil responses in Cuba as early as the Aponte Rebellion in 1812 and then a century later in 1912, when Afro-Cubans formed the Black Peoples' Independence Party as a way of promoting the social and political rights of Cuba's prerevolution black citizenry. A political forerunner to the 1920s Afrocubanismo cultural movement, this twentieth-century

party was deemed illegal and officially outlawed in Cuba, inciting upris-
ing and rebellion among black Cubans. As a result, the Afro-Cuban leader
Evaristo Estenoz was publicly hanged, and scholars estimate a minimum
of fifteen thousand and as many as thirty-five thousand people were killed
during these uprisings.[163] In the postrevolutionary period of the 1960s,
the perception was that race and racial tensions had been transcended
in Cuba and that the populace was now unified under the national and
trans-racial banner of *Cubano*. Juan Almeida Bosque echoed the general
ideological sentiment on race in the 1960s when he stated that "there are
neither 'whites' nor 'blacks' in Cuba, only Cubans whose skin is lighter
and darker. The Revolution has put an end to all issues of 'race' or 'color,'"
which in many ways was an echoing of the words of José Martí a century
earlier: "More than white, more than black, we are Cubans."[164] Therefore, in
stark contrast to the social esteem given blackness and Africa within conceptions of nationhood among many of the black citizenry of the United
States, the secretary general of the Cuban Foreign Ministry, Juan Otero,
declared, "Cuba is not Africa and we *will not allow* any Negro to pretend
he is African. Cuban Negroes are *Cubans*; period! Those who are not happy
with being simply Cubans, preferring instead to be Negroes, may pack up
and go to Mississippi where they will be treated as such!"[165]

This national conception of socialist reform and racial democracy was
in complete opposition to that of the United States in the 1960s, when race
and racial ideology were the source of fermenting national and social discourse. Migration immediately following the island's revolution enabled
these Cuban racial and social tensions to be transplanted to the United
States and played out in ambiguous social contexts. Designating this immigrant group along racial lines, the 1970 U.S. Census stated that 93.5 percent
of Cubans in the United States self-identified as white as opposed to
6.5 percent who self-designated as black.[166] Residential patterns in the
United States would closely mirror these racial distinctions, with Anglo-
Cubans preferring to live in the Miami–Fort Lauderdale areas in Florida
(where less than 0.8 percent of Afro-Cubans resided by 1970) and most Afro-
Cubans statistically repopulating themselves in New Jersey and New York,
with the state of New York serving as home to "approximately 35 percent of
all black Cuban-Americans" or "the largest single concentration of black
Cuban-Americans in the United States."[167] Related to this issue, scholars
such as Heriberto Dixon estimate that the Cuban-American middle class in

the United States is approximately 92 percent white and conclude that this group, as opposed to Afro-Cubans, has been "more able than certain other Hispanic groups to align itself racially with the dominant cultural groups in the United States."[168]

Patterning the behaviors of previous immigrant groups to the United States, Cubans attempted to reestablish their religious identities by largely integrating themselves within existing religious communities in America and in particular American Roman Catholic parishes. This uneasy integration often meant that Cuban immigrants, particularly those in New York City, found themselves "extremely uncomfortable in the Irish- and Italian-dominated Catholic Churches. Discrimination, poverty, the language barrier, and the paucity of real efforts by the church to reach out and embrace them led many Cubans to view the church as rigid, unresponsive, and unable to help them in their daily ordeals."[169] In addition, the American Roman Catholic Church did not fully represent the complex religious identities many Cuban immigrants held, so as Miguel A. De La Torre explained, there was a sharp "difference between what was done at the Irish church down the street and what was done in our apartment."[170]

The religious orientations many Cubans transplanted often included the popular spiritual practice known as Santería. According to Steven Gregory, there were some tens of thousands of devotees of the Afro-Cuban religion on the island of Cuba.[171] Because of the religion's clandestine practice, however, it is difficult to state precisely what percentage of Cuba's Santería practitioners migrated to the United States, and to New York City in particular. What is certain, however, is that Santería or Ocha and its devotees began to make a visible imprint on the religious culture of New York City by the 1950s. De La Torre cautions scholars that before rushing to analyze Santería as a derivative of Nigerian Yoruba, a black Atlantic religious complex, or the resource for modern movements of religious recovery and re-Africanization, Santería must first be locally contextualized and seen as an "indigenous symbol of cultural resistance" and as a "genuinely Cuban religion rooted in the violent contact of separate religious faiths" that "contributes to a Cuban worldview on its own terms."[172] It is also a "popular religious complex" that shares religious space in Cuba alongside Roman Catholicism, Spiritism, Palo, and a lesser known Muertería or rituals communicating with the dead.[173] Moreover, as De La Torre, Hugh Thomas, and Carlos Moore document, Santería was also a force in Cuban sociopolitics before its arrival in the United States. In fact, it played a religious role during the Cuban Revolution as Pres. Fulgencio Batista in 1958 gathered all the prominent priests of Santería in Guanabacoa "at which many cocks and goats were sacrificed to appease the 'demon of war' believed to be spearheaded by Fidel Castro's army."[174]

The widespread presence of Santería in the United States is attributed directly to the four waves of Cuban immigration, with the first before 1959; the second between 1959 and 1962, resulting in an influx of 280,000 Cuban immigrants; the third from 1965 to 1973, with the arrival of an additional 273,000 Cubans; and the fourth from April to October 1980, which delivered some 125,000 Cubans (close to 40 percent black and mulatto) from Port Mariel.[175] Alternatively, Robert Farris Thompson characterizes the history of Yoruba-derived traditions in the United States by way of Cuban hosts as a "tale of triple diaspora" from Africa to Cuba and eventually through multiple migrations to North America.[176] For Thompson, North American exposure to the specific Afro-Caribbean religious culture of Santería began as early as the 1930s with Desi Arnaz, along with his musical devotion to the orisa deity, Babalu Aye. During this pre-1959 period, Portuguese native Carmen Miranda can be added to Arnaz as one of the musical pioneers in Afro-Cuban jazz: Tito Puente, Julio Collazo, and Chano Pozo, who were early forerunners in exposing Santería elements to a North American audience.[177] In fact Cuban percussionists Julio Collazo and Francisco Aguabella, who originally came to the United States to perform in the Katherine Dunham Dance Company, were viewed as among the few people in the United States "during the 1950s who understood the deeper intricacies of *bata* drumming."[178] Collazo is often viewed as "the catalyst for the development of ceremonial drumming in New York."

The earliest known *"ile* or house of Orisa worship" in New York City came with the arrival of Cuban babalawo Pancho Mora (Oba Ifa Moroti— "Ifa's knowledge pushes aside difficulty") in 1946.[179] Mora was among the estimated fifty thousand Cuban nationals who lived in the United States before the Cuban Revolution.[180] According to Stephen Gregory, Mora "reported that he had been charged by the *Asociación de San Francisco*, an organization of *babalawos* . . . in Havana, with bringing the religion to the United States during the 1940s."[181] Mora arrived in New York City in 1946 and remained there until his death some forty years later.[182] According to Brandon, "In 1954, Mora initiated the first *santera* in Puerto Rico.

He is credited with holding the first American *Santería* drum-dance in 1964, and he initiated priests as far away as Venezuela, Colombia, and Mexico."[183] He was one of among a first generation Cuban-initiated priesthood that included Juana Manrique Claudio, Leonore Dolme, Mercedes Nobles, Asunta Serrano, and José Manuel Ginart. Marta Vega gathered the following information from Mora during an interview shortly before his death:

> Ifa Moroti (Pancho Mora) was a practicing priest in Cuba before arriving in New York City. In an interview with Pancho Mora that I conducted in 1981, he indicated that he started practicing *Ifa* in New York City in 1950. His belief in this ancient tradition and his desire to maintain his belief system motivated his commitment to founding the first *orisa* community in New York City. He noted that his pioneering work was the base from which the tradition has grown to include thousands of initiates from all walks of life and ethnic groups. When interviewed, he had initiated several thousand godchildren from varied professions who reflect an international community. He traveled extensively to Latin America and nationally to perform rituals spreading the practice of *Santería*.[184]

Pancho Mora and his wife, Myrta Burgess, emerged as major figures in the larger Cuban orisa community in New York City and became the leaders of a religious house, or ile, with a vast, extensive membership. With their female counterpart, Mercedes Nobles, they were committed leaders of multiethnic religious houses whose membership included Cubans, Puerto Ricans, and African Americans.[185] Because of his level of ethnic openness, Adefunmi would later come to recognize Pancho Mora as his "Cuban godfather" and spiritual mentor in the United States.[186]

What is distinctive about early devotees of Santería, like Mora, is that they attempted to transfer the religious practices of their old religion to a new American space while simultaneously maintaining geographical, theological, and ritual loyalty and allegiance to Cuba. Throughout the 1950s and 1960s, Cuba remained the georeligious center of Santería's authority, even as its religious landscape steadily expanded throughout the United States.[187] Adefunmi would greatly challenge this authority. In the next chapter, I continue this discussion and posit that competing with the symbol of Cuba among its expatriates was the emerging cultural symbol of Africa among African Americans in Harlem. Africa, for nationalists like Adefunmi, became the symbolic core of a pervasive "protest culture" in Harlem while at the same time becoming a new theocratic center upon which religious identity and nationhood could presumably rest.[188]

CHAPTER THREE

Harlem Yoruba, Orisha-Vodu, and the Making of "New Oyo"

ৡৢৢৢৢ

"IT WAS OLIANA that first introduced me distinctly and definitely to Yoruba religion," reflected Adefunmi. Before meeting Christopher Oliana in 1959, Adefunmi's ritual and ceremonial practices represented an eclectic sampling of African cultural and religious customs derived through texts, travels, and the Order of Damballah Hwedo. After encountering Oliana and Cuban Santería, Adefunmi refashioned his cultural and religious practices based on his new understandings of Africa. The resulting reformulation eventually became "Orisha-Vodu," which combined an Africanized Santería with an Americanized racial nationalism. According to Adefunmi, "Among the Dahomeans, who subscribed to Yoruba religion during the reign of King Tegbesu, the Orisha are called the Vodu or Vudu," hence the derivation of Orisha-Vodu.[1] Orisha-Vodu was, in actuality, what Baba Medahochi labeled a "pan-African ritualistic system" that "equally incorporated" and "equally accepted" African sacred rituals and practices from Yoruba-Dahomean and Congo traditions.[2]

This socially indigenized understanding of Cuban Santería in America emphasized racial solidarity, racialized iconography, and ritual innovation.

Collectively the ritual, cultural, and esoteric practices in Shango and Yoruba Temples, the literary writings of Oseijeman Adefunmi, and later the creation of Oyotunji African Village became expressions of a new Yoruba traditionalism in North America. I devote this chapter to an exploration of this emerging new public and ritual traditionalism and its implications for fielding larger questions of religious nationalism, the institutionalization of religion, and contested notions of religious ownership and authority.

North American Initiates, Cuban Initiations

In Santería, Adefunmi saw a powerful connection between the Atlantic world and Africa and envisioned religion as an effective vehicle for harnessing this power. As Adefunmi would later explain, "Every culture is sustained by the religion of its people. For religion . . . is the ritual capsule containing the history, the laws, the customs, the cuisine, and the interpretation of cosmic and environmental phenomena of a people. . . . It is for this reason that the priests, or ministers, of every religion are in fact the custodians of a national heritage, including the religion, the local heroes, the arts, the political ideals, the architecture, even the vital geographical features of the lands of the particular spiritual allegiance."[3]

For Adefunmi, Santería offered access and opportunity to "re-enter the priesthood of the Gods of Africa."[4] Santería provided for Adefunmi, as a black North American, a deep existential knowing that extended beyond America, for, as Obatala priest and dancer Oladepo Adeyemi remarked, "Before slavery there was Africa."[5] As Joseph Murphy insightfully points out, for "Oseijeman Adefunmi and many African Americans, spiritualities from Africa offer a return to roots, an authentic religion for black men and black women that will free them from the tyrannies of white cultural values."[6] In many ways it was less of a return than a summoning—African Americans were not traveling to Africa to encounter the orisa deities; rather the deities themselves were summoned to North America to become the core of a new religious, cultural, and later institutional reflection for Adefunmi and Yoruba Temple.

In 1959, Adefunmi decided to undergo a formal initiation ceremony in Cuba in order to solidify his religious commitment to Santería, and Oliana, who had not been fully initiated, made a decision to initiate as well.[7] Oliana and Adefunmi arrived in Havana, Cuba, in 1959 and made their way to Matanzas, a center of Afro-Cuban culture. There they met Sonaga, the priest who would initiate them into the religion of Santería/Lucumi/Ocha and whose spiritual lineage traced back to the renowned Cuban Ferminita Gómez.[8] Oliana returned the following year later in 1960 accompanied by another African American from Harlem, Edward James, who would also undergo initiation and become a priest of Obatala.[9] Several years later, Adefunmi recounted the details of his initiation as one of the first black, non-Hispanic North Americans:

> When [Adefunmi] arrived at Havana, he was driven to Matanzas, which is known as "little Africa" because of the intensity of the Lucumi, Dahomean, and Congolese religions preserved there. From that moment on, his great spiritual sojourn took him into a mysterious labyrinth of occult tunnels and corridors through which a man must pass in search of a Racial Soul. For this former black Christian American, the journey "back to Africa" began with a ritual death during which he was snatched by a Cuban priest and wrapped in a white shroud and told to become speechless. He was then taken to the simulated graveyards to greet his family ancestors and to thus consider himself a spirit. As a spirit he was guided in the night to a river where a fowl was sacrificed and the blood drained over a dish of food which was offered to the Spirit of the River. He was then literally stripped naked by priests who tore his clothes to shreds, and casting them to the river, commenced to wash away all of his previous life. When he emerged from the dark river, he was guided (shrouded from head to ankles in white cloth) back along a winding dusty road to the temple of the African God who was to "resurrect" him, and give him a new life with a new purpose.[10]

Adefunmi's initial reaction to his initiation in Cuba was one of bewilderment and nescience. According to Carl Hunt, one of the North American Yoruba movement's earliest chroniclers:

> The shock did not come until after the ceremony because [Adefunmi] could not really see everything while he was being initiated. He could see the bringing in of goats, rams and pigeons

to make up the various gods and the blood being poured in and on objects. But he could not see what was in the pot given him containing his gods. . . . "I remember the shock after the initiation rituals were over and we were preparing to leave the Temple and return to America, our God father told us to open our pots and see what we had and there was nothing in them but stones. And I thought, Oh My God! You mean I spent two thousand dollars for some stones to take home to my wife; and there was embarrassment and shock at the same time." Although this was a setback, it proved to be only momentary. He was too deeply involved, and the enthusiasm of the crowd was so great when they were leaving the Temple with their singing and chanting, that he realized he had found what he had been seeking.[11]

When Adefunmi returned, a novice in the religious world of Santería, he was no longer exclusively a member of an African American racial community in Harlem. He was now a part of a wider Cuban religious lineage and spiritual priesthood.

As an African American born in the United States of non-Hispanic origin, Adefunmi faced two major challenges upon his return from Cuba. The first was the difficulty of receiving religious training and tutelage in the United States, and the second was the barrier of language that estranged him from the local Cuban priesthood. In Cuba the person who facilitated one's initiation became one's "godparent" and would assume responsibility for the initiate's religious education and spiritual development. Newly initiated North Americans into Santería were often separated from their godparent(s) by considerable distance. As a possible solution to this problem, Oliana directed Adefunmi to Pancho Mora, whom Adefunmi came "to regard . . . as a kind of American godfather."[12] Because the Spanish language was so deeply inscribed within the religion, however, African Americans in the United States were potentially alienated from its inner knowledge and complex theological workings. In his analysis of language and nationalism, Benedict Anderson concluded that "bilingualism meant access," and in the case of Santería the absence of bilingualism meant that deeper access to Santería was often blocked to Anglophone African Americans.[13] Adefunmi therefore commenced to engage in rigorous self-teaching. According to Adefunmi, "Oliana taught me a system of using the

merindinlogun system, but adding four more *odus* to it, which made it sixteen, which meant that we could read sixteen different *odus*. They weren't
precisely the *odus* that I use now. But I did make myself on one occasion
use four pieces of coconut shell because anyone slated to be a *babalawo*
couldn't use cowrie. . . . So I made myself a crude *opele* and with *opele* then
I began to train myself how to read the sixteen different falls of those pieces
of coconut."[14]

Adefunmi stated that despite these early obstacles, the experience of
initiation gave him a feeling of liberation and brought concrete meaning
to his spiritual and former literary quest for an African God. Ultimately,
he realized that "all revelations would not come from an academic study
of African religion, no matter how exhaustive; rather they would gradually be discovered through the actual practice of the rituals and lifestyle of
an African civilization."[15] Adefunmi envisioned new possibilities for his
newly found religion, believing that "if African American people were to
embrace it, it would fire up the mind, imagination, economic, and political
system thereby transforming us into becoming a new dynamic people."[16]
In 1959, Adefunmi's efforts helped to bring about a "segmentation of the
religious community along new ethnic and social lines forging a space for
African Americans in the world of African gods."[17] Working collabora-
tively with Oliana, they established new North American religious institutions that served to honor the Africa gods they had received in Cuba.

Shango Temple: Competing Ideals of the Orisa

In 1959, Christopher Oliana and Oseijeman Adefunmi established Shango
Temple at 71 East 125th Street, whose mission was to "bring the Gods of
Africa to the people of Harlem."[18] They transformed space in a Harlem
brownstone into a ritual site where they could introduce the orisa deities
to the Harlem community.[19] Within Shango Temple, Adefunmi and Oliana
wore the colors and beads associated with their particular African deity
and performed several basic ceremonies and services. Given their novice
status, however, they were unwilling to perform full initiation rites for
new devotees. Those interested in being initiated into the religion through
Shango and later Yoruba Temples were directed to santeras like Mercedes
Nobles and Asunta Asunción Serrano.[20] Serrano, who self-identified as an
Afro-Puerto Rican, was a priestess of Obatala who migrated from Puerto

Rico and resided in New York City. A divination reading given to her at the time of her initiation in 1958 indicated that she was destined to initiate non-Hispanic black North Americans into the religion.[21] During the 1960s, she initiated many African Americans in New York into Santería, in addition to several white Americans, most notably Judith Gleason.[22] Like Pancho Mora and Mercedes Nobles, who initiated close to three dozen people in the United States, Serrano went on to form thriving multiethnic and multiracial spiritual houses in New York that served both Hispanic and African American communities.[23] Serrano, along with Mercedes Nobles, Leonore Dolme, and Juana Manrique Claudio, were Latina priestesses who remained committed to the initiation of non-Hispanic U.S.-born African Americans.

Through the combined efforts of Oliana, Adefunmi, and Serrano, Shango Temple was becoming a concrete religious institution in Harlem, where African American nationalists and supporters like Lloyd Weaver could obtain African names and gain important knowledge of the orisa.[24]

FIGURE 2. Entrance to King Shango.
The figure of Shango was an important source of inspiration
in Harlem. Photograph courtesy of Klytus Smith.

Adefunmi and Oliana did not fully agree, however, on Shango Temple's focus and direction. Adefunmi was in many ways unyielding in his vision that Shango Temple should link African Americans in the United States to the gods and culture of their ancestral homeland, Africa. As such, the temple's emphasis should be on Africa and African gods, not on Cuba and cloaked Roman Catholic saints. Oliana, of Cuban descent, was not so willing to discard Cuban influences that had so heavily defined the religious culture. With its overall vision and purpose unresolved, Shango Temple closed its doors to the Harlem community in less than a year. Despite disagreement, Oliana and Adefunmi would continue to sustain a relationship of collaboration and support in the future. By 1960, Adefunmi went in search of a new spiritual home in Harlem devoted to an African God and its spiritual manifestations. With the rising tide of 1960s black political mobility worldwide, Adefunmi began to seek deliberate, purposeful ways to infuse black-nationalist philosophies with a determined spiritual and cultural orientation toward Africa.

Religion, Race, and Africa of the 1960s

More than forty years ago, historian of religion Charles H. Long began laying the intellectual foundation for serious scholars of religion to interrogate "Africa" as both historical reality and religious image in African American religious life. "Africa," when examined as an interpretive framework for theorizing black religion, probes complex themes of ancestral origins, religious and racial meaning, and prophetic models for black rehumanization. Throughout the centuries leading up to the 1960s, African Americans had looked to Africa as the ultimate symbolic source for racial validation and affirmation, territorial authority, and religious inspiration.[25] Long contends that "the image of Africa, an image related to historical beginnings, has been one of the primordial religious images of great significance. It constitutes the religious revalorization of the land, a place where the natural and ordinary gestures of the blacks were and could be authenticated."[26] From the earliest movements to the 1960s, Long concludes that "one can trace almost every nationalistic movement among blacks and find Africa to be the dominating and guiding image."[27]

Over time, Africa became for African Americans part of a larger system of symbols involving primordial origins, historical subjectivism, and ontological authentication. For nationalists like Adefunmi, this system provided expanded notions of lineage and genealogy, a renarrativized history, and a deepened ancestral association. The geo-symbolism and meaning of Africa created a unique "homeland-diaspora mode of existence" arguably dissimilar from that of other American immigrant communities in that the homeland was not one specific nation or state but an entire continent.[28] As descendants of diasporaed captives, the understanding, as Michael J. C. Echeruo explains, is that African Americans "once had a home of their own, a nation, if you like, but nevertheless a convenanted forever home, a site . . . which is theirs, inalienably."[29] In line with Charles H. Long's theoretical reflections, Echeruo concludes that "this home, this land is not important only as a physical space; it is even more important as the source, root, final location for a determinable lineage. No person can claim to be part of a diaspora who cannot, however improbably, claim also to be traceable by descent to a lineage and (hence) to a place."[30]

The Africa of Adefunmi and 1960s Yoruba Americans was not quite the same Africa as that of their nineteenth-century predecessors, who saw in the distant continent potential for racial uplift, black economic development, and Christian sovereignty. Both nationalist generations negotiated the ambiguous question of indigeneity, which allowed for the validation of ancestral birthright, the legitimization of transnational belonging, and the normalization of cultural ingenuity. Adefunmi's Africa, however, grew firmly out of the context of 1960s expressions of black nationalism, which required at that time no mass exodus to the continent, but instead the mining of its cultural, religious, and psychical resources in order to rehumanize and rehistoricize blackness in North America.

Determinations of how meaning would be expressed toward Africa would largely be "shaped by voids as well as solids."[31] The void representing historical cleavage from Africa would be symbolically solidified by employing cultural selectivity, rehistoricizing one's identity, and establishing new processes of traditionalization.[32] Adefunmi sought to bring new meaning to the history and culture of Africa and illustrate its immediate relevance to African Americans in Harlem. He engaged in deliberate institutional, ritual, and literary ways of "traditionalizing" Yoruba culture in the United States, exemplifying Dell Hymes's belief that in "unofficial cultural processes people validate practices, ideas, and activities by naming them traditions from a heritable, shared past."[33] Adefunmi's challenge, however, was in developing a nationalist strategy based on new modes of African traditionalism that would be attractive to an American black constituency, most of whom, according to Robert Hood, only a decade previously in the 1950s "could not name an African country or territory on the continent."[34]

Given the broad range of black nationalism, it is difficult to precisely locate Adefunmi along a territorial, cultural, or revolutionary continuum, particularly given his positioning of religion as a fundamental ingredient of his political and cultural nationalism. He explained: "The reason I had gone into Voodoo was based on my nationalist philosophy in which I had conceived the notion that it is through religion that a people preserve their culture."[35] Driving much of Adefunmi's interpretation of Santería was "an attempt to culturalize the black-nationalist movement."[36] As an emerging cultural leader, Adefunmi viewed Africa as a source of religious and territorial inspiration, placing him in a succession with African Americans who for centuries had related to Africa in fundamentally nationalist ways.

Understanding the African American Yoruba movement as an aspect of religious nationalism encourages scholars to rethink and to retheorize black nationalism beyond the traditional sociopolitical frameworks. Moreover, what is of great interest to me in a discussion of religious nationalism is how African Americans in the 1960s used religion along with their symbolically reclaimed African identities as a theoretical canvas for encoding black nationalism within the context of a Yoruba movement. I identify at least five critical ways in which Adefunmi and his followers were able to formulate important geographical, bodily, hermeneutical, and literary sites for reinscribing their nationalist selves. First, group origins and identity were rehistoricized and navigated away from slavery and America and toward Africa. Second, African Americans became bodily hosts of visual and material culture. Natural hairstyles, African garb, African bodily ornaments, and African religious rites became physical indictors of African distinctness. Third, America in the 1960s became what Charles H. Long calls a "hermeneutical situation" out of which African Americans began to explore and juxtapose new models of sacred reality and nationhood.[37] Fourth, African Americans subverted pejorative categories of race so that race no longer existed as a category of exclusion from American society but as a signifier of inclusion into a wider African community. Finally, new literatures of protest were created as a way of challenging old orthodoxies and encoding new historical identities. The latter point I address in more detail in the next chapter.

Religion, nationalism, race, culture, and new ways of historicizing became inseparable in Adefunmi's thinking. He sought to develop "a religion of revolution" and embodied the challenge Hayward Henry Jr. put forth a few years later: "How do we nationalize the black spirit (spiritual Nationalism) into an institutional form . . . that speaks to the need for black revolution?"[38] In many ways, Adefunmi overlapped with previous black-resistance movements that historically organized their protest and nationalist platforms around religion.[39] What distinguished Adefunmi, however, was his firm belief that African-based religions, not Christianity or Islam, were the sole, redemptive spiritual resources for African American people. Through the use of symbol, style, history, literature, dress, hair, language, music, culture, and religion, and an emphasis on the radical interconnections of race, religion, and nationalism, Adefunmi attempted to generate a new system of meaning through Yoruba Temple that would revalue Africa, revive its culture, and spiritualize its traditions.[40]

Yoruba Temple, Orisha-Vodu, and the Localization of the Orisa Tradition in Harlem

In 1960, the establishment of Yoruba Temple at 28 West 116th Street in Harlem marked the beginning of a new era of African American agency within the orisa tradition and provided the institutional legitimacy through which African Americans "claimed their right to embrace African culture."[41] It was no secret that Yoruba Temple interpreted Cuban Santería broadly, adapting the pan-Yoruba religious tradition for specialized local use. In August 1961, Harlem's *Amsterdam News* called Yoruba Temple the "Center of African Culture."[42] "In addition to Voodoo ceremonies held every Friday night," the article related, "the Temple offers courses in African language, history, dance, drums, and African singing."[43] Yoruba Temple's vision of intentional indigenization of Yoruba religion in the United States appeared to Adefunmi's Anglo-Cuban counterparts as an attempt to dislodge the reins of religious authority out of Caribbean and Hispanic hands into that of black North Americans, symbolically elevating Africa and African-style culture to a place of standardized authority within the tradition.[44]

FIGURE 3. Bus advertising Harlem's Yoruba Temple.
Photograph courtesy of Klytus Smith.

Therefore, Yoruba Temple in some ways stood at the heart of religious contestation between Cuban and African American communities in Harlem and emerged as an important local attempt at autonomy and institutional agency. Through the activities of cultural production, public ceremony and ritual, divination, and print media, Yoruba Temple began the process of localizing the African gods in Harlem. Its primary task was to ritualize and propagate for its African American followers an identity, culture, and religion that emphasized what Djisovi Ikukomi Eason calls its preslave, rather than a slave-associated, past.[45]

By 1960, Yoruba Temple was officially incorporated as the African Theological Archministry Inc. An official charter was drawn up by Trinidadian lawyer Counselor Butts,[46] notarized by Isaac G. McNatt, approved by New York Supreme Court justice Edgar J. Nathan Jr., and endorsed on February 27, 1960, by the following signatories: Oserjeman King (Adefunmi), Clarence Robins, Henry J. Maxwell, Royal G. Brown, Richard Washington, Mary Bennett, and Christopher Oliana.[47] Also among the original temple founders was Mama Keke, but because she was a foreign national of Barbados, she could not officially endorse the legal charter.[48] For a filing fee of forty dollars, the organization was incorporated under article nine of the Religious Corporations Law of the State of New York in 1960. According to its original act of incorporation, the African Theological Archministry Inc. had a fourfold purpose:

> (a) To study and propagate the indigenous religion and philosophy of Africa, especially as developed by the Yoruba philosophers; (b) to teach and promote the ideal of the One Supreme Being who rules the Universe, and who manifests himself through Great Souls and in various forms of Nature; (c) to organize, develop, and maintain temples of worship in various parts of the United States and other countries; and (d) to create and foster the development of various religious orders, either of priests or of laymen, for the furtherance of the other purposes expressed in this certificate.

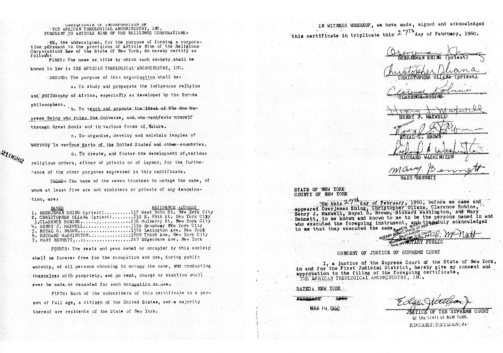

FIGURE 4. Original certificate of incorporation of the African Theological Archministry Inc., February 1960. Courtesy State of New York Department of State.

As a subsidiary of the African Theological Archministry, Adefunmi also formed an educational component known as the Yoruba Academy. Under the auspices of the academy, classes were offered at Yoruba Temple in African languages, Yoruba sociology, Orisa culture (both Nigerian and Dahomean), the cultures of Edo and Akan, and the study of Yoruba marriage and polygamy.[49] They read texts such as E. A. Ajisafe Moore's *Laws and Customs of the Yoruba People*, which became "une sorte de livre sacré," or sacred text of culture in Yoruba Temple.[50] Equipped with official legal status, the priesthood of Yoruba Temple, along with its founder, Adefunmi, set about the task of forging a new era in Harlem's black religious history that paid tribute to the gods of Africa and sanctioned its ancient cultural productions.

Adefunmi immediately launched a campaign to make Harlem the center for a "New Africa" in America. In order to engrave this "New Africa" into the minds of African Americans, Adefunmi declared in 1960 that the upper East and West sides of Harlem, New York, would be renamed "New Oyo." Naming Harlem after an ancient Nigerian kingdom enabled it to become a new "metaphoric landscape" for resisting the negative ascriptive identity of blackness in America.[51]

Benedict Anderson sheds an interesting light on this complex notion of reinscribing physical geographies as "new." He documents among Europeans the complex phenomenon of designating physical spaces or emerging nations as "new" in the hopes of establishing a renewed sense of historical connection and continuity. According to Anderson, "In the sixteenth century Europeans had begun the strange habit of naming remote places, first in the Americas and Africa, later in Asia, Australia, and Oceania, a 'new' versions of (thereby) 'old' toponyms in their lands of origins. . . . It was not that, in general, the naming of political or religious sites as 'new' was in itself new. . . . But in these names 'new' invariably has the meaning of 'successor' to, or 'inheritor' of, something vanished."[52] The naming of Harlem as New Oyo symbolized for Adefunmi the restoration of the "vanished" ancient Yoruba kingdom of Oyo in West Africa. Years later, when asked why he privileged Oyo over other Nigeria provinces (for example, the spiritually endowed Ile-Ife), Adefunmi responded, "Well, mainly because of all the books that I had gotten a hold of in the . . . 1960s. I had gotten a hold of [Samuel] Johnson's *History of the Yoruba*, and of course his whole treatise was based on Oyo, since he was an Oyo man and his *History of the*

Yoruba was mainly the history of Oyo and its conquests. So that was what instilled in my mind that this was the great capital and the focus of glory of the Yoruba. So if we wanted Harlem to become the same kind of thing, a great citadel of Yoruba culture, well then I should call it New Oyo."[53]

New Oyo would be the seat of cultural recovery for the millions of Americans of African descent who had systematically lost their identity during slavery and assumed the nonhistorical identity of "Negro." Adefunmi found it quite unsettling that "in America, all Africans, whether from Ashanti, Dahomey, Yoruba or Congo, were termed negroes."[54] To him, the label "Negro," as haphazardly conferred upon "Africans" in America, was devoid of a concrete historical connection, for it fostered an identity among North American blacks that left them totally alienated from Africa. He therefore made a conscious decision to "avoid the use of the term 'Negro' to designate Africans," describing it as "being of vulgar origin and representing no true cultural or anthropological type."[55] After African Americans received knowledge of the gods of Africa and the culture of the African continent, it was Adefunmi's understanding that a restored African subjectivity would replace that of the American "Negro" and his inferiorized social status. New Oyo would thus provide the landscape from which a new community would emerge, "constructed symbolically" around a new set of assumptions surrounding both Africa and America.[56] In renaming Harlem's landscape he hoped, as R. J. Zwi Werblowsky similarly argues in *Sacred Space, Shrines, City, Land*, to figuratively transform the meaning of Harlem's local cosmography and landscape in the "mindscape" of African Americans.[57]

Harlem's Yoruba Temple fostered a complex group of members, clients, participants, and audience. On some occasions as many as several hundred people were in attendance at its rituals, ceremonies, and rallies,[58] including a small supportive group of Afro-Cubans and Afro-Puerto Ricans who frequented the temple, appreciative of its vision of reorienting the religion toward Africa and embracing their spiritual heritage.[59] Along with Adefunmi, temple members coordinated ceremonies, developed an academic curriculum of courses, engaged in drumming and dance performances, executed rituals, and saw to the daily maintenance of the temple. Although membership records of Yoruba Temple are sketchy, one source described a core membership and ardent supporters of fifty persons, some of whom included Mama Keke, Orisa Mola Akinyele Awolowo, Bonsu, Olanyan, Adeyemi, Phiankhi

Akinbaloye, Kuma Omolade, Olobunmi Adefunmi, Majile Olafemi, Asunta Serrano, Abiodun, Abiola Sinclair, Alfred Davis, Lionel Scott, John H. Clarke, Conrad S. Peter, and Queen Mother Moore.[60]

What is most symbolic about Yoruba Temple was its ability to attract a richly diverse diaspora constituency represented by places such as the United States, Barbados, Panama, Cuba, Haiti, Trinidad, and Puerto Rico. Although these disapora locales did not exactly mirror the racial politics of the United States, they nonetheless were historical and social contexts where complex modes of discrimination had in some way been enacted against people of African ancestry. Thus, North America's Yoruba Temple could appeal to someone like Yeyefini Efunbolade, who was born in Panama and suffered under the local association of "Chombo" or "nigger," which she said "signified shame and social alienation that was associated with my dark complexion." For her, affinities to African and Yoruba culture offered her "liberation from the feelings and thoughts that kept me trapped in a 'Negro' world of insecurity, shame, guilt, and confusion."[61]

During the temple's ten-year life-span, the number of African Americans who formally underwent initiation was relatively small. According to Adefunmi, "There were only three or four of us at the most . . . [who] had gotten initiated in the early sixties." José Manuel Girat, who migrated to New York from Cuba in 1959, "estimates that there must have been about thirty people he knew at the time initiated into the religion."[62] Initiation was not the only way to access the religion of Yoruba Temple, though; many in the New York community and beyond felt comfortable tapping into its cultural, ceremonial, and spiritual resources without it.

Adefunmi's religious and cultural message of African nationhood proved extremely attractive to African Americans involved in the political and social dimensions of black nationalism. Like Adefunmi, prominent black nationalists such as Malcolm X of the Black Muslim movement and Trinidadian-born Stokely Carmichael of the Black Power movement championed this connection of African Americans to Africa in the larger American arena. In a speech given in October 1969, in honor of the Malcolm X Liberation University in Durham, North Carolina, Carmichael declared: "Now, we must recognize that black people, whether we are in Durham, North Carolina; San Francisco, California; Jamaica, Trinidad, Brazil, Europe—or on the mother continent, that we are all an African people, we are Africans, there can be no question about that. We came

FIGURE 5. Chief Orisa Mola Akinyele Awolowo, original member of
Harlem's Yoruba Temple, who would later become one of the first initiations
performed at Oyotunji African Village. Photograph courtesy of University
of North Texas Press. Originally reproduced in Rod Davis, *American Vodou:
Journey into a Hidden World* (Denton: University of North Texas Press, 1998).

from Africa, our race is African. The things that always distinguish us from
white people—Europeans—are all African things."[63] As J. Lorand Matory
explains, "The Black Power Movement of the 1960s, resurrected and popu-
larized Africa-centered idioms of Black political unity," and Yoruba Temple
flourished in this trend.[64]

Overall, however, in the 1960s Yoruba Temple was part of a larger black-
nationalist "counter-movement" that sought to move "away from subordination to independence, from alienation . . . to self-affirmation."[65] African
American Yoruba priestess Majile Olafemi Osunbunmi recalled that what
led her to Adefunmi's Yoruba Temple in Harlem and later to initiation
was a simple inner affirmation that she knew "she was just African." As
Kim D. Butler insightfully suggests in theorizing this phenomenon within
black diaspora communities of the New World, "African identity became
an articulation of personal choice, rather than an indicator of birthplace."[66]
By the mid-1960s, African Americans had embraced the maxim W. E. B.

Dubois had put forth some four decades earlier in *The Crisis*—"Off with these thought-chains . . . let us train ourselves to see beauty in black."[67] To African Americans in the 1960s, dashikis, drums, dance, Afros, ancestors, art, history, land, language, and global independence struggles came to signify acts of culturalism that were considered beautiful and African.[68] These forms of cultural representation marked the demise of "dis-Africanization" declaring that "Black is Beautiful," celebrating black bodily and phenotypic aesthetics and cultivating African cultural revivals.

Being African in the 1960s also involved joining newly developed African dance and drumming companies; forming political parties and organizations in support of African independence struggles; and establishing black art forums. These elements of black "expressive culture" provided an important "opportunity to gauge the character, scope, and orientation of a movement" that placed Africa at the center of its cultural and sacred reflections.[69] It was never singularly any one of these elements, but an intricate composite of all these elements, that embodied Africa, normalized blackness, and reshaped "the social meanings of race" in America.[70] It was, therefore, no mere coincidence, then, that many African Americans in Harlem who pursued their quest for Africa through art, music, dance, or politics also found themselves at Yoruba Temple.

Yoruba Temple offered a space where the black body could be the lived site of religious practice. Conscious of their slave past of humiliation through objectification and nakedness, African American Yoruba transfigured the black body into a subjectively clothed being of meaning and wholeness. In analyzing African modes of expression, Babatunde Lawal suggests that the body is often transformed into a "canvas" on which religion, politics, and culture can be mapped and emblematized.[71] The natural hair of Africans, traditional-style African wear and fabric, head and body adornment, and the beaded eleke necklaces collectively formed a "pictogram" or "image text" Yoruba Temple members created that allowed for "theologizing with the body."[72] With dress and hair as an image text with a definitive readable code, African Americans used their bodies as a forum for expressing the meanings that Africa and their African heritage held for them. Members of the African American priesthood like Marjorie Baynes Quiñones would be among the first to make this African attire and African adornment sacred in rituals of formal orisa initiation in the United States.[73]

Members of the Harlem Black Arts movement, who saw this new cultural resource as complementing their goals, made regular appearances at Yoruba Temple. As its participants conceptualized it, the Black Arts movement was the "spiritual sister" of Black Power. Exhibiting the commonly felt need to define the universe on their own terms, the poets, dramatists, and artists of the late sixties and early seventies sought to foster black empowerment through "a radical reordering of the western cultural aesthetic." Their major goal was to spur the growth of a dynamic, functional black aesthetic that emphasized the distinctiveness of African American culture—along with its unique symbols, myths, and metaphors; extolled the virtues of black life-styles and values; and promoted race consciousness, pride, and unity. If successful in this quest, they would bring about the "destruction of the white thing," putting an end to the "alien sensibility" that had long tainted black creative expression. No longer limited by "white ideas, and white ways of looking at the world," both the artists and their audience would move several steps closer to complete mental liberation.[74]

Within the context of the Black Arts movement, "the attempt to construct a new black culture was deeply intertwined with the search for religious alternatives to mainstream Christianity, a search that included not only Islam, but also a renewed interest in the signs and symbols of pre-Islamic and traditional African religions (such as the Yoruban religion)."[75] Although poetic, literary, and theatrical, the Black Arts movement fostered what could in some sense also be seen as a religious nationalist agenda offering "a religiously-infused narrative as empowering myth" and "constructing an alternative nation . . . with its own sense of spirituality and political vision."[76]

As with most black-nationalist groups of that time, the Black Arts movement was greatly influenced by the rapid decolonization of Africa and embraced the notion that someday African Americans in the United States would experience their own "decolonization." Amiri Baraka recognized the effect of African independence upon the Black Arts movement and welcomed its influence. In his autobiography, he stated: "The emergence of the independent African states and the appearance of African freedom fighters, fighting guerrilla wars with white colonialism, was destined to produce young intellectuals (and older ones too) who reveled in the spirit of defiant revolution and sought to use it to create art. An art that would reach the people, that would take them higher, ready them for war and victory . . . That was our vision and its image kept us stepping, heads high and backs straight."[77] Although Baraka was not a regular member, he often found himself attracted to the work of Harlem's Yoruba Temple and had Adefunmi officiate over his wedding ceremony. The temple for Baraka and other black artists was a window for viewing an African world in a constructed tapestry of African dress, music, culture, religion, and politics.

In addition to support from Black Arts, prominent women figures such as Queen Mother Moore, Mama Keke, and Asunta Serrano participated widely in implementing and sustaining the temple's vision. In a black-nationalist arena whose scholarly history has largely been masculinized, it has become easy to overlook the support that women such as Audley Moore supplied. Moore, widely known as Queen Mother Moore, the matri-arch of the pan-African movement, was perhaps one of the premier black female nationalist figures of the 1960s. She was best known for establishing the Reparations Committee for the Descendants of United States Slaves, but was also the founder of the African American Cultural Foundation, the Universal Association of Ethiopian Women Inc., and the Eloise Moore College of African Studies, "where the people could come . . . from all over the world to be de-colonialized and de-Negroized."[78] According to Adefunmi, Moore was a dedicated supporter of his work as a nationalist and as leader of the Yoruba Temple.[79] Although her personal religious affili-ation was more closely connected to Egyptian and Ethiopian spirituality, in an interview before her death, Moore revealed that she "always felt a special kinship with the Yoruba."[80] Adefunmi remarked that "she wasn't too much interested in the religion but she thought it [Yoruba Temple] was a step for-ward."[81] Like countless other African Americans, Queen Mother Moore received a Yoruba name from Adefunmi, Iyaluwa, fittingly interpreted as "Mother of our Town" and "Mother of the People."

Another prominent woman crucial to the work of Yoruba Temple was Mama Keke. An African Caribbean from Barbados, she had been a sup-porter of Adefunmi in the 1950s when he first established the Order of Damballah Hwedo and loyally supported Adefunmi throughout his vari-ous evolutionary approaches to the African God. An entrepreneur in her own right, Mama Keke was known for her Moremi Book Store and African Market.[82] Adefunmi affectionately credits her with being his "most ardent supporter" and years later made Oyotunji African Village the final resting place for her remains. Referring to Mama Keke, Adefunmi stated: "Every place we went she stayed with us. She . . . profoundly believed in everything we were doing. She was born in Barbados so she had some sense of racism and nationalism, which seemed to fit with our philosophies. Then she began to get deeper and deeper and more interested and involved in the religion."[83] Mama Keke was one of the original founding members of Yoruba Temple, and Adefunmi attributed much of the temple's development in those early years to her commitment and support. According to Oloosa Lloyd Weaver, it was Adefunmi, Keke, Quiñones, Oliana, and this first generation of Yoruba Americas who helped to "make sense of Orisa in the New York context."[84]

Private Consultations as Public Service in Harlem's Yoruba Temple

Throughout the 1960s, Yoruba Temple became a place where African Americans could bring their private concerns before the gods of Africa. The priests and priestesses of Yoruba Temple communicated with the African gods, offered advice, performed offerings and animal sacrifices, and used divination to provide healing to the numerous African American clients who sought their assistance. Divination, or readings, was part of a vast world of spiritual technology by which humans were able to communicate with the African orisa gods, allowing "for two-way communication with spirits and deities."[85] Priests and priestesses of Yoruba Temple performed divinations for African American clients to help alleviate their physical and spiritual ills. By 1963, the demand of the African American clientele in Harlem for readings was so great that Adefunmi had no other employment outside the temple. According to Carl Hunt, "He was so busy making readings and sacrifices for people he could not keep a job."[86]

The Harlem community's positive reception to these spiritual consultation services did not develop in a vacuum. Since the period of enslavement, African Americans in the United States have accessed the esoteric healing worlds of the supernatural. These traditions, often called voodoo, hoodoo, rootwork, or conjure, were spiritual world views that offered its suppliants both explanation and intervention. Albert Raboteau called conjure a "theory for explaining the mystery of evil" but "also a practice for doing something about it."[87] Within the context of southern slavery, Raboteau explained, "conjure was a method of control: first, the control which comes from knowledge—being able to explain crucial phenomena, such as illness, misfortune and evil; second, the control which comes from the capacity to act effectively . . . third, a means of control over the future through reading the 'signs'; fourth, an aid to social control because it supplied a system whereby conflict, otherwise stifled, could be aired."[88] Communicating within a context of spiritual negotiation and mediation enabled African Americans to transcend fixed notions of human destiny. African mystical technologies supported human agency in the temporal world and subverted fixed Protestant notions of predestination and fate. For the price of five dollars, African Americans were able to come to Yoruba Temple and hear what advice the gods of Africa could offer for alleviating the challenging conditions of their American lives.

In order to perform spiritual readings at Yoruba Temple, Adefunmi used methods of divination ranging from cowrie and coconut shells (which he learned to "read" from Oliana) to the use of a rough replica of a Yoruba opele, or divining chain, that he crafted himself. The heart of the reading involved an exploration of the individual's personality, a search for the spiritual source of the client's affliction, and an identification of an orisa deity for whom to make supplications. After the reading, Adefunmi offered written prescriptions to the individual of possible remedies, which ranged from various food offerings and animal sacrifice to the wearing of or avoidance of certain objects. Remedies requiring sacrifices usually called for a goat, chicken, pigeon, or guinea fowl. Sacrifices were made for clients primarily at the temple but often at the home of Adefunmi as well. In addition, Adefunmi instructed clients on the creation of ancestral altars in their private dwellings or would often carve representations of African deity for clients to take with them to assist in their spiritual work and healing.[89]

Members of Yoruba Temple, like Mama Keke, believed in the healing capabilities of the performed divinations. In one instance, Mama Keke's daughter had become afflicted, and she decided to take her to Adefunmi for a reading. In order to help the daughter, Adefunmi suggested that certain *ebo*, or sacrifices, be made to the orisa spirit. As Adefunmi recounted the event, "Keke and myself were astonished at the changes that took place . . . after the ebo. So then after that Keke was convinced that I was the spiritual leader she needed. She stood with me ever since."[90]

Clients were able to obtain spiritual readings from Adefunmi and regular members of the priesthood of the temple, which included Puerto Rican santera Asunta Serrano. The spiritual readings Serrano performed at the temple were somewhat different from those of Adefunmi. Serrano's method of divination and the ways in which she communicated with the supernatural world would include trances and séances that resembled Espiritismo, a form of popular spiritualism in Puerto Rico that at times included Cuban orisa spirits in the pantheon of spirits summoned during spirit communication.[91] Divination readings became an important way to attract African Americans to Yoruba Temple. They were convinced that the gods of Africa the Yoruba Temple celebrated represented efficacious power, and despite their own religious affiliations, they were willing to access this power in order to address the needs and afflictions of their daily lives.

Nearby African Americans from the Bronx and Brooklyn, and from as far away as Philadelphia, Chicago, Washington, New Jersey, Connecticut, and Indiana, came to receive information and spiritual consultation from the temple. Noted among these spiritual sojourners were Obalumi Ogunseye, Iya Omowunmi Ogundaisi, and Oladepo Adeyemi (Arthur Hall) from Philadelphia; and Baba Medahochi (who was known as Omowale) and Chief Adeyemi from Gary, Indiana. Reflecting on these earlier days, Adefunmi stated that "the Yoruba Temple, which subsequently spawned Yoruba Temples in Philadelphia,[92] Indiana,[93] and Chicago,[94] mainly served as a dispensary of information and acquaintance with African religion." In a 1976 interview with *Sepia* magazine, Chief Ogunseye reflected on this period. "I came under the influence of Efuntola at his temple in Harlem and he pointed the way. I and some other young people did our own research, and we found a basis of continuity from West Africa to the Caribbean and even to the U.S., a sound foundation to renew our identity. My zeal and enthusiasm radiated to my wife, and she began finding answers in it too. My wife's name was Laura Fernandez, and it is now Omow[un]mi, which means, "I love and adore my children."[95]

Many who came to the temple first heard about it through the American media. Baba Medahochi, for example, journeyed to New York City from Gary, Indiana, after reading an article in *Hep* magazine on Adefunmi and seeing him on television playing drums in a display of African culture. Arriving in New York without a precise address, Medahochi inquired at Micheaux's Bookstore in Harlem, where he was directed to Adefunmi. At this initial meeting, Medahochi recalls, were Adefunmi and Nana Dinizulu, the African American leader of the American Akan movement. Reflecting some sixty years later on this initial encounter Medahochi stated, "When I met Baba [Adefunmi], my life changed."[96] As a result of this initial encounter, Adefunmi later traveled to Indiana along with Mama Keke to preside over seven ceremonies, such as the giving of the sacred orisa beads or elekes and the spiritual conferring of several "warrior" deities such as Elegba and Ogun.[97] Adefunmi returned to Indiana several times, and a Yoruba Temple was eventually established in 1962 in this midwestern region.[98] Medahochi, who first initiated in the 1960s into Cuban Palo and then again in 1970 at Oyotunji African Village, admitted that Adefunmi was "very influential" upon him, changing his "whole way of thinking."[99]

Members of the Black Muslim community of the Nation of Islam also sought help from the gods of Africa, often doing so in the strictest of confidence, according to Adefunmi. One event that has become an important part of African American Yoruba lore occurred according to Adefunmi's recollection on February 19, 1965. On that day, Adefunmi says he was approached by several Black Muslims in order to conduct a spiritual reading concerning Malcolm X.[100] Yoruba Temple and the Nation of Islam had a mutual working relationship in Harlem, having shared rally spaces and, in some instances, members.[101] Adefunmi admits that Malcolm X may not have been aware that this reading was being requested. The outcome of the reading revealed great misfortune and that Oya, the Yoruba goddess who presides over the cemetery, was hovering around Malcolm X. As was standard with most readings, Adefunmi said he prescribed the performance of several sacrifices in order to assuage the orisa and offset any malady. He advised that two black hens be sacrificed to Oya in order to ward off death. Adefunmi says he remembers the uneasiness on the part of the Black Muslim clients to endorse the use of animal sacrifice. According to Adefunmi, the sacrifice was never administered, and several days later, according to Adefunmi's account, the world learned of Malcolm X's assassination.[102] More than three decades later, in 1999, Baba Songodian Ifatunji of Chicago State University corroborated Adefunmi's story at the Sixth World Congress of Orisa Tradition and Culture in the Republic of Trinidad and Tobago. While participating on one of the conference's panels, Baba Ifatunji stated, "He [Malcolm X] sent several of his lieutenants to Oba Adefunmi to seek advice, and I'm told that His Highness [Adefunmi] divined and discovered that he was child of Oya and that he had some serious ebo [sacrifice] that he needed to do. His Highness prescribed the ebo, and they didn't do it; they were just seeking advice . . . He [Malcolm X] was going to pass if they did not complete the ebo. The Odu, I think, was Osa Meji . . ."[103] In general, divination readings performed in Yoruba Temple served to bring healing and regeneration to willing African American clients in need of African-inspired spiritual intervention. These divination services became a private means of affirming Yoruba Temple's growing public importance and legitimacy.

Yoruba Temple and the Theology of the Streets

In the 1960s the streets of Harlem functioned as an allegorical space for acting out the tensions, frustrations, and triumphs of African American people. Neither a neutral nor benign public space, the streets of Harlem promoted religious and cultural activities, were used as a mechanism for public access and recognition, and served as a powerful intermediary link between nationalist organizations and an African American populace. With Yoruba Temple, the streets of Harlem were transformed into an active site of pilgrimage, ceremony, and ritual, a sacred public space where African Americans poured out their expressions of honor and celebration, of anger and protest, of disappointment and grief.[104] Baraka recalls how the streets of Harlem served as the dramatic stage for nationalist empowerment:

> There were all kinds of other nationalists. The street-corner variety, which included not only the Garveyites but folks like Eddie "Porkchop" Davis, who was on the ladder daily giving white people hell. There were the cultural nationalists like the Nation of Islam, the Yoruba Temple, and even smaller cults and the orthodox or Sunni Muslims, who also had many variations, and the black Jews or Hebrews, the Egyptian Coptics, and various other "conscious-raising" religious cults and sects. . . . There were also the basic working people, moving out of Harlem most times to work and struggle and then returning at night to the indignities of ghetto life.[105]

Motivated by these public street orations, African Americans inadvertently joined nationalist organizations, embraced new political philosophies, and encountered new gods.

Disruptions in the social lives of African Americans often played themselves out in the streets. From the civil rights streets of the South to the

FIGURE 6. Oseijeman Adefunmi at a street rally in Harlem.
Photograph courtesy of Klytus Smith.

streets of the urban North, African American movement and mobilization theories and philosophies were given public voice as part of a collective African American voice of protest throughout the 1960s. In Harlem,
demonstrations ranged from rallies to riots in response to instances of
police brutality, the bombing of black churches, and the assassination of
black leaders such as Malcolm X and Martin Luther King Jr. During these
moments, the streets of Harlem embodied the rage as well as the mourn-
ing and grief of the people. Similar to the 1917 "Silent Parade" in New York,
which "responded to the massacre of black people in East St. Louis," where
black children had been being thrown into raging fires, members of Yoruba
Temple participated in a public grief processional adorned in all white when
four black girls were burned in the 1963 church bombing in Birmingham,
Alabama.[106] Thus, the streets could bear the public grief of a community
as well as create a "spiritual atmosphere" with the ability "to stir in participants and spectators as well."[107]

As a site of resistance, subversion, and social critique, the streets have a
long resonance in African American public and political history that dates

as far back as the early eighteenth century.[108] Historian William Piersen in his book, *Black Yankees: The Development of an Afro-American Subculture in Eighteenth-Century New England*, describes that by the mid-1700s, enslaved Africans used festivals, pageants, processionals, and parade culture to both invert and subvert prescribed socio-political norms of public power. Over the course of that century, public forums such Negro Election Day, Pinkster, General Training, and Jonkonnu were public sites for African cultural proliferation in North America and gave occasion to African indigenous social and cultural self-expression.[109] These public street venues became outlets where Africans could give expression, "each in their own tongue, after the customs of several nations in Africa."[110] Objects of African material culture such as the Guinea drum were crafted and played, and practices like the Guinea dance were readily observed. According to one nineteenth-century white observer of the public Guinea dance, the "chief musician" was "dressed in a horrid manner [and] rolling his eyes and tossing his head with an air of savage wildness."[111] He was reportedly dressed in "feathers and cow tails," and the accompanying drummers created according to this observer "sounds of frightful dissonance."[112] Africans reportedly joined in the Guinea dance according to how "the spirit moved him or her to do so."[113] The observer posited that these were "twisting, wriggling histerical [*sic*] slaves who, for the first time, were thousands of miles away in the heart of superstitious Africa" and that within these moments of cultural freedom it was "not unusual for this wild dance to continue through two days."[114]

Over the course of the eighteenth and nineteenth centuries, public street parades, festivals, and processionals had a threefold effect upon African and African American life: First, they allowed those of African descent (both enslaved and free) to enact and control public representations of themselves against those of Anglo-Americans. Second, they were used by early African communities as a vehicle of social cohesion to "foster unity among an increasingly disparate black population."[115] Finally, in the postbellum era of contested citizenry, "they proclaimed to a skeptical and often hostile white audience that blacks were no longer slaves and that as American citizens they, too, had a right to the streets."[116]

Historians of public ceremonial and urban public culture such as Susan Davis examine festivals and parades as a genre of street drama that embedded within them a "relationship to the social contexts in which it was performed" and ultimately an outlet to "propose new ideas about social relations."[117] They in some sense "ritualize a wide range of social questions and relations," ultimately making larger social commentaries on "class, race, ethnicity, power, . . . legitimacy[,]" and historical memory.[118] Historically, these public displays on the part of enslaved and free African Americans "communicated group presence, conviction, and solidarity" and were perceived as ominous and a foreboding, and very real, threat to the status quo.[119] Therefore, while America's streets enabled African Americans a public way to "participate in the discourse of the American republic" and engage in social critique, the streets were also potential sites for social chaos, where racial brawls, mob violence, and riots could readily occur. The future streets of the 1960s would embody these same powerful dualities and possibilities.

Parade, oratory, and rally culture as mapped on to public streets became important indicators of agency for African Americans as they aimed "to establish their own right to public urban space."[120] Within American popular culture, "the streets enabled workers, poor people, and racial minorities to broadcast messages to large numbers of people."[121] Historically, African Americans took full advantage of these opportunities, particularly as they used processional parades as a form of "vernacular communication."[122] These parades functioned both as expressions of social protest as well "as tools for building, maintaining, and confronting power relations."[123] According to Shane White, the "parade rapidly developed into an important cultural form" and "an important site on which cultural tensions within the African-American community were worked out."[124]

For African Americans, parade and rally expressions can ultimately be viewed as "rituals of empowerment" that enact social meaning, utility, and purpose. On the Harlem streets of the 1960s, public parades and rallies represented "one of a large range of urban communicative events" that included "orations, lectures, sermons . . . and political meetings."[125] More specifically, Yoruba Temple sought ways to tap into the various sources of power that urban streets held. One way this was accomplished was through cooperative rallies, parades, and religious drum ceremonies, or bembes. On several occasions, Yoruba Temple participated in rallies and parades alongside other popular nationalist organizations, such as the Nation of Islam and the Black Arts Theatre. Through these joint ventures they were able to address the people of Harlem by means of prestigious street platforms such as those adjacent to Louis Michaeux's Bookstore

FIGURE 7. Oseijeman Adefunmi leading parade in Harlem along with Mama Keke and Queen Mother Moore. Photograph courtesy of Klytus Smith.

on 125th Street, where people such as Malcolm X, historian J. A. Rogers, Louis X (now Louis Farrakhan), and Dr. Yosef A. A. ben Jochannan (Dr. Ben) graced the street podium. On these occasions, Adefunmi was given an opportunity to tell the people of Harlem of the mission of Yoruba Temple and the religion of Orisha-Vodu, making a plea to summon them back to their ancestral traditions.

Adefunmi and Yoruba Temple also regularly collaborated on ceremonial activities with high-profile personalities such as renowned Nigerian percussionist Michael Babatunde Olatunji. Olatunji's local notoriety was heightened among African Americans because of his Harlem-based Olatunji Center of African Culture located at 43 East 125th Street, an effort that was largely funded by the monthly support of African American jazz musician John Coltrane.[126] While a young man, Olatunji attended Morehouse College and during his first encounter with African Americans in Harlem and Atlanta remarked, "My goodness, these people are Africans but they don't realize it."[127] This sparked Olatunji's initial vision to create an African cultural center and make the following declaration: "I must return to Harlem one day. This was the place where I would need to start a program that would help people reclaim their identity with Africa, so that one day they would be able to embrace Africa, as the other ethnic groups that made up this country have embraced their homelands. Not until then would they become better citizens of America and of the world."[128] Olatunji understood his Center of African Culture as "revitalizing interest in African culture, and helping to destroy the ugly image of Africa that had been planted in the minds of millions of Americans through Hollywood movies and so many books and articles about Africa and Africans."[129] The Harlem center offered classes in music, drumming, dance, language, folklore, and the history of Africa.[130]

Olatunji and his famous Drums of Passion performed in the 1964–1965 New York World's Fair African Pavilion, as did Adefunmi and several members of Yoruba Temple.[131] For several decades, Olatunji went on to record with noted artists and performers such as Herbie Mann, Max Roach, Randy Weston, Quincy Jones, Taj Mahal, Stevie Wonder, Abbey Lincoln, Mickey Hart, Carlos Santana, and Tupac Shakur.[132] One of Olatunji's master drummers, James Hawthorne Bey (a student of Isamae

FIGURE 8. Nigerian drummer Babatunde Olatunji featured along with James Brown at the Apollo Theater in Harlem. Photograph courtesy of Klytus Smith.

Andrews), became well known among the New York African American Yoruba community as Chief Bey, an accomplished ceremonial drummer.[133] Bey's own recording career included a litany of great performers such as Cab Calloway, Art Blakely, Herbie Mann, Harry Belafonte, and Leontyne Price. Olatunji taught Chief Bey many chants in honor of Yoruba deities that were eventually recorded on Olatunji's 1960 *Drums of Passion* album. He said of Chief Bey that "his deep voice really demonstrated how our people have utilized their African heritage in this country, as in the call and response of gospel music."[134]

In 1960, Olatunji organized an Ngoma Festival in New York in celebration of Adefunmi's Yoruba Temple. Olatunji commissioned Arthur Hall's (Oladepo Adeyemi) Philadelphia-based dance company to perform a dance for Adefunmi's orisa, Obatala. At this occasion of celebration, performance, libations, and animal sacrifice, Adefunmi in turn gave Hall a carved mask of Obatala as an expression of his deep gratitude and "to acknowledge that the spirit of Obatala was now in America."[135] Olatunji was a Nigeria Yoruba who took seriously the expression of Africa represented by Yoruba Temple. There were, however, other Nigerian Yoruba who viewed Yoruba Temple as "silly" and as mere "entertainment for those people who knew nothing about Africa."[136] Nevertheless, Yoruba Temple spilled out into the streets of Harlem through parades and religious drum ceremonies, or bembes, enacting what historian Alessandra Lorini calls "rituals of race." Robert Anthony Orsi estimated that "Harlem had more parades than any other ethnic community except the Italians."[137] These parades became a "peculiar text" scripted by "multiple authors" who, like their forebears, collectively performed a "noble vengeance" against established American public, social, and cultural norms of blackness.[138]

Within a larger Protestant American context, bembes represented transgressive discursive spaces in their honoring of Africa gods. They were important public-ritual moments where one could witness Yoruba American theology at work. As a general overview, bembes ritually employ a "multisensorial" approach to libations, chants, drums, dances, sacrifice, and trance-possession whereby "divinity is transformed into a mode that is safe for human contact."[139] In Yoruba Temple, they were held largely on the weekends, especially on Fridays. African Americans would attend these bembes in public parks in Harlem, at the Ujamaa Market that Adefunmi founded in 1962, or on the public streets in front of the temple.

When Yoruba Temple began hosting bembes, the temple had strong ties
to Oliana, and the ceremonies tended to be somewhat Cuban in style and
content, with some 130 people, including professors and college students,
as well as members of the working-class community in Harlem in attendance.[140] When asked to describe a bembe at Yoruba Temple, Adefunmi
remarked:

> They were the standard Cuban type thing, since [Oliana], being
> more knowledgeable, conducted them, and so gradually I learned
> how he did it and what was the system and approach. You take
> care of the dead first, and they used to put some little thing in
> the corner, place a candle there, a glass of water, and some pieces
> of coconut, and that was for the dead. We always did that first.
> Then he would come out into the main floor . . . and then he did
> his Mojubas—that standard mojuba used by all people in Cuban
> Santería. And then after that he would begin to chant to Elegba,
> and he would encourage everybody to dance, and he would show
> them what the simple steps were to each one of the dances, and
> after Elegba was usually Ogun and Ochosi. But later we were on
> our own. We African Americans were on our own.[141]

Gradually, Adefunmi relied on distinct African American modes of public empowerment and eventually shifted from a dependence on Cuban
religious knowledge and ritual interpretation to a reliance on African
American creative agency. The following is a description of an innovative
African American ritual reformulation from a firsthand account in 1969:

> At Friday night bembe (service), the priest babalosha Oseijeman
> Adefunmi is always the last to arrive. . . . Rites begin with offerings—
> usually fruit—to the gods whose night it is for worship. . . . Then
> there are the salutations, made to a list of black militant saints who
> span the globe and range through a sizable chunk of history. While
> the Ogboni stamp out metallic rhythms . . . Baba chants in Yoruba:
> "[M]Ojuba (we bow down to you) Malcolm . . . . [M]ojuba, Patrice
> Lumumba . . . [M]ojuba, W. E. B. Dubois." There are [M]ojubas for
> Harriet Tubman, Nat Turner, Langston Hughes, even figures more
> obscure, like the Haitian revolutionary Jean Jacques Dessailines.

Marcus Garvey, as a pioneer black nationalist, is never left out. Sometimes, there is a sacrifice. A cock is used . . . There is always the dancing and the singing, into the smoky hours of the morning, when the drummers are sapped of their strength and Baba bids farewell.[142]

By 1969, Adefunmi along with his followers of North American and Caribbean descent had established Yoruba Temple as a vibrant space for religious and cultural expressions of Africa. Despite struggles for authority that developed among his Cuban peers, Adefunmi embraced his role as the "Chief Priest of the Yoruba Temple, Dean of the Yoruba Academy and Chief of the Yoruba Nation of North America."[143] He saw himself as creating "culturally revived institutions" and enduring forms of public ritual culture. For example, in the 1960s, Adefunmi established an Oshun Festival in Harlem, which became a forerunner to the nationally recognized Odunde Festival that commenced in Philadelphia a few years later. Similar to Odunde, this 1960s festival honored Oshun as the goddess of the river. Adefunmi would lead a public processional through the streets of Harlem to New York's Hudson River and "make offering[s] to the goddess there."[144] With this, Adefunmi was not only localizing a specific African American ritual interpretation of the orisa but through new "relational changes with nature" was quite profoundly consecrating Harlem's local geography as sacred spaces for African American religious observances.[145] Addressing this new theory of nature and geography, one practitioner argued that once the deities "crossed the Atlantic Ocean and reached the Western hemisphere, their domains changed" and "no longer were they exclusively associated with finite physical locations."[146] Therefore, Oshun became associated with new "geographical place-names," such as New York's Hudson River and Philadelphia's Schuylkill River, and sacrifices for Yemonja and Olokun could be offered at new sacred sites such as New York's Coney Island Beach and other North American geographies.[147]

In the end, neither the Africanization of Yoruba Temple nor the indigenization processes of Cuban Santería Adefunmi enacted occurred without consequence. As a result of these processes, some Cuban immigrants and African American practitioners developed relationships fraught with ambiguity, creating moments of conflict as well as new avenues for continued cooperation.[148] According to Adeyemi, Adefunmi "came back from

Cuba, went to New York, started a house among African Americans, and that is where the shit hit the fan."[149] The sections that follow will continue to explore this complicated dynamic of divergence and alliance among Cubans and African American devotees. The next chapter will explore the ways Adefunmi sought to give textual legitimacy to African American interpretations of the orisa gods and impart a new sense of history and identity to an African American readership. Chapter 5 will then revisit the complex reactions of Cuban practitioners as they responded to an emerging African American authority that sought to transform the religion they understood as La Regla de Ocha/Santería/Lucumi into new interpretations of race, power, and nationhood.

CHAPTER FOUR

"Indigenous Literacies" and the African Library Series

A Textual Approach to History, Nation, and Tradition

Ꮆ᠍ᎬᎧᎬᎧ

Religious nationalism in many ways "represents the return to text" and a "renarrativization of the nation."[1] Texts within this milieu become authoritative sources of "timeless truths" that provide "a basis for the narration of contemporary history."[2] In this chapter, I engage what David D. Hall calls "the politics of texts" and how text making became an important way of renarrativizing African American primordialism and its global citizenry.[3] Within the context of 1960s African American Yoruba, I explore "the social dimensions of reading" and the ways "religious communities use texts to sustain their religious practice," often doing so while resisting and subverting canonized scripts and representations.[4]

In the 1960s, black-nationalist organizations produced written texts in the form of pamphlets, leaflets, and books as a means of cultivating a renewed sense of personhood and fostering a new sense of tradition and nation among African Americans in the United States. These "indigenous literacies" functioned as countertextual models to Western forms of scholarship and mediaship that imprisoned Africa and Africans in malignant tropes of the uncivilized primitive and the cultureless, historyless slave.[5]

To use J. Lorand Matory's conceptual category, these texts were in many ways an attempt to "unslave" the history and culture of African peoples.[6] As insider texts, they were in an imperceptible dialogue with an unnamed body of Western literature that represented Africa and its traditions as historically meaningless and culturally unsalvageable. What was ultimately at stake in creating new literatures was the ability to recover African American corporality from the fixed somatic, ontological, and unhistorical category of slave in the Americas and establish the narratability and cosmological significance of Africa.

In his appeal to a reputed African American nation, Oseijeman Adefunmi generated a print genre that created a new soteriology for African American audiences through a reinvestment in the religious philosophies of Yoruba/Fon Orisha-Vodu; the cultural restoration vision of Yoruba Temple; and the sociocultural and religious expectations of an African global citizenry. Through Adefunmi's world of print, readers were able to glimpse the politics of the day and the "text-making that flowed from it."[7] His written works became forerunners to what has now expanded into a vibrant, contemporary African American literature in North American Yoruba culture and tradition. Collectively, these insider texts provide an important gaze into the meaning of a specific interpretation of Yoruba and African identity in North America and the lenses of lived experiences that reflect it.[8]

According to black theologian James Cone, "When white people enslaved Africans, their intention was to dehistoricize black existence, to foreclose the possibility of a future defined by the African heritage."[9] Thus, the substance of Adefunmi's early texts posited a "redemptive historical framework" that freed African Americans from a condemned history ending only in a slave past.[10] These texts reinforced the notion that "before slavery was Africa," serving as written platforms for a nationalist summoning of African Americans to reclaim their original African selves.[11]

Meant to inform African American Yoruba life by rooting identity and personhood in a renewed historical self, Adefunmi's texts introduced new cultural institutions and countered the historical rupture of slavery with Africa's religious recovery. African American readers were provided access to a cohesive African world and united into a critical body of North American African citizenry. In his texts, Adefunmi would foster a re-ethnification of black North Americans based on African ancestry that superseded an amorphous slave or Negro identity.[12] Texts and culture would form a union of meaning for "re-visioning history and geography" and for constructing "a moral and spiritual basis for contemporary affiliations and identity."[13] Collectively, they would transform a pejorative black subject that had been historically crafted from objectified chattel, racialized mythology, and American social pathology into a reclaimed, re-owned, and revalued African. Texts functioned as a way of supplanting an overarching "narrative of displacement" that dominated black diasporic identity and perpetuated its historical marginalization.[14]

African Americans continually wrestled with the problem of a "divided historical consciousness" that kept them suspended between a "tyrannical 'white' historiography" and a desired "history of the 'black world' created anew."[15] Thus, the Yoruba movement in America, like other ethnic revival movements, cultivated "historical awareness, based on a new reconstruction of their history" and furnished "the collective with a shared historical past."[16] These efforts at rehistoricizing helped to deepen the black "national consciousness," reinforce self-worth, provide "legitimacy for territorial and political aspirations," and present new "paradigms of culture" in America.[17] With Africa as a new "existential perspective," Oseijeman Adefunmi attempted to rewrite the national history of African Americans as "a measure crucial in creating a new understanding of the black person as an integral element in the history of the United States."[18] The understanding was that African people were not only important on the world stage of civilization and culture, but contrary to "white" historiography, they were also vital participants in the historical development of America. His texts restructured the boundaries with regard to who would have authority to write the historical narratives of African Americans, publish and distribute them, and control the mechanisms of their content.[19]

Similar to the early nationalist philosopher Marcus Mosiah Garvey, Oseijeman Adefunmi introduced his readership to new theological conceptions of black divinity, innovative historical and cultural interpretations of Africa, and future possibilities of black autonomous nationhood. More important, this textual medium served to inform African American Yoruba self-awareness in three key ways. First, it provided a historicized sense of identity and personhood rooted within a textured African self. Second, it introduced social and cultural institutions and new governing principles and philosophies that would accompany this novel African identity. Third, it treated and transcended the sore spot of ontological, spatial, and cultural rupture inherited through slavery and systematically moved toward renewed reconciliation and recovery through the religion of the Yoruba. Engaging a "nationalist historical understanding," Adefunmi formulated new symbols of authentic identity for his American readership within "the theater of history" where the "performance of identity" is most commonly rescripted and plotted.[20] Both Oseijeman Adefunmi and Marcus Garvey strategically dispensed printed literature as a means of reshaping African American self-understanding and procuring widespread African American support for a territorial nation. This "print-language," some scholars contend, is what "invents nationalism" and is vital to creating national associations and belongingness across seemingly impermeable boundaries.[21] Through this written medium Garvey and Adefunmi, in addition to using local public platforms and oratory stages in Harlem, were able to distribute their nationalist theories more widely.

Textuality, particularly among African American Yoruba, served as a critical agent for disseminating and localizing a new religious consciousness. Texts united African Americans readers not only within the context of a modern national populace but also within a reputed historical lineage of ancient nationhood. For Adefunmi, textual production and the "politics of writing" were closely tied to the larger 1960s black-nationalist philosophies, which advocated authoring and reclaiming one's history. His distinct contribution was in promoting the legitimacy of Africa as a cultural, civic, and religious point of reference.

Judson L. Jeffries in his book, *Black Power in the Belly of the Beast*, describes the importance of "heightening Black people's consciousness" through historical production.[22] History was a powerful vehicle for "untellings" as well as a central catalyst for cultivating political, cultural, and religious awareness among African Americans.[23] For many African American nationalists like Adefunmi, the move toward autonomous black nationhood in the twentieth century was somehow directly linked to the historical lineage of sovereign African nation-states of times past. Adefunmi's texts sought to "rehabilitate" the historical past of African Americans by "reviving cultural assets from their classical or pre-classical periods," establishing them as exclusive descendants of the historical place of Africa as opposed to descendants of the historical processes of slavery.[24] Through his texts, Adefunmi navigated multispatiality and time, "collapsing, ultimately, the rigid demarcation of the prescriptive past, present, and future of linear time."[25]

Within the context of an oral global Yoruba tradition, Adefunmi's proliferation of counter-mainstream literature in American Yoruba history cannot be easily overlooked. Collectively, Adefunmi's texts sought to return to a "first creation," or primordial identity, that would subsequently dissolve all externally imposed definitions of African Americans.[26] What becomes truly subversive about Adefunmi's historical agency is his creation of a textual counternarrative whereby black North Americans envisaged their existence before America and re-presented themselves as historically, authentically, and ancestrally African.[27] In the end, through African literary tracts, movements such as Garvey's in the early twentieth century and the American Yoruba movement decades later created an opportunity "for rapidly growing numbers of people to think about themselves, and to relate themselves to others, in profoundly new ways."[28]

Adefunmi's texts commonly commenced in Africa in the midst of historical and cultural moments of symmetry, harmony, and cooperation. They inevitably include major transitional disruptions such as warfare, European domination, and slavery, setting the stage for social upheaval and the impending creation of a scattered black diasporic community in the West. They often concluded by stressing the continued need for African American communities in the United States to recover the viable cultural model of Africa. A close textual analysis of five of Adefunmi's key texts in the African Library Series—*Orisha: A First Glimpse of the African Religion of Brazil, Cuba, Haiti, Trinidad and now U.S.A.; The Gods of Africa; Tribal Origins of the African-Americans; The African State;* and *An African Marriage*—will illuminate these points more fully.

Orisha: A First Glimpse

As early as 1959, immediately following his initiation, Adefunmi began to generate his own written explications of Yoruba religion, circulating them through Shango, and later Yoruba, Temples. *Orisha: A First Glimpse of the African Religion of Brazil, Cuba, Haiti, Trinidad and now U.S.A.* was Adefunmi's first literary introduction of the African God and its emergence in the United States. This and subsequent texts became part of a larger "rhetorical strategy of recovery" aimed at reconnecting African

Americans to lost identities.[29] In *Orisha*, Adefunmi proclaimed because "Africans born in America were persuaded to renounce their Ancestors and their ancient rites," the result was a "rapid degeneration into crime, immorality, and inertia," culminating in the tragic "loss of cultural identity."[30] Through his writings, Adefunmi offered, as Michael J. C. Echeruo explains, a way of engaging in ethnic self-determination in response to this new alien Atlanticism.[31] Adefunmi's work was designed to combat a narrative of complete tragic loss and exile by offering opportunities for metaphorical return.

A diasporic treatise illustrated with images of the orisa African deity, the text announced that the newly established Shango Temple would serve as the institutional resource "of a rising African-American priesthood to rank Harlem with Agbomey, Ife, Benin, Bahia, Port au Prince and Matanzas as a citadel of West African civilization."[32] Adefunmi identified himself as "one of the first two Afro-American savants to return to the priesthood of his Ancestral religion" through an initiation conducted "in one of the oldest Yoruba Temples in Matanzas, Cuba." He introduced his readers to "the mystic science of divination, the secret rituals of the Obatala Priesthood, Yoruba Theology, Sacred Drums, Yoruba, Ashanti, and Dahomean history."[33] Adefunmi's *Orisha* hoped to appeal to an African self-consciousness he assumed among his African American readership. Textually, he made overtures to an African diasporic self that collectively functioned as a subjective self, a public self, and a peripheral self in the Americas and the Caribbean.[34] This was a self that Adefunmi was able to "manipulate within history" using it, therefore, as a way not simply to "create" identity but to "restructure" it.[35] Adefunmi saw himself and coinitiate Christopher Oliana as catalysts for a mass return of African Americans from their "degeneration" and "inertia" to a more authentic place of cultural and religious Africanity. As dispersed citizens, African Americans identified with "this inalienable right to wish a return, to reclaim connections to a lineage, however fractured, that makes one individual a part of a diffuse and disparate collection of persons we call the Diaspora."[36]

Theorizing the meaning of being African for Adefunmi meant not simply adopting and adhering to a rigid set of social or cultural requisites but was in many ways "a historical and contingent reality, the experience of its historicity being the context of many parables of fluctuating identities."[37] Adefunmi's written texts brought coherence and solidity to these fluctuating identities and provided "a concept of the self whose unity resides in the unity of [the] narrative."[38] The natural progression of the historical narratives he detailed in his texts always reinscribed the need for African Americans to recover "the source of all African culture," which he rooted firmly in religion.[39] These texts ultimately provided a platform that "allowed African Americans to identify themselves historically and theologically" with Africa and not be eternally circumscribed as a victimized community in America.[40] In many ways, Adefunmi offered an intertextual response to a body of Western texts he saw as misrepresenting Africa and its descendants.

A year after the publication of *Orisha*, Adefunmi formed the African Library Series, published under the auspices of Great Benin Books. The series comprised several Yoruba Temple publications, all authored by Adefunmi, describing the new Yoruba- and Dahomean-based religion of Orisha-Vodu along with its theology, anthropology, culture, and polity. All texts were copyrighted to Oseijeman Adefunmi, "Babalosha (Chief Priest)," designated "a production of the Yoruba Temple Research Division," and based in "New Oyo (Harlem), New York" and later Oyotunji African Village. The series defined the tenets of the Yoruba expression he named Orisha-Vodu, expounded upon his philosophy on racial origins, developed his treatise on the merits of African social and cultural practices such as Ogboni and polygamy, and outlined the institutions needed to sustain and ritualize an African understanding of the world. Through the use of these texts, Adefunmi provided African Americans with a new paradigm and set of boundaries from which to redefine and negotiate race, religion, culture, and American society. He made these publications available for purchase at Yoruba Temple in Harlem at a nominal cost of around a dollar. An African American priestess who worked with Adefunmi in the 1960s saw him as a "key molder of black readers' perceptions," and remarked some forty years later that given the scarcity of reliable books on Africa in the 1960s, Adefunmi's texts became one of the most effective ways that African Americans acquired information about African sacred traditions.[41] She attests to an overwhelmingly positive reader reception by an African American audience who felt that access to positive literature on Africa and their connection to its heritage had been severely lacking.

Careful readings of Adefunmi's texts clearly divulge his complex notions of Africa. His texts functioned as "a system of representations."[42] With a certain ideal of Africa, emphasizing its stable ancient kingdoms, cradles of civilization, and ontological currency as the primordial homeland of formerly enslaved black people in America. He did so at a time in the 1960s when Africa was experiencing constant flux because of rapid independence and colonial transitions.

In his texts, Adefunmi employs a narrative of slavery in which African Americans were spiritually severed from their ancient African gods, but now in the 1960s, the "ancient ways" of the African gods were being "filtered down to the present generation" and reentering the lives of African Americans. Yoruba Temple, the "first purely African institution," as opposed to the Christian church or Muslim mosque/temple in the United States, would commit itself to the task of facilitating the reconciliation of African Americans with their ancient deity. Within the emerging "renaissance of African culture," descendants of African slaves in the United States could now restore the "traditions of ancient ways" and create a new "cultural identity" as a "monument" to those Africans who perished in the slave trade.

In seeking to restore the "traditions of ancient ways," African Americans would, in fact, create new ways of traditionalizing Yoruba cultures in America. Adefunmi believed that the gods of Africa had a special purpose for the race of Africans in America and that this purpose would be articulated through Yoruba Temple and the religion of Orisha-Vodu. In his writings, Yoruba religion and Orisha-Vodu were often used interchangeably. For example, Adefunmi states, "Yoruba Temple of New York refers to the religion of the Yoruba as Orisha-Vodu. Orisha is the Yoruba word for the Gods or Saints. Among the Dahomeans, who received their religion from the Yoruba, the Gods are called Vodu (Vudu or Voodoo), hence Orisha-Vodu."[43] A close examination of Orisha-Vodu in many ways reveals an underlying fusion of Adefunmi's textual knowledge of the vodun, or gods, from Herskovits's *Dahomey* and Adefunmi's experiential knowledge of the Cuban orisa spirits. Rather than a rigid or fixed recasting of traditional Yoruba theology, he was intentionally trying to create a distinct religious interpretation for African Americans "based upon the environment in which they lived."[44] For black North Americans, the lived expressions of Orisha-Vodu would be made manifest within the contours of the United States, not in Africa or even Cuba.

The Gods of Africa

Adefunmi's *The Gods of Africa* became the first official text in the new African Library Series of Yoruba Temple. Published in 1960, it explored the history of the Yoruba people in Africa and the transmission of its religion, which Adefunmi labeled Orisha-Vodu, to the Americas. It outlined the theological tenets of Orisha-Vodu, introduced African Americans to specific gods of Africa and their natural attributes, and articulated the long-term goals of Yoruba Temple and the function of its priesthood. Although the original text did not include citations and bibliographical information, it appears to have drawn heavily from the works of Yoruba Christian scholar Samuel Johnson and American anthropologist Melville Herskovits.[45] Adefunmi found the works of these two scholars especially insightful given their interests in African antiquity on the one hand and African continuity on the other.

Samuel Johnson's historical work focused specifically on the ancient culture of Oyo. Johnson himself was born in Sierra Leone and was the son of a "recaptive African" whom the British navy had rescued from a slave ship.[46] Johnson claimed direct Yoruba descent from the Alaafin Abiodun of Oyo. Especially useful to Adefunmi was the degree to which Johnson detailed cultural, religious, and ritual practices of the Yoruba in West Africa, which Adefunmi transmitted to African Americans as genuine expressions of African culture. As we shall see in chapter 6, Johnson's book provided one of the primary resources of cultural production and practice that later came to shape Oyotunji African Village. (In Adefunmi's textual and cultural appropriations of Johnson, he does not question Johnson's status as an Anglican priest or how this lens might have influenced his reading of Yoruba history and cultural praxis. Instead, Adefunmi considers Johnson an authority based on his identity as an ethnic Yoruba.) It was Melville Herskovits, however, who provided the tangible evidential linkage that geographically connected African cultural practices to those of Africans in the Americas. Because Herskovits's texts stressed issues of continuity, survivals, synthesis, and reinterpretation, Adefunmi was able to construct careful textual boundaries that minimized the cultural distance between Africa and America.

In an attempt to sketch a history of what he understood as Yoruba theology, Adefunmi introduced readers to the sacred landscape of the Yoruba, the orisa deity, and the practice of ancestral veneration. *The Gods of Africa* specifically challenged the intentional "Europeanization" of African religion and culture as well as the understandable, yet contestable, use of Roman Catholic iconography to represent the divinities Cuban immigrants in the

United States promoted. For Adefunmi, such use reflected "the white man's concept" of the orisa, while also serving as cloaks of resistance under which "priests continued the worship of [the] orisha."[47] As a result, the enslaved African priests began to appropriate the images of Roman Catholic saints in order to maintain the worship of the orisa.[48] Despite the necessity for this practice during the times of enslavement, however, Adefunmi felt the time had come to "re-Africanize" all white Roman Catholic representations.[49]

This re-Africanization process inevitably required an extended history that authenticated Yoruba religion before its Cuban context. Therefore, when African Americans opened the pages of *The Gods of Africa*, they were introduced to the ancient history of "Yoruba Kingdom" dating back as far as the eighth century. Adefunmi impressed upon his African American readership that "this was 1,000 years before the United States was founded."[50] Readers went on to examine Adefunmi's historical speculations on the original home of the Yorubas in Upper Egypt and Kush and their migration to West Africa after Muslim invasion. In their new space in West Africa, according to Adefunmi, settlements in Ile-Ife and Oyo (located in present-day Nigeria) were developed under great Yoruba kings and princes such as Oduduwa, Oranmiyan, and forty-one other divine successors. Adefunmi highlighted the skill and brilliance of the Yoruba as statesmen and militarists who created "the foundations of the Yoruba Empire, which stretched from Eastern Nigeria across Dahomey and Togoland, as far as Accra in what is now Ghana."[51] He also included a brief description of traditional Yoruba government that explained the role of the Ogboni council of elders and the role of the Oba, or king, who served as political leader and as spiritual representative of the ancestors.

To connect the history of African Americans to the ancient Yoruba, Adefunmi told of the waning of the "Golden Age of the Oyo Dynasty" and its downfall to foreign invaders following the arrival of the Europeans, who were reportedly "fomenting civil wars to capitalize in the slave trade."[52] Although he glosses the participation of African accomplices in this destabilization process, he squarely places blame on "the arrival of the Europeans" and states that as a tragic consequence, "each year thousands of Yoruba were captured and taken to the West Indies and to South and North America, where they became cotton pickers and house servants in North and South Carolina, Georgia, Alabama, Mississippi, Louisiana, Virginia, etc. and even as far as New Jersey, New York, and Rhode Island."[53] In recounting this seemingly linear trajectory "from Egypt, Nubia and Kush, to Nigeria, and then to America," Adefunmi was constructing a new Yoruba religious history that included the presence of African Americans. The narrative resumed in the New World context where the forces of "Europeanization" and processes of cultural alienation and de-ethnicization burgeoned.[54] According to Adefunmi:

> In America, all Africans, whether from Ashanti, Dahomey, Yoruba or Congo, were termed "negroes." When the American Civil War ended slavery, some 4 million Africans, many of them half breeds, found themselves in a foreign country, among a foreign people, with all manners of foreign customs. The Americans made no attempt to restore West African cultural institutions which would have given the Africans a national foundation upon which to rebuild. Instead they proceeded to Europeanize them.[55]

In order to counter the continued Europeanization of Africans still "struggling in many ways to find themselves," Adefunmi's pamphlet declared that Yoruba Temple in New York had now "begun laying the foundations of West African culture in America."[56]

The Gods of Africa functioned as a textual exercise in recovery. Adefunmi saw his work as reintroducing African Americans to the estranged gods who had been systematically and forcefully relinquished during slavery. Embracing the religion of the Yoruba would initiate a theological recovery of Olodumare, the Supreme Creator, the orisa deities of the Yoruba that emanated from this supreme source, the ancestors from whom African Americans descended, and the practice of divination to maintain spiritual communication. The orisa were described as some 401 divine energies emanating from Olodumare and often identified as personifications of nature and ecology.[57] Adefunmi stressed that the practice of divination or spiritual consultations was an essential component of Orisha-Vodu theology. Ifa-Orunmila presided over the "vital science of foretelling events."[58] Moreover, not only was divination described as a medium of communication between humans and the African gods, it was also based on a body of sacred oral literature that displaced the Western canonical authority of a written text. "Divination by shells, nuts, bones, pebbles or whatever, is the method African priests and worshippers use to correspond with the Gods and interpret their will. It takes the place of the 'holy book' used by literate religions. Divination permits the worshippers to have instant answers and information on any subject which confronts him. The *Ifa* system consists of 4,086 poetic references which serve as a description for the problems encountered by the client."[59]

In addition, Adefunmi outlined the practice of ancestor veneration, which he described as vital to this movement of recovery and religious return. "All civilized people worship their ancestors either through special memorial days, public statues, portraits in oils or photographs, and many other methods" and for the Yoruba, ancestors were venerated through elaborate masquerades, the maintenance of shrines, and the pouring of libations.[60] Explicating the continuity of African culture, Adefunmi maintained that through ancestor veneration "the culture of the Yoruba continues, for by keeping alive their memory, their traditions, dress, language, organizations, laws and customs, they preserve their total civilization."[61] The veneration of ancestors was valued as an essential component of Orisha-Vodu because it provided African Americans with a connection to ancestors beyond North America.

Finally, Adefunmi offered African American readers practical instructions on how to ritually honor their ancestors in their private dwellings. African Americans were encouraged to create small ancestor altars in their homes. Dressed with offerings of fruit, flowers, water, and an Egungun ancestor figure, these shrines would create for African Americans an ancestral association that could be continually reinforced. Adefunmi concluded his literary treatise on Orisha-Vodu with a brief overview of Harlem's Yoruba Temple and the African cultural practices instituted therein, the "revolutionary innovations" of religion and culture the temple offered the African American community, and the ultimate vision of an African "Yoruba state" in North America.[62]

Tribal Origins

With *Tribal Origins of the African Americans* (1962), Adefunmi published perhaps his most ambitious explication of the "pre-American" origins of African Americans. Inspired by the chapter "The Search for Tribal Origins" in Melville Herskovits's *The Myth of the Negro Past*, Adefunmi set about the task of tracing African American cultural and religious origins back to

Africa. Although Adefunmi held heavily racialized conceptions of African religious identity, he was able to use scholarship by white Americans and Europeans such as Ulli Bier, Melville Herskovits, Pierre Verger, and Basil Davidson as sources of textual authority to corroborate the cultural, religious, and primordial links he made to Africa.

Tribal Origins begins with a passionate, somber foreword emphasizing U.S. African Americans' pre-American origins and pleading for their cultural and religious "reendowment":

> There is no tragedy which has caused a deeper personal conflict in the mind and spirit of the black American than the question of his pre-American origins. Nothing fills the average American born black with more discomfort and embarrassment than a discussion about Africa. The two basic reasons for his severe attack of inferiority on those occasions is firstly, his complete lack of accurate knowledge about the regions of his pre-American origins, and secondly, his even greater ignorance of any of the aspects of his ancestral civilization. Thus it is unthinkable that real, honest progress and purpose can be brought into the lives of a people who have no idea or measurement to judge their progress by. Briefly stated, "it is impossible to know where you are going if you do not know where you have been," or "You cannot tell whom you can become if you do not know who you are." For years therefore, Africa and people derived therefrom, have been subjected to every conceivable ridicule and humiliation. With no society to defend its culture, it is inevitable that for every person of African origin, Africa became a badge of shame. It is therefore the purpose of this booklet and the Yoruba Temple to begin the re-endowment of every African-born-in-America with confidence and appreciation of his origins and culture.[63]

Equipped with charts, illustrations, and a map of Africa entitled "Our Ancestral Land," Adefunmi attempted to make historical linkages between African Americans in the United States and the ancient communities of West Africa. He commends Melville Herskovits's landmark text, *The Myth of the Negro Past*, for vital contributions to the study of African American cultural origins, dispelling theories of the scattered origins of

African Americans, identifying geographical clusters, and recognizing the Dahomean and Yoruba influences within many of the cultural retentions in the Americas. Adefunmi also tried to explain why, "if African culture remained so strong in certain New World regions, its outward forms nearly vanished from North America."[64] Adefunmi cited the geographical diversity of slavery in the New World; the fact that Protestantism dominated North America; the "western deprecation of African religion with its Gods, dancing and drums"; and the elite, anti-African education received by U.S. blacks after emancipation.[65]

According to Adefunmi, even in the absence of outward survivals among black North Americans, "It goes without saying that the student of African cultures can easily recognize that the *character* of the African-American is extremely *African*."[66] Outwardly visible cultural practices, such as those seen throughout South America and the Caribbean, did not negate the fact that "an African-American well trained in his ancestral culture can see dozens of instances weekly whose underlying character is unquestionably African."[67] Therefore, in the case of black North Americans, Adefunmi argued only the "outward forms of certain characteristics reflect European influences" with the inward forms still distinguishably African.[68] Adefunmi's goal, then, was to remold the outer features of African Americans using African sociocultural and religious practices so that they would correspond with their "unquestionably African" inner core.

At the close of *Tribal Origins*, Adefunmi responded to the question, "What will the increased knowledge of tribal origins and the liberation and nationalism of Africa itself produce among the African-Americans?" He predicted that African Americans would reject the Christian and Islamic traditions currently being practiced within their communities and would instead seek a religion that would complement their African origins. He interpreted the nationalist fervor of the 1960s as "a great reaction against Christianity and a searching for something African to identify within the realm of spiritual matters."[69] He believed that the African American affiliation with the Honorable Elijah Muhammad and the "superficially intellectual association with Islam" would be short-lived, because Islam "was not indigenously African to begin with" and also because Adefunmi found it "difficult to imagine that the black majority in America will allow themselves to exchange one foreign culture for another both of which are basically the same and equally antagonistic to African culture."[70]

Adefunmi's goal, however, was exposure and promotion, reversion, not conversion. As he would state in his next publication, *The African State*, "The idea of one religion converting peoples of other nations, races, and regions is arrogant, imperialistic, and unsuitable, because each religion is based upon geographical peculiarities, their customs and philosophies of a people and legends handed down to them by the Ancestors. To convert one people then to the religion of another people is to interrupt the natural continuity of self knowledge, history and culture of a people."[71] *Tribal Origins* was an important link in helping restore the "natural continuity" of African Americans with Africa and their reversion to Orisha-Vodu. With Orisha-Vodu, African Americans could discard their "cultural amnesia" and engage in the "restoration" of a "true identity" based solely on their "own cultural progenitors."[72]

The African State

The purpose of *The African State* was to describe the complex institutional structures and cultural configurations, along with religion, that maintained African society. Central to African society was a "sacred state" that united the institutions of economy, the home, and religion. This state was like a monarchy, with the king-priest receiving his divine status from the orisa. His highest-ranking wife was the Iya-Oba, or the "king's official mother," who functioned as the most powerful female in the state. Economically the state organized itself under a system of communal socialism. According to Adefunmi, within "such a system so devoutly respectful of the interdependence and dignity of humans, capitalism with its extreme emphasis on selfish competition and ambition and where one or a small group of individuals might control the means of survival of the entire community, seems animal, and savage in its truest sense, and destructive to the natural group instinct and co-operativeness which supposedly raises man above beast."[73] Agriculture and small trade dominated the economy of communal socialism, and for Adefunmi, it was not until the arrival of Europeans in Africa and the transatlantic slave trade that this economy was severely disrupted:

> At this same period in world history similar scenes of horror and degradation could be found everywhere Europeans had appeared. It was as if an age of apocalypse had dawned upon the universe

and a malevolent God had caused a scourge of white men to spill out of Europe to despoil and degrade all of mankind in a plague of destruction in which entire civilizations would be wrecked, whole races would be ravished and nearly wiped out, and their depopulated continents occupied by a sea of uncouth invaders. When the slave trade declined, West Africa had lost one half of its population, only a trifle remained of the former splendor of its Kingdoms. Europeans by virtue of superior weapons had commenced the conquest of the continent and the economy had collapsed and industrial incentive rapidly perish[ed] due to the importation of cheap manufactures from Europe. It was at this period and from this time that most of the false impressions of Africa were formed.

Adefunmi's goal was to reeducate African Americans about the culture of their ancestors and teach them the foundational structures of African nationhood. Borrowing from the Africa of antiquity as well as from post-colonial Africa provided Adefunmi and his supporters with a wide range of cultural and religious capital from which to choose. Adefunmi was aware to some degree that he was fashioning a Yoruba culture that would not be a strict facsimile. Given his broader interests in Dahomean and Egyptian cultures, it would for him undoubtedly remain African.

Ultimately, *The African State* was part of a larger social philosophy that Adefunmi called the African Cultural Restoration Plan. The plan had goals ranging from procuring an autonomous land base in the United States to transforming the cultural and religious contours of African American life. *The African State*, coupled with *An African Marriage*, was in many ways published as an instructional guidebook to assist in the implementation of this plan. For Adefunmi, it was the social, cultural, political, economic, and familial institutions of the African state that would in essence provide the necessary protection for the preservation of an integral and aggregated African self.

An African Marriage

Family and home were two important institutions in the realization of his African Cultural Restoration Plan. Related to this, Roger Friedland in his article, "Religious Nationalism and the Problem of Collective

Representation," argues that religious nationalists consider "the loving family, not the autonomous individual, as the elemental unit of which the social is composed."[74] Reinforcing the centrality of the African family, Adefunmi published a short pamphlet entitled *An African Marriage*, specifically detailing the meaning of the institution of marriage. The cover was illustrated with a picture of a young black woman in African attire whose outstretched hands were grasping two smiling children. Over their heads read the title, *An African Marriage*. The conspicuous absence of the African husband from the picture offered its readers a glimpse into Adefunmi's perceptions of the African marriage and gendered notions of the home. The booklet conveyed African cultural practices through the fictional narrative of Ewumi, a prototypical African wife and mother. According to the pamphlet, Ewumi's journey began in the town of Ede in Nigeria. As a child, "Ewumi seldom saw her father, and he played no part in her life. Only the mother was ever present."[75] Ewumi's life unfolded within a network of women that included her mother, her grandmother, and her aunts, who provided the "solid framework within which she could feel secure."[76] Ewumi's extended maternal network and family present a stark contrast to the nuclear family of the West. In the text's gendered representations of Ewumi, she was taught the roles and responsibilities related to the domestic sphere. As a young girl, she learned to "cook, wash clothes, to grind pepper, and pound maize and dried yam slices in the mortar."[77] Ewumi also took part in "the town's religious festivals, especially in the four-day festival of the new yams in July in honour of the Orishas (the gods) and the seven-day festival in honour of the god Shango at the end of the rainy season."[78]

According to the story, Ewumi grew up to be a fine girl and was soon ready for marriage. She received expensive gifts from her prospective husband and a bride price of thirty-nine dollars was set. The booklet sought to clarify misconceptions about African dowry, explaining that "the bride price was not so much a contract between two individuals as the symbol of two families being joined together."[79] Ewumi entered her husband's household as part of a polygynous marriage, with one husband and many wives. The pamphlet sought to bring definition and texture to the polygynous unit and espoused the efficacies of a marital system often deemed oppressive to women. Women benefited from polygyny, the pamphlet argued, because household responsibilities were shared. Also, in terms of power dynamics, "divorce is easy for a woman; almost impossible for man. Wives like Ewumi were responsible for meals and received conjugal visits from their husband on a rotating cycle of five days."[80] "Morals in Yoruba society, and the rules derived therefrom . . . tend to ensure the production of many children and . . . guarantee that no women will be left to die as spinsters."[81]

Adefunmi presented polygyny as an important practice in the African restoration process in America. Adefunmi most likely anticipated a gender critique as he thought to explain that any deference African women exhibited to their husband "does not imply the contempt nor disregard for women so characteristic of Islamic society. . . . A Yoruba husband may increase the number of wives in his household only after considerable consultation, and the approbation of his first wife. He may increase his wives, but not decrease them, for once he has taken a woman he is expected to provide [for], protect, and respect her till death."[82] According to Amiri Baraka, "The idea of polygamy was 'new' and 'black' so we went for it."[83] By 1965, Adefunmi had divorced from his Dutch wife, and along with several other male temple priests, adopted a polygynous life-style. Although plural marriage was not recognized under American civil law, he advocated it as a valid African social and cultural alternative to monogamous Western Christian marriage. Ceremonially recognized polygyny eventually became an option in the 1960s that continues to be exercised in the twenty-first century among members of the African American Yoruba priesthood throughout the United States.

Africa, for Adefunmi, was held together within symbiotic relationships of religion, culture, government, economy, the home, and marriage. These institutional networks of support were for Adefunmi integral cornerstones in building an African nation and tradition in America, and his early texts served as an important literary medium through which their knowledge would be disseminated.

Textuality and Tradition

Tradition or the ongoing process of "traditionalizing" in which Adefunmi and African American Yoruba were engaged should not be viewed as static but as what J. Lorand Matory calls a "shifting gestalt" placed in correspondence with a dynamic set of assumed religious and cultural practices that predate America.[84] Through his texts, Adefunmi sought to transform the ancient cultural traditions of Africa into a "living tradition" in America.

"Living traditions," according to Alasdair MacIntyre "continue a not-yet-completed narrative," and they "confront a future whose determinate and determinable character . . . derives from the past."[85] Tradition in this sense is no longer about "time-honoured orthodox doctrines that have been fossilized" or a "repository" for "relics" but is seen as "dynamic, current, and responsive to change."[86] History, nation, selfhood, and tradition became integral to understanding Adefunmi's broader religious and cultural project of rewriting African Americans into a new historical framework that included a preenslaved, pre-American moment in Africa that countered former conflicting representations. As Thomas Eriksen theorizes in *Ethnicity and Nationalism*, "People are more liable . . . to reflect upon and objectify their way of life as a culture or as a *tradition*, and in this way they may become *a people* with an abstract sense of community and a presumed shared history."[87] This newly constructed notion of "traditional" culture provides, as Paul Gilroy explains, a new way "to articulate personal autonomy with collective empowerment."[88] Thus, Adefunmi's task was not simply historical; it was what John Ernest labels "metahistorical," in that he challenged the very "terms of history and the politics of historical writing."[89]

Adefunmi's use of textual language revived new images of antiquity and encoded new historical self-references for African Americans that transcended the slave motif. With the use of textual support, the ontological meaning of African American-ness would no longer rest within the bounded, objectified category of slave but would appropriate the textured identity of African. Charles H. Long argues that for the African American "to normalize the condition of slavery would be to deny his existence as a human being. The slave had to come to terms with the opaqueness of his condition and at the same time oppose it. He had to experience the truth of his negativity and at the same time transform and create *an-other* reality."[90] Thus, diasporic communities understood that the creation of "*an-other*" reality meant making "sense of the trauma of the decentering and destruction of their cultures" and coming "to terms with the fact that *their cultures would never be the same.*"[91] As diasporic populations began to create "on the level of . . . religious consciousness," Long argues, "not only did this transformation produce new cultural forms, but its significance must be understood from the point of view of the *creativity of the transforming process itself.*"[92] Within this larger context, Adefunmi's writings, the formation of Shango and Yoruba Temples, his cultural reproductions of

Africa, and later Oyotunji African Village become critical examples of "the creativity of the transforming process" through which African Americans formulated their own vernacular expression of Yoruba identity and tradition. What matters most is not to determine whether the substance of what they created was quantifiably African, but how we might best understand its various layers of meaning, innovative formulations, and creative discourses involved in this "transforming process."

If tradition can be viewed as what Jeffrey Stout calls "a discursive practice considered in the dimension of history," then one could see Adefunmi's literary works and institutions as fostering a new tradition among the "many trans-Atlantic manifestations" of Yoruba.[93] African American Yoruba to some degree sought to express their notion of tradition as James Baldwin did, as coming "out of the battle waged to maintain their integrity" and reflective of "the long and painful experience of a people."[94]

Oseijeman Adefunmi's texts foreshadowed a larger textual movement among American Yoruba practitioners and scholars that extended into the twenty-first century. J. Lorand Matory posits that written texts have emerged as important "vehicles of trans-Atlantic Yoruba identity" and "black Atlantic cultural transmission."[95] Although Adefunmi's texts never reached the status of canon, they were nevertheless crucial in offering African Americans a useable image of Africa that could "create a unity of vision" among its North American descendants.[96] Within the world of Adefunmi's texts, Africa became the primary impetus for theorizing identity, ritualizing culture, advancing tradition, and engaging in what Gesa Mackenthun calls "national self-invention."[97] Moreover, Adefunmi was able to do this at a critical time in American social history when the wider American populace wrestled with issues of political inclusion, racial difference, and global sovereignty.

Ultimately, Adefunmi's "authorship" was predicated on providing African Americans with a "narrative concept of selfhood"[98] that was rooted not in what MacIntyre calls "the unity of a narrative embodied in a single life" but in a self that found meaning within a collective journey of history.[99] What Adefunmi's texts most profoundly reveal is that "texts are always moments in conversation."[100] For African American Yoruba, localization and legitimacy were constantly being negotiated, were often unstable, yet always enduring, even within a larger religious arena characterized by the inevitable "contested construction" of tradition.[101] Cuban devotees often challenged acts of religious agency by African American Yoruba, leading to moments of conflict between African American and Hispanic Yoruba communities in New York City over wider issues of orthodoxy and orthopraxy, authority and hierarchy. The sources of these conflicts are the subject of the next chapter.

CHAPTER FIVE

"This Religion Comes from Cuba!"

Race, Religion, and Contested Geographies

☙❧

Why are we trying to recapture our experience by going through the Caribbean? The only link that we have through anything African is directly straight across the water to Africa.

—Chief Adenibi Edubi Ifamyiwa Ajamu

A S LATE AS the mid-1990s, words still echoed in Oseijeman Adefunmi's head that were spoken to him some thirty years ago at a bembe drum ceremony. He and another African American devotee found themselves in conversation with a Cuban santera regarding the origins of the tradition Adefunmi called Yoruba. Adorned in a dashiki (an African-patterned multicolored shirt commonly worn in the 1960s), Adefunmi was approached by the Cuban santera, who inquired, "Why are you dressed like that?" Coming from a tradition where Cuban male *santeros* customarily wore white, European-style shirts, pants, and head coverings and female santeras wore white skirts, blouses, dresses, and head wraps, this Cuban santera considered Adefunmi rather oddly attired for the sacred ritual occasion. Adefunmi's response must have seemed equally perplexing: "Well, this is the way that they dress in Africa." To which the santera immediately responded, "Africa has nothing to do with this." Adefunmi then explained, "But the gods and goddesses are all Africans." Overhearing the exchange, another devotee interjected, "Well, you know the religion comes from Africa." The Cuban santera immediately brought the conversation to a screeching halt, emphatically pronouncing, "What are you talking about? This religion comes from *Cuba!*"[1]

Cuban immigrants brought to America distinct interpretations of Yoruba religion that had been cultivated in the social, cultural, and political milieu of Cuba. African Americans, by contrast, wanted to emphasize their ancestral claims to Africa as well as their distinct national and racial interpretations of the religion as informed by their immediate U.S. context. Rather than debate the harrowing intricacies of authentication, I seek to unveil the growing sectarianism that resulted from the diverse ways in which the African American and Cuban communities sought to legitimize their claims to the orisa tradition.[2] In the end, religious authority in North America was established not from a single transliteration of Yoruba religion but through ethnically competing discourses.

From 1960 to 1970, incidents of convergence as well as of conflict emerged between African American and Cuban orisa communities in New York City.[3] This was the formative decade that produced a distinct African American imprint within the North American Yoruba movement, beginning with the establishment of Yoruba Temple in Harlem and culminating with the formation of Oyotunji African Village in South Carolina. During this decade, the two communities' divergent cultural heritages created what Aina Olomo called "a chasm of alienation."[4] One major cause of this chasm was the infusion of black-nationalist politics into the religion and in Adefunmi's case through his affiliations with black territorial nationalist groups such as the Republic of New Africa. Other areas of contestation between the two groups centered on the use of representational iconography from Roman Catholicism and Yoruba Temple's very public display of orisa sacred ceremonies. At the very core of these religious tensions lay an inability of both groups to agree on how best to localize interpretations of Yoruba religion in the United States and at the same time maintain standardized criteria for religious authority. According to Beatriz Morales, "Cuban priests and priestesses resented the movement not only because it played down the role of the Catholic saints but also because it questioned the legitimacy of Christian influences."[5]

In this chapter, I seek not to simply iterate a narrative of religious conflict between African American and Cuban communities in the United States. As Babalosa John Mason, an active participant in this early Yoruba American history, cautions both scholars and practitioners, one should not rigidly polarize the relationship between the two communities, for, as Steven Gregory observes, their "ethnic differences were mitigated, to a large extent, by the complex relations of ritual kinship that bind practitioners together in culturally active religious groups."[6] Instead, this chapter examines an outgrowth of this ambiguous relationship of cooperation and conflict: the assertion of a "self-determined legitimacy" on the part of African Americans.[7] With a growing yet precarious reliance on their own sense of agency, African Americans reshaped religious standards of orthodoxy and authority while adopting racial identity as a legitimate lens for meaning making within the tradition.

Cubans and African Americans shared social and religious space in Harlem, New York. Yet what they did not share was a unified vision of how this religion should be localized within a North America U.S. context. For the newly arriving Cubans, the religion provided a living connection to a specific cultural place, a home in the Caribbean symbolically linking them to an old world of memory, family, and history. As Steven Gregory explains, santería's "convivial ritual kinship networks, performative tradition, and collective forms of social spiritual support . . . provided important cultural resources for affirming and negotiating their identities as Latinos in North America."[8] For Cubans in North America, it was not necessary to spiritualize Africa; instead, they looked to Cuba for their spiritual sustenance. According to Pancho Mora, "I haven't lost anything in Africa, I don't need to go back to Africa . . . [This religion] came from my father's house and my father's house is in Cuba." In contrast, the religion symbolized for African Americans a trans-American history and reconnection to Africa, a possibility for a post-Christian culture, and potential for a renewed self-representation in America. It symbolized something "unambiguously African . . . whose survival and development in the New World offered proof of the tenacity of African cultures in spite of the horrors of the slave trade and centuries of racial subordination."[9] Functioning alongside and in tandem with each other both communities engaged in the "contested construction" of what North American Yoruba "tradition" would become.[10]

In short, what both communities were seeking were ways of demarcating "place" and "space" for themselves amidst North America's diverse religious and social landscape. According to Dolores Hayden in *The Power of Place*, communities within North America have continuously sought to create both physical and transcendent places out of which they construct their daily lives. They inculcate these places with religious, social, and political meaning, creating a unique lens through which their immediate reality is lived. Self-representation and identity are "intimately tied to memory: both . . . personal memories (where we have come from and where we have dwelt) and . . . the collective or social memories interconnected with the histories of our families, neighbors, fellow workers, and ethnic communities."[11]

This interplay of personal, social, and collective identity is helpful in understanding both the Cuban and the African American Yoruba communities in Harlem during the 1960s. On the one hand, the Cuban community was a direct product of immigration, largely after the Cuban Revolution. Like other immigrant communities, it attempted to adjust to the contours

FIGURE 9. Cuban immigrants in Harlem welcome the visit of President Fidel Castro in 1960. Photograph courtesy of Klytus Smith.

of American life while negotiating a deep sense of displacement and reconstructing institutions of meaning. Cuban nationals in the United States wrestled with the transformations occurring on their island, some in political support of President Fidel Castro, while others in complete disavowal and renunciation of the revolution's agenda.

According to Cuban psychologist Mercedes Sandoval, "Uprootedness . . . affected [Cuban] exiles with prevalent feelings of loss, ambivalence, lack of control, and frustration."[12] Memories of home in Cuba and an enduring emphasis on geographical origins helped to remedy their sense of uprootedness and exile.

African Americans, on the other hand, possessed an ambiguous national identity where for both black and white Americans race was often ranked over collective citizenry. African Americans lived with the historical fact that although North America had been the place of African-descendant births and repopulation since the sixteenth century, it took a Constitutional amendment in the nineteenth century to naturalize their citizenship. These conflicting interpretations of religion, community, and civil identity profoundly shaped the content of engagement between African Americans and Cubans in both communities' efforts to localize Yoruba religion.

William A. Christian Jr. in *Local Religion in Sixteenth-Century Spain* provides a useful model for understanding the processes of religious localization and indigenization by popular religious communities. In his study of sixteenth-century Roman Catholicism in Spain, Christian concluded that "two levels" of Roman Catholic religious identity were in practice.[13] One level involved what he called the "Church Universal," with its traditional orthodoxy and established clerical authority based in a far-removed geographical center. The other level involved the popular religion of local communities and its symbiotic yet autonomous development in relation to the center. Local interpretations of religion were reshaped around "particular sacred places, images, . . . idiosyncratic ceremonies, and a unique calendar built from the settlement's own sacred history."[14] In celebrating local sacred histories, communities created religious meaning and authority based on interpretations primarily "embodied in the home landscape."[15] Similarly, African Americans reformulated Yoruba religion into "a religion in which the *local* was of primary significance."[16] Informing this local religious consciousness was their historical separation from Africa and their acute self-consciousness as a racialized body in the United States, as evidenced by their continuous social dislocation.

Christian's study supports the validity of local interpretations of religion even as they diverge from established centers. He helps us understand that "religious customs may be similar or different, they may start by inspiration or by diffusion, but by definition they have one thing in common: they are tied to a specific place and a historical constituency" and form in essence a "little tradition" that has "taken root in a particular place."[17] Through this interpretive lens, African American Yoruba religion represents not a deviation from a presumed orthodoxy but an innovative expression rooted in local meanings.

Revisiting Yoruba Temple: A Case Study in Lived Autonomy

According to historian Lawrence Levine, "It is not necessary for a people to originate or to invent all or even most of the elements of their culture. It is necessary only that these components become their own, embedded in their traditions, expressive of their world view and life style."[18] Cubans and African Americans indeed labored to make this religion become their own in North America. Cuban practitioners were concerned with orthodoxy and concealment, while African American devotees became public and nationalist. Over time, religious worlds collided in Harlem, and Adefunmi's public activities at Yoruba Temple and plans for Oyotunji African Village stood at the heart of this collision. Yoruba Temple altered the face of what Cuban practitioners were calling Santería and Ocha by infusing it with specific interpretations of culture, race, and nationalism. With its new starting point residing in what Brandon calls an "orientation toward Africa," the Cuban community no longer recognized the religion of their Caribbean home as its black North American practitioners paraded through the streets of Harlem, transformed the iconography, adorned themselves in African clothing, married polygynously, and communicated in black-nationalist rhetoric.[19]

The public ritual displays of Yoruba Temple and its exclusive focus on Africa exacerbated tensions between Adefunmi and his Cuban counterparts. Fissures erupted widely and rapidly over the place of African culture within the religion, the appropriateness of indigenously American philosophies of race within the religion, and the temple's public exposure

FIGURE 10.
Oseijeman
Adefunmi performs
a ritual for the
ancestors outside
of Yoruba Temple.
Photograph courtesy
of Klytus Smith.

of sacred rituals. George Brandon labeled this period of African American agency and autonomy within the religion as the "second new formation of Santería."[20]

Adefunmi recalls that "the idea of Orisha temples, publicly displayed, shocked the older Cuban priests who had emerged from a long tradition of clandestine practice and persecution in Cuba."[21] Cubans held strong notions of ritual orthopraxy, which Adefunmi's Yoruba Temple challenged. To institutionalize the worship of the orisa gods in a public temple in Harlem went against very deep religious proclivities of Cuban immigrants. How could ceremonies designed for initiates and believers become public exhibitions for all to see? How could the sacred shrines and sacred vessels that housed the gods be on display for public viewing? How could the sacred praise songs, chants, and drum rhythms be allowed to fall on the ears of common observers? How would the orisa respond to these innovations? How would U.S. officials and civil authorities respond, and could intolerance and persecution be avoided? These were the questions that plagued Cuban santeros and santeras in Harlem in the 1960s as a result of the activities of Yoruba Temple. This concern about public ritualization and media coverage would continue to persist for large numbers of North American Cubans for several decades, until the public notoriety of Ernesto Pichardo's Church of Lucumi Babalu Aye (established 1974) in Hialeah, Florida, and its successful Supreme Court victories on behalf of the religion in 1993.

Despite ideological divisions that arose between the two communities, Adefunmi was extremely indebted to Cuban practitioners, such as Pancho Mora, who facilitated his early introduction to Yoruba religion and credited them as supporters of Yoruba Temple activities. Throughout the 1960s, Adefunmi possessed deep affection and respect for Mora, and they maintained an amicable relationship despite their divergent perceptions of the religion. In fact, Mora owned one of the first botanicas, or spiritual stores, in New York City located near Amsterdam Avenue, where he sold religious artifacts and offered divination readings for clients. During that time, Adefunmi lived within walking distance of the botanica, where he would often go to visit Mora to discuss issues regarding the religion. Occasionally, Adefunmi would seek spiritual guidance and request divination readings from Mora.[22] Their cordial friendship and apparent spiritual relationship did not prevent philosophical tensions between the two men on the question of religious practice, however. Adefunmi confesses that his Latino counterparts openly "objected to his flamboyant Yoruba attire," his "television appearances" with "temple drummers and members in ceremonies to the Gods," his public advertisements of Yoruba Temple, his obtaining a legal "charter of incorporation" for Yoruba Temple, and his open polygyny.[23]

As other scholars have indicated, it was clear that "the African nationalist ideology and objectives of the Yoruba Temple conflicted both with the esoteric conditions of *Santería* and with the assimilationist goals of many Cubans."[24] Many Cubans had a growing concern about how Adefunmi's public expressions might affect their immigrant status. The perception was that African Americans were drawing their own distinct boundaries around notions of the Yoruba sacred and were increasingly violating the veil of secrecy that characterized the religion in Cuba. Adefunmi invoked race in ways that Cuban immigrants perceived as alienating and exclusive.

In publicizing the religion in Harlem through public rallies, bembes, and parades, Adefunmi breached the code of secrecy by inviting newspaper and media personnel to Yoruba Temple and exposing the tradition in potentially vulnerable ways through television. In a speech some twenty-one years later at the International Conference on the Orisa Tradition, spearheaded by the Caribbean Cultural Center in New York and hosted in Nigeria in 1981, Adefunmi reflected on these earlier tensions: "An alarm . . . had been set off among the Cuban-American establishment which had always operated in the utmost obscurity. They feared the Afro-Americans, dressed in Yoruba attire, boldly conducting drum ceremonies and openly advertising their location and activities would attract police interference.[25] This had often been the case in Cuba. But the Afro-Americans were in no mood to conceal the discovery of their long-lost culture. Instead, they proceeded to broadcast on radio the legends of the Orisha. They appeared on television repeatedly announcing the 'return of the Gods and Goddesses of Africa!'"[26] The religio-nationalist strategies of Yoruba Temple, while facilitating the presumed needs of the African American community, continually widened the orthopraxic gap between them and their fellow Cuban adherents. According to Adefunmi, African Americans had discovered their "long-lost culture," and combined with religion, this ideological sentiment held huge nationalist currency within a racialized America.

Religion and the Politics of Race

As explained in previous chapters, the influx of Latino immigrants possessing ambiguous notions of race introduced great complexity to the American racial equation. Latin Caribbean communities represented a vast phenotypic range, and African Americans' experiences of them often varied, according to the phenotypic spectrum. As early as 1940, J. A. Rogers had begun to probe the complex Latino response to American racial politics and typologies. Rogers satirically remarked, "If you don't want a fight on your hands don't mention 'Negro' blood to the average Cuban or Puerto Rican in the United States even if he is three-fourths black."[27] He sardonically referred to this complex phenomenon, ubiquitous throughout the Americas and the Caribbean as "hushing up Negro ancestry."[28]

Analyzing the intersection of race and religion, Marta Vega contends that "the racist attitudes of the Cuban and Puerto Rican communities were . . . manifested when African Americans began initiating into the Yoruba tradition in New York City."[29] According to Vega, "Language and cultural differences, in addition to racist attitudes, and the attempt to maintain control over the information on Yoruba practice caused dissension among these two communities."[30] Vega's insightful fieldwork revealed that "the divisions between the African Americans and Latino communities due to oppressive, racist attitudes our communities had internalized were confronted as African Americans actively sought to incorporate the Orishas of Cuba . . . into the Black Power Revolution."[31] As an initiate of Lloyd Weaver and Marjorie Baynes Quiñones, Oseye Mchawi reflects on this period remembering that "the relationship between the Latino community and African American community at that time was often strained but acceptable . . . The African Americans had to deal with a certain amount of prejudices to gain information, and they did . . . They were often ostracized, there was a language barrier."[32] She assesses that the current relationship between both groups has transformed significantly and that "there is now a closer relationship between the Latino community and African American community. There is now a more open exchange and relationship."[33]

Conflicting notions of race and how it informed self-identity proved to be a constant barrier between Cuban and African American orisa communities. According to Gayle McGarrity and Osvaldo Cárdenas, the concept of race played an intricate role in Cuban society. Designations for "white" in Cuba were extremely complex and not determined solely by biology. Unlike in the United States, the nebulous category "socially white," which provided access to elite privileges, was a viable option even for Cubans who possessed some African ancestry.[34] Many Cuban immigrants entering the racialized context of the United States would have clung to shifting perceptions of whiteness, which, McGarrity and Cárdenas argued, were ultimately "more important than fact."[35] In contrast, African Americans were socialized in the United States, where whiteness and blackness were rigidly and legally defined.

The racial experiences of African American Yoruba determined their view of the use of white saints and conceptions of purity. As Steven Gregory states, "Members of the Temple rejected the association of the Yoruba orisa with Catholic saints, as well as other symbolic or terminological traces of

Christianity within Afrocuban religious practice. An emphasis was placed on reconstituting 'pure' Yoruba religious traditions by going directly to West African sources. Ironically, these sources were often to be found in anthropological literature."[36] Notions of racial and religious purity posed a conceptual paradox. Both African American and Cuban communities developed their religious philosophies physically removed from the tradition's initial source in Africa. Yet both sets of practitioners held firm views on the degree to which the religion's parameters of ritual purity could and could not be challenged.

Throughout the 1960s, Adefunmi's energies were largely devoted to redirecting the symbolic center of the religion from Cuba to Africa. He began a radical erasure of the images Cubans offered the religion in the form of saints and began to replace them with his own African-inspired iconography. According to Adefunmi, African American refusal to continue the syncretism between the Orishas and the Roman Saints, which had been so necessary during the slave era, but which now they regarded as an anachronism, deeply frustrated and angered their Afro-Cuban mentors.[37] For many Cubans, the orisa inhabited Cuba and were summoned to the United States via immigration. Therefore, Mercedes Cros Sandoval argues that these immigrants brought with them a "transculturalized, Cubanized" interpretation of Yoruba religion.[38] Africa and racial interpretations did not figure as prominently and as self-consciously for Cubans as they did for African Americans. Sandoval contends that for many Cuban santeros and santeras it was not until many years later that "the study of academic literature opened a window to Africa, to the very roots of the religion they were practicing."[39] According to Christine Ayorinde, even in the twenty-first century, "for most "Cuban *santeros* . . . being 'Yoruba' does not mean being or wanting to be African."[40] From Adefunmi's point of view, "the Cuban priests and myself were worlds apart. Our whole life-style had changed, we had introduced a racism into the religion that didn't exist among the Cubans. They didn't have the race problem that we had in the United States, and, of course, they couldn't understand my extremely severe racial attitudes at that time. So that naturally alienated a lot of them."[41]

Many scholars like Marta Vega, Steven Gregory, Mercedes Cros Sandoval, and Pedro Pérez Sarduy argue, however, that Cuba did, in fact, have its own racial challenges that were subsequently played out in the North American religious arenas of Santería. From the revolutionary period of the late 1950s to the early 1980s, "blacks constituted less than 5 percent of Cuban immigrants."[42] Cros Sandoval argues that because of the disproportionate number of white Cubans who immigrated to the United States before the Mariel boatlift in 1980, "many white *santeros* achieved positions of preeminence in diasporic *Santería*," resulting in "the perception of a 'whitening' trend within the religion."[43] An added dimension of U.S. versus Cuban Santería is the claim of sociologist Harry G. Lefever that white Cuban babalawos enjoyed a numerical majority in the United States, which was far less typical in Cuba.[44] This "whitening trend," according to Sandoval, deemphasized in the United States the important function of Santería as the "core of ethnic identity," "roots," and "heritage" many black Cubans held, noting that "among whites . . . this function has never been meaningful."[45]

In the United States among African Americans and primarily Anglo-Cubans, questions of ethnic identity, roots, and heritage focused primarily on the issue of religious authority. African American practitioners in the 1960s were very much concerned that "white Cubans owned the Orisas" and that "for white Cubans to 'own' an African religion was absolutely ridiculous."[46] From the point of view of many white Cuban practitioners, Adefunmi did not have the legitimacy to implement innovations in the religion. Furthermore, according to the Cuban system, Adefunmi lacked priestly authority under which special religious rites could be performed. Although his divination reading in Cuba revealed he was to become a babalawo or priest of the Ifa divination method, he had not undergone such initiatory rites by Cuban religious standards.[47] In Adefunmi's opinion, his African ancestry afforded him open access to the "gods of Africa." He therefore established Yoruba Temple and performed divination readings based not on Cuban priestly authority but on a self-proclaimed, African ancestral authority. Adefunmi had self-consciously transformed his ritual "descent" from Cuban practitioners into a ritual "dissent" from them.

Cuban practitioners were keen to point out how the temple diverged from their entrenched interpretations of orthodoxy. Steven Gregory, referencing Sandra Cohn's early research, notes that what resulted from this contested interaction was that "the legitimacy or authenticity of the religious practice of the Yoruba Temple was challenged by some Cuban practitioners. In particular, the Cubans denounced the *bembes*, or religious festivals, sponsored by the Temple, noting that the drums used were not properly consecrated and that participants in the ceremonies were never possessed by the Orisha—a sure sign, they argued, of their lack of authenticity."[48] It was inferred that because Yoruba Temple did not have a lineage of possession priests, their ceremonies were not valid according to Cuban ritual standards yet to the contrary, there exists firsthand documented accounts of Yoruba Temple ceremonies that report "frequently dancers went into trances of possession."[49] Scholars such as Harry G. Lefever, Raul Carnizares, and Mercedes Cros Sandoval argue that "fewer trance-possessions" characterized U.S. Santería in general "because consecrated *bata* drums, the playing of which are essential for possession, either are not available or are not played in order to avoid negative reactions from neighbors."[50] The issue of Adefunmi and Yoruba Temple's legitimacy was in some ways grounded in a much broader politics of legitimacy being played out in the discourse of black nationalism. Amiri Baraka argues that "legitimacy" was in fact determined by a complex "association of symbols" and that to "control the symbolism and imagery" of and for African Americans translated for Adefunmi into figurative power.[51]

This power of symbolic naming or renaming spoke to larger issues of identity formation. Naming became an important way African Americans re-owned their historical past in Africa. Adefunmi sparked major controversy by dispensing African names to noninitiated persons. For him, African names were tied to a larger black-nationalist movement that felt the need to replace the "white man's" or "slave" name. He therefore not only offered African Americans new names but also encouraged them for their children, developing a "Yoruba naming ceremony for the newly born" in an effort to reconnect African Americans to African cultural practices.[52] For Cuban practitioners, these African names held significant sacred meaning and were reserved primarily for those who had undergone initiatory rites into the religion. Adefunmi, in contrast, saw them as a form of cultural currency through which African Americans could acquire a stronger link to Africa and its traditions. In spite of these differences, according to John Mason as well as Steven Gregory, there was always some cooperation between the black and Afro-Hispanic communities in particular. Some Afro-Cubans, although fewer before the 1980s Mariel era, were very much interested in the African roots of the tradition, and their presence complicated the boundaries that seemed to polarize the two communities. Adefunmi in fact acknowledged that the Afro-Cuban community "were secretly sympathetic to the aspirations of the Yoruba Temple" and admitted that "through them, vital information concerning rituals and potent articles flowed back to the Temple."[53]

By the late 1960s, Adefunmi revived his efforts to construct a blueprint for building a black homeland in the United States for African Americans. This idea was very much a continuation of Adefunmi's neo-Garvey affiliations in Harlem and also closely related to his 1962 role as deputy prime minister in the African Descendants Nationalist Independence Partition Party, which later held a conference on slavery reparations in Philadelphia.[54] Another leader of the organization was its minister of foreign affairs, Queen Mother Moore, who with Adefunmi, affirmed the organization's emphasis on "African names and African garb."[55] A forerunner to the Republic of New Africa formed six years later in 1968, the African Descendants Nationalist Independence Partition Party quickly established under its jurisdiction the United African Peoples Provisional Government, which instead of advocating emigration to Africa, demanded domestic sovereignty in America in "all land south of Delaware to the southwest corner of New Mexico." Adefunmi's 1960s activism also included the founding of the Harlem People's Parliament, where Adefunmi served as prime minister, Orisa Mola Akinyele Awolowo as minister of information, and Kenya's first president, Jomo Kenyatta, as minister of arts and culture.[56] Adefunmi's involvement with this organization and later with the Republic of New Africa was critical in laying the groundwork for a new homeland, distancing himself even further from his Cuban counterparts. While first-generation Cuban immigrants were adjusting to resettlement in their newly adopted country, Adefunmi was laying the foundation for a new partitioned nation-state for African Americans.

The Republic of New Africa: A Precursor to Black Nationhood

Oseijeman Adefunmi's nationalist platform experienced a profound evolution resulting from his membership in the territorial nationalist organization, the Republic of New Africa (RNA). Similar to other paramilitary and black territorial organizations of the 1960s, the Republic of New Africa was concerned largely with the prospect of a separate black nation, which it saw as "the government for the non-self-governing blacks held captive within the United States."[57] This black-separatist discourse was very much in line with its contemporaries such as the Nation of Islam, the Black Panthers, the

Congress on Racial Equality, and the Student Non-Violent Coordinating Committee, all of which expressed similar sentiments of separatism as a viable solution for the social and racial problems of the time.[58] The Republic of New Africa was part of a movement of territorial nationalists, then, who from 1968 to 1974 called for the geographical secession of African Americans from the United States of America.[59] It advocated a separate nation for "New Afrikan" people who specifically were the "descendants of persons kidnapped from Afrika and held here against their will, currently residing in the United States . . ."[60] The RNA's philosophical axiom rested on the premise that the United States had engaged in deliberate acts of "domestic colonialism" against its black citizenry.[61] Therefore, upon securing geographical sovereignty within the borders of the United States, the RNA would establish a "government in exile" in order to preside over its black populace. Its early financial sustenance would come from an estimated $400 billion in U.S. government reparations and its future maintained by a collective adoption of Ujamaa, "the Tanzanian model of cooperative economics and community self-sufficiency."[62] The RNA also saw separation as an act of "racial peace" and not, as their documents indicate, "limitless or unreasoning animosity toward America."[63] Their ultimate premise was that "reasonable men" should never be placed in a position "to accept permanent hostility and dislocation."[64] By January 1969, Milton Henry had pronounced that the RNA had purchased "a hundred acres in Mississippi" for its "base headquarters" and was asking each "black citizen" to "buy one-hundred-dollar Malcolm X land certificates" in order to launch the new republic.[65] More specifically the RNA demanded from the U.S. government a minimum of ten thousand dollars for every African American within its borders and "reparations were to be paid in fulfillment of the 'promise' by some Reconstruction-era politicians to freedmen of 40 acres, $50, and a mule."[66] The treasury amassed through reparations would then be used "to eliminate poverty, dependence, and crime through programs that raised self-esteem and achievement."[67]

In 1968, the leading African American magazine, *Ebony*, featured a story on the Republic of New Africa describing its recent formation and its ideological connections to its historical predecessors. The article stated:

> Some 200 black persons across the country, convening in Detroit
> this spring, gave birth to the Republic of New Africa, the newest

and perhaps boldest innovation in the history of black separatism. The Republic of New Africa is not a militant civil rights group seeking equality with white Americans, but in the words of the conferees (or delegates as they came to be called) a black nation—a government with its own elected officials. New African delegates signed a Declaration of Independence declaring black people of America "forever free and independent of the jurisdiction of the United States." Incredible? At first glance, perhaps, but the Republic of New Africa is in fact, only the contemporary aspect of a vision that has long been endemic to America's racial reality.[68]

The physical, structural, and ideological groundwork for the imminent New Africa was laid by the organization's visionaries, Milton and Richard Henry (later known as Gaidi and Imari Obadele). The first president was Robert Williams; first vice president, Milton Henry; ministers of culture, Baba Oseijeman Adefunmi and Amiri Baraka; minister

FIGURE 11. Executive leadership of the Republic of New Africa. Originally published in *Esquire Magazine*, January 1969. Photograph courtesy of Adger Cowans.

of education, Maulana Karenga; ministers of defense, H. Rap Brown and Baba Medahochi; minister of finance, Raymond Willis; treasurer, Obaboa Alowo; deputy minister of state, Wilber Grattan; as well as a prominent female leadership, namely minister of health, Queen Mother Moore; minister of justice, Joan Franklin; and second vice president, Betty Shabazz, widow of Malcolm X.[69]

After returning from his travels in the early 1960s, Milton, a Yale-trained lawyer, became increasingly convinced that African American separation was essential.[70] Along with his brother Richard, a journalist, he therefore proposed that the five southern states of South Carolina, Georgia, Alabama, Mississippi, and Louisiana should be set aside for African Americans. These states would be wrested from the hands of the American government by RNA members either as reparations from the U.S. government, by "outvoting whites county by county, city by city, state by state . . . ," or by military seizure by the RNA's Black Legion.[71] As a first step, in May 1968, "Gaidi mailed to President Nixon and handed two State Department officials a note demanding $400 billion in reparations, the designated five states, and the beginning of negotiations between the United States of America and the Republic of New Africa."[72] No evidence documents that the U.S. government ever acknowledged this note.[73] In the meantime, members of the organization were expected to devote themselves fully to the development of an all-black territory within the United States and were required to pledge the following "Oath of Allegiance" to the Republic of New Africa: "For the fruition of black power, for the triumph of black nationhood, I pledge to the Republic of New Africa and to the building of a better people and a better world, my total devotion, my total resources, and the total power of my mortal life."[74]

The Republic of New Africa attempted to realize the vision of black separation and self-governance of many of its twentieth-century predecessors such as Garvey's United Negro Improvement Association and Oscar Brown's National Movement for the Establishment of a 49th State.[75] It quickly established itself in the late 1960s as the new "provisional government" for all African Americans in the United States,[76] forming "consulates" in New York, Baltimore, Pittsburgh, Philadelphia, Washington, Chicago, Cleveland, San Francisco, and Los Angeles.[77] Mirroring the sentiments of the UNIA some five decades earlier, the RNA adopted Garvey's notion of a provisional black government, his idea of an African republic, and his creation of a paramilitary wing.[78] Whereas Garvey's goal was to form an independent black nation on the continent of Africa, however, the RNA's was a new diaspora republic in the land of its dispersal.

The Republic of New Africa was a twentieth-century response to the historical symbiosis between racialized blackness and landlessness. It fused the nineteenth-century notion of racial uplift and racial autonomy with a twentieth-century respect for African cultural values and the possibility of an independent black settlement in America. As a result of this fusion, the RNA was able to create an opportunity for "African" emigration on American soil while redesignating all black North Americans as "New Africans" and thus automatic citizens of the republic.[79] Like other sovereign nations, nonresidents would require temporary entry visas to the independent black homeland. Americans who intended to reside in the Republic of New Africa were expected to renounce their American citizenship and commit themselves fully to uplifting the new black sovereign nation.[80]

Interestingly enough, the literature of the Republic of New Africa resounded with profoundly American themes of a "frontier," "limitless opportunity," "hard work," and "ambition."[81] In "The Anti-Depression Program of the Republic of New Afrika," Obadele argued that because of discrimination, African Americans in the United States "never had a frontier" and the Republic of New Africa would provide "a place whither a man can go and be respected and rise as high as hard work, ambition, and ability can carry him."[82] In many ways, Obadele was theorizing a dual interpretation of America's racialized frontier. The first occurred for "the white American" who embraced the "*idea* of building a new world on virgin land," and the other was the twentieth-century Republic of New Africa and the ability of its "sovereign black nation" to "release lush and long-lived creativity for black people."[83]

As the organization's minister of culture, Oseijeman Adefunmi advocated "a completely separate nation mentally, spiritually, politically, even in ways of marriage and burials."[84] Adefunmi's membership in the Republic of New Africa had a significant impact on the ways in which he would conceptualize Oyotunji African Village a few years later. His main focus was on the transformative possibilities of culture and the vision to live it out within a sovereign state. Adefunmi disagreed with the organization's paramilitary thrust, and indeed the organization eventually experienced intense ideological tensions over the location of the new republic, the establishment of an armed militia, and the use of force in acquiring territory. By 1970, the Henry brothers had become estranged, the organization had split, and legal discrepancies arose concerning the actual ownership of a plot of land in Mississippi that the RNA had consecrated El Malik, or the "capital of the still unliberated nation" in honor of the slain black leader Malcolm X.[85] The demise of the Republic of New Africa was hastened in the early 1970s as the result of a violent police and FBI confrontation at the organizational headquarters that led to the imprisonment of several key members of the organization, including one of the Henry brothers. The organization was left unable to fulfill its promise of a New Africa, and an independent black nation never materialized. The Republic of New Africa's important legacy, however, would rest on its ability to propose a "new understanding of citizenship" to African Americans.[86] Adefunmi would take this unfulfilled vision of a black nation, couple it with a religious and cultural mission, and devise the early plans for Oyotunji African Village.

With the RNA's failed attempts at a homeland, Adefunmi viewed the tradition as being at a crossroads in New York City and was unsure whether his differences with Cuban practitioners could be resolved. Immigration, religious harassment in Cuba, and clandestine worship were important issues that affected the mode of Cuban practice of Santería in the United States. Issues of race, nationhood, and Africa most heavily dominated the practices of African Americans who were committed nationalists. Adefunmi understood, as Cros Sandoval so readily points out, that "many converted American Blacks feel that through *Santería* they have known the gods they think might have been worshipped by their ancestors, even though they might not know if they themselves are of Yoruba ancestry. *Santería* offers them a source of ethnic/racial identity, . . . is a link to Africa, to their long forgotten roots."[87]

Adefunmi desired a land base to symbolize these "forgotten roots." Growing increasingly disenchanted with urban life in New York City, Adefunmi therefore believed the time was ripe for laying the foundation for the new nation. In theory, much of the membership of Yoruba Temple agreed that African Americans were in need of an all-black space that would enable them to live in religious, cultural, political, and social autonomy. As one Yoruba Temple attendee recalls, though, members had important concerns: "Were black people prepared to run a country? Had we educated ourselves enough to run a country? The continent of Africa was having problems at the time in its adjustment from colonialism, what effect would that have on the new nation and why would their North American settlement be any easier?"[88] Ultimately, disagreement on where the new nation should be erected began to splinter the membership.

The three compelling possibilities for black nationhood were to form a black homeland in Harlem, relocate to Africa or the Caribbean, or find a land base in America's South.[89] Because Yoruba Temple had established itself as an important religious and cultural institution in New York City, some members saw Harlem as the logical place for the independent black space. Many members raised questions, however, regarding the likelihood of maintaining an African cultural and religious life-style in an urban setting. Many members imagined the African life-style they sought to recover as rural and pastoral, much like the one they believed their enslaved ancestors left behind. Competing with this image, though, was the reality of a postcolonial Africa characterized by the cosmopolitanism and urbanism of Accra, Lagos, and Dakar.

By 1969, Adefunmi had come to believe that "Yoruba Temple had reached the limits to which its culturally revived institutions could compete with the dominant Euro-American cultural institutions of New York City."[90] According to Carl Hunt, "The members of the Yoruba Temple realized that their culture could be practiced in an urban area, but they did not believe the cities were the place to solve the problems of American Blacks. They found that the architecture of the American cities was not conducive to the organization of the African family. They realized also that their jobs would not allow them to live their African lifestyle on a daily basis. They could practice their religion only on the weekends."[91]

Repatriation to Africa was still seen in the 1960s as an option for northern black nationalists. As a continent, Africa was rapidly decolonizing and gaining its independence at a time when racism was still pervasive throughout America. In 1961, the African Nationalist Pioneer Movement (ANPM) headed by former Garveyite Carlos Cooks, of which Adefunmi was a member, revived the question of African resettlement among America's black population. Born in the Dominican Republic, Cooks, like many of his nationalist contemporaries in Harlem, despised the self-effacing processes by which "Africans were converted into Negroes," which he saw as "zombified Caste creatures whose loyalty is permanently married to the white race; whose God and idolatry status is white..."[92] In an article entitled "Would Resettle Africa to Solve U.S. Problem," Professor Waldo Williams, a spokesperson for the ANPM, stated that "the history of our (the Negro's) association with the white man has convinced the intelligent elements of our race that the black man has no permanent future in white America." As a result, Williams concluded, the "only practical solution was a 'repatriation program' under which Africa would absorb millions of dark skinned Americans."[93] In 1965, an editorial appeared again in the *New York Amsterdam News* by David Kenyatta suggesting that the U.S. "government should set up agencies to resettle the Black People in Africa on a volunteer basis," for "this would solve the racial problem and the so-called Negroes will attain their freedom."[94]

After much deliberation, however, Adefunmi abandoned the option to emigrate to Africa for pragmatic and philosophical reasons. According to Hunt, Adefunmi "believed the time for returning to Africa was long past." Adefunmi believed that if Yoruba Americans returned to Africa, they would be unable to fulfill their responsibilities to the descendants of Africa in diasporic contexts. Adefunmi's agenda had been largely preoccupied with the diasporic Africans in North America and their religious and cultural redemption. Unlike the vision his parents held under Garveyism decades earlier, Adefunmi did not feel it necessary to return, but remain.

Adefunmi believed that the strength of Africa's descendants had to be proven in America. Having witnessed how Africans were displaying their physical courage and spiritual fortitude by fighting colonialism throughout the continent of Africa and in the Caribbean, he felt that Africans in North America needed to show the same fortitude and self-determination within their own domestic colonial context. He concluded that "if [African Americans] went back to Africa with their tails between their legs, all history would record that they had been stripped of their culture. They would not be regarded as real men."[95] North America was where African Americans must launch their fight and build their nation.

As early as 1962, Adefunmi had announced during a Harlem rally that within the next ten years, African Americans would have the option of residing in an independent African nation, a space in the United States that would legitimize the religious and cultural traditions of Africa and provide a land base for America's historically dispossessed black communities. In 1969, Adefunmi selected the American South as the location for the new black homeland. When looking at the South, Adefunmi believed that with the exception of New Orleans, the low country of South Carolina was the most culturally African in its religio-cultural orientation because of its history of conjurers and rootworkers.[96] Not everyone agreed, however, with Adefunmi's decision to develop a black nation in the South, and some chose to remain behind in New York City. Regarding the fate of the remaining members, Steven Gregory explains that eventually "many of the black Americans who had been involved with the Yoruba Temple of Harlem formed their own religious communities or houses" in New York City, where the tradition continues to thrive among African Americans until this day.[97] Asunta Serrano predicted early on that Adefunmi was in many ways creating another system with a new set of organizing principles within the New World Yoruba tradition. Adefunmi's hope was to actualize this alternative system in a landed community that would later become Oyotunji African Village. He thought it virtually impossible to establish a separate nation within an urban context and that there was something inherently alienating about a congested urban context for a religion that held the power and animation of the natural world in highest esteem. Therefore, in July 1969, Adefunmi and a handful of his supporters, including his wife Majile Osunbunmi and Omiyeye Wesihuni, left New Oyo, New York, bound for the American South, determined to build Oyotunji African Village, where Oyo would once more rise again.

PART TWO

African American Yoruba Since 1970

CHAPTER SIX

Oyotunji African Village

A Diaspora Experiment in African Nationhood

ରେଚ୍ଚ

Here in America we have been briefly conquered by European culture, but we are Africans nonetheless.

—Oba Oseijeman Adefunmi I

OYOTUNJI AFRICAN VILLAGE is a twenty-seven-acre diaspora interpretation of Africa in North America. The physical road to Oyotunji leads travelers down 95 South from Charleston to local Highway 17, running through South Carolina's scenic low country. From the town of Sheldon, South Carolina, a narrow dirt road twists and turns to the entrance of Oyotunji. Wooden signs nailed to trees along the road indicate to first-time visitors that they are drawing nearer to America's African Village. At the entrance to Oyotunji African Village, travelers behold a new material, aesthetic, and visual culture based on "traditional Yoruba prototypes from Nigeria and Benin Republic."[1] A deliberate indicator of "boundary maintenance" demarcates the physical and spiritual boundaries of Oyotunji African Village from the broader American world:[2]

You are leaving the U.S. You are entering the Yoruba Kingdom. In
the name of His Highness Efuntola, peace[. W]elcome to the sacred
Yoruba Village of Oyotunji. The only village in North America built
by priests of the Vodun cults as a tribute to our ancestors. These
priests preserve the customs, laws and religion of the African race[.]
Welcome to our land!

Entering the African world of Oyotunji, you are placed, as one visitor
stated, "in another context altogether."[3] The figurative transition from the
United States to an African village in North America immediately mani-
fests itself as visitors encounter the shrine of the Yoruba deity, Esu-Elegba.
Esu is one of the many public shrines in Oyotunji Village constructed on
"artistic epistemologies" of West Africa.[4] Esu-Elegba is the divine trickster
in the Yoruba pantheon who stands at the crossroads and mediates between
the mundane world and the world of spirit. At Oyotunji African Village,
Esu-Elegba stands at the crossroads, symbolically mediating between a
contested world of North America and a conceptual world of Africa.

FIGURE 12. Welcome sign written in Yoruba and English
demarcating the borders between the United States and
Oyotunji African Village. Photograph courtesy of author.

Oyotunji African Village exists today as evidence of an alternative community of African American nationalists seeking over four decades ago to express their religious and cultural interpretations of Yoruba society. They constructed an African-style village to summon Africa to them in their diaspora environs. Adefunmi and the residents of Oyotunji combined the historical and racial complexities of their lived American experience with their knowledge of Africa to create a "new Yorubaland" in the low country of South Carolina. They sought to promote a new "sacred nationality" among African Americans in the United States.[5] According to Mikelle Smith Omari-Tunkara, "Oyo Tunji testifies to the agency and activity of African Americans in the diaspora,"[6] and in Oyotunji this agency has concentrated on the "creation of African American males and females in the Yoruba likeness."[7]

FIGURE 13. Shrine of Esu-Elegba, the orisa of the crossroads, at the entrance of Oyotunji African Village. Photograph courtesy of author.

In theory, Oyotunji African Village is an experiment in the "historical ontology of the present."[8] It is a space that envisages living out of an
ontological reality rooted in history and antiquity while negotiating a lived
identity in the present. Oyotunji Village navigates a cultural and religious
epistemology that takes a "backward glance"[9] in "redeploy[ing] certain
indigenous idioms"[10] of a Yoruba past while at the same time charting a
relevant present and future. It conveys a time-origin-space paradigm that
is motivated by pre-Atlantic moments rooted in Africa and culturally executed in North America. Africa firmly rests at the center of Oyotunji's philosophies, cultivating what Kim D. Butler calls an "oppositional identity"
in a Western Hemisphere of symbolic exile.[11] According to its founder,
Oba Efuntola Oseijeman Adelabu Adefunmi I, Oyotunji Village stands as
a "tiny Yoruba enclave,"[12] a "full life-style alternative" struggling to survive
in twenty-first-century North America.[13] Its founder envisioned Oyotunji
African Village in South Carolina "as a monument to their Africa[n] past."[14]
It does not pretend to be an exact replication of a village in West Africa
but instead is a religious and cultural redaction or "rearticulation of the
'African'" in North America. It patterns itself on the enduring structures
and sacred expressions of ancient and modern Yoruba-Fon traditions in
Nigeria, the Benin Republic, and their diaspora,[15] and what Mikelle Smith
Omari-Tunkara rather insightfully recognizes as a "traditional hieratic
Yoruba conception."[16] Oyotunji residents negotiate a notion of paradoxical citizenship, for "they . . . are citizens of the United States and residents
of the state of South Carolina and . . . regulated by federal and state laws."[17]
Yet they negotiate this paradoxical citizenship in the midst of the arduous
challenge of creating "a relatively autonomous village . . . that is free from
the constraints of the outside world."[18]

With "shifting articulations" of Oyotunji Village as both Yoruba and
African, Oseijeman Adefunmi attempted to radically transform the modes
of religion, culture, and society that governed African American life in
the United States.[19] Village residents self-identify as Yoruba, although the
larger "conceptual frame of reference is in reality all of Africa," according
to Lefever, for it draws its influence and meaning from Yoruba as well as the
Fon, Akan, and Egyptian cultures.[20] They hold in deep respect the sacred
philosophies that represent the diverse ethnicities that created the Atlantic
diaspora. Yet they most highly esteem the Yoruba or "canonized them as
the preeminent classical standard of African culture in the New World,"

FIGURE 14. Arched entranceway to Oyotunji
African Village. Photograph courtesy of author.

as do so many black Atlantic communities.[21] They see the Yoruba deities
as having "survived the bitter nightmare of the slave trade" and understand that in the diaspora, their "worship has supported the retention of the
priesthood, folk tales, music, politics, food, art and language."[22]

When His Royal Highness Oseijeman Adefunmi I established it
in 1970, Oyotunji African Village was consecrated to the Yoruba deities
Obatala and Oshun, who were considered "the first of the Gods of Africa
to return for the redemption of the souls of Afro-Americans."[23] Honoring
the ancient African kingdom of Oyo as a sacred symbol of Yoruba religion
and culture, Adefunmi named the village, Oyotunji, or "Oyo rises again."
Speaking as its appointed Oba and monarch and first in a new royal lineage, Oseijeman Adefunmi stated in 1975, "The king I have come to destroy

is the decadent Western world led by the United States."[24] African royalty and monarchical discourse function in Oyotunji philosophy in place of a lineage that ends abruptly in American slavery. Civic and social appropriations of monarchal rule at Oyotunji also raise important metaquestions concerning the symbolic redefinition of power, the inversion of political power, and the shifting of national allegiance in the face of an ominous American society.

At its founding in 1970, Adefunmi envisioned Oyotunji African Village as a symbol of spatial resistance where black-nationalist paradigms of the 1960s would wed African American conceptions of Yoruba religion and nationhood. Clearly, Oyotunji's inception was inspired by a particular understanding of ancient African religious tropes. It was also, however, inspired by the modern political desire to "recreate the power of the African

FIGURE 15. Founder of Oyotunji African Village, His Royal Highness Oseijeman Adefunmi I. Photograph courtesy of *Milwaukee Courier.*

state, a desire expressed throughout postcolonial Africa in the 1960s by nations that had literally been reconstituting themselves."[25]

Adefunmi visualized Oyotunji as a place where Yoruba religion would be expressed through the "intimate marriage of theology and science" in a universe where "extreme contradictions . . . abound."[26] One of the obvious contradictions Oyotunji faced was the process of trying to territorialize Africa within the borders of America. In conventional forms of religious nationalism and territorialization, there is generally a "tendency on the part of a religious collectivity to claim that a specific territory is its exclusive homeland."[27] The geographical mapping of Oyotunji African Village in North America complicates this understanding because Oyotunjians must acknowledge their ancestral homeland (Africa) while conceptually trying to reproduce it in their birth land (America). Given this paradox, as an exceptional exercise in the "cultural translation of practices," Oyotunji Village is what Velma Love calls "a New World redemptive strategy . . . in an effort to normalize history and identity."[28] In their daily lives, village residents integrate a cohesive living philosophy of religion, culture, and nationhood contextualized within a rural communal setting. As a conflation of "Yoruba culture with Black racial unity,"[29] its "identity-building features" translate into a place where an African-expressed religious world view is enacted, philosophies of race codified, and a bounded black space engraved onto the American landscape.[30]

Oyotunji has made a broad appeal to African Americans across class and education lines. Many current and past residents have attended college, with some holding advanced degrees and doctorates. Many have been participants in grassroots movements, committed to wedding their political activism with their endeavors regarding Africa. Statistically, Oyotunji consists of some twelve families, with a total population of close to three dozen people. In the past, the village has housed as many as 250 African American residents at the height of black-nationalist enthusiasm.[31] Oyotunji's numbers, however, in no way indicate the vast influence and symbolic meaning the village has held since 1970. For example, although the current community is small, the national community of priests and priestesses affiliated with Oyotunji Village and the African Theological Archministry numbers in the thousands. Through a core group of African American priests who were originally initiated at Oyotunji, there exists a host of "grandchildren" and "great-grandchildren" who trace their spiritual lineage back to Oyotunji. In 1992, Adefunmi estimated that some 435 people had been initiated into the Yoruba priesthood through Oyotunji. By the mid-1990s, that number had grown to nearly 600, and more initiations have continued to take place in the twenty-first century.[32]

Oyotunji's community is defined in broad, yet select, terms and consists of resident priests and devotees, past resident and nonresident chiefs; hundreds of practitioners whose initiations or godparents' initiations were performed at Oyotunji; scholars, researchers, and investigators who assume temporary residence in the village; daily tourists; an ephemeral body of clients or suppliants who regularly seek medicinal and curative services; and an array of spiritual entities to whom they regularly communicate and supplicate. Anglo-Europeans and Anglo-Americans are welcome in Oyotunji Village as tourists and may receive advice through divination. The Oyotunji priesthood restricts residency and initiation rites to those of African descent, however, as evidenced either biophenotypically or spiritually.[33] Residency is panethnic and open to all people of African descent. Therefore, over the years, Oyotunji has been home not just to North American–born African Americans but also to blacks born on the continent of Africa, South America, and the Caribbean.[34] In the end, according to Adefunmi, "It is a fact that the Yoruba [at Oyotunji] have indeed succeeded in fashioning in their tiny community a place in point and time where each night they lie down in a world governed by African rules and awake each morning to a world governed by African forms."[35]

Chief Akintobe has lived at Oyotunji Village since 1977 and has established himself as a respected chief and loyal citizen. When I interviewed him, he openly assessed the tensions and challenges that Oyotunji has faced over the past forty years, yet remains loyally devoted to the Oyotunji ideal for three primary reasons. First and foremost, he awakes each day with the assurance that he lives in the only place within North America where a "Black Flag" waves freely in honor of African nationhood. Reflecting Oyotunji's multiple associations with Africa, its flag is decorated with the Ethiopian colors of red, gold, and green and adorned with an Egyptian Ankh or symbol of life. Chief Akintobe hopes to demonstrate to African Americans in his nearby home community of St. Helena Island, South Carolina, that the religious life in Oyotunji Village affords them an African alternative to Christian faith and a Western style of living: "I was determined because of my belief of what I was doing for them—for all of the

FIGURE 16. Oyotunji African Village residents and chieftains.
Featured are Chief Ajamu (1940–2009), Chief Akintobe,
Chief Olaitan, and Iya Osadele. Photographs courtesy of author.

people on the islands—that's why I continued to maintain myself here. I wasn't just representing myself. I was representing all of the people on the islands—to show them that Christianity was not [the way]. . . . It was that spirit in me telling me that I must do this."[36] He goes on to say that although Oyotunji Village has experienced many challenges throughout the years, its residents have continued to "put the Nation first."[37]

Her Royal Grace Iyashanla, disenchanted with life in rural Virginia and the Christian orientation of her family, joined both the Black Panther Party and the Black Liberation Army in the 1960s. She decided, however, that "after she got through running around with guns and all that kind of stuff" and the death of several of her friends, she was attracted to the religious and communal life-style Oyotunji Village offered.[38] After reading an article in the African American magazine *Sepia* in June 1975, Iyashanla decided to relocate to the village. The article described a group of African Americans who had ventured to South Carolina five years earlier in order to create an "African Kingdom" in the United States. The group had purchased several acres of land, developed a marketplace, established a school, erected outdoor shrines and altars to orisa deities, and performed divinatory works of prediction and healing. Its leader, Oseijeman Adefunmi, characterized African Americans in the United States as a "colonized people, powerless to control their destiny" and offered Oyotunji Village as a means of redirecting this destiny.[39] She was drawn to the village because its residents had committed themselves to what the article called the "culturization of African Americans to the heritage of the motherland."[40] She was especially interested in Adefunmi's strategic rejection of the "concept of militancy" because he did not believe African Americans were equipped at that time to win a "military revolution."[41]

Less than four months after the publication of this article, Iyashanla found herself en route to Oyotunji Village to assume residence among African Americans who had committed themselves, "with the help of the gods," to saving "their people" from the "decadence and degeneration of the Western world."[42] Vividly recalling her first encounter with Oyotunji Village, Iyashanla remembers: "I tell you when we came down that night, we got to South Carolina about nine that night. When we were coming down that dirt road there, the trees like came together—you know, trees on this side of the road and trees on that side; they joined at the top. I said, 'I'm leaving here in the morning. This is the boondocks! But I woke up at five o'clock in the morning to go to the pump to get some water, and it was so quiet and peaceful and just so serene. I said, 'Wow, this is really nice.' And I just fell in love with Oyotunji just like that. . . . When I found this, it was really just a calling."[43] Iyashanla experienced a special connection to Oyotunji and has remained a devoted resident since 1975. "I found my custom, my tradition. I found that this is really what my heart relates to."[44]

Finally, Baba Akintunde, a native of New Rochelle, New York, and former resident and chief at Oyotunji, lived in the village for nearly a decade. During our interview, he revealed that his journey to Oyotunji had begun in the 1960s during his undergraduate career as a student member in the Yorubas of Shaw University. When asked why his journey led him to Oyotunji Village, he simply responded, "Because I've always wanted to be free!"[45] When I inquired how he understood the seemingly paradoxical concept of an "African" nation within America, Akintunde explained, "Oyotunji Village is the most profound living experiment of African culture in the Western Hemisphere. As far as African Americans are concerned, there has never been an attempt like this to incorporate African tradition in a daily life-style—NEVER, and this is phenomenal! The Oyotunji experiment—it's an experiment on life."[46]

The narratives of Akintobe, Iyashanla, and Akintunde provide distinct windows through which to examine the interconnections between religion and nationalism as well as African American notions of autonomy and freedom. African Americans arriving at Oyotunji Village did so as political, territorial, and cultural nationalists seeking an alternative to the racial, social, and political turmoil that dominated American society in the 1960s and early 1970s. They believed in the possibilities of black nationhood as well as in the power of African American religious and cultural transformation. As an intentional social experiment, Oyotunji sought to build a residential community based on interpretations of African religious traditions, traditions that were themselves part of a larger moral universe placed in dynamic rapport with the natural, social, and political worlds around them.[47] This chapter is devoted to examining the multiple dimensions of religion, nationhood, and healing as culturally theorized in Oyotunji African Village. It maintains that despite the array of choices, conflicts, and ambiguities circumscribing Oyotunji's interpretations of Africa, it nonetheless exists in North America as a localized, indigenized example of African American religious and cultural agency in the wider Yoruba tradition.

Village Polity, Social Infrastructure, and Gender Construction

Historian Kim D. Butler, in *Freedoms Given, Freedoms Won*, offers insightful analysis on the ways members of the African diaspora in Brazil and other places have chosen black alternative communities or "separatist collectives" as strategies of countercitizenship.[48] In keeping with this counter-civic impulse, Butler argues that these communities, and Oyotunji can be considered one of them, have managed to coexist "with the mainstream as an alternative" space, often without relinquishing inhabitants' "constitutional rights and protections as citizens of the larger society."[49] Diasporic communities attempt to "create an insular world" that cultivates "such intangibles as dignity and self-worth, denied in the mainstream." They seek to develop "supportive infrastructure and institutions" that materialize not necessarily as "direct retentions of homeland cultures" but often as "creoles and blends" that either "incorporated indigenous elements" or "patched together aspects of a variety of African cultures."[50] Butler views these structural attempts to reproduce a "black world" in the diaspora as a consistent component of broader "patterns of black response" that have, since slavery, developed among communities in the Afro-Atlantic world.[51] Thus, in many ways, Oyotunji African Village can be understood as both profoundly diasporic and profoundly American.

Critical to the multiple contextualizations of Oyotunji African Village is the fact that it has had important diaspora antecedents in both North and South America. Historically, one cannot examine Oyotunji's twentieth-century Yoruba Village without recognizing the first legally established "African enclave" in North America by those who were largely of Yoruba origin and ethnicity. Its founders were African-born survivors of the last slave ship entering North America, the *Clotilda*, which arrived in Alabama in the year 1860. After enduring five years of enslavement, these survivors established Africa Town in postslavery America sometime between 1866 and 1868, which represented a deliberate territorial effort on the part of these first-generation West Africans to "recreate Africa where they were."[52] Sylvaine Diouf's *Dreams of Africa in Alabama: The Slave Ship Clotilda and the Story of the Last Africans Brought to America* is an outstanding documentary history of these Yoruba-descended Africans who "tried to recreate their own Africa on the soil of Alabama."[53] Although there had been earlier studies of this community conducted by others, including Zora Neale Hurston in the 1920s, it is Diouf's work that stands as the most comprehensive study of Africa Town, tracing the origin of its founders to the slave port of Ouidah in Dahomey; chronicling the voyage of the slave ship *Clotilda* on which they were taken as captives; narrativizing their lives as enslaved persons in Alabama; recounting their unsuccessful attempts at return to Africa; and historicizing the development of the North American African settlement, Africa Town.

Kupollee, Adissa, Omolabi, Kehounco, Abile, Oluale, Kolssola, Fabumi, and the others, a total of 110 persons, arrived in Alabama near Mobile in July 1860, never to return to the place of their ancestral birth.[54] Following emancipation, a group of these original captives settled on a few acres of land in Alabama as a sign of communal, cultural, and Yoruba linguistic solidarity. Gathered in this community were West Africans with vivid memories of their home villages and families, monarchical rulers and chieftaincy, the violent massacres surrounding their capture, the trauma of a Middle Passage journey, and the religious traditions and initiatory rites of their communities. Many of this group who disembarked in North America in 1860 "had scarifications on the face and/or body" and cheeks as well as other "distinctive marks" like those of Kupollee, whose "two front teeth had been pecked off to form an inverted V" and wore his original "small hoop" earring in each ear.[55] Diouf states there is also evidence of Orisa initiation rites having been performed before arrival as well as initiation "into *oro*, the Yoruba secret society."[56] She contends that this group of displaced Africans in many ways founded a settlement that was "a black town on the surface and an ethnic one at its core."[57] According to Diouf, "Their languages, their modes of verbal and nonverbal communication; the manner in which they perceived the others; their understandings of hierarchy, age and gender relations, and family structures, their cultural practices that valued community over individuality; their conception of lineage and ethnicity; and their longing for their homelands were among the most significant elements that set them apart."[58] Over time, some members of the group struggled to maintain a semblance of their traditional and Muslim identities, while others eventually became Protestant Christians. Diouf argues, however, that "they viewed and called themselves Africans and willfully maintained this identity with all the attendant manners, languages, behaviors, and practices that sustained it."[59] For noted African American leaders like Booker T. Washington, Africa Town pejoratively signified Africans who chose to "cling to the memories and traditions of their savage life in Africa, and may be said to represent the limits . . . of negro progress during the last half century."[60] However, the inhabitants of Africa Town, U.S.A., ultimately saw themselves and their legacy as a community of remembrance designed to foster a sense "of belonging to a land and a people far away" who willingly chose to give "their descendents the same sense of family, of belonging to a place, of being part of a distinctive community."[61]

Like Africa Town, U.S.A., Oyotunji African Village was to symbolize a space of belonging, community, and place for people of African descent. As such, Adefunmi was careful not to pattern Oyotunji on a rigid conception of African life.[62] He was content with an African mosaic of cultural elements that would make the village identifiably Yoruba. As he began the task of fashioning a Yoruba-inspired Oyotunji, Adefunmi used resources that had served him well for religious and cultural production—texts.[63] He immediately went to those works that had previously done the job, especially Samuel Johnson's *The History of the Yorubas* (1921), Olumide Lucas's *The Religion of the Yoruba* (1948), and N. A. Fadipe's *The Sociology of the Yoruba* (1970).[64]

From these resources, Adefunmi attempted to develop an African system of governance, political hierarchy, and social structure for Oyotunji. He endeavored to create a "total social system" where "religion becomes an integral part of political relations" and permeated kinship ties, relationships of hierarchy, and social interaction.[65] Among the many elements holding this system in place at Oyotunji were a set of etiquettes and rules and a "respect for parents, age, and seniority of rank."[66] To create an alternative system of governance, Adefunmi established a "monarchical socialism,"[67] a chieftaincy, men and women's societies, an ancestral society, a legal body, an educational system, and marriage institutions that became the means through which Oyotunji residents were able, as Roger Friedland states, to "recode themselves" and "thereby create new worlds" of nationhood.[68]

Adefunmi established an ancient African-style monarchy in which the Oba, or king, assumed the primary responsibility for governing the community. A chieftaincy was established to support the leadership of the Oba by managing the daily operations and affairs of Oyotunji and providing counsel to the Oba in matters of governance. Finally, Adefunmi instituted a governing body of elders called the Ogboni Society. Carl Hunt understood Oyotunji's Ogboni Society as patterning "one of the oldest and most widespread secret societies in Nigeria . . . called, 'Ogboni.' Devoted to the worship of the Earth divinity, it encompasses family heads, chiefs and priests of various orisa. . . . In many kingdoms," Hunt explained, "it counterbalances the authority of the king."[69] To the Ogboni Society, Adefunmi delegated the responsibility of administrative, legal, and judicial matters in the village.[70] It balanced and regulated the monarchy, and the only established authority capable of superseding traditional law was revelation divulged through the divination system of Ifa.[71]

For the governance of social codes and behaviors, Adefunmi instituted the Akinkonju and Egbebinrin societies. These male and female societies examined issues of family, marriage, and appropriate gender roles for Oyotunji inhabitants. In addition, spiritual behavior in Oyotunji was governed by the Igbimolosha, which was responsible for the training of the Yoruba priesthood and the veneration of the ancestors through the Egungun Society. Central to Adefunmi's plan to restore African culture in North America was the institution of the Egungun Society, which oversaw funerary rites, honorary masquerading, and the ancestors.[72] According to Adefunmi, "[A]ll power for the resurrection and the safeguarding of the Afrikan people comes via the ancestors," which made the "resurrection and restoration of the powerful *Egungun* worship" absolutely necessary at Oyotunji Village.[73] By elevating the ancestors in this way, Adefunmi estranged himself even further from his Cuban colleagues in New York. According to Adefunmi, "My emphasis was on the worship of the dead, and they found that very interesting, but also very objectionable, the Cubans did."[74] Adefunmi had much more to gain by reclaiming an ancestral connection than did Cuban immigrants, for in this connection African Americans authenticated themselves and reestablished ties with the "ancestors . . . buried in the soil of West Africa."[75] With the exception of two sites in Brazil, Oyotunji's Egungun Society still remains one of the few in the Western Hemisphere.[76]

After thirteen years of inscribing a new Yorubaland in New York City and South Carolina, Adefunmi visited Ile-Ife, Nigeria, for the first time in 1972, a symbolic journey between "Yorubalands" that had profound effects upon Oyotunji Village after Adefunmi's return.[77] Adefunmi had been invited to accompany an African American dance troupe to Ghana led by his friend and noted black-nationalist leader of the African American Akan movement in North America, Nana Dinizulu.[78] After his stay in Ghana, Adefunmi made his way to Nigeria, where in Abeokuta he was initiated into the Yoruba priesthood of Ifa by the Oluwa of Ijeun, making him among the first Nigerian-initiated African American babalawos, or priest of divination, in the United States.[79] Benefiting from Adefunmi's visit to Nigeria, Oyotunji Village began to undergo rapid structural evolutions. New statutes and ordinances were enacted in the village, making African attire standard, knowledge of African history compulsory, and tribal marks mandatory for all residents.[80] Addressing this issue, the laws of Oyotunji's Ogboni clearly stated, "Be it hereby known to all and sundry that the King has said that it is an insult to the spirit of our ancestors and disrespectful to the people of Yoruba Village for Yorubas to be seen outside their homes in non-Yoruba dress styles. . . . The only exception is the use of Western made winter or rain wear. Any Yoruba seen improperly dressed out of doors is liable to a fine . . ."[81] In addition, because Oyotunji Village used the ancient Oyo Empire as inspiration, Oyotunji residents were to receive facial marks, or *abaja*, that resembled those of Yoruba people in Oyo, Nigeria. Marks were made either with a razor blade or a sharp knife and carved according to the specifications of Samuel Johnson's 1921 illustrated publication of *The History of the Yoruba*.[82] These facial markings became an important distinguishing feature Oyotunji residents used to designate their new identity as Yorubas in America. Adefunmi then turned his efforts to strengthening the institutions of culture, religion, economy, family, and education in order to reinforce Oyotunji's Yoruba identity.

As a distinct community, the village worked diligently to acquire the necessary legal certification to ensure that the education of Oyotunji's children would be exclusively controlled by its own educated priesthood. Chartered by the state of South Carolina, the Yoruba Royal Academy was established in 1973 as the primary educational institution in Oyotunji. Children enrolled at Oyotunji Village's Yoruba Royal Academy began their day with the following pledge: "I am compelled by a spiritual force I cannot resist to swear my eternal allegiance to the king and the flag of the Yoruba nation. I also solemnly swear to do everything in my power and use every means conceivable for the welfare of my people and the preservation of the culture and tradition of my ancestors. So let it be, oh, ye gods of Africa."[83] After reciting the pledge, the children explored an educational curriculum consisting of Yoruba language, English, mathematics, African history and culture, the history of the African American Yoruba movement, the history of Oyotunji Village, herbology, astrology, ritual and worship, and arts and

FIGURE 17.
Young Oyotunji
dancer and drummers
perform for tour
groups. Photograph
courtesy of author.

crafts.[84] The academy existed as an essential means of socializing Oyotunji children into the alternative world of African consciousness. Although not immune to the influences and icons of contemporary popular culture in the United States, the year-long Akinkanju and Egbobirin rites of passage for boys and girls and the proliferation of daily cultural cues were ritual reminders of their distinct North American Yoruba identity.[85]

Matters of gender, family, and marriage, like education, were also interpreted at Oyotunji along flexible African cultural norms. Often within contexts of religious nationalism, Roger Friedland argues, "religious nationalists give primacy to the family . . . as the social space through which society should be conceived and composed."[86] Embedded within this "familial discourse" are conceptions of national loyalty and a "program of comportment" along gender lines that to some degree offers "a mechanism of social control of men," a control that some scholars argue only subtly masks "masculine privilege."[87]

Within the Oyotunji Village, family networks and gendered notions of power have often been played out within the complex marital partnering practice of plural marriage.[88] Polygyny as a legitimately recognized form of West African marriage had been practiced to a limited degree in Harlem during the early years of Yoruba Temple, but it was much more openly practiced as a choice in social experimentation in Oyotunji Village, with the founding Oba having multiple wives and close to two dozen children over the course of his lifetime.[89] The state of South Carolina has never legally recognized these polygynous units, although Chief Olaitan (Alagba) stated some time ago that the village was "in the process of negotiating with the authorities to recognise our marriages contracted in the Yoruba traditional way."[90] Regardless of its legal status, polygyny has held considerable cultural meaning within the Oyotunji community. According to the village's king, "Under the system of polygyny at Oyotunji a man is allowed to marry as many wives as he can afford. If a man does marry more than one wife, there are certain obligations he has to meet. The law at Oyotunji states that when a man marries a woman he has to build her a house to live in, a cook shed, an ancestor worship house, a toilet and give her enough money to start some kind of business of her own."[91] Whereas many African cultures viewed polygyny as a sign of wealth and prosperity, Adefunmi maintained that, in Oyotunji, polygyny functioned much more pragmatically as a means of increasing the family unit, dividing labor responsibilities, protecting women from childlessness, and ensuring African posterity.[92]

I once asked an Oyotunji chief how he would respond to contemporary womanist and feminist critiques that polygyny is a potentially exploitative institution for women. Embedded in his responses were gendered interpretations of responsibilities, duties, and tasks and a normative understanding of heterosexual partnerships. Responding openly, the chief remarked, "Well, it only exploits women, if women feel that they are being exploited. If it's done in a cultural context, then they are not being exploited because we feel that a woman needs help and so she should go out and find help by bringing in other co-wives into the family to have children, to help her with the chores, where everything can be shared. This is how the African mind works, when there are more women who would be without a man. That was the main factor: that no woman should be without a man."[93]

Within this context of gendered responses, I found most revealing the responses of African American Yoruba women in Oyotunji who comment on the choice to engage in plural marital contexts. For example, one Yoruba woman who lived largely in an urban context before residing at Oyotunji stated that before she became a priestess, more often than not the men she dated "always had somebody on the side." She eventually decided when entering the Yoruba tradition, "Why fool myself? At least polygyny is in the open. You know what you're dealing with. You know the men usually don't want nobody else because in the Yoruba culture they can only take as many wives as they can afford. . . . So I figure what the hell, I'm gonna try it . . ."[94] Oyotunji's HRG Iyashanla spoke favorably about her own experience with polygyny. She valued having space to explore her own pursuits and never really liked for a man to be "all up under her all the time." This sentiment, coupled with the fact that she was not a "possessive" person, made a polygynous relationship conducive to her independent life-style.[95] In addition, Iya Yeyefini Efunbolade, who spent fifteen years in Oyotunji and was married to Adefunmi at a time in the 1970s when she was one of seven wives, is clear on articulating the real challenges women within the context of plural marriage faced. Yet, she was also able to reflect on the ways women sought their own means of empowerment through gaining access to political and social authority, forming lasting bonds as co-wives, cooperative systems of support, spiritual mentorship, and "cohesiveness and camaraderie."[96] Some North American priestesses, however, ultimately view polygynous marital configurations as a form of sociospiritual control with the ability to lessen women's spiritual potentiality, potency, and opportunities to be unfettered priestly specialists. Despite these views, at Oyotunji African Village, plural marriages are said to function as a part of a larger political, cultural, educational, economic, and social infrastructure put to solidify the village's world views.

Gender identity and dynamics, in general, are quite complex in their negotiation at Oyotunji. At the start of my research in the mid- to late 1990s, a core group of capable and compelling women resided at the village, among them Her Royal Grace Iyashanla, Her Royal Grace Iya Orite, Her Royal Grace Osunbemi, Iya Onisegun, and Iya Osadele. These women, who lived amidst a population of several younger women at Oyotunji, were thoroughly integrated into the governing bodies of the village. They served as chiefs, sat on governing boards, and participated in major decisions that shaped the direction of the village.

This display of female power did not emerge accidently, however. It was the direct result of a concerted women's movement that was launched at Oyotunji Village from 1974 to 1975 under the leadership of one of Adefunmi's wives, Iyalode Majile Olafemi Osunbunmi, who protested against the constructed "servile status" of Oyotunji's women residents.[97] She, along with another of the Adefunmi's wives Yeyefini Efunbolade, highlighted women's issues such as the challenges in multiwived families, "the unfair treatment and expectations of women," the financial challenges facing mothers in the village, loneliness, and the nature and quality of educational futures for their children.[98] Several of Oyotunji's first-generation male residents had been former Black Muslims and as such had carried over into Oyotunji strong conceptions of masculinity and inflexible norms of male dominance and gender hierarchy. The women in the village challenged what they understood was the structural institutionalization of their powerlessness. As a result, new laws were enacted that granted expanded rights to women, banned compulsory polygyny after 1974, and gave women the right to own property.[99]

Less than two decades later, the women of Oyotunji mobilized once more, this time to fight for equal spiritual access to the ritual tools of Ifa divination normally restricted to men. According to Dijsovi Ikukomi Eason, "In the early 1990s, pressure from the Oyotunji women would lead to a radical development in African American women eventually being accepted into the *Ifa* divining priesthood. Traditionally, they had been restricted to the role of *apetibis*, female priests who are relegated to the inferior roles in the *Ifa* priesthood and who do so much of the difficult work for initiations and other rituals within the movement."[100] As a result, several members of the Oyotunji female priesthood traveled to the Republic of Benin in 1992 and were "initiated into the Fon Fa priesthood as equals to their male counterparts" in the cult of the Bokano at Atendehu Hoca.[101] Analyzing this innovation, George Brandon states:

> Over the years the African Theological Archministry has shown a concern with gender roles and especially with the roles of women in the context of an African structure adapting to the situation of African Americans in the U.S. In some cases this has led to a greater degree of gender equality and to an extension of roles to women which they would not have been eligible to assume within Santeria. An important innovation of this kind in the U.S. context

is the initiation and instruction of women into *Ifa* divination. This is not done by the Santeria priesthood, which excluded women from full initiation into *Ifa*. Once it was learned that women could be initiated into *Ifa* in Nigeria and in Benin, Adefunmi began to encourage and implement it, including taking some priestesses to Benin for initiation.[102]

At Oyotunji, one now finds women in the priesthood freely using what were designated traditional male-divination tools to assist them in their readings for clients, directly subverting certain gender configurations in other global Yoruba communities. This gendered understanding of the Ifa priesthood several years earlier caused much concern among Cuban American orisa communities. According to Juan J. Sosa, "*Santeros* of Miami caused a great uproar in 1980 when a Nigerian *babalao*, while visiting Miami's priests, suggested that in Miami—as in Nigeria—women should be admitted to take part in the high priesthood of the religion."[103] In the twenty-first century, Oloye Aina Olomo, states that "right now, in the United States there are more Iyanifas, women initiated into the priesthood of Ifa, than have been recorded being seen in Nigeria."[104]

Alongside these gender advances in Oyotunji, however, modes of traditional decorum and expectations were put in place to govern female behavior. For example, although child rearing was communal to some degree, mothers, not fathers, were still expected to be the primary caregivers to their children. In addition, strict social regulations governed the behavior of unmarried women and their social interactions with men. Finally, women were expected to conduct themselves in compliance with the teachings learned in the Egbemoremi Women's Society. Oyotunji women are seemingly subject to no more restrictions than males, however. The village has a fixed sense of what is proper, and this is not always determined along gender lines. Oyotunji women enjoy the freedom to travel beyond the village and given appropriate accountability can remain outside of the village for extended periods of time. There appears a deeper complexity regarding women's identity at Oyotunji that at times seems difficult to penetrate, though. One often senses that although the women at Oyotunji are fiercely independent in thought and deed, their performed postures are deeply rooted in African-inspired gender expectations that respect males as the head of families and compounds. Gender dynamics, then, along with gendered identity and gendered cultural politics at Oyotunji, are among those many areas subject to constant reinterpretation, translation, and renegotiation. As Carl Hunt astutely concludes, "The cultural aspects of life at Oyotunji are not static, neither is traditional Yoruba culture." It is this dynamism that permeates the organizing structures of Oyotunji.

Oyotunji Daily Life

Oyotunji African Village is governed by a "lived philosophy" that structures daily life.[105] The village pursues its goals within a "new economy of time" based on right relations with the orisa through shrines and monthly festivals, providing healing services to an afflicted public, and committing itself to structures of governance and well-being that ensure the enduring future of the nation of Oyotunji. At Oyotunji Village, the day commonly begins at eight in the morning. At this time the village drum is sounded, summoning the residents of the village to their daily obligations. The Oyotunji national flag is raised in honor of the nation, and residents then turn to their designated work. As general ground rules, all residents must wear African attire at all times; all men are required to work on *dokpwe*, or community projects, and within three months, all permanent residents must undergo facial scarification and receive tribal marks.[106]

Both adults and children of the village are responsible for daily tasks that assist in its maintenance. These range from raking the village grounds to feeding and maintaining the various shrines.[107] Following morning tasks, children from the village and from surrounding areas come together with the priests and priestesses of Oyotunji for the daily educational activities of the Royal Yoruba Academy. Adult members of the village not assigned to teach at the academy organize one of the many monthly public festivals and religious ceremonies held at the village. Tasks include spiritually cleansing various areas of the village in ceremonial preparation; acquiring various animals and ritual supplies; and publicizing the festival. The Oba in his capacity as spiritual ruler often participates in these ritual functions. In addition, Oyotunji adult residents up until 1991 also engaged in publishing *Inside Oyotunji*, a bimonthly newsletter now available electronically on YouTube.[108]

Baba Medahochi especially advocated efforts in African language training for daily use in village life. For Medahochi, a major component

of re-Africanizing American diaspora identity was freedom from linguistic, mental, and cultural imperialism by learning an African language.
According to Medahochi:

> A language is indicative of a culture . . . The first thing that
> Africans are supposed to do in the re-afrikanization of ourselves
> should be to try to acquire an African language because we must
> redefine our whole world . . . I can't explain the feeling you have
> when you are able to express your opinions and your view of the
> world in an African language . . . You cannot re-afrikanize your-
> self in English or Arabic or Dutch or Chinese . . . In order to be
> an African, you must have an African expression to define your
> world. Once you get the opportunity to study an African language,
> we should take advantage of that . . . I'm opposed to ebonics and
> patois, creolization of languages the same way I'm opposed to eat-
> ing chitterlings. I will eat it if that's all the food that's available
> but there's no excuse at this time . . . when we got over thousand
> African languages available . . . The first thing that the captive per-
> son must get back is his language . . .[109]

Oyotunji, therefore, seeks to cultivate familiarity with the Yoruba language
among its residents. This is mostly visible in greetings, informal social
exchanges among residents, and in structured religious activities. Thus,
although not all residents are fluent, they are, nonetheless, expected to employ
a form of Yoruba vernacular as a part of daily ritual and social protocol.[110]

In Oyotunji's black nation, there is no private land ownership. The
"state" owns all property, and it is "portioned out by the Ogboni society
(the governing body) to married men or single female heads of household
according to the size of their families."[111] Residents are required to pay a
nominal rent fee and a general tax for the continual development of the village. Residents are also responsible for their own health care. For the most
part Western medicine is not stressed in the village, and healing is initially
attempted using spiritual and herbal pharmacopoeia. Residents are not,
however, averse to supplementing traditional methods with Western medicine, consulting local African American doctors, when necessary.

Since 1970, America's federal and local judicial systems have not been unaware of Oyotunji African Village and its subsequent cultural innovations.

In 1972, the Federal Bureau of Investigation (FBI) arrested Adefunmi on "suspicion of bigamy, polygamy, and tax evasion."[112] The African American periodical *Jet Magazine* reported on the incident and stated that following the arrest "there was no defense fund, no bond fund, or legal fund of any kind—just the sacrifice of a goat to Obatala. No one knew what would become of Baba or how long he would be kept by the federal officials. There was a brief panic and then resignation that things would work themselves out. Two days later, all charges were dropped."[113] Again in the early 1980s, the local sheriff of Beaufort County, South Carolina, Morgan McCutcheon, was urged to convene a grand jury to investigate Oyotunji Village on two indictments: ritual scarification as a form of child abuse and the illegality of plural marriages being practiced in the village. The village was cleared in both investigations, with the jury ruling in favor of "religious freedom; but the practice only should be undertaken by consenting adults."[114] The village argued that "scarring is a religious practice and the children are proud of the mark" and that it "is no more child abuse than the painful injections which all American children receive."[115] The village was also cleared on the plural-marriages charges, with officials stating that "the marriages aren't recorded in the county courthouse and therefore aren't illegal."[116]

In addition to these legal challenges, one consistent challenge facing village residents over the years has been that of economic sustainability. In his early years, Adefunmi was very much inspired by the nationalist work of nineteenth-century leader Martin Delaney in South Carolina. According to Lefever, "Adefunmi knew that shortly after the Civil War, General Sherman had set aside land in eastern South Carolina for ex-slaves. Delaney, then an agent of the Freedmen's Bureau in South Carolina, used his position to persuade numerous ex-slaves to accept the offer to become economically [self-]sufficient landowners."[117] Also, within the W. E. B. Dubois/ Booker T. Washington debate, Adefunmi viewed the platforms of Booker T. Washington as much more expedient for African American communities. Adefunmi II explains, "My father always said we should have went with the route of Booker T. Washington who wanted to corner the southern agricultural market for African Americans and create industry . . . So if we would have taken that route as opposed to the political route [of Dubois], then we would be, I'm sure, in a different fashion."[118]

Maintaining a philosophy of economic nationalism, Oyotunji encourages black entrepreneurship and the pursuit of independent sources of revenue as markers of self-sufficiency and autonomy from American institutions. Seeking full-time employment outside the village or applying for food stamps (which villagers view as "foreign aid"[119] or "reparation payments for the years of labor that their forefathers gave America without pay"[120]) are measures of last resort, particularly since Oyotunji believes in economic self-determination. Any government assistance villagers acquired was interpreted as repayment of its debt to African Americans. As Adefunmi stated, "We know the United States owes us a living because we supplied them a living. . . . We built their foundation and we didn't get a damn thing but a crack across the back and the rape of our women. . . . We would not be in this condition if it were not for the American slave state. And if it weren't for the 300 years of free labor, American wouldn't be as far along as it is now."[121] Related to this, in 1971, one year after the village's inception, a reporter for the *News & Courier* tried to satirically underscore the issue of food stamp usage at the Oyotunji stating, "The village shows that black man can function without the man around. Life without 'the man' does not, however, exclude his food stamps."[122] Adefunmi responded with a written editorial entitled "Pay for Slavery." The editorial read as follows:

To The News and Courier:

Your editorial quip "Without the Man" (Nov. 9), regarding the use of U.S. government food stamps at Yoruba Village represents one of those short-sighted but influential remarks responsible for so much mischief in common race relations, and much vicious legislation on professional levels. For our temporary dependence on the U.S. Department of Agriculture represents a miserable and grudging return for the 250 years of free labor and ideas which Yorubas supplied to that department during its infancy and ignorance. Rather than limit your readers to a prejudiced conclusion, you could have reminded them in a few lines more that the making of America, especially the South, was desperately dependent on having human aid from the Yoruba and other West African Kingdoms. Otherwise why continue slavery for so long a time? You could have reminded all Americans that having gotten something for nothing, it's time to pay back; also, that an honorable people, rather than hide behind guilty welfare programs, would be paying the blacks unconditional reparations in cash, land, technology and material. For indeed, if true justice prevailed, some 15 million white Americans and their offspring in perpetuity should be committed to work free for blacks until the year 2221. If the American power structure is not ready to comply with such measures to liquidate its debt to us, then spare us your proud prejudices, and let us hear no more suggestion that the Yorubas are getting something for nothing. Oseijeman Adefunmi (Chief Baba, King of the Yorubas) Box 51, Sheldon.

Given the reality of financial pressures, however, Oyotunji's philosophy of self-sufficiency cannot always be adhered to in every instance. Sustainability is thus a process and a goal at Oyotunji, constantly renegotiated by its committed group of residents.

The primary sources of income at Oyotunji Village are revenues obtained through tourism; proceeds generated from the African marketplace; honoraria from lectures or workshops or special appearances like the Oyotunji dancers in Alex Haley's widely acclaimed *Roots* miniseries; revenues generated from rental fees when used as a movie set depicting Africa; as well as fees generated from spiritual consultations. Spiritual consultations, in particular, provide revenues that help to sustain the individual lives of village priests.[123] As with other sightseeing attractions, tourist season at Oyotunji is inconsistent and unstable, and the income generated from it often fluctuates. Divination, however, provides a more consistent form of income.

Oyotunji Village has published and disseminated an array of what J. Lorand Matory calls "tourist orientation materials."[124] Oyotunji Village is prominently featured in tourist literature advertising the Gullah Sea Islands and South Carolina in general and has increasingly become an added attraction for large family-reunion itineraries.[125] Visitors are introduced to various religious and cultural aspects of Oyotunji's traditions. They are escorted to each of the eight public shrines, provided with a brief theological explanation of the concept of each of the displayed orisa, and informed of the various public ceremonies and private ritual practices available to visitors. Depending on the time of year, visitors might witness a public ceremony or festival in honor of the orisa spirits. Its recent brochure describes Oyotunji as "North America's only authentic African Village," where visitors are provided "an opportunity to make a 'pilgrimage to Africa in America.'"

" A Pilgrimage to Africa in America..."

Founded in 1970,

The Kingdom of Oyotunji African Village is modeled after the ancient Yoruba Kingdoms of Nigeria. It is the first and only community dedicated to the redemption and restoration of African Culture in North America. The culture of the Village is based

on the traditional religion, customs, and art forms of the Yoruba people of Southwest Nigeria, Southern Dahomey, Togoland, and regions adjacent to the City of Accra in Ghana. The African Villager is thus, a settlement of persons interested in the study and practice of such cultural traditions.

In 1980,

the directors of the Oyotunji African Village were granted a religious charter in the name of the African Theological Archministry, Inc. The activities of the Village have remained in subsequent years, a project of the A.T.A. The A.T.A.'s essential activities are the dissemination of printed and verbal knowledge and information concerning the origins of the African-American population; the religious and cultural traditions practiced by their ancestors; and to de-emphasize negative stereotypes concerning African traditions, customs and religions.

The Oyotunji African Village allows visitors an opportunity to make a "pilgrimage to Africa in America." The aspects of Yoruba culture to which visitors are introduced include art, architecture, cuisine, language, attire, education and spiritual devotion. The Village is replete with temples and shrines to ancient as well as contemporary ancestors , and to the deities of the Yoruba religion.

OYOTUNJI OFFERS:

• *Monthly annual festivals, opened to the public and filled with entertainment and information about the missing link in the lives of African Americans.*

• *Weekly religious services of worship for residents and for the general public who may attend regularly.*

•*The Yoruba Temple Dancers, Drummers, and Singers featuring costumed presentations, including the Rites of Passage program.*

•*Special benefits to "Friends of the African Village"*

FIGURE 18. Tourist brochure featuring Oyotunji African Village.

The Internet also provides publicity for Oyotunji African Village. Its official website, www.oyotunjiafricanvillage.org, features a brief history of Oyotunji, an annual calendar of Oyotunji events, news and updates concerning the village, the annual Ifa divination "Reading of the Year," historic photos, registration forms for applying to the Yoruba Royal Academy boarding school for children, and an electronic link to *Inside Oyotunji*, a monthly webcast on YouTube.

Finally, since its inception in 1970, Oyotunji has not been immune from intragroup tension and external challenges. Within tightly bounded communities, crisis and controversy abound within its lived everyday moments. Kamari Clarke's exceptional ethnographic work on Oyotunji Village provides keen analytical insight into the sources of village contestations. Like most monarchical societies, there were, early on, unsuccessful coup attempts, and Adefunmi's authority was "challenged during an armed insurrection which was led by a disgruntled priest and a few followers."[126] Also, in one instance the police suspected the village of willingly harboring fugitives. Adefunmi believed that the village was offering religious asylum, or "social shelter," stating "when people come into the Village they reform. . . . As a priest it is my duty to help and protect my people. Just as the Catholic priest must keep secret any confession given to him, I must do likewise."[127] Moreover, there have been multiple occasions of public critiques by former residents who have left, dissatisfied with various aspects of village life and governance.[128] Because it is virtually impossible for Oyotunji African Village to create hermetically sealed borders around its polity, religion, and culture, the village constantly battles both internal and external tests and the challenges of a tradition continuously in the making.

"When I Came Here I Felt Something": Narratives from Oyotunji Village and the South Carolina Gullah Region

In 1996, J. Lorand Matory challenged scholars of the African diaspora "to be more self-conscious in their assumptions about the relationship between diasporas and the classical origins they claim and more attentive to the interested nature of insiders' narratives."[129] The insiders' narratives from Oyotunji Village provide a useful lens for analyzing the assumed African origins that shape religious and cultural meaning in the village. Through a constructed world of Africa at Oyotunji Village, residents engage in acts of self-representation and self-narration, reform identity, reclaim ancestors, and reinterpret religious boundaries. Residents find coherence in Oyotunji Village because Africa is regarded as a "sacred symbol" in the Geertzian sense, functioning to "synthesize a people's ethos—the tone, character, and quality of their life, its moral and aesthetic style and mood—and their world view—the picture they have of the way things in sheer actuality are, their most comprehensive ideas of order."[130] In this sense, Africa as sacred symbol and as world view invoke in Oyotunji Village "a basic congruence between a particular style of life and a specific . . . metaphysic" that become mutually sustainable and logical in the daily lives of the residents.[131]

Oyotunji insiders' narratives express ambivalence toward North America and its inability to embrace Americans of African descent as full citizens and cultural contributors. African symbolism, therefore, functions as a metaphor of both protest and of freedom. Throughout our interviews, insiders ordered their narratives in similar ways: they first detailed their family history and background along with their former religious affiliations, then they described a nationalist conversion moment, and finally an eventual turning toward African traditions. Most of the narrators were ardent black nationalists who were often committed members to black-nationalist organizations in the 1960s, when they had a fervent desire to transform American society by revolutionizing the political, social, cultural, and religious condition of blacks. Believing that many of these goals were unrealized in the 1960s, they saw in Oyotunji Village a chance to provide closure to their ambivalence toward North America by engaging in the community's creative approach to Africa.

"What I saw when I arrived was an African society in bloom . . . I got a chance to see African people being themselves. . . ."[132] This was Chief Olaitan's first impression of his new home when he arrived at Oyotunji Village in 1978. Before 1978, Olaitan was a disc jockey for WUFO in his native Buffalo, New York. Olaitan characterizes his behavior during the late 1960s and early 1970s, as "militant," and he was often seen as rebellious, particularly when he and another African American disc jockey took over the radio station in protest of a new mandate that they play "white" songs during their black radio program. Olaitan recalls, "The whole day we did the format we thought a black radio station should be about—news, information and black music."[133] Olaitan's spirit of rebellion carried over into his organizational affiliations. In 1975, he and a handful of African Americans in Buffalo established the Yoruba Foundation. Inspired by Adefunmi's Yoruba Temple in Harlem in the 1960s and his work in Oyotunji Village, the Yoruba Foundation sought to provide historical, cultural, and religious resources to the African American community in Buffalo. The upstate New York organization established a working relationship with Oyotunji African Village that included an internship program for its members as well as conferences on Yoruba religion and culture. The Yoruba Foundation made conscious attempts to live up to what Olaitan calls Buffalo's "history of resistance," which he says proudly began with the Underground Railroad. It was not solely his affiliation with black nationalism that led Olaitan to the gates of Oyotunji, however. He felt that many African American nationalist groups were based on a "failed logic" to overthrow the government or establish a military army or engage in armed warfare. Instead, the collective philosophy of the Yoruba Foundation reflected the assumption that "we [were] in a war for the minds, hearts, and souls of our people. . . . That is where we saw the struggle being."[134]

What eventually led Olaitan to Oyotunji Village was the unfolding of his own spiritual philosophy. Although he grew up Baptist, he recalls that at an early age he "began to wander around or to question." This then guided him to affiliate with a host of religions including the African Methodist Episcopal Church, the Roman Catholic Church, and the Nation of Islam. Throughout this time, he found himself posing questions particularly to his peers in the Nation of Islam: "What was our culture? What was our religion before the arrival of the Muslims? Didn't we have something before they came, and what was it if we did?" Olaitan admits that it was the search for answers to these questions that ultimately led him to Oyotunji African Village. On July 4, 1976, Olaitan recalls making a decision that he was going to wear African clothes exclusively from that moment on and states, "So that was the day I declared my independence." This sense of independence made him feel as though he had escaped from American cultural imperialism and entrapment. Less than two years later, he found himself at Oyotunji Village with hopes of exercising this new cultural freedom in a black nation he saw as "up and going."

For many African American residents, Oyotunji's religious orientations were not inherently new but were an extension of the historical African-diasporic expressions and healing practices to which they had previously been exposed in their indigenous Southern communities. Louisiana and South Carolina were the homes of several Oyotunji residents, both areas rich in voodoo lore. Voodoo religiosity permeated Louisiana communities, and voodoo priestess Marie LaVeau epitomized the pervasiveness of voodoo cultural expression in Louisiana. My introduction to Elegba priest Chief Eleshin (Yuseff Abdulla) and former resident began when he remarked, "There was a lot of African influence [in my family], a lot of traditional medicine. My great grandmother was a medicine woman. I had a great grandfather who was a medicine man, and they said he was the best in the area."[135] Chief Eleshin brought with him to Oyotunji Village a rich tradition of healing and folk medicine from rural Louisiana. Louisiana had what Eleshin called "natural cultural-ness," a rich "voodoo tradition," and "a great deal of history about Africanisms."[136] Eleshin understood Louisiana as having a "real cultural root type history." Influenced by Louisiana's "root" culture, Eleshin admits that he lived his life before Oyotunji "dibbling and dabbling" in various religious traditions. His religious journey is chronicled in a recent A&E documentary, *Voodoo Rituals*.[137] At one point in his life he was very much involved with the Islamic faith, eventually becoming an imam and helping to establish the Islamic Party of North America. Dissatisfaction with Islam gradually set in, and Eleshin remarked that his "spirit was looking for more in a religion, not just prayers or a building."[138] Given his background in Louisiana and his early exposure to the orientations of Africa there, Eleshin found himself in 1975 saying, "I wanted more Africanisms, and as I grew older I felt, 'What does a true African do?'"[139] He had a brief affiliation with Akan religion, but it was not until he went to Oyotunji that his African spiritual desires were fulfilled. After meeting Adefunmi, he decided to make Oyotunji his new home. As he reflected, "When I came here I felt something. My spirit clicked with the Oba. From dreams or from visions, I had envisioned studying under some wise man, so I chose the Oba to be that wise man."[140]

Oyotunji African Village was settled, it is important to note, amidst the richly diverse spiritual community of the Gullah in South Carolina and existed alongside the religious world of the southern Gullah/Geechee people. Although Adefunmi ultimately came seeking to restore connections to a lineage much more geographically primordial, the American South was an important historical and cultural symbol of African American life. Adefunmi had in many ways returned "to the South Carolina roots of his family" through his own maternal lineage traceable to nearby Anderson County, South Carolina.[141] According to Cohn, the South represented "a return to the earth and to roots, to a 'homeland' and to a past. These roots are merged in various pasts which connect individuals to Africa; the South is the home of the ancestors, immediate (parents and grandparents) and remote (African slaves); here the soil is said to be 'baptized with the blood of ancestors'; and it is here where African gods were first brought to America and where they are, it is felt, most accessible."[142]

Oyotunji's geographical location in the Gullah/Geechee American South offered dialogical opportunities for deep religious interaction. Village residents found themselves among a community of black southerners for whom cultural and religious claims to Africa were not in any way new. What emerged, particularly within the context of divination and healing, were overlapping orientations that gave occasion for Oyotunji, with its new African divinatory practices, to interact with a community whose practices represented a historical continuum that went back to their enslaved African ancestors. Divination became a mediatorial language through which Gullah and Oyotunji communities connected. Both communities largely understood the divinatory healing arts as a "cooperative struggle of the divinity and human person to achieve a good end" in one's daily life.[143] Therefore, the spiritual encounters between Gullah clients and Oyotunji diviners provided an opportunity to link the past with the present, offering a range of curative meanings and possibilities.[144]

In *A Peculiar People*, Margaret Washington Creel examines the religious and cultural history of this low-country region and argues that the spiritual lives and folk customs of the Gullah were largely informed by religious orientations toward Africa.[145] Because of the region's geographical isolation and minimal contact with the outside world, Creel makes the case for the "retention of traditional African provenance" throughout the southern South Carolina and Georgia Gullah region.[146] According to Creel, "In their isolation, the Gullahs remained an uprooted people whose acceptance of Christianity was sometimes outward, selective, and subject to reinterpretations which would not force them to relinquish old ways entirely."[147] The Gullah tradition can most readily be viewed as a convergence of complex cultural orientations that over time affected their religious cosmology, linguistic expression, and production of material culture. Influencing the formation of these cultural orientations were what Patricia Jones-Jackson calls "African stylistic devices"[148] that have endured in distinctly American ways. Moreover, Charles Joyner, in *Down by the Riverside: A South Carolina Slave Community*, understands this South Carolina cultural geography as having undergone a "transformation of diverse African cultures into an Afro-American culture."[149] With Oyotunji's presence in the region, South Carolina's "religious tapestry" continued to be an important site for what Preston L. McKever-Floyd calls "religious pluralism."[150] In many ways, Oyotunji's spiritual philosophy, with its practice of conjuration/divination, rootwork, herbalism, system of offerings, and amulet and charm production, was similar to that of its Southern neighbors. Over time a degree of respect and reciprocity developed between Oyotunji and the Gullah. According to Hunt, "It was not long before they accepted the Villagers warmly, and they soon realized that they had some things in common. The Blacks who live along the Georgia and South Carolina Sea Islands are probably the most voodoo conscious people in the United States. When they learned that the use of divination and root medicines were a part of the Yoruba lifestyle, most of their fears disappeared and the villagers began to visit them occasionally and attend their parties, homecomings, funerals and weddings."[151]

In fact, the historical Gullah traditions in South Carolina overlapped so much with the world of Oyotunji that it was not uncommon for local Gullah clients to disclose to Oyotunji priests during a reading or spiritual prescription, "Grandma used to say that, great-grandma used to say that," revealing a sense of familiarity with the expressed spiritual orientations. Adefunmi and other Yoruba practitioners understood that "the residue of African religious beliefs continues among older black Americans in their belief in prophets, diviners, astrologers, spiritualists, fortune tellers, root doctors, and obeah or voodoo doctors (mistakenly called 'witch doctors' by Western people)."[152] According to Adefunmi, "African people in the Americas still believe in these things because these people actually practice some of the sciences of which real religion is made, unlike the preachers and so-called priests of Western religions who can do nothing more than . . . comment on old miracles, prophesies and religious news made thousands of years ago."[153]

Similarly, Oyotunji's Chief Akintobe, a native of the St. Helena Gullah community in the South Carolina Sea Islands, remembers how the "sociology of the people" was deeply connected to the spiritual world of Africa they retained in their culture. Akintobe recalls, "As a young boy many of the African traditions could still be seen like the charms, the anklets, the dime or the penny on the ankle. . . . The sort of things they would say to us . . . just the words like 'puttin mouth on you' which was putting a curse on you. Many people had the [gift of seeing spirits]."

Akintobe first heard of Oyotunji Village back in 1971 while an enlisted officer in the army in Germany. Because of its proximity to his home, he immediately paid a visit to Oyotunji when he returned to the United States in 1973. His first response to the village was, "This all looks familiar; this really reminds me of the past." In 1977, after returning from Africa, having traveled to Liberia, Ghana, Togo, Benin, and Nigeria, Akintobe decided to enter the African village in America. He said for him it was not difficult to make an adjustment to the village because it so closely recalled the Gullah tradition.

Like Akintobe, Oyotunji's Shango Omuyiwa Akinwon was also from the Gullah region. During our interview, Akinwon readily described the richness of the Gullah religious environment that immediately surrounded him growing up as a child: "Beaufort is really deep. This place is known for

what we call here in the village, voodoo, or what you call juju, root workers. I know a lot of root workers. I knew plenty of root workers in Beaufort
before I knew anybody [at Oyotunji.]"[154]

The narratives of both Akinwon and Akintobe on the religious folk
beliefs of the Gullah region culminated in numerous recollections of South
Carolina's famed root doctor and conjurer, Dr. Buzzard, and the many religious specialists who would continue to assume his name. A Sea Island
resident, Cornelia Walker Bailey recounts in her book, *God, Dr. Buzzard,
and the Bolito Man*, that "the first Dr. Buzzard got off the boat and began
practicing root in St. Helena, South Carolina. He was said to be as powerful
as a buzzard and to have the patience of a buzzard, and that's how he got
his name. Ever since then, rootworkers in the Sea Islands have been known
as Dr. Buzzard and it always has been said that the ones in South Carolina
have the strongest root of all."[155] Both Akinwon and Akintobe attest to the
widespread notoriety of the Dr. Buzzard of the 1940s. Akinwon remarked,
"I knew of Dr. Buzzard back in the forties. His son now runs the program.
But back in the forties he got his name by saying he made a buzzard row a
boat across the Beaufort River so then they started calling him Dr. Buzzard.
But he was a very powerful root doctor. He learned from his ancestors who
came from Africa. He learned how to use them roots . . . He used the herbs
to heal people; he used the herbs to help people. . . . The herbs got magical
powers, 'cause you know the tree live just like we live. He was like, what we
would say, a diviner; he was just like a diviner."[156]

The specialty in rootwork and "counter-cunjur" of Stepheney Robinson
(also known as Dr. Buzzard) earned him the respect of both black and white
South Carolinians as an esteemed member of the "root brotherhood."[157]
Such "doctors were accorded during their day the status of 'experts'" and
were "left to build up their remunerative practices, exempt from the Law
and pretty much free from interference."[158] Southern customary law accommodated their presence as long as they "operated within their proper prov-
ince of root spells" and avoided identifying themselves part of the "legally
recognized" profession of "materia medica."[159]

By the late 1940s, Dr. Buzzard had amassed a tremendous amount of
wealth. As a diviner and root doctor, he was especially known for his reputed
skills to influence judges and juries in the Beaufort County Courthouse.
While court was in session, it was said "he could chew the root and affect
the outcome of the case." In addition, "He also used another procedure in

affecting the result of trials. He concocted a powder by grinding together certain materials, and he sprinkled the powder on the desks, tables, and chairs in the courtroom. After the powder had been scattered about the courtroom, Dr. Buzzard said the room and been 'rooted,' and the course of the trial in progress would change."[160] By his own admission, he was someone gifted with "the Sight" and did not practice his spiritual abilities in a way antithetical to the region's black church culture. In fact, in one instance, when one black Christian community was torn apart by internal schisms and the mysterious burning down of the church, it was Dr. Buzzard who lent assistance. A 1949 account of the event stated, "Of his prosperity there could be no question. . . . When the Baptist Church of Frogmore split upon some fine point of dogma and, shortly after the schism, burned to the ground, it was Stepheney Robinson, who rebuilt it with a $3,000 loan in ready cash."[161]

Oyotunji's Chief Akintobe revealed his own personal affiliation with the famed doctor as well: "My neighbor was Dr. Buzzard. He was a root doctor . . . I saw him as a little boy. . . . All of this, at the time I didn't know it, was leaving an impression in me."[162] The reputation of Dr. Buzzard's power in the realm of the spirits transcended the geographical borders of South Carolina. Akinwon and Akintobe remember that many clients came from far and wide to seek healing services from Dr. Buzzard, and although his reputation as a spiritual worker was quite public, his clients sought to remain clandestine. Some practitioners of rootwork contend that secrecy determines the effectiveness of the root and ultimately the healing or harming powers of the spiritual work performed. According to Peter Henry, a contemporary of Dr. Buzzard, "Everything about roots is kept mysterious. Colored people won't talk about them or show them. Root doctors say that if a root is seen, it will 'turn on' its owner. Negroes using roots usually keep them hidden beneath their clothes or sewed in seams. Secrecy is part of the power of suggestion that makes roots work."[163] Thus, people went to see root doctors and diviners like Dr. Buzzard under the cloak of secrecy.

In a lengthy illustration of this point, Akinwon recalled an occasion when one of Dr. Buzzard's Northern clients traveled to the South to employ his spiritual services:

> I remember one time I was at the bus station, and this old guy got
> off the bus. He was like dressed down. I think he was from New

York. He was clean, had on one of them top hats and all this. Me and my mother was standing there about to ride the bus, and he came over and asked us, "Where's the Doctor, can you help me find the Doctor?" And then at first we looked at each other and said, "Doctor? This time of evening?" Because it was like five o'clock in the evening. "Doctor, what doctor?" We said, "No doctor's office located down here." And he said. "Oh no, not *that* type of doctor." And then it clicked to us. And then we said, "Ooh, you talking about Dr. Buzzard!" And he was like trying to keep it quiet. It wasn't that much people around, but he still kept trying to keep it quiet. A lot of people when they go to a root doctor or a diviner, they try to keep it quiet, and African people should never try to keep that quiet because back in the time when our people used to live in Africa everybody went to a diviner, even the king, for what they had to deal with in everyday life. Say for instance you had to go to another tribe or village, they would always get a reading. If a child is born, you get a reading. If somebody died, they got a reading. If there was a wedding, they got a reading. So you see now, working from that time back into Africa till all the way into Beaufort, South Carolina, these Africans still keep that tradition. They didn't lose that tradition.[164]

The religious history of South Carolina's low country and the spiritual legacy of rootworkers like Dr. Buzzard greatly influenced the ways in which Akinwon and Akintobe embraced Oyotunji. Coming from a Gullah/ Geechee world informed by multiple approaches to spiritual healing, Oyotunji's approaches felt familiar to them. Although Oyotunji introduced new methods of divination and conjuration of spirits, it tapped into a long historical tradition of healing among African Americans in the Gullah region. Both Dr. Buzzard of the past and Oyotunji's priesthood of the present were called upon to invoke the spirits on behalf of the socially, physically, and spiritually afflicted.

Like the clients of Dr. Buzzard, Oyotunji's spiritual petitioners came from afar to witness the invisible healing power of the spirits, often shrouding themselves in secrecy and invisibility as well. Public religious respectability in the South was very much tied to Christianity in the 1970s, not to African rootwork, and Oyotunji's clients often feigned public adherence to Christianity while turning to other spiritual traditions to fulfill private needs. In the past, church membership and participation did not preclude entry into the worlds of conjure, rootwork, and Dr. Buzzard. As one local Gullah resident explained, "Let's say I tried the church and that didn't work . . . I need to do something a little more drastic. I'll try Dr. Buzzard."[165] Continuing this function today, Oyotunji Village provides an important resource for African American clients seeking therapeutic consultations, medicinal solutions, and restorative remedies, even if they feel they must pursue these alternative curative modes surreptitiously.

Divination and the Sociology of Healing

African American clients look to the priests and priestesses of Oyotunji as mediums for healing. For these clients, members of the priesthood "function as doctors as well as psychologists and are in charge of esoteric and detailed religious healing and knowledge concerning the *orisa* they serve."[166] Clients come to Oyotunji not necessarily to join the Yoruba tradition but to solicit the African gods for help with the pressing matters of daily life. Typically, when other measures of relief and amelioration have been exhausted, clients look to Oyotunji Village as discrete and discretionary providers of "African" healing. Their orientation toward these practices comes less from a contemporary desire to seek out specifically Yoruba or Ifa diviners per se and more from a past Southern cultural orientation toward black folk medicine, healing, and divinatory systems of conjuration.

As specialists in spiritual technology, Oyotunji's priesthood provides its services as a "private practice" away from the ceremonial gaze of public ritual.[167] For Oyotunji's clientele, many of who are Christian, it is a space where religious boundaries are relaxed, rigid orthodoxies suspended, justice issues expanded, and healing alternatives welcomed. Like other divinatory epistemologies, these services expose clients to a new orientation toward sacred power and possibility. They also provide "an explicit, culturally specific way of thinking and talking about cause, effect, power, and agency, and as a practical, creative process of mobilizing spiritual and material resources to address problems and to effect change."[168]

Within the realm of divination, several critical questions arise regarding the sociology of healing and the comingling of religious worlds. According to Kristina Wirtz, "people facing health problems or a wide variety of other personal, familial, economic, or legal difficulties often seek spiritual help and herbal remedies by shopping around across ostensibly distinct traditions."[169] One Oyotunji priest summed up the practice of divination as the moment when "your past makes your future" within a complex ritual web that includes the client; the diviner specialist; the revealed oracular knowledge; and the sacrifice and offerings of appeasement, petition, cleansing, or thanksgiving.[170] When accessed as "a system of alternative medical care,"[171] this divinatory "priestcraft" offers services analogous to Western medicine's examination, consultation, diagnosis, and prescriptions.[172] Divination consultations between priests and clients are intensely private, regarded as "priestly counsel," and according to Mary Cuthrell Curry, are like "a session between a therapist and a patient."[173] Sacred instruments are often "cast" and examined by diviner specialists that assist in administering a diagnosis and proper consultation to the client.

Joseph Murphy carefully points out that the "Yoruba ritual core is oracular," and as such, clients are introduced to a world of symbols, stories, and metaphors from sacred oracles such as Ifa that help to divulge the source of the client's problems.[174] Within this sacred exchange, clients are transported through chants and stories, or Odus, to earlier moments in history when divinations were performed for Orunmila or other sacred

FIGURE 19.
Oba Adefunmi
performing Ifa
divination with *ikin*
in the late 1970s.
Photograph courtesy
of Oyotunji African
Village and Kamari
Clarke.

personalities in the Yoruba world. Orunmila's former divinations then help
to bring light to clients' present-day afflictions, placing them along a shared
continuum of human trials and challenges and solutions. Through the figurative metaphors of Ifa divination, priests engage in a process of analogizing as a way of providing answers and solutions to clients' problems. Some
diviners have referred to the Odu as a "living entity which is talking to the
diviner" on behalf of the client. After the client's situation is satisfacto-
rily diagnosed, prescriptions are made to achieve restorative results in the
client's life. Prescriptions might include herbal medicine for ingestion or
bathing, topical salves, healing soaps, incantations and prayers, food offering, animal sacrifices, and, in some instances, initiation.[175] Huntington
reveals that within this tradition human bodies as the site for healing "are
implicated deeply in the holistic healing of Orisha as they embody the
everyday lived and experienced nexus of the spiritual, biological, social
and emotional worlds, in which we are understood to exist."[176]

Although the "medical heritages" associated with Africa have often
been maligned as evil, devil work, black magic, witchcraft, or sorcery, they
are, in fact, ethically sophisticated systems governed by strict behavioral
and moral edicts, precepts, and codes.[177] Members of Oyotunji's priesthood are reluctant to engage in practices that promote harm over healing,
injury over health, or offense over protection. Connected to their spiritual
obligation is a responsibility to impart moral and ethical counsel to their
clients as they help them understand the gravity and power of the spirits
whom they have consulted for intercession on their behalf. As a divining
priesthood, they are ideally bound by Yoruba-espoused moral principles of
good character, inner coolness and balance, and ethical responsibility.[178]

Velana Huntington's interviewees in her study, "Bodies in Contexts:
Holistic Ideals of Health, Healing, and Wellness in an America Orisha
Community," offer an insightful look into the ethical obligations of Yoruba
American divining priests. According to Oshunfemi, "We try not to judge
a person, client, or member by their situation and [we] make every effort to
be completely honest in a sensitive and unconditional manner as it relates
to whatever their spiritual challenge. . . . Our culture and spiritual beliefs
are our foundation of thought and reference. People trust us because confi-
dentiality is crucial, although all of this varies due to the spiritual personal
character of a priest."[179] She speaks to an implicit code of ethics and adds,
"I am spiritually responsible to do the right thing for them as to the best

of my knowledge or [to] have the humility to refer them to someone better equipped to assist them."[180] Similarly, in Olosunmi's own experience,
he says, "We are called upon to provide advice and direction in the areas
of marriage, employment, and for any number of psychological and social
interaction problems" and as priests, "are required to act as social workers
or counselors in every phase of human life."[181] In addition, Ifagbemi sees
the priestly function in divination as "reading your environment, reading what's going on around you and how you are affected and how you
affect."[182] For both priests and clients, spiritual consultations inadvertently
become avenues of opportunity to impart Yoruba religion's understanding of an "anthropocentric ontology" where "existence . . . is viewed in
terms of its connection to humans" and where human agency is a chief
negotiator with the natural and spiritual worlds.[183] Divination deals with
accessing modes of human healing, but Adefunmi also saw it as a way "to
discover . . . one's character, one's aptitudes, one's odds and to set diligently
to work."[184]

    As a religious practice, ritual divination and theurgical practices
are not exclusive to African-based traditions but have been shared by
many global religious traditions throughout the centuries. William A.
Christian Jr. argues that "the desperation of people seeking help" creates a religious moment where humans are "relatively flexible and open
to new options" in healing and spiritual resolution.[185] Within his study
on the Roman Catholic tradition, Christian speaks of the presence of this
phenomenon in the sixteenth century, when "lay professionals circulated
through the Castilian countryside selling their services to individuals or
communities to ward off disease, locusts, other insect pests, or hailstorms
by magical methods,"[186] concluding that "religion in the form of bargains
with the gods provided a means of social control over these disasters."[187]
Within the context of American society, "nonmedical healing," a term
sociologist Meredith McGuire coined, has become a growing phenomenon
across racial, class, and religious lines.[188] As McGuire explains, alternative
healing occurs within the context of "an entire system of beliefs and practices."[189] This is especially true for Yoruba-patterned forms of divination at
Oyotunji. Priestly diviners enter into a consultatory world where for clients,
"wellness and illness fall between the very real crossroads of biology and
culture" and according to Huntington, "are physical, emotional, and mental states that are affected by people's everyday realities and perceptions."[190]

Illness in Yoruba cosmology is not easily definable in completely natural terms but often falls into the realms of the unnatural and the supernatural. One does not simply seek a cure for illness; one seeks an explanation of its origin. As Yvonne Chireau indicates, it is not so much that African Americans dismiss "scientific etiologies or material explanations when identifying sickness . . . Rather their views of the causes of a sickness were more inclusive of what one might call metaphysical agents."[191] At Oyotunji, I encountered clear religious spaces where people come with their "everyday contradictions, memories, problems, and hardships," weaving a multivalent hermeneutic around what Jacob Olupona calls the "theory of disease" and what I would refer to as the origins of affliction.[192] In this space, one entered into a complex world of healing based not exclusively on medical diagnoses or Western pharmacopoeia but on the praxis work of spirit(s), ritual, offerings, and results. This was a space where "in times of physical, emotional, or spiritual crisis," people maneuvered a world *between practices* and across belief systems, seeking not just a cure from affliction but an *explanation of its origin* allowing "multiple interpretive frames and discourses" to illumine the "illness event."[193] According to Jacob K. Olupona, "Because traditional Yoruba theories of sickness tend to relate more to nonnatural causes, the Yoruba seek diagnosis, explanation, meaning, and treatment of disease through the lens of divination practices."[194] Human illness and misfortune are remedied spiritually because they speak directly to "a state of disequilibria with the spirit world."[195] As Susan Starr Sered and Linda Barnes explain in their series foreword, as one engages "the study of religion and healing," it is essential to examine "how individuals, communities, and religious traditions diagnose and interpret causes of illness and the sources of affliction, as well as notions of what constitutes health, both ideally and pragmatically."[196]

At Oyotunji Village, divination technology mirrors that of other Yoruba practitioners and can assume a variety of forms.[197] A basic form of divination uses four pieces of coconut or *obi* fruit sections that render affirmative and negative responses. The two most common approaches are either by throwing sixteen cowrie shells, which is a form of Yoruba divination called *eerindilogun*, or by casting a divining chain or the ikin used in the Yoruba divination system of Ifa, which also references the deity as well as Ifa-Orunmila.[198] Other Oyotunji priests have been known to use additional methods, such as tarot cards, palmistry, numerology, and

astrology.[199] Divining tools such as the cowrie or the chain are then interpreted or "read" according to a body of sacred Yoruba oracular allegories
that relate to the client's problem. From the instruments that are cast, the
diviner is able to discern "a pattern from some visual configuration of signs
that is restructured . . . in terms of meaning."[200] According to Huntington,
"A person's spiritual beliefs and practices, family life, friendships, occupa-
tion, education, income, and physical health all interact as a synchronous
and holistic context" out of which clients are read.[201] After the source of
the problem is revealed by oracular interpretation, a spiritual solution is
sought. The orisa or ancestors that arise in the reading are summoned as
"agencies of well-being" to assist the client in the process toward healing.[202]
Therefore, offerings are commonly administered so that the orisa gods or
ancestral spirits may invoke favor, embracing both spirits and clients into
a larger "ethic of reciprocity."[203]

Judy Rosenthal, in her research on Ewe Voodoo, discloses that animal sacrifice is viewed in "terms of reciprocal services and gift giving"
and is considered sacred because the animals "are given to the gods as a
feast." Kola Abimbola interprets sacrifice as a "code of communication; it
is a means of exchange in which one communicates with the supernatural
realm of existence in expectation of receiving something else."[204] Ebo is
also a communion between the person who offers it and those who partake in it.[205] Last, it is common that animals used in the sacrifice are eaten
"so that the eater may become like [the gods] and share in the communal
maintenance of divinity."[206]

Animal sacrifice among Yoruba Americans is not as rampant and
unbridled as Hollywood might suggest. It is viewed quite solemnly, one
African American babalawo explains: "I looked at the bird that had just
died for me and I knew then that this was a serious thing . . . Whatever
it was that I was to do, it had to be taken seriously."[207] In addition to animals, which are used when more acute forms of affliction are identified,
offerings can take the forms of candles, incense, flowers, fruit, constructions, and shrines. Joseph Murphy argues that divination and sacrifice are
the prominent sites where "humans beings and spirits interact"[208] in an
exploration of the "spiritual aspects of wellness."[209] Within this ritual context, clients can discover "chosen destinies," learn "a code of ethics that
brings a change in direction," and ultimately "restore spiritual and natural
equilibrium."[210] The Oyotunji priesthood has a prominent position in the

elaborate systems of consultation, appeasement, healing, and restoration. Their roles mirror that of their African American conjurer and root doctor forebears who were traditionally consulted on "mundane matters of health, marriage, and . . . reputed to be able to read signs, effect herbal and spiritual healings, interpret dreams."[211]

Clients enter Oyotunji seeking a new sociology of religious knowledge that helps to decode the inexplicable and indecipherable. They enter with their "everyday contradictions, memories, problems, and hardships," weaving a multivalent epistemology around the origins of affliction.[212] According to one priest, the moment clients make up their minds to come to Oyotunji, they have already conditioned themselves to accept its possible diagnosis and ritual prescriptions. Huntington, in her wonderfully rich text on the body and wellness in the orisa tradition, states that "it is more common than not for people to move between practices or beliefs since, in times of physical, emotional, or spiritual crisis, people may be more willing to explore other healing options."[213]

Many African American clients come to Oyotunji with "basically either problems with the law[214] or problems with work, health, or love: "I want my man. I want to get rid of my man. I want my woman. I want to get rid of my woman. I'm having problems on my job. Can you help me? My nature's down."[215] Clients also consult Yoruba diviners with more severe problems such as employment and terminal illnesses such as cancer and HIV/AIDS.[216] Anthropologist Karen McCarthy Brown speaks of a similar phenomenon among practitioners and healers of Haitian vodou. According to Brown, "Many different kinds of problems are amenable to treatment within the Vodou system—love, family, work, and money problems as well as physical maladies. . . . Because relational networks extend beyond the living to include the dead and the [spirits], the Vodou healer must explore a vast, tangled web of relations to find the troubled strand putting stress on the whole fabric."[217]

African American women, in particular, disproportionately sought answers regarding love relationships, family and domestic affairs, and matters of physical health. As Stephanie Y. Mitchem highlights in her chapter, "Healing Hearts and Broken Bodies: An African American Women's Spirituality of Healing," healing for African American women "is not just about curing physical ills but necessarily includes healing the past, the present, work, income, family, community, spirit, mind, and emotions."[218] Moreover,

female clients widely covered the spectrum of economic classes ranging from
the working class to the professional elite, and for both Oyotunji's male and
female clientele, the Christian faith was the dominant religious affiliation.

Christianity, the Art of Divination, and the Power of the "Work"

Clients who come to Oyotunji for spiritual "Work" are overwhelmingly
African Americans who profess Protestant Christianity as their primary
religious affiliation. That priests and priestesses of Oyotunji Village readily admit that most of their clients self-identify as "Christian" raises interesting questions concerning the fluidity and permeability of African
American religiosity in the South as well as the ways Christian identities
are negotiated alongside black esoteric clandestine traditions. Margaret
Washington Creel offers historical insight on this issue when she argues
that "African beliefs, where these remained, accommodated the slave situation just as Christianity, to some extent, accommodated African religion and philosophy. Where Protestantism did not tolerate Africanity as a
separate expression, Africanisms sometimes continued through secretive-
ness or by finding a place at the center of Protestantism."[219] Oba Adefunmi
understood this phenomenon as an important historical "aspect of Afro-
American folk behavior."[220] He found most intriguing the "persistence
with which Afro-Americans continue to patronize 'readers' to discover
the cause or solution to all manner of troubles whether spiritual, domestic,
medical, economic, or otherwise" while observing that though they may
"devoutedly profess Christianity with its injunctions against 'soothsay-
ers,' this in "no way seem[s] to restrain the need to respond to the occult
instinct."[221] For Adefunmi, Christianity and these esoteric practices have
never been mutually exclusive for African Americans in the United States,
and he cites as an example the fact that "numerous Afro-American preachers have devised or inherited from slaves in cultural transition various
techniques of using the King James Bible in divination processes" and that
what ultimately connected these Christian preachers to the "Root Man" or
the "Hoodoo or Voodoo man or Lady" was their shared commitment to do
"Work."[222] The power of the "Work," according to Adefunmi, has led not
the stereotypically defined masses of "so-called ignorant or 'uneducated'
blacks" to the diviners of Oyotunji, but rather the "politicians, teachers,
policemen, college students, executives, and in one instance, an FBI agent"

seeking the "human religious approach" and sacred counsel that Oyotunji divination specialists offer.[223]

Within this network of black folk praxis, services for the "Work" are not readily advertised or publicized; people learn of practitioners from clients who testify to the efficacy of their actions. Some priests, however, print business cards or brochures that are distributed to clients. In these publications, priests like Odunfonda Adaramola might self-identify as "Diviner, Astrologer, Counselor." Dr. Yefin D. D. self-identifed on a business card some twenty years ago as "Herbalist, Reader, Spiritual Advisor, Specialist in Herbal Baths, Charms & Divine Medicine (African System) Located in the World Famous OYOTUNJI AFRICAN VILLAGE."[224] The late Chief Ajamu described himself as "Professional Practitioner of African Science." Chief Alagba Olaitan provides a wider range of spiritual services: "Ancestral ceremonies, Naming ceremonies, funerals, weddings, Male Rites of Passage programs and Spiritual divination."[225]

Although eager to seek out this work, many Christian clients still "sneak in and sneak out" of the village for fear of being seen by fellow church parishioners. Chief Akintobe states that many of his Christian clients provide insight into this bifocal religious consciousness. One client stated, "I read my Bible last night but I still want to get that traditional medicine and that traditional healing." She confessed to the diviner "if it wasn't for you *and* the Lord, I wouldn't know what to do." Within the "complementary strengths" and "practical blending" of both traditions, clients are provided with what Wirtz calls "a complete package of spiritual protection."[226]

The pliability of religious boundaries is evident throughout the Caribbean as well as in Oyotunji's low-country location. Scholars who study communities of African descent throughout the Caribbean document religious practitioners' ability to choose from Protestant and Roman Catholic forms of Christianity as well as the Afro-healing traditions. According to one informant anthropologist Francio Guadeloupe interviewed, "Of course I visit an Obeah doctor, plenty of times. Anybody tell you they never do that, they are lying. When things go wrong and the doctor can't help, the priest can't help, well, then, it is the Obeah man you turning to. . . . So I am going to believe all the things that suit me, even though I was baptized in the Catholic Church."[227]

Local low-country clients, like those in the Caribbean, rely on many sources of spiritual power. Those from the Gullah and Geechee regions of

South Carolina and Georgia attest to the fact that "the old people didn't put their faith in God alone. God had his place, but so did Dr. Buzzard."[228] Within their cosmological understanding of the world, divination offers alternative economies of time: "I'm gonna pray to God but God takes his time to answer, so I'm also gonna consult Dr. Buzzard and use this magic potion which will bring me faster results."[229] The Christian God is posited as slow and patient in rendering spiritual results, whereas the orisa and the ancestors respond with more immediacy, according to the urgency of the problem. According to one client, "Jesus makes you wait . . . You can go to this kind of spiritual consultation and not have to wait. . . . You can be empowered. . . . You can receive information that allows you to make change in your life immediately and in the near future." Like the clients of Oyotunji, practitioners of the low-country culture found they could reconcile these lived cosmologies because ultimately "they knew and the Good Lord above knew too that they needed some *extra luck*," making room for a flexible and additive spiritual epistemology.[230]

What is most pronounced in this context is that rigid distinctions between Christian and non-Christian boundaries are profoundly elastic in matters of healing. Residents of Oyotunji recount numerous stories regarding their Christian clients and the fervor with which they seek the power of the African gods. Analyzing this phenomenon, one practitioner remarked, "Even though [African Americans] profess this allegiance to Christianity, that is not where their hearts and souls go when they're at a crossroads. . . . What becomes privileged is what I would call African religion or African resources that help us tap into those [African] spiritual powers."[231] Within healing and therapeutic contexts, Yoruba divination offers Protestant Christians an alternative theology of the tragic that allows them to "navigate through the tragic," drawing on diverse spiritual resources and curative time frames.[232]

Even ordained Christian clergy seek out divination. As priest Shango Omuyiwa Akinwon recalls, "Even today you get those people who go to the churches, these big preachers. He'll have a congregation of about four or five hundred people, but if he gets a little problem—Oh, Lord—he be pulling right on up here with a sign on his car that says, 'Buckle up for Jesus'—coming to get him a reading from the king or one of these priests and priestesses because he knows the deal."[233] In an interview Velma Love recorded in 2001, Oyotunji's Chief Ajamu described that some Christian clients "would come after dark, but others were bolder" and "would come on Sunday afternoon still dressed up in their church clothes."[234] He stated that Oyotunji diviners "used to get more business on Sunday than any other time, but now people come all during the week as well."[235] Chief Ajamu, who lived in Oyotunji in the 1970s, was himself no stranger to the Christian tradition and had at one time "studied to be a Catholic priest."[236] Ajamu, however, abandoned Christianity for the Yoruba tradition, unlike many of his clientele who chose to make spiritual voyages between the two. Nigerian babalawo Dr. Wande Abimbola attests to this phenomenon even among the Yoruba of Nigeria, where Christians and Muslims will come at night: "Please divine for me" or "Please, give me a talisman to put in the soil so that many people will come to my church or mosque," with an openness to animal sacrifice and a willingness to "build bridges" with regard to religious practice.[237] The moment of priest-client interaction within the context of divination is for many a "religious experience."[238] According to one client, "When I'm getting a divination reading . . . this is religious experience. It's beyond just a spiritual consultation" particularly because of "the way sacrifice plays a role." For this client, divination incorporates "prayer, ritual sacrifice, chanting, healing prescriptions" in ways that are not often as accessibly tangible in traditional Protestantism or Islam.[239] Despite these clandestine and efficacious encounters, though, few Christian clients are ever willing to participate in public expressions of ecumenism or public acts of defense or advocacy on behalf of Africa's traditional religions.

The priesthood of Oyotunji comprehends divination work not as fortune-telling but as a healing service, or what the late Chief Awolowo called a "mission" for the larger African American community beyond the Yoruba faith. Within the context of their priestcraft, diviners understand themselves as "helpers and counselors to peoples who may suffer the problems and frustrations of trying to express and sometimes repress their African essence."[240] Oba Sekou Olayinka understood his role as a diviner as imparting to clients a sense that "there is always hope. There's always a chance that this can right itself. There's something that can be done."[241]

For Christians, Yoruba divination offers a theological epistemology of spiritual surrogacy and advocacy that are not rooted in notions of divine suffering.[242] The orisa and the ancestors did not necessarily have to undergo suffering as a redemptive act. Divine intercession on the part of orisa/ancestor spirits for humans is based more on ritual gifts and acts of reciprocity than messianic tropes of suffering. In addition, Christian clients are offered a sense of human agency and responsibility that in many ways confounds Protestant notions of providence, fate, and destiny. In Yewande's observations, Christian clients "need answers and help that Jesus is not giving them, that Jesus is not providing for them. . . . You get a chance for self-reflection. . . . They're going to tell you narratives or stories or interact with you about your life in a way that forces you to be reflective about choices you've made, about choices other people are making that are impinging upon you. . . . It's not about leaving your burden at the feet of some god-man who's going to take it away from you."[243]

Another benefit of Yoruba services to Christians is that one "can actually interface with the divine."[244] As Olayinka observes, "The Christians always say that Jesus is coming back, and I always say that the orisas come back all the time either at bembes or drum celebrations or even in divination we can interface and communicate with our God."[245] Reflecting on the divinatory arts of the tradition he explains, "A prayer is not just hoping and not even just believing . . . but knowing [that] I made my prayers, I made my offerings and sacrifices, now I'm gonna go out and do the work, and it will manifest. . . . It will manifest in this lifetime. What could be better!"[246]

Finally, clients have demonstrated that the need to seek healing and spiritual answers transcends all denominational or religious barriers. Accessing divination services at Oyotunji Village in no way interferes with traditional church membership or replaces primary faith affiliations. For the most part, Christian clients engage in temporary spiritual encounters and do not seek an enduring or sustaining relationship with the orisa tradition. Huntington asserts that "healing does not require religious conversion" and as such "resonate[s] with people in their everyday spiritual existence and their well-seeking practices."[247] In general, priests do not see themselves as proselytizers to their clientele but view their "mission" as committing themselves to addressing clients' immediate needs in the most effective ways possible, even if it means making payment arrangements with clients who are unable to meet the initial financial obligations. This proved ideal for one African American mother who was seeking spiritual intervention on behalf of her son, whom she believed was falsely accused of murder. According to the priest, "She put up her house, she mortgaged everything, trying to help her son before coming to Oyotunji."[248] Spiritual readings, then, function as a religious practice with important social implications. To understand their efficacy is to understand the presence of a larger "social arena" with which these readings interact and engage.[249]

The economic catastrophe of 2008 caused a rapid surge in the number of clients seeking the services of Oyotunji. Clients began to come "not because the diviners can work a miracle for them" but because "they want to hear somebody talk to them about their lives, about how to handle situations. The priesthood of Oyotunji often feels that their spiritual credentials are only part of what they need to confront the challenges that often plague their clients' lives. They are also required to be "a shrink, an anthropologist, a sociologist, a security guard" in order to keep "people secure." As one priest said, "You gotta be everything to be able to understand the way the world is now" and assist the clients who navigate their lives within it.[250]

Oyotunji's First Forty Years: Global and National Reflections

Oyotunji Village has for over the past forty years invested in the vision of an African God and an African nation in America. Its vision was not so much to reconstitute the Old World of Africa but to provide diasporic African Americans in this hemisphere with a sense of spatial ownership in North America. Since its inception in 1970, Oyotunji Village has helped to shape the history of African American Yoruba thought through its written texts, its black-nationalist ideologies, and its strong racial philosophies. It developed out of a tradition of dissent that challenged American models of religion, politics, and nationhood. In 1976, Adefunmi called Oyotunji the embodiment of this dissent: "We are launching a spiritual attack to undermine the moral, political, and social control this country maintains over persons of African background."[251] Symbolically, Oyotunji Village functions as a discursive space from which African Americans are able to critically address America's Protestant hegemony, its historical assumptions about race, and its restricted notions of citizenry and nationhood.

Since 1970, Oyotunji Village has also bequeathed to black North Americans a complex legacy of African nationhood with black dynastic rule. Oyotunji residents are acutely aware that this legacy has often been a source of contestation among African American practitioners, and feelings of ambiguity often surround the ways that Oyotunji situates itself in relation to other African American Yoruba in North America. As one of the earliest known non-Hispanic African American males in the United States initiated into the orisa tradition, Adefunmi understood himself as a pioneer and elder of the tradition in North America. His status as elder-king was the presumed authorities of divination, coronation, and primogeniture. This initial platform of authority rested on the revealed message of a divination reading that Adefunmi received during his initial initiation in 1959. According to the diviner, Adefunmi was "a King sent to destroy a King." Adefunmi interpreted the first king as himself and the second king as the religious and cultural hegemony of America. The second source authorizing his kingship derived first from his 1972 crowning by a group of "Yoruba-American pioneers who joined him in his forest foothold in South Carolina" and then from a 1981 ceremony that Adefunmi received while attending the International World Congress of Orisa Culture and Tradition in Ile-Ife, Nigeria.[252] In a photograph highlighting this Yoruba ceremony, the following words were captioned:

> CORONATION AT IFE, NIGERIA (WEST AFRICA). King of South Carolina's African Village of Oyotunji . . . Adefunmi's coronation on June 5, 1981[,] at the palace of African King Okunade Sijuwade Olubuse II, The Oni of Ife, marked the first time a non-Nigerian had been crowned a traditional king.

This ceremony highlights a new phenomenon that has emerged in the past two decades whereby African ruling elders in Nigeria have conferred chieftaincies and titles upon African Americans in the diaspora. Adefunmi was named a *bale* (king or town ruler) or Alashe by the Ooni of Ife in Nigeria and was given "a sword as a symbol of his office and authority."[253] For Adefunmi, this Nigerian-conferred ceremonial title helped to further legitimize his leadership in Oyotunji and in North America. As one resident of Oyotunji explained, "the Oba did not make himself King. The Oba was taken to Nigeria by Marta Vega. I believe they had some type of conference. The Oba went there just to attend this conference, and the Ooni [of Ife] was so impressed by the accomplishments of the Oba that he told his king makers to make this man bale [king] . . .[254]

Adefunmi publicly addressed the ambiguities surrounding his North American rulership and Nigerian title at an Ifa Conference in New York City in 1993:

The question has also been put to us, how does Oyotunji appoint itself the cultural authority to rule on who has the right to preside over New World Yoruba revivals. Our response to that is, firstly by virtue of primogeniture. Oseijeman Adefunmi was the first of the African Americans to lay claim to the legacy of his ancestors through initiation into the priesthood of Obatala. He was the first known African American to return to the priesthood of Orunmila. The Yoruba Temple of New York and the settlement of Oyotunji were the first public havens for the reception of the ancestral gods and goddesses. The *Bale* of Oyotunji is the first African American to be handed a sword of state by the reigning *Ooni* of Ife, His Divine Majesty Okunade Sijuwade Olubuse II, and to swear allegiance to that king of the Yoruba nation. Adefunmi I was the founder of the African Theological Archministry, the first instrument for restoring the religious institutions of Africa. In conclusion, Adefunmi is an African himself and he was appointed by the ancestors in a séance at Matanzas, Cuba, held in 1960. He was told that he was "a King sent to destroy a King!"[255]

Finally, interesting questions of legitimacy, authenticity, and religious exchange have emerged within black Atlantic communities, particularly as diaspora practitioners return to Nigeria for spiritual initiations, and the Oonis, past and present, tour major diaspora sites, such as the United States, Cuba, Trinidad, and Brazil. Despite the externally conferred titles, however, populations of urban African American devotees did not uniformly support Adefunmi's claims of Yoruba sovereignty. According to one North American Yoruba priest, "In that village, I give him the respect of being the Oba of that village. Outside of that village, he is just another priest. He is my elder, and he is the first African American to be initiated in Cuba and bring it back here."[256] In the United States, some African Americans question the function of a separate black monarchical, theocratic nation in today's society. Critics argue that embedded in the notion of kingship are two inherent problems in that kingship "doesn't set a place where women can rule" and that "the idea of monarchy goes against our tradition [in the diaspora]," especially when one views the rulership of "powerful women in Brazil."[257] Another African American priest was much more critical, citing Adefunmi's unwillingness to "in line" behind other elders. This priest sympathized with Cubans in the 1960s who felt Adefunmi should have been much humbler in his activities, given his spiritual age in orisa. Adefunmi, it seemed, wanted to "reorder the seating arrangements" in the orisa priesthood, "putting himself first" in the religion where he would not have to "kowtow to anyone."[258] Within such a complex discourse of authority, offices and titles Nigerian Yoruba exogenously conferred clearly complicate the politics of local Atlantic Yoruba communities.

In the end, many practitioners throughout North America express their deep gratitude for the Oyotunji experiment. As one priestess states, "I think of Oyotunji as the Yoruba University. I think it has served us well. I'm proud of the people who have come through Oyotunji, the pioneers who took whatever they could of the religion and tried to work with it and keep it alive."[259] Other national priests, although disagreeing with the need for an established kingship or monarchy, argue that Oyotunji "in its own way . . . was a brilliant move in the sense that [it] gave dignity and royalty and grace and style . . . back to African people, that we can be kings and queens, too, even if only symbolically. Understanding the '60s and '70s. I think that was necessary."[260] Despite mixed sentiments toward Oyotunji, one scholar ultimately concludes that even if Oyotunji African Village survives "only as history, they should be remembered and studied as significant expressions of Black nationalism in the late 20th and early 21st centuries."[261]

Oyotunji African Village and Oba Adejuyibe Adefunmi II: Visions for the Twenty-first Century

In an American society where the life-span of most African American nationalist groups and intentional religious communities has been relatively short, the question remains forty-two years later: what will ensure Oyotunji's survival in the future? With the passing of Oyotunji Village's original founder, Oba Oseijeman Efuntola Adefunmi I, in 2005, the village continues to exist today under the leadership of the Oba's son, Adejuyigbe Adefunmi II. Having celebrated in 2009 the fiftieth anniversary of the original Oba's initiation in Cuba in 1959, Oyotunji African Village and its residents find themselves at a unique crossroads, reflecting on its past while envisioning the future in the twenty-first century. With many of its elder residents nearing or older than sixty, they look to an Oyotunji that can endure beyond their years. Chief Akintobe remarks, "We hope that we [will] leave a foundation that those behind us can continue, where they don't have to figure out too much, because the pattern has been set; the groundwork has been laid. All they [will] have to do is keep extending it, keep paving, get the rough edges out, and through changes and time and environment and attitudes, make adjustments, . . . compromises."[262]

Oyotunji residents, including the first Oba, have always been honest in addressing their personal disappointments over the years. One of the residents responded: "The greatest disappointment to me, I guess, is some of the reasons why people move. Some people run away because they wanted their freedom to do as they choose, to sleep as late as they wish, to come and go as they please. Once they left it was like a burden lifted off of them: They didn't have to come to meetings; they didn't have to pull guard duty at night; they didn't have to come to the male work force; the women didn't have to get up in the morning to rake, to have rotation, rotating basis of cooking, to serve people, and to make money."[263] Oyotunji's first Oba revealed that one of his own disappointments over the years had been the fact that "there is not enough close contact between Oyotunji and the vast number of people that have been initiated and that many of them still haven't understood the concept, the Yoruba concept, that they are obligated to take care of their parent, their parent temple. So that's regrettable, but we hope to be able to increase that contact as the years go on. . . . I think that according to Ile-Ife—Ile-Ife meaning the Yoruba history—things develop very slowly, and of course there is a very common saying that Rome wasn't built in a day; Oyotunji wasn't either."[264] In spite of their disappointments, there still remains a committed cadre of villagers who vow to remain loyal to the vision of Oyotunji. From the point of view of its residents, the ability to resurrect "African civilization in the midst of the United States" has been Oyotunji's symbolic gift of physical and spiritual resistance to the modern Western world.[265] To those who have lived inside the transformative world of Oyotunji, it must be seen as "the living shrine" that sought to "offer an alternative for African Americans—who had lost knowledge of Africa—so as to help them reclaim African traditions."[266]

In reflecting on his mission with respect to Oyotunji, Adefunmi I remarked, "We never intended to go back to 16th century Nigeria. We began this way out of necessity and to learn how to survive. We want to develop as the ages develop."[267] Adefunmi I revealed that his vision of Oyotunji was always much larger than himself and he knew that for Oyotunji to evolve into "a great center for learning" for African American Yoruba in North America would take longer than his own lifetime. Adefunmi saw himself standing in the huge cultural gap for African culture amidst a larger Western world and hoping that by its hundredth year in existence, Oyotunji village would have, in his own words, "made our impression against the Christian world and reduced its importance as well as its effect on us."[268] In general, Oyotunjians in no way professed to be a utopian society in the traditional apocalyptic, millenarian sense of the word. One resident remarked that he hoped that anyone who would read this work would "realize that Oyotunji is not a utopian society. It's like any other developing nation starting from the beginning."[269] Despite its shortcomings, residents of Oyotunji look back over some forty years of existence and reflect, "Through our own hands we were able to build a 'nation' that still stands . . ."[270]

Moreover, in summarizing the legacy and efforts of Oba Adefunmi I, Adaramola, an Oyotunji resident, compared Adefunmi's historical role in the shaping of Yoruba religion and culture in North America to the creative power of the orisa Obatala: "Adefunmi was born into an African American world devoid of a coherent African identity or culture. From this chaos, Adefunmi began to create males and females in the 'Yoruba likeness.' His creative potential continued as he created the tradition's basic necessities: shelter in Yoruba Temple; African literature and carvings, and introduced a new language with which to communicate to the new gods."[271] Today's Oyotunji Village has fashioned itself into a Yoruba likeness of religious and cultural meaning that is an expression of African-descended North Americans. "The major concern," according to Christopher Antonio Brooks, "should not be with the authenticity of this village, but with the degree of devotion and commitment of those to whom the tradition is meaningful." In 1970, he continued, Oyotunji sought to "fulfill a cultural and historic void." Thus for many of its elder residents, such as Iya Igberohinjade Oludoye, "this is Africa . . . It's a bridge *home*."[272]

As Oyotunji positions itself within a wider, twenty-first-century Yoruba culture in North America, its new Oba and king, Adejuyigbe Adefunmi II, hopes to build on the legacy and foundation of his father while providing new and innovative ways for propagating an African cultural consciousness beyond the physical compounds and shrines of Oyotunji Village. A young Oba in his midthirties, Adefunmi II grew up in the age of technology, electronic information, visual media, and hip-hop. For the new Oba, "Oyotunji is not just this nine acres anymore. Oyotunji is the cyber-space. Oyotunji is a style of dress. Oyotunji is a mind-set."[273] He increasingly finds himself less concerned with the number of America's Yoruba priesthood who actually reside in Oyotunji and more with the questions of how many people have been affected by Oyotunji and what the meaning of that effect is.[274]

Although one can detect a quality, a tone, that hints at the older Adefunmi (and throughout our interview Adefunmi II would stop himself and say, "I sound like my dad now"), it is evident that the younger Oba sees Oyotunji as more than a nationalist land base, considering it more broadly as a comprehensive "sociology," a "cultural ethnic" philosophy, a resource for Nigerian babalawo immigrating to the United States who find themselves divining for African Americans. His goal is also to position Oyotunji as an advocate and center for "ground-level" organizing and

FIGURE 20.
Oba Adejuyibe
Adefunmi II. A
photograph of his
father, Adefunmi I,
hangs in the back-
ground. Photograph
courtesy of author.

outreach programs to combat the social ills that continue to plague African Americans in America's urban environments.

For the new Oba, Oyotunji as "sociology" embodies a particular way of life governed by a set of shared principles and views inferred from Yoruba philosophies and applied in a North American diaspora context. According to Adefunmi II, "Serious . . . ethics and laws and rules . . . still exist . . . in Oyotunji. . . . As small as it is, it's a state because you have a parliament, you have a king, you have a chieftaincy, you have a whole breakdown of a state, and we control our affairs in our kingdom."[275] The sociology of Oyotunji, however, is constantly negotiated within a wider network of American statehood and political geography. These blurred national boundaries allowed for the senior Adefunmi to be king and head priest of Oyotunji while a registered voter in the American general election. The crucial difference between Oyotunji and the rest of North America is not one of land but of psychology and spirituality. Adefunmi II acknowledges that "Oyotunji is another land psychologically and spiritually. . . . Of course we're not a different country. The psychology, above all, is what is different—'You're leaving the United States.' But physically—no. We're in South Carolina. We're definitely a part of America."[276]

Oyotunji's "cultural ethnic" philosophy continues to persist in the twenty-first century despite current rhetorical appeals to post-racialism and multiculturalism. Oyotunji remains faithful to its original oath that they "do not initiate Europeans." It is open to entering into "cross-cultural exchange" with all global participants but ultimately believes that "individual cultures have to have a love and respect for their own."[277] According to Oba Adefunmi II, the distinction Oyotunji is making is "not a racial distinction, it's a cultural distinction." Oyotunji informs individuals that they "do not initiate Europeans" with "a lot of diplomacy, plenty of diplomacy," for they do not see their position as "an arrogant or boastful thing."[278] An example of this level of diplomacy extended to those of European ancestry is as follows: "We would be doing you a disservice. We would be disrespecting our ancestors. You are disrespecting your English ancestors because prior to Christianity, you had a pagan heritage. You might not subscribe to it, but the Yoruba pagan heritage is not going to fit you. We might believe in the same aspects of paganism . . . God of fire, God of water, et cetera, but the way we approach it, the way we celebrate it, it is different. We want to see what you do. . . . You may have the same thing, but it's not Yoruba,

it may be Druidism . . ."[279] The village priesthood has also found ways to
address the potential "one-drop" person who is phenotypically European
yet has African ancestry. They ask for material evidence, and if ancestry
cannot be determined by that, then, according to the Oba, "We go to Ifa"
divination to determine ancestral roots and lineages. In the event that no
African ancestry is revealed during divination, they advise clients to turn
to their "own traditions" for spiritual sustenance.

In another vein, Oyotunji as a twenty-first-century social resource for
divining Nigerian babalawo priests is quite a fascinating concept in that it
views spiritual divination as sociologically rooted and deeply connected to
the social and historical contexts of the clients. The view is that in order
to read with precision and prescribe with care and accuracy for African
Americans in the United States, it is imperative that the diviner understand the chronology of lived experiences that contextualize their requests
for healing and amelioration. Oyotunji's new Oba contends that "to be a
traditional Yoruba priest in America and to be able to divine for African
Americans . . . you're gonna have to get into sociology. You're gonna have
to get outside just the basic Ifa Yoruba rituals and get into some deep psychological stuff—trauma—that has happened to these people and be able
to work within that."[280] With the migration of Nigerian Yoruba priests,
new cross-cultural diviner-client relationships have developed throughout
North America. Yet Adefunmi II recognizes that the problems of African
Americans do not emerge in a vacuum but within a set of social, historical,
and psychological experiences that result from being experientially racialized as black in the United States. Because difficulty and crisis, although
seemingly personal in nature, can often be influenced by larger social fac-
tors, Adefunmi II advises, "Nigerians should check in with Oyotunji first
because they don't have a clue as to the deep trauma that African Americans
suffer from, the psychological things we suffer from." A comprehensive and
effective diviner, he believes, must be "sensitive to that."[281]

Today, the ties between Nigeria and Oyotunji continue to be fluid. On
the one hand, Oyotunji's connection with a spiritual Nigeria in the form
of access to, collegial relations with, and mutual respect and reverence for
the Ooni of Ife and members of the Nigerian Yoruba priesthood remains
quite strong. In Oyotunji, the Ooni of Ife is considered a "grand patron"
and a "prime example of the supremacy of . . . royalty and monarchy."[282] In
2006, in response to an invitation the Ooni of Ife extended, Adefunmi II

traveled to Nigeria to appear in the Ooni's royal court following his own coronation as the new Oba of Oyotunji Village. The secular, everyday, experiential Nigeria, however, often poses obstacles and challenges for North American Oyotunjians who attempt to travel there. Even Adefunmi II while in Nigeria with an entourage of approximately twelve, reports that he was falsely "busted for cocaine, and I didn't have an ounce, a drop, a bit of cocaine on my person, but it's the system."[283] He says the incident occurred largely because they were "African Americans in [traditional] dress claiming Yoruba culture, claiming to be a Yoruba king," to which the Nigerian authorities responded, "Yeah, well, you speak like an American. You speak like a white guy. You look like a white guy."[284] Adefunmi II ultimately viewed the incident as "an experience" that in no way diminished his respect for the current Ooni of Ife, Alafin of Oyo, or the sacred geographical home of the religion and culture he and other Oyotunjians venerate as Yoruba.

As the twenty-first century progresses, the walls between Oyotunji and the rest of the African American world will become even more permeable

FIGURE 21. Oba Adefunmi and Oyotunji chiefs meet with the
Ooni of Ife, His Majesty Oba Okunade Sijuwade, Olubuse II, 1996.
Photograph courtesy of Oyotunji African Village and Kamari Clarke.

as the village continues its ongoing webcast, launches a cable show, expands video production, and prepares for a national tour to promote the message of unity amongst Yoruba Americans, unity among all African Americans, and the continued celebration of fifty years of Yoruba culture and initiation among black North Americans. Although small in number, Oyotunji residents look confidently to the success of these endeavors, citing that the village's very existence and its legacy rests on a bold step made by just one man.

Assessing the legacy and influence of Oseijeman Adefunmi, the African Theological Archministry, and the "Yoruba Revitalization Movement," George Brandon documents an extensive "network of at least nineteen centers affiliated with the movement throughout the northeast, the south and the Midwest with possibly as many as 10,000 members. The movement has links to Nigeria and Benin; prints books and a newsletter; and some members have developed school and youth programs, including rites of passage for African American youth and adolescents."[285] Brandon documents that its practitioners, who are "primarily U.S. born African American and . . . predominantly female," are largely responsible for furthering this legacy in the twenty-first century.[286]

This legacy of twentieth-century boldness inherited from Oseijeman Adefunmi I exists as a source of constant inspiration in the twenty-first century for many African American practitioners and for his son. When asked what he most wanted readers to understand about Oyotunji African Village's forty-two-year existence, Oba Adefunmi II responded, "Oyotunji represents a bold step in this whole African redemption of Africans in America from slavery to now. . . . Whether it is here for another hundred or another ten years, it will go down in history because it happened and it's a bold step."[287]

CHAPTER SEVEN

"That's Alright . . . I'm a Yoruba Baptist"

Negotiating Religious Plurality and "Theological Openness" in African American Yoruba Practice

ᏮᏇᏇᏇ

We'd go to church, we'd shake hands and we'd sing spirituals when I was growing up, but we believed in God, Dr. Buzzard, and the Bolito Man.

—Cornelia Bailey

IN THE SACRED ORACULAR literature of Ifa, the thirteenth Odu, Otura Meji, recounts the story of Orunmila, the Yoruba god of knowledge, wisdom, divination, and destiny, who consented to his children's practice of an auxiliary religious faith.[1] Within the narration of the Odu, as trained philosopher and babalawo Kola Abimbola translated it, Orunmila teaches his children "how to divine with the sacred palmnuts," "how to print the signatures of each Odu onto sand," and "how to prescribe and effectively perform sacrifices."[2] The Odu states that Orunmila's children "mastered" these traditional Yoruba practices, yet "on one memorable day," Orunmila saw them performing the religious practices of another tradition:

They took their father's (agbada) garments;
They took their mother's (gele) headdress;
They wore the agbada garments;
They turbaned themselves with the gele headdress;
They erected four pillars as supporting posts for a structure;
They went inside the structure they had erected;
They started to mutter inaudible words to themselves;
They were touching the floor with their foreheads;
They were standing up;
They were kneeling down;
They were getting up.
[Orunmila] was just observing them in amazement.
They were performing these rituals five times a day.
Orunmila then remembered the Ifa . . .
That the diviners from the divination practice had chanted to him,
And he did not quarrel with his children.[3]

What had been divined for Orunmila was "Lekeelekee-eye-Imole; To-ba-si-lori-opoto, A-ba-lori-oronbo, A-maa-fi-gbogbo-ara-kuwu-elewu-kiri," or "The-cattle-egret, bird-of-Muslims; Takes-flight-from-atop-the-opoto-tree, Then-perches-atop-the-lime-tree, But-also-gains-a-lot-of-wisdom-in-the-process."[4] The Odu then ends favorably for Orunmila and concludes, "We are seeking a good end to our lives."[5] Hermeneutically, the Odu, Otura Meji, reveals that in seeking a "good end" to human life, Yoruba traditionalists may engage a plural approach to the sacred.

According to Kola Abimbola, a "theological openness" and a "principle of elasticity" are "central to understanding the Yoruba Diaspora."[6] As a trained Nigerian babalawo, Abimbola contends that "the theme of openness to virtues from other cultures and religions" can readily be evidenced throughout Yoruba's sacred Ifa literature.[7] Yoruba devotees may willingly negotiate an amalgam of sacred knowledges that collectively enable them, as the Odu suggests, to gain "a-lot-of-wisdom-in-the-process." This sense of "cognitive openness" allows for multisourced notions of divine power to coexist in sustaining, fulfilling, and beneficial ways for Yoruba practitioners. In many ways this is evident in present-day Nigeria, where orisa worship "coexists in complementary tension" with the imported traditions of Islam and Christianity.[8]

Elizabeth Isichei in *The Religious Traditions of Africa* describes this notion of religious expansionism as "an enlargement of scale *within* traditional religions."[9] Like Oyotunji's clients in the previous chapter, several African American practitioners maintain Yoruba theological integrity amidst contiguous frames of religious reference.[10] As one priestess observed, concerning Yoruba religious practice in North America, "There is a lot of infusion of Native American influence, on the Spiritual level, Palo influence in Yoruba, New Age philosophy, crystals."[11] This, she reasons, is "due to the Yoruba priest becoming more comfortable in the context of what Yoruba tradition is. That you can add to it without diluting it. That it is an embellishment. It is not devaluing Yoruba tradition. . . ."[12]

Because Abimbola argues that Yoruba traditions are strongly pragmatic and efficacious, he maintains that they are "not merely concerned with faith and the afterlife, but also with practical guidelines on how to live together in a diverse, multi-cultural, global, and cosmopolitan world."[13] Hence, in their unique navigation of a multivalent world, New World expressions of Yoruba do not "demand exclusivity," but, as Mercedes Cros Sandoval recognizes, "tolerate, welcome, and accept other avenues of access to the sacred."[14] Similarly, anthropologist Karen McCarthy Brown speaks of "cultural *bricolage*," the ability, for example, of Vodou devotees in North America to live "in the midst of religious and cultural pluralism" and simultaneously sustain multiple "religious commitments" to Haitian Vodou, Puerto Rican Santería, and Vatican II Roman Catholicism.[15] In many ways, diasporic expressions of Yoruba religion defy traditional boundaries and orthodox typologies by engaging in a self-selecting religious bricolage, making use of sacred practices "that effectively [blur] such dichotomies . . . in the study of religion as the official and vernacular."[16]

For black North Americans, a dominant religious presence that has existed alongside what Janet Cornelius calls "black cosmologies" in the United States has been Protestant Christianity. Since the height of the Second Great Awakening and the spread of plantation missions from the 1820s to the 1860s, Protestant Christianity has featured prominently within the religious personality of African Americans.[17] Its theological orientations have informed understandings of slave religion in America, the rise of black independent Christian churches and denominations, and the philosophies of many postbellum movements of black social resistance and activism. Throughout these periodizations, however, Protestant Christianity has always had to theologically engage in a creative interplay with non-Christian orientations that collectively formed the multiple identities of African American religiosity.[18] As Yvonne Chireau's important and compelling work illustrates, enduring religious expressions such as conjure, hoodoo, voodoo, divination, and rootwork formed a meaningful and effectual partnership with black Christian Protestantism. Chireau's mentor, historian of religion Albert Raboteau, previously examined this notion of religious synergy within the context of slavery, observing, "conjure and Christianity were not so much antithetical as complementary." According to Raboteau, "Conjure could, without contradiction, exist side by side with Christianity in the same individual and in the same community because, for the slaves, conjure answered purposes which Christianity did not and Christianity answered purposes which conjure did not."[19] Raboteau's and Chireau's works thoughtfully avoid narrowly circumscribing the boundaries of black religious expression at the expense of eclipsing moments of religious parallelism, overlap, and coexistence. According to Chireau, "Most interpreters set 'Christian' and 'non-Christian' traditions *against* each other, with little regard for the *range of relationships* that might exist between them" and adds "while it may be useful for academic interpreters, a rigid dichotomy between Christian and non-Christian expressions in black folk traditions belies practitioners' own experiences."[20]

Within lived negotiations of the sacred, there exist moments that disprove the seemingly "theoretically irreconcilable," attest to the permeability of religious practice, and recognize the shadings of religious meaning.[21] According to Oyotunji's Chief Akintobe, "All through time, people have always went to the witchdoctor or the medicine man for help. That's not going to stop. And more and more people although they be Christian or whatever, they're gonna sneak and find out somebody to go to get some work done and will be right in church Sunday morning with their Bible."[22] This phenomenon of symbiotic religiosity, with traditions functioning not in direct tension or contradiction but in contemporaneous pragmatic coexistence, has been what Matory calls an important "constituting dynamic" within African American Yoruba expression, particularly in North America.[23] Religious boundaries that rigidly differentiate the "spiritual personages" of Yoruba and Christianity remain pragmatically lenient, allowing space for dialogue, exchange, and cooperation.[24] In the Atlantic world, Karen McCarthy Brown readily attests, there is a recognizable "historic confluence between

Christianity and the religions of West Africa."[25] This allows for African peoples to engage in the phenomena that theologian Adam Clark identifies as
"double belonging" without inherent conflict or contradiction.[26]

This confluence between Christianity and the religions of West Africa
specifically as it relates to Yoruba traditions has been a transnational phenomenon and can also be seen in the 1930s and 1940s within the context
of Nigerian nationalism and anticolonial resistance in the movements
of Orunmlaism (Orunlaism) and Ijo Orunmila Adulawo. According to
James S. Coleman in *Nigeria: Background to Nationalism*, "These separatist
movements were remarkably early manifestations of protest against white
domination and the status of inferiority" faced under British colonial
rule.[27] Movements such as Orunmlaism sought to reinterpret European
Christianity in light of Yoruba traditional principles. As a religious nationalist movement, it decried the foreignness of missionary Christianity, challenged European racialization of Christian iconography, and developed
biblical exegetical frameworks based on a new symbiotic hermeneutic of
Odu Ifa.

Supporting the theological underpinnings of Nigerian Christian
nationalism was A. F. Beyioku's *Orunmlaism, the Basis of Jesuism*, published in Lagos in 1943. Beyioku called for the rejection of "these multifarious imported religions" and their "foreign mode of prayers," for he
believed it was impossible for Nigerians to have "political emancipation
without spiritual emancipation."[28] Beyioku radically redefined traditional
Christian doctrines relating to salvation, divine revelation, and Christology
through his reading of Odu Ifa and traditional Yoruba principles. He urged
his Nigerian readership subjected under colonial rule to "paint God as an
African, paint the Angels as Africans, paint the Devil by all means in any
colour than an African, then believe in Orunmla and thou shalt be saved
and all thine house."[29] Within Orunmlaism, the divine authority of the
Bible as interpreted within Euro-Christianity was subverted: "We shall
begin on the hypothesis that the Bible is an Ifa Book."[30] Orunmlaism's pre-
decessor movement, Ijo Orunmila Adulawo, which A. O. Oshiga founded
in 1934, also juxtaposed the Christian Bible and Ifa texts. In Ijo Orunmila
Adulawo, there was "a collection of the stanzas of Ifa from which lessons
were read and texts taken for sermons."[31]

Finally, within both movements, traditional European Christology was
systematically dismantled, making Jesus an "Ifa Priest" who freely engages

in the art of divination. According to Beyioku's reading, "Divination is not a foreign teaching in the Christian Bible, there are Urim and Thummin, Joseph's Divination Cup, the Ephod.... We read of Jesus practicing Geomancy by writing with His finger on the ground and divining thereafter." He concluded, "I should like to see the Bible re-written with a view to introducing Yoruba Philosophic and Theosophic terminologies therein."[32]

Thus, Orunmlaism in Nigeria provides a historical antecedent in the twentieth century for the placing of Yoruba traditions in dialogical rapport with Euro-Christianity in the diasporan Americas and Caribbean. Countless devotees throughout North America, the Caribbean, and South America have located themselves comfortably within the interstices of these multiple religious worlds. According to Mercedes Cros Sandoval, "Manifestations of mixed religious beliefs and behavior co-existed" and were "practiced concurrently" throughout Cuba.[33] In defining his dual allegiant identity, one Afro-Brazilian priest remarked, "I am like a deacon in a Candomblé house. I am a Catholic. I've never stopped being that. I study Candomblé. I am strongly tied to it day and night. But I never stop coming to Mass whenever I can."[34] Religious correspondences between the two traditions converge, resulting in creative new understandings: "In Africa, in authentic African rituals, what is the strongest moment, equivalent to the bread and wine? The moment of receiving the energies of the ancestors. Or the spirits."[35] Similarly, one African American devotee in North America found herself practicing among Puerto Ricans who were both ardent adherents to the orisa and practicing Roman Catholics. On one occasion, this devotee witnessed several Puerto Rican practitioners "come to a bembe and decide, 'Okay, got to go because Mass starts in about an hour. . . .'"[36] Finally, akin to Lusophone, Hispanophone, and Anglophone diaspora contexts, anthropologists Richard and Sally Price in their research on the Afro-healing tradition of quimbois in Francophone Martinique confirm that practitioners were often like the "cane cutter who, to cure a malady, goes to Catholic mass in the morning, participates in a Hindu ceremony in the afternoon, and consults a black *quimboiseur* in the evening."[37]

Like Cros Sandoval, Miguel De La Torre contends that "throughout the Americas the widespread occurrence of cultural groups simultaneously participating in two diverse, if not contradictory, religious systems continues to exist."[38] As one Cuban practitioner, Wilfredo Fernandez Jr. posits, the "orichas did not demand exclusivity" and are accepting of the posture "the more gods the more power."[39] In contrast, some African Americans in the Yoruba priesthood adhere to stricter boundaries, as one Latino Yoruba priest from the Bronx noticed: "African Americans have gotten away more from church. They've gotten away from the Catholic or from the Baptist or whatever they were and they're more concerned with the African. Whereas the Latino still goes to Catholic Church, still has the baby baptized, still has to get married in the Catholic Church."[40] In this world of sacred duality and dynamic pluralism, the overall sense among many diasporic practitioners is that because there is "imminent power in the universe," there are infinite opportunities for spiritual compatibility and efficacy.

This discussion in no way prefaces an extensive discussion on religious syncretism. Instead, I would like to examine a phenomenon that allows sacred realities to coalesce in a coherent network of religious parallelism for several African American Yoruba in the United States. This alternative orientational framework accommodates the presence of multiple religious worlds, or what Monica Coleman theorizes as "multiple religious belonging" that operate in dialogically supportive, nonsyncretic, associations.[41] For many African American Yoruba, the religious importation of other sacred philosophies like Protestant Christianity into their lived Yoruba practice creates a multilayered and polysemous system of meaning that informs and enhances their religious identity in significant, valuable ways. Through several narrative vignettes, readers will explore throughout this chapter how African American Yoruba in North America have made cross-traditionality and bireligiosity an integrative, workable, and meaningful orientation of religious plasticity.

Ayoka, Yemoja, and the Episcopal Priesthood

I first met Ayoka in the early 1990s at a professional conference where she attended each session as a bodily religious text, her eleke necklaces prominently and openly displayed around her neck. Virtually unnoticed by the thousands of professionals around us, these visible material symbols immediately signaled to me her invisible devotion to the orisa. Through her biaxial religious identity as a Yemoja priestess and an ordained member of the Episcopalian priesthood, Ayoka forged a religious alliance between what might be perceived as competing spiritual entities.

Ayoka says she "grew up religiously in that kind of nebulous popular Christianity—Christmas and Easter."[42] She was an infrequent church-goer and remembers only occasionally attending vacation Bible school in the summers. Despite any enduring institutional church affiliations, Ayoka says she always felt an innate sense of spirituality. "I think I was naturally spiritual as a child. . . . I was always from the time I was eight, nine, ten years searching religiously. . . . From the time I was very young I was . . . wondering what I'm doing here on earth. I thought . . . that it had to do with spirituality."[43] Her early spiritual journey assumed various paths. At a young age, she began reading texts on Buddhism, Judaism, Taoism, Islam, and Baha'i and eventually attended a Quaker college in Pennsylvania. While in seminary, her spiritual attraction to ritualization and religious practice led her first to the Episcopal Church and later to the Yoruba orisa tradition.

While attending the Episcopal Church, Ayoka felt a deep calling to its priesthood and enrolled in seminary to commence the process of study and ordination. After baptism in the Episcopal Church and beginning the preliminary procedures for ordination, Ayoka encountered the orisa. As a seminarian, she was required to do a praxis internship that consisted of working in a local New York church among several Latina women who practiced various healing arts. During her field praxis, Ayoka says she "met a woman, who is my godsister now, who said I should go to have a reading." Close to one year later, Ayoka went for the divination reading. According to Ayoka, "I wasn't sure what this whole thing was about, but I was getting more connected to this circle of women who were healers, and one of the things they all had in common was some connection to orisa. They were acupuncturists, massage therapists, psychotherapists, community organizers. . . ."[44] Although Ayoka was fully immersed in the ordination process for the Episcopal priesthood, she felt herself drawn to the spiritual world of the women she was interning among. During a visit to their Yoruba ile gathering, she began to feel an increasing spiritual connection to Africa as well as an awareness of a strong ancestral presence. She recalls, "I . . . felt I was home there. . . . I think I was really yearning for a connection to African-ness, and I really felt that the spirituality we were engaging in was very, very powerful. There was a power there that I don't find in the Christian tradition, a rootedness. . . . I think my ancestors have always been with me. . . . And I really believed that they wanted me to be there."[45]

Shortly after this mystical experience, Ayoka completed the ordination process in the Episcopal Church and almost immediately thereafter began pursuing the initiation process into the Yoruba priesthood. I asked her to reflect on what it meant to negotiate these dual initiation rites in such close proximity. Ayoka responded, "Part of me feels that the priest that I was supposed to be, I misinterpreted," implying that she was perhaps destined to be a part of the Yoruba, not the Episcopal, priesthood. Although not contradictory for her, she does admit that maintaining allegiance to both traditions does at times raise unavoidable ambivalence. She ponders, "There's so much to know in the orisa tradition, why am I spending my time doing something else?" She also finds that when she chooses to access spiritual power on her behalf, she more readily consults the Yoruba resources at her disposal: "When I really need a path to be opened, [I go to] orisa. I more and more struggle with Christianity. I'm not calling on Jesus to do anything; the real power is not there."[46]

Other African American Yoruba practitioners I worked among held similar unsettling concerns about the compatibility of Yoruba religion and Protestant Christianity. They wrestled with the traditional theological exclusivity of Christianity and the ways in which it was historically used within systems of slaveocracy and colonialism as a weapon of religio-cultural genocide. According to one Yoruba participant, "I think it becomes even more complicated by colonialism and racist Christianity and sexist Christianity. I think when you add all of that on it makes me even more adamant that it doesn't work for me, and my perspective is that it would not be the most useful doctrine to heal us as a people. . . . It's an exclusivist notion that ends on leading to sexism, heterosexism, patriarchy, racism."[47] This informant believed that unlike the Yoruba tradition, which celebrates human agency and authority supported by orisa and ancestral spiritual power, Christianity ultimately posits "an exclusivist notion that does not celebrate human diversity as having authority."[48] Although Ayoka's view is not as strong and she still remains active in both Christian and orisa priesthoods, she nonetheless feels compelled to commit to a single priestly tradition in the future. Ayoka concludes in the final analysis, "I think I'm going to need to make a decision. I think that has always been apart of my odu— that a dog with four legs can't walk in two paths. . . . . see in the future a need to make a commitment one way or the other, and it probably will be for orisa because that's just a rich tradition that needs to be preserved on its own."[49]

The Bible, Ifa, and Yoruba Theological Mergence

A singular spiritual path is not always a necessary choice for African American practitioners who wish to negotiate the religious worlds of both Yoruba and Christianity. Some, in fact, choose both and find the internal tensions Ayoka identified significantly less pronounced. One African American priestess, Adejoke, proudly celebrates her descent from African American Baptist leader, feminist, activist, and Virginia native Nannie Helen Burroughs, a lineage she traces through her great-grandfather, whom she identified in our interview as a sibling of Burrough's father.[50] Adejoke's adherence to both Yoruba and Baptist traditions is not unique. According to Velma Love, "A large percentage of Orisha worshippers in America are Christian . . . Baptist."[51] Adejoke occupies the formal religious space of an initiated Yoruba priestess who honors the traditions of her African heritage while also serving as an ordained Christian minister at a prominent Baptist church.

Adejoke gathers much inspiration from the model of Nannie Helen Burroughs and her tireless work in the early 1900s as a founder of the Woman's Convention within the National Baptist Convention.[52] According to historian Evelyn Brooks Higginbotham, during Burroughs's first year as corresponding secretary, "she labored 365 days, traveled 22,125 miles, delivered 215 speeches, organized a dozen societies, wrote 9,235 letters, and received 4,820."[53] The achievement that directly influenced the course of Adejoke's life was Burroughs's contribution to African American education and her affiliation with the National Training School for Women and Girls in Washington, DC. In 1909 as its first president, Burroughs diligently implemented the school's philosophy of uplift and self-help through industrial training. Burroughs understood the concept of "work" as twofold, corresponding to compensated labor and the ability to sustain oneself autonomously and responsibly. "Work," for black women, also included "race work" or exercising one's additional "responsibility to the collective cause of African Americans."[54] Although this space does not allow for a comprehensive treatment of Nannie Helen Burroughs and her contributions to African American religious and secular institutions, it is fair to say, as Evelyn Brooks Higginbotham points out, that her role was so significant to this early black denominational history that "no scholar of the black church can overlook or disregard her presence and influence. [Burroughs] stands among the finest representations of the black Christian tradition."[55]

Adejoke describes her family as "traditional Baptists" and as "old-line church founders in Orange Country and Madison, Virginia." She understands the Baptist Church as the "church of my ancestors" and is active in many of its activities relating to women and children. At the time of our interview, she was completing a doctoral degree in education and was the director of an after-school educational and tutorial program for black children that she founded. In many ways, Adejoke sees the life of Nannie Helen Burroughs as a guide for her own:

> She had a great faith. She built her school on a hill and she called that school, "Zion's Holy Hill." She believed that she could have this school in a time where black folks were not doing well economically and she had very little in terms of financial resources, but she had a big vision and a faith in God. . . . In the old days, it was a school that served an international clientele from Africa, the Caribbean islands, et cetera, and had a boarding part to it. . . . I believe I have inherited some of her visionary spirit and great faith that all things are possible through the power of God.[56]

Adejoke fully embraces both of her Yoruba and Christian worlds. Her first exposure to Yoruba religion was through a Christian minister who negotiated a similar space of Yoruba and Methodism. In terms of her own religious duality she explains, "I don't seem to see a problem with it. It seems to fit well into my life. I am in the church seeking a closer relationship with Olodumare, and I am seeking a closer relationship with God Almighty. I use the term interchangeably because they both mean the same to me. My reason for being is to get closer to God."[57] For Adejoke, the traditions coexist in a harmonious dialogical compendium of sacred beliefs. Unlike Ayoka, she never feels as though she will need to choose one tradition over the other. In fact, on several occasions, divination consultations in the Yoruba tradition have encouraged her continued participation in her black Christian tradition, revealing to her the synergy and cooperation between them. Adejoke does not attempt to maintain a culture of secrecy around her Yoruba priesthood. Although many have not found it necessary, or perhaps even appropriate, to preach Ifa in a Christian venue or directly announce it from the pulpit, those congregants literate in symbolic iconography could easily read the bodily tapestry of colors or neck, wrist, and ankle adornments, finding visible evidence of the orisa.

Throughout our discussions, I invited Adejoke to reflect on the distinct ways in which Yoruba religion, which she calls Ifa, has influenced her theological understanding of traditional Christian teachings and doctrines. Three organizing themes anchoring these discussions were the theological concept of sacrifice, the question of Christology, and the concept of biblical hermeneutics. Merging her strong Baptist roots with an African American Yoruba consciousness theologically enhanced Adejoke's understanding of sacrifice. She is comfortable with the ritual sacrifice of animals in the Yoruba tradition and feels that there exists a theological "common ground" on the question of sacrifice between the two traditions. According to Adejoke, "If we trace back into the history of Christianity, there is always the breaking of the bread. The communion service . . . represents the breaking of the body of Christ and the drinking of his blood. In Ifa, those similarities are the same in that it is a blood sacrifice. We are taught that the largest Christian sacrifice that was ever paid was the life of Jesus—his body and his blood."[58] I marveled at Adejoke's ability as an African American practitioner to create theological interstices that coherently coalesced the Christian notion of blood with an ancestral understanding of blood. This symbiotic dance of Yoruba and Christian theology invites into the discussion the notion that Jesus was not the only blood shed for diasporic African persons. Within the theological consortium of Yoruba and Christianity, there is space and an allowance for the recognition and acknowledgment that the sacred blood of Jesus, the sacred blood of the ancestors in the Middle Passage and during slavery, and the sacred blood shed during the propitiating moment of animal sacrifice can all be revered in their own right.

Adejoke is open to the theological correspondence between the two traditions and also open to the ways they may mutually inform one another. For example, Adejoke's participation in the Yoruba tradition as a priestess has significantly affected her understanding of Jesus Christ. When asked how she situates the notion of Christology within her Yoruba religious world view she explained, "[Jesus] was a prophet, and I understand that he was not the only prophet that we have had on earth. He was one of the prophets that was lifted up by the Christian church but there are others. Even Jesus himself says that he has come to show us how to do these things and that we too can do what he has done, and more. It was like he expected us to attain his level and to go beyond him. . . . I guess I am still seeking [this level] through the power of God, through the power of the orisa, lifting me up."[59]

Several African American practitioners readily share Adejoke's theological interpretation as it relates to the nature of human anthropology. Among African American Yoruba the views of original sin, natural depravity, and the essentialist posture of human nature as inherently sinful are wholly rejected. Instead, the emphasis is placed on actualizing the depths of human agency and potentiality and sacralizing black humanity. Using a biblical analogy, Shango priest Baba Medahochi explains: "As a human being, you have the capacity to become divine. And this divinity that is within you has the capacity to be given birth. . . . [Jesus] said, and I can't quote it, . . . it's in the Bible, 'Marvel not at the things that I do. The things that I do, you can also do and greater things can you also do.' That's a challenge. If someone can heal the sick, if someone can raise the dead, if someone can feed five thousand, then so can we."[60] For those like Medahochi and Adejoke, there is a link, a connection, that unites the human being with other spiritual entities and lessens the presumed ontological distance between them. Thus, many African Americans are attracted to Yoruba religion because it resists the dichotomous, "anti-somaticism" of Christianity and instead sacralizes both human body and spirit.[61]

Radically reconfiguring traditional theological notions of Christology, incarnation, and special revelation are Adejoke's reinterpretation of Jesus as the Son of God and her understanding that, like Jesus, "all humans are sons and daughters of God, or *omo-Oludumare*, children of Olodumare."[62] Her sentiments echo those of African Americans from a previous generation like James Baldwin, who presumably did not have contact with Yoruba American traditions while in his native Harlem, but who in his own way similarly challenged the traditional notion that Jesus's essence was somehow different than that of all human beings. In 1965, Baldwin posed a series of compelling questions about traditional Christian doctrinal philosophies: "What is wrong with a man and a woman sleeping together, making love to each other and having a baby like everybody else? Why does the son of God have to be born immaculately? Aren't we all the sons of God?"[63] Both Baldwin and Adejoke quite emphatically expand the

Christian notion of Jesus as "divine enfleshment" to ultimately include the sacralized humanity of African Americans and all other humans within this theological configuration.[64]

Moreover, Adejoke and Baldwin's doctrine of humanity radically alters traditional Christian notions of salvation and destiny as they relate to human substance and human agency.[65] Theologian Clarence Hardy III recounts Baldwin's thinking on this front as Baldwin "declares that religious teachings that claim Jesus is the 'Son of God' are 'a revelation and a revolution' not because he is the sole son of God but because 'it means that we are all the sons of God.' Because everyone has equal status as children of God, the relationship between Jesus and God is only revelatory when it confirms that all human beings and not just a single pious Jew from Nazareth can claim the divine power necessary to define our own lives. . . . We are responsible for our soul's salvation, not the bishop, not the priest, not my mother. . . . God's only hope is us. If we don't make it, he ain't going to make it either."[66]

Unlike Baldwin, however, Adejoke reinforces her radical engagement with biblical hermeneutics through a comparative analysis of the sacred texts of Christianity and of the Ifa oral teachings in Yoruba religion. She draws spiritual sustenance from both bodies of text:

> I believe in the holy scriptures because even Ifa has holy scriptures. . . . Studying the Bible you know there is something called the concordance, and that helps you to have an even greater understanding of the word that is written in the scriptures. So, too, the power of the Ifa tradition helps you to open up an even greater world of the Bible. . . . Ifa has something which is called the Odu . . . These are the holy scriptures of Ifa. . . . The Odu are the scriptural verses of Ifa, and each Odu has its scripture in that they tell you how to become elevated, how to live your life, how to respond in a way that is in more alignment with Olodumare, with the power of God working through you for the betterment of not only yourself, but the uplifting of society. . . . The Odu is becoming more accessible to people now. There are books that if you want to read it on your own, you can, but it is better to study with a spiritual teacher or guide, high priest or babalawo.

According to Adejoke, a movement codifying the oral teachings of Ifa is well under way, particularly with the publication of several landmark texts such as Wande Abimbola's *Ifa: An Exposition of Ifa Literary Corpus*, William Bascom's *Ifa Divination: Communication Between Gods and Men in West Africa*, Afolabi Epega and Philip John Neimark's *The Sacred Ifa Oracle*, and Maulana Karenga's *Odu Ifa: The Ethical Teachings*. The mounting textualization in the current era makes previously oral forms of knowledge accessible to a number of American communities. Wande Abimbola is cautious about the move to rigidly textualize the Ifa corpus, though: "When you write down the Ifa text, there is the danger of making it so fixed that it becomes very difficult to change anything there, even in the areas where the *babalawo* had been allowed to use his own words. So it ceases to be something that is performed and enjoyed."[67] While safeguarding the need to have a written sacred text like the Bible to gauge religious legitimacy, probing questions are also raised regarding the ways Yoruba religion has perhaps been subtly influenced by the scriptural dominance of religious traditions in the West, a question that scholars of comparative sacred literature might do well to explore more fully.

Emergent in several narratives similar to Adejoke's was an open receptivity to spiritual symbiosis and reciprocity, as well as an apparent willingness to engage in expanded moments of religious ecumenism. For example, devotees like Obatala priestess Iya Omalewa Eniolorunopa see Yoruba's capacity to engage in dialogical relationship with other traditions as important because it creates possibilities to draw upon the restorative traditions of both Africa and African America, creating what Bishop Turner aptly referred to as a highway "across the Atlantic" that merges both Old and New World faith traditions. According to Iya Omolewa, "I have no trouble going to the Christian church. They singing to Jesus, I'm singing to Esu. I know in my mind we singing to the same person. I can go to the mosque and have no difficulty because I know in my mind Allah and Olodumare are one and the same. . . . I'm kind of happy wherever I am but I choose to practice the religion of my ancestors, which is Ifa."[68] This sense of theological correspondence among traditions allows some practitioners to make meaningful analogies between the physical "rock" that represents Esu and the symbolic "rock" represented by Jesus ("Jesus is the cornerstone, the rock"). Jesus and Esu both make people "open their eyes to the important things of life . . . Esu is the one who makes sure our prayers get to heaven, similar to Jesus."[69] What grounds such theological fluidity is a profound understanding that within the context of spirituality and spiritual practice, "all knowledge works together."[70]

It is important to note, however, that some African American Yoruba such as Aina Olomo approach such dual theological integration with caution. Olomo is careful to warn "Yoruba-based practitioners with Christian Core Beliefs" against a "colonized spirituality" in which "converts to Yoruba spiritual paths continue to glorify Olodumare in the same manner that they worshipped God-the-Father, Jesus, and Allah. The name has changed, but not the conceptual understanding."[71] She is concerned that without a "spiritual re-positioning" of "previous beliefs," the language, symbolism, and "theological premises" of traditions that have historically engaged people of African descent in contexts of "slavery and colonization" will become "superimposed" onto Yoruba practice.[72] Olomo, however, is sympathetic to the reasons many African American Yoruba might continue to "integrate the religious practices, which they have grown up with, into their newly embraced religious system."[73] She understands that they "bring with them spiritual methodologies and archetypes from other religions."[74] In making a transition from a background in Christianity and Islam into Yoruba, Olomo says of her own experience, "I did not have to throw away or completely ignore the religious tenets that had given my family spiritual solace for generations. Because of ancestral veneration I could integrate them into my African spirituality."[75] She is careful not to disregard the sacred traditions of the black American ancestors, concluding that "it does nothing for the already damaged self-esteem to belittle or dismiss the religious beliefs of our immediate fore-parents."[76]

The narratives of Ayoka, Adejoke, and others illustrate the ways African American Yoruba practice flexibility regarding the spiritual exchange and cross-fertilization of their religious worlds. Defending the integrity and efficacy of a dual spiritual reservoir, Adejoke concludes, "It helped me to become grounded on a spiritual level that all things are truly possible through the power of Olodumare, God Almighty, his orisa, and his emissaries working in my life. I don't have to fight battles alone. . . . Sometimes Christianity makes you feel alone, but with [Ifa], I have a broader depth of understanding. . . . My ancestors are now more vibrant to me. I know that their energy is pulling for me to make it, those old souls, old Africans."[77]

"That's Alright . . . I'm a Yoruba Baptist"

The ability to integrate old familial traditions with new African spiritualities is exactly what affords author and journalist Afi-Odelia Scruggs the freedom to define herself comfortably as a Yoruba Baptist. For Scruggs, both Yoruba conceptions and Baptist orientations inform her immediate spiritual identity and the ways she conceptualizes the ancestors, the Bible, notions of sacrifice, and the identity of God. Growing up in Nashville, Tennessee, during the civil rights era, Scruggs experienced the black Christian church as "an organizing tool" and as "the one institution that black people controlled."[78] Her foray into Yoruba traditions came as a result of what she saw as the black Baptist church lacking an institutionalized, ritualized way of revering the Egun (ancestors). According to Scruggs, "Christianity did not have a way for me to honor Egun. That was what was missing."[79] Leaving the church was not, however, imperative or necessary in order to "commune" with her ancestors. She thought that had she "just stayed in a traditional Christian church," exclusively experiencing the "life-altering" presence of her ancestors would not be possible.[80]

A decisive moment in Scruggs's life sparked a deeper connection to the ancestors. While engaging in what she termed "ancestral work," which included both researching her family history and working professionally as a freelance writer on an assignment covering southern plantations, Scruggs recalls researching a story on a Virginia tobacco plantation. A powerful spiritual incident ensued when she realized it was owned by Thomas Prosser, the legal slave master of the 1800 insurrectionist Gabriel Prosser. While on the plantation, Scruggs recounts, "Every little brick was like somebody shouting at me, 'You are walking on your history and you don't even know it.' 'You want your history, you are in the midst of your history, you are looking at your history.'"[81] This mystical encounter, coupled with the influence of living in Washington, DC, during the rise of the Afrocentric movement of the late 1980s and early 1990s, produced, for Scruggs, an "awareness of different ways to worship, different ways to relate to the ancestors."[82] She immediately set about the task of constructing an ancestral altar in her home as a space for meditation and communion. She reflects, "I got Luisah Teish's book, *Jambalaya*, and I set up my little altar and I didn't worry about whether it was right or wrong. I just set it up . . . I decided I'm gonna talk to my ancestors. I was really talking to them and acknowledged, 'I really want to do something for you. I feel your presence. Show me what to do.'"[83]

Scruggs's ritual veneration of the ancestors and growing awareness of the orisa did not come without challenges to her Baptist faith. She acknowledges that there was "some difficulty in terms of transition" within and between the two traditions. According to Scruggs, "You did not have a sacred place in your house if you were Protestant. You had a sacred space in the church."[84] She wrestled with notions of "idolatry," realizing that "a hard-core Christian would tell you, 'You worshipping idols.'"[85] Magnifying this concern for her were the ways in which "the altars for the orisa, especially at a bembe, were so elaborate."[86] What eventually helped to assuage these challenges was her exposure to the Trinidadian Spiritual Baptist tradition. Mother Taylor's temple in Washington, DC, and her transnational initiatory rites in Trinidad exposed Scruggs to a new way of being both Baptist and Yoruba. While in Trinidad, she found the baptism and mourners rites of the Spiritual Baptists as powerful and meaningful as the rites of Trinidad's Shango orisa ceremony.

Moreover, informing Scruggs's ultimate understanding of sacrifice and the nature of God are both Christian and Yoruba beliefs. After a Yoruba divination reading revealing the need for her to perform animal sacrifice in order to alleviate the issue she was then confronting, she said she could grasp more fully in Christianity the sheer immensity of Abraham's decision to sacrifice his son, Isaac, and Jesus's self-sacrifice. In the following passage, Scruggs reflects on how witnessing the sacrifice of animals in the orisa ritual revealed the powerful interconnections between both traditions:

> After having to kill a goat, when I went back and read Abraham and Isaac, I really had a much different picture in my mind. . . . If you have seen [a sacrifice] you know how horrible Abraham must have felt that he had to tie his son up and do this ritual with his son. I mean it is a horrifying passage. . . . The crucifixion [of Jesus] became much more meaningful . . . because I have seen [sacrifice] . . . I might not have understood the mercy of that had I not gone through a [Yoruba] sacrificial tradition. You're actually there when the blood is being spilled and you realize that something has given its life for you in a real way because you see that life go. . . . It's not something you walk into lightly and I think . . . you just need to do right [be]cause you don't want anything to have to

give up its life because you did some trifling stuff. If it's because of
a situation outside your control then that's different . . .

The strength of Scruggs's personal theology rests in an unfettered pragmatism, "People make compromises, and people make connections and really
that's what I have done."[87] Scruggs links her Yoruba and Baptist faiths to
forge a path that helps her approach the vastness and mystery of God, the
orisa, and the ancestors in epistemologically compelling ways. She contends that because of the vastness of God, "you just can't say there's a single
way. . . . I don't really think God can be understood; I think we try. . . . God
cannot be contained so there are different ways and different paths to the
knowledge of God."[88] Given human diversity, she acknowledges that "some
people need a more constricted path, some people need a wider path."[89]

For her own spiritual journey, Scruggs has chosen the wider path,
where sacred knowledge is dialogical, ritual and belief are interconnected,
and religious identity is fluid and permeable. She credits the orisa tradition
with giving her an abundance of spiritual insights involving the nature of
God, including "a real respect for the wrath of God." This insight radically
differed from her Christian upbringing, which stressed "God is good all
the time."[90] According to Scruggs, "The Yoruba don't say that. The Yoruba
say, 'Look, there are two sides to the orisa, and you want to stay on the good
side."[91] Moreover, Scruggs adds that "because of orisa, I read the Bible dif-
ferently . . . Legba is Galatians, Be not deceived, God is not mocked, and in
my Bible it says don't be misled, nobody makes a fool out of God. So when
you understand Legba, you have to realize that God has a sense of humor,
just make sure the joke's not on you. That's how you approach Elegba."[92]

The orisa tradition has provided Scruggs with new insight into what
she calls "Old Testament Christianity," particularly the ways the practices
of plural marriage and sacrifice and the role of taboos function within both
traditions. Navigating both traditions simultaneously, she chooses not to
live in constant fear of the Christian church's judgment upon her, and in
her own words accepts that "there are different ways of worship, and you
can incorporate things in your own practice that are fulfilling to you without necessarily feeling that you violating, that you're gonna go to hell, or
that the demons are gonna attack."[93]

Not unlike the historical nature, character, and expression of African
American religiosity in the United States, Scruggs's narrative demonstrates

a fluidity of view in accessing broader bases of spiritual power. Because of this, Scruggs's innovative approach to biblical hermeneutics and her theological openness make her resistant to liturgical rigidity, strict fundamentalism, and tightly bounded ritualism when they surface in Yoruba and in Christianity. She maintains the spiritual improvisations of her African American Baptist roots as opposed to the meticulous ceremonial orthodoxy of some Yoruba Americans, believing that "if the spirit say so, well then we need to say so . . ."[94] She is often disheartened at the unyielding approach to ritual performance practices as observed by some African American Yoruba who reprove, "You didn't sing the songs right. You didn't do the prayers right. You not pronouncing the words right."[95] In response to this ritual inflexibility, Scruggs's ultimate fluid posture and orientation is, "That's alright. You know. Hey, I'm a Yoruba Baptist. If I want to put 'Wade in the Water' to sing to Yemoja, she don't have a problem with it; she let me sing it."[96]

Jesus, the Orisa, and "This Double Consciousness of Faith"

Scruggs's multivocal view continues to manifest itself in practitioners like Oluweri Egundyao Onisegun, who also engages orientations to the sacred in lithe and meaningful ways. Oluweri Egunyao Onisegun, using his "names of power" for this study, is a university professor, pastoral theologian, ordained Baptist minister, and an initiated priest of Ogun who has found a "sense of spiritual fulfillment" as he embraces the mutual compatibility of these multiple realities. For Onisegun, his current identity as a Baptist minister and an Ifa priest, along with his expertise in pastoral care and counseling, provide many opportunities for sacred cross-pollination. He traces his openness to religious synthesis to his childhood and the spiritual resources of black Southern lore. Onisegun says that his journey to the orisa began when he was an undergraduate major in the discipline of anthropology, when he first began to conduct research on a paper entitled, "Transformative and Transcendental: African Rites of Passage as a Psychological Study in Growth and Development." This early scholarly trajectory would follow him throughout his doctoral research and eventually be transformed into a personal spiritual quest.

Onisegun holds fond memories of his grandmother, affectionately called Big Mama, and the spiritual ways she used her Afrosouthern orientations to live out her Christian identity. Onisegun admits, however, that

Big Mama's ways "might raise some questions" for orthodox Christians. According to Onisegun, "Big Mama . . . literally had a closet upstairs in her house in one of the bedrooms. In the closet, there was a table, a chair, and on the table were incense sticks, the Seven Magical African Powers candle, cards for numerology, a book on eugenics, a Bible, and . . . some dolls" along with "authentic African art pieces."[97] "If any of us got sick or when anything was wrong," Onisegun recalls, "the verse talks about entering into a closet (Matthew 6:6, 'But thou, when thou prayest, enter into thy closet, and when thou hast shut thy door, pray to thy Father which is in secret; and thy Father which seeth in secret shall reward thee openly.')." Big Mama "took it literally and entered into a closet and would perform all types of work."[98] Onisegun remembers the rich iconoclasm and sacred instruments, the diverse pharmacopoeia, and the corpus of healing remedies that often involved "herbs that smelled real bad," which she'd put "around my neck on a string" or instead of a crucifix, a "round plastic blue-like little half saucer" with a "picture of Jesus in the manger and Mary and Joseph . . . and on the end of it was ribbon and the back was smeared with some kind of oil." He was cautioned to "leave it above your door to keep all evil away from you."[99]

It is this southern orientation he brought to his journey to Yoruba traditions, which, for Onisegun, began largely within the context of academia. While he was a graduate student, a professor prompted him to enhance his scholarly life by writing on what he was "most passionate about." Onisegun was able to frame a project that brought together interests in physical anthropology, religious and theological studies, and psychology. He wanted to begin from the premise that "if in fact we were to help African American . . . people in general," we "needed to pool all African cultural resources, spirituality, and religiously to inform the praxis of pastoral care."[100] More specifically, he found in "Yoruba religious thought and culture foundations for pastoral theology" and diverse spiritual resources for psychological wellness.[101] Undergoing initiation while still in graduate school, Onisegun said he was told by an Ifa priest, "Now you have permission to do the research that others cannot do" and that this new sacred knowledge would "inform . . . the final product that you will defend."[102] Because of the open posture he assumed between his priestly and scholarly identities, the religious boundaries often drawn between the professional and the private and the academic and the esoteric were, in lived practice, quite synergistic and functioned much more seamlessly.

Concerning his initial experiences as a new initiate, Onisegun candidly discloses, "I will admit the journey has not been easy—the transition, and as I like to sometimes say, wedding of the two [traditions] did not start off as a happy marriage."[103] He reflects on his early years in Christian seminary where there was little room for African spiritual thought to cohabitate. According to Onisegun, "Any of us, especially those of us who headed by the way of seminary on our journey to whatever work we were doing, we were never given the permission, nor did we take the permission, to bring to the table our other conversation that may have included some other traditions."[104] He exposes his deep inner wrestling in his early years in trying to reconcile his ordained Christian ministry with the ongoing commitment he felt to African spiritualities:

> I found for many of us raised in one faith tradition and that's all
> we've ever been exposed to, when we are presented with another,
> it probably causes an internal conflict. There's a war and a struggle
> that begins to take place. In one sense you want to be faithful to
> that which you have always known. In another sense, . . . you also
> want to be true to the information you have now received . . . I have
> always wanted to try and reconcile how I can be in [Christian]
> ministry and how do I bring this [Ifa] to the table so that I don't feel
> that either I am compromising or I am not being true to who it is
> that I am. And that for a while presented a great challenge to me.[105]

Onisegun admits that it was not until a conversation with a noted Ghanaian scholar and professor of pastoral care, theology, and counseling, Emmanuel Lartey, that he was able to imagine nonconflicting avenues for cohesive coreligiosity. Lartey wisely remarked, as Onisegun paraphrases, that "the African mind has no problem with going to the mosque on Friday, stopping by the synagogue on Saturday, singing in the church on Sunday, and paying homage at an ancestral shrine on Monday. That is how the African mind works. In the Western mind, it has to be one or the other, and the fluidity is not there; there are strong lines of demarcation."[106]

Emmanuel Lartey's words express a phenomenon readily found in Africa and its diaspora. Francio Guadeloupe's recent work, *Chanting Down the New Jerusalem*, speaks with a similar resonance about those individuals in St. Martin whom the author typologizes as religious *bricoleurs*.[107]

During his fieldwork, Guadeloupe discovered that a "devout Catholic, also attended the Seventh-day Adventist Church and had no qualms about visiting Obeah sessions."[108] His informants desired religious boundaries that could be elastic and amenable to their range of needs. Guadeloupe was told, "Caribbean people in general, do not like too much discipline."[109] Therefore, the interviewee further explained, "They do not want to be a *total* Christian, because there are certain expectations. So they rather be on their own and take in bits and use it to their own convenience."[110] Within this Caribbean context, to be a Christian for many often defied the traditional "boundaries of denominational exclusiveness" and did not necessarily preclude extensive borrowing "from non-Christian religions."[111]

In reflecting on his conversation with Emmanuel Lartey, Onisegun was ultimately able to ascertain that "traditions are not hermetically sealed; they borrow, interpenetrate, and mutually transform," as William D. Hart aptly explained in his book *Black Religion*.[112] Furthermore, Onisegun came to realize more fully that to "blur the line" and dismantle the rules governing strict Christian orthodoxy requires "coming to a place of understanding that yes, I can do that," knowing that "it requires courage; it requires some honesty; and it requires faith—not in the traditional sense of the word faith, but faith in what it is you have recently now discovered and come to realize that what you are looking at never felt wrong."[113]

Being able to bring an understanding of religious porousness to his professional pastoral care and counseling has proven richly rewarding for Onisegun. He notes, "I bring to the table those spiritual resources that normal pastoral counseling may not use." In his own consultative philosophy, he finds that what has been quite effective is "having an understanding of our people culturally prior to slavery helps us as we try to help move them through whatever it is they are going through."[114] Within the context of his ministries of counseling and preaching, Onisegun has also committed himself to "use this kind of understanding of African spiritual traditions as a hermeneutical lens by which I am going to reinterpret the Christian faith—not in the sense where I am in the pulpit coming off dogmatic or condemnatory or highly critical of those who don't believe this but hopefully coming off in such a way that it informs what I'm doing."[115]

By placing Yoruba religion in conversation with Christianity in ways that foster "deep, mutual, boundary-bending transformation," Onisegun has unearthed new meaning to traditional understandings of the church, the Bible, the Eucharist, sacrifice, and Jesus.[116] The black Christian church no longer represents a site of conflict for this priest of Ogun but instead a set of "different symbols at work" that he then decodes in light of his dual African-Protestant religious positioning:

> I walk into the church, and I can imagine the community. I can hear the beats of the talking drum. I can see the elders, and the priests, and the priestesses. The wise people and the healers are all there . . . You can read some texts, and they'll talk about an orisa riding someone, and I would liken that to someone in the church catching the Holy Spirit and the orisa riding him or her in the church . . . We are, in some sense, still doing it. The clothes have changed, the songs have changed, the language has changed, but to a certain extent I think we are still there. The more we understand what we used to do, the better we'll understand what we do today.[117]

Onisegun is able to view the black Christian church through a bilateral gaze of "practical harmonies."[118] Thus, rather than experience their religious lives through conflict and ambiguity, practitioners like Onisegun are able to live out of what Lee H. Butler Jr. calls an "embodied harmony," thereby assuming a relational posture toward the divine through plurality.[119]

Both the natural world of the Yoruba and the ecclesiastical structure of the black Christian church become transformative sites where "life itself is ritualized."[120] Onisegun finds in both traditions a meaningful devotion to uphold the "efficacy of sacrifice" and although within his professional academic context white colleagues have made comments and jokes reinforcing stereotypical popular notions of "cutting off the heads chickens," Onisegun, like many practitioners, engages the ritual of sacrifice with great reverence and respect.

As it relates to the contexts of Yoruba initiation and healing, Onisegun speaks with great solemnity of the ritual practice of animal sacrifice. According to Onisegun, "There is almost a transference in the blood rite of the sacrifice," a "transference of energy onto the individual."[121] Animal sacrifice is a ceremonial rite, a sacrament, which comes with great "expectation."[122] In one instance he witnessed a sacred head-cleansing rite where the blood of a lamb was used as emblematic power to wash away "some of the internal problems he was having."[123] Onisegun stated that during this ritual, he "often thought of when we sing in church about being washed in the blood of the lamb" remarking that "we actually do it" in Yoruba religion.[124]

Onisegun stated most directly, "I am not fond of taking the life of an animal. I want to be clear about that." He is not open to animal sacrifice, or ebo, "just for the sake of killing" but understands that the Ashe "found in the blood" is an extremely powerful energy with a profound ability to "facilitate someone's transformation."[125] Finding resonance with the Communion rites of black Christian churches, Onisegun reflects on "why the celebration of Communion or the Eucharist was so important for African Americans" and its ability "to hold a very special place in our hearts to the point people start crying. . . ."[126] For Onisegun, this metaphorical materiality of blood becomes a sacred theological site where the two traditions converge:

> It's something about blood. I remember . . . a book, Joanne Terrell's, *Power in the Blood* and started thinking about what is this power in the blood? . . . So many of us who were captured during slavery came directly out of West Africa, where these water rites and blood rites were so often a part of everything we did. And so for us to relive Communion and imagine that we are symbolically partaking of the blood of Christ, the body of Christ . . . I think it fits well within that framework we once knew . . . I see it as the same thing. The power of the blood that is in the sacrifice or the ritual, I say, is the power of the blood that we recognize when we talk about the blood of Jesus. The power is the same. The names have been changed to protect the innocent, so to speak, but the power is the same, and that is one thing that has helped me where I don't see a conflict now when I'm in church.[127]

This theological exercise in shifting recontextualization plays out within the context of biblical hermeneutics and Christology as well. First, Onisegun, like many practitioners of dual Yoruba and Christian traditions, tends to soften the rigid theological boundaries that associate the Christian Bible with the exclusive word of God. Onisegun is of the understanding that "words are special, are sacred, and the Bible is one particular culture's understanding, presentation, expression, and interpretation of that word."[128] Therefore, to value the Christian revelatory scriptures exclusively over other cultural revelations, he would argue, "in some sense deifies this text and culture over everyone else's."[129] In his work in Christian ministry, Onisegun is able to identify biblical stories as important and "to communicate that story to people so that they walk away with a balanced understanding of it as important, but it is not the only story."[130] Thus, textual sacrality and authority for many jointly or multiply positioned practitioners is most often complex and multifaceted, and Onisegun is no exception. This is quite evident when he places the Christian Bible in dialogue with Yoruba Ifa Odu. According to Onisegun, "Within Ifa, we have the Odu Ifa, and these stories are also just as sacred and important. Depending upon those scholars who speculate, Ifa is about seven to eight thousand years old, which actually . . . predates many other biblical stories. What do we do with that? I mean, is one more sacred than the other? No. I think it's all sacred, and it's all special, and they're all powerful, depending on how we use that ability, how we use those stories."[131]

For Onisegun, "The Bible still becomes problematic for many of us, even those who teach it (whether it be New or Old Testament), those of us who teach theology, those of us who come to these institutions. We still have not come to a place where we can take the text and find where it is we are going to preach without encountering those bumps and bruises along the way."[132] It is Onisegun's ability, however, to engage in theological recontextualizations that ultimately informs his praxis as both a Baptist minister and a Yoruba priest. He highlights, for example, the biblical verses John 9:6–7, which state: "When [Jesus] had thus spoken, he spat on the ground, and made clay of the spittle, and he anointed the eyes of the blind man with the clay, And said unto him, Go, wash in the pool of Siloam, (which is by interpretation, Sent.) He went his way therefore, and washed, and came seeing."[133] In Onisegun's role as both minister and priest, he engages in hermeneutical overlay whereby Jesus "looks like an African healer, or a babalawo, making use of the resources of the earth which includes all of nature and pharmacopeia in order to facilitate an act of healing . . . I see Jesus operating within that particular context of a healer, the context of a sage, the context of an advisor . . . I see Jesus as this kind of composite, of not only the Son of God . . . but also as healer, a sage, or as in African theology, an ancestor par excellence. That helps me to better interpret his life so that it makes meaning for me."[134] He argues, though, that those who live out their sacred identities within these composite spaces must first give

themselves "permission to do that" without fear of compromise or persecution. He advises, "We have to give ourselves permission to do that . . . I
think for me that was the biggest challenge, and that's what I have been
able to do. It's a struggle because I serve the chapel at the university I teach
at, and even there it was rough starting but working with the students . . . I
am able to slowly bring some things to the table that do not frighten them
away—or the administration."[135]

In addition to biblical interpretation, the question of Christology continues to be a challenging aspect in Yoruba/Christian interactions. Alleviating the challenge that Christology raises in bilingual religiosities has
been the ability to employ Jesus as a strategy, as a "skillful way" of deepen-
ing one's knowledge of another tradition, as William D. Hart insightfully
suggests.[136] When Jesus is methodologically understood as strategy, one is
then able to observe the complex ways practitioners like Onisegun engage
in fluid recontextualizations, situating Jesus within larger theological contexts that "emerge out of Africa," as well as locating Jesus's humanity and
divinity within a larger universal context where "all of our births are special and all of us come to earth for a particular purpose and reason."[137]
Upon further analysis, Onisegun states, "we have taken this particular
story and elevated him beyond humanity so that when we see [Jesus] doing
what he does, only he can do it, and if only he can do it, then what is my
purpose for being here?"[138] Onisegun continues, "It doesn't impress me
that Jesus walked on water thousands of years ago. I am trying to walk on
water today, how to navigate through this society . . . And so that's why
I struggled with that. It was why I had to . . . recontextualize and try to
understand [Jesus] in another light, and that has been helpful."[139]

Negotiating the biblical Jesus as one religious strategy within a divinely
fluid world rather than as a fixed and exclusive incarnation affords practitioners a sense of freedom and agency to adopt a flexible Christology
while alleviating the anxieties of disavowing strict Christian doctrinal
orthodoxy. It provides opportunities for theological affinities to develop
without sacrificing the epistemological richness and distinctness of either
tradition. In its absence, however, practitioners would be somewhat destined to wrestle with what Onisegun calls a "kind of double consciousness of faith."[140] Invoking W. E. B. Dubois's poignant metaphor of "double
consciousness" within this context speaks to negotiating religious identities that are constantly warring and irreconcilable and forever plagued by

an irrevocable two-ness. In contrast, Jesus as strategy allows for the malleability and plasticity of the figure of Jesus and provides opportunities for a friend who is an Olokun priestess and Roman Catholic to suggest to Onisegun with "our people and our obsession with Jesus, why don't we just make Jesus an orisa . . . That's what we got to do, just make Jesus an orisa because as much as we call on him, as much as we mention his name, as much as we invoke his presence, it's just like him operating as an orisa."[141] For Onisegun, this and the ability to extemporize theology make for a richly textured, ritually pliable, and extraordinarily sinuous approach to religious identity. For this male of African descent born in a North American diaspora, it is his complex religious dimensionality that empowers Onisegun and other practitioners to "fill the void" and ultimately, to "put some pieces back together."[142]

"I Was Born Again—Truly": First Afrikan Church and an Afrocentric Christian Ministry

Throughout their religious history, African Americans have drawn elastic boundaries around religious beliefs and expressions in order to accommodate their shifting sociopolitical and spiritual needs in North America. In more recent years, churches like First Afrikan Church in the suburbs of Atlanta, Georgia, have emerged as institutional representations of these elastic boundaries. First Afrikan Church's liturgical and theological openness includes a reverence for traditional black Christian rites while embracing traditional African spiritual and cultural sensibilities. Sharing the multifaith religious consciousness of Ayoka, Adejoke, Scruggs, and Onisegun, the pastor of First Afrikan Presbyterian Church, the Reverend Baba Mark Ogunwale Keita Lomax, is both an ordained Presbyterian minister with a doctoral degree and a fully initiated Yoruba priest of Ogun.

Even with his formal background in Pentecostalism and Presbyterianism, Lomax admits that he unknowingly lived the embodiment of Ogun long before he gained knowledge of the orisa tradition: "The Ogun I know has always been who I am—always been the one unafraid to make a difference, unafraid to open the door, to clear the path for a new idea. . . . The one who will go into a battle not knowing the outcome but go in anyway. . . . Who is a loner . . . I've always liked to go to the forest, go to the mountains, go to the woods and spend time. Then there's a deep passionate part—deep profoundly sometimes frightening passion—that people are both compelled and repulsed by, and I think that's also Ogun."[143]

Negotiating spiritual liminality as both Ogun priest and ordained Presbyterian minister, Lomax speaks of the "beautiful struggle" it has been to wed the best of the black Christian liberation tradition with "African culture and spirituality." According to Lomax, there exist "two different kinds of religious sensibilities in the black community"[144]—"The survival tradition arose primarily among the slaves as an . . . expression of their dogged refusal to totally resign their humanity in the face of dehumanization. The Africans' use of conjuration, magic and voodoo and hoodoo, properly called *vodun* and *obeah*, was an attempt to survive the Christian brainwashing that accompanied their physical bondage. The liberation tradition grew out of the free Black community of the North. Its emphasis was on personal and social evaluation, moral behavior, and political liberty rather than sheer survival."[145]

Andrea Abrams, in her important, full-length study of First Afrikan Church written in 2006, uses the work of theologian James H. Cone to theorize the theological negotiation of African and Christian identities in the United States. According to Cone, "It was the African side of Black religion that helped African Americans to see beyond the White distortions of the gospel and to discover its true meaning as God's liberation of the oppressed from bondage. It was the Christian element in Black religion that helped African Americans to reorient their African past so that it would become more useful in the struggle to survive with dignity in a society that they did not make."[146] Given the complexities of this black religious legacy, Lomax calls his work an "Afrocentric Christian Ministry" that "utilizes the histories and cultures of African descended peoples as sources for biblical reflection and interpretation, ministry development and implementation, and evangelism in the community context where we exist."[147]

Lomax's personal journey begins in Akron, Ohio. He was raised in a household with an African American mother and a father descended from Cherokee ancestry who had survived forced removal along the historic Trail of Tears. While Lomax's mother was spiritually rooted in the sanctified holiness tradition of the Church of God, Lomax's father remained largely unchurched and instead deeply rooted in the traditions of healing, herbalism, and nature spirits of his Cherokee ancestry. Collectively, his parents shared both a profound reverence for Africa and an intense

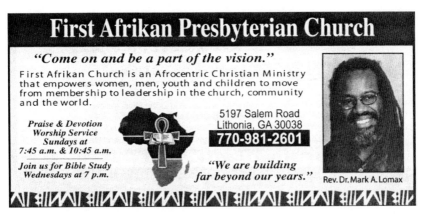

FIGURE 22. Advertisement for First Afrikan Church with Reverend Mark Ogunwale Lomax. Photograph courtesy of First Afrikan Church.

critique of America. According to Lomax, "We were never taught or told that we needed to love America for any particular reason. . . . My parents were crystal clear about where we came from. They were intent upon making sure that we understood that our reality did not begin in enslavement, our reality began in freedom somewhere on the continent of Africa."[148] During his childhood, Lomax was designated as a "special child," gifted with the spiritual ability of second sight to "see." He states, "As a child, I was the closest one to a 'seer' in my family. I saw stuff all the time, but I never did feel comfortable talking about it. I heard stuff all the time, but I never did feel comfortable sharing it."[149]

Despite the testimonies of both family and strangers that he was spiritually a "special child," the social realities of blackness in America often negated their voices. According to Lomax, "I never knew what they were talking about nor did I ever believe it. Being a dark-skinned person coming up in the fifties and sixties, it was hard to accept, hard to hear because my reality did speak to something different when other people would stop and say, 'Eeeel' and talk about your skin color or people would come up and spit in my face . . ."[150] Although Lomax's early Pentecostalism could not protect him from these inter- and intraracial onslaughts, it did provide him passage into a dynamic religious world he experienced as African. Mirroring scholars of religion and anthropology such as Melville J. Herskovits, who made some of the earliest associations between Pentecostal and African religious practice, Lomax similarly reflected on his experiences in his Church of God house of worship with its ritual assemblage of shouting, falling out, being slain in the spirit, speaking in tongues, and dancing counterclockwise. In his opinion, "Those things seem to be very African," and he felt that "if you trace religious practices in North America back far enough, you'll end up in Africa. Counter to E. Franklin Frazier and others, I don't think that we lost our memory in the Middle Passage; I think [to say] that is to denigrate the African genius..."[151]

Before the official formation of First Afrikan Church in 1993, Lomax said, the "notion of marrying Christianity to African culture and spiritual- ity" began to "consume" him. He admits that in its embryonic stages, he did not possess full clarity on what this religious symbiosis would look like, but states, "What I did have clarity about was that I had to do the work as pas- tor/scholar of both gathering a community of people who were interested not only in becoming Christian but also in becoming African."[152] Lomax developed philosophy of what would eventually become First Afrikan Church over several years of reflection, and in 1996 it became the subject of his doctoral dissertation at United Theological Seminary, "The Effects of an Afrocentric Hermeneutic in a Developing Congregation."

The institutional focus of what became First Afrikan Church is the cel- ebration of "African genius" as specifically expressed in America and as it is inspired by a wealth of spiritual resources from ancient Kemet, West and Central Africa, the African American Nguzo Saba, African American folk wisdom, and the black Christian liberation tradition. Because First Afrikan Church espouses a distinct understanding of Christian origins that locates the roots of early Christendom and the identity of Jesus Christ in north- east Africa, African and Christian identities are obviously seen as comple- mentary.[153] Unfortunately, the belief in an allied African-Christian identity was not widely shared among Lomax's ministerial cohort of local Atlanta preachers. Shortly after the formation of First Afrikan Church, Lomax was professionally ostracized from an alliance of Atlanta clergy. According to Lomax, "The whole preaching community cut me off, and the word out there was that I had lost my mind, that I had become an African and that I was going to hell... I was going to hell! I had turned away from Jesus and had become an African.... In other words, you can't be African and Christian. You can only be Christian if you deny the fact that you're African."[154]

Within the wider religious landscape of Atlanta, First Afrikan Church exists as an anomaly amidst a growing ecclesial megachurch movement of

African Americans headed by figures such Crefloe and Taffi Dollar, Bishop Eddie Long, the former copastorate team of Juanita Bynum and Thomas W. Weeks III, and T. D. Jake's annual MegaFest.[155] Standing in stark contrast to what he calls the "spiritualized capitalism" of the megachurch movement, Lomax sees the mission of First Afrikan as one of *kujichagalia* derived from the Kawaida tradition or the Nguzo Saba principle meaning self-determination. This understanding of self-determination is deeply rooted in a collective notion of community empowerment and transformation. Institutionally, First Afrikan attempts to embody this principle by providing an array of religious offerings to the Atlanta community, including Sunday worship services, ancestral remembrance ceremonies, rites of passage classes, Juneteenth celebrations, a community bookstore, Uhuru community Caregivers, Camp Taifa summer youth programs, Shabbat meditations, and ancestral ritual walks on the Chattahoochee River. Moreover, it operates a private educational facility for children, Kilombo Pan-Afrikan Institute, whose commitment is to "produce students, teachers and families who will possess the skills, knowledge and understanding to work and to live in such a way that honors our Creator, our Ancestors and the best of our traditions as African peoples."[156] Several years ago, the church also partnered with fourteen other nearby congregations and collaborated on constructing 345 residential housing units for poor and working-class African Americans in Southeast Atlanta.

Aesthetically, First Afrikan's visual culture reflects a deliberate affirmation of African and African American iconography. Prominently displayed is an ancestral shrine commemorating famous African Americans; an ankh representing the Egyptian principle of eternal life; an array of African masks, fabric, and black artistic paintings; as well as a representation of an ancestral Egungun on the pulpit. First Afrikan's commitment is not to physically transport millions of African Americans to a specific geographical location in Africa but instead to transport African Americans to a level of African religious consciousness in order to live boldly and unapologetically as a historical people of African descent in America.

Because Lomax is in agreement with Molefi Asante that "all religions rise out of the deification of someone's nationalism," the religion of First Afrikan intimately reflects the nationalism and deification of the sacred in African-descended communities.[157] It garners its inspiration from both ancestral religious legacies in America and the wisdom traditions of Africa.

First Afrikan is a place where congregants sit in the pews with eleke neck-laces prominently around their necks representing the orisa spirits, the King James Version of the Bible in their hands, and with quiet reverence proceed to consume the sacramental "body and blood" of Jesus Christ dur-ing the holy Communion ritual. This polygonal lived praxis is common among a population of devotees and represents a new kind of orthodox fluidity that seeks to make sense of what it means to be of African descent, removed from the original source of diaspora, steeped in a North American history of evangelical Protestantism, while ultimately desiring to live out of a "particular conception" that reconciles these multistranded entities.

Theologically, one finds the true meaning of "salvation" in locating oneself as first African, and then secondarily exhibiting an openness to the spiritual practices (inclusive of black Christianity) that emerged among African-descended people in Africa and in the diaspora. According to Lomax, "If you can attain this, then maybe you'll get something in the next life that looks like salvation."[158] He enters into the Christian theological dis-course with expansive innovation, locating the salvation of black humanity within a much broader context than traditional Euro-Christian evangeli-cal notions of Jesus Christ. At First Afrikan, Lomax uses the "call of Jesus" and the "model of Jesus" as dual paradigms for a larger discourse on black liberation, where the ultimate goal rests in black self-actualization and self-empowerment in an American context he figuratively refers to as "Empire." Lomax contends, "I'm trying to understand the message of Jesus and what it means for my people or whether it has meaning. If it doesn't, then I have to leave it alone."[159] Lomax's commitment lies not in a simple reverence for the humanity and divinity of Jesus but most importantly in how this Jesus figure can build reverence for the integrity, dignity, and divinity of black humanity. According to Lomax, "I don't think Jesus is God in any sense of the word—not any more than you or I. . . . His life did serve as a model for how one could live with such authenticity in the world that the divine in you can come out through the Holy Ghost."[160] Lomax urges his congre-gants toward a "God-consciousness" that centers on social action, collective empowerment, and the cultivation of the divine nature within them, ulti-mately rejecting rigid notions of Trinitarianism or Calvinist understand-ings of total depravity that anchored early Presbyterianism.

As First Afrikan's leader, Lomax skillfully navigates a complex reli-gious identity as both black Christian pastor and initiated Yoruba babalosa.

He recognizes the spiritual diversity of his congregation and acknowledges that "there are people sitting up here who have joined this ministry because they know I've been initiated," as well as "those who are still fundamentalist, who are evangelical."[161] Lomax views his own dual religious identity not as an "either/or" but as a "both/and" approach to spiritual embodiment and empowerment.

Lomax's journey to the Yoruba component of his composite identity began more than twenty years ago. As he reflected on his religious background in the sanctified church and tried to understand the source of the spiritual power in these ecstatic experiences, Lomax felt more and more drawn to what he saw as its African religious expressions. He recalls, "I knew there was something deeper, something more powerful. I didn't believe then nor do I believe now that you could tap into that through American evangelical kinds of Protestantism. I thought that there had to be something more akin to African spirituality."[162]

Lomax soon realized that what he searched for extended well beyond Christianity and eventually came to acknowledge that "there was power in African traditional religions." Unsure of how to access this power, he turned to reading texts and to discussions with a friend who was a practicing Ifa priest in the Yoruba priesthood. Lomax was then introduced to the elder Yoruba priest, Baba Medahochi. In 1996, Lomax speaks of experiencing an inner knowing that he had waited until he "couldn't hold out any longer" and decided to undergo full initiation as a priest of Ogun. Because First Afrikan had only been formed three years previously, Lomax understood that his initiation might place his pastorship in imminent jeopardy. He recalls, "You're talking at that junction about risking losing everything that I built over the last years, but I said if I don't, I'm gonna die. I felt that. And so I did it, and what a powerful transformation . . . took place in my life."[163]

This transformation was immediately apparent to his parishioners at First Afrikan Church. According to Lomax, "Everybody who could see it, could not believe it because I was born again—truly."[164] In contemplating the best way to introduce his new priestly identity to First Afrikan congregants, Lomax decided on the following:

I never made a broad announcement from the pulpit, but people were actually able to see the transformation I had gone through. People asked me what [the initiation] meant for my prayer life.

Initially I was still trying to work that out, but now I am pouring my libations; I am honoring Esu and Ogun and Oshun in my
prayer life. I do have a shrine. I got my machete with the red rope
around it. I got my Ogun pot. I mean, Yeah, you come to my house,
and you are going to see it. You are going to see the black stone at
the door because I'm a practitioner. And I'm a practitioner because
this way has opened up some stuff for me, deep inside of me, that I
knew was there, and I can just draw on these sources like ancestors
and spirits in ways that I have never been able to draw on. It has
opened up another world for me, and that can only be of benefit
for this community.[165]

Lomax brings his spiritual resources both as preacher and as baba to bear
at First Afrikan. His ministry at First Afrikan Church embodies a W. E. B.
Duboisian conception of the historical black preacher who finds his antecedents in the African priest or medicine man of African traditional religions. According to Dubois:

And yet some traces were retained of the former group life, and
the chief remaining institution was the Priest or Medicine-man.
He early appeared on the plantation and found his function as
the healer of the sick, the interpreter of the Unknown, the com-
forter of the sorrowing, the supernatural avenger of wrong, and
the one who rudely but picturesquely expressed the longing, disappointment, and resentment of a stolen and oppressed people.
Thus, as bard, physician, judge, and priest, within the narrow limits allowed by the slave system, rose the Negro preacher, and under
him the first Afro-American institution, the Negro Church. This
church was not at first by any means Christian nor definitely organized; rather it was an adaptation and mingling of heathen rites
among the members of each plantation, and roughly designated
as Voodooism.[166]

Whereas for Dubois the African priest or medicine man had an evolutionary relationship with the Negro preacher, Lomax instead occupies a
space of cultural fusion, drawing upon the spiritual technologies of both
traditions to enhance and inform his ministry. As a committed pastor

and *babalosa*, Lomax devotes himself to "reading" the "sacred text" of his ministry, which he defines as the diverse congregants in the pews of First Afrikan Church. When training young African American clergy in the classroom at Johnson C. Smith Theological Seminary, he asks, "Do you know how to read the sacred text?" His students often respond, "You talking about the Bible?" To which Lomax then explains, "No, I'm talking about the pew, that's your sacred text."[167] Moreover, through his expertise in homiletics, Lomax draws upon both his African American Christian and his Yoruba traditions to theorize on the efficacy of orality within black religious contexts. He compares preaching with the art of divination and states: "Preaching is a kind of type of divining. You know you have preached well when people can say, 'You were in my house last week'; or 'You were on my street'; or 'You have stepped on my toes.' Those are codes for saying, 'Yeah, you were on the right spiritual path. You understood and discerned my situation, and you spoke to it today.' That Bible is the Odu. Those stories right there. I be reading the spirits—the spirits of the ones who are in front of you, the spirit of the community. And you're speaking to it and of it in ways that people can really truly identify with in an existential way."[168]

For Lomax, both traditions provide a wealth of resources and insightful points of reference as he engages in an African American sacred moment at First Afrikan Church. Although his sermons rarely refer to the specific deities or theological intricacies of Yoruba religion, Lomax has mastered the art of utterance, innuendo, and nuance to reference important tenets in Yoruba cosmology. For example, in his Sunday sermons, he weaves biblical stories such as Luke 16:19–31 on Lazarus's ascendancy with Yoruba's conception of ancestor veneration and Olorun. With a radical exegetical lens and a close reading of biblical texts, Lomax jolts his listeners out of traditional black Church readings of the Bible, boldly asserting to his parishioners "that when Lazarus died, he didn't go to heaven—that's not what this text says. He went to be with his ancestor, Abraham. To be gathered to his ancestor was heaven."[169] Anticipating theological resistance, Lomax continues, "Some of us don't like ancestor talk, but here it is in your Bible. He went to be with his ancestor. You can call that heaven if you want to, but that ain't what the Bible says."[170] Although possessing a critical stance, African American Yoruba practitioners like Lomax find themselves slow to denigrate the Christian traditions of their ancestors and black predecessors in North America. There is a recognition that within the distinct expressions and meanings that African Americans fashioned out of Christianity lies a sustaining power that enabled them to resist America's historical attempts at social and ontological annihilation.

Despite this, practitioners like Lomax share an understanding that Christianity cannot represent the only black religious signifier while Africa and its spiritual resources go completely eclipsed. They are unafraid to enter into what have traditionally been academic debates on the question of African religious cultures in North America, explicitly referencing and countering claims of scholars such as E. Franklin Frazier, who argued, "It is impossible to establish any continuity between African religious practices and the Negro church in the United States"; or Eugene Genovese, who argued that slavery "crushed much of the specific African religious memory"; or Albert Raboteau, who, although often misunderstood in this debate, stated, "In the United States the gods of Africa died."[171] African American Yoruba practitioners like Lomax are firm in their positions in this debate and look with more favor on viewpoints like those of Gayraud Wilmore, who is more sympathetic to the provenance of African orientations amidst an emerging and evolving black Christian consciousness in America. For example, in *Black Religion and Black Radicalism: An Interpretation of the Religious History of Afro-American People*, Wilmore argues that "the slaves were not completely divested of their belief systems" in America and that the "African religious background . . . provided a rapidly disintegrating but persistent base upon which the institutions of the slave were erected."[172] For Wilmore, enslaved Africans "maintained the basic ontological and soteriological emphases" of African traditional religions, thus emphatically contending that "Christianity alone . . . could not have provided the slaves with all the resources they needed for the kind of resistance they expressed. . . ."[173] It had to be enriched with the volatile ingredients of the African religious past . . ."[174]

Wilmore, however, candidly acknowledges the complicated, implicit complexities regarding the webbing debate on African retentions. He is fully aware of the way source availability, data reliability, and even personal ideology have made such arguments problematic. Of his own scholarly leanings, he transparently discloses:

Drawing on the works of Du Bois and Herskovits rather than E. Franklin Frazier and Stanley Elkins, I have attempted to show

the indomitable humanity of the slaves and the credibility of the
African background thesis in plantation America. In an area of
scholarly dispute where the primary source materials are sparse
on either side, ideological leanings are all too apparent. There is
no disguising the fact that I have chosen to lean in the direction
of the strength of the African inheritance rather than the puta-
tive irresistibility of the Euro-American acculturation process as
it supposedly works in contact with "less civilized" cultures. There
is as much evidence that certain retentions from Africa persisted
in Afro-American religion in the South as there is that the slaves
collapsed before the juggernaut of evangelicalism and were revived
in the pure white garments of Euro-American Christianity.[175]

Lomax, like Wilmore, concedes that the "the polytheistic aspect of traditional African religion had to be surrendered under great duress despite
the fact that the idea of a Supreme Being was not foreign to Africans. This
resulted in the taking on of more and more of the language, ritual trappings, and symbolization of Christianity until the old African religions
were overpowered."[176] This appropriation of Christian symbolization, however, or what Dianne M. Stewart identifies as christianisms, did not necessarily lead to the conclusion that the gods themselves "ultimately. . . . died."
Instead Lomax, with theological support from Wilmore, posits an alternative position in this debate. Agreeing with Wilmore that the African spiritual entities became "disembodied and depersonalized," Lomax argues
that in the encounter with Protestant Christianity, the spiritual attributes
and features of the "disembodied and depersonalized" African spirits were
then collectively rehoused within the single sacred host figure of Jesus.[177]
Lomax's contention, in other words, challenges the analytical shortcomings
of anthropologists and religionists who accept correspondences between
African gods and Roman Catholic saints as proof of cultural retentions,
yet are unwilling to apply the same scholarly methodology to a Protestant
Christian framework where the attributes of various African gods could
create an association with Protestantism's single saintly figure of Jesus
Christ. This hypothesis takes into consideration African Americans' inability to openly practice and thereby sustain their complex traditions during
slavery and concludes that with their historical encounter with evangelical Protestantism in the United States, African Americans poured a lot of

their "African spiritual content into the person of Jesus."[178] Lomax makes
the fascinating claim that although Africans may have arrived with religious associations connected to specific spirit entities such as *nkisi*, *orisa*,
or *vodun*, these spiritual associations became translatable into North
American Protestantism as they did to Roman Catholicism. Lomax argues
compellingly that "in so many ways we have poured the content of the
orisa (we're talking about Yoruba) and also other African spiritual traditions into one person. [Jesus] becomes all of that for us and then more."[179]
In our interview, Lomax theorizes this intriguing claim of religious correspondence in more detail:

> Jesus is the orisa in the West that encompasses all other orisa. Jesus
> is the Waymaker—that's Ogun; Jesus will fight your battles. Jesus is
> also a lover—that's Oshun. Jesus will show you the Way—He's like
> Esu. He stands at the crossroads and shows you the Way . . . Jesus
> is also Shango. Jesus will see you through the storm. Shango is the
> storm, but Jesus will help you through it. . . . He'll create a storm
> for you too because if you want to deal with somebody—pray for
> them in Jesus's name. . . . I think that's part of the reason we still
> resonate with Jesus. Man, Jesus is something else in the African
> consciousness of America. . . . We pray everything to God, but we
> say, "In Jesus Name." So there is this recognition that there is this
> one overarching High God, this Creator of us all, and then there's
> this powerful one and only orisa—Jesus. . . . That's all you need.
> And that's how I work it out theologically.[180]

Within this complex theological premise, the Jesus of the African diaspora becomes the vessel holding the vast attributes that African-descended
people formerly ascribed to the many deities of the Africa pantheon. In the
absence of this pantheon in North America, the deities' multifarious sacred
embodiments and attributes were vested in the single host of Jesus. John
3:16 and the evangelical doctrine of salvation therefore is radically transformed, and Jesus becomes a portal, a gateway, a strategy, reconstituted
and reincarnated as a manifestation of the many attributes and correspondences of Yoruba orisa deity: Jesus absorbs Esu's ascription as Waymaker;
Babaluaye and Osanyin's properties as healers; Ifa-Orunmila's divinatory
capacities as He divines in the sand; Ogun, Oshosi, and Osun's warrior

abilities to fight your battles; Shango's power as a mighty battle axe, the power of Oya as He quiets the storm winds and walks on top of water; Oshun and Yemoja's nurturance as He suffers the little children to come unto him, and the power of Obatala through Jesus's theologically conterminous presence with God the Creator.

As a religious studies scholar teaching at a major seminary, Jim Perkinson in his work on the Yoruba orisa Ogou (Ogun) provides insightful theorization on what he believes "the supplement of a figure such as Ogou in particular (and diaspora possession activity in general) might add to the history of Jesus."[181] Within the context of a liberation paradigm, he poses the following compelling question: "In the colonial and postcolonial histories of conflagration that have engulfed African-heritage peoples, where might we expect to discover the sources for an authentic Christology, rendering the presence and activity of Jesus among the oppressed not so much intelligible for evaluation as available for use?"[182] In an effort to outdistance the historical legacy and oppressive tyranny of Christian supremacy, he suggests that diaspora communities might engage in a process of "creative creolization" and amalgamation, whereby "if Ogou, for instance, is an indigenous West African form increasingly efficacious in articulating the experience of the diaspora, first in the grip of enslavement, then in the wars for political freedom, and finally in a postcolony fraught with social struggle and economic entropy, Christianity might need to wonder in our day about Jesus *Ogou* rather than Jesus *Christ*."[183] Perkinson's suggestions ultimately raise important questions about why African diasporic notions of Jesus should be any more sacrosanct and sacred than African orisa such as Ogun, particularly as they relate to theological articulations of liberation paradigms.[184]

Thus, Lomax, like Perkinson, finds analogizing useful when explaining the theological contours of Yoruba religion to his congregants. As he states, "I try to meet the people where they are. . . . So when I start talking about my understanding of Ifa, people asking me particular questions, I bring it back to Jesus and try to help people see all of what I said in our minds today is concentrated in this one person."[185] Scruggs echoes this sentiment when she maintains that it is the practice of this unique relational connection to Jesus that African Americans "bring to" Yoruba religion. She argues that this gets translated into a personal connection to the orisa, which in many ways "comes from the meaningful personal relationships that African Americans have had with divinity and spiritual entities such as Jesus."[186]

Historian of religion James A. Noel, in his study of African American religion, insightfully postulates, "We can conjecture that African divinities became identified, initially, with Old Testament figures in the United States, and finally, with Jesus."[187] In many ways Noel, Scruggs, and Lomax attempt to dismantle traditional academic theories of hybridity and syncretism that are largely analyzed within the context of Roman Catholicism by positing revealing the buoyancy of Protestantism as it absorbs and is transformed by diaspora religious processes.

Lomax's theological openness to both the Jesus of black Christianity and the orisa of the Yoruba tradition is a direct reflection of his adherence to what Baba Medahochi refers to as "Afrikan Spiritual Unity," a concept more fully explored in the next chapter. Lomax resists drawing fixed theological boundaries around access to the spirit at First Afrikan Church. In his own words he states, "I try to respond to what I perceive as the need to bring it all together. It's unity and diversity. I'm not asking anybody to give up where you are. So at First Afrikan fundamentally you find practitioners of Ifa ... you find fundamentalist Christians, you name it you'll find the whole gamut here. The one thing that we have in common is we believe that there is an intelligence which we most frequently call God."[188] Andrea Abrams study of First Afrikan Church concludes that "the church has been deliberate in choosing those aspects of African culture and history which best speak to their current circumstances and which are flexible enough to be interpreted by a diverse group of individuals."[189] Furthermore, she adds, "the church leadership takes care to explain from what cultural traditions and in what time periods mores and practices are borrowed and continuously encourages the congregation to learn as much as possible both in and out of the church."[190] The result is a complex theology, ritual tradition, and religious practice that reflects the spiritual currency of Africa, the liberation theology of black Protestantism, and the grassroots political activism of black-nationalist social movements.

As Presbyterian pastor and African priest at First Afrikan Church, Lomax expends considerable effort cultivating a religious consciousness that valorizes Africa and venerates its ancestors as a spiritual weapon against what Gayraud Wilmore calls "the black magic of white oppression."[191] Lomax admits the difficulty of living "boldly" and "unapologetically" in this regard, especially as he navigates a broader North America among "folks who are confused enough to destroy themselves."[192] Yet he perseveres in his calling both as a Yoruba and as a Presbyterian, committing his ministry to cultivating a liberation consciousness among Atlanta's African Americans. He concludes: "That's my burden. That's my mission. That's my pain—but also my pleasure. I don't feel as obligated to any other people [as to] African people."[193]

Supporting Lomax's ministry at First Afrikan Church before his transition in 2007 in profoundly committed ways was his spiritual godfather in the orisa tradition, Baba Medahochi. Because of Baba Medahochi's recognition of the rich spiritual traditions of African Americans in the United States, he could readily appreciate the religious significance of an institution like First Afrikan Church. Under the visionary leadership of his spiritual godson, Baba Medahochi revealed in our interview, "First Afrikan community is an answer to my prayers forty years ago. I prayed that there would be a community of African Americans who would recognize who we are and not be exclusive about who we are and accept all of what we are."[194] Although Medahochi would not religiously self-identify as Christian, his formal membership in the church was a way of affirming the cultural and institutional contributions that First Afrikan Church made to the African American religious landscape. According to Medahochi, "It's just like they say. It is an Afrikan-centered Christian church. They have Africanized Christianity as much as they can. . . . I think it's very progressive, and I think it's the right way to go. I don't necessarily use that as my reference— Christianity—but I don't see anything wrong with what they are doing."[195] Medahochi specifically resonated with First Afrikan because his own personal travels had led him in 1978 to Ghana, Togo, and Senegal, where, especially in Senegal, he was deeply impressed by the ways in which West Africans could domesticate, Africanize, and locally indigenize religious traditions like Islam. In fact, throughout his life Medahochi often quipped, "I tell people, Islam is my girlfriend and African religion is my wife."[196]

A senior elder in the American Yoruba priesthood, Medahochi felt fully accepted by the First Afrikan congregation. He vividly recalls the moment when he stood up in church to become a member of the community: "The fact is they didn't ask me 'Do you accept Jesus?' or I would have told them, 'No . . . I'm not joining to be saved, I'm already saved.'"[197] Baba Medahochi's spiritual father, Oseijeman Adefunmi, was theologically clear in his own teachings on this issue. According to Adefunmi, "Salvation is in your own family if you celebrate *Egungun* (ancestor veneration)."[198]

Therefore, Baba Medahochi was most impressed with First Afrikan's inclusion of ancestral veneration and the fact that several among its membership maintained personal ancestral shrines in their homes. In turn, First Afrikan members respected Baba Medahochi's dedicated commitment to the religious traditions of Africa. He was often called upon to give the church's Mbongi, or teaching lesson. According to one of the church elders, Reverend Will Esuyemi Coleman:

> [Baba Medahochi] has taught us by his presence and also in his teachings that it is not difficult to remember our ancestors. . . . And that is just one gift that he's given us. . . . The fact that he joined First Afrikan Church is also an expression of the expansiveness of his consciousness but he realizes (and he teaches us as a babalawo, as a bakono) that we are first Africans and then we are what enslavement has made us a consequence of—then we're Presbyterian, and then we're Christian, and then we're Muslim . . . And because we are first Africans, we can be united in what we do in recovering our ancestral memory and power. So we say *Ashe, Ashe, Ashe-O.*

Baba Medahochi, a key proponent of the philosophical concept of Afrikan Spiritual Unity discussed at greater length in the next chapter, understood that the recovery of "ancestral memory and power" began with the African ancestors. This also included the ancestors of North America; as a result, he could never totally exclude Christianity or any expression of African people's faith traditions in this hemisphere. In reflecting on her husband, Djisovi, who was a godchild of Baba Medahochi, Lillian Ashcraft-Eason adds, "Djisovi thought, as do some other New Yorubas, that he and I should participate in the Protestant religions of our African-American ancestors. We joined Methodist and Baptist churches and performed in pageants and took part in other programs. Pastors often welcomed our offers to teach about African traditional cultures and religions. These churches afforded us opportunities to learn, serve, and teach."[199] It is virtually impossible that all Africans captured in the transatlantic slave trade were ethnically and religiously Yoruba, but the ability of African diasporic people to unify traditions and view the world through a religious kaleidoscope enables them to tap into the best of the traditions of Africa as well as the best of the New World Afrikan expressions of Christianity.

Conclusion

What we see as fixed identities, many West Indians see as "coats"
they put on or take off, depending on the context.

—Francio Guadeloupe

As African American Yoruba practitioners navigate lived religious worlds
that coalesce, they employ what Guadeloupe calls a "flexibility and pragmatism" that are not available through either Yoruba exclusivism or Christian
fundamentalism.[200] As one African American Yoruba priestess stated,
"Knowledge should be inclusive of all the different avenues."[201] Yoruba
practitioners often view past affiliations with mainstream Christian faiths
as "too restrictive," and they savor the freedom to be able to "move between"
several different traditions.[202] As Huntington's informant Maria explained,
"All the paths, they meet. All is God."[203] Some members of the African
American Yoruba priesthood have chosen to give direct theological expression to this inclusivity by participating in interfaith dialogues. One such
priestess believes that "there's only one Supreme Deity, and we call that
deity Olodumare; they call it Jehovah, Allah, Brahma. . . . Whatever the
name, it's talking about the one architect of the universe."[204]

For a sizeable portion of practitioners, however, their initiations into
Yoruba religion meant a definitive choice to sever the ties of previous (often
Christian) religious identities and engage in what they see as the exclusive
"boundary-maintaining practices" of the Yoruba tradition.[205] These practitioners contend that the "Black Church" does not address the "African culture of our ancestors," that Christianity is an "imposed religion that did not
come from African culture," and that Christianity "was a tool of oppression
used against my people." Finally, unlike Christian church services, they
point out that in Yoruba drumming ceremonies "the *orixas* might come up
and touch, or give you a personal message."[206] In spite of these concerns,
a growing number in the African American Yoruba priesthood ultimately
take their cue from nineteenth-century voodoo priestess Marie Laveau,
who in New Orleans made both Congo Square and the Roman Catholic
Church her sacred ritual domains, or Zora Neale Hurston, who reconciled
the Baptist faith of her preacher father with her six-fold initiations into
voodoo.[207] In contemporary times, we can turn to Iyanla Vanzant, who
locates her spiritual ministry within both the Yoruba priesthood and the
Unity Church remarking, "I learned to combine the universal principles I

was learning through Unity with the cultural principles I had learned in Yoruba."[208] What has emerged among this representative group of practitioners is the opportunity for "a theological embrace of diasporic possession practices that places those activities in a modality of *reciprocal hermeneusis* with Christian self-understanding."[209] Rejecting static and inflexible religious orthodoxies, the testimonies of these devotees attest to the ways Yoruba religion and allied religious traditions have afforded access to new sacred meanings of multiple power with profound efficacy and remarkable coherence.

CHAPTER EIGHT

"Afrikan Americans in the U.S.A. Bring Something Different to Ifa"

Indigenizing Yoruba Religious Cultures

ᕲᗡᑉᑫᕂ

I'd jump up dar and den and holler and shout and sing and pat, and dey would all cotch de words and I'd sing it to some old shout song I'd heard 'em sing from Africa, and dey'd all take it up and keep at it, and keep a-addin' to it. . . .

—Narrative of a former slave

B EGINNING IN THE late 1950s and onto the twenty-first century, African Americans have carved out their own distinct interpretations of the Yoruba world. The North American social context has yielded a surplus of new meanings for African Americans who "keep a-addin' to" the global Yoruba tradition. As historian Kim D. Butler observes, "Each diaspora has unique historical circumstances," and its "choices of identity."[1] Although specific ethnic communities might try to confer strictures of orthodoxy and orthopraxy upon the orisa, it is their sinuous, porous, and supple nature that accommodates innovation, resourcefulness, and local indigenizations.

In this chapter, indigenizing Yoruba religious culture is defined not so much in terms of primordial origins as it is in terms of the intricate processes that bring about ritual, cultural, theological, and literary mechanisms of localization. Peter Hulme's concept of indigeneity is "an avowal of ethnic distinctiveness and national sovereignty based on the historical claim to be in some sense the descendants of the earliest inhabitants of a particular place." I use it here to examine the complex paradox that while Yoruba indigeneity occurs in North America, it is the descent from the "particular place" of Africa that bestows authority in these efforts.[2]

Since the late 1950s, four basic influences have helped to determine the ways Yoruba practice has been indigenized on North American soil. First, Yoruba religion assumed powerful new religious and social meaning within a diasporic American context where identity had long been heavily racialized. Social meanings of blackness and whiteness in North America form relevant subtexts that often define Yoruba religious identity in America. Yoruba religion has allowed ancestral connections to be reestablished, restored, and renewed for native-born black North Americans in a context where racialized identity is multifunctional.

Second, the proliferation of religious literatures and texts has influenced the indigenization of African American Yoruba. Most practitioners possess extensive libraries that supplement their religious practice, challenging conventionally held notions of Yoruba religion as an exclusively oral tradition. These libraries provide informational accessibility to the tradition and include volumes on the divinatory stories of Ifa, the personalities and characteristics of the orisa, the complexities of divination, and the fundamentals of Yoruba language and ritual song. Third, the boundaries circumscribing Yoruba American identity often possess an elastic quality that readily accommodates both metaphysical sciences and other global traditions such as Christianity and Eastern practices. As discussed in chapter 7, this permeability has enabled African Americans to create religious systems that fluidly engage Yoruba and other spiritual traditions. Finally, as an important part of their indigenizing efforts, African American Yoruba seek to revere and affirm the legitimacy of the spiritual practices of their ancestors born not only in Africa but in North America. These North American cultivated practices are often embraced within a larger vision of what Baba Medahochi labels Afrikan Spiritual Unity, which celebrates and selectively draws from both African and black diasporic sacred knowledge. Working in tandem with the many efforts to rehumanize the meaning of blackness in this Atlantic basin, African Americans in the final analysis indigenized Yoruba religious practices and kept "a-addin' to it" in order to accommodate their immediate social, theological, and ritual needs in America. According to Philadelphia priest Oba Sekou Olayinka, the results were an array of innovative, creative contributions to the orisa tradition in North America—what he fittingly terms African Americanisms.[3]

Yoruba Religion and American Racial Discourse

God dreamed of heroes, wise men, and powerful women
She sang of genius, sorcerer, and inventress
Our Race was born.

—John Mason, *Orin Orisa*[4]

Often used as a mode of religious and cultural authority, race discourse has shaped the ways that notions of authenticity, legitimacy, orthodoxy, ownership, inclusion, and exclusion are negotiated within American Yoruba identity politics. In the twentieth century, race emerged as a dominant theme in the relationship between African American and Anglo-Cuban devotees. In the twenty-first century, this racial ethos persists as Yoruba religion in North America expands its practitioner base and accommodates the rising number of Euro-American initiates into the tradition.

As discussed in previous chapters, in the late 1950s and early 1960s, the African American and Anglo-Cuban communities each possessed their own distinctive interpretations of race and ethnicity that controlled the politics of access to the religion. For African Americans, one source of ambiguity rested in where to place Cuban immigrants along the spectrum of American racial designations. Early Cuban immigrants to the United States came from a country where privilege was connected to the process of whitening or *blanqueamiento*.[5] Within this complex racial process in prerevolutionary Cuba, mixed-raced persons could evolve into the coveted "white" category, and blacks could elevate their social status to that of mixed raced. Upon arrival in the United States, Cubans, much like post-apartheid South Africans, found themselves quickly immersed in yet another complex racial context where social access and privileges were allotted according to distinct phenotypic designations. Many pre-Mariel Cubans were deemed "white" within this complex American racial theater, and Adefunmi contends that for the most part his surrogate Cuban godfather in New York eschewed relationships with darker-skinned African Americans. According to Adefunmi, "I guess because of my complexion he thought I looked more Cuban and so it was easy for me to pass. He was a couple of hues darker than I was, but he thought like a white Cuban might in any case. And so he disregarded the African Americans, thinking they would never understand, that they would never make it."[6]

Conversely, as self-proclaimed Africans within the geographical contours of the United States, African American Yoruba nationalists not only sought to expunge external white, Roman Catholic iconography but to radicalize Yoruba theology. For example, within the West African context of Dahomey, a Yoruba was thought to have three souls, which Herskovits described as the guardian spirit, the personal soul, and the intuitive soul.[7] William Bascom characterized these three souls as the ancestral guardian soul associated with the head, the vital force of breath, and the shadow, "which has no function during life but simply follows the living body about."[8] Nigerian theologian E. Bolaji Idowu collapsed these multiple souls into two, ori and emi, representing the spiritual head and human breath.[9] Because of the strong racial conundrum in which African Americans found themselves negotiating in the 1960s, Adefunmi expanded the two human souls to nine.[10] Of the nine souls, the "racial soul," the "national soul," and the "ancestral soul" were chief innovations. The concept of the racial soul was deeply rooted in an American understanding of race that ascribed certain essential attributes, traits, and characteristics to a particular group. According to Adefunmi, the racial soul "governs the particular race a person is born into. This soul gives different races the certain talents they are noted for."[11] The national soul, according to Adefunmi, "makes you part of a particular heritage. This soul is represented by the type of clothes you wear, the food you eat, etc." Finally, the ancestral soul was what linked African Americans to Africa. For Adefunmi, "A person maintains the heredity chain by worshipping his ancestors." For many African Americans, race coupled with ancestry reinforced historical linkages to Africa. According to one African American Yemoja priestess, "There is definitely a tie to African-ness and I think that for black folks that is racial."[12]

Since the 1960s, this self-proclaimed African-ness inspired African Americans toward self-reliance in the Yoruba tradition. Adefunmi, along with other African American priests like Baba Medahochi, promoted religious autonomy and self-sufficiency for African Americans. Adefunmi recounts: "[Medahochi] says, 'Baba you've read that the Cubans have worked out their own system of the African religion, the Brazilians have worked out their own system, the Haitians have worked out their own system as they needed it, and we, African Americans, should do it too. And you're the only one that knows anything about what it is we're doing, and so I think that you really have an obligation . . . that you should begin to initiate.' And so, since he was presenting such an invincible argument, I then agreed and I began to initiate."[13] Adefunmi recalled that "Cubans were extremely incensed over [this move toward ritual, theological, and institutional self-reliance], and they said that they . . . were not going to recognize the people that we initiated . . ."[14]

At that time, African American practitioners found themselves rethinking Yoruba religion in permissive ways that reflected their own specific immediate racial, historical, and social proclivities. According to Lloyd Weaver:

> Black Americans . . . had to find ways to make Orisha worship relative to them in ways that were not real concerns for their Cuban elders. We were interested in the religion as an alternative to Western Christianity. Many of us had turned to Islam in this search but others of us, wanted something that was more specifically ancestral. And having found it we were not as inclined, as had been the Cubans, to hide our religion. We staunchly refused to keep Christian artifacts in our shrines as disguises and could never begin to refer to Orishas as "saints" even though we totally respected and appreciated the fact that if the Cubans had not done these things, instructed by Orisha itself, we would not have authentic ashe of Orisha that is in our heads today. Our respect for those Cuban priests of the Caribbean will never cease, nor will our gratitude.[15]

In the late twentieth and twenty-first centuries, the strained relations between African American and Latino communities have somewhat diminished. Examples of alliance and cooperation can be found throughout places like New York and Miami. Cuban babalawos such as Ernesto Pichardo have played an important part in this intercultural bridge building both in Miami and also in Oyotunji African Village and at one point even encouraged the village to consider a presence in Miami in order to have greater access to the African Americans there.[16] Many local Yoruba houses minimize racial differences and now foster a multicultural approach to religious community. With an active black-nationalist agenda largely dissolved, not all African American adherents feel an urgent need for exclusively black houses of worship.

Among some African Americans today, however, race has become crystallized on the initiation of Anglo-Americans who lack a "bio-hereditary membership" in the racial world of Africa-descended people.[17] Although this was not an initial focus of my research, I found that African Americans born in the United States tended to oppose the initiation of whites quite strongly and were more likely to question its appropriateness than their Caribbean or West African counterparts. A common perception I found among many African Americans was that white initiates have used race and money to negotiate access and prominence within the religion. Moreover, some African American devotees fear that whites may have the tendency to "exoticize" the religion, viewing the tradition as nothing more than another African adventure: "Got to go to Kenya to save them animals; got to go to Nigeria to get them orisas."[18] It is along this North American racial black/ white spectrum where the goal of religious unity often begins to fissure.

Conversely, I found Nigerian-born Yoruba to be much more receptive to a multiracial approach to Yoruba religious community. Like Nigerian theologian Idowu, they argue theologically that "Ile-Ife, according to the beliefs of the Yoruba, is the earthly origin and fountain of all; it is also the earthly end to which all must return. . . . Ile-Ife is the origin and center, not only of the Yoruba world but also of the whole world of nations and peoples."[19] Given this understanding of the world, Nigerian Yoruba often hesitate to construct boundaries of exclusion or impose restrictions based primarily on racial designations. According to Wande Abimbola, "We believe in the brotherhood of mankind. In this culture, in this religion, in this thought system, there is no room for hate. There is no room for discrimination."[20] Likewise, Nigerian scholar Femi-Ojo-Ade stated, "The depositories of the tradition in the Diaspora must be praised for their perseverance and their Africanness, which should not be confused with blackness. For among the believers of Orisha are found many people of many shades and, in certain centers, it might even shock the observer that many a black has nothing to do with Orishas, whereas a Caucasian worships Ogun, Yemaja, and other deities."[21] African Americans in the United States, however, have a vested interest in maintaining what they see as the racial integrity of Yoruba religion in ways that Nigerian or many Latino practitioners are reluctant to publically endorse.

Symbolizing Whiteness in African American Yoruba Thought

African American concerns about white initiation date back to the early days of Oba Oseijeman Adefunmi and other African American nationalists. They developed a racialized hermeneutic surrounding white American presence within Yoruba religion that coupled complex readings of human creation, history, and theology with analytical discourses on power and privilege. The backdrop of American social history most immediately informed this hermeneutic and directly influenced how African Americans understood issues of race, hegemony, and status. In an early 1966 study of Harlem's Yoruba Temple, Adefunmi was quoted as saying, "There is no room for racism in our religion. If the religion is valid for blacks, it applies to whites as well. We teach that when an Afro-American has self-respect, he has no need to fear or hate the white man."[22] However, Adefunmi's initiatory practices were largely incongruous with this statement. More representative of Adefunmi's thought was a lecture he gave in 1993 at Columbia University, where it is evident that his views on white initiation were directly informed by discursive reflections on slavery. In this lecture, Adefunmi states, "We have heard that all humans were created at Ile-Ife . . . Black, white, red, yellow. . . . And so, they are all entitled to know the mysteries of the ancestors of the Yoruba. Our response to that is that when one member of the human family betrays another through enslavement, or selling or genocide, then the offended family may repudiate the offending member; who by his betrayal of the family forfeits his right of inheritance to the family fortune or the family legacy, or in our case the family secrets."[23] In mythologizing the historical encounter between Africans and Europeans, Adefunmi argued that although Europeans may have descended from Ile-Ife, the transgressive act of chattel enslavement caused them to forfeit their inheritance rights and as a result lose access to the "secrets" of the religion of their original human lineage. One Oyotunji chief restated it this way:

[Ife-Ife] was the cradle of civilization of man. All men of all colors were created in Ife and then went out into the world. . . . As far as what the Nigerians are saying that all men were created in Ife so, therefore, Ifa should be a universal religion . . . We are opposed to that because we know the nature of the European. He suppressed religions in Africa, came to divide them. . . . How can you impose your religion on another race of people, you see? There's some misunderstanding, even with the Nigerians. [Nigerians] have also been exposed to Christianity and Islam to a great degree, and where now we [African Americans] have denounced that, they still accept it. They just now coming around to practicing in North America the rituals and divinations.[24]

To be sure, African American Yoruba practitioners are far from consensus on the initiation of whites. Dissenting voices view religion and religious identity as less bounded by the category of race. According to one view, "I don't think I should try to judge who should be in this religion and who shouldn't be. If they feel like they are led to be a part of this . . . I'm not going to go around asking people for their birth certificates. I figure the divinities will take care of that. If Tina Turner want to be a Buddhist or Sammy Davis want to be Jewish, I have no problem. They have to follow their Ori, and I don't think I should try to judge one way or the other."[25]

Great suspicion, speculation, and distrust remain regarding Anglo-Americans motivations for entering the religion. Some cite "the current popularity of New Age religion and health treatments," others see it as an attraction to "psychic abilities," while still others see it as a desire for power in all forms.[26] Regardless of their motivations, many Euro-Americans feel a spiritual connection to the practices of Africa's Yoruba. Some are trying to make sense of their history, as one African American priestess explained: "White Americans in the United States who are practitioners of this tradition, no matter how controversial their presence, share our history on this side of the Atlantic Ocean. They too have memories of the enslavement of Africans and indentured servitude; sweat shops, ghettos and overcoming the guilt of the actions of their fore parents. Our collective memory unites us regardless of which role our ancestors played."[27] She advises that practitioners "move beyond" the self-imposed "walls" that divide.[28] Because there are "many tributaries in the memories of our bloodstream" including

European ancestry, the religion for her represents a space of historical transcendence and is, in essence, "one of the first times a spiritual tradition provides the opportunity for people in the Western hemisphere to overcome the boundaries established by the dominant culture."[29]

I would be misrepresenting the data if I portrayed Adefunmi's viewpoints as a mere isolated case. His viewpoint is not universally embraced. Yet, a good many African Americans feel strongly that Yoruba religion is a reflection of the socially defined ethnic and racial heritage of people of African descent and that the maintenance of that heritage is their exclusive responsibility. For them, Africa functions not just as a national geography of citizenship but as a genealogical indicator of racial ancestry.

Some members of the African American priesthood strongly contend that "if you're not African, you cannot be in the tradition. . . . If you're an African, this is your birthright. That's how I teach it. That's how we present it."[30] During the course of her field research in New York City, Marta Vega interviewed a senior African American priest who "registered concern over the increase of European Americans being initiated," and in his own words pointedly addressed the issue: "White initiation is another way of colonizing us, using the privilege of race."[31] He expressed a fear that the racial discrimination and unequal power dynamics that African Americans have historically and socially endured in America could easily be mapped onto the Yoruba religious sphere. Another African American priest agreed: "Once those Europeans who are getting initiated become powerful, they are going to try to suppress those smaller houses. . . . They're going to try to take Yoruba from our children and incorporate their godchildren into their houses."[32]

Like Adefunmi, many wrestle with how to embrace this position without appearing prejudiced and antiwhite. A plea for African Americans to be "*supremely* African," it is argued, should not be read as "anti-white" but instead as a call for comprehensive immersion into the "mysteries of the African genius for its direct descendants":[33]

> We African Americans find that it is not necessary that we be anti-white, but it is necessary that we be very pro-Yoruba, very pro-African. It is necessary that we be *supremely* African, indeed. We must be conscious of who we are. We are a people who have returned to the most vital and sensitive mysteries of the African

genius. We are able to do this gracefully and successfully because we are the direct descendants of the thinkers and occultists who expounded it. Yet we have often stood silently by while another ethnic people have co-opted, usurped and capitalized on everything that our ancestors have discovered or revealed.[34]

Mercedes Cros Sandoval states that although issues of "racial and cultural heritage" may appeal to practitioners of African descent, "among whites . . . this function has never been meaningful."[35] On many levels, it is difficult to disaggregate the views of African Americans on white initiation from their historical legacy of white racism in America. For one African American priest, white initiation was an issue "not just of race but of advantage. There's a certain advantage tied into him being white and a certain disadvantage tied into me being black."[36] Another priest commented that white attraction to the Yoruba tradition involved "a very simple answer—power. Europeans are attracted to anything that has power . . . That's what it's all about."[37]

The question of white initiation is, therefore, not simply a religious issue for African Americans but a sociopolitical one as well. I discovered that interpretations of white Yoruba participation are almost always foregrounded with socioracial terminology. Like many other prominent priests, John Mason, though not rigidly dogmatic about the exclusion of white Americans, argues that given the racial geography of America and the "many generations white folks have been free to accumulate wealth," white Americans "have to at least acknowledge the fact they have profited beyond the reasonable expense of others. That's all I'm asking. Once you admit that, then we can at least make a move to how then do we use your advantage, your position, to help others gain parity."[38] Mason ultimately argues that issues of "redressing" and "retribution" are "what white initiates must be addressing."[39]

Related to this is a reluctance on the part of some members of the African American priesthood to initiate white non-Hispanic Americans. For example, Baba Medahochi recalled an extremely uncomfortable moment at a bembe when an African American priestess became possessed and told a white woman that she needed to be initiated. Medahochi remembers his ambivalence. "The priestess who was there asked the spirit who is supposed to do this? And the spirit said, 'Medahochi.' Now if I accept Obatala is supposed to be possessed in this woman then what am I supposed to do it? Say I'm not gonna do what Obatala said?"[40] On another occasion Medahochi was present during the initiation of a white person but distinctly remembers a member of the Oyotunji priesthood leaving the room.

Theologically, the residents of Oyotunji Village oppose the initiation of whites into the religion. Strong evidence of their black-nationalist heritage permeates their position. As one priest remarked, "The reason why we don't have white people in Oyotunji is because at some point we don't want their *egun* [ancestors] with our egun. We don't want to have no shit because you see his grandfather enslaved my grandfather."[41] Another Oyotunji resident summed up the official position of the village on the initiation of white Americans into the Yoruba priesthood in this way: "We despise it. We despise it because we know how aggressive the whites are and how in ten, twenty years, how they can change [the] whole complexion of our tradition, of the religion. And that is the reason we do not initiate whites and when we initiate someone this is an oath that we take—that we will not initiate anyone who is not of the African race."[42]

Oyotunji priests are not alone in their views on white initiation. Other African American–headed spiritual houses support this position, stating that they would never initiate white devotees and that those who do are "being dishonoring and disloyal to our ancestors."[43] African American practitioners were clear in their articulations that their resistance was rooted not in ideology and rhetoric but in history and experience. According to one priest, "My thing is this—if you were really interested in African traditions, you could have come to Africa three, four, five hundred years ago and gotten it. . . . Why was it necessary to come all the way to Africa to colonize it? Enslave it? Just to end up all these centuries later saying, 'Oh, wow, you've got something awesome.' Had you had your way, you would have stamped it out . . . it would have been all gone. But because of the resilience of African people . . . it still exists even in Africa and the New World. And now you are here to partake of it, but not because of anything you've done to help save it. If anything, your ancestors have tried to destroy it . . ."[44] This same priest added that he was "actually quite ashamed to say that white people are a part of this tradition because of the history of what they've done."[45] He concluded that "if they had been successful in what they were trying to do, there would be no Lucumi; there would be no Shango Baptist; there would be no Ifa."[46] In decoding this provocative issue within American Yoruba discourse, there often remains very little distance between the politics of religion and the politics of socioracial perspectives.

In recent years with the rise of electronic communication, the issues of race and initiation have been the subjects of much debate on various orisa websites on the Internet. Iya L'Orisa Yeye Olashun OladeKoju Lakesi, a graduate of Fisk University, priestess of Oshun, and author of *Iya Mi O* asks, "Shall Africans now casually join hands with their Caucasian 'brethren' on a level playing field of peace in the circle of Orisha worship?"[47] Her article quite sharply admonishes white devotees: "You, who claim to 'love' the Orisha so much. . . . Do you not realize that these are African Gods with black skin, thick lips, kinky hair, voluptuous frames. . . . Has it ever occurred to you that African people are the genetic descendants, i.e., 'chosen people' of Orisha who were created by Orisha? How deep is your love for the African Orisha whom you have never seen, when you witness the racism of your own people against African children in the incarnate world?"[48] This article conveys an overall uneasiness about the way discussions of race in America are either negated or neutralized. Lakesi also seems to challenge a perceived dissonance between the ways the meaning of whiteness is religiously negotiated in the orisa community and sociopolitically negotiated in American society.

Throughout my interviews, many African Americans accused white initiates of adopting "purist" platforms with respect to religious practice, in that they perceived continental African initiations as much more authentic than those performed in the diaspora. According to one African American priestess, many white devotees adhere to "this purist African stuff [as if] the . . . real religion . . . comes directly from Africa. A lot of whites in the religion want to have a pure African experience. If they are going to make Ocha, they're going to make Ocha in Nigeria. There is this idea that they couldn't possibly make Ocha in the United States. So there is a real kind of purity that in their minds gives a kind of superiority because [they] made Ocha on African soil . . ."[49]

Slightly nuancing this perspective, African American Yoruba contend that while the "real" may indeed have come from Africa, North American diasporic religious vocabularies of the twenty-first century are as valid as their antecedents. Within these conversations on white initiation, purity and authenticity are imbued with geographical significance located in Africa. The common perception is that white Americans entering into the tradition qualitatively measure purity, authenticity, accessibility, and acceptability and find these more readily in continental Africa, specifically Nigeria. J. Lorand Matory cites a similar phenomenon among Anglo-Brazilians, where it can be interpreted that "they have chosen to jump the queue, seeking their authorization and models directly from the African source" rather than submit to African Brazilian spiritual authority.[50]

The complicated ingredients of race and spiritual authenticity make for feelings of deep ambivalence among North American practitioners. As one practitioner remarked, "That's where the prejudice comes in because if you're practicing Santería or Lucumi or a brand that has come through the diaspora, [it] is not seen as legitimate as if you go . . . to an Ifa priest from Nigeria or a babalorisa from Africa to make your Ocha."[51] The practitioner then went on to add, "I've never been to Nigeria . . . but I wonder if you have the selling of spirituality . . . [to those who are] trying to . . . have this authentic experience and trying to buy something that really isn't for sale."[52] Another practitioner felt that although many white Americans found themselves more in initiating contexts with African Yoruba, "the deep spiritual things, the Nigerians are not giving that to the white people they're initiating" and perhaps not "giving it to African Americans either."[53] Overall, more often than not, African Americans view white initiation with great distrust and ambivalence, seeing it as a threat to the "African" integrity of Yoruba religion, undermining of the legitimacy of diaspora religious authority, and a knotty conflation of religion, race, privilege, and power in the Atlantic world. Although this phenomenon could be viewed solely as another form of North American racism and exclusivism, a more nuanced reading would view racial selectivity by African Americans as part of a larger symbolic rehumanizing stratagem that seeks to bracket any and all symbols of white presence, power, and external gaze.

Throughout my research on Anglos' practitionership in Yoruba religion, a name that resurfaced was that of Anglo-American Ifa priest Philip John Neimark, or Oluwo Fagbamilia, founder of the Ifa Foundation of North America and Ifa College. Although Neimark's textual resources can readily be found on the shelves of private devotion libraries, some African American practitioners find themselves ambivalent about his Yoruba institution-building efforts in the United States.

Despite these concerns, which are well known to them, Neimark and his wife Vassa Neimark (Iyanifa Olufadeke) have managed to create Ola

Olu, or what they deem a meaningful "Sacred land" on ten acres of land in Florida for spiritual retreats, the performance of initiations and ceremonies, and housing a teaching center. According to their web page, Neimark and his wife "have created a totally private space allowing for all ceremonial work to be done with absolute freedom on Sacred land and in Sacred Spaces upon that land. Because of this, your connection with the *Orisa* is pure and potent."[54] Referencing their narrative of Ola Olu, they contend that part of what makes this land sacred is that it remained "almost untouched, as the Native Americans used it hundreds of years ago. This area was where the runaway slaves from Georgia, Alabama, and other states found refuge with the Seminole Indians of Central Florida."[55] They go on to say that "the mixture of these cultures, historically known as Maroons, created a unique blending of Native American spirituality and the ancient spirituality of the escaped African slaves."[56] By calling 877-IfaOracle, one can gain access to the institutions, texts, and spiritual resources offered at Ola Olu. Services to the American orisa community include divination readings by e-mail or phone, initiation rites, guidance and instruction to the incarcerated, workshops and spiritual retreats, and spiritual tools imported directly from Africa or handmade by the Iyanifa herself. Their website photos ultimately depict a multiracial affiliation and clientele.

Philip John Neimark was by social profession a financial analyst and by spiritual profession a babalawo, or high priest, of Ifa.[57] A millionaire by the age of thirty, Neimark encountered the tradition by way of Santería/Lucumi in the 1970s, when, his niece recounts, he was told in a spiritual reading "that someday he must become a babalawo or die."[58] While living in Chicago, he recalls that his curiosity and interest led him to place a call to noted anthropologist and author of several Yoruba-related texts, Dr. William Bascom. According to Neimark, "After an hour on the phone, I finally blurted out, 'Dr. Bascom, you sound as if you believe in it!'" to which Bascom responded, "Mr. Neimark, all I can tell you is, it works."[59] By his own admission, Neimark does not see Santería/Lucumi as an "adaptation of *Ifa*."[60] When asked in an interview if he viewed such religions as "Voodoo, Candomble and Santeria" as being "based upon Ifa," Neimark responded, "This is simply not true. Parts of each, less than you might think, are based on Ifa's principles. The rest is a potpourri of Catholicism, French Spiritism, Fon and Congo."[61] Neimark and his wife were instead interested in finding the "roots" of Ifa, a journey which they say "resulted in re-discovering Ifa in the African Tradition . . ." and developed a close affiliation with the late Nigerian Yoruba Dr. Afolabi Epega, whom Neimark affectionately identifies as his "original mentor."[62] Since that time, Neimark has become known for his contributions to the Yoruba print genre and for his establishment of the Ifa Foundation of North America and the Ifa College, both now located in Florida. He is the author of one text on Yoruba religion, *The Way of the Orisa: Empowering Your Life Through the Ancient African Religion of Ifa* and a coedited text with Dr. Afolabi Epega, *The Sacred Ifa Oracle.* In the foreword to *The Way of the Orisa*, Epega, a "Yoruba of Africa," establishes Neimark's legitimacy as a leader among Yoruba practitioners in America, stating that "another growing group of Ifa practitioners, of which the author of this volume is a leader, encompasses members of every race and cultural background, *just as the Yoruba of Africa would have it.*"[63]

Although he is often viewed by African Americans through racialized lenses, Neimark's literary self-representation does not directly engage the issue of race. In *The Way of the Orisa*, Dr. Epega, the coeditor of Neimark's second book, discusses race primarily in the book's introduction. Epega establishes his own religious authority as a "fifth-generation African babalawo" and as the grandson of the babalowo who initiated William Bascom into the Ogboni Society in Ile-Ife, Nigeria.[64] He is related to the late David Epega, Christian minister and author of the 1931 text *The Mystery of the Yoruba Gods.*[65] Epega says of his first meeting with Neimark, "It was as if our coming together had been preordained by the orisa."[66] According to Epega, "Some wonder about the propriety of a white man participating at the highest levels of a 'black religion.' They should not question this. Ifa is not a black religion, it is an African religion originating from Ile-Ife in what is now the nation of Nigeria."[67] Having asserted the religion's origins in Ile-Ife and the ways the "Yoruba of Africa would have it," Epega seeks to assert the legitimacy of Neimark and other white devotees within the religion, using Yoruba mythology to support his view: "Oosanla, or Obatala as he is better known in the West, one of our most important orisa, was white. Ifa teaches that people of all colors were born into the earth from Ile Ife. To attempt to secularize the religion, either for personal or political purposes is to deny the teachings of Ifa and separate yourself from the reality of the makeup of the world. Ifa teaches integrating with the world in every aspect. To segregate any part is to stray from the path. . . ."[68] Epega speaks as though to a veiled audience whose protests nonetheless permeate his responses. Several African Americans have accused Epega of exploiting his identity as a Nigerian Yoruba and a direct descendant of Nigerian babalawos to lend authority to his support of white initiation. One practitioner I interviewed had strong responses to Epega's position:

> What I don't understand is members of the African priesthood turning their back on history (and in effect "the sacrifice of their Ancestors") and offering the control of Yoruba in North America to a white man. . . . Has history taught us anything about ourselves and these people? Every non-white culture on this planet has been approached by this "wolf in sheep's clothing" and paid the price of giving him their trust. Today's circumstances are no different than those of the past. The constant in-fighting that is taking place in the Yoruba community is once again opening us up to outside interference, which will inevitably lead to us losing control of our cultural heritage. I'm not saying there is no place for white people in Yoruba. I'm saying, as a matter of fact, they cannot be allowed to control the culture of another people . . . again.[69]

Another African American responded more directly to Neimark's literary influence within the tradition: "Now we have . . . the whites being initiated, writing books, like Neimark and saying he's an authority on Ifaism, an advisor. The book is a very nice book, but he didn't discover anything that was said in there; that's been passed from father to son for centuries. He just put it into a book form. . . . Now he's the founder of the first Ifa institution in America."[70]

Neimark's perceived status as a white authority figure on Yoruba, along with a growing symbolic number of white participants in the religion, has forced African Americans to interrogate the definitions that for them define Yoruba religion as African and to explore issues of status and authority. One African American Obatala priest remarked of Neimark, "He's opted for Orisha but in that he has seen himself as some messiah. He's cast himself not in a small role but in a large role. He basically has crowned himself. He has placed this crown upon his head. It's a very interesting way in which history sort of repeats itself. . . . He uses the Judeo-Christian model and then puts an African face on it . . ."[71]

In the midst of this racially charged discourse, Neimark, however, positions himself and his wife as American practitioners who seek to restore inclusiveness to Yoruba religion citing in their own past how they have both "objected to the racial, sexual and gender discrimination" they previously encountered in Santería/Lucumi. They expressed their commitment to counter "the Eurocentric/Afrophobic viewpoint of most of Academia" concerning the tradition.[72] The couple consider themselves forerunners in a movement called "American Ifa," which they say "is the result of more than 25 years of study and examination of the ancient philosophy of the Yoruba culture of West Africa."[73] According to the Neimarks, one of the major tenets of America Ifa is that "Timeless and Universal Truths must apply to *all* people, regardless of race, nationality, gender or sexual orientation, in order to be valid."[74] Within American Ifa, they are deliberately "stripping away the Nationalism, fear, dependence and contradictions that have adhered themselves like barnacles to the hull of this beautiful and powerful philosophy. It is about effectively freeing these basic universal truths to function in the Western society we are part of." Neimark and his wife credit the Ifa Foundation of North America for having "initiated the first female Iyanifa, the first openly gay Babalawo" in an effort "to restore Ifa to the inclusive world view it was created to provide."[75] In the heterogeneous world of American Yoruba, however, these messages are not received without contestation and scrutiny. In spite of the many perceptions of Neimark, he remains among the growing number of prosperous Anglo-Americans who, through the spiritual lineage of Neimark and others, now participate in North America's Yoruba religious cultures.

Finally, within this discussion it is important to mention those moments of approval over the course of my research when names of white devotees of a previous generation were favorably invoked and these believers had distinguished themselves as strong advocates of the tradition. Among them were Judith Gleason, who was initiated by Asunta Serrano and is said to be the first white non-Hispanic initiate in North America; Susan Wenger, a German artist who helped to restore the sacred groves of Osun in Oshogbo, Nigeria; and Robert Farris Thompson, a scholar who has made significant contributions to Yoruba religious and historical studies. Scholars such as William Bascom, Maya Deren, and Robert Farris Thompson were all initiated during the course of their research.[76] After reading Thompson's work, one African American priest recalled his initial response: "How can you stand there and talk about these words that I have been wanting to hear all of my life? . . . God, I wish he was black. But, of course, he is not. But I love the guy anyhow."[77] Another African American Yoruba priest said of Robert Farris Thompson, "Well, you know that brother should have been born black."[78] What these comments most revealed was a sense of respect and integrity they attributed to Robert Farris Thompson for his works and active ceremonial and ritual presence within the Yoruba tradition throughout the years. Similar sentiments were voiced about the "respectful dialogue" posture of scholars such as John Pemberton III, Pierre Verger, Ulli Bier, and William Bascom.[79] According to one practitioner, "The literary contributions to Orisha worship of Bascom, Verger, Bier, and Thompson are noteworthy, but history documents that these *Oyimbo* are a rare breed among their people, and an unusual exception rather that the rule."[80]

Because social and geographical locations are ultimately never inseparable from modes of religious expression, Yoruba identity has come to embody new meaning in the United States. It is a site where the symbols of what it means to be "white" and "black" and "African" are constantly in flux and negotiated through American social cues, norms, and beliefs. The section that follows will examine the role of ancestral veneration and its function within this challenging terrain of racialized positioning and African American re-ownership.

Ancestor Veneration and the Re-Ownership of Africa

For many African Americans, ancestor veneration substitutes for genealogical precision, providing an anterior lineage beyond the United States. Through valuing the ancestors or the "divinized dead," African Americans are able to symbolically re-own Africa in powerfully spiritual and metaphorical ways.[81] The Africa that most held spiritual currency among African Americans was not modern and contemporary Africa, but ancient Africa—the Africa that their ancestors had inhabited and were snatched away from, whose sacred religious systems predated Christianity and Western modernity.

Ancestral re-ownership of Africa links twenty-first-century African Americans to a historically complex physical, spiritual, and racial geography. According to Adefunmi, ancestors are the "racial parents" of African

Americans and are the vital source of their reconnection to Africa.[82] For Yoruba Americans, ancestors are understood as the known and unknown departed spirits of those who have gone before them within a direct familial lineage. These ancestors, or egun, as practitioners refer to them, are bound in a spiritual relationship with their descendants and provide them with guidance and protection in their lives. They are seen as the foundation of communal identity and the moral arbiters of community affairs. In all, they are spiritual beings from the past who have a hand in shaping present conditions and future destinies. According to Adefunmi, "The ancestors are important because for a society to survive, to manage itself, and to decide what is good for it or what is bad for it, one has to consult those who lived previously."[83]

Because the ancestors are the spiritual mediators between an American present and an African past, African Americans place a great deal of emphasis on their reverence, linking them to destiny, community, and identity. According to Adefunmi, "Whatever an individual is to become, we attribute to our ancestors. . . . Our ancestors are our makers, our creators. And for [this] reason, then the ancestors become sacred if we preserve their customs, their laws, their ideals, their cuisine, their attire, all these things they discovered, they advanced, and they developed for the benefit of their descendants. If those things are lost, then of course, that community of people are going to suffer."[84]

I once asked Adefunmi what aspect of the Yoruba tradition most appealed to him, to which he quickly replied, "Of course, the worship of ancestors, because this explains who we really are as a people."[85] Along similar lines, Oyotunji Village's Chief Akintobe remarked, "One of the most important things that people should get out of this is ancestral custom and tradition: . . . How are we going to govern ourselves? And how are we going to allow ourselves to be governed? And by what dictates? By our own personal whims . . . or by summoning our ancestors back. . . . We're still searching for a certain identity which is not superimposed on us by anyone."[86]

In Yoruba cosmology, the ancestors and the moral order are interconnected. Issues of morality, honor, ethics, and virtue are governed largely by the ancestors. According to African American Yoruba priest Baba Ifa Karade, ancestors "provide the ethics and worldview by which adherents to the culture must abide . . . for the development of the self and culture."[87]

FIGURE 23.
Egungun ancestor masquerade dancer at Oyotunji African Village. Photograph courtesy of author.

African American practitioners I encountered constructed ancestral shrines as mediums of sacred power.[88] According to John Mason, "the shrine serves as a definite meeting place between the deceased and his or her family. At the shrines, loved ones leave offerings, speak with the dead, and ask for special favors."[89] According to African American priestess Luisah Teish, for African American practitioners the ancestral shrine "becomes 'sacred space,' a place between the physical and spiritual world where the Ancestors and the living can communicate in peace."[90] Complex issues of identity and origin are resolved spiritually through sophisticated understanding of the ancestors. Thus, many African Americans in the United States confess a sentiment similar to that of African American Yoruba priestess Iya-Sokoya Onayemi Karade, who asks: "What country in Africa did I come from? Who were my people? What was their religion? These are but a few questions we can ask about our origin. Sadly, these and many other inquiries regarding our ancestry will go unanswered forever, due to the crushing blows of slavery; blows which have severed the umbilical cord of African descendants from the womb of Mother Africa."[91]

For African Americans, the ritual veneration of ancestors, both known and unknown, helps to reattach the severed genealogical cord from Africa. For African American Yoruba, ancestors embody the power of transcendence, the power to reconnect to an original moment in Africa that predates its diaspora. Africa thus functions as an originary space of authenticity before the amputating effects of slavery caused dismemberment and separation. The ancestors, therefore, become vital in the complex process of reattaching African American Yoruba to their distant beginnings. One practitioner summed it up this way: "Molefi Asante said if you're gonna worship anybody as a black person, worship your ancestors, and that's something I firmly believe. I think we need to overemphasize ancestral rituals and create new ones for the diaspora. I think that would help us to be reborn. That rebirth that we're looking for in Christianity—that never really happens anyway—I think if we really begin to design rituals around ancestors and really took the authority to do it, we would be reborn."[92]

The relationship between African American Yoruba and their ancestors can be complicated by the need to disaggregate the ancestors into what Aina Olomo calls the "elder ancestors" of Africa and those of the diaspora.[93] Olomo believes that historically there were "elder ancestors" who maintained an uninterrupted lineage on the continent of Africa, escaping slavery, and those who did not. The memories of African Americans' New World ancestors "are not shared with the ancestors who stayed on the continent of Africa."[94] African American Yoruba are acutely aware that their dual communities of ancestors are not experientially synonymous. According to Aina Olomo, "The pain and sorrows of the African holocaust, slavery, loss of name, family and culture are not part of the genetic memory of Yoruba born on African soil; nor is the will and strength it takes to re-build, re-gain, and re-establish our spiritual heritage imprinted on the collective soul of our brothers and sisters who remained at home."[95]

One of the most innovative contributions African Americans have made to Yoruba practice has been the divinatory ritual of the roots readings. Performed under the auspices of Ifa divination,[96] a roots reading is said to determine "where an individual's ancestors came from."[97]African American Yoruba who have had these readings performed say that they trace lineage connections back to Africa and identify specific ethnic origins of a person's ancestry. An early researcher of Oyotunji African Village stated at the outset of his study that "they have attempted to legitimize their ancestry, not by strict genealogical means, but by identifying with traditional Yoruba practices and customs which they have to some degree defined."[98] This is true in part because spiritual roots readings have in many ways helped to provide an important avenue for legitimizing African ancestry. As anthropologist Kamari Clarke insightfully remarks, the goal of roots readings is to "recover client ancestral histories. . . . It reproduces a canon of Yoruba divinatory structure while reshaping the terms by which Yoruba history is re-signified in new locations."[99]

The power of these roots readings lies in how priests and priestesses incorporate the outcomes of these readings into ancestral discourses on lineage and embrace the multiple ethnic identities revealed that link them to Africa. Roots readings function as a divinatory forum for addressing these probing genealogical questions. Within the context of roots readings they participate in a ritual contract where the genetic hybridity of African Americans (which may include European ancestry but is not emphasized) is disaggregated, allowing African ethnicities to become sacrosanct. For example, after receiving a roots reading, Baba Medahochi understood his ancestral ethnicity as follows: "Mother's side—Ewe from Togo. Father's side—Lipe people from northern Nigeria. I'll accept that. It may not be accurate but it's satisfactory."[100] Medahochi's approach to the ritual of roots readings, like many African American Yoruba, embodies a spiritual pragmatism that enables him to be both practical and judicious in his lived approach to religious knowledge.

Reflecting on the complex origins of African American ancestry, J. Lorand Matory argues that for many African Americans in the New World, the exclusive emphasis on African ancestors is by and large a choice that is made in order to inscribe an African identity that is often maintained more by ideological than by biological truths.[101] Despite this inherent tension, roots readings support the efforts of African American Yoruba to see themselves through what Baba Ifa Karade calls "ancestral eyes" and use this concentrated lens to understand themselves as African in the Atlantic world.[102] It represents a diasporic consciousness rooted in transcendence. By tracing their ancestors back to a time before their New World encounter, they are able to transcend America as the ultimate source of identity and replace it with a primordial preslavery Africa with alternative possibilities. For Karade, as for most African American Yoruba, Africa speaks to the healing of "ancestral rupture." As an African American ontologically displaced from Africa, Karade revealed, "I felt the horrid depths of slavery. It existed beyond the academic, beyond the revolutionary, beyond the inspired hatred toward the enslavers. Beyond it all I found the deepest aspect of my African self."[103] Ultimately Karade attests, "I have to know not only about Africa, I have to know who my people are. All of this is . . . what makes it possible for us to say that we can link ourselves to a definite past . . . something that's outside of the cultural context of that country called America. We're no longer Americans in that sense . . ."[104]

John Mason, Yoruba Reversionism, and the African American Textual Movement Since Adefunmi

Through his early texts in the 1960s, Adefunmi offered an interpretation of Yoruba religion he hoped would be useful in shaping a new religious identity for African Americans in the United States. These works were among the earliest treatises on Yoruba religion an African American authored for an African American readership in the United States. Today, African American Yoruba literature has grown to include the works of dozens of scholars and scholar-practitioners, such as Babalosa John Mason, Baba Ifa Karade, Mikelle Omari-Tunkara, Mary Cuthrell Curry, Luisah Teish, Marta Vega, Iyanla Vanzant, Lionel Scott, Ra Ifagbemi, Lloyd Weaver, Ayobunmi Sangode, Diedre Badejo, Oluweri Egundyao Onisegun, Djisovi Ikukomi Eason, and many others. Collectively, they provide an African American Yoruba textual hermeneutic that is informed by a distinct American social location, transatlantic sensibility, and diasporic consciousness.

As discussed in chapter 4, texts have become central to the transmission of Yoruba-related information in the diaspora. Scholars such as J. Lorand

Matory and Mercedes Cros Sandoval acknowledge the influence these texts have not only for North American practitioners but also for those in Brazil and Cuba. Matory acknowledges that "the priests and followers of the Yoruba-Atlantic traditions frequently own and read books . . . written by university-trained scholars."[105] More important, Matory makes a profound case for the ways texts can influence religious practice and devotee orientation. According to Matory:

> The degree to which . . . books become catechisms or procedural guides is variable, but it is clear that many priests use the information that scholars bring, particularly when those scholars possess a credible claim to information from the African "motherland." . . . Our analyses are often employed as models of African "tradition," which can be used to include and elevate particular segments of New-World religious communities. Therefore, our analyses can be used to marginalize other segments of those communities and to de-legitimise existing practices. Our influence can be powerful, whether we are committed to studying our field sites honestly, or we are committed to misrepresenting them as allegories of some ideal that we are recommending to an audience unable to check our facts.[106]

Similar to Matory, Cros Sandoval argues that "academic literature . . . opened new avenues for priests and priestesses to learn about their religion in a nontraditional manner."[107] She contends that the proliferation of practitioner texts in the forms of "books, manuals, newspapers, and newsletters," combined with the organization of formal conferences, has enabled orisa devotees to participate in a larger "literary tradition" whereby "they communicate, learn, and expand their knowledge about Santeria, the Yoruban religion, and their practices."[108]

In more recent years, texts have also been seen as important vehicles of cultural preservation. Their distribution and use by some practitioners have in many ways resisted a fixed, romantic ethos that definitively classifies Yoruba religion as essentially an oral tradition. One practitioner commented, "I just don't think we have the luxury not to be writing things down, not to participate in certain forms of modern Western culture when it comes on to this. People say, 'Oh we're an oral culture, and we'll lose something.' I just think we will really lose if we don't participate in some of these media for preserving culture and heritage and for passing down a legacy and a tradition."[109] Other African American practitioners worry that in the United States the religion might assume a traditional American denominational structure.[110] Thus, the growing textualization of Yoruba religious practice and information, some believe, may entrench orthodoxy within the tradition. There exists a degree of fear about becoming a "print-based theology."[111] Scholars such as Olabiyi Babalolo Yai are concerned that "book knowledge" may be an insufficient source of "religious knowledge" because for him "it is void of ase," or "vital life force," and may possess "misunderstandings, mistranslations, and Eurocentrism."[112] He shares the fear of several practitioners that an increasing textualization of the tradition may have "doctrinaire and even dogmatic consequences."[113] Coupled with one practitioner's sentiments on the challenges of textuality were concerns over what I call cultural orthodoxy within the tradition particularly as it related to bodily aesthetic representations of Africa. According to Priestess Ayoka, "We don't need to . . . dress in an African way to claim legitimacy as people who follow orisa . . . I would hate to see that become some sort of orthodoxy because . . . this religion is not only about the outward, the physical. African-ness and orisa is not the clothes you wear. What I worry about is the same reason I worry about Afrocentrism: who is defining what it means?"[114] Biblical scholar Velma Love explores the concern of some practitioners that "Yoruba religion in the West might become another book religion."[115] Love quotes an African American priestess who reveals the emerging religious practice of "reading books and quoting oracles as if they were biblical scriptures."[116]

Baba Ifatunji, like other Yoruba priests, is able to draw more fluid connections between his Baptist upbringing and orientation toward the Bible and his current capacity as an Ifa diviner. He sees the Odu of Ifa not as a "fixed entity" but similar to the ways in which his Baptist father saw the Bible, as a "roadmap."[117] For Ifatunji, both bodies of sacred literature enable African Americans to interpose their "actual experiences," within these texts, making them "pertinent to us as African people in America."[118] Ifatunji says he was taught that "every time the Odu fell on the map, the story continues" and can be "retold," perhaps ultimately welcoming the adding of new diaspora odus to the existing Ifa divination corpus.[119] Ifatunji, like Djisovi Ikukomi Eason, understands Ifa texts as "mythohistorical" and "transcultural belonging to the collective memory of Yoruba and New World peoples."[120] Whether it is a new interpretation of the odus of Ifa literature or the application of Apatakis and proverbial stories of the orisa as strategies for the African American psychological healing and development, as clinical psychologist and Obatala priest Lionel Scott suggests, members of the African American priesthood are committed to a distinct African American hermeneutic in interpreting Yoruba literature.[121]

Serious discussions on the production of New World orisa sacred literature must include that of scholar-practitioner Babalosa John Mason, 1999 recipient of the distinguished John Simon Guggenheim Memorial Foundation Fellowship. Mason is an important scholar and priest who has both authored and coauthored close to a dozen texts that challenge rigid conceptions of Yoruba orthodoxy or what he calls Ifaism. He finds great value in recording and documenting New World ritual practices as valid traditions of Yoruba expression. His books have made a powerful textual impact on the diasporic world and can be found on the shelves of priests and scholars from New York City to Salvador de Bahia.

Speaking biographically, Mason once stated, "I was going to be a [Roman Catholic] priest before I became a *real* priest." Within his capacity as a priest of Obatala, he has written numerous texts that emphasize the historical, theological, and ritual aspects of Yoruba's New World expressions.[122] Anthropologist Sandra Barnes says fondly of John Mason that he is an "insider-intellectual" who "writes prolifically and movingly of the historical and contemporary meanings of religious experience taken from his own training in Afro-Cuban and African American faiths."[123] In 1985, his *Four New World Yoruba Rituals*, which explores Afro-Atlantic ritual performance, ushered in a new generation in African American Yoruba literature.[124]

For more than two decades, Mason has attempted to shed light on the cross-fertilization of the orisa tradition from Cuba to the United States.[125] He particularly emphasizes the importance of the Afro-Cuban cultural heritage, one he personally shares, in the development of the tradition in the United States. At the same time, Mason seeks to dispel the myth that "Spanish" as opposed to "African" culture is Cuba's dominant resource. According to Mason, for Cuba, Yoruba traditions are "the only culture worth exporting. . . . What they export besides tobacco and sugar is African culture."[126] Conceptually, Mason understands his work as

"Yoruba Reversionism." According to Mason, "You go back to your history, your institutions and rules of engagement, decorum. . . . You take those institutions and structures and set them in place with whatever adjustments . . . and in the current context ask, 'How are we going to make that work in this arena?' And how do we then keep vigilant so that we constantly keep it fresh and fulfilling the needs?"[127]

Adefunmi and Mason each established a publishing institution to facilitate the publication of their work. Adefunmi founded African Theological Archministry in the early 1960s, and Mason founded the Yoruba Theological Archministry over a decade later in the late 1970s. Both archministries function as important institutional resources committed to disseminating printed materials, providing lecture series and classes, conducting workshops, and offering language instruction. Adefunmi chose the panethnic designator African, rather than Yoruba, for his archministry because, in his own words, "I knew that many [African] religions were gathering together . . . and so I didn't think that we should be incorporating and excluding any of the African religions. And so, if we wanted any kind of indigenous African religion, we would be ready and prepared to accept it and to propound it so. Hence, the African Theological Archministry."[128] According to Mason, the goal of the Yoruba Theological Archministry is to "produce the best information for the orisa communities, here and wherever, who are interested in knowing about orisa traditions as they've been maintained especially between Cuban and the United States—that's our prime objective—documenting and using that information as a base for activism in terms of changing injustice. . . ."[129] Mason attributes his early interest in the world of texts to his spiritual godfather and mentor, Christopher Oliana, who was an ardent reader and whose extensive library Mason later came to inherit. Mason's publishing agenda is part of his "life's work of creating new images of the Orisa."[130] As "New World traditionalists," African Americans like Mason are continually reshaping the contours of the Yoruba tradition to meet the needs of their local American context.[131]

In *Black Gods: Orisa Studies in the New World*, published in 1985, Mason acknowledges the multilingual challenges many New World devotees, especially African Americans, encountered early on. English-speaking African Americans quite often found themselves at a disadvantage when trying to learn from Spanish-speaking devotees. Gary Edwards describes this quandary: "The religion had passed through many languages. Prayers, ceremonies, and songs had been somewhat altered by the demands of Spanish-speaking Cubans, which presented little problem if you spoke Spanish, but a large problem if you spoke only English."[132] In partial response to this dilemma, Mason, who is fluent in both English and Spanish, has dedicated his works to bridging many of the linguistic barriers faced by non-Latino African Americans in the United States. For example, *Orin Orisa: Songs for Selected Heads* provided African Americans with *orisa* songs that had been previously inaccessible.[133] Mason sees his corpus of books as resources, not as commodities, and thus is steadfast in his commitment not to "treat religion as a business." Ultimately he avows, "Religion is what I believe, not what I sell."[134]

In his works, Mason intentionally emphasizes the diasporic context and not Africa, focusing on Yoruba religion in the New World, because, he argues, African Americans have been in the New World some four hundred years. He makes a compelling case that the local heritage of African Americans is rooted in the diaspora, therefore, the "link in terms of orisa people in the United States is between Cuba and here."[135] Above all else, Mason is seeking to leave a textual legacy that will endure. He explains his literary goals: "I don't write these books to try and proselytize people. These are textbooks for my community. And it's not as though this is the law. I say, 'Read this'; now this gives a basis for asking intelligent questions, as Chris [Oliana] used to say. All you want to do is help people ask intelligent questions."[136]

Mason is ultimately interested in ways of reconstituting "spiritual authenticity" and making it work practically within African American communities.[137] For Mason, this spiritual authenticity lies in Yoruba traditions and their ability to offer African American communities a new set of "master symbols" that emphasize not their innate depravity, as does Western Christianity, but their inherent divinity.[138] In his work, Mason hopes to help African Americans exercise their own sense of purpose and agency and establish a foundation from which to expand the boundaries of the tradition while simultaneously challenging the ownership of Yoruba religion by any single ethnic discourse.

Orisa and Astrology:
A North American Improvisational Expression

As we will see in the sections that follow, theological innovations such as astrological interpretations of the orisa, religious plurality, and unbounded admixture of African spiritualities often work together to form a cohesive, textured, and flexible expression of orisa devotion in North America. Although it is not a dominant theological vocabulary with which all African Americans articulate their Yoruba identity, astrology is present within the North American tradition and is worthy of examination. Oseijeman Adefunmi very early on began to associate orisa energy with astronomical and astrological entities. Yoruba religion, as understood by Adefunmi was "an African form of astrology. . . . All of the prototypes of the gods are traceable to astrological powers and astrological characteristics."[139] He believed that because "all religions are based upon astronomy and astrology," one could infer certain corresponding characteristics between the orisa and astrological entities.[140] When asked to speak at the historic hundredth anniversary of the World's Parliament of Religion in Chicago in 1993, Adefunmi declared, "All religions are based upon astrology, deeply encased in the ethnology of the nation or tribe which created [the religion] as a means of cultural preservation."[141]

African American practitioners who find these associations meaningful are able to gain insightful information from pairing the twelve astrological sun signs with a corresponding orisa. They seem able to make more textured assessments of human and orisa attributes and personalities if astrological, planetary, and in some instances, numerological couplings are known: Babaluaiye (Capricorn/Saturn/13); Oya (Aquarius/Uranus/9); Olokun (Pisces/Neptune/7); Shango (Aries/Mars/6); Osun (Taurus, Libra/ Venus/5); Yemonja (Cancer/Moon/7); Ifa-Orunmila (Leo/Sun/16); Esu-Elegba (Gemini, Virgo/Mercury/1 or 3); Ogun (Scorpio/Pluto/3); and Obatala (Sagittarius/Jupiter/8).[142] For many African American Yoruba, Yoruba religion and astrology overlap. Many contend that astrological systems and religious systems seemingly rooted in the sacred sciences of Africa are in fact complementary.

For African American practitioners, astrology is understood as North African and Egyptian in origin, and because this metaphysical system was historically understood as a system for divination, one practitioner was able to view astrology "just as valuable as the Odus" of the Ifa divination system.[143] Adefunmi, like African American priestess Luisah Teish, affirms the historical importance of astrology within the African American Yoruba tradition. In her discussion of Voodoo priests in eighteenth- and nineteenth-century New Orleans, Teish remarks that "these Nago, Fon, Ibo, and Congo worshippers both aided and handicapped by Creolization knew the rudiments of astrology, the curing properties of herbs, and divined with pebbles and bones."[144] In her work, Teish uses astrology to periodize historical moments and contends that we are now living in the transitional era between the "Piscean" and "Aquarian Ages." In her understanding this means that "much of the past must die" and that "some ancient practices must be revised and made useful in the present."[145]

Moreover, astrological principles have expanded to Yoruba interpretations of racial designations and characteristics, which can be understood through planetary correspondence. For example, Adefunmi posits that Africans are a "Piscean" race. Governed by the astrological water sign of Pisces and what he sees as its Yoruba counterpart Olokun, the orisa of deep waters, the African race is as a consequence more inclined toward things of the spirit.[146] According to astrological principles as understood by Adefunmi, "Neptune or Olokun is the planet of intuition, hypersensitivity, imagination. . . . It signifies those of an artistic, mystical, or highly sensitive nature. . . ."[147] Conversely, the planetary nature of the European or Caucasian race is supposedly rooted in the planet Mars and ruled by the sun sign of Aries. Ogun, or the *orisa* of iron and war, is the Yoruba correspondent in this configuration and as such, "As the God of War, Mars represents Passion, Desire, Energy, Assertiveness, Courage, Initiative. It signifies young men, those in the Armed Forces or the police or those who work with Fire, Iron or Steel. . . . Its action is to Energize, Stimulate, Intensify, Inflame, Aggravate. . . . Its glyph represents the cross of materiality oriented in a definite direction, exalted over the circle of the spirit."[148] Because Neptune and Mars are understood as cosmic opposites in character and nature, its accompanying African and European racial correspondents are cosmic opposites in nature as well. Adefunmi deduces, "The differences between these two signs and their planets are so profound and so contrary that a harmonious, common cultural or political destiny by their subjects is totally unrealizable."[149] His fundamental conclusion is that "the transformation from cosmic energy through astronomical mythology to racial image is how we may trace religion in general and the Yoruba religion in particular."[150]

Throughout my research, I found it quite useful to peruse the libraries of African American Yoruba practitioners as a way of gauging their literary orientation to the religion. On many of their bookshelves, works such as *The Complete Astrologer*; Grant Lewis' *Astrology for the Millions*; Ronald Davison's *Astrology*; Geraldine Thorster's *God Herself: The Female Roots of Astrology*; Thelma Balfour's *Black Sun Signs: An African American Guide to the Zodiac*, and numerous related texts often sat side by side with books on orisa thought and practice. According to African American Yoruba priest and diviner Akintobe, "There's a similarity, if you read up on astrology. If you have a good foundation in astrology, then the orisa is not that much different. So in divination you'll have a good knowledge on how to divine and combinations, per se, because you have a knowledge of astrology. Some people can just look at you and say, you're a Pisces, you're a Virgo and they start running things down."[151] Even in newsletters published by African American Yoruba practitioners, one may find advertisements offering such astrology services such as constructing "natal charts, progressions, etc. . . ."[152] Moreover, early on Adefunmi devised a way of providing offerings to the Orisa through astrological energies. For example, when Adefunmi was in need of money to further the vision of Oyotunji Village, he formulated a ritual that "began by drawing a big zodiac on his living room floor and then [he] took certain of the gods and placed them in positions on the zodiac which corresponded with the money positions in astrology. He then lit some candles and began a chant while he offered the Orishas some wine and other spirits" and in the end "received favorable answers" and "was firmly convinced the Orishas worked."[153]

The inclusion of astrology alongside Yoruba religious concepts has been met with uncertainty by some practitioners. For example, in the introduction to John Mason's text, *Black Gods*, he writes: "Some people believe that Yoruba religious belief has a definite relationship to astrology. However, the authors of this study could find no evidence in any of the literature that explicitly proves that Yoruba religious belief, or tradition, has any substantial link to astrology."[154] Mason does admit that the Yoruba cosmic view of the world includes "consideration of the sun, the moon, the comets, the stars, the rainbow, and all other phenomena that appear in the firmament, but these elements are not dealt with in the same way that one would deal with the heavenly bodies in astrology."[155]

Within lived Yoruba religious contexts, the vocabulary of astrology is often present in vernacular conversations that reflect the interchangeability of orisa and devotee personalities. For example, I witnessed such references as "You know she'll change on you in a minute; she's so Oya," or "Don't let him get mad at you because you know he's Shango," or "You know them Elegbas can be so two-faced," or "Girl, you better watch your man around that Oshun." Within this interplay, the orisa deities replace the astrological sun signs, not in some trite and superficial way, but by becoming complex indicators and associations of human personality and nature.

In my fieldwork and studies of the Yoruba in Nigeria, I uncovered no concrete evidence that Nigerian Yoruba adopt astrological or planetary correspondents as a way of gaining greater understandings of human or orisa personalities.[156] J. Lorand Matory, in his article "Purity and Privilege in a Black Atlantic Nation: Yoruba 1930–1950," was one of the few studies I found briefly referencing a connection between Nigerian Yoruba and astrology: "Ifa is a corruption of the ancient Religions and Astrology."[157] Along with Matory, Abayomi Cole, in "Astrological Geomancy in Africa," examines the relationship between the Yoruba form of divination, Ifa, and astrology. According to Cole, "This accounts for the sixteen palm nuts used in Yoruba divination—all corresponding to the twelve houses of the heavens and two geomantic witnesses and one geomantic judge and one grand judge obtained by the permutation of the judge, the fifteenth figure, with the figure of the first house, all equal to sixteen figures."[158] Wande Abimbola, however, contends that astrology "was never an important part of our own religion in Africa" and that "to be sure, we have some rudimentary ideas about the stars and the moon, but they are not an important part of our belief and divination system."[159] Because my interests in astrology and orisa were by and large not comparative, my North American observations do not preclude the fact that astrology and planetary phenomena may indeed play into the world view of other global diaspora Yoruba communities. I wanted, however, to highlight its complementary use and that of other metaphysical philosophies alongside African American Yoruba religious thought in North America.

Because religious traditions have such permeable boundaries, according to Donald Cosentino, "the flirtation of African religions with European mysticisms has been largely unanalyzed, neglecting a major influence on the evolution of Vodou and Santeria, and a fascinating field of comparison with parallel flirtations in Yoruba culture."[160] These religious "flirtations" surface in Yoruba American practice in the form of Eastern mysticism as well. The New Jersey Ile Tawo Lona of Baba Ifa Karade is perhaps one example where Hindu chakra concepts, yoga, meditation, and Chinese

Tai Chi martial art forms are cultivated as essential components of a disciplined Yoruba life. Karade's godson in the tradition, Baba Akinkugbe Karade, recognizes that "others may have difficulty with Tai Chi as part of an Ifa Temple," but "when one notes the purpose of Ifa is to place one in a state of alignment with [one's] Ori, its purpose within the Ifa contexts becomes apparent."[161] African American Yoruba like those in Karade's Ile Tawo Lona demonstrate that although Yoruba religion is the central axis of religious orientation for them, it is not at the exclusion of Eastern mystical knowledge or Central African Bakongo practices such as "scratching" that impart additional spiritual significance and wisdom.[162] As we will see in the next section, in this posture of openness, African Americans are able to find "unity in diversity" as they draw upon a multilayered wealth of theological resources and ritual practices that ultimately inform their own distinct meaning of Yoruba religion in North America.

"Finding Unity in Diversity": Toward a Vision of Afrikan Spiritual Unity

"Our ancestors have made a way out of no way; we brought together everything we could to continue our survival. . . . Nobody can tell me that some of the things our ancestors did (i.e. synchronizing/blending/creating spiritual systems) was wrong, because it was effective."[163] Baba Medahochi's conceptual notion of Afrikan Spiritual Unity seeks to acknowledge and affirm the rich diaspora spiritual legacies created and maintained over centuries by African Americans throughout and beyond enslavement. Although a part of the Yoruba priesthood, he and his supporters are not willing to discard those spiritual traditions produced by black North Americans as forms of sustenance, resistance, and survival against internal dehumanization. Because diasporaed Africans were able to engage in their own forms of religious agency in North America, Baba Medahochi wants to ensure that African Americans see the black southern "seer" as valid as the Yoruba babalawo or the African American root doctor as valid as the trained Yoruba herbalist and that the American ancestors of African Americans be comparably venerated and revered as those in Africa.

This philosophy, which Medahochi shares with his spiritual teacher, Oba Oseijeman Adefunmi, involves the freedom to draw upon the diverse sacred resources of both the continent of Africa and those produced by the African diaspora as a way of creating a venerated corpus of religious practices. The concept of "Afrikan" or "New Afrikan" has become a crucial trope for theorizing the complexity of African American Yoruba identity in the twenty-first century. For many African American Yoruba, the concept affirms a connection to the continent of Africa while at the same time establishing a distinct Afrikan identity that acknowledges the Middle Passage, enslavement, displacement, diaspority, the blending of many ethnicities, and religious and cultural localism, as well as issues of rupture, transplantation, amalgamation, and innovation often accompanied by a longing for reconciliation. New Afrikan also denotes social location outside the continent of Africa and awareness that a new transethnic identity must be negotiated from a position of geographical exteriority. Afrikan Spiritual Unity unites people of African descent across diverse religious boundaries with a central goal of what Medahochi calls the "retribalization" of African diasporic people throughout the Atlantic.[164]

African people experienced what historian of religion Sterling Stuckey calls a "strange detribalizing process" in the Atlantic world. Stuckey believes this allowed black communities in the diaspora "for the first time in their history to think of the oneness of African peoples and to perceive practically the whole of the African continent as a single entity."[165] Similarly, theologian Dianne Stewart argues that diasporic people who arrived on slave ships were "the *first* Africans" in the modern world:

> African identity emerged first among those populations that became enslaved laborers in the Americas and the Caribbean between the early 16th through the late 19th century. Africans who remained on the continent, for the most part, were not forced to reckon with identities beyond their familial, clan, and ethnic identities until the colonial period set in across the continent during the 19th century. However, Africanness meant something very specific to the groups of captives who were racialized as "African," "Negro," or "Black" people commencing much earlier than the 19th century. The enslaved and their descendants did not only have to reckon with this identity as one thrust upon them; they actively claimed an African identity very early as can be seen in the monikers they chose for their clubs, organizations, institutions, movements, etc. How else do we understand Maria Stewart's pleas to her

"fellow sons and daughters of Africa" in her famous speeches, or the appearance of the identifier *African* in the names of so many church denominations, literary clubs and social movements? They shaped a diasporic identity both out of their shared experience of compelled alienation from Africa and collective resistance to the sources of that alienation. This diasporic African identity transcends ethnicity and even race for it encompasses the two and much, much more that emerges from what can only be called a dynamic and at times elusive experience of being Black in the Americas and the Caribbean.[166]

Historian Evelyn Brooks Higginbotham makes a similar observation when she argues, "In the crucible of the Middle Passage and American slavery, the multiple linguistic, tribal, and ethnic divisions among Africans came to be forged into a single, common ancestry."[167] Thus, the concept of Afrikan Spiritual Unity embraces the multiplicity of religious world views that these ethnically diverse Africans transported to the New World. In a radical inversion of former notions that viewed tribal and ethnic diversity as sources of contention and division, Afrikan Spiritual Unity posits an alternative orthodoxy that emphasizes spiritual pluralism and what Medahochi calls mystical retribalization.

One of Baba Medahochi's primary claims is that as a diasporic people descended from "at least 100 different ethnic groups stolen from the motherland," it is unrealistic to expect that "'doing work' strictly from one Afrikan spiritual tradition is the only way to activate the healing, transformation, and ascension of the Afrikan-American spirit."[168] For this reason, Afrikan Spiritual Unity remains flexible, dynamic, and adaptable to the contemporary needs of African Americans in the United States. Within the movement for Afrikan Spiritual Unity, there is no pretense that an exact replica of an ancient African spirituality is possible. Instead, it values "collective wisdom" and honors the "diversity and spiritual power" of diaspora ancestors' capacities "not only to survive but also to thrive in what were once strange cities and plantations."[169] More important, since continental ancestors were also historical victims of the same atrocities of slavery, Middle Passage, and diaspora, Afrikan Spiritual Unity allows Nigerian Yoruba to orient themselves around this inclusive spiritual framework through valuing the spiritual traditions of those in the diaspora who would also be a part of their ancestral lineage.

By the twenty-first century, the black Atlantic discourse surround-
ing African-expressed spiritual traditions concentrated largely on Brazil
(Candomblé), Haiti (Vodou), and Cuba (Santería/Lukumi). As a result,
North America (including Canada) has often been undervalued as a vital
participant in these Afro-Atlantic discussions. Before his passing in 2007,
Baba Medahochi championed the sacred currency of North American–
born ancestors and their spiritual resources. In "The Memoirs of an Old
Swamp Priest," Baba Medahochi reflects on the African American spiritual
traditions that nourished his own religiosity. Raised in rural Murfreesboro,
Tennessee, Medahochi grew up in a world that valued the spiritual expertise of the "root doctah" and the herbal pharmacology or "secret doctor-
ing tradition of the Afrikan American south."[170] Medahochi also included
among ancestral spiritual traditions cultivated in the United States conjure,
the spiritualist church, and Holy Ghost and ancestral spirit possession. In
Medahochi's spiritual house, or Egbe Ifa Oyelagobo, he emphasized "as a
New Afrikan people, the experience of our Ancestors in Virginia, Tennessee,
Arkansas, Louisiana Mississippi, Alabama, Georgia, the Carolinas, et al.

FIGURE 24.
Baba Medahochi
Kofi Omowale
Zannu (1923–2007),
initiated into the
traditions of Palo
Mayombe, Ewe
Afa, Vodun, the
priesthood of
Shango, inducted
into the Ogboni
Iledi Akesan, and
a member of First
Afrikan Church in
Lithonia, Georgia.
Photograph
courtesy of First
Afrikan Church.

must be deified to spiritually empower us and to elevate the spirits of those who struggled in this hemisphere before us."[171]

Baba Medahochi attributes his first adult consciousness of New Afrikan spirituality to his early exposure to these ancestral traditions and to a book by Stephen Vincent Benet, *Freedom's a Hard Bought Thing.* In the book, the protagonist, Koffi (whose name Medahochi chose as his first African name), an African enslaved in the United States, goes to consult a known seer and spiritual advisor for the slave community. For Medahochi, the ability of his U.S. ancestors to rely on their "own spiritual light to discern what was useful and what was not" in the making of these sacred traditions exemplifies the richness of an American "New Afrikan" identity.[172]

Medahochi's New Afrikan identity also included the cultural, philosophical, and hermeneutical productions of African Americans. Given this, he was very supportive of Maulana Karenga's cultural creation of Kwanzaa, his accompanying ethical system of Kawaida, and his Kawaidaic interpretation of Yoruba Ifa odu literature as important diaspora contributions of Africanity.[173] According to Karenga:

> We have in a real sense begun to build a Kawaida or African American form of Ifa tradition in the same sense that forms of the way of Ifa have evolved in Brazil as Candomblé, Cuba as Lukumí, Haiti as Voudun, and Puerto Rico as Lukumí. Again, then, we approach our tradition—continental as well as diasporan tradition—not simply as a context or process in which we come, but also as an ongoing product of our efforts to understand and engage it and constantly enrich and expand it as a living, valuable and instructive way of being human in the world . . . The fundamental thrust of the Kawaida interpretation of the Odu Ifa is to shift the almost exclusive focus on divination by adherents and scholars to an essentially ethical focus.[174]

Like Karenga, Baba Medahochi's position was one strongly in favor of indigenization. In support of this position, he never traveled to Nigeria to undertake any of his formal priestly initiations. For him, diaspora indigenization included not only initiating on one's own authority but also the use of "native resources" so that all authentic ritual material culture would not always rest in Nigeria.[175] Ultimately, Medahochi believed that the spiritual resources of African Americans in the United States must become an integral part of an Afrikan sacred canon.

The Egbe Sankofa Kingdom of the Gods of Afrika in Philadelphia, which Oba Sekou Olayinka heads, is a twenty-first-century exponent of the New Afrikan philosophy. Through the spiritual lineage of his father, Baba Obalobi Obailumi Ogunseye, Baba Sekou Olayinka claims Oba Oseijeman Adefunmi as his "spiritual grandfather." Olayinka was born and raised in the Yoruba tradition from childhood by his father Baba Obalobi Obailumi Ogunseye and his mother Iya Omowunmi Ogundaisi, both of whom had direct spiritual linkages to Oseijeman Adefunmi's (Kabiyesi's) Yoruba Temple in Harlem. Olayinka is a part of a second generation of U.S.-born African American practitioners who was not raised in the traditional black Christian church. As far as he can remember in his childhood, "his elekes were on him."[176] He recalls that instead of playing with the traditional American GI Joe toys, his play involved Shango envisioned as an action figure and that of other Yoruba orisa warriors. In early documentation, one can find Olayinka as a child featured in national media publications such as *Sepia Magazine*, along with his parents and some three to four hundred Yoruba practitioners in Philadelphia, processing to the Schuylkill River for a Yemoja ceremony in celebration of Odunde and the Yoruba New Year, alongside other photos that include Oseijeman Adefunmi in Oyotunji Village. In the 1976 article, a young Sekou is seated with other children, all with elekes prominently worn about their necks, above a caption reading, "Children of the Ogunseye's are being brought up in African religious traditions and all have African names. They are Sekou, 10, Osagyefo, 10, Obawajumi, 5, Omorishanla, 6, and Iyatunde, 7, seated in their living room next to fertility figure that guards over the house."[177]

Olayinka now heads his own African American Yoruba community, Egbe Sankofa. He envisions the source of African sacred knowledge resting in both Africa and America and says he and his members are "structuring the Egbe according to what we need over here."[178] The concept of Afrikan informs his liturgy—in addition to Yoruba chants, drumming, and Odu lessons, the Egbe also includes the commemoration of important African American ancestors such as Marcus Garvey, Malcolm X, John Hendrick Clarke, and W. E. B. Dubois; embodies a respect for the spirituals of African American ancestors; and includes the singing of James Weldon Johnson's "Lift Every Voice and Sing" with *djembe* accompaniment.

FIGURE 25. Members of Egbe Sankofa Kingdom of the
Gods of Afraka at a ceremony on the New Jersey shore
for the orisa Yemoja. Photograph courtesy of author.

Within his Egbe, Baba Olayinka uses the theme of Sankofa, the Akan word meaning to go back to the source and retrieve to move forward.[179] As Sankofarians, they believe in a "Pan-Afrikan World Union," emphasizing that "the ancestral spirits must be remembered and honored, and consulted by the living."[180] Although drawing from African and African American religious traditions, the Egbe's socioeconomic and political vision is solidly rooted in America. It offers a wide range of spiritual resources and services for its religious membership, such as collective weekly religious ceremonies, annual predawn festivals for Oshun at Philadelphia's Schuylkill River, Odunde ceremonial offerings, Olokun festivals at the New Jersey shore, membership classes, Oriki classes, Yoruba classes, Odu Ifa studies, prayer lists, divinations, and initiation. The Egbe also functions as a public resource for the surrounding Philadelphia African American community. Outreach activities include organizing Juneteenth activities; hosting an annual Master, Scholar, Teacher Service that commemorates and honors outstanding teachers and scholars in various disciplines; facilitating manhood and womanhood preparation programs; organizing Martin Luther King Jr. services; and conducting workshops on emergency preparedness and the legal system.

In the twenty-first century, Baba Olayinka maintains that the challenge of his generation's priesthood entails "African Americans . . . defining themselves." They must find creative ways to do so in a North America that now functions as a major global host for the dynamic diversity of Yoruba ethnic pluralism—an arena in which Nigerians, African Americans, Euro-Americans, Puerto Ricans, Cubans, Dominicans, Panamanians, and others have forged a spiritual kinship bound together by the orisa. As practitioners in this global religious tradition, African Americans in the United States have been able "to take it and keep at it and to *keep a-addin' to it*," as suggested in the opening epigraph. Thus, African American self-definition must ultimately encompass the ability to establish a tradition germane to them as contemporary social beings in America and, most important, meaningful for them as ancestored Africans in the diaspora.[181]

Conclusion

"What We're Looking for in Africa Is Already Here"

A Conclusion for the Twenty-first Century

☙❧

My observation among the practitioners of African religion is that
African Americans don't have enough confidence in ourselves and
we always take a backseat for somebody to teach us as though we
are blank, a chalkboard that don't have anything written on it.
Anyway, I think the world is waiting on our contribution to it.

—Baba Medahochi Kofi Omowale Zannu

AFRICAN AMERICAN YORUBA did not physically return to the Old
World of Africa but instead engaged in a "reinterrogation of the
meaning of that Old World from the point of view of the New World."[1]
Wrestling with questions of meaning, identity, and geosocial location, they,
along with their diaspora counterparts, struggled to bring form and substance to the modern human complex Charles H. Long identifies as the
"trans-Atlantic African."[2] With this novel identity evolved a new "defining
reality," one that included race, social experience, and dehumanizing resis-
tors as meaningful components of religious reflection.[3] More important,
Long posits, "The Atlantic world introduces us to the globalization of the

meaning of humanity."[4] For Americans of African descent, their Atlantic world journey began with captivity and dehumanization and culminated in legal chattelization. Given their historical status as nonhuman property, one of the underlying goals of black religious-nationalist movements has been to inevitably find ways to rehumanize black materiality and resist the supremacy and dominance of a sanctioning Anglo *imago dei.*

Approaching the study of African American Yoruba in North America as a religious historian has led me to view the quest for the religious meanings of Africa as acts of rehumanization, reenculturation, and revaluation in the diaspora. Since slavery, African Americans in the United States have used religion to combat moral bankruptcy, resist social brutality, and maintain human integrity. Because of the egregious apparatus of dehumanization visited upon African Americans throughout most of American social history, African Americans have consistently sought resistance strategies to rehumanize their social and spiritual selves. Within the context of Yoruba religion, these strategies included transforming images of Africa; reconfiguring national identity, creating new histories, identifying new origins, rethinking cultural norms; producing textual legacies; and reconstituting religious meaning.

In the twentieth century, black religious nationalism became the space in which American social history, redefinitions of humanity, and divine meaning converged. Its theological conundrums were not new, and for diasporic blacks the antecedents rest in a time when, according to Charles H. Long, new orientational questions had to be asked: "To whom does one pray from the bowels of a slave ship? To the gods of Africa? To the gods of the masters of the slave vessels? . . . To whom does one pray?"[5] For Long, "From the perspective of religious experience, this was the beginning of African American religion and culture."[6] As active agents in this history and religious culture, African American Yoruba since 1959 have chosen to pray to "the gods of Africa"—not African gods left behind in a perpetual ancient stasis, but transportable African gods who could be summoned to help navigate the "complex ambiguity of the Atlantic world."[7] In many ways Yoruba religion has become a metacultural phenomenon and "can no longer be conceptualized as confined to a provincial ethnic tradition."[8] African Americans in North America have come to represent one of the many communities of global orisa articulations engaging in a "protean improvisation" on Yoruba meaning in the twenty-first century.[9]

They became not simply practitioners of a fixed historic Yoruba but major players in a dynamic contemporary global reorientation of orisa religious traditions. In a tradition that reveres 400+1 orisa divinities, there is continuous room for African American improvisation and perhaps even the contribution of its own North American feminine and warrior orisa (Marie Laveau, Nina Simone, Harriet Tubman, James Baldwin, Nat Turner, and so forth) to the orisa pantheon.

For more than five decades, they have developed the orisa tradition in North America into an important repository for the spiritual *"repossession of what they deemed their rightful inheritance—Africa."*[10] At the same time they have enabled the "socialization" of a new religious order that included America.[11] What distinguishes African Americans in the Yoruba tradition is their ability to approach the gods of Africa through their "lived experience of blackness" in America.[12] African Americans are living examples of Baba IfaTunji's idea that "Ifa is not a fixed story" but that like the sacred odu, its power and meaning are newly manifested with each recasting and interpretation.

As we enter into the second decade of the twenty-first century, several African American religious iles, egbes, priests, and practitioners have begun to consider the future of Yoruba/Ifa in North America and the ways its practice can be further indigenized. My concluding remarks are devoted to inviting new discussions on the future of African American Yoruba in North America as they contemplate the challenges of globalization, institutionalization, collective political activism, gender authority, polysexual orientations, environmentalism and eco-spirituality, religious vernacularism, and home and belonging.

"Yoruba Religion is a World Religion Without a World Structure": Yoruba Traditions and the Challenge of Globalization

In a speech given before an audience of orisa practitioners from Nigeria, the United States, Cuba, Brazil, Puerto Rico, Venezuela, Trinidad and Tobago, and Argentina gathered at the First World Conference on the Orisa Tradition held June 1-7, 1981, in Ile-Ife, Nigeria,[13] Nigerian Ifa priest and Awise Ni Agbaye, Dr. Wande Abimbola, stated, "Yoruba religion is a world religion without a world structure."[14] For more than two decades, Abimbola has concentrated on providing global practitioners of Yoruba

religion with a "world structure" and a "coherent theology." He regularly
spends half of each year in his African home in Oyo, Nigeria, and the
other half teaching and servicing the spiritual needs of orisa communities throughout the African diaspora, often from a small base in Atlanta,
Georgia. As an elder babalawo and authoritative scholar in Yoruba studies,
Abimbola provides countless spiritual services such as divinations, initiations, language instruction, and ritual training to an expansive clientele
broadly based throughout the United States, Cuba, Brazil, Venezuela, and
Trinidad. Abimbola is a pivotal figure in discussions of the future of Yoruba
globalization. He eschews a rigid notion of the tradition and understands
that "Yoruba culture has been transformed in the Americas" among whom
he calls *"Diaspora Africans."*[15]

For the growing international community of orisa practitioners, the
notion of globalization entails geographical expansiveness, cross-cultural
contact, global communication and information exchange, cultural trans-
portability, and transnational networks. Although some believe that along
with globalization should come a form of "standardization" for the "very survival of the tradition," there is no consensus on this among orisa devotees.[16] In
fact, of all the aspects of globalization, efforts toward standardization appear
the most challenging for local practitioners who currently practice multiple
forms of hierarchy and authority, varied stylistic and linguistic norms, in
diverse social and historical settings. There is some resistance to "homogenization" or to reducing "things, people, and cultures to common denomi-
nators."[17] Angela Jorge instead suggests emphasizing shared commonalities
over shared differences as a unifying force within the global tradition:

> Although there are differences, such as language, the common
> bond as Africans in the Diaspora is a strong one. It is a bond that
> needs to be emphasized. It is important for me . . . as a Puerto Rican
> of African ancestry to be aware of what has happened and is hap-
> pening to Brazilians of African descent, to Venezuelans of African
> descent, to Trinidadians of African descent, to all Africans in the
> Diaspora. . . . We must transcend national and geographic bound-
> aries and understand that our experience is a collective experience.
> We must accept that our commonalties and our differences are
> the result of our unique experience as Africans in the Diaspora.
> They are part of our past and present reality and it is from our

commonalties and differences that we must, that we will, forge a new future in the New World.[18]

While open to engaging the commonalities of a world religion, some practitioners are deeply committed to preserving the integrity of their local structures of meaning and support what theologian Josiah U. Young, calls a more "transcontextual perspective" that "focuses on diverse situations and seeks to transform them in praxis that does not annul [the] distinctiveness of those situations."[19] For Yoruba practitioners, transcontextuality would mean maintaining the integrity of the local while participating in a wider global discourse. From the perspective of some practitioners, because Yoruba religion in the twenty-first century is far from an "unchanging 'traditional' religion," imposing standardizations or regulatory processes may not only suppress the dynamic innovations of local expressions but complicate the authority of local religious leadership.[20]

Strong proponents of local sovereignty, such as Trinidadian scholar and Ogun priestess Molly Ahye, directly challenge Nigerian Yoruba who try to position themselves as elevated authorities within the tradition. In response to a Nigerian Yoruba who intimated in the 1981 Orisa World Congress that diaspora practitioners had "come home to correct a few points," Ahye boldly asserted, "I would like to say that we shouldn't be corrected. We should leave to oursel[ves] the way we worship because I'm not sure that you are correct or we are correct. I think it's not a matter of *correction*, but to *exchange* ideas."[21] Moreover, as recently as June 2010, the Lukumi Council of Oba Oriates of South Florida, which Ernesto Pichardo and others of the "Lukumi religion in its traditional Cuban form" represent, ratified the Miami Lukumi Accord.[22] Supported by a multiethnic constituency, this document was formulated in response to local conflicts between the Santería/Lukumi priesthood and "practitioners of the so-called Traditional Yoruba Religion" over the issue of reordination or initiation of priests from the former tradition. The eleven-point Accord emphasized a fidelity to the diaspora ancestors of Lukumi practice (as opposed to that of West Africa); a rejection of "coercive mechanisms of reformative traditions foreign" to "Lukumi customs"; a resistance "to modify, rectify, justify, modernize" or "abandon the theological principles" of Lukumi's current practice; and a pronouncement of Lukumi and so-called Traditional Yoruba Religion as "unequivocally different" and "incompatible." It sought to render each expression "an autonomous tradition" that is "unequivocally separate and independent of each other." A major point of action within the accord was the ruling that "any and all persons that convert to the Traditional Yoruba practices will lose any and all rights in our [Lukumi] tradition." What seemed ultimately at stake from the accord were three fundamental issues: one, given the document's opening with a paraphrase of the First Amendment of the U.S. Constitution, the right to complete religious autonomy amidst competing traditions of the Orisa in North America; two, the right to religious authority in conferring priestly legitimacy, as well as the right to refuse recognition to those who "abandon Lukumi worship to adopt those of the Yoruba Traditionalists"; and third, the right to restrict access to private religious ceremonies solely to those "persons properly and ritualistically ordained and/or consecrated in the priesthood, following the patterns bequeathed to us by our Lukumi ancestors." Thus, within this discursive space of diaspora religious legitimacy and authenticity, "Yoruba Traditionalists," as represented by the practices of Nigerian Yoruba, wrestle for religious traction in North America.

While outside Nigerian borders Yoruba religious expression has experienced exponential growth, the tradition struggles to compete with Christianity and Islam for adherents within its internal boundaries. One practitioner who traveled to Nigeria expressed her disappointment at having to "search out traditional Orisha worship" while "in the meantime loudspeakers speaking about Allah and Jesus Christ are very open and significant."[23] Thus, the recovery of Yoruba traditional conventions in the diaspora may coincide with a time that many West African Yoruba in Nigeria are engaged in "counter-movements against the traditional."[24] Wande Abimbola has also on occasion expressed a deep sense of disappointment at the comparative difference in fervor between Orisa worship's practice in Nigeria and in the Caribbean and Americas. Directing his comments toward Nigerian Yoruba, Abimbola remarked:

> Wherever we go in the Americas and in the other parts of the world people remind us of our traditional culture. People do not even know that many of us have forsaken our culture. What we are saying is not that we should return to a culture of one thousand years ago. What we are saying is that every generation must learn how to . . . revitalize the culture of the society which gave

birth to the generation. . . . We have almost completely turned our backs to our own traditional culture especially our traditional religion. . . . All over the African diaspora wherever you go . . . you encounter people who have devoted their lives to the propagation of Orisha culture. But alas! In Africa which is the birthplace of this religion, many of the people of our generation have turned their back to their own culture.[25]

In a similar vein, Wale Ogunlola, upon his return from Oyotunji African Village in 1998, wrote in a column entitled, "Africa Abroad," that "Nigerian Yoruba might well feel ashamed that he or she has not taken all these matters perfectly seriously—as if they were of no value."[26] Despite a contemporary religious and cultural climate in Nigeria that often prevents public affiliations to orisa traditions, communities on this side of the Atlantic are instead experiencing the proliferation of orisa "vernacular spaces."[27] John Pemberton III asserts that "the extraordinary and imaginative adaptation of Yoruba peoples, not only in West Africa but also in Brazil, Cuba, Haiti, and the United States" as well as the "enlarging" of their "vision" is "a gift given by the orisa."[28] Within the multifarious vernacular spaces of Africa and the diaspora, local geographies and expressions of the orisa predominate.

"We Have to Establish Our Own Kinds of Institutions": African American Yoruba and the Challenge of Institutionalization

As Nigerian Yoruba wrestle with the place of orisa traditional culture in contemporary society, African American Yoruba seek to find ways of ensuring its continued, yet innovative, preservation within North America. Shortly before his passing, Baba Medahochi remarked, "There are certain aspects of the traditions that must be protected, respected, and upheld with the highest integrity," allowing "room for creativity, expansion, and evolution."[29] In the wake of the 1994 Supreme Court case involving the Church of the Lukumi Babalu Aye and the issue of animal sacrifice, Cuban-born priest Ernesto Pichardo remarked of orisa practice in the United States, "To make it in this society, you have to be institutionalized. You have to be a force that protects its own interests."[30] As Pichardo and African American Yoruba envision ways to achieve effective institutionalization, they often find themselves employing traditional ecclesiastical models of American religious organization and structure. As Pichardo's choice of name for his Miami-based organization (Church of the Lukumi Babalu Aye) reveals, orisa practitioners have long had to navigate American's public terrain of religious respectability in order to avoid marginalization and persecution.

Stereotypical images of African religion as evil and malevolent still abound within the United States. African religions are said to be "filled with the devil," and anyone participating in them "demon possessed." Most often a source of deep disappointment and frustration is that even the larger African American populace in the United States participates in such denigration, calling traditional religion "spooky shit" or that "voodoo stuff."[31] One African American priestess, reflecting on the disparaging gaze often directed at the religion, said, "I think it's a beautiful religion and I get very upset sometimes when either the press, or people that really don't know what it's about, condemn it . . . Lots of times it's negative, it's derogatory—you know, the A.S.P.C.A. and organizations like that. They say that there's religious freedom in this country, but you know you question it . . . I can't understand an organization like the A.S.P.C.A. They're a humane organization, supposedly, but a lot of the animals that they have they have to kill because they can't place them. That's not humane to me."[32]

Many African Americans are often respectful and tolerant of other global faith traditions while disdaining religions of Africa. As one priestess observed, "And yet [African Americans] can go right past the Buddha shrine with the incense burning, the water, the flowers, going to the Chinese restaurant, and they will even make offerings—throw pennies at the Buddha in the little water. . . . They have no problem with Buddhism, but anything African is scary . . . because we were brainwashed that nothing good came out of Africa and Africa had nothing to offer. We were told that everything about us was wrong, including our religion."[33] Such self-denigration belittles and devalues an important aspect of the historical African past. Therefore, the challenge of appealing to a wider African American community that is not primarily African affirming but is largely Christian socialized becomes not only one of effective institutionalization but also one of dismantling religious and cultural stereotypes.

Regarding institution building, elders like Baba Medahochi argued that because African Americans have been so "congregationally oriented" in their religious orientations in the United States, orisa practitioners might pragmatically have to adopt more of an ecclesiastical structure of worship:

"We need to recodify how we present African religion to our people. We are congregationally oriented people. We're used to having someone standing in front of us. That's why [T. D.] Jakes can have a MegaFest. We can have a Mega-IfaFest . . . but we haven't organized it in that way . . . In the Ifa faith system . . . [we] can have a little service, people sitting down in chairs and listening to somebody . . . preach from the odu. That's how the Honorable Elijah Muhammad established the Nation of Islam—by teaching."[34] Medahochi attempted to offer a pragmatic structural approach to orisa religious organization without compromising its content. His institutional model builds upon the existing structural model of individual iles and egbes, broadening them to accommodate an even larger American constituency base.

Related to this larger institutional vision are discussions among some African American Yoruba about forming national seminaries and religious academies in the United States for the accreditation and intensive study of Yoruba traditions. Nigerian babalawo Wande Abimbola, who expressed such a plan nearly two decades ago, shares this vision. A chief proponent in these discussions today is Oba Sekou Olayinka of Philadelphia, who is concerned that the recent passing of key African American Yoruba elders like Baba Alfred, Baba Bernard, Mama Keke, Oba Oseijeman, Baba Medahochi, Chief Bey, Iya Barbara Kenyatta Bey, Chief Ajamu, and several others has created a major void in the transmission of religious and ritual knowledge. With Olayinka's vision of the Ifa Theological Seminary and Orisha Studies Academy and its accompanying Sankofa Village, his hope is to offer up to four years of specialized Yoruba studies, in addition to providing needed social services to the surrounding African American communities of Philadelphia. He summarizes his vision of the academy: "To be a priest, you can't master it all . . . you have to choose an area to major in. We want to develop priests who major in being Obas, we want to develop priests who major in Ita, the Odus, herbs, drums, songs, incantations, Orisa food, Egun. . . . We need to formalize ourselves and create institutions that become the repositories of all the collective knowledge that we have, and people can go there and glean the knowledge of other people that have come before them and add to that knowledge."[35]

With the direct social and spiritual needs of African Americans in mind, Oba Olayinka roots his philosophy in "ReAfrakanization," or the process of "rediscovery, reclamation, and re-identification with traditional cultures, values and morals" whereby African Americans come to understand their identity.[36] Olayinka's vision also includes the future creation in North America of what he calls Sankofa Village. Unlike Oyotunji African Village's rural context, Sankofa Village will not have a residential component but instead will be a comprehensive urban conglomeration comprised of an Orisa temple, meeting space, community center, recreation center, and business center. It would offer a wide range of social and cultural outreach services such as daycare, adult education and GED classes, tutorials, meeting spaces for Narcotics and Alcoholics Anonymous, private educational facilities for children, drumming and dance classes, and grassroots community organizing space. Olayinka sees this as a long-range plan to ensure that African American Yoruba institutions become comprehensively serviceable to the spiritual, cultural, and social needs of African American communities throughout the United States. Because of its grand scale, he speculates that he "probably won't see the end of it," but what is most important for him is that he sees "the beginning of it."[37] Oba Olayinka's vision of Sankofa Village and an Orisa Seminary and Academy speak to the many ways the future of Yoruba indigenization might be secured in America.

"If We Were the Ausar Auset, We'd Own Half of Bed-Stuy": Toward a Vision of Political Activism and Collective Responsibility

The African American Yoruba of the generations of Oba Oseijeman, Baba Medahochi, Chief Bey, Mama Keke, and even those younger like John and Valerie Mason, coupled their Yoruba spirituality with concrete sociopolitical activism on behalf of actual black communities. While participating in orisa traditions, many of this generation saw the necessity for participation in secular black-nationalist movements and grassroots organizations that worked on behalf of a wider, dispossessed African American population in the United States. Over the years, this activist enthusiasm appears to have waned. Several orisa practitioners express deep concern that political activism is no longer central to African American Yoruba identity and that African American Yoruba are not always committed to organizations, movements, or causes that alleviate the suffering of African-descended people domestically or African people globally. In recent years, for example, how would one locate the collective orisa national agenda or their organized efforts on behalf of victims of South African apartheid; Rwanda's ethnic genocide; Congo's civil war and sexual war against women; the violence in Darfur; or the collective national agenda regarding the aftermath of Hurricane Katrina; the devastation of African and African American communities resulting from HIV/AIDS; the ravaging of men, women, and children because of black-on-black homicide; or the alarming rate of male and female incarceration in America's prison industrial complex? Moreover, in 2007 and 2008, when Democratic presidential candidate Barack Obama met with the American Israel Public Affairs Committee and the National Jewish Democratic Council, as well as Christian evangelicals, at the Saddleback Valley Community Church, reassuring these religious-based organizations of his commitment to their domestic and foreign concerns, could Obama have easily identified an orisa organizational counterpart with a national governing structure that could position thousands of orisa practitioners as an equally powerful political constituency? Finally, although there have been commendable efforts on the part of the National African Religion Congress in Philadelphia, one practitioner wondered when there would be an international African/Orisa Anti-Defamation League, an organization that would fight exclusively "against anti-Africanism, against the pejorative attacks on African religions."[38]

John Mason laments that "activism has somehow or another gone by the by[way]."[39] He states emphatically, "The orisa community does itself a disservice by thinking that all we have to do is make parties. We have . . . to accommodate a bigger agenda. We don't need any more bembes, not to say they are not wonderful places to . . . showcase all kinds of art and cultural retention, but they're not being active."[40] Mason would advocate in addition that orisa practitioners "establish our own kinds of institutions," even museums, to house the important visual and material culture of the tradition. Challenging members of the North American orisa community to engage in broader platforms of social and community activism is, for Mason, getting them to see that "it's about empowerment."[41]

Mason's vision of activism is collective and community based, yet also comes from a deeply personal concern. He reflects on the condition of African American men in the United States and worries about his own sons as potential "fodder to be grist for the mill" of American society. He sees African American communities as under siege and in a "danger zone" and urges orisa practitioners, in addition to their religious endeavors, to "look for some social cures."[42] For Mason, pressing social issues like protecting African American children and communities and providing jobs to the unemployed are unquestionably religious concerns and must be addressed as such.[43] Mason and his wife, Valerie, both longtime community activists in Brooklyn, New York, would ultimately agree that in addition to being an honorable and knowledgeable member of the orisa priesthood, "you want to be an activist . . . to help strengthen your community."[44]

Yoruba priests like John Mason and Oba Sekou Olayinka, who find themselves within northern urban cities like New York and Philadelphia, stress the engagement of orisa communities in grassroots community activism. For these priests, the plight of African American communities is at the center of any discourse that connects Yoruba religion and politics. Oba Olayinka argues that orisa communities must organize themselves into a political bloc, making themselves known as an important national constituency to be reckoned with. In the end, he willingly conflates religion and politics, saying, "I vote my interests. I don't vote Democrat or Republican. I vote EGBE. I'm not loyal to the Democratic Party, and I'm not loyal to the Republican Party. I'm loyal to my community!"[45] For Olayinka, it is ultimately the gathered spiritual community structure of the Egbe and its collective political needs that warrant political primacy.

Finally, although Sheldon, South Carolina, is not a major center of urban violence and community decay, residents of Oyotunji African Village still see themselves as advocates for grassroots organizing around the many urban challenges that face the larger African American populace of the United States. A skilled mason in the construction profession, the new Oba Adefunmi II expresses deep indignation over the physical conditions of African American communities. One might refer to these neighborhoods as "Africa Town," given their large preponderance of residents of African descent; however, physically and aesthetically he says of these urban spaces, it "looks like a bomb hit it; the other side of town looks like Baghdad . . . because we've lost the sociology, the camaraderie" that once wove these communities together.[46] He sees Oyotunji not as an isolated entity but as an integral part of a complex network of African American communities throughout North America. Therefore, for the most desolate of African American communities, Adefunmi II proposes the following plan:

We got to take the communities and reface them, make them African looking. Put things in them that represent who we are. We gotta work. We have to get on the ground and do these things. We should be in communities—active—in Liberty City, in the West side of Atlanta, East St. Louis, in the communities where African Americans are having a hard time. . . . Don't say it can't be done because I see the Mormons do it. I was in Jamaica [and] saw two Mormons riding on a bike, white shirts, going to do their Mormon business . . . whether they were going to watch an old lady, or to rake her yard, or to say a prayer, whatever they were doing there. We're not saying go out and take religion to the people. We're saying go out and help the people.[47]

For this reason, Oyotunji African Village, under its new leadership, is committed to an organized plan of outreach for the twenty-first century. It hopes to continue its programs with inner-city urban schools and local prisons, extending these efforts to historically black colleges and universities as well as local orisa houses throughout the United States. Some forty years after its formation, Oyotunji African Village still sees itself as existing within "the belly of beast" with a mission to create an ongoing challenge to Western culture.[48] Although the United States is currently governed by the first African American president, Barack Obama, the Oba believes that one "African American in politics doesn't really change much for African American people because you get into politics [and] you're for everybody" and must ultimately "further the national American agenda."[49] The new Oba believes that African Americans must fight for themselves. As African American Yoruba devotees define the future of their religion in the United States, they must decide, as did their nationalist predecessors, what should be their collective political response to the challenges of being black in a changing American societal landscape. In looking to the future of these and other visionary endeavors in the twenty-first century, it is important to examine how the voices of women play a role in these discussions and developments.

"Whatever's Gonna Happen, It's Gonna Be African American Women": Gender Empowerment and Gendered Identities in the Future of African American Yoruba

In an interview with Yewande in 2006, I asked why she, as a North American woman, found herself attracted to the orisa tradition. She replied that she did not want to be a part of any religion that did not allow her to honor her female ancestors and needed a religion that enabled her to preserve their gendered authority and presence in her life. For Yewande, it was also important to be a part of a tradition where female orisa deity governed "areas of knowledge and sources of knowledge" that both men and women needed "not just to survive, but to thrive."[50] Like many African American women, she was drawn to what she viewed as alternative sources of women's empowerment, leadership, and authority. Contrasting her Christian background, she states, "When you're coming from parts of the diaspora where women can't even stand in a [Christian] pulpit," the orisa tradition marks a "significant shift in the role of women in the leadership and in the ritual life of the community."[51] Yewande emphatically contends that the orisa tradition challenges the disempowerment of women and provides complex gendered models of "authority, power, representation, and visibility."[52] As the twenty-first century progresses, African American Yoruba women, like their diaspora counterparts, are becoming prominent leaders of religious houses and important conveyers of spiritual knowledge in the American orisa community. Olabiyi Babaloloa Yai contends that "much of the orientations of the orisa tradition, much of the tenor of the new syncretisms" and in essence, the fate of this global tradition, will rest largely upon "whether African women occupy the center of the process or are relegated to its periphery."[53]

Yet, while African American women occupy multiple arenas of power within the orisa tradition, they also make it known that gender authority is still a contested matter in the twenty-first century. Women find themselves often confronting rigid gender hierarchies, bounded gendered spaces, and fixed gendered identities. For some, philosophical ideologies such as "gender balance and complementarity" and their rhetorical uses are often subtle forms of sexism that strategically cloak authority in discourses of the "traditional."[54] The "traditional" and "tradition" can become at times sites for the performance of hypermasculine identities and rigidly defined feminine roles often rationalized as "African." One woman reflects on this in the following way: "Women in the diaspora who are joining these traditions might be facing a certain kind of black masculinist nationalism that is oppressive to women, and I think that it is important for women to recognize that there are indigenous traditions within Yoruba and other African cultures that challenge that masculinist approach . . ."[55] African American Yoruba women like Afi-Odelia Scruggs recall feeling that there was very little "respect for the intellectual power of women" on the part of some male leadership.[56] Women who had come from religious backgrounds (including Christian) where women were spiritual heads, established healers like Miss Irene, and ordained church leaders like Mother Taylor, found these gendered negotiations of power extremely unsettling.[57]

Women also revealed that subtle forms of restriction were placed on their access to specialized ritual knowledge and praxis. According to one senior priestess, "Women have the opportunity to get initiated, but they will not be taught by the men. It won't happen. That's why I started a group where women can come together and women can teach women . . . but the men will not teach the women."[58] She often felt that in some religious houses male priests formed what she called a "boys' club," putting in place invisible yet impenetrable gender boundaries that relegated women to the service (versus philosophical and praxis) components of orisa worship. She states, "I've been trying to get the odus and get the women to study the odus, but the men keep us busy cooking goat and STUFF and STUFF and STUFF. Women doing anything beyond the menial jobs is not encouraged in Ifa. Just sit up and look good, look cute."[59] There appear to be few male priests like Djisovi Ikukomi Eason who openly "argued in support of the feminist cause in the Ifa priesthood."[60]

As an institutional gendered response in support of the concerns of women, one African American priestess, Iya Omolewa Eniolorunopa, founded the Egbe Odu Ifa Sacred African Literary Society in 2000 in Atlanta, Georgia, "a women's group of interfaith leaders, scholars, and friends dedicated to comparing 'sacred' world literature for discussion and enlightenment."[61] Its ecumenical mission is "to provide a forum for discussion and comparative research of universal themes, timeless topics from all genre of spiritual wisdom (Odu Ifa, Bible, Koran, Torah, Bhagavad-Gita, Upanishad, etc.); to expose our members to ancient, West African theology; to explore the ingenuity required for an ancient, nonliterate (not illiterate) people to develop, preserve, and disseminate their beliefs—through the centuries—without the art of writing; and to consider and respect all viewpoints . . . celebrating religious similarities."[62]

In line with this, women's narratives also contain strong voices of dissent and critique on the practice of plural marriage, with some viewing it as a way of limiting women's spiritual potential. One woman analyzed polygyny in the North American Yoruba tradition as follows: "I think it's a way of

keeping women in check because they are constantly fighting over the attention from the men or making sure their children get their fair chance. . . . We
are kept talking about earthly things. . . . We are never really allowed to delve
into our spiritual [side]."[63] In her own experiences, she said she has repeatedly observed that "women who have been elevated spiritually, men really
seem to want to pull them into a polygamous thing to cut their wings."[64] For
her, polygynous arrangements along with the frequency with which women
are relegated to roles of religious domesticity pose major impediments to
African American women's full and equal participation in the advancement and transmission of orisa knowledge and thought in the United States.
As she reflects on the gendered future of Yoruba religion, she concludes,
"African American women are the only women on the planet that don't take
orders from their men, so whatever's gonna happen, it's gonna be African
American women, . . . but with the polygamy and stuff here trying to keep
us down . . . we won't have time to study our sacred literature."[65]

As the voices of African American Yoruba women continue to gain
prominence and equal standing on the wider American orisa stage, they
will no doubt prove vital forces in the tradition's future preservation and
sustenance. A trend that is already gaining great momentum is that of
African American Yoruba women using the print media to disseminate
and encode gendered power and influence. As we look to the future, following the models of prominent Yoruba priestesses such as Iyanla Vanzant,
Luisah Teish, Ayobunmi Sangode, Marta Vega, Aina Olomo, and others,
African American women will continue to use both the published text,
the electronic superhighway, the ile, the classroom, and the kitchen table
to transmit their valuable experiences of the orisa to a new generation of
national and international priestesses, devotees, and seekers.

"If I Worry About Somebody Being Homosexual and Not Worry About that Person Being Mistreated as a Human Being, Then I've Missed the Point": African American Yoruba and the Challenge of Polysexual Identities

"The gods don't discriminate. People do."[66] This has more often than not
been the experience of practitioners who have dared to challenge the perceived heteronormativity of the orisa tradition. Randy P. Conner and David
Hatfield Sparks discuss the ways in which notions of "gender diversity" and

"sexual complexity" confront a sense of gender normativity within diaspora orisa traditions, unveiling the invisibility that nonheterosexual devotees often feel. The world of the Yoruba orisa provides for many a gateway into a "multidimensional reality" that is "inclusive of divinities and/or spirits, the ancestral dead, and animals, plants, stones, and other entities and objects expressing various forms of consciousness, all interacting in one way or another with human subjects/agents."[67] As Randy P. Conner rightly points out, many of these "human subject/agents" enter the world of the orisa as "multifaceted selves" bringing "sexual and/or gender complexity" to the orisa tradition that is expressed through lesbian, gay, bisexual, transgender, queer, and intersex (LGBTQI) subjectivities.[68] Conner and Hatfield include the voices of several African American practitioners who seek to have all their layers of identity, "including African American and lesbian, be acknowledged."[69] In breaking this silence, one African American practitioner remarked, "It's important for people to know that there are lesbians and gays who are involved in this religion."[70]

"Gender variant" devotees who are lesbian, gay, bisexual, transgender, intersex, self-selecting cross-dressing, and those transitionally awaiting or in various stages of anatomical change, offer creative definitions and new views on the meanings of gender identity, orisa personality, and sacred unions.[71] Within open and accepting religious houses, such devotees are welcomed and embraced. In more muted and nonembracing spaces, they are often subject to ritual prohibitions, heteronormative theology, and limited structural access and resources. Although gay practitioners are seen as "very intuitive" and powerful, the narratives Conner and Sparks collected reveal that LGBTQI devotees are denied initiation; not recognized as validly initiated if the initiating spiritual parent was gay; compelled to choose between heterosexual men and women's societies without gender-complex options; forced to endure allegations of ritual "impurity" and "contamination"; denied spiritual services; and prevented from entering specialized priesthoods or handling sacred objects.[72] According to one African American priestess, "A lot of African Americans who practice this tradition would rather not see any white involved in it, and there are those who would like to see no gay or lesbian or transgender involved. . . . I have heard there are houses in which African Americans and other people of color take an oath not to initiate any white people or any gay people."[73] She concludes by saying, "Spirit don't look at who you're sleepin' with. Spirit looks at what's within your heart."[74] For many devotees, the primary source of prejudice and intolerance rests not with the orisa deities but among their human community of fellow devotees.

A powerful trope frequently used to prevent the full participation of LGBTQI devotees in the orisa community involves the normative authority and discourse of the traditional. Nonheterosexual practitioners are often viewed outside the scope of ancient African gender traditionalism with its presumed normative practices of heterosexual marriage, biological reproduction, and clearly demarcated masculine and feminine roles determined primarily by physical anatomy.[75] The authority of Yoruba traditional society is often upheld based on subjective interpretations of culture, social codes, gender roles, and sacred literature. Within a dominant heterosexual orisa populace, these collective sources of authority are often used to regulate sexual orientation and identity. M. Jacqui Alexander aptly points out that "within the Yoruba system Olodumare, god, is not gendered," and that "moving from neutered conceptualization to the engendering of Sacred praxis maps a complex journey from energy to embodiment constitutive of a masculinization of the social organization of the Sacred, but it need not carry the immediate presumption of women's subordination," nor, I might add, of that of anyone else's.[76]

Despite this, the LGBTQI orisa community does have heterosexual supporters, defenders, and allies who openly critique homophobic attitudes, behaviors, and practices and defend their right to coexist within the tradition. Vodu priestess, now Yoruba-initiated priestess, Mama Lola professes to having "godchildren who are gay, who are lesbian, who are interested in Vodou or orisha."[77] On the issue of sexual orientation within these traditions, she explains: "We do spiritual work together, then you close your door, and I do not interfere. I'm not interested in their private lives, what they do behind closed doors. You do whatever you want with your body. That's not my business. And what I do is not others' business. That's *my* life. *I'm a mother, not a private detective!* In Vodou, everybody's equal. In *orisha*, we're equal."[78] Similar to Mama Lola, prominent Obatala priest John Mason finds the recent divisive discourse on the presence of gays and lesbians in the orisa tradition to be a distraction from forging meaningful coalitions and stronger alliances within America's orisa community. Because in the twenty-first century, Mason argues, "the ground is changing so quickly in terms of gender and gender power bases," he refuses to participate in the perpetuation of homophobic attitudes within Yoruba American circles.[79]

Like John Mason, noted Nigerian Ifa priest Wande Abimbola and his son Kola Abimbola are nondiscriminatory and supportive allies against homophobic efforts within the Yoruba tradition. The elder Abimbola, who also critiques gender discrimination and supports the initiation of women into the Ifa divining priesthood, feels that on the issue of homosexuality, "Who are we to probe into the personal life of another person?"[80] Following suit, the younger of the two babalawos, Kola Abimbola, contends, "Simply put, *orisa* religion is founded upon respect and openness" and for him this includes the diversity of sexual orientations. He concludes, "To the best of my knowledge, Ifa, the holy scriptures of Orisa Religion, is silent on precisely those sexual orientations that some people find offensive. If there are no Ifa poems that deal with these issues directly, all we can do is to extrapolate and offer interpretations. But whatever one's interpretation is, one should always remember *Iwapele* [good character], the ultimate guiding principle of Orisa religion."[81]

The challenge of inclusion with regard to sexual identity extends well beyond the borders of the United States. Gay men and women in Cuba and Brazil also seek to find full acceptance in the orisa tradition. One Cuban woman remarked, "I am who I am. . . . You shouldn't love or not love someone because he is or is not homosexual. Likewise, if you go to the saints with a problem that you want resolved, the saint is not going to consider whether or not you're homosexual before he or she helps you. They don't look at you as 'a homosexual.' They look at you as a human being."[82] Similarly, an Afro-Cuban gay male sees his relationship with the "Orisha" as "very personal." He goes on to say, "I think there's room for innovation. My personal opinion is that as long as you love *Orisha*, you respect *Orisha*, *Orisha* doesn't care about your sexuality."[83] Unlike most other orisa locales, gay practitioners in Brazil openly created organizational networks of support such as Ade Dudu, whose mission is to affirm the "sexually variant practitioners" of the Candomblé community.[84]

Despite the challenges surrounding inclusivity, LGBTQI devotees manage to carve out important sites of meaning within the orisa tradition. They seek to bring their whole selves to the tradition and cultivate networks of support that include the orisa, godparents, as well as same-sex unions and partnerships. Orisa deities such as Oxumare (who was identified as homosexual), Oshun, Yemaya, Obatala, Olokun, Yewa, Oya, Inle, Logunede, Pomba Gira, and Orunmila LGBTQI devotees find exceptionally affirming.[85] In witnessing moments of trance possession, LGBTQI priests and priestesses can occasionally glimpse the complex and fluid gender boundaries of orisa that they themselves may negotiate. In these moments, male orisa can easily employ a female host, and female orisa can readily use a male host in ways that anthropomorphize and blur their gendered characteristics. This spiritual "gender shifting" provides practitioners with the assurance that they, like the orisa, resist strictly gendered boundaries and instead adopt more fluid approaches to sexual typologies.

As LGBTQI practitioners find personal connection and meaning with their orisa deities, they also have been able to cultivate meaningful love relationships among themselves. Within Yoruba American orisa communities, same-sex unions are becoming more and more prevalent, offering important alternatives to the heterosexual marriages and polygamous units found within the orisa tradition. These "ceremonies of union" and "same-sex commitment ceremonies" are performed by a member of the orisa priesthood who offers divinations, prayers, and sacrifices.[86] Often conducted in the presence of a supportive community, these ceremonies symbolize a dual commitment to both the spirit world of orisa and the ancestors and to their loving human partnerships. They speak to the creative ways in which orisa practitioners structuralize spiritual meaning and, as Conner and Sparks insightfully reveal, how they ultimately balance "eros, gender, and the sacred in their lives."[87]

"Ecology is Simply Honoring What is Sacred": Yoruba American Environmentalism and Eco-Spirituality for the Twenty-first Century

As America "goes green" in the twenty-first century in an effort to curb global warming and detoxify the environment, some African American Yoruba have called upon practitioners to become more ecologically aware of the ways orisa ritual practice may affect the natural environment. Efforts among Yoruba Americans can be linked to a larger eco-spiritual understanding that asserts that "humans are part of a moral order that extends beyond the human species" and that this commitment exhibits itself through "ethical, moral, or religious tendencies that relate to ecological issues."[88] Because there is a spiritization of nature within orisa cosmology, practitioners are urged to regard the natural world as a sacred site for power and medicinal healing. For Wande Abimbola, because "Yoruba religion is based on a profound respect for the natural environment due to an ancient covenant between humans and all other creatures and objects of nature," the challenge in the twenty-first century is to maintain such a covenant "in the face of the excessive greed, capitalism, materialism, militarism, and wanton exploitation of the earth, the forests, the oceans, animals, and other creatures of nature in contemporary times."[89] In other words, the larger issue rests within a complex theological understanding of "interspecies relations" and how one brings to bear "elements of ancient African thought on the subject matter of the environment."[90]

Amanda Holmes's research on Yoruba religion and eco-spiritualism insightfully reveals a cosmology where "nature" is understood "as a community of intersubjective beings" and an "embodied landscape" that encourages "environmentally respectful behaviors."[91] According to Holmes, the orisa "inhabit" complex "ecosystems" that are understood as "extended community" and possess "a spirit or an anthropomorphic consciousness that people must respect."[92] Given this understanding, eco-spiritual advocates in North America such as Shango priestess Aina Olomo urge Yoruba practitioners to engage in responsible forms of "ritual ecology," keeping in mind that "it is the natural world that allows the human race to experience and access the sacred."[93] For Olomo there is a theological correlation between the condition of the natural world and its ability to provide restorative energy to orisa practitioners. Writing to an audience of orisa priests, Olomo describes their interrelatedness between humans and nature at length:

As we practice our spirituality, making sound ecological decisions influences the intensity of our spiritual contact. During rituals, prayers, and other ceremonies we generate energy. . . . The force of what we generate has the potential to propel us into the realms of the divine. I have learned that how we care for the planet influences the depth of our divinities receptiveness and the amount of their divine energies that they send to us. . . . As practitioners of an earth-based theology, our spiritual beliefs reinforce our link to the natural world. . . . We honor the wind, oceans, rain, forests, and rivers; thunder and lightning, tornadoes, and mountains are some of the natural elements that are also venerated in Yoruba religious rituals. Since nature is the object our devotions, it is imperative that our spiritual practices replenish the earth, and its inhabitants.[94]

For Olomo, because it is in nature that much of divine energy resides, orisa practitioners and ritual specialists have an implicit obligation to ensure that the natural world remains balanced, nourished, and free from pollutants and toxins. Compromising the ecological ethics of this obligation, for example, places in peril plant and herb life of Osanyin needed in healing pharmacopoeia.

Because divination and sacrifice are so pronounced in the religious world of orisa priests and their clients, practicing forms of environmental ethics become essential. Olomo raises a crucial question (one that received national attention over a decade ago in Florida's Hialeah County) concerning the public discarding of ritual sacrifices. According to Olomo,

FIGURE 26. Recycle receptacle at Oyotunji African Village. Receptacle reads, "Keep Oyotunji Beautiful." Photograph courtesy of author.

practitioners must discard their ritual items "in ways that honor the divinities," and divining elders must practice "spiritual and natural ecology" in order to guarantee this.[95] The challenges of urban living have made this issue even more exigent for orisa practitioners. Therefore, Olomo calls upon members of her fellow priesthood to be exceedingly diligent in disposing of ritual sacrifices, particularly those that were used for the removal of "negative energies," which she warns can be easily transferable in public spaces. Speaking to her priestly contemporaries, Olomo states:

> Unfortunately, most of us give little consideration to the effect that some of our rituals have on the ecological balance of the places where we leave the leftovers of our ceremonies. In cities where there are large numbers of Yoruba-based practitioners, it is not uncommon to see large plastic garbage bags that smell of rancid and decaying foodstuffs. Passing through cities, I have often encountered the discarded leftovers of rituals: candle wax, coconuts, fruit, money and other items used in sacrificial ceremonies. Parks, residential streets, subways, buses, courtrooms, cemeteries, and street corners are just some of the locations that have been defiled by items left carelessly to decompose. Discarding these items without taking any precautions or steps to re-connect them with the earth's life cycles is inconsistent with the connections that we seeks with the divine forces when we conduct rituals.[96]

Incorporating ecologically friendly practices into one's ceremonial life broadens the definition of orisa ritual to include not only where one dispenses with ritual items but how. Olomo makes a final plea for orisa practitioners to "use biodegradable items whenever possible" and "bury and burn things in an earth friendly manner" in an effort to "maintain the ecological balance of nature."[97] It is her hope that an ecologically minded orisa priesthood and clientele will be vigilant in their efforts to prevent the release of toxins to an earth practitioners ultimately regard as sacred.

Over the course of the twenty-first century perhaps these ecological convictions may ultimately become a part of a larger movement Dwight N. Hopkins labels Black Environmental Liberation Theology.[98] This would couple practitioners' efforts with the need to frame "environmental racism within the context of holistic environmental and social sickness" stressing the "need of holistic healing, especially for communities of color."[99] Collectively, these initiatives will not only yield profound social outcomes regarding African Americans and environmental health but will also prove effective in preserving the ethnobotanical resources, restorative energy, and curative properties of the earth.[100]

"I Don't Think There Has to Be One Way or the Other; There's Room for All of Us": Expressing an African American "Dialect" in a Yoruba Global Culture

In 1998, Egbe Omo Obatala Incorporated hosted a national conference in upstate New York in which prominent members of the African American orisa priesthood, Oseye Mchawi, Stephanie Weaver, Sauda Smith, Baba Alfred, and others, expressed to their largely African American audience that in the orisa tradition, "There are so many dialects and yours is one. You should be proud."[101] African American attendees were encouraged to value and appreciate the contributions they had made to the global orisa tradition and respect the integrity of their particular historical journey in America: "You should stop saying you lost your heritage. This is history beginning *here*. This is *another* Yoruba . . ."[102]

Many African American Yoruba acknowledge that the continent of Africa and the island of Cuba will always be important geo-symbolic and spiritual references for how they engage Yoruba practice. There is, however, a growing recognition that African Americans possess their own religious vernacularism and offer a valuable point of view to the orisa tradition. Although rooted in the United States, African Americans, like other global practitioners, feel they, too, can affirm the sacredness of their local geography. According to Oba Olayinka, "Harlem, New York, for this tradition is Ile-Ife, and it spread out from there . . . for African Americans. . . . We see ourselves as uniquely African in our own way here in this country."[103]

As African American Yoruba in the United States have increasingly embraced their distinct interpretation of the orisa, their need to seek out external sources of religious knowledge has lessened. In the twenty-first century, one finds a deliberate reconfiguring of religious authority, indigeneity, and authenticity among African American Yoruba. Within this larger discourse of authenticity, one important view emerges, "Everybody says we must come to the source. I don't agree with that. The source becomes that country."[104] Aini Olomo notes that "African Americans have been conditioned to think that everybody else's way is superior to our own" and that African Americans must look outside of their own resources in order to find the "real thing."[105] She wonders why African American practitioners choose to travel internationally "in hopes of finding authenticity and validation" instead of "consulting the elders amongst us"[106]:

> Yoruba tradition, as it is presently evolving in North America among English speaking people, has its own variety, encompasses elements from its environment, history and culture. This is the same way Yoruba traditions developed in Africa. The belief system incorporates the ancestral and genetic memories and collective wisdom that accumulate from the struggles unique to the ethnic group. . . . Traveling all the way to Nigeria, Cuba, or Brazil in search of spirituality because we think what is practiced in other countries is "the real thing" . . . keeps North Americans from focusing on the internal work that needs to be done, and from experiencing the beauty and value of the spiritual development that is taking place within our own group as our own collective consciousness solidifies.[107]

Oba Olayinka, like Olomo, believes that there is validity in the ways African Americans in the United States engage orisa. They believe in the integrity of the unique historical, social, and cultural contributions that African Americans have made to the tradition since the twentieth century. According to this philosophy, just as the continent of Africa has been vital to how global orisa identity is understood, so has the continent of North America emerged as a new, productive, and generative site for orisa reflection. According to Olayinka, "I just feel that it is very, very important that we don't look to anybody but ourselves. . . . In the tradition, a lot of us look to the Cubans almost to the point of worship, and even those who look to the traditional side of the culture, everything is Africa, Africa, Africa . . . [They] spend so much time running back and forth to Africa."[108] In fact, as Olayinka explains, "African Americans are the fuel. The reason why this tradition is growing and why it's thriving is because of African Americans. We have given this tradition life in America, both with our love and appreciation and respect for it, with our money and with our time and our strong desire to master the various nuances of this vast, vast tradition."[109]

In recent years, Nigeria's Ooni of Ife conferring of titles and chieftaincies to people of African descent throughout the diaspora, while symbolizing powerful associations between West African and black Atlantic orisa communities in places like North America, South America, and the Caribbean, have also come to complicate local hierarchies and politics of authority. However welcome these titles have been to local diaspora communities, some question the exogenous authority they seem to confer. As one African American priest remarked, "People running over to Africa and getting chieftaincies but yeah you a chief over there but what are you over here? . . . This is where you're at. I believe that if I want to be a chief, then my people here need to make me one. . . . It's given by the people that you work with and work amongst and the people that you persuade and influence. African chieftaincies are like getting an honorary chieftaincy. It's like getting an honorary doctorate. In order to get a real doctorate you've got to earn it . . . and you've got to earn it where it counts."[110] Where it counts for many African American Yoruba is more and more being defined as North America. In the end, Olayinka would argue that while he respects the international honors and titles bestowed upon African Americans from the United States, he asserts the importance of local authority and the local conferring of religious status within the tradition. Baba Alfred Davis of New York City stated well over a decade ago, "Authority is based on how it's done in that family," making explicit the potency of local and not international authority. Increasingly, African American Yoruba, while admitting that Africa will always be an important spiritual reference for how they engage Yoruba practice, insist that an African American priesthood must determine the legitimacy of these practices. Oba Olayinka justifies the authority of African American priests by positioning twenty-first century African American Yoruba as descendants of a lineage that began with practitioners like his parents and Oseijeman Adefunmi. He concludes that "every African American . . . no matter what house you're in, be it a Lucumi house or a Yoruba house, owes a debt of gratitude to Oba Oseijeman as a spiritual ancestor." Beginning with Yoruba Temple, through his leadership "he dropped the gauntlet as to what was going to be acceptable and what wasn't going to be acceptable."[111]

In the twenty-first century, Africa is now heralded as one location among many geographical locations that possesses sacred knowledge of the orisa. Because questions of authenticity are continually at work within these geoplural sites, African American practitioners are at times ambiguous as to how they should relate to their African counterparts and whether the relationships forged are truly dialogically equal. An example of this ambiguity emerged for one African American practitioner while participating in the Orisa World Congress in San Francisco in 1997. In observing what began to seem a pattern, the practitioner remarked, "I resented the fact that the Nigerians did not go to any of workshops to hear the papers unless it was somebody [Nigerian] they knew . . . In other words, nothing good comes from America."[112] Several practitioners felt that Nigerian devotees positioned themselves as authorities, as teachers who "correct" African American Yoruba, rather than being receptive to their distinct contributions. Such African American practitioners contend that New World traditions must begin to rest on their own legacies of tradition building and diasporic authority. They believe the relationship between Africa and the diaspora should be one of reciprocity, not hierarchy. "We have much to learn from our African brothers, and they have much to learn from us," remarked one practitioner. Similarly, when John Mason is asked about his affiliations with Nigeria and why he did not go there for his priestly credentials, he responds, "Why would I go to Nigeria? All my people are here. . . . We've been here for four hundred years."[113] Baba Akinkugbe Karade similarly remarks, "In the final analysis, it matters not how you worship or how your initiation was done. What really matters is what the initiate does with the ashe."[114]

Geographical as well as ethnoautonomy seem best to characterize recent leanings in the global orisa tradition. More than two decades ago prominent Nigerian babalawo Wande Abimbola posited an umbrella movement that would include all global orisa practitioners. This seems to have been replaced for some African American devotees by an investment in their own indigenously American interpretations and expressions. For example, Yewande argued the main challenge involves "who gets to determine what is orthodox?"[115] In light of this challenge, she is cautious with regard to the umbrella concept and wary if, for example, one single ethnic group is seen "as the head of it and becomes the pope of all orisa people."[116] Ernesto Pichardo echoes a similar sentiment and contends that in the New World there exists a very strong resistance against the idea of pope of the religion.[117] Even when notions of African Yoruba are elevated within Cuban orisa practice, Pichardo argues, as is the case for Ilé Tuntún, it is the region of Oyo and not Ile-Ife and the Ooni that are prominent.[118] Therefore, equally as challenging as the fear of ritual homogenization is the fear of hegemonization whereby a priestly vanguard may emerge among Yoruba traditions. The preference among many African American Yoruba as well as Cuban Americans is a space where the celebration of difference may be respected.

For Yewande, it is not necessary for the orisa community in the twenty-first century to delimit areas of ritual and worship but to devote efforts to implementing social strategies that protect and ensure the longevity and well-being of both its national and international priesthood. For example, she suggests that institutional bodies like the World Congress can be active in instituting insurance plans for priests and priestesses; fostering efforts so that the initiated priesthood can be licensed and registered to perform legal marriage rites; developing an institution as a depository for records and archives; establishing an electronic networking service and database to link global devotees; and acting as a liaison body for coordinating opportunities for dialogue among traditional diviners, healers, and priests and other local social bodies.[119] Yewande contends that this new form of global collectivizing may provide a future space for coming together based on common goals that further the orisa community in North America and worldwide.

In the twenty-first century, North America is viewed as a new important locus for the development of orisa traditions. It is the site where religious authority is leveled and vernacular Yoruba traditions thrive. According to Iya Omalewa, "I think each group has their way of doing things, neither way is wrong. . . . If it's working for the people who practice it, it's good."[120] Within North America, orisa religious diversity is increasingly being cultivated, and according to Karade, "These differences have given birth to denominations."[121] This denominational understanding has enabled African American Yoruba to recognize their tradition in self-legitimizing ways and recognize, as Baba Medahochi suggested, that African Americans have their own "spiritual foundation" in the United States. Baba Olayinka makes it clear that "in America, you can do it all. You can do it privately, and you can do it publicly, and the only way you can do that is because of the sacrifices and efforts that African Americans have made."[122] Olayinka's position represents that of many African American devotees, especially those who credit Oseijeman Adefunmi and New York's Yoruba Temple with having paved the way for public orisa practice. Priestess Igberohinjade

Oludoye vividly remembers a time when the religion in North America had to be practiced "in the basement or closet" and insists that "no matter what people think they have, . . . had [Adefunmi] not come and boldly in the streets of New York and everywhere, wore his dashiki, said this is our culture and I'm in it all the way," North American practitioners would not be enjoying many of the public religious freedoms they now possess in orisa.[123]

Unlike any other international locale in the twenty-first century, North America is now the site where multiple orisa "dialects" (African American, Nigerian, Cuban, Brazilian, Trinidadian, Honduran, Dominican, Panamanian, Venezuelan, Puerto Rican, and so forth) thrive and interact. Although these varying orisa geolocales possess distinct "histories without a common past" regarding how they may have developed, North America now forges the possibility for a new path with a common future.[124] "America is New Africa," claims Oba Olayinka. Replete with thriving orisa communities, numerous priestly traditions and resources, and a wealth of diverse sacred knowledge, North America has now evolved into the most diverse orisa locality and vital global center for orisa activity. As Baba Medahochi said less than a year before his passing, African Americans in this tradition no longer need to look yearningly to Africa for religious sustenance and validation: "What we're looking for in Africa is already here."[125]

"I Think It's Home with a Capital 'H'; I Think It Says My Humanity as a Person of African Descent Matters": A Movement Toward Closure

As I bring this book to a close, I devote my final reflections to the ways African American Yoruba refer to this tradition as a symbol of ile, or home. The politics of home and belonging and the subsequent alienation of diasporicity have been adequately theorized in scholarly studies elsewhere. What is important to recount here is the longing of African American Yoruba in North America and their basic plea for a rehumanized existence and an ontological home. Home as metaphor is twofold in that for some, as M. Jacqui Alexander points out, it is within the sphere of private domesticity, not public ecclesial structure, where the orisa reside. In this sense, home is "multiply valenced, a space and place in which Time centers the movement of Sacred energies; a place where those who walk with you—Orisha, Lwa, Spirit—live and manifest (drop in) apparently impromptu, or when called to work."[126] Thus, the domestic sphere of one's private physical home is subsequently transformed into a sacred space where the orisa are "fed, celebrated, and honored . . . because they reside there. It is one of the many places where they reside, whereas it may be the only place that we reside. Home is a set of practices . . . and at the heart of those practices are those that mark its conversion in a spiritual workplace."[127]

Functioning alongside this materiality of home, however, is the ontology of home, where many North American practitioners analogize their devotion to orisa and their fidelity to Africa. Baba Mark Ogunwale Keita Lomax says, "Since childhood I've been on the path of going home."[128] For him this search for home cannot be located geographically, for home rests not in the physicality of land. Instead, as Ogunwale recognizes, black North Americans are trying to find "African roots" that "really are [more] spiritual . . . than geographic."[129] Iya Omolewa similarly wrestles with the ambiguity of a geographical home and is resistant to the idea that it rests exclusively in North America, which she states is "not really our home . . . when they were hanging us, lynching us."[130] In this she echoes the voices of American ancestors of African descent that resonate within her spirit, "Y'all can kill our body but you can't kill me—the real me—because I'm going home."[131] For Iya Omolewa, "This world is just a marketplace; Orun (heaven) is our home."[132] Yoruba traditions offer her a spiritual path toward this home. Velma Love's 2003 interview with an Obatala priest revealed similar sentiments: "This religion is home for me. I know nothing better. This was here before I started going to church. This was here while I was going to church and this was here when I stopped going to church. If I decide to go back to church this will still be here. This is where my heart is. This is home."[133]

Oluweri Egundyao Onisegun embraced this tradition not just as a rejection of "something we perceive to be handed down to us by someone else," but an acceptance of "something now within my soul that resonates with this."[134] Ritually, he reflects, "when I got my first ancestral shrine, as I would start off every day, I would stop and kneel at the shrine, pour libations, set some food there, and I walked away feeling fulfilled, that I could start the day now with a sense of empowerment, a sense of purpose, and a sense of mission, and it was nice. And it is nice."[135] This ancestral shrine is for him a symbolic "act of remembering. . . . Our ancestors continue to live as long as we speak their names."[136] What Onisegun ultimately derives from Yoruba religion is "a sense of spiritual fulfillment, and that's something that is never talked about. This sense of spiritual fulfillment is a place that I can now call home."[137]

Finally, for practitioners like Yewande, Yoruba religion is "Home with a Capital H" and a space of belonging where her "humanity as a person of African descent matters and is not determined by anything White."[138] While rooted in a North American diaspora context, Yewande says Yoruba religion offers her a chance to reclaim an Africa that is "good in and of itself" and a vital "source of healing, rich knowledge, and imagination."[139] As a rehumanizing motif, Yoruba traditions ontologically translate for Yewande like this: "Africa is good enough, and therefore I'm good enough."[140] For her, the "quintessential depiction" of this can be found in the movie *Amistad*, when the main character, Cinque, a shipwrecked African in a North American world, stands up and declares, "I want free." In reflecting on these words, Yewande grieves as she acknowledges "And even I don't know what

FIGURE 27. Processional of North American Yoruba practitioners at Harlem Day Parade in New York City. Photograph courtesy of author.

that means as a descendant of enslaved persons . . . I felt chills inside me when Cinque said 'I want free' and that's what we want. We want free. We want just to be normal human beings. We want not to be broken. We want to be free from being beggars at the table of a religion [Christianity] that sanctioned our destruction. . . . We want to be delivered from that. African religions do that for us."[141] The challenge, according to the current Oba of Oyotunji African Village, is that African Americans have to be "convinced to be free."[142] He contends that in the twenty-first century, Oyotunji African Village is "doing essentially what our ancestors did in the form of a Harriet Tubman who had to convince people of their situation . . . so that they can be liberated . . . as Africans and African people."[143]

With hopes of finding home as whole beings, African American Yoruba in the United States carry with them lived North American diaspora realities of racial blackness, social genderedness, and sexual subjectivities that they bring to each and every encounter with the orisa. According to Iya Omolewa, African Americans had "only one orisa when we got off those slaves ships and that was our Ori."[144] Since 1959, this Ori, this inner head, has guided many African Americans to a rich, dynamic approach to the African gods, creating along the way their own "improvisational sense of the tradition."[145]

Well into the twenty-first century, many African Americans have no plans to return permanently to the continent of Africa. They practice Yoruba traditions with the awareness that "one is mysteriously shipwrecked forever, in the Great New World."[146] Thus, as James Baldwin confesses, "One can neither assess nor overcome the storm of the middle passage"; it placed us in *another condition* where African Americans are forever meted an amputated destiny where this "missing identity aches."[147] Yoruba religious traditions and cultures ultimately help to heal these aches for a "missing identity" and a missing African home several centuries removed.

In the end, *Yoruba Traditions and African American Religious Nationalism* is my attempt to tell the history of African American Yoruba as Babalosa John Mason encouragingly advised—with "a little humanity brought to the table"—for as he explained to me over a decade ago, it is a story with "a wonderful cast of characters; a story worth telling. It's as simple as that."[148] Ashe.

NOTES

Foreword

1. For a succinct statement of Victor Turner's description and analysis of religious pilgrimage, see his *The Center Out There: Pilgrim's Goal*. History of Religions, vol. 12, no. 3 (Feb. 1973), pp. 191–230.
2. Andrea Wilson Nightingale, *Spectacles of Truth in Classical Greek Philosophy: Theoria in its Cultural Context* (New York: Cambridge University Press, 2004).
3. Nightingale, 42.

Preface

1. Ifa-Orunmila is well revered among Yoruba practitioners as the orisa deity who governs divination and human destiny.
2. Mike Crang and Ian Cook, *Doing Ethnographies* (Los Angeles: SAGE Publications, 2007), 9; Gesa Mackenthun, "The Transoceanic Emergence of American Postcolonial Identities," in *A Companion to the Literatures of Colonial America*, ed. Susan Castillo and Ivy Schweitzer (Malden, MA: Blackwell Publishing, 2005), 336.
3. Kim D. Butler, "Africa in the Reinvention of Nineteenth-Century Afro-Bahian Identity," in *Rethinking the African Diaspora: The Making of a Black Atlantic World in the Bight of Benin and Brazil*, ed. Kristin Mann and Edna G. Bay (London: Frank Cass, 2001), 151.
4. Butler, "Africa," 149; also see Russell T. McCutcheon, "Africa on Our Minds," in *The African Diaspora and the Study of Religion*, ed. Theodore Luis Trost (New York: Palgrave MacMillan, 2007), 229–38.
5. Charles H. Long, *Significations: Signs, Symbols, and Images in the Interpretation of Religion* (Philadelphia, PA: Fortress Press, 1986), 1–9, 173–84.

6. Tatsuo Murakami, "Asking the Question of the Origin of Religion in the Age of Globalization," in *Religion and Global Culture: New Terrain in the Study of Religion and the Work of Charles H. Long*, ed. Jennifer I. M. Reid (Lanham, MD: Lexington Books, 2003), 18.

7. Amy Gutmann, *Identity in Democracy* (Princeton, NJ: Princeton University Press, 2003), 156; Charles H. Long, "The History of the History of Religions," in *A Reader's Guide to the Great Religions: Second Edition*, 2nd ed., ed. Charles J. Adams (New York: The Free Press, 1977), 469; Ernst Cassirer, *The Philosophy of the Enlightenment* (Princeton, NJ: Princeton University Press, 1959), 159.

8. Maritza Quiñones Rivera, "From Trigueñita to Afro-Puerto Rican: Intersections of the Racialized, Gendered, and Sexualized Body in Puerto Rico and the U.S. Mainland," *Meridians*, no. 1 (2006): 166.

9. Miguel A. De La Torre, "Ochun: (N)Either the (M)Other of All Cubans (n)or the Bleached Virgin," *Journal of the American Academy of Religion* 69, no. 4 (December 2001): 837–38.

10. Jacob K. Olupona and Terry Rey, introduction to *Orisa Devotion as World Religion: The Globalization of Yoruba Religious Culture*, ed. Jacob K. Olupona and Terry Rey (Madison: University of Wisconsin Press, 2008), 3; Louis Djisovi Ikukomi Eason, *Ifa: The Yoruba God of Divination in Nigeria and the United States* (Trenton, NJ: Africa World Press, 2008), xix.

11. Olupona and Rey, introduction to *Orisa Devotion as World Religion*, 3; Kristina Wirtz, *Ritual, Discourse, and Community in Cuban Santería: Speaking of a Sacred World* (Gainesville: University Press of Florida, 2007), 28.

12. Olasope O. Oyelaran, "From Local to Global: Rethinking Yoruba Religious Traditions for the Next Millennium" (Florida International University, December 9–12, 1999).

13. J. Lorand Matory, *Sex and the Empire That Is No More: Gender and the Politics of Metaphor in Oyo Yoruba Religion* (Minneapolis: University of Minnesota Press, 1994), 66.

14. Eugenio Matibag, *Afro-Cuban Experience: Cultural Reflections in Narrative* (Gainesville: University Press of Florida, 1996), 99.

15. Olupona and Rey, introduction to *Orisa Devotion as World Religion*, 21.

16. Olabiyi Babalola Yai, "Yoruba Religion and Globalization: Some Reflections," in *Orisa Devotion as World Religion: The Globalization of Yoruba Religious Culture*, ed. Jacob K. Olupona and Terry Rey (Madison: University of Wisconsin Press, 2008), 242.

17. Christopher Antonio Brooks, BM, MM, "Eku Odun: A Yoruba Celebration" (master's thesis, University of Texas at Austin, 1984), 53.

18. W. E. B. Dubois, review of *The Negro in Africa and America*, by Joseph Alexander Tillinghast, *Political Science Quarterly* 18 (December 1903): 695.

19. Hortense Spillers et al., "'Whatcha Gonna Do?': Revisiting 'Mama's Baby, Pap's Maybe: An American Grammar Book': A Conversation with Hortense Spillers, Saidiya Hartman, Farah Jasmine Griffin, Shelly Eversley, & Jennifer L. Morgan," *Women's Studies Quarterly* 35, nos. 1/2 (Spring–Summer 2007): 305.

20. Joyce Fleuckiger, *In Amma's Healing Room: Gender and Vernacular Islam in South India* (Bloomington: Indiana University Press, 2006), xi; Jim Perkinson, "Ogu's

Iron or Jesus' Irony: Who's Zooming Who in Diasporic Possession Cult Activity," in *Religion and Global Culture: New Terrain in the Study of Religion and the Work of Charles H. Long*, ed. Jennifer I. M. Reid (Lanham, MD: Lexington Books, 2003), 102; Spillers et al., "'Whatcha Gonna Do?'," 305.

21. Thomas A. Tweed, "Between the Living and the Dead: Fieldwork, History, and the Interpreter's Position," in *Personal Knowledge and Beyond: Reshaping the Ethnography of Religion*, ed. James V. Spickard, J. Shawn Landres, and Meredith McGuire (New York: New York University Press, 2002), 65.

22. Although dated, such projects in religious studies might still be worth undertaking today if lessons can be learned from past attempts with a mindfulness toward bracketing overdetermined sociological analyses of slavery and exposing "the political motives behind . . . assertions about cultural genealogy." Scholars would need to interrogate honestly the Western Christian biases often embedded in the theoretical methods of black religious studies and confess more openly Frazieran leanings regarding the North American cultural complex, adopting more fluid boundaries around what it means to be African rather than accepting a delimited geographical literalism, intellectual fundamentalism, or scholarly fear that often accompany such studies. Scholars would have to work as well with the assumption of sufficiency rather than scarcity when assessing documentary sources, believing that primary data, though still buried, can be unearthed in local historical societies, embarkation records, plantation records and ledgers, newspapers, judicial records, missionary societies, colonial dispatches, diaries, journals, letters, travel accounts, or narrative biographies throughout the diaspora.

23. Henry John Drewal and John Mason, *Beads, Body and Soul: Art and Light in the Yoruba Universe* (Los Angeles: UCLA Fowler Museum of Cultural History, 1998), 246.

24. C. R. Hallpike, "Social Hair," in *Reader in Comparative Religion: An Anthropological Approach*, ed. William Lessa and Evon Z. Vogt (New York: Harper and Row, 1972), 98.

25. Steven Gregory, *Santería in New York City: A Study in Cultural Resistance* (New York: Garland Publishing, 1999), x–xi.

26. George Brandon, *Santeria from Africa to the New World: The Dead Sell Memories* (Bloomington: Indiana University Press, 1993), 2.

27. Brandon, *Santeria from Africa to the New World*, 2.

28. bell hooks, "Postmodern Blackness," in *Colonial Discourse and Post-Colonial Theory: A Reader*, ed. Patrick Williams and Laura Chrisman (New York: Columbia University Press, 1994), 426.

29. www.virginiafoundation.org/roots/background.html.

30. Kim D. Butler, *Freedoms Given, Freedoms Won: Afro-Brazilians in Post-Abolition São Paulo and Salvador* (New Brunswick, NJ: Rutgers University Press, 1998), 226; Butler, "Africa," 139.

31. J. Lorand Matory, *Black Atlantic Religion: Tradition, Transnationalism, and Matriarchy in the Afro-Brazilian Candomblé* (Princeton, NJ: Princeton University Press, 2005), 273–74.

32. James Baldwin, *The Evidence of Things Not Seen* (New York: Henry Holt and Company, 1985), 45–46; and *The Price of the Ticket: Collected Nonfiction 1948–1985* (New York: St. Martin's Press, 1985), xix.

33. For a more extensive analysis of anti-Africanness, see Dianne M. Stewart, *Three Eyes for the Journey: African Dimensions of the Jamaican Religious Experience* (New York: Oxford University Press, 2005), 172, 178–81.

34. Oyebanji Awodinni Morawo (Baale Morawo), personal interview with the author, July 21, 1995.

35. E. U. Essien-Udom, *Black Nationalism: A Search for Identity in America* (Chicago, IL: University of Chicago Press, 1971), 20.

36. Harry G. Lefever, "When the Saints Go Riding In: Santeria in Cuba and the United States," *Journal of the Scientific Study of Religion* 35, no. 3 (September 1996): 323; Mary Ann Clark, *Santería: Correcting the Myths and Uncovering the Realities of a Growing Religion* (Westport, CT: Praeger Publishers, 2007), 26; Oloosa Lloyd Weaver, "Notes on Orisa Worship in an Urban Setting: The New York Example" (paper, International Conference on Orisa Tradition, Ile-Ife, Nigeria, July 1–6, 1986), 14.

37. Matory, *Black Atlantic Religion: Tradition*, 315; Karen McCarthy Brown, *Mama Lola: A Vodou Priestess in Brooklyn* (Berkeley: University of California Press, 2001), xi.

38. I am indebted to Marta Moreno Vega, founder of the Caribbean Culture Center in New York City, who has done an outstanding job in ensuring that many of these names do not slip into obscurity.

39. Judy Rosenthal, *Possession, Ecstasy, and Law in Ewe Voodoo* (Charlottesville: University Press of Virginia, 1998), 1.

40. Dexter B. Gordon, *Black Identity: Rhetoric, Ideology, and Nineteenth-Century Black Nationalism* (Carbondale: Southern Illinois University Press, 2003), 71.

41. Lee H. Butler Jr., *Liberating Our Dignity, Saving Our Souls: A New Theory of African American Identity Formation* (St. Louis, MO: Chalice Press, 2006), 5.

42. Yaacov Shavit, *History in Black: African-Americans in Search of an Ancient Past* (London: Frank Cass Publishers, 2001), xii.

43. Stephan Palmié, *Africas of the Americas: Beyond the Search for Origins in the Study of Afro-Atlantic Religions* (Leiden, Netherlands: Brill, 2008), 2; Fran Markowitz, "Claiming the Pain, Making a Change: The African Hebrew Israelite Community's Alternative to the Black Diaspora," in *Homelands and Diasporas: Holy Lands and Other Places*, ed. André Levy and Alex Weingrod (Stanford, CA: Stanford University Press, 2005), 324.

44. Palmié, *Africas of the Americas*, 12; Baldwin, *Evidence*, 50.

45. Palmié, *Africas of the Americas*, 10; Bernard J. Wolfson, "African American Jews: Dispelling Myths, Bridging the Divide," in *Black Zion: African American Religious Encounters with Judaism*, ed. Yvonne Chireau and Nathaniel Deutsch (New York: Oxford University Press, 2000), 44.

46. Patricia Williams Lessane, "Tell My Feet I've Made it Home: African-American Imaginings of Home and to Find the Orixas" (PhD diss., University of Illinois at Chicago, 2005), 91.

47. Palmié, *Africas of the Americas*, 32; James Baldwin, "White Man's Guilt," in *The Price of the Ticket: Collected Nonfiction 1948-1985* (New York: St. Martin's Press, 1985), 411.

48. Stuart Hall, "Cultural Identity and Diaspora," in *Colonial Discourse and Post-Colonial Theory: A Reader*, ed. Patrick Williams and Laura Chrisman (New York: Columbia University Press, 1994), 399; Baldwin, *Price of the Ticket*, xix.

49. Hall, "Cultural Identity and Diaspora," 399; Charles H. Long, "Indigenous People, Materialities, and Religion: Outline for a New Orientation to Religious Meaning," in *Religion and Global Culture: New Terrain in the Study of Religion and the Work of Charles H. Long*, ed. Jennifer I. M. Reid (Lanham, MD: Lexington Books, 2003), 178.

Introduction

1. In 1986 the first documented cross of light was reported to have made an appearance in Southern California. The Pierce family attested to seeing "the brilliant image of a cross shining through the bathroom window." Since that time, cross of light sightings have been reported throughout California, Florida, New York, Louisiana, and Tennessee, appearing ironically in both church and bathroom windows. Moreover, not exclusive to North America, crosses of light have been documented globally in France, Germany, New Zealand, Slovenia, and the Philippines. The Crosses of Light Archive (http://miracles.mcn.org/crossesz.htm) chronicles that the first reported cross of light in New York City appeared in 1998 to a Hispanic community on West 113th Street. If my uncle, Johnny Speller, whom we affectionately called Uncle Spip, were alive today, however, he would give testimony to the crosses of light that were revealed to African Americans in a Harlem window two and a half decades earlier.

2. See Yvonne P. Chireau, *Black Magic: Religion and the African American Conjuring Tradition* (Berkeley: University of California Press, 2003), 141-43.

3. Andrea Honebrink, "Yoruba Renaissance: The Religious Teachings of a Great African Civilization Attract New Followers," *Utne Reader*, November/December 1993, 46.

4. Kola Abimbola, *Yoruba Culture: A Philosophical Account* (Birmingham, UK: Iroko Academic Publishers, 2006), 36-37; Clark, *Santería*, 2; Mary Ann Clark, "¡No Hay Ningún Santo Aquí! (There Are No Saints Here!): Symbolic Language within Santería," *Journal of the American Academy of Religion* 69, no. 1 (March 2001): 23.

5. Lefever, "When the Saints Go Riding In," 322.

6. George Brandon, "Hierarchy Without a Head: Observations on Changes in the Social Organization of Some Afroamerican Religions in the United States, 1959-1999 with Special Reference to Santeria," *Archives de Sciences Sociales des Religions* 117 (Janvier-Mars 2002): 165; Velana Annemarie Huntington, "Bodies in Contexts: Holistic Ideals of Health, Healing, and Wellness in an American Orisa Community" (PhD diss., University of Iowa, 2002), 124-25.

7. Wirtz, *Ritual, Discourse, and Community in Cuban Santería*, 46.

8. Patrick Manning, *The African Diaspora: A History Through Culture* (New York: Columbia University Press, 2009), 341.

9. Stephan Palmié, ed., *Africas of the Americas: Beyond the Search for Origins in the Study of Afro-Atlantic Religions* (Leiden, Netherlands: Brill, 2008), 27.

10. J. Lorand Matory, *Black Atlantic Religion: Tradition, Transnationalism, and Matriarchy in the Afro-Brazilian Candomblé* (Princeton, NJ: Princeton University Press, 2005), 39.

11. Matibag, *Afro-Cuban Experience*, xiv.

12. Charles H. Long, *Significations: Signs, Symbols, and Images in the Interpretation of Religion* (Philadelphia, PA: Fortress Press, 1986), 7; David D. Hall, ed., *Lived Religion in America: Toward a History of Practice* (Princeton, NJ: Princeton University Press), viii.

13. J. Lorand Matory, *Sex and the Empire That Is No More: Gender and the Politics of Metaphor in Oyo Yoruba Religion* (Minneapolis: University of Minnesota Press, 1994), 221.

14. Crang and Cook, *Doing Ethnographies*, 14; Marion S. Goldman, "Voicing Spiritualities: Anchored Composites as an Approach to Understanding Religious Commitment," in *Personal Knowledge and Beyond: Reshaping the Ethnography of Religion*, ed. James V. Spickard, J. Shawn Landres, and Meredith B. McGuire (New York: New York University Press, 2002), 161; Joseph Miller, director, "Roots: African Dimensions of the History and Cultures of the Americas Through the Trans-Atlantic Slave Trade" (NEH Summer Seminar for College Instructors, Virginia Foundation for the Humanities and Public Policy Charlottesville, VA, June 8–July 10, 2009).

15. Gordon, *Black Identity*, 96.

16. Armin W. Geertz, "As the Other Sees Us: On Reciprocity and the Mutual Reflection in the Study of Native American Religions," in *Personal Knowledge and Beyond: Reshaping the Ethnography of Religion*, ed. James V. Spickard, J. Shawn Landres, and Meredith B. McGuire (New York: New York University Press, 2002), 233–34.

17. James V. Spickard, "On the Epistemology of Post-Colonial Ethnography," in *Personal Knowledge and Beyond: Reshaping the Ethnography of Religion*, ed. James V. Spickard, J. Shawn Landres, and Meredith B. McGuire (New York: New York University Press, 2002), 243.

18. Karen McCarthy Brown, *Mama Lola: A Vodou Priestess in Brooklyn* (Berkeley: University of California Press, 2001), xi.

19. Karen McCarthy Brown, "Writing about 'the Other,' Revisited," in *Personal Knowledge and Beyond: Reshaping the Ethnography of Religion*, ed. James V. Spickard, J. Shawn Landres, and Meredith B. McGuire (New York: New York University Press, 2002), 133.

20. Crang and Cook, *Doing Ethnographies*, 14.

21. Victor Anderson, *Creative Exchange: A Constructive Theology of African American Religious Experience* (Minneapolis: Fortress Press, 2008), 43.

22. Stephan Palmié, *Wizard and Scientists: Explorations in Afro-Cuban Modernity and Tradition* (Durham, NC: Duke University Press, 2002), 4.

23. Joyce Flueckiger, "Roundtable: Anthropology, Ethnography, and Theology" (Ethnography and Theology, Emory University, Atlanta, GA, March 4–6, 2009); Long, *Significations*, 175–76.

24. With the revised edition of Benedict Anderson's *Imagined Communities* in 1991, "imagined," "imaginary," and "imagination" have emerged as dominant categories of analysis among social scientists and humanists whose areas of expertise include diaspora studies, black nationalism, African American religious traditions, and broader New World religious and cultural phenomena. Despite the popularity of these categories, few scholars give critical insight into their limitations in their direct application to black communities in the Americas and the Caribbean. Moreover, even fewer scholars provide sufficient analyses of why Anderson's understanding of nation-states with their roots in dynastic empires and his strong emphasis on Southeast Asian communities is a useful theoretical lens for understanding the ways in which black communities in the New World have historically gone about their productions of identity, religion, and culture. J. Lorand Matory, one of the few exceptions, insightfully applies Anderson's category of the "imagined" to the religiosocial context of Brazil while at the same time framing its major limitations and shortcomings. Given Anderson's oversight, Matory contends that not only were descendants of Africa present in the New World development of "territorial nations," but they were also "neither passive nor marginal" to this formation. Moreover, Anderson neglects the ways in which Africa and its descendants in the New World were creating trans-Atlantic conceptions of community through multiple mediums of exchange. Matory challenges the lack of elasticity of Anderson's imagined nation-state and its reduction to a homogenized "territorially nationalist imagination" that replaced multiple conceptions of imagined citizenship. He also critiques Anderson for privileging the printed text as the dominant transmission of nation-ness to the exclusion of "ritual, musical, and bodily practices." Finally, Matory challenges Anderson on his lack of emphasis on the dialogical relationship between "indigenism and diasporism," which often simultaneously mediated the identities of national communities; see Matory's *Black Atlantic Religion*.

25. Susan L. Taylor, "Courage to Love with Cornel West," *Essence: The Men's Issue*, November 2005, 162–64.

26. Curtis J. Evans, *The Burden of Black Religion* (New York: Oxford University Press, 2008), 127.

27. Hall, "Cultural Identity and Diaspora," 395.

28. Hall, "Cultural Identity and Diaspora," 395.

29. Matory, *Black Atlantic Religion*, 73.

30. Paul Gilroy, "Urban Social Movements, 'Race' and Community," in *Colonial Discourse and Post-Colonial Theory: A Reader*, ed. Patrick Williams and Laura Chrisman (New York: Columbia University Press, 1994), 416; Roberta S. Gold, "The Blacks Jews of Harlem: Representation, Identity, and Race, 1920–1939," *American Quarterly* 55, no. 2 (June 2003): 205.

31. Jayne O. Ifekwunigwe, "Scattered Belongings: Reconfiguring the 'African' in the English-African Diaspora," in *New African Diasporas*, ed. Khalid Koser (New York: Routledge, 2003), 62.

32. Hall, "Cultural Identity and Diaspora," 397.

33. Jonathan Z. Smith, *Imagining Religion: From Babylon to Jonestown* (Chicago: University of Chicago Press, 1982), 20. Smith's full citation reads, "For a student of religion such as myself to accept willingly the designation 'historian of religion' is

to submit to a lifelong sentence of ambiguity. I cannot think of two more difficult terms than 'history' and 'religion.'"

34. Long, *Significations*; James A. Noel, *Black Religion and the Imagination of Matter in the Atlantic World* (New York: Palgrave MacMillan, 2009), ix–xi, and chapters 1–3.

35. Benedict Anderson, *Imagined Communities: Reflections on the Origin and Spread of Nationalism* (New York: Verso, 1991), 141–54.

36. Anderson, *Imagined Communities*, 148–49.

37. Anderson, *Imagined Communities*, 118.

38. John Ernest, *Liberation Historiography: African American Writers and the Challenge of History, 1794–1861* (Chapel Hill: University of North Carolina Press, 2004), 8.

39. Data for this study were also gathered from consulting multiple sources, including microfiche texts from the 1950s and 1960s from the Library of Congress and the Schomburg Center for Research in Black Culture, photographic and historical archives, audio recordings, the Joseph E. Holloway collection, newspapers, popular journals, material-culture sources, private photographic collections, scholar-practitioner texts and narratives, web and Internet resources, secondary literature, unpublished dissertations, and oral history.

40. Marta Vega, "Yoruba Philosophy: Multiple Levels of Transformation and Understanding" (Ann Arbor: UMI Dissertation Services, 1995). In chapter 5, "Yoruba Orisa Tradition in New York City," Vega provides a comprehensive overview of the major figures, influences, and evolutions that occurred in the development of the tradition in New York City; see pages 86–109.

41. Honebrink, "Yoruba Renaissance," 48.

42. Noel, *Black Religion and the Imagination of Matter*, 7.

43. Olupona and Rey, *Orisa Devotion as World Religion*, 24.

44. Hilary E. Wyss, "Indigenous Literacies: New England and New Spain," in *A Companion to the Literatures of Colonial America*, ed. Susan Castillo and Ivy Schweitzer (Malden, MA: Blackwell Publishing, 2005), 387–401.

45. Marion Berghahn, *Images of Africa in Black American Literature* (Totowa, NJ: Rowman and Littlefield, 1977), 19; see specifically, "The 'White' Image of Africa During the Period of Slavery" and "The Role of Africa in the Self-Image of Afro-Americans."

46. Berghahn, *Images of Africa*, 20.

47. Berghahn, *Images of Africa*, 19–20.

48. Berghahn, *Images of Africa*, 20.

49. Palmié, *Africas of the Americas*, 17, 164.

50. Nicholas D. U. Onyewu, "An Approach to African Politics," *African Studies Review* 13, no. 1 (April 1970): 9–16 (emphasis mine).

51. McCutcheon, "Africa On Our Minds," 29.

52. Palmié, *Africas of the Americas*, 11.

53. Palmié, *Africas of the Americas*, 14.

54. Eason, Louis Djisovi Ikukomi, *Ifa: The Yoruba God of Divination in Nigeria and the United States* (Trenton, NJ: Africa World Press, 2008), xxv.

55. This concept of the re-ownership of Africa was in part developed because of my own experiences of the way in which the boundaries of "African" identity are often circumscribed and negotiated in the United States among African nationals and African Americans. On the one hand, there is the moment in a New York City taxicab when a Ghanaian taxi driver asks me where I am from, and I tell him that I'm "African American," to which he responds, "You're not 'African.'" On the other hand, these are individuals who identify themselves as "black" rather than as "African American" because in their self-understanding they are "not African." The theoretical rubric of re-ownership presupposes a primordial moment of initial origin. It thus reminds the Ghanaian taxi driver and American "blacks" that the authority to negate Africanity lies not exclusively in ideology, but in genealogy. African American Yoruba clearly understood this point and, when necessary, strategically collapsed both ideology and genealogy in order to reinforce it.

56. Evelyn Brooks Higginbotham, "African-American Women's History and the Metalanguage of Race," *Signs* 17, no. 2 (Winter 1992): 254.

57. "Discovery and Invention: Religions in Contact in the Americas," in *Harvard University Center for the Study of World Religions* 1, no. 1 (Fall 1993), 5.

58. Henry John Drewal and John Mason, *Beads, Body and Soul: Art and Light in the Yoruba Universe* (Los Angeles: UCLA Fowler Museum of Cultural History, 1998), 244.

Chapter One

1. Gayraud Wilmore, *Black Religion and Black Radicalism: An Interpretation of the Religious History of Afro-American People* (New York: Orbis Books, 1993), 122, 125.

2. Wilmore, *Black Religion and Black Radicalism*, 125.

3. Wilmore, *Black Religion and Black Radicalism*, 125.

4. Wilmore, *Black Religion and Black Radicalism*, 125.

5. Wilmore, *Black Religion and Black Radicalism*, 124–25.

6. Wilmore, *Black Religion and Black Radicalism*, 125.

7. Wilmore, *Black Religion and Black Radicalism*, 123.

8. Wilmore, *Black Religion and Black Radicalism*, 125.

9. James H. Cone, *Martin and Malcolm and America: A Dream or a Nightmare* (New York: Orbis Books, 1991), 160.

10. Baba Akinkugbe Karade, *Path to Priesthood: The Making of an African Priest in an American World* (New York: Kanda Mukutu Books, 2001), 10.

11. Baba Ifa Karade, panelist, International Congress of Orisa Tradition and Culture, Trinidad, W.I., August 19, 1999.

12. Gilroy, "Urban Social Movements," 407.

13. Robert E. Hood, in particular, speaks to the "layers of meaning" of blackness in the West and in the United States, namely historical/cultural, as when speaking of Africa or African descendants in the diaspora; physical, as when speaking of Negroid or Africanoid physical traits such as wooly or kinky hair, broad noses, thick lips, skin color, and even sexual organs; racial, as in hierarchies classifying

and "declassifying" all humankind in early anthropology, comparative anatomy, and Egyptology; biological, as used to distinguish "African/black blood" codes of identity from "European/white blood" in European countries and their respective colonies; and ideological, as in pan-Africanism and Afrocentrism over against what many call Eurocentrism and the ideology of Afrikaner South Africa. Robert E. Hood, *Begrimed and Black: Christian Traditions on Black and Blackness* (Minneapolis, MN: Fortress Press, 1994), xi.

14. Sylvester A. Johnson, *The Myth of Ham in Nineteenth-Century American Christianity: Race, Heathens, and the People of God* (New York: Palgrave Mac-Millan, 2004), 5.

15. Petrine Archer-Straw, *Negrophilia: Avant-Garde Paris and Black Culture in the 1920s* (New York: Thames and Hudson, 2000), 11–18.

16. James W. Perkinson, "The Ghost in the Global Machine: Categorical Whiteness as 'Religious' Violence" (Religion, Social Conflict and Peace Group, American Academy of Religion, Ontario, Canada, October 31, 2010).

17. Joseph R. Washington, *Anti-Blackness in English Religion 1500–1800* (New York: E. Mellen Press, 1984), xiii.

18. Washington, *Anti-Blackness in English Religion*, xvi–xvii.

19. Washington, *Anti-Blackness in English Religion*, xiii.

20. Washington, *Anti-Blackness in English Religion*, xiii.

21. Johnson, *Myth of Ham*, 21.

22. Johnson, *Myth of Ham*, 21.

23. Johnson, *Myth of Ham*, 21.

24. Johnson, *Myth of Ham*, 12.

25. Johnson, *Myth of Ham*, 13.

26. Eddie S. Glaude Jr., *Exodus!: Religion, Race, and Nation in Early Nineteenth-Century Black America* (Chicago: University of Chicago Press, 2000), 114.

27. Karen Ho and Wende Elizabeth Marshall, "Criminality and Citizenship: Implicating the White Nation," in *Race Consciousness: African-American Studies for the New Century*, ed. Judith Jackson Fossett and Jeffrey A. Tucker (New York: New York University Press, 1997), 210. Similarly, James Noel in chapter 6 of *Black Religion and the Imagination of Matter* also works with the theme of transubstantiation, arguing, "What African American slaves developed were covert practices of reverse transubstantiation whereby they were recreated and reconstituted as human beings."

28. Evans, *Burden of Black Religion*, 105.

29. Toni Morrison, "Unspeakable Things Unspoken: The Afro-American Presence in American Literature," in *The Black Feminist Reader*, ed. Joy James and T. Denean Sharpley-Whiting (Malden, MA: Blackwell Publishers, 2000), 47.

30. Morrison, "Unspeakable Things Unspoken," 48.

31. Morrison, "Unspeakable Things Unspoken," 48–49.

32. Hood, *Begrimed and Black*, 182.

33. Hood, *Begrimed and Black*, 182.

34. Hood, *Begrimed and Black*, 185.

35. Hood, *Begrimed and Black*, 187.

36. Hood, *Begrimed and Black*, 187.

37. Washington, *Anti-Blackness in English Religion*, 125.

38. Colette Guillaumin, "Race and Nature: The System of Marks," in *Racism*, ed. Leonard Harris (Amherst, MA: Humanity Books, 1999), 219–36.

39. M. Jacqui Alexander, *Pedagogies of Crossing: Meditations on Feminism, Sexual Politics, Memory and the Sacred* (Durham, NC: Duke University Press, 2005), 296.

40. Johnson, *Myth of Ham*, 21.

41. Winthrop Jordan, *White Over Black: American Attitudes Towards the Negro, 1550–1812* (Chapel Hill: University of North Carolina Press, 1968), 5.

42. Curtis Keim, *Mistaking Africa: Curiosities and Inventions of the American Mind* (Boulder, CO: Westview Press, 1999), 11.

43. Lee H. Butler Jr., *Liberating Our Dignity, Saving Our Souls: A New Theory of African American Identity Formation* (St. Louis: Chalice Press, 2006), 14.

44. Jordan, *White Over Black*, 23.

45. Jordan, *White Over Black*, 23.

46. Hood, *Begrimed and Black*, 95 (emphasis in quote is mine).

47. Washington, *Anti-Blackness in English Religion*, 112.

48. Washington, *Anti-Blackness in English Religion*, 123.

49. Jordan, *White Over Black*, 24.

50. Washington, *Anti-Blackness in English Religion*, 118.

51. Washington, *Anti-Blackness in English Religion*, 131.

52. Washington, *Anti-Blackness in English Religion*, 171.

53. Jordan, *White Over Black*, 20.

54. David Crosby, Roots: African Dimensions of the History and Cultures of the Americas Through the Trans-Atlantic Slave Trade (NEH Summer Seminar for College Instructors, Virginia Foundation for the Humanities and Public Policy, Charlottesville, VA, June 8–July 10, 2009).

55. Hood, *Begrimed and Black*, 96.

56. Hood, *Begrimed and Black*, 23–24; Washington, *Anti-Blackness in English Religion*, 536.

57. Washington, *Anti-Blackness in English Religion*, 133.

58. Hood, *Begrimed and Black*, 21; Washington, *Anti-Blackness in English Religion*, 131.

59. Washington, *Anti-Blackness in English Religion*, 140.

60. Washington, *Anti-Blackness in English Religion*, 133.

61. Long, *Significations*, 1986, 91; also see Noel, *Black Religion and the Imagination of Matter*, 5.

62. Jordan, *White Over Black*, 4.

63. Matthew Frye Jacobson, *Whiteness of a Different Color: European Immigrants and the Alchemy of Race* (Cambridge, MA: Harvard University Press, 1998).

64. Jordan, *White Over Black*, 15.

65. Jordan, *White Over Black*, 13–16.

66. Jordan, *White Over Black*, 16.

67. Jordan, *White Over Black*, 16.

68. Jordan, *White Over Black*, 17.

69. Washington, *Anti-Blackness in English Religion*, 19.

70. Washington, *Anti-Blackness in English Religion*, 19.

71. Hood, *Begrimed and Black*, 89.

72. Hood, *Begrimed and Black*, 89.

73. Hood, *Begrimed and Black*, 85.

74. Hood, *Begrimed and Black*, 78.

75. Jordan, *White Over Black*, 7.

76. Hood, *Begrimed and Black*, 73.

77. Jordan, *White Over Black*, 24.

78. Jordan, *White Over Black*, 17.

79. Jordan, *White Over Black*, 18.

80. Hood, *Begrimed and Black*, 152.

81. Gordon, *Black Identity*, 56.

82. Gordon, *Black Identity*, 55.

83. Lee H. Butler Jr. "Loving . . . Body and Soul Together" (Chicago Theological Seminary Convocation, Chicago, IL, December 2004).

84. Washington, *Anti-Blackness in English Religion*, 127.

85. Hood, *Begrimed and Black*, 149.

86. Hood, *Begrimed and Black*, 156.

87. Hood, *Begrimed and Black*, 89.

88. Washington, *Anti-Blackness in English Religion*, 132.

89. Cynthia Dobbs, "Toni Morrison's Beloved: Bodies Returned, Modernism Revisited," *African American Review* 32, no. 4 (Winter 1998): 564.

90. Susan Nance, "Mystery of the Moorish Science Temple: Southern Blacks and American Alternative Spirituality in 1920s Chicago," *Religion and American Culture* 12, no. 2 (Summer 2002): 138; Jordan, *White Over Black*, 9; Hood, *Begrimed and Black*, 88.

91. Riggins R. Earl, *Dark Symbols, Obscure Signs: God, Self, and Community in the Slave Mind* (Knoxville: University of Tennessee Press, 2003), 51.

92. Jordan, *White Over Black*, 17.

93. Hood, *Begrimed and Black*, 139.

94. Cotton Mather, *The Negro Christianized: An Essay to Excite and Assist the Good Work, the Instruction of Negro-Servants in Christianity* (Boston, 1706); Tracey E. Hucks, "The Black Church, Invisible and Visible," *The Encyclopedia of American Cultural and Intellectual History*, ed. Mary Kupiec Clayton and Peter W. Williams (New York: Scribner, 2001), 229.

95. Hood, *Begrimed and Black*, 140.

96. Hood, *Begrimed and Black*, 140.

97. Nell Irvin Painter, "Was Marie White? The Trajectory of a Question in the United States," *The Journal of Southern History* 74, no. 1 (February 2008): 22.

98. Painter, "Was Marie White?," 23, 30.

99. Painter, "Was Marie White?," 4.

100. Washington, *Anti-Blackness in English Religion*, 22; Hood, *Begrimed and Black*, 82.

101. Hood, *Begrimed and Black*, 87, 147; Jordan, *White Over Black*, 24.

102. Victor Anderson, *Beyond Ontological Blackness: An Essay on African American Religious and Cultural Criticism* (New York: Continuum Publishing, 1995), 13.

103. Hood, *Begrimed and Black*, 153.

104. Roger Friedland, "Religious Nationalism and the Problem of Collective Representation," *Annual Review of Sociology* 27 (August 2001): 136.

105. Lena Delgado De Torres, "Reformulating Nationalism in the African Diaspora: The Aponte Rebellion of 1812," *The New Centennial Review* 3, no. 3 (Fall 2003): 41–42.

106. Melani McAlister, "One Black Allah: The Middle East in the Cultural Politics of African American Liberation, 1955–1970," *American Quarterly* 51, no. 3 (1999): 650.

107. Jeffrey Stout, "Theses on Black Nationalism," in *Is It Nation Time?: Contemporary Essays on Black Power and Black Nationalism*, ed. Eddie S. Glaude Jr. (Chicago: University of Chicago Press, 2002), 245.

108. Jeffrey Stout, *Democracy and Tradition* (Princeton, NJ: Princeton University Press, 2004), 45.

109. Manning Marable, *Race, Reform and Rebellion: The Second Reconstruction in Black America* (Jackson: University Press of Mississippi, 1984), 59.

110. Wilson Jeremiah Moses, *Classical Black Nationalism: From the American Revolution to Marcus Garvey* (New York: New York University Press, 1996), 5.

111. William L. Van Deburg, *New Day in Babylon: The Black Power Movement and American Culture 1965–1975* (Chicago: University of Chicago Press, 1992), 153.

112. Wilson Jeremiah Moses, *The Golden Age of Black Nationalism 1850–1925* (New York: Oxford University Press, 1978), 17.

113. Moses, *Classical Black Nationalism*, 5.

114. Van Deburg, *New Day in Babylon*, 171.

115. Patricia Hill Collins, "Black Nationalism and African American Ethnicity: The Case of Afrocentrism as Civil Religion," in *Ethnicity, Nationalism, and Minority Rights*, ed. Stephen May, Tariq Modood, and Judith Squires (New York: Cambridge University Press, 2004), 97.

116. Collins, "Black Nationalism and African American Ethnicity," 97.

117. Collins, "Black Nationalism and African American Ethnicity," 98; Kim D. Butler, *Freedoms Given, Freedoms Won: Afro-Brazilians in Post-Abolition São Paulo and Salvador* (New Brunswick, NJ: Rutgers University Press, 1998), 1.

118. Collins, "Black Nationalism and African American Ethnicity," 105.

119. Thomas Hylland Eriksen, *Ethnicity and Nationalism* (London: Pluto Press, 2002), 106–7.

120. Eriksen, *Ethnicity and Nationalism*, 107; Hank Johnston, "Religio-Nationalist Subcultures under the Communists: Comparisons from the Baltics, Transcaucasia and Ukraine," *International Studies in the Sociology of Religion* 54, no. 3 (Autumn 1993): 237–55.

121. Gold, "The Black Jews of Harlem," 216; Friedland, "Religious Nationalism," 126.

122. Friedland, "Religious Nationalism," 134, 142.

123. Zillur R. Khan, "Islam and Bengali Nationalism," *Asian Survey* 25, no. 8 (August 1985): 834.

124. John H. Bracey Jr., August Meier, and Elliott Rudwick, *Black Nationalism in America* (Indianapolis: Bobbs-Merrill Company, 1970), xxvii.

125. J. Deotis Roberts, "Afro-Arab Islam and the Black Revolution," *Journal of Black Religious Thought* 28, no. 2 (Autumn–Winter 1971): 95–111.

126. Milind Wakankar, "Body, Crowd, Identity: Genealogy of a Hindu Nationalist Ascetics," *Social Text* 45 (Winter 1995): 46.

127. Brian Porter, "The Catholic Nation: Religion, Identity, and the Narratives of Polish History," *The Slavic and East European Journal* 45, no. 2 (Summer 2001): 294.

128. Greg Gaut, "Can a Christian be a Nationalist? Vladimir Solov'ev's Critique of Nationalism," *Slavic Review* 57, no. 1 (Spring 1998): 83.

129. Cone, *Martin and Malcolm and America*, 16.

130. R. Drew Smith, "Black Religious Nationalism and the Politics of Transcendence," *Journal of the American Academy of Religion* 66, no. 3 (Autumn 1998): 538.

131. Smith, "Black Religious Nationalism," 538.

132. Smith, "Black Religious Nationalism," 538.

133. Josiah U. Young, *A Pan-African Theology: Providence and the Legacy of the Ancestors* (Trenton, NJ: Africa World Press, 1992), 56.

134. Young, *Pan-African Theology*, 74.

135. Gordon, *Black Identity*, 105.

136. Hood, *Begrimed and Black*, 163.

137. Hood, *Begrimed and Black*, 189.

138. Young, *Pan-African Theology*, 57.

139. Gordon, *Black Identity*, 36.

140. Gordon, *Black Identity*, 95–96.

141. Gordon, *Black Identity*, 149, 172.

142. Dianne Stewart, "Response," in *The Ties that Bind: African American and Hispanic American/Latino/a Theologies in Dialogue*, ed. Anthony B. Pinn and Benjamin Valentin (New York: Continuum, 2001), 202.

143. Tunde Adeleke, *UnAfrican Americans: Nineteenth-Century Black Nationalists and the Civilizing Mission* (Lexington: University Press of Kentucky, 1998), 9.

144. Wilmore, *Black Religion and Black Radicalism*, 124–25.

145. Adeleke, *UnAfrican Americans*, 137.

146. Simon Gikandi, "Culture and Reasonableness," *Contemporary Literature* 34, no. 4 (Winter 1993): 779; Glaude, *Exodus!*, 162.

147. Johnson, *Myth of Ham*, 12.

148. Adeleke, *UnAfrican Americans*, 116.

149. Lewis R. Gordon, *Existentia Africana: Understanding Africana Existential Thought* (New York: Routledge, 2000), 140.

150. Adeleke, *UnAfrican Americans*, 121.

151. Hood, *Begrimed and Black*, 170.

152. Hood, *Begrimed and Black*, 170.

153. Long, *Significations*, 175–76.

154. Hood, *Begrimed and Black*, 23.

155. Shavit, *History in Black*, x.

156. Stewart, *Three Eyes for the Journey*, 144.

157. Michael J. C. Echeruo, "An African Diaspora: The Ontological Project," in *The African Diaspora: African Origins and New World Identities*, ed. Isidore Okpewho, Carole Boyce Davies, and Ali A. Mazrui (Bloomington: Indiana University Press, 1999), 16.

158. Jacob K. Olupona, "Globalization and African Immigrant Religious Communities," in *Religion and Global Culture: New Terrain in the Study of Religion and the Work of Charles H. Long*, ed. Jennifer I. M. Reid (Lanham, MD: Lexington Books, 2003), 84; Ifekwunigwe, "Scattered Belongings," 56; David Leeming, *James Baldwin: A Biography* (New York: Knopf, 1994), 197.

159. Butler, *Freedoms Given, Freedoms Won*, 4.

160. Thomas C. Holt, "Slavery and Freedom in the Atlantic World: Reflections on the Diasporan Framework," in *Crossing Boundaries: Comparative History of Black People in Diaspora*, ed. Darlene Clark Hine and Jacqueline McLeod (Bloomington: Indiana University Press, 1999), 37.

161. McAlister, "One Black Allah," 625.

162. Patricia Williams Lessane, "Tell My Feet I've Made It Home: African-American Imaginings of Home and to Find the Orixas," (PhD diss., University of Illinois at Chicago, 2005), 203.

163. Ernest, *Liberation Historiography*, 9.

164. Lessane, "Tell My Feet I've Made It Home," 203.

165. Harvard University Center for the Study of World Religions, *NEWS* 1, no. 1 (Fall 1993): 3–4.

166. Harvard University Center for the Study of World Religions, *NEWS* 1, no. 1 (Fall 1993): 3.

167. W. E. B. Dubois, *The Souls of Black Folk* (New York: Bantam Books, 1989), 6.

168. Ho and Marshall, "Criminality and Citizenship," 214.

169. Lessane, "Tell My Feet I've Made it Home," 140.

Chapter Two

1. Oba Efuntola Oseijeman Adelabu Adefunmi I, personal interviews with the author, August 1994, January 1995, August 1996, and August 1997.

2. Sidney J. Lemelle and Robin D. G. Kelly, eds., *Imagining Home: Class, Culture and Nationalism in the African Diaspora* (New York: Verso, 1994), 7.

3. Robert Anthony Orsi, *The Madonna of 115th Street: Faith and Community in Italian Harlem, 1880–1950* (New Haven, CT: Yale University Press, 1985), xxii.

4. Hall, *Lived Religion in America*, x.

5. Gold, Roberta S., "The Blacks Jews of Harlem: Representation, Identity, and Race, 1920–1939," *American Quarterly* 55, no. 2 (June 2003): 216–17.

6. David D. Hall, *A History of the Book in America* (Cambridge: Cambridge University Press, 2001), 9.

7. During World War I and succeeding decades, Detroit was a popular destination for African American migrants from the South. The first trickle of migrants began in 1915 when 1,000 blacks arrived each month from such states as Georgia, Alabama, South Carolina, and Arkansas. Whereas only 5,741 blacks lived in the city in 1910, comprising a little more than 1 percent of the total population, by 1920 the African American community had swelled to 40,838 or 4.1 percent of the aggregate. By 1930 with the onset of the Depression and the temporary cessation of the Great Migration, 120,066 blacks resided in Detroit, forming 7.6 percent of the populace; see Claude Andrew Clegg III, *An Original Man* (New York: St. Martin's Press, 1997), 14.

8. John Hope Franklin and Alfred A. Moss, *From Slavery to Freedom: A History of African Americans* (New York: McGraw-Hill, 1994), 398.

9. Stephen C. Clapp, *A Reporter at Large: African Theological Arch-Ministry, Inc.* (New York Public Library, Schomburg Collection, 1966), 10.

10. Franklin and Moss, *From Slavery to Freedom*, 473.

11. Oba Efuntola Oseijeman Adelabu Adefunmi I, personal interviews with the author, August 1994, January 1995, August 1996, and August 1997.

12. Carl Hunt, *Oyotunji Village: The Yoruba Movement in America* (Washington, DC: University Press of America, 1979), 21; Eason, *Ifa*, 83.

13. Oba Efuntola Oseijeman Adelabu Adefunmi I, personal interviews with the author, August 1994, January 1995, August 1996, and August 1997.

14. Oba Efuntola Oseijeman Adelabu Adefunmi I, personal interviews with the author, August 1994, January 1995, August 1996, and August 1997.

15. Oba Efuntola Oseijeman Adelabu Adefunmi I, personal interviews with the author, August 1994, January 1995, August 1996, and August 1997.

16. Oba Efuntola Oseijeman Adelabu Adefunmi I, personal interviews with the author, August 1994, January 1995, August 1996, and August 1997.

17. Oba Efuntola Oseijeman Adelabu Adefunmi I, personal interviews with the author, August 1994, January 1995, August 1996, and August 1997. This is a phonetic spelling of the name.

18. Oba Efuntola Oseijeman Adelabu Adefunmi I, personal interviews with the author, August 1994, January 1995, August 1996, and August 1997.

19. Daryl Pinckney, *Out There: Mavericks of Black Literature* (New York: Basic Civitas Books, 2002); also, www.everygeneration.co.uk/profiles/jarogers.htm.

20. www.everygeneration.co.uk/profiles/jarogers.htm.

21. Oba Oseijeman Efuntola Adelabu Adefunmi I, personal interviews with the author, August 1994, January 1995, August 1996, and August 1997.

22. J. A. Rogers, *Sex and Race: Negro-Caucasian Mixing in All Ages and All Lands* (New York: H. M. Rogers, 1967).

23. Oba Efuntola Oseijeman Adelabu Adefunmi I, personal interviews with the author, August 1994, January 1995, August 1996, and August 1997.

24. Oba Efuntola Oseijeman Adelabu Adefunmi I, personal interviews with the author, August 1994, January 1995, August 1996, and August 1997.

25. Oba Efuntola Oseijeman Adelabu Adefunmi I, personal interviews with the author, August 1994, January 1995, August 1996, and August 1997.

26. Oba Efuntola Oseijeman Adelabu Adefunmi I, personal interviews with the author, August 1994, January 1995, August 1996, and August 1997.

27. George Washington Williams, *History of the Negro Race in America, 1619–1880* (New York: Arno Press and the New York Times, 1968), 19.

28. Williams, *History of the Negro Race*, vi–vii.

29. Williams, *History of the Negro Race*, vi–vii.

30. Williams, *History of the Negro Race*, vii.

31. Williams, *History of the Negro Race*, 552.

32. Williams, *History of the Negro Race*, 114.

33. Williams stated in his text that "there is not a more promising mission-field in the world than Africa, and yet our friends in America take so little interest in this work!" Williams, *History of the Negro Race*, 108–14.

34. Mbonu Ojike, *My Africa* (New York: John Doubleday Company, 1946), xiii.

35. Ojike, *My Africa*, xiii.

36. Ojike, *My Africa*, 3.

37. Henry M. Stanley, *Through the dark continent or, The sources of the Nile around the great lakes of equatorial Africa and down the Livingstone River to the Atlantic Ocean* (New York: Harper & Brothers, 1878); David Livingstone, *Livingstone's Africa* (Philadelphia: Hubbard Brothers, 1872); William Winwood Read, *Savage Africa; being the narrative of a tour in equatorial, southwestern, and northwestern Africa; with notes on the habits of the gorilla; on the existence of unicorns and tailed men; on the slave trade; on the origin, character, and capabilities of the negro, and on the future civilization of western Africa* (New York: Harper, 1864); J. G. Wood, *The uncivilized races of men in all countries of the world; being a comprehensive account of their manners and customs, and of their physical, social, mental, moral and religious characteristics* (Hartford, CT: J. B. Burr and Company, 1871).

38. Leo Frobenius, *The Voice of Africa* (London: Hutchison and Co. 1913); George W. Ellis, *Negro Culture in West Africa* (New York: Neale Publishing, 1914); Melville Herskovits, *Dahomey: An Ancient West African Kingdom*, 2 vols. (New York: J. J. Augustin, 1938); W. E. B. Dubois, *Black Folk Then and Now* (New York: Holt & Co., 1939); James Weldon Johnson, *Native African Races and Culture* (Charlottesville, VA: The Michie Company, 1927); HRH Prince Akiki Nyabongo, *African Answers Back* (London: Routledge, 1936); George Padmore, *Africa and World Peace* (London: Secker and Warburg, 1937); W. Tete-Ansa, *Africa at Work* (New York, 1930); Prince A. A. Nwafo Orizu, *Without Bitterness* (New York: Creative Age Press, 1944); Samuel Johnson, *History of the Yoruba* (London: Routledge, 1921); Alain Locke, *The Negro in Art* (New York: Hacker Art Books, 1940, 1968); Eslanda Robeson, *African Journey* (New York: John Day Company, 1945); Carter G. Woodson, *The African Background* (New York: Negroes Universities Press, 1936).

39. Ojike, *My Africa*, 182.

40. Ojike, *My Africa*, 192.

41. Ojike, *My Africa*, 193.

42. Ojike, *My Africa*, 196.

43. Oba Efuntola Oseijeman Adelabu Adefunmi I, personal interviews with the author, August 1994, January 1995, August 1996, August 1997.

44. For a more comprehensive look at Long's hypothesis on Africa and its connection to African American religiosity, see "Perspectives for a Study of Afro-American Religion in the United States" in Long, *Significations*, 173–84.

45. Long, *Significations*, 136.

46. Hans A. Baer and Merrill Singer, *African-American Religion in the Twentieth Century: Varieties of Protest and Accommodation* (Knoxville: University of Tennessee Press, 1992), 118–19.

47. Clegg, *An Original Man*, 19.

48. Nance, "Mystery of the Moorish Science Temple," 146, 138.

49. Susan Nance, "Respectability and Representation: The Moorish Science Temple, Morocco, and Black Public Culture in 1920s Chicago," *American Quarterly* 54, no. 4 (December 2002): 628–29; Nance, "Mystery of the Moorish Science Temple," 131.

50. Baer and Singer, *African-American Religion in the Twentieth Century*, 118.

51. Baer and Singer, *African-American Religion in the Twentieth Century*, 118.

52. Gold, "The Black Jews of Harlem," 212; Joseph R. Washington, *Black Sects and Cults* (Garden City, NY: Doubleday and Company, 1972), 128.

53. Nance, "Respectability and Representation," 628.

54. Baer and Singer, *African-American Religion in the Twentieth Century*, 119.

55. Baer and Singer, *African-American Religion in the Twentieth Century*, 119.

56. Arthur Huff Fauset, *Black Gods of the Metropolis: Negro Religious Cults in the Urban North* (Philadelphia: University of Pennsylvania Press, 1944, 1971), 47.

57. Fauset, *Black Gods of the Metropolis*, 47.

58. Fauset, *Black Gods of the Metropolis*, 42–43.

59. Larry Murphy, J. Gordon Melton, and Gary L. Ward, *Encyclopedia of African American Religions* (New York: Garland Publishing, 1993), 31.

60. Fauset, *Black Gods of the Metropolis*, 42; Murphy, Melton, and Ward, *Encyclopedia of African American Religions*, 31.

61. Murphy, Melton, and Ward, *Encyclopedia of African American Religions*, 31.

62. Nance, "Respectability and Representation," 624.

63. Nance, "Mystery of the Moorish Science Temple," 136.

64. Oba Efuntola Oseijeman Adelabu Adefunmi I, personal interviews with the author, August 1994, January 1995, August 1996, and August 1997.

65. By assuming the surname Bey, King's father was very much in line with the members of the Moorish Science Temple. According to Gayraud Wilmore, "Many of these groups continued the practice of changing the names of believers, or attaching 'el' or 'bey' to their given names as a sign of Asiatic nationality"; see Wilmore, *Black Religion and Black Radicalism*, 160.

66. During a tape-recorded interview with the author, King described in detail how "it was there that I first saw a photograph—I have never forgotten it—a picture of some people at the pyramids of Giza in Egypt and it was a man and he was sitting on a camel . . . on the card it says, 'Brother Roy King Bey, Here I is where I has longed to be.' And that was the full text of the postcard. Because it was very impressive, I asked my mother about it and she said that not only was your father a Mason, but he was a follower of Drew Ali . . ." Oba Efuntola Oseijeman Adelabu

Adefunmi I, personal interviews with the author, August 1994, January 1995, and August 1996.

67. Fauset, *Black Gods of the Metropolis*, 48.

68. Murphy, Melton, and Ward, *Encyclopedia of African American Religions*, 294.

69. James Turner, "The Sociology of Black Nationalism," *The Black Scholar* 1, no. 2 (December 1969): 25.

70. Murphy, Melton, and Ward, *Encyclopedia of African American Religion*, 293. Maroons were formerly enslaved Africans who escaped to the mountainous regions of Jamaica and other Caribbean islands and formed free communities.

71. Butler, *Freedoms Given, Freedoms Won*, 225.

72. Murphy, Melton, and Ward, *Encyclopedia of African American Religion*, 294.

73. Randall Burkett, *Black Redemption: Churchmen Speak for the Garvey Movement* (Philadelphia: Temple University Press, 1978), 9. The Declaration of Rights was a lengthy document that contained a preamble, fifty-three declared rights for the race worldwide, and ended with the following summation before the signatory section: "These rights we believe to be justly ours and proper for the protection of the Negro race at large, and because of this belief, we, on behalf of the four hundred million Negroes of the world, do pledge herein the sacred blood of the race in defense, and we hereby subscribe our names as a guarantee of the truthfulness and faithfulness hereof in the presence of the Almighty God, on the 13th day of August, in the year of our Lord one thousand nine hundred and twenty." John Henrik Clarke, *Marcus Garvey and the Vision of Africa* (New York: Vintage Books, 1974), 443–51.

74. Burkett, *Black Redemption*, 3.

75. Burkett, *Black Redemption*, 3.

76. Burkett, *Black Redemption*, 3.

77. Franklin and Moss, *From Slavery to Freedom*, 358.

78. Burkett, *Black Redemption*, 34.

79. Burkett, *Black Redemption*, 34.

80. Burkett, *Black Redemption*, 7–8.

81. Burkett, *Black Redemption*, 7–8.

82. Murphy, Melton, and Ward, *Encyclopedia of African American Religions*, 294.

83. Clarke, *Marcus Garvey*, 4.

84. E. U. Essien-Udom, *Black Nationalism: A Search for an Identity in America* (Chicago: University of Chicago Press, 1971), 36.

85. Duse Mohammed Ali, *In the Land of the Pharaohs: A Short History of Egypt* (London: Stanley Paul & Co. 1911), xx.

86. Ali, *In the Land of the Pharaohs*, 1.

87. Ali, *In the Land of the Pharaohs*, 356.

88. Ali, *In the Land of the Pharaohs*, 354.

89. Anderson, *Imagined Communities*, 168.

90. Anderson, *Imagined Communities*, 152–53.

91. *African Times and Orient Review* 4, no. 5 (May 1917): 99.

92. Clarke, *Marcus Garvey*, 156.

93. Robert A. Hill, ed., *The Marcus Garvey and Universal Negro Improvement Association Papers, Volume 1, 1826–August 1919* (Berkeley: University of California Press, 1983), 116.

94. Hill, *The Marcus Garvey and Universal Negro Improvement Association Papers*, 1:118.

95. Milton C. Sernett, *Bound for the Promised Land: African American Religion and the Great Migration* (Durham, NC: Duke University Press, 1997), 81.

96. Oba Efuntola Oseijeman Adelabu Adefunmi I, personal interviews with the author, August 1994, January 1995, and August 1996.

97. Hunt, *Oyotunji Village*, 22.

98. Hunt, *Oyotunji Village*, 22.

99. Oba Efuntola Oseijeman Adelabu Adefunmi I, personal interviews with the author, August 1994, January 1995, August 1996, and August 1997.

100. Oba Efuntola Oseijeman Adelabu Adefunmi I, personal interviews with the author, August 1994, January 1995, August 1996, and August 1997.

101. Oba Efuntola Oseijeman Adelabu Adefunmi I, personal interviews with the author, August 1994, January 1995, August 1996, and August 1997.

102. Oba Efuntola Oseijeman Adelabu Adefunmi I, personal interviews with the author, August 1994, January 1995, August 1996, and August 1997.

103. Oba Efuntola Oseijeman Adelabu Adefunmi I, personal interviews with the author, August 1994, January 1995, August 1996, and August 1997.

104. Marta Moreno Vega, "The Dynamic Influence of Cubans, Puerto Ricans, and African Americans in the Growth of Ocha in New York City," in *Orisa Devotion as World Religion: The Globalization of Yoruba Religious Culture*, ed. Jacob K. Olupona and Terry Rey (Madison: University of Wisconsin Press, 2008), 326.

105. Claude Levi-Strauss, foreword to the French edition of *Dances of Haiti* by Katherine Dunham (Los Angeles: Center for Afro-American Studies at UCLA, 1983), xv.

106. Levi-Strauss, foreword to the French edition of *Dances of Haiti*, ix–x.

107. Vega, "Yoruba Philosophy," 108–9.

108. Oba Efuntola Oseijeman Adelabu Adefunmi I, personal interviews with the author, August 1994, January 1995, August 1996, and August 1997.

109. Oba Efuntola Oseijeman Adelabu Adefunmi I, personal interviews with the author, August 1994, January 1995, August 1996, and August 1997.

110. Babatunde Olatunji, *The Beat of My Drum: An Autobiography* (Philadelphia: Temple University Press, 2005), 34–35.

111. Oba Efuntola Oseijeman Adelabu Adefunmi I, personal interviews with the author, August 1994, January 1995, August 1996, and August 1997.

112. Oba Efuntola Oseijeman Adelabu Adefunmi I, personal interviews with the author, August 1994, January 1995, and August 1996.

113. Oba Efuntola Oseijeman Adelabu Adefunmi I, personal interviews with the author, August 1994, January 1995, August 1996, and August 1997.

114. Oba Efuntola Oseijeman Adelabu Adefunmi I, personal interviews with the author, August 1994, January 1995, August 1996, and August 1997.

115. Hunt, *Oyotunji Village*, 24.

116. Oba Efuntola Oseijeman Adelabu Adefunmi I, personal interviews with the author, August 1994, January 1995, August 1996, and August 1997.

117. Sernett, *Bound for the Promised Land*, 205.

118. Hunt, *Oyotunji Village*, 24.

119. Stephen Palmié, "Against Syncretism, 'Africanizing' and 'Cubanizing' Discourses in North American Orisa Worship," in *Counterworks: Managing the Diversity of Knowledge*, ed. Richard Fardon (New York: Routledge, 1995), 78.

120. "Damballah-wedo is a benevolent snake spirit who haunts the springs and climbs on trees . . . [He] is most commonly seen as the rainbow. He is a being with a dual nature, both male and female. Coiled in a spiral round the earth, he sustains the world and prevents its disintegration. As he revolves around the earth, he sets in motion the heavenly bodies. Because his nature is motion, he is also water." Alfred Metraux, *Voodoo in Haiti* (New York: Schocken Books, 1972), 361.

121. Brown, *Mama Lola*; see chapter entitled "*Danbala*," 271–310.

122. Herskovits, *Dahomey*, 1:207–8.

123. Oba Efuntola Oseijeman Adelabu Adefunmi I, personal interviews with the author, August 1994, January 1995, August 1996, and August 1997.

124. Oba Efuntola Oseijeman Adelabu Adefunmi I, personal interviews with the author, August 1994, January 1995, August 1996, and August 1997.

125. Oba Efuntola Oseijeman Adelabu Adefunmi I, personal interviews with the author, August 1994, January 1995, August 1996, and August 1997.

126. Hunt, *Oyotunji Village*, 25.

127. George Brandon, *Santeria from Africa to the New World: The Dead Sell Memories* (Bloomington: Indiana University Press, 1993), 114–15.

128. Hunt, *Oyotunji Village*, 25. For the remainder of the book, I will use Oseijeman Adefunmi to refer to the former Walter King.

129. Oba Efuntola Oseijeman Adelabu Adefunmi I, personal interviews with the author, August 1994, January 1995, August 1996, and August 1997.

130. Oba Efuntola Oseijeman Adelabu Adefunmi I, personal interviews with the author, August 1994, January 1995, August 1996, and August 1997.

131. Oba Efuntola Oseijeman Adelabu Adefunmi I, personal interviews with the author, August 1994, January 1995, August 1996, and August 1997.

132. Oba Efuntola Oseijeman Adelabu Adefunmi I, personal interviews with the author, August 1994, January 1995, August 1996, and August 1997.

133. Hunt, *Oyotunji Village*, 25.

134. Hunt, *Oyotunji Village*, 25.

135. Robert Weisbord, *Ebony Kinship: Africa, Africans, and the Afro-American* (Westport, CT: Greenwood Press, 1973), 186.

136. Gold, "The Black Jews of Harlem," 212.

137. Mary Elaine Curry, "Making the Gods: The Yoruba Religion in the Black Community" (Ann Arbor, MI: UMI Dissertation Services, 1991), 171. The spread of the Akan religion among African Americans in the United States has largely been attributed to Nana Yao Opare Dinizulu, who was known as the chief priest of Akan in America. Dinizulu's travels to Ghana in the 1960s exposed him to the Akan

tradition and motivated him to spread these teachings among African Americans. See the video recording of "Voices of the Gods" for an extended interview with Dinizulu and representations of Akan ceremonies in the United States.

138. Curry, "Making the Gods," 171.

139. Gregory, *Santería in New York City*, 30.

140. Oba Efuntola Oseijeman Adelabu Adefunmi I, personal interviews with the author, August 1994, January 1995, August 1996, and August 1997.

141. Oba Efuntola Oseijeman Adelabu Adefunmi I, personal interviews with the author, August 1994, January 1995, August 1996, and August 1997.

142. Oba Efuntola Oseijeman Adelabu Adefunmi I, personal interviews with the author, August 1994, January 1995, August 1996, and August 1997.

143. Oba Efuntola Oseijeman Adelabu Adefunmi I, personal interviews with the author, August 1994, January 1995, August 1996, and August 1997.

144. Palmié, "Against Syncretism," 78.

145. Oba Efuntola Oseijeman Adelabu Adefunmi I, personal interviews with the author, August 1994, January 1995, August 1996, and August 1997.

146. Tracey E. Hucks, "From Cuban Santeria to African Yoruba: Evolutions in African American Orisa History, 1959–1970," in *Orisa Devotion as World Religion: The Globalization of Yoruba Religious Culture*, ed. Jacob K. Olupona and Terry Rey (Madison: University of Wisconsin Press, 2008), 343.

147. Steven Gregory quotes one scholar as saying there were at least 50,000 Cubans in the United States by 1959. Other scholars argue for an even higher number and estimate that between the time Fidel Castro assumed power in January 1959 and the Cuban Missile Crisis in October 1962, some 280,000 Cuban immigrants entered the United States. This number increased steadily over the years. By 1979, Brandon says the Cuban population in Dade County, Florida, alone had reached some 500,000 people. The following year, in 1980, 120,000 more Cubans arrived in the United States during the Mariel boat lift. Currently, far more than 1 million Cubans reside in the United States; see Steven Gregory, "Santería in New York City: A Study in Cultural Resistance" (Ann Arbor, MI: UMI Dissertation Series, 1986); Brandon, *Santeria: From Africa to the New World*; Heriberto Dixon, "Cuban-American Counterpoint: Black Cubans in the United States," *Dialectical Anthropology* 13, no. 3 (1988), 227–39.

148. "Cuban Refugees: The Preferred Minority," *Sepia*, June 6, 1970, 9.

149. Irene B. Taeuber and Conrad Taeuber, *People of the United States in the 20th Century* (Washington, DC: Government Printing Office, 1971), 93–99.

150. Nancy A. Denton and Douglas S. Massey, "Racial Identity among Caribbean Hispanics: The Effect of Double Minority Status on Residential Segregation," *American Sociological Review* 54, no. 5 (October 1989): 790–808.

151. Clifford Krauss, "Blacks Praise Cuban Revolution's Benefits," *The Wall Street Journal*, July 9, 1986.

152. Krauss, "Blacks Praise Cuban Revolution's Benefits."

153. Delgado De Torres, "Reformulating Nationalism in the African Diaspora," 30–31.

154. Krauss, "Blacks Praise Cuban Revolution's Benefits"; Carlos Moore, *Castro, the Blacks, and Africa* (Los Angeles: University of California Center for Afro-American Studies, 1988), 15 (emphasis is mine).

155. Carlos Moore, "Afro-Cubans and the Communist Revolution," in *African Presence in the Americas*, ed. Carlos Moore, Tanya Sanders, Shawna Moore (Trenton, NJ: Africa World Press, 1995), 15.

156. Marianne Masferrer and Carmelo Mesa-Lago, "The Gradual Integration of the Black in Cuba: Under the Colony, the Republic, and the Revolution," in *Slavery and Race Relations in Latin America*, ed. Robert Brent Toplin (Westport, CT: Greenwood Press, 1974), 361.

157. Dixon, "Cuban-American Counterpoint," 230.

158. Dixon, "Cuban-American Counterpoint," 232.

159. Hugh Thomas, *Cuba: The Pursuit of Freedom* (New York: Harper & Row, Publishers, 1971), 1117.

160. Masferrer and Mesa-Lago, "The Gradual Integration of the Black in Cuba," 381.

161. Dixon, "Cuban-American Counterpoint," 233.

162. De La Torre, "Ochun: (N)Either the (M)Other of All Cubans," 841.

163. Masferrer and Mesa-Lago, "The Gradual Integration of the Black in Cuba," 360.

164. Moore, *Castro, the Blacks, and Africa*, 224; also see http://www.afrocubaweb.com/maceo.htm.

165. Moore, *Castro, the Blacks, and Africa*, 224.

166. Benigno E. Aguirre, "Differential Migration of Cuban Social Races: A Review and Interpretation of the Problem," *Latin American Research Review* 11, no. 1 (1976): 104.

167. Dixon, "Cuban-American Counterpoint," 234–35; Aguirre, "Differential Migration of Cuban Social Races," 114.

168. Dixon, "Cuban-American Counterpoint," 229.

169. Brandon, *Santeria from Africa to the New World*, 106.

170. De La Torre, "Ochun: (N)Either the (M)Other of All Cubans," 837–38.

171. Gregory, *Santería in New York City*, 55–56.

172. De La Torre, "Ochun: (N)Either the (M)Other of All Cubans," 845, 841.

173. Wirtz, *Ritual, Discourse, and Community in Cuban Santería*, 30; Mercedes Cros Sandoval, *Worldview, the Orichas, and Santería: Africa to Cuba and Beyond* (Gainesville: University Press of Florida, 2006), 324.

174. Thomas, *Cuba: The Pursuit of Freedom*, 1122.

175. Dixon, "Cuban-American Counterpoint," 230–31.

176. Robert Farris Thompson, "The Three Warriors: Atlantic Altars of Esu, Ogun and Osoosi," in *The Yoruba Artist: New Theoretical Perspectives on African Arts*, ed. Rowland Abiodun, Henry J. Drewal, and John Pemberton III (Washington, DC: Smithsonian Institution Press, 1994), 225.

177. Thompson, "The Three Warriors," 226–27.

178. Steven Harry Cornelius, "The Convergence of Power: An Investigation into the Music Liturgy of Santeria in New York City" (Ann Arbor, MI: UMI Dissertation Service, 1989), 53–54.

179. Drewal and Mason, *Beads, Body and Soul*, 128; Huntington, "Bodies in Contexts," 18.

180. Dixon, "Cuban-American Counterpoint," 230.

181. Gregory, *Santería in New York City*, 57.

182. Brandon, *Santeria from Africa to the New World*, 106.

183. Brandon, *Santeria from Africa to the New World*, 106.

184. Vega, "Yoruba Philosophy," 87.

185. Brandon, *Santeria from Africa to the New World*, 106-7.

186. Oba Efuntola Oseijeman Adelabu Adefunmi I, personal interviews with the author, August 1994, January 1995, August 1996, and August 1997.

187. Gregory, *Santería in New York City*, 57; Aguirre, "Differential Migration of Cuban Social Classes," 103. For example, initiatory rites for devotees were commonly performed in Cuba until the time U.S.-Cuba travel became severely restricted in the early 1970s.

188. Adeleke, *UnAfrican Americans*, 5.

Chapter Three

1. HRH Oseijeman Adefunmi I, "Notes on the Return of the Gods of Africa and the Rising of Oyotunji," *Sagala, A Journey of Art and Ideas* 2, no. 1 (December 1988): 40.

2. Eason, *Ifa*, 93.

3. Adefunmi, "Notes," 38.

4. Adefunmi, "Notes," 38.

5. Arthur Hall, founder of Afro-American Dance Ensemble of Philadelphia, personal interview with the author, November 27, 1993.

6. Joseph Murphy, "Santería and Vodou in the United States," in *America's Alternative Religions*, ed. Timothy Miller (Albany: State University of New York Press, 1995), 293.

7. Oba Oseijeman Efuntola Adelabu Adefunmi I, personal interviews with the author, August 1994, January 1995, August 1996, and August 1997. According to Adefunmi, after the divinatory revelation that counseled him to seek initiation into the tradition, his immediate response was, "Well, if I should go to Cuba then and get initiated as you're advising me, would I be a Voodoo priest?" Adefunmi was able to filter much of his new interpretations of Santería through the Haitian/Dahomean lenses to which he had been formerly exposed. He goes on to describe this decision in greater detail, "And I said, 'OK then, I'm going.' . . . [Oliana] decided that he would get initiated because though he had been raised in the tradition of Santería, he had never really been fully initiated . . . Both of us got initiated the same day. Naturally being Obatala, I went first . . . and they initiated [Oliana] into the god, Aganju."

8. Stefania Capone, *Les Yoruba du Nouveau Monde: Religion, Ethnicité and Nationalism Noir aux États-Unis* (Paris: Éditions Karthala, 2005), 130.

9. Vega, "Yoruba Philosophy," 272.

10. Adefunmi, "Notes," 39. It was also revealed during initiation that Adefunmi's "cosmic mother" in the Orisa pantheon would be Oshun.

11. Hunt, *Oyotunji Village*, 27.

12. Oba Oseijeman Efuntola Adelabu Adefunmi I, personal interviews with the author, August 1994, January 1995, August 1996, and August 1997.

13. Anderson, *Imagined Communities*, 116.

14. Adefunni cites two texts by Bascom that were helpful resources in learning the techniques of divination; see William Bascom, *Ifa Divination: Communication between Gods and Men in West Africa* (Bloomington: Indiana University Press, 1991) and *Sixteen Cowries: Yoruba Divination from Africa to the New World* (Bloomington: Indiana University Press, 1993).

15. Adefunmi, "Notes," 38.

16. Adefunmi, "Notes," 38.

17. Cornelius, "The Convergence of Power," 6.

18. Vega, "Yoruba Philosophy," 185.

19. For an illustration of these paintings on the walls of Shango Temple see Oseijeman Adelabu Adefunmi, *Orisha: A First Glimpse of the African Religion of Brazil, Cuba, Haiti, Trinidad and now U.S.A.* (New York: Great Benin Books, 1959).

20. Oseijeman Adelabu Adefunmi, "Building a Community," *Caribe* (Fall/Winter 1981): 10.

21. Vega, "Yoruba Philosophy," 137.

22. "*Oya* spoke and claimed me," was Judith Gleason's explanation for the initiation into the religion. According to Gleason, while in a state of possession a priestess of Candomblé in Brazil told her she was Oya, the goddess of the wind and the cemetery. Gleason said when she returned to New York, Sunta became her guide into Santería. According to Gleason, "All the divinations said I should be initiated. Most people wouldn't have followed through, but I felt it was fate. It was a very deep religious obligation. I see my initiation in terms of learning to serve a powerful and potentially disintegrating force. It can't abandon you, and you don't dare break the contract with it—it can blow you apart." See Tracy Cochran, "Among the Believers: Converts to Santeria," *New York*, October 12, 1987, 33–34.

23. Vega, "Yoruba Philosophy," 137.

24. Drewal and Mason, *Beads, Body and Soul*, 130.

25. See Long, *Significations*, 175–76.

26. Long, *Significations*, 176.

27. Long, *Significations*, 176.

28. Yaacov Shavit, *History in Black: African-Americans in Search of an Ancient Past* (London: Frank Cass Publishers, 2001), x.

29. Echeruo, "An African Diaspora," 13.

30. Echeruo, "An African Diaspora," 13.

31. Susan Davis, *Parades and Power: Street Theatre in Nineteenth-Century Philadelphia* (Philadelphia: Temple University Press, 1986), 17.

32. Davis, *Parades and Power*, 17.

33. Davis, *Parades and Power*, 16.

34. Hood, *Begrimed and Black*, 164.

35. Oba Oseijeman Efuntola Adelabu Adefunmi I, personal interviews with the author, August 1994, January 1995, August 1996, and August 1997.

36. Oba Oseijeman Adelabu Adefunmi, *Oyotunji SHANGOFEST* (Sheldon, SC: African Theological Archministry, n.d.), 12.

37. Long, *Significations*, 141.

38. Henry Hayward Jr., "Toward a Religion of Revolution," *The Black Scholar* 2, no. 4 (December 1970): 28.

39. Baer and Singer, *African American Religion in the Twentieth Century*. The work of Hans Baer and Merrill Singer has been important in documenting this historical phenomenon, particularly as it emerged among black North Americans in black Protestant sects and churches.

40. Long, *Significations*, 7.

41. Kim D. Butler, "Africa in the Reinvention of Nineteenth-Century Afro-Bahian Identity," in *Rethinking the African Diaspora: The Making of a Black Atlantic World in the Bight of Benin and Brazil*, ed. Kristin Mann and Edna G. Bay (London: Frank Cass, 2001), 136.

42. "Temple Center of African Culture," *New York Amsterdam News*, August 12, 1961.

43. "Temple Center of African Culture."

44. Butler, "Africa," 137.

45. Ikulomi Djisovi Eason, "A Time of Destiny: Ifa Culture and Festivals in Ile-Ife, Nigeria and Oyotunji African Village in South Carolina" (Ann Arbor, MI: UMI Dissertation Services, 1997).

46. Oba Oseijeman Efuntola Adelabu Adefunmi I, personal interviews with the author, July 1994, January 1995, August 1996, and August 1997.

47. Hunt, *Oyotunji Village*, 22.

48. Oseijeman Adefunmi, *The Gods of Africa*, African Library Series (New York: Great Benin Books, 1960), 16.

49. Oloosa Lloyd Weaver, "Notes on Orisa Worship in an Urban Setting" (paper presented at the International Conference on Orisa Tradition, Ile-Ife, Nigeria, July 1–6, 1986), 13; "The World Conference on Orisa, Ile-Ife, Nigeria, June 1–7, 1981: A Special Report," *Caribe* 5, no. 4 (Fall/Winter 1981): 11.

50. Capone, *Les Yoruba du Nouveau Monde*, 147.

51. Gold, "The Black Jews of Harlem," 214–15.

52. Anderson, *Imagined Communities*, 187.

53. Oba Oseijeman Efuntola Adelabu Adefunmi I, personal interviews with the author, August 1994, January 1995, August 1996, and August 1997.

54. Adefunmi, *The Gods of Africa*, 3.

55. Oseijeman Adefunmi, *The African State* (New York: Great Benin Books, 1962), 1.

56. Gilroy, "Urban Social Movements," 415.

57. Kedar and Werblowsy, *Sacred Space*, 9–17.

58. Amiri Baraka, *The Autobiography of LeRoi Jones* (Chicago: Lawrence Hill Books, 1984), 217; Abiola Sinclair, *The Harlem Cultural/Political Movements, 1960–1970: From Malcolm X to "Black is Beautiful"* (New York: Gumbs and Thomas Publishers, 1995), 110.

59. Oba Oseijeman Efuntola Adelabu Adefunmi I, personal interviews with the author, August 1994, January 1995, August 1996, and August 1997.

60. Sinclair, *Harlem Cultural/Political Movements*, 110; Vega, "Yoruba Philosophy," 188.

61. Yeyefini Efunbolade, "The Living Shrine: Life and Meaning in Oyotunji," in *Women and New and Africana Religions*, ed. Lillian Ashcraft-Eason, Darnise C. Martin, and Oyeronke Olademo (Santa Barbara: ABC-CLIO, 2010), 60.

62. Oba Oseijeman Efuntola Adelabu Adefunmi I, personal interviews with the author, August 1994, January 1995, August 1996, and August 1997; Vega, "Yoruba Philosophy," 191.

63. Sinclair, *Harlem Cultural/Political Movements*, 16.

64. Matory, "Man in the 'City of Women,'" 397–98.

65. Turner, "The Sociology of Black Nationalism," 18, 22.

66. Butler, "Africa," 149.

67. Bracey Jr., Meier, and Rudwick, *Black Nationalism in America*, 278.

68. Hall, "Cultural Identity and Diaspora," 392.

69. Gilroy, "Urban Social Movements," 404.

70. Ifekwunigwe, "Scattered Belongings," 60; Kim D. Butler, "Up From Slavery: Afro-Brazilian Activism in São Paul, 1888–1938," *The Americas* 49, no. 2 (October 1992): 180.

71. Babatunde Lawal, "Art and Architecture, History of African," in *Encyclopedia of African History Volume 1 A-G*, ed. Kevin Shillington (New York: Fitzboy Dearborn, 2005), 103–8; Babatunde Lawal (NEH Roots 2009 Seminar Lecture, University of Virginia, Charlottesville, VA, June 19, 2009).

72. Babatunde Lawal (NEH Roots 2009 Seminar Lecture, University of Virginia, Charlottesville, VA, June 19, 2009); Jim Perkinson, "Ogu's Iron or Jesus' Irony: Who's Zooming Who in Diasporic Possession Cult Activity," in *Religion and Global Culture: New Terrain in the Study of Religion and the Work of Charles H. Long*, ed. by Jennifer I. M. Reid (Lanham, MD: Lexington Books, 2003), 108.

73. Capone, *Les Yoruba du Nouveau Monde*, 213.

74. Van Deburg, *New Day in Babylon*, 181.

75. McAlister, "One Black Allah," 638.

76. McAlister, "One Black Allah," 642.

77. Baraka, *The Autobiography of LeRoi Jones*, 204.

78. Ruth Edmonds Hill, *The Black Women Oral History Project from the Arthur and Elizabeth Library on the History of Women in America, Radcliffe College* (London: Mechler, 1990), 198–99.

79. Sinclair, *Harlem Cultural/Political Movements*, 92.

80. Hill, *Black Women Oral History Project*, 175.

81. Oba Oseijeman Efuntola Adelabu Adefunmi I, personal interviews with the author, August 1994, January 1995, August 1996, and August 1997.

82. Efunbolade, "The Living Shrine," 60.

83. Oba Oseijeman Efuntola Adelabu Adefunmi I, personal interviews with the author, August 1994, January 1995, August 1996, and August 1997.

84. Weaver, "Notes on Orisa Worship in an Urban Setting," 15.

85. Wirtz, *Ritual, Discourse, and Community in Cuban Santería*, 38.

86. Hunt, *Oyotunji Village*, 30. Adefunmi's income sources during this period, before he pursued full-time employment as a diviner, were somewhat obscure. It is known

that one of his major income sources came from Ujamaa Market. Created in 1966 as an endeavor in black entrepreneurship, Ujamaa Market embodied Adefunmi's vision of an African marketplace and restaurant selling various oils, incense, clothing, and foods.

87. Albert Raboteau, *Slave Religion: The "Invisible Institution" in the Antebellum South* (New York: Oxford University Press, 1978), 276.

88. Raboteau, *Slave Religion*, 286.

89. Hunt, *Oyotunji Village*, 30–31.

90. Oba Oseijeman Efuntola Adelabu Adefunmi I, personal interviews with the author, August 1994, January 1995, August 1996, and August 1997.

91. The roots of Espiritismo lie in the philosophy of the Frenchman Hippolyte Leon Denizared Rivail, more commonly known by his pseudonym of Allan Kardec. Kardec "believed that spiritual progress must be physically achieved through a series of progressive incarnations and that each person has a group of guardian angels and spirits who guide him or her through the 'tests' of life (pruebas)." Kardec's most influential texts included *The Book of the Spirits* and *The Gospel According to Spiritism*, also known as *El Evangelio*; see Andres Isidoro Perez y Mena, *Speaking with the Dead: Development of Afro-Latin Religion among Puerto Ricans in the United States: A Study into the Interpenetration of Civilizations in the New World* (New York: AMS Press, 1991).

92. See "African Cultural Restoration in Philadelphia: 1963–1982," in George Howard, *Gifts from Ile Ife: Africa's Impact on the Americas* (Philadelphia: Black History Museum Committee, 1982), 82.

93. Shango Temple was established in Gary, Indiana, in 1962 after two African American came to Harlem to ask for Adefunmi's assistance in forming a Yoruba community in the South.

94. Baba Songodina Ifatunji established the Songo Temple in Chicago, Illinois.

95. Leonard Lear, "An Old African Religion Makes a U.S. Comeback," *Sepia*, November 1976, 24.

96. Baba Medahochi Kofi Omowale Zannu, personal interviews with the author, August 7, 2006, and August 23, 2006.

97. Ikuloma Djisovi Eason, "Historicizing Ifa Culture in Oyotunji African Village," in *Orisa Devotion as World Religion: The Globalization of Yoruba Religious Culture*, ed. Jacob K. Olupona and Terry Rey (Madison: University of Wisconsin Press, 2008), 281.

98. Eason, "Time of Destiny," 88–91; Hunt, *Oyotunji Village*, 29.

99. Baba Medahochi Kofi Omowale Zannu, personal interviews with the author, August 7, 2006, and August 23, 2006.

100. Oba Oseijeman Efuntola Adelabu Adefunmi I, personal interviews with the author, August 1994, January 1995, August 1996, and August 1997.

101. Hunt, *Oyotunji Village*, 31.

102. Hunt, *Oyotunji Village*, 30.

103. Baba Ifa Tunji included a discussion of this event as a part of his larger conference paper given at the Sixth Annual Conference on Orisa Tradition and Culture in Port of Spain, Trinidad, in 1999. Velma Love, in her doctoral thesis, "Odu Outcomes:

Yoruba Scriptures in African American Constructions of Self and World," corroborates this story and cites a videotape of Oseijeman Adefunmi that is housed in the holdings of the Caribbean Cultural Center in New York City.

104. Orsi, *Madonna of 115th Street*, 219. Physical geography was localized to suit the needs of Harlem's political, cultural, and religious nationalists creating an analytical space—"the streets"—to become what Robert Anthony Orsi has identified as an important hermeneutical opportunity "to read the theology of a people."

105. Baraka, *The Autobiography of LeRoi Jones*, 220.

106. Alessandra Lorini, *Rituals of Race: American Public Culture and the Search for Racial Democracy* (Charlottesville: University of Virginia Press, 1999), 208, 243–44.

107. Lorini, *Rituals of Race*, 247.

108. Shane White, "'It Was a Proud Day': African Americans, Festivals, and Parades in the North, 1741–1834," *The Journal of American History* 81, no. 1 (June 1994): 30.

109. White, "'It Was a Proud Day,'" 20.

110. White, "'It Was a Proud Day,'" 19.

111. White, "'It Was a Proud Day,'" 23.

112. White, "'It Was a Proud Day,'" 24.

113. White, "'It Was a Proud Day,'" 24.

114. White, "'It Was a Proud Day,'" 24.

115. White, "'It Was a Proud Day,'" 50.

116. White, "'It Was a Proud Day,'" 50.

117. Davis, *Parades and Power*, 3–4.

118. Davis, *Parades and Power*, 155.

119. Davis, *Parades and Power*, 156.

120. White, "'It Was a Proud Day,'" 34.

121. Davis, *Parades and Power*, 33.

122. Davis, *Parades and Power*, 15.

123. Davis, *Parades and Power*, 5.

124. White, "'It Was a Proud Day,'" 42–43.

125. Davis, *Parades and Power*, 14.

126. Olatunji, *Beat of My Drum*, 11.

127. Olatunji, *Beat of My Drum*, 107.

128. Olatunji, *Beat of My Drum*, 102–3.

129. Olatunji, *Beat of My Drum*, 173.

130. Olatunji, *Beat of My Drum*, 172.

131. Olatunji, *Beat of My Drum*, 171.

132. Olatunji, *Beat of My Drum*, 23–24.

133. Olatunji, *Beat of My Drum*, 11.

134. Olatunji, *Beat of My Drum*, 140.

135. Arthur Hall, founder of Afro-American Dance Ensemble of Philadelphia, personal interview with the author, November 27, 1993.

136. Capone, *Les Yoruba du Nouveau Monde*, 254.

137. Sinclair, *Harlem Cultural/Political Movements*, 87; Orsi, *Madonna of 115th Street*, 219–31.

138. Lorini, *Rituals of Race*, 3–4.

139. Chirevo V. Kwenda, "Mthunzini (A Place in the Shade): Religion and the Heat of Globalization," in *Religion and Global Culture: New Terrain in the Study of Religion and the Work of Charles H. Long*, ed. Jennifer I. M. Reid (Lanham, MD: Lexington Books, 2003), 76.

140. Oba Oseijeman Efuntola Adelabu Adefunmi I, personal interviews with the author, July 1994, January 1995, August 1996, and August 1997.

141. Oba Oseijeman Efuntola Adelabu Adefunmi I, personal interviews with the author, August 1994, January 1995, August 1996, and August 1997.

142. George Goodman, "Harlem's Yorubas: A Search for Something to Believe In," *Look Magazine*, January 1969.

143. Gregory, *Santería in New York City*, 32.

144. Howard, *Gifts of Ile-Ife*, 83. The Oshun Festival in Harlem later became the inspiration for the Oshun Festival, now Odunde Festival, enacted in Philadelphia some years later in the early 1970s.

145. Huntington, "Bodies in Contexts," 110.

146. Aina Olomo, *The Core of Fire: A Path to Yoruba Spiritual Activism* (New York: Athelia Henrietta Press, 2002), 48.

147. Cornelius O. Adepedgba, "Associated Place-Names and Sacred Icons of Seven Yoruba Deities: Historicity in Yoruba Religious Tradition," in *Orisa Devotion as World Religion: The Globalization of Yoruba Religious Culture*, ed. Jacob K. Olupona and Terry Rey (Madison: University of Wisconsin Press, 2008), 107.

148. Palmié, "Against Syncretism," 77.

149. Arthur Hall, founder of Afro-American Dance Ensemble of Philadelphia, personal interview with the author, November 27, 1993, 15.

Chapter Four

1. Friedland, "Religious Nationalism," 145.

2. Friedland, "Religious Nationalism," 145.

3. Hall, *A History of the Book in America*, 40–49, 169.

4. Hall, *A History of the Book in America*, 169.

5. Wyss, "Indigenous Literacies," 387.

6. J. Lorand Matory, "Free to Be a Slave: Slavery as Metaphor in the Afro-Atlantic Religions," in *Africas of the Americas*, ed. Stephan Palmié (Leiden: Brill, 2008), 356.

7. David D. Hall, *Ways of Writing: The Practice and Politics of Text-Making in Seventeenth-Century New England* (Philadelphia: University of Pennsylvania Press, 2008), 172.

8. Eriksen, *Ethnicity and Nationalism*, 106.

9. James H. Cone, *The Spirituals and the Blues* (New York: Orbis Books, 1971), 23.

10. Smith, "Black Religious Nationalism," 534.

11. Arthur Hall, founder of Afro-American Dance Ensemble of Philadelphia, personal interview with the author, November 27, 1993, 7.

12. T. K. Oommen, "Religious Nationalism and Democratic Polity: The Indian Case," *Sociology of Religion* 55, no. 4 (Winter 1994): 457.

13. McAlister, "One Black Allah," 642.

14. Hall, "Cultural Identity and Diaspora," 392.

15. Shavit, *History in Black*, 4.

16. Shavit, *History in Black*, 255.

17. Shavit, *History in Black*, 255.

18. Shavit, *History in Black*, 5, 255.

19. Hall, *Ways of Writing*, 2, 158.

20. Ernest, *Liberation Historiography*, 24–27.

21. Anderson, *Imagined Communities*, 134.

22. Judson L. Jeffries, ed., *Black Power in the Belly of the Beast* (Urbana: University of Illinois Press, 2006), 8.

23. Ernest, *Liberation Historiography*, 37.

24. Shavit, *History in Black*, 255.

25. Alexander, *Pedagogies of Crossing*, 292.

26. Long, *Significations*, 170.

27. Anderson, *Imagined Communities*, 153.

28. Anderson, *Imagined Communities*, 36.

29. Gordon, *Black Identity*, 20.

30. Adefunmi, *Orisha*, 14.

31. Echeruo, "An African Diaspora," 5.

32. Adefunmi, *Orisha*, 15.

33. Adefunmi, *Orisha*, 15.

34. Echeruo, "An African Diaspora," 13.

35. Echeruo, "An African Diaspora," 13–14.

36. Echeruo, "An African Diaspora," 14.

37. Echeruo, "An African Diaspora," 17.

38. Susan Moller Okin, *Justice, Gender, and the Family* (New York: Basic Books, 1989), 56.

39. Adefunmi, *Orisha*. There was no page number for this citation. It appeared on a page demarcated, "About the Author."

40. Ernest, *Liberation Historiography*, 11.

41. Nance, "Mystery of the Moorish Science Temple," 142.

42. Gabriel Josipovici, *Text and Voice: Essays 1981–1991* (New York: St. Martin's Press, 1992), 181.

43. Adefunmi, *The Gods of Africa*, 4.

44. Adefunmi, *Orisha*, 3.

45. An original copy of *The Gods of Africa* may be found on microfilm at the Schomburg Library for Research in Black Culture in New York City. Since 1960, Adefunmi made three additional reprintings of this text, which has been revised

and updated to include information on Oyotunji Village. The most recent printing in 1987 is still devoid of references.

46. http://www.dacb.org/stories/nigeria/johnson_1samuel.html.

47. Adefunmi, *The Gods of Africa*, 4.

48. Adefunmi, *The Gods of Africa*, 10.

49. Murphy, "Santería and Vodou in the United States," 293.

50. Adefunmi, *The Gods of Africa*, 1.

51. Adefunmi, *The Gods of Africa*, 3.

52. Adefunmi, *The Gods of Africa*, 3.

53. Adefunmi, *The Gods of Africa*, 3. In recent years scholars have challenged this "fantastic history," arguing that very few Yoruba actually entered the United States and that it is more than likely that "the North American mainland . . . took less than three percent of African arrivals" directly into the United States; David Eltis, "The Volume and Structure of the Transatlantic Slave Trade: A Reassessment," *William and Mary Quarterly* 58, no. 1 (2001): 17–46.

54. Adefunmi, *The Gods of Africa*, 3.

55. Adefunmi, *The Gods of Africa*, 3.

56. Adefunmi, *The Gods of Africa*, 4.

57. In *The Gods of Africa*, Adefunmi explained the attributes of specific orisa such as Eshu-Elegbara, the messenger god of all the Orisha-Vodu, representing the "unpredictable element in life"; Yemoja the goddess of the sea and the venerated mother of the orisa; Ifa-Orunmila, the god of divination; the gods of hunting and of war, Oshosi and Ogun; the god of lightning and the goddess of beauty and fertility, Shango and Oshun; the divine twins, Ibeji; the goddess of wind and the cemetery, Oya; the god of the wilderness, Aganju; and the god of smallpox, Shopona or Babaluaiye.

58. Adefunmi, *The Gods of Africa*, 7.

59. Adefunmi, *The Gods of Africa*, 6.

60. Adefunmi, *The Gods of Africa*, 12.

61. Adefunmi, *The Gods of Africa*, 12.

62. Adefunmi, *The Gods of Africa*, 16.

63. Oseijeman Adefunmi, *Tribal Origins of the African-Americans* (New York: Great Benin Books, 1962), i.

64. Adefunmi, *Tribal Origins*, 9.

65. Adefunmi, *Tribal Origins*, 9–10.

66. Adefunmi, *Tribal Origins*, 9.

67. Adefunmi, *Tribal Origins*, 9.

68. Adefunmi, *Tribal Origins*, 9.

69. Adefunmi, *Tribal Origins*, 11.

70. Adefunmi, *Tribal Origins*, 11.

71. Adefunmi, *The African State*, 15.

72. Adefunmi, *Tribal Origins*, 10.

73. Adefunmi, *The African State*, 3.

74. Friedland, "Religious Nationalism," 137.

75. Oseijeman Adefunmi, *An African Marriage* (New York: Great Benin Books, n.d.), 1.

76. Adefunmi, *An African Marriage*, 2.

77. Adefunmi, *An African Marriage*, 6.

78. Adefunmi, *An African Marriage*, 7.

79. Adefunmi, *An African Marriage*, 7.

80. Adefunmi, *An African Marriage*, 9.

81. Adefunmi, *An African Marriage*, 17.

82. Adefunmi, *The African State*, 7.

83. Baraka, *The Autobiography of Leroi Jones*, 321.

84. Matory, *Sex and the Empire That Is No More*, 61–62.

85. Alasdair C. MacIntyre, *After Virtue: A Study in Moral Theory* (Notre Dame, IN: University of Notre Dame Press, 1981), 223.

86. Abimbola, *Yoruba Culture*, xv.

87. Eriksen, *Ethnicity and Nationalism*, 85.

88. Gilroy, "Urban Social Movements," 418.

89. Ernest, *Liberation Historiography*, 4.

90. Charles Long, "Perspectives for a Study of Afro-American Religion in the United States," *History of Religions* 11, no. 1 (August 1971): 59.

91. Long, "Perspectives for a Study," 108.

92. Long, *Significations*, 177 (emphasis is mine).

93. Stout, *Democracy and Tradition*, 135.

94. Leeming, *James Baldwin: A Biography*, 325.

95. J. Lorand Matory, "The English Professors of Brazil: On the Diasporic Roots of the Yoruba Nation," *Comparative Studies in Society and History* 41, no. 1 (January 1999): 95–97.

96. Alasdair MacIntyre, *Three Rival Versions of Moral Enquiry: Encyclopaedia, Genealogy, and Tradition* (Notre Dame, IN: University of Notre Dame Press, 1990), 216.

97. Gesa Mackenthun, "The Transoceanic Emergence of American Postcolonial Identities," in *A Companion to the Literatures of Colonial America*, ed. Susan Castillo and Ivy Schweitzer (Malden, MA: Blackwell Publishing, 2005), 337.

98. MacIntyre, *Three Rival Versions of Moral Enquiry*, 217.

99. Echeruo, "An African Diaspora," 3.

100. MacIntyre, *Three Rival Versions of Moral Enquiry*, 196.

101. Matory, *Black Atlantic Religion*, 209.

Chapter Five

1. Oba Efuntola Oseijeman Adelabu Adefunmi I, personal interviews with the author, August 1994, January 1995, August 1996, and August 1997. Another African American attests to having had a similar conversation several decades ago with the Cuban babalawo, Pancho Mora, as well.

2. John Pemberton III, postscript to *Orisa Devotion as World Religion: The Globalization of Yoruba Religious Culture*, ed. Jacob K. Olupona and Terry Rey (Madison: University of Wisconsin Press, 2008), 570.

3. Christopher Antonio Brooks, "Eku Odun: A Yoruba Celebration" (master's thesis, University of Texas at Austin, 1984), 52.

4. Olomo, *Core of Fire*, 39.

5. Beatriz Morales, "Returning to the Source: Yoruba Religion in the South," in *Religion in the Contemporary South: Diversity, Community, and Identity*, ed. O. Kendall White Jr. and Daryl White (Athens: University of Georgia Press, 1995), 126.

6. Gregory, "Santería in New York City," 65.

7. Long, *Significations*, 176. Within the historical context of slavery, Long argues that "by being slaves, black persons were isolated from any self-determined legitimacy in the society of which they were a part and were recognized by their physiological characteristics. This constituted a complexity of experience revolving around the relationship between their physical being and their origins. So even if they had no conscious memory of Africa, the image of Africa played an enormous part in the religion of the blacks."

8. Gregory, "Santería in New York City," 100.

9. Gregory, "Santería in New York City," 100.

10. Matory, *Black Atlantic Religion*, 209.

11. Dolores Hayden, *The Power of Place: Urban Landscapes as Public History* (Cambridge, MA: MIT Press, 1995), 9.

12. Mercedes Cros Sandoval, "Afro-Cuban Religion in Perspective," in *Enigmatic Powers: Syncretism with African and Indigenous Peoples' Religions Among Latinos*, ed. Anthony Stevens-Arroyo and Andres Perez Y Mena (New York: Bildner Center for Western Hemisphere Studies, 1995), 93.

13. William A. Christian Jr., *Local Religion in Sixteenth-Century Spain* (Princeton, NJ: Princeton University Press, 1981), 3.

14. Christian, *Local Religion*, 3.

15. Christian, *Local Religion*, 20.

16. Christian, *Local Religion*, 22.

17. Christian, *Local Religion*, 178.

18. Lawrence Levine, *Black Culture and Black Conscious* (New York: Oxford University Press, 1977), 24.

19. Brandon, *Santeria from Africa to the New World*, 114.

20. Brandon, *Santeria from Africa to the New World*, 114.

21. Adefunmi, *The Gods of Africa*, 16.

22. Oba Oseijeman Efuntola Adelabu Adefunmi I, personal interviews with the author, August 1994, January 1995, August 1996, and August 1997.

23. Adefunmi, "Notes," 42.

24. Gregory, "Santería in New York City," 30.

25. This fear was not unfounded. There were several incidents of police and ASPCA intrusions on ritual ceremonies in New York and Miami during this time; see "A Once-Hidden Faith Leaps Into the Open: After Years of Secrecy, Santería is

Suddenly Much More Popular. And Public," *New York Times*, January 27, 1997, and for a more recent account, "The Yoruba Tradition and the Law" in Vega, "Yoruba Philosophy," 224–34.

26. "The World Conference on Orisa," 10–12.

27. J. A. Rogers, "The Suppression of Negro History, 1940," in *Modern Black Nationalism from Marcus Garvey to Louis Farrakhan*, ed. William L. Van Deburg (New York: New York University Press, 1997), 72.

28. Van Deburg, *Modern Black Nationalism*, 72.

29. Vega, "Yoruba Philosophy," 136.

30. Vega, "Yoruba Philosophy," 136.

31. Vega, "Yoruba Philosophy," 104.

32. Vega, "Yoruba Philosophy," 197.

33. Vega, "Yoruba Philosophy," 197.

34. Gayle McGarrity and Osvaldo Cárdenas, "Cuba," in *No Longer Invisible: Afro-Latin Americans Today*, ed. Minority Right Group (London: Minority Rights Publications, 1995), 97.

35. McGarrity and Cárdenas, "Cuba," 97.

36. Gregory, "Santería in New York City," 61–62.

37. "The World Conference on Orisa," 11.

38. Cros Sandoval, *Worldview, the Orichas, and Santería*, 332.

39. Cros Sandoval, *Worldview, the Orichas, and Santería*, 334.

40. Christine Ayorinde, "Writing Out Africa: Racial Politics and the Cuban *regal de ocha*," in *The African Diaspora and the Study of Religion*, ed. Theodore Louis Trost (New York: Palgrave MacMillan, 2007), 159.

41. Palmié, "Against Syncretism," 79.

42. Denton and Massey, "Racial Identity Among Caribbean Hispanics," 794.

43. Cros Sandoval, *Worldview, the Orichas, and Santería*, 332.

44. Lefever, "When the Saints Go Riding In," 323.

45. Cros Sandoval, *Worldview, the Orichas, and Santería*, 333.

46. Arthur Hall, founder of Afro-American Dance Ensemble of Philadelphia, personal interview with the author, November 27, 1993, 15–16.

47. Oba Oseijeman Efuntola Adelabu Adefunmi I, personal interviews with the author, August 1994, January 1995, August 1996, August 1997.

48. Gregory, "Santería in New York City," 62.

49. Capone, *Les Yoruba du Nouveau Monde*, 135; Clapp, *A Reporter at Large*, 6–8.

50. Harry G. Lefever, "Leaving the United States: The Black Nationalist Themes of Orisha-Vodu," *Journal of Black Studies* 31, no. 2 (November 2000): 323; Raul Canizares, *Walking with the Night: The Afro-Cuban World of Santería* (Rochester, VT: Destiny Books, 1993), 33; Cros Sandoval, *Worldview, the Orichas, and Santería*, 61.

51. Imamu Amiri Baraka (LeRoi Jones), "The Pan-African Party and the Black Nation," *The Black Scholar* 2, no. 7 (March 1971): 28.

52. Adefunmi, "Building a Community," 11.

53. Adefunmi, "Building a Community," 11.

54. Jeffrey O. G. Ogbar, *Black Power: Radical Politics and African American Identity* (Baltimore, MD: Johns Hopkins University Press, 2004), 132.

55. Ogbar, *Black Power*, 133.

56. Ogbar, *Black Power*, 179–80.

57. Bracey Jr., Meier, and Rudwick, *Black Nationalism in America*, 518.

58. Raymond Hall, *Black Separatism and Social Reality: Rhetoric and Reason* (New York: Pergamon, 1977), 135.

59. Projects: "Contention in Space-Time—The Republic of New Africa, 1967–1974," http://www.cidcm.umd.edu/projects/rip/rightframe.htm.

60. Imari Obadele, "An Act to Stimulate Economic Growth in the United States and Compensate, in Part for the Grievous Wrongs of Slavery and the Unjust Enrichment which Accrued to the United States Therefrom," in *Modern Black Nationalism from Marcus Garvey to Louis Farrakhan*, ed. William L. Van Deburg (New York: New York University Press, 1997), 335.

61. Wilbur Grattan, "Republic of New Africa Denounces Ron Everett (Karenga)," *The Black Panther*, May 11, 1969, or http://www.etext.org/Politics/MIM/bpp/bpp110569a_p7.htm.

62. William L. Van Deburg, ed., *Modern Black Nationalism: From Marcus Garvey to Louis Farrakhan* (New York: New York University Press, 1997), 197.

63. "From the Anti-Depression Program of the Republic of New Africa," in *Modern Black Nationalism from Marcus Garvey to Louis Farrakhan*, ed. William L. Van Deburg (New York: New York University Press, 1997), 198.

64. "From the Anti-Depression Program," 198.

65. Bracey Jr., Meier, and Rudwick, *Black Nationalism in America*, 518.

66. Donald Cunnigan, "The Republic of New Africa in Mississippi," in *Black Power in the Belly of the Beast*, ed. Judson L. Jeffries (Urbana: University of Illinois Press, 2006), 98.

67. Donald Cunnigen, "The Republic of New Africa in Mississippi," in *Black Power in the Belly of the Beast*, ed. Judson L. Jeffries (Urbana: University of Illinois Press, 2006), 103.

68. David Llorens, "Black Separatism in Perspective: Movement Reflects Failure in Integration," *Ebony*, September 1968, 88–95.

69. Llorens, "Black Separatism in Perspective: Movement Reflects Failure in Integration," 88.

70. Hall, *Black Separatism*, 132.

71. Hall, *Black Separatism*, 220.

72. Hall, *Black Separatism*, 129–32.

73. Hall, *Black Separatism*, 129–32.

74. Van Deburg, *New Day in Babylon*, 132.

75. Wilson Record, "The Negro Intellectual and Negro Nationalism," *Social Forces* 33, no. 1 (October 1954): 18.

76. Hall, *Black Separatism*, 129.

77. Hall, *Black Separatism*, 130; Van Deburg, *New Day in Babylon*, 145.

78. Hall, *Black Separatism*, 129.

79. "From the Anti-Depression Program," 199. Imari Obadele projected that "ten million black people in America wish to be a part of an independent new Africa . . ." He remarked that "no one will be coerced or made to come to New Africa, nor will the ten million who choose New Africa constitute all of the black poor, all of the oppressed or hope-lost . . . Many others will be the gifted, the well stationed, the ordinary man and woman with a desire for a life better."

80. According to the RNA, reparations from the United States government would constitute a large portion of the republic's revenues. Gayraud Wilmore argues that the earliest documented demand for black reparations came from Bishop Henry McNeal Turner. Turner saw reparations as a feasible means of financing a mass emigration effort to Africa in the nineteenth century. In 1900 Turner tried to persuade African American leaders to ask for $100 million "to go home" and estimated that the United States owed African Americans some $40 billion in total; see Hall, *Black Separatism*, 136–38, and Wilmore, *Black Religion and Black Radicalism*, 122–29, for a more detailed discussion on the RNA and Turner's understanding of reparations.

81. Van Deburg, *Modern Black Nationalism*, 201–2.

82. Van Deburg, *Modern Black Nationalism*, 201–2.

83. Van Deburg, *Modern Black Nationalism*, 202.

84. Hall, *Black Separatism*, 138.

85. Cunnigen, "Republic of New Africa," 100; Imari Abubkarai Obadele, "The Struggle of the Republic of New Africa," *The Black Scholar* 5, no. 9 (June 1974): 22.

86. Cunnigen, "Republic of New Africa," 112.

87. Cros Sandoval, "Afro-Cuban Religion in Perspective," 95–96.

88. Barbara Cherry, telephone interview with the author, February 1996.

89. Hunt, *Oyotunji Village*, 35.

90. "The World Conference on Orisa," 11.

91. Hunt, *Oyotunji Village*, 35.

92. Carlos Cook, "Speech on the 'Buy Black' Campaign," in *Modern Black Nationalism: From Marcus Garvey to Louis Farrakhan*, ed. William L. Van Deburg (New York: New York University Press, 1997), 85.

93. "Would Resettle Africa to Solve U.S. Problem," *New York Amsterdam News*, March 31, 1962.

94. David Kenyatta, "Letter of the Week," *New York Amsterdam News*, September 4, 1965.

95. Adeleke, *UnAfrican Americans*, 6.

96. Oba Oseijeman Efuntola Adelabu Adefunmi I, personal interviews with the author, August 1994, January 1995, August 1996, and August 1997.

97. Gregory, "Santería in New York City," 65.

Chapter Six

1. Mikelle Smith Omari-Tunkara, "Oyo Tunji: A Yoruba Community in the USA," in *African Folklore: An Encyclopedia*, ed. Philip M. Peek and Kwesi Yankah (New York: Routledge, 2004), 328.

2. Eriksen, *Ethnicity and Nationalism*, 111.

3. Rod Davis, *American Voudou: Journey into a Hidden World* (Denton: University of North Texas Press, 1998), 179.

4. Omari-Tunkara, "Oyo Tunji," 329.

5. Matory, "English Professors of Brazil," 89.

6. Omari-Tunkara, "Oyo Tunji," 329.

7. Odunfonda I., Adaramola, "Obatala: The Yoruba God of Creation" (Sheldon, SC: African Theological Archminitry, n.d.), 17.

8. Wakankar, "Body, Crowd, Identity," 69.

9. Michael George Hanchard, *Orpheus and Power: The* Movimento Negro *of Rio de Janeiro and São Paulo, Brazil, 1945–1988* (Princeton, NJ: Princeton University Press, 1994), 79, 164.

10. Wakankar, "Body, Crowd, Identity," 45.

11. Butler, "Africa," 151.

12. Oseijeman Adefunmi, "Keynote Address" (Ifa Festival, Columbia University, New York, January 16, 1993), 8.

13. Drewal and Mason, *Beads, Body and Soul*, 246.

14. Velma Love, "Odu Outcomes: Yoruba Scriptures in African American Constructions of Self and World" (Ann Arbor, MI: UMI Dissertation Services, 2007), 236.

15. Gordon, *Black Identity*, 35.

16. Mikelle Smith Omari, "Completing the Circle: Notes on African Art, Society, and Religion in Oyotunji, South Carolina," *African Arts Magazine*, July 1991, 74.

17. Lefever, "Leaving the United States," 189.

18. Lefever, "Leaving the United States," 189.

19. Wakankar, "Body, Crowd, Identity," 47.

20. Lefever, "Leaving the United States," 186.

21. Matory, "English Professors of Brazil," 81.

22. Adefunmi, *Oyotunji SHANGOFEST*, 12.

23. Oseijeman Adelabu Adefunmi, ed., *Oshoun Festival* (Sheldon, SC: Great Benin Books, n.d.), 19.

24. Milton Jordan, "African Kingdom in South Carolina," *Sepia*, April 1975, 24; Omari-Tunkara, "Oyo Tunji," 329.

25. Imamu Amira Baraka (LeRoi Jones), "The Pan-African Party and the Black Nation," *The Black Scholar* 2, no. 7 (March 1971): 26.

26. Adefunmi, "Notes," 40.

27. Oommen, "Religious Nationalism and Democratic Polity," 457; also see Friedland, "Religious Nationalism," 125–52.

28. Love, "Odu Outcomes," 233, 37.

29. Matory, "English Professors of Brazil," 89.

30. Eriksen, *Ethnicity and Nationalism*, 111.

31. For discussions on past population statistics, see Lear, "An Old African Religion"; Dolly Carlisle, "King or Con Man: The Controversial Ruler of Yoruba, S.C. is really just Walter from Detroit," *People*, October 12, 1981, 16; Jordan, "African Kingdom in South Carolina"; Omari, "Completing the Circle," 67; J. Gordon Melton, ed.,

Encyclopedia of American Religions, 3rd ed. (Farmington Hills, MI: Gale Research Inc. 1989), 801–2.

32. Frank Hefin, "The Oyotunji African Village, Founded a Sovereign Nation, is Still an Enigma," *The Lowcountry Ledger*, February 23, 1992.

33. Omari, "Completing the Circle," 75; HRG Iya Orite (Iyale Imole) Olasowo, "The Relationship Between Ifa and Osun," in *Oshoun Festival*, ed. Oseijeman Adelabu Adefunmi (Sheldon, SC: African Theological Archministry, 1980), 17.

34. Davis, *American Voudou*, 195.

35. Oba Ofuntola Oseijeman Adelabu Adefunmi I, *Olorisha: A Guidebook into Yoruba Religion* (Sheldon, SC: Great Benin Books, 1982), back cover.

36. Chief Akintobe, personal interview with the author, August 1996.

37. Chief Akintobe, personal interview with the author, August 1996.

38. Her Royal Grace Iyashanla, personal interview with the author, August 1996.

39. Jordan, "African Kingdom in South Carolina," 18.

40. Jordan, "African Kingdom in South Carolina," 18.

41. Jordan, "African Kingdom in South Carolina," 23.

42. Jordan, "African Kingdom in South Carolina," 25.

43. Her Royal Grace Iyashanla, personal interview with the author, August 1996.

44. Her Royal Grace Iyashanla, personal interview with the author, August 1996.

45. Baba Akintunde, personal interview with the author, August 1995.

46. Baba Akintunde, personal interview with the author, August 1995.

47. Jacob K. Olupona, "Owner of the Day and Regulator of the Universe: Ifa Divination and Healing among the Yoruba of Southwestern Nigeria," in *Divination and Healing: Potent Vision*, ed. Michael Winkelman and Philip M. Peek (Tucson: University of Arizona Press, 2004), 104–6.

48. Butler, *Freedoms Given, Freedoms Won*, 220.

49. Butler, *Freedoms Given, Freedoms Won*, 222.

50. Butler, *Freedoms Given, Freedoms Won*, 220–21.

51. Butler, *Freedoms Given, Freedoms Won*, 219, 221.

52. Sylviane A. Diouf, *Dreams of Africa in Alabama: The Slave Ship Clotilda and the Story of the Last Africans Brought to America* (New York: Oxford University Press, 2007), 3.

53. Diouf, *Dreams of Africa in Alabama*, 5.

54. Diouf, *Dreams of Africa in Alabama*, 6.

55. Diouf, *Dreams of Africa in Alabama*, 32, 44.

56. Diouf, *Dreams of Africa in Alabama*, 43.

57. Diouf, *Dreams of Africa in Alabama*, 156.

58. Diouf, *Dreams of Africa in Alabama*, 181.

59. Diouf, *Dreams of Africa in Alabama*, 232.

60. Diouf, *Dreams of Africa in Alabama*, 181.

61. Diouf, *Dreams of Africa in Alabama*, 232.

62. Joe Drape, "African Village in the Carolinas: Home is where Yoruban Heart Is," *The Atlanta Journal and Constitution*, April 23, 1991.

63. Jordan, "African Kingdom in South Carolina," 18.

64. Matory, "Man in the 'City of Women,'" 156–58. According to Matory, "The Oyo-born and British educated C.M.S. missionary Samuel Johnson and others as well helped to establish a Yoruba literary canon, including not only a Yoruba translation of the Bible but grand narrations of the Yoruba supposedly shared Oyo legacy."

65. Sandra Cohn, "Ethnic Identity in New York City" (master's thesis, New York University, 1973), 13.

66. Cohn, "Ethnic Identity in New York City," 14.

67. Hunt, *Oyotunji Village*, 69.

68. Friedland, "Religious Nationalism," 132.

69. Hunt, *Oyotunji Village*, 81–82.

70. Hunt, *Oyotunji Village*, 69.

71. Her Royal Grace Oshunbemi Abimbola (public lecture, Swarthmore College, Swarthmore, PA, November 20, 1997).

72. Hunt, *Oyotunji Village*, 81.

73. Adefunmi, "Keynote Address," 3.

74. Oba Oseijeman Efuntola Adelabu Adefunmi I, personal interviews with the author, August 1994, January 1995, August 1996, and August 1997.

75. Oba Oseijeman Efuntola Adelabu Adefunmi I, personal interviews with the author, August 1994, January 1995, August 1996, and August 1997.

76. Brandon, *Santeria from Africa to the New World*, 156.

77. Hunt, *Oyotunji Village*, 50.

78. Hunt, *Oyotunji Village*, 51.

79. Hunt, *Oyotunji Village*, 52.

80. Hunt, *Oyotunji Village*, 56.

81. Hunt, *Oyotunji Village*, 56; also see Ogboni Book at Oyotunji African Village.

82. Johnson, *History of the Yoruba*, 104–9. See these pages for the guidelines used for facial markings at Oyotunji Village.

83. Adefunmi, "Keynote Address," 14.

84. Hunt, *Oyotunji Village*, 60.

85. HRG Odufunade Adaramola, *Rites of Passage: An Explanation of the Cycles and Stages of Human Growth and Development* (Sheldon, SC: Great Benin Books, 1991), 10–15.

86. Friedland, "Religious Nationalism," 135.

87. Friedland, "Religious Nationalism," 133–36.

88. Debra Mubashshir Masjeed (lecture, Society for the Study of Black Religion, Washington, DC, March 26, 2009).

89. Efunbolade, "The Living Shrine," 68.

90. Chief Wale Ogunlola, "A Yoruba Village in America (II)," *West Africa*, February 2–8, 1998.

91. For a fuller discussion of polygyny at Oyotunji, see Hunt, *Oyotunji Village*, 93–100.

92. Hunt, *Oyotunji Village*, 93–100.

93. Chief Olaitan, personal interview with the author, August 1996.

94. Anonymous priestess, personal interview with the author, July 1994.

95. Her Royal Grace Iyashanla, personal interview with the author, August 1995.

96. Efunbolade, "The Living Shrine," 68–69.

97. Hunt, *Oyotunji Village*, 108.

98. Efunbolade, "The Living Shrine," 64–65.

99. Hunt, *Oyotunji Village*, 72, 108, 110; Eason, *Ifa*, 100.

100. Eason, "Historicizing Ifa Culture," 284.

101. Eason, "Historicizing Ifa Culture," 284.

102. Brandon, *Santeria from Africa to the New World*, 162.

103. Juan J. Sosa, "La Santería: An Integrating, Mythological Worldview in a Dis-integrating Society," in *Orisa Devotion as World Religion: The Globalization of Yoruba Religious Culture*, ed. Jacob K. Olupona and Terry Rey (Madison: University of Wisconsin Press, 2008), 384;

104. ason, *Ifa*, xxiv.

105. Andrew Apter, "Que Faire? Reconsidering Inventions of Africa," *Critical Inquiry* 19, no. 1 (Autumn 1992): 92.

106. Hunt, *Oyotunji Village*, 56.

107. Morales, "Returning to the Source," 127.

108. Omari, "Completing the Circle," 74.

109. http://adiama.com/medahochi.

110. Zillur R. Khan, "Islam and Bengali Nationalism," *Asian Survey* 25, no. 8 (August 1985): 837.

111. Lefever, "Leaving the United States," 174.

112. "African Affairs: An Africa Village in South Carolina," *Jet Magazine*, January 3, 1974, 52.

113. "African Affairs: An Africa Village in South Carolina," 52.

114. Debra Butterworth, "Oyotunji Attracts Tourists, Criticism for African Ways," *The Beaufort Gazette*, July 19, 1982.

115. Butterworth, "Oyotunji Attracts Tourists."

116. Butterworth, "Oyotunji Attracts Tourists."

117. Lefever, "Leaving the United States," 186.

118. Oba Adejuyibe Adefunmi II, personal interview, September 19, 2008.

119. Brooks, "Eku Odun," 11.

120. Hunt, *Oyotunji Village*, 63.

121. Thomas M. Hunter, "Blacks Seeking Lost Heritage," *News & Courier*, July 21, 1971.

122. Hunter, "Blacks Seeking Lost Heritage"; editorial, "Without 'The Man,'" *News & Courier*, November 9, 1971; Oseijeman Adefunmi, "Pay for Slavery," *News & Courier*, November 9, 1971.

123. Hunt, *Oyotunji Village*, 63; Palmié, "Against Syncretism," 89.

124. Matory, "Man in the 'City of Women,'" 361.

125. Lefever, "Leaving the United States," 191; Jim Polson, "Back to the Land?," *Beaufort Gazette*, April 7, 1981.

126. Brooks, "Eku Odun," 14.

127. Hunt, *Oyotunji Village*, 44–45, 50; Brooks, "Eku Odun," 53.

128. Brooks, "Eku Odun," 51.

129. Matory, "Revisiting the African Diaspora," 169.

130. Clifford Geertz, *The Interpretation of Cultures* (New York: Basic Books, 1973), 89.

131. Geertz, *The Interpretation of Cultures*, 90.

132. Chief Olaitan, personal interview with the author, August 1996.

133. Chief Olaitan, personal interview with the author, August 1996.

134. Chief Olaitan, personal interview with the author, August 1996.

135. Chief Eleshin, personal interview with the author, August 1996.

136. Chief Eleshin, personal interview with the author, August 1996.

137. *Voodoo Rituals* (New York: A&E Home Video, 2002), DVD.

138. Chief Eleshin, personal interview with the author, August 1996.

139. Chief Eleshin, personal interview with the author, August 1996.

140. Chief Eleshin, personal interview with the author, August 1996.

141. Lefever, "Leaving the United States," 185.

142. Cohn, "Ethnic Identity in New York City," 9.

143. Maulana Karenga, *Odú Ifá: The Ethical Teachings* (Los Angeles: University of San-kore Press, 1999), vii.

144. Loudell Snow, *Walkin' Over Medicine* (Boulder, CO: Westview Press, 1993), 270.

145. Margaret Washington Creel, *A Peculiar People: Slave Religion and Community-Culture Among the Gullahs* (New York: New York University Press, 1989), 2.

146. Creel, *A Peculiar People*, 1.

147. Creel, *A Peculiar People*, 325.

148. Patricia Jones-Jackson, "Let the Church Say 'Amen'": The Language of Religious Rituals in Coastal South Carolina," in *The Crucible of Carolina: Essays in the Development of Gullah Language and Culture*, ed. Michael Montgomery (Athens: University of Georgia Press, 1994), 115–32.

149. Charles Joyner, *Down by the Riverside: A South Carolina Slave Community* (Urbana: University of Illinois Press, 1984), xix.

150. Preston L. McKever-Floyd, "Masks of the Sacred: Religious Pluralism in South Carolina," in *Religion in South Carolina*, ed. Charles H. Lippy (Columbia: University of South Carolina Press, 1993), 153, 165.

151. Hunt, *Oyotunji Village*, 60.

152. Lear, "An Old African Religion Makes a U.S. Comeback," 23.

153. Lear, "An Old African Religion Makes a U.S. Comeback," 23.

154. Chief Akintobe, personal interview with the author, August 1996.

155. Cornelia Walker Bailey, *God, Dr. Buzzard, and the Bolito Man: A Saltwater Geechee Talks about Life on Sapelo Island* (New York: First Anchor Books Edition, 2001), 190.

156. Shango Omuyiwa Akinwon, personal interview with the author, August 1994.

157. Samuel Hopkins Adams, "Dr. Bug, Dr. Buzzard, and the U.S.A.," *True*, July 1949, 69.

158. Adams, "Dr. Bug, Dr. Buzzard, and the U.S.A.," 69, 71.

159. Adams, "Dr. Bug, Dr. Buzzard, and the U.S.A.," 69.

160. Nancy Rhyne, *Tales of the South Carolina Low Country* (Winston-Salem, SC: John F. Blair, 1982), 72–73.

161. Adams, "Dr. Bug, Dr. Buzzard, and the U.S.A.," 71.

162. Chief Akintobe, personal interview with the author, August 1996.

163. Michael Soper, "Voodoo Flourishes on Sea Island," *Beaufort Gazette Sunday Magazine*, April 9, 1961.

164. Shango Omuyiwa Akinwon, personal interview with the author, August 1994.

165. Bailey, *God, Dr. Buzzard, and the Bolito Man*, 187.

166. Omari, "Completing the Circle," 71.

167. David H. Brown, "Conjure/Doctors: An Exploration of a Black Discourse in America, Antebellum to 1940," *Folklore Forum* 23, no. 1/2 (1990): 4.

168. Charles H. Long, "Bodies in Time and the Healing of Spaces: Religion, Temporalities, and Health," in *Faith, Health, and Healing in African American Life*, ed. Stephanie Y. Mitchem and Emilie M. Townes (London: Praeger, 2008), 43; Brown, "Conjure/Doctors," 5.

169. Wirtz, *Ritual, Discourse, and Community in Cuban Santería*, 39.

170. Huntington, "Bodies in Contexts," 185.

171. Brown, "Conjure/Doctors," 4.

172. Brown, "Writing about 'The Other,'" 128.

173. Mary Cuthrell Curry, *Making the Gods in New York: The Yoruba Religion in the African American Community* (New York: Garland Publishers, 1997), 57.

174. Joseph Murphy, "Afro-American Religion and Oracles: *Santeria* in Cuba," *Journal of the Interdenominational Theological Center* 8, no. 1 (Fall 1980): 87.

175. Huntington, "Bodies in Contexts," 7–8.

176. Huntington, "Bodies in Contexts," 180.

177. Huntington, "Bodies in Contexts," 11.

178. Huntington, "Bodies in Contexts," 116, 193.

179. Huntington, "Bodies in Contexts," 179.

180. Huntington, "Bodies in Contexts," 179.

181. Weaver, "Notes on Orisa Worship in an Urban Setting," 18.

182. Huntington, "Bodies in Contexts," 145.

183. McKever-Floyd, "Masks of the Sacred," 155.

184. Adefunmi, *Olorisha*, 14.

185. Christan, *Local Religion*, 22.

186. Christian, *Local Religion*, 29.

187. Christian, *Local Religion*, 176.

188. Meredith McGuire, *Ritual Healing in Suburban America* (New Brunswick, NJ: Rutgers University Press, 1988). Chapters specifically helpful for this study were "Middle-Class Use of Nonmedical Healing," "Healing in Christian Groups," and "Psychic and Occult Healing."

189. McGuire, *Ritual Healing in Suburban America*, 6.

190. Huntington, "Bodies in Contexts," 44.

191. Yvonne Chireau, "Natural and Supernatural: African American Hoodoo Narratives of Sickness and Healing," in *Faith, Health, and Healing in African American Life*, ed. Stephanie Y. Mitchem and Emilie M. Townes (London: Praeger, 2008), 12.

192. Huntington, "Bodies in Contexts," 129; Olupona, "Owner of the Day," 111.

193. Huntington, "Bodies in Contexts," 44.

194. Olupona, "Owner of the Day," 112.

195. Olupona, "Owner of the Day," 113.

196. Stephanie Y. Mitchem and Emilie M. Townes, eds., *Faith, Health, and Healing in African American Life* (London: Praeger, 2008), xii.

197. Olomo, *Core of Fire*, 40.

198. Judy Rosenthal speaks of a similar divination system among the Ewe called Afa, which is also consulted for advice and healing. According to Rosenthal, "One of the operations in Afa divination is to find out who or what is acting on a person or situation (kin, affines, spirits, ancestors, vodus, one's own ignorance or past, and so forth) and how this agency is to be interpreted broadly in categories of good (well-being) and evil (misfortune), happiness and unhappiness, or of evenness (coolness) and unevenness (heat). In the Ewe version of Afa (Dzisa), these agencies and effects of agency are divided into seventeen sorts of happiness, good fortune, well-being, and enjoyment; they are divided into only five kinds of evil, misfortune, suffering, bad luck, and unhappiness (Surgy's empechement—blocking—of energy, power, or strength)." Judy Rosenthal, *Possession, Ecstasy, and Law in Ewe Voodoo* (Charlottesville: University Press of Virginia, 1998), 224; see also Olupona's "Owner of the Day," 103–17.

199. Omari-Tunkara, "Oyo Tunji," 329.

200. Noel, *Black Religion and the Imagination of Matter*, 85.

201. Huntington, "Bodies in Contexts," 138.

202. Rosenthal, *Possession, Ecstasy, and Law*, 224.

203. Rosenthal, *Possession, Ecstasy, and Law*, 234.

204. Abimbola, *Yoruba Culture*, 69.

205. Wande Abimbola and Ivor Miller, *Ifa Will Mend Our Broken World: Thoughts on Yoruba Religion and Culture in Africa and the Diaspora* (Roxbury, MA: Aim Books, 1997), 82.

206. Rosenthal, *Possession, Ecstasy, and Law*, 236.

207. Karade, *Path to Priesthood*, 22.

208. Murphy, "Santería and Vodou in the United States," 292.

209. Huntington, "Bodies in Contexts," 138.

210. Olomo, *Core of Fire*, 122–23.

211. McKever-Floyd, "Masks of the Sacred," 158.

212. Huntington, "Bodies in Contexts," 44.

213. Huntington, "Bodies in Contexts," 129.

214. Regarding the legal system, a large number of Oyotunji clients are either mothers coming to the village on behalf of incarcerated black males or black males themselves petitioning the gods of Africa through Oyotunji for spiritual

NOTES TO PAGES 209–14

intervention in their condition. Chief Akintobe, personal interview with the author, August 1996.

215. Personal notes from field notebook, August 1996.

216. Oba Sekou Olayinka, personal interviews with the author, August 2003 and September 2003.

217. Brown, *Mama Lola*, 344–50.

218. Stephanie Y. Mitchem, "Healing Heart and Broken Bodies: An African American Women's Spirituality of Healing," in *Faith, Health, and Healing in African American Life*, ed. Stephanie Y. Mitchem and Emilie M. Townes (London: Praeger, 2008), 184.

219. Creel, *A Peculiar People*, 325.

220. Adefunmi, "Notes," 41.

221. Adefunmi, "Notes," 41.

222. Adefunmi, "Notes," 41.

223. Adefunmi, "Notes," 41.

224. Adefunmi, *Oshoun Festival*, 13.

225. Chief Alagba Olaitan, *Ancestor Veneration* (Sheldon SC: African Theological Archministry, n.d.), inside back cover; Davis, *American Voudou*, 278.

226. Wirtz, *Ritual, Discourse, and Community in Cuban Santería*, 40–41.

227. Francio Guadeloupe, *Chanting Down the New Jerusalem: Calypso, Christianity, and Capitalism in the Caribbean* (Los Angeles: University of California Press, 2009), 81.

228. Bailey, *God, Dr. Buzzard, and the Bolito Man*, 189.

229. Bailey, *God, Dr. Buzzard, and the Bolito Man*, 189.

230. Bailey, *God, Dr. Buzzard, and the Bolito Man*, 189.

231. Yewande, personal interview with the author, August 23, 2006.

232. Yewande, personal interview with the author, August 23, 2006.

233. Shango Omuyiwa Akinwon, personal interview with the author, August 1994.

234. Love, "Odu Outcomes," 74.

235. Love, "Odu Outcomes," 74.

236. Davis, *American Voudou*, 277.

237. Abimbola and Miller, *Ifa Will Mend Our Broken World*, 7.

238. Yewande, personal interview with the author, August 23, 2006.

239. Yewande, personal interview with the author, August 23, 2006.

240. Adefunmi, *Oshoun Festival*, 9.

241. Oba Sekou Olayinka, personal interviews with the author, August 2003 and September 2003.

242. Oba Sekou Olayinka, personal interviews with the author, August 2003 and September 2003.

243. Yewande, personal interview with the author, August 23, 2006.

244. Oba Sekou Olayinka, personal interviews with the author, August 2003 and September 2003.

245. Oba Sekou Olayinka, personal interviews with the author, August 2003 and September 2003.

246. Oba Sekou Olayinka, personal interviews with the author, August 2003 and September 2003.
247. Huntington, "Bodies in Contexts," 183.
248. Chief Akintobe, personal interview with the author, August 1996.
249. Brown, "Conjure/Doctors," 5.
250. Oba Adejuyibe Adefunmi II, personal interview with the author, September 19, 2008.
251. Lear, "Oyotunji Village," 18.
252. Adefunmi, *Olorisha*, 3.
253. Adefunmi, *Olorisha*, 3; Smith, *Imagining Religions*, 96; Eason, *Ifa*, 282.
254. Chief Akintobe, personal interview with the author, August 1996.
255. Adefunmi, "Keynote Address," 17–18.
256. Babalosa John Mason, personal interview with the author, December 11, 1997.
257. Babalosa John Mason, personal interview with the author, December 11, 1997.
258. Anonymous priest, personal interview with the author, January 1998.
259. Iya Omolewa Eniolorunopa, personal interview with the author, July 2006.
260. Oba Sekou Olayinka, personal interviews with the author, August 2003 and September 2003.
261. Lefever, "Leaving the United States," 193.
262. Chief Akintobe, personal interview with the author, August 1996.
263. Chief Akintobe, personal interview with the author, August 1996.
264. Oba Oseijeman Efuntola Adelabu Adefunmi I, personal interviews with the author, August 1994, January 1995, August 1996, and August 1997.
265. Baba Akintunde, personal interview with the author, August 1995.
266. Efunbolade, "The Living Shrine," 70.
267. Joe Drape, "African Village in the Carolinas: Home Is Where the Yoruban Heart Is," *The Atlanta Journal and Constitution*, April 23, 1991.
268. Oba Oseijeman Efuntola Adelabu Adefunmi I, personal interviews with the author, August 1994, January 1995, August 1996, and August 1997.
269. Chief Akintobe, personal interview with the author, August 1996.
270. Efunbolade, "The Living Shrine," 70.
271. Adefunmi, *Orisha*, 17.
272. Brooks, "Eku Odun," 54; www.oyotunjiafricanvillage.org/news.htm; Adefunmi, *Olorisha*, ii.
273. Oba Adejuyibe Adefunmi II, personal interview with the author, September 19, 2008.
274. Oba Adejuyibe Adefunmi II, personal interview with the author, September 19, 2008.
275. Oba Adejuyibe Adefunmi II, personal interview with the author, September 19, 2008.
276. Oba Adejuyibe Adefunmi II, personal interview with the author, September 19, 2008.
277. Oba Adejuyibe Adefunmi II, personal interview with the author, September 19, 2008.
278. Oba Adejuyibe Adefunmi II, personal interview with the author, September 19, 2008.
279. Oba Adejuyibe Adefunmi II, personal interview with the author, September 19, 2008.
280. Oba Adejuyibe Adefunmi II, personal interview with the author, September 19, 2008.
281. Oba Adejuyibe Adefunmi II, personal interview with the author, September 19, 2008.
282. Oba Adejuyibe Adefunmi II, personal interview with the author, September 19, 2008.

283. Oba Adejuyibe Adefunmi II, personal interview with the author, September 19, 2008.
284. Oba Adejuyibe Adefunmi II, personal interview with the author, September 19, 2008.
285. Brandon, *Santeria from Africa to the New World*, 160.
286. Brandon, *Santeria from Africa to the New World*, 160.
287. Oba Adejuyibe Adefunmi II, personal interview with the author, September 19, 2008.

Chapter Seven

1. Abimbola, *Yoruba Culture*, 101–2.
2. Abimbola, *Yoruba Culture*, 102–3.
3. Abimbola, *Yoruba Culture*, 103.
4. Abimbola, *Yoruba Culture*, 103.
5. Abimbola, *Yoruba Culture*, 104.
6. Abimbola, *Yoruba Culture*, 101.
7. Abimbola, *Yoruba Culture*, 101.
8. Wirtz, *Ritual, Discourse, and Community in Cuban Santería*, 29.
9. Elizabeth Isichei, *The Religious Traditions of Africa: A History* (Westport, CT: Praeger, 2004), 8.
10. Brown, "Conjure/Doctors," 10.
11. Vega, "Yoruba Philosophy," 203.
12. Vega, "Yoruba Philosophy," 197.
13. Abimbola, *Yoruba Culture*, 102.
14. Cros Sandoval, *Worldview, the Orichas, and Santería*, 351.
15. Brown, *Mama Lola*, xi–xii. Brown states that Mama Lola "gifted in the art of cultural *bricolage*, that is, making use of whatever cultural elements serve to support her and her family, regardless of whether they are Haitian or 'American' or come from any of the other peoples and cultures she routinely encounters in New York City. Her current religious commitments include Haitian Vodou and Puerto Rican Santeria, as well as Vatican II Catholicism as interpreted by first-generation Irish-immigrant priests."
16. David D. Hall, "Review Essay: What is the Place of 'Experience' in Religious History?," *Religion and American Culture* 13, no. 2 (Summer 2003): 249.
17. See Janet Cornelius, *Slave Missions and the Black Church in the Antebellum South* (Columbia: University of South Carolina Press, 1999), 23–102.
18. Brown, "Conjure/Doctors," 10.
19. Raboteau, *Slave Religion*, 287–88.
20. Chireau, *Black Magic*, 4.
21. Brown, "Conjure/Doctors," 10.
22. Chief Akintobe, personal interview with the author, August 1996.
23. Matory, *Sex and the Empire That Is No More*, 62.
24. Yvonne Daniel, "The Potency of Dance: A Haitian Examination," *The Black Scholar* 11, no. 18 (November/December, 1980): 72.
25. Brown, *Mama Lola*, 343.

26. Adam Clark, "Black Theology, Afrocentricity, and the Womanist Challenge" (Black Theology Group, American Academy of Religion, Atlanta, GA, October 30, 2010).

27. James S. Coleman, *Nigeria: Background to Nationalism* (Berkeley: University of California Press, 1958), 177.

28. Geoffrey Parrinder, *Religion in an African City* (London: Oxford University Press, 1953), 127.

29. Parrinder, *Religion in an African City*, 126–27.

30. Parrinder, *Religion in an African City*, 127.

31. Brandon, "Hierarchy Without a Head," 157.

32. Parrinder, *Religion in an African City*, 127.

33. Cros Sandoval, *Worldview, the Orichas, and Santería*, 324.

34. *Bahia, Africa in the Americas*, directed by Geovanni Brewer (Berkeley: University of California Extension Media Center, 1988), VHS.

35. John Burdick, *Blessed Anastácia: Women, Race, and Popular Christianity in Brazil* (New York: Routledge, 1998), 192.

36. Afi-Odelia Scruggs, personal interview with the author, April 2007.

37. Richard and Sally Price, "Shadowboxing in the Mangrove," *Cultural Anthropology* 12, no. 1 (1997): 12.

38. De La Torre, "Ochun: (N)Either the (M)Other of All Cubans," 858–59.

39. Cros Sandoval, *Worldview, the Orichas, and Santería*, 351.

40. Oba Osunkunle, personal interview with the author, New York City, October 16, 1997.

41. Monica A. Coleman, "The Womb Circle: A Womanist Practice of Multiple-Religious Belonging," *Practical Matters: A Transdisciplinary Multimedia Journal of Religious Practices and Practical Theology*, no.4 (Spring 2011): 8.

42. Ayoka, telephone interview with the author, March 2, 1998.

43. Ayoka, telephone interview with the author, March 2, 1998.

44. Ayoka, telephone interview with the author, March 2, 1998.

45. Ayoka, telephone interview with the author, March 2, 1998.

46. Ayoka, telephone interview with the author, March 2, 1998.

47. Yewande, personal interview with the author, August 23, 2006.

48. Yewande, personal interview with the author, August 23, 2006.

49. Ayoka, telephone interview with the author, March 2, 1998.

50. Adejoke, telephone interview with the author, February 1, 1998, and March 22, 1998.

51. Love, "Odu Outcomes," 75.

52. Evelyn Brooks Higginbotham, "Religion, Politics, and Gender: The Leadership of Nannie Helen Burroughs," in *This Far By Faith: Readings in African-American Women's Religious Biography*, ed. Judith Weisenfeld (New York: Routledge, 1996), 142.

53. Higginbotham, "Religion, Politics, and Gender," 143.

54. Evelyn Brooks Higginbotham, *Righteous Discontent: The Women's Movement in the Black Baptist Church, 1880–1920* (Cambridge, MA: Harvard University Press, 1993), 211.

55. Higginbotham, "Religion, Politics, and Gender," 154.

56. Adejoke, telephone interview with the author, February 1, 1998, and March 22, 1998.

57. Adejoke, telephone interview with the author, February 1, 1998, and March 22, 1998.

58. Adejoke, telephone interview with the author, February 1, 1998, and March 22, 1998.
59. Adejoke, telephone interview with the author, February 1, 1998, and March 22, 1998.
60. Baba Medahochi Kofi Omowale Zannu, personal interviews with the author, August 7, 2006, and August 23, 2006.
61. Dr. John Kinney, "State of Black Religion" (Society for the Study of Black Religion, Washington, DC, March 28, 2009).
62. Adejoke, telephone interview with the author, February 1, 1998, and March 22, 1998.
63. Clarence Hardy III, *James Baldwin's God: Sex, Hope, and Crisis in Black Holiness Culture* (Knoxville: University of Tennessee Press, 2003), 59.
64. Sallie McFague, *The Body of God: An Ecological Theology* (Minneapolis: Fortress Press, 1993), 207.
65. Hardy, *James Baldwin's God*, 59.
66. Hardy, *James Baldwin's God*, 59–60.
67. Abimbola and Miller, *Ifa Will Mend Our Broken World*, 89.
68. Iya Omolewa Eniolorunopa, personal interview with the author, July 2006.
69. Iya Omolewa Eniolorunopa, personal interview with the author, July 2006.
70. Iya Omolewa Eniolorunopa, personal interview with the author, July 2006.
71. Olomo, *Core of Fire*, 108.
72. Olomo, *Core of Fire*, 15–16, 108–9, 112–13, 156.
73. Olomo, *Core of Fire*, 15.
74. Olomo, *Core of Fire*, 18.
75. Olomo, *Core of Fire*, 16.
76. Olomo, *Core of Fire*, 28.
77. Adejoke, telephone interview with the author, February 1, 1998, and March 22, 1998.
78. Afi-Odelia Scruggs, personal interview with the author, April 2007.
79. Afi-Odelia Scruggs, personal interview with the author, April 2007.
80. Afi-Odelia Scruggs, personal interview with the author, April 2007.
81. Afi-Odelia Scruggs, personal interview with the author, April 2007.
82. Afi-Odelia Scruggs, personal interview with the author, April 2007.
83. Afi-Odelia Scruggs, personal interview with the author, April 2007.
84. Afi-Odelia Scruggs, personal interview with the author, April 2007.
85. Afi-Odelia Scruggs, personal interview with the author, April 2007.
86. Afi-Odelia Scruggs, personal interview with the author, April 2007.
87. Afi-Odelia Scruggs, personal interview with the author, April 2007.
88. Afi-Odelia Scruggs, personal interview with the author, April 2007.
89. Afi-Odelia Scruggs, personal interview with the author, April 2007.
90. Afi-Odelia Scruggs, personal interview with the author, April 2007.
91. Afi-Odelia Scruggs, personal interview with the author, April 2007.
92. Afi-Odelia Scruggs, personal interview with the author, April 2007.
93. Afi-Odelia Scruggs, personal interview with the author, April 2007.
94. Afi-Odelia Scruggs, personal interview with the author, April 2007.
95. Afi-Odelia Scruggs, personal interview with the author, April 2007.
96. Afi-Odelia Scruggs, personal interview with the author, April 2007.

97. Oluweri Egundyao Onisegun, personal interview with the author, March 26, 2009.
98. Oluweri Egundyao Onisegun, personal interview with the author, March 26, 2009.
99. Oluweri Egundyao Onisegun, personal interview with the author, March 26, 2009.
100. Oluweri Egundyao Onisegun, personal interview with the author, March 26, 2009.
101. Oluweri Egundyao Onisegun, personal interview with the author, March 26, 2009.
102. Oluweri Egundyao Onisegun, personal interview with the author, March 26, 2009.
103. Oluweri Egundyao Onisegun, personal interview with the author, March 26, 2009.
104. Oluweri Egundyao Onisegun, personal interview with the author, March 26, 2009.
105. Oluweri Egundyao Onisegun, personal interview with the author, March 26, 2009.
106. Oluweri Egundyao Onisegun, personal interview with the author, March 26, 2009.
107. Guadeloupe, *Chanting Down the New Jerusalem*, 81.
108. Guadeloupe, *Chanting Down the New Jerusalem*, 81.
109. Guadeloupe, *Chanting Down the New Jerusalem*, 82.
110. Guadeloupe, *Chanting Down the New Jerusalem*, 82.
111. Guadeloupe, *Chanting Down the New Jerusalem*, 81.
112. William D. Hart, *Black Religion: Malcolm X, Julius Lester, and Jan Willis* (New York: Palgrave Macmillan, 2008), 194.
113. Oluweri Egundyao Onisegun, personal interview with the author, March 26, 2009.
114. Oluweri Egundyao Onisegun, personal interview with the author, March 26, 2009.
115. Oluweri Egundyao Onisegun, personal interview with the author, March 26, 2009.
116. Hart, *Black Religion: Malcolm X*, 179.
117. Oluweri Egundyao Onisegun, personal interview with the author, March 26, 2009.
118. Hart, *Black Religion: Malcolm X*, 180.
119. Butler, *Liberating Our Dignity, Saving Our Souls*, 71.
120. Oluweri Egundyao Onisegun, personal interview with the author, March 26, 2009.
121. Oluweri Egundyao Onisegun, personal interview with the author, March 26, 2009.
122. Oluweri Egundyao Onisegun, personal interview with the author, March 26, 2009.
123. Oluweri Egundyao Onisegun, personal interview with the author, March 26, 2009.
124. Oluweri Egundyao Onisegun, personal interview with the author, March 26, 2009.
125. Oluweri Egundyao Onisegun, personal interview with the author, March 26, 2009.
126. Oluweri Egundyao Onisegun, personal interview with the author, March 26, 2009.
127. Oluweri Egundyao Onisegun, personal interview with the author, March 26, 2009.
128. Oluweri Egundyao Onisegun, personal interview with the author, March 26, 2009.
129. Oluweri Egundyao Onisegun, personal interview with the author, March 26, 2009.
130. Oluweri Egundyao Onisegun, personal interview with the author, March 26, 2009.
131. Oluweri Egundyao Onisegun, personal interview with the author, March 26, 2009.
132. Oluweri Egundyao Onisegun, personal interview with the author, March 26, 2009.
133. John 9:6-7 (King James Version).
134. Oluweri Egundyao Onisegun, personal interview with the author, March 26, 2009.
135. Oluweri Egundyao Onisegun, personal interview with the author, March 26, 2009.
136. Hart, *Black Religion: Malcolm X*, 178.
137. Oluweri Egundyao Onisegun, personal interview with the author, March 26, 2009.
138. Oluweri Egundyao Onisegun, personal interview with the author, March 26, 2009.

139. Oluweri Egundyao Onisegun, personal interview with the author, March 26, 2009.

140. Oluweri Egundyao Onisegun, personal interview with the author, March 26, 2009.

141. Oluweri Egundyao Onisegun, personal interview with the author, March 26, 2009.

142. Oluweri Egundyao Onisegun, personal interview with the author, March 26, 2009.

143. Mark Ogunwale Keita Lomax, personal interview with the author, August 4, 2006.

144. Mark Ogunwale Keita Lomax, personal interview with the author, August 4, 2006.

145. Andrea Abrams, "Who I Am and Whose I Am: Race, Class, Gender and Nation in an Afrocentric Church" (Ann Arbor, MI: UMI Dissertation Services, 2006), 65.

146. Abrams, "Who I Am and Whose I Am," 66.

147. Abrams, "Who I Am and Whose I Am," 3.

148. Mark Ogunwale Keita Lomax, personal interview with the author, August 4, 2006.

149. Mark Ogunwale Keita Lomax, personal interview with the author, August 4, 2006.

150. Mark Ogunwale Keita Lomax, personal interview with the author, August 4, 2006.

151. Mark Ogunwale Keita Lomax, personal interview with the author, August 4, 2006.

152. Mark Ogunwale Keita Lomax, personal interview with the author, August 4, 2006.

153. "For these contemporary congregations, the origin of Christianity finds its home in Africa. It yields a spirituality that connects them geographically, historically, biblically, and ancestrally as a people of exile. They acknowledge the establishment of the first African church in 42 CE by the Cyrenian Jew John Mark, who was also the companion of Paul and the author of the second gospel. They celebrate the planting of Christianity in the Upper Nile Valley by Judich, the Ethiopian eunuch spoken of in Acts 8:36–40, and the later adoption of Christianity in Ethiopia by the fourth century. They are also aware of the solid presence of Christianity among the native Copts of Egypt and the strength of their church." Julia Speller, *Walkin' the Talk: Keepin' the Faith in Africentric Congregations* (Cleveland, OH: The Pilgrim Press, 2005), 105.

154. Mark Ogunwale Keita Lomax, personal interview with the author, August 4, 2006.

155. The greater Atlanta area is a major center for megachurch activities such as T. D. Jakes's MegaFest and also for large megacongregational churches pastored by Crefloe Dollar and Juanita Bynum. Eddie Long's New Birth Missionary Baptist Church grew from three hundred members in 1987 to twenty-two thousand in 2001; see Tamelyn Norene Tucker, "Bringing the Church 'Back In' Black Megachurch and Community Development" (Ann Arbor, MI: UMI Dissertation Services, 2002), 83.

156. Abrams, "Who I Am and Whose I Am," 109.

157. Molefi Kete Asante, *Afrocentricity* (Trenton, NJ: Africa World Press, 1988), 2.

158. Mark Ogunwale Keita Lomax, personal interview with the author, August 4, 2006.

159. Mark Ogunwale Keita Lomax, personal interview with the author, August 4, 2006.

160. Mark Ogunwale Keita Lomax, personal interview with the author, August 4, 2006.

161. Mark Ogunwale Keita Lomax, personal interview with the author, August 4, 2006.

162. Mark Ogunwale Keita Lomax, personal interview with the author, August 4, 2006.

163. Mark Ogunwale Keita Lomax, personal interview with the author, August 4, 2006.

164. Mark Ogunwale Keita Lomax, personal interview with the author, August 4, 2006.

165. Mark Ogunwale Keita Lomax, personal interview with the author, August 4, 2006.

166. Dubois, *The Souls of Black Folk*, 123.

167. Mark Ogunwale Keita Lomax, personal interview with the author, August 4, 2006.

168. Mark Ogunwale Keita Lomax, personal interview with the author, August 4, 2006.

169. Mark Ogunwale Keita Lomax, personal interview with the author, August 4, 2006.

170. Mark Ogunwale Keita Lomax, personal interview with the author, August 4, 2006.

171. Eugene Genovese, *Roll, Jordan, Roll: The World the Slaves Made* (New York: Pantheon, 1974), 211; Raboteau, *Slave Religion*, 43–92.

172. Wilmore, *Black Religion and Black Radicalism*, 11, 14–15.

173. Wilmore, *Black Religion and Black Radicalism*, 11.

174. Wilmore, *Black Religion and Black Radicalism*, 27.

175. Wilmore, *Black Religion and Black Radicalism*, 26.

176. Wilmore, *Black Religion and Black Radicalism*, 26.

177. Mark Ogunwale Keita Lomax, personal interview with the author, August 4, 2006.

178. Mark Ogunwale Keita Lomax, personal interview with the author, August 4, 2006.

179. Mark Ogunwale Keita Lomax, personal interview with the author, August 4, 2006.

180. Mark Ogunwale Keita Lomax, personal interview with the author, August 4, 2006.

181. Perkinson, "Ogu's Iron or Jesus' Irony?," 118.

182. Perkinson, "Ogu's Iron or Jesus' Irony?," 117.

183. Perkinson, "Ogu's Iron or Jesus' Irony?," 117 (emphasis mine).

184. Perkinson, "Ogu's Iron or Jesus' Irony?," 118.

185. Mark Ogunwale Keita Lomax, personal interview with the author, August 4, 2006.

186. Afi-Odelia Scruggs, personal interview with the author, April 2007.

187. Noel, *Black Religion and the Imagination of Matter*, 13.

188. Mark Ogunwale Keita Lomax, personal interview with the author, August 4, 2006.

189. Abrams, "Who I Am and Whose I Am," 179–80.

190. Abrams, "Who I Am and Whose I Am," 179–80.

191. Wilmore, *Black Religion and Black Radicalism*, 26.

192. Mark Ogunwale Keita Lomax, personal interview with the author, August 4, 2006.

193. Mark Ogunwale Keita Lomax, personal interview with the author, August 4, 2006.

194. Baba Medahochi Kofi Omowale Zannu, personal interviews with the author, August 7, 2006, and August 23, 2006.

195. Baba Medahochi Kofi Omowale Zannu, personal interviews with the author, August 7, 2006, and August 23, 2006.

196. Baba Medahochi Kofi Omowale Zannu, personal interviews with the author, August 7, 2006, and August 23, 2006.

197. Baba Medahochi Kofi Omowale Zannu, personal interviews with the author, August 7, 2006, and August 23, 2006.

198. Vega, "Yoruba Philosophy," 188.

199. Eason, *Ifa*, xv.

200. Guadeloupe, *Chanting Down the New Jerusalem*, 81.

201. Iya Omolewa Eniolorunopa, personal interview with the author, July 2006.

202. Huntington, "Bodies in Contexts," 130–31.

203. Huntington, "Bodies in Contexts," 131.

204. Iya Omolewa Eniolorunopa, personal interview with the author, July 2006.
205. Wirtz, *Ritual, Discourse, and Community in Cuban Santería*, 45.
206. Lessane, "Tell My Feet I've Made it Home," 137.
207. Zora Neale Hurston, *Mules and Men* (Bloomington: Indiana University Press, 1963), 207–8.
208. Tracey E. Hucks, "Burning With a Flame in America: African American Women in African-Derived Traditions," *Journal of Feminist Studies in Religion* 17, no. 2 (Fall 2001): 102; Iyanla Vanzant, *Yesterday, I Cried: Celebrating the Lessons of Living and Loving* (New York: Simon & Schuster, 1998), 247.
209. Perkinson, "Ogu's Iron or Jesus' Irony?" 100.

Chapter Eight

1. Butler, *Freedoms Given, Freedoms Won*, 226.
2. Peter Hulme, "Survival and Invention: Indigeneity in the Caribbean," in *Text and Nation: Cross-Disciplinary Essays on Cultural and National Identities*, ed. Laura García-Moreno and Peter C. Pfeiffer (Columbia, SC: Camden House, 1996), 49.
3. Oba Sekou Olayinka, personal interviews with the author, August 2003 and September 2003.
4. John Mason, *Orin Orisa: Songs for Selected Heads* (Brooklyn: Yoruba Theological Archministry, 1992), 1.
5. Minority Rights Group, ed., *No Longer Invisible: Afro-Latin Americans Today* (London: Minority Rights Group, 1995), 94.
6. Oba Oseijeman Efuntola Adelabu Adefunmi I, personal interviews with the author, August 1994, January 1995, August 1996, and August 1997.
7. Herskovits, *Dahomey*, 233.
8. Bascom, *The Yoruba of Southwestern Nigeria* (New York: Holt, Rinehart and Winston, 1937), 71.
9. E. Bolaji Idowu, *Olodumare: God in Yoruba Belief* (London: Longsman, 1962).
10. Hunt, *Oyotunji Village*, 87.
11. Hunt, *Oyotunji Village*, 87.
12. Ayoka, telephone interview with the author, March 2, 1998.
13. Oba Oseijeman Efuntola Adelabu Adefunmi I, personal interviews with the author, August 1994, January 1995, August 1996, and August 1997.
14. Oba Oseijeman Efuntola Adelabu Adefunmi I, personal interviews with the author, August 1994, January 1995, August 1996, and August 1997.
15. Curry, *Making the Gods in New York*, 160.
16. Capone, *Les Yoruba du Nouveau Monde*, 203.
17. Olupona and Rey, *Orisa Devotion as World Religion*, 9.
18. Anonymous priestess, personal interview with the author, June 1997.
19. Idowu, *Olodumare*, 14.
20. "The World Conference on Orisa," 7.
21. "The World Conference on Orisa," 13.

22. Lefever, "Leaving the United States," 181: Clapp, *Reporter at Large*.

23. Oseijeman Adefunmi, "Keynote Address," 17.

24. Chief Akintobe, personal interview with the author, August 1996. As an aside, this statement makes explicit that the practice of Yoruba religion in the United States by African Americans has in some way affected the religious lives not only of other African Americans but of Nigerians as well, a theme that could be fruitfully pursued in a future study. According to Adefunmi, "We have perceived also that Oyotunji is having an immense impact on the Yoruba of Nigeria . . . Many of them come here as Christians with little or no knowledge of their own culture or of their own religion. . . . Once they discover us here, many of them have actually gone back into their own priesthood and are professing their own religion. . . . The last couple of times we went to Nigeria, we were greatly celebrated because of our work here in the United States. And so a great influence from the African American is being extended all the way to Nigeria . . ."

25. Iya Omolewa Eniolorunopa, personal interview with the author, July 2006.

26. Cornelius, "Convergence of Power," 7.

27. Olomo, *Core of Fire*, 28.

28. Olomo, *Core of Fire*, 148.

29. Olomo, *Core of Fire*, 29.

30. Oba Sekou Olayinka, personal interviews with the author, August 2003 and September 2003.

31. Vega, "Yoruba Philosophy," 272.

32. Anonymous priest, personal interview with the author, August 1996.

33. Adefunmi, "Keynote Address," 9.

34. Adefunmi, "Keynote Address," 9.

35. Cros Sandoval, *Worldview, the Orichas, and Santería*, 333.

36. Babalosa John Mason, personal interview with the author, December 11, 1997.

37. Chief Akintobe, personal interview with the author, August 1996.

38. Babalosa John Mason, personal interview with the author, December 11, 1997.

39. Babalosa John Mason, personal interview with the author, December 11, 1997.

40. Baba Medahochi Kofi Omowale Zannu, personal interviews with the author, August 7, 2006, and August 23, 2006.

41. Anonymous resident, personal interview with the author, August 1996.

42. Chief Akintobe, personal interview with the author, August 1996.

43. Oba Sekou Olayinka, personal interviews with the author, August 2003 and September 2003.

44. Oba Sekou Olayinka, personal interviews with the author, August 2003 and September 2003.

45. Oba Sekou Olayinka, personal interviews with the author, August 2003 and September 2003.

46. Oba Sekou Olayinka, personal interviews with the author, August 2003 and September 2003.

47. Iya L'Orisa Yeye Olashun OladeKoju Lakesi, "Racism and Racists in Ifa Orisha Religion," OrishaNet, http://www.orishanet.org/. OrishaNet is a website.

48. OrishaNet, http://www.orishanet.org/.

49. Ayoka, personal interview, March 2, 1998.

50. Matory, *Black Atlantic Religion*, 226.

51. Ayoka, personal interview, March 2, 1998.

52. Ayoka, personal interview, March 2, 1998.

53. Anonymous priestess, personal interview, July 1999.

54. http://www.ifafoundation.org/library_show.php?tableID=46.

55. http://www.ifafoundation.org/library_show.php?tableID=46.

56. http://www.ifafoundation.org/library_show.php?tableID=46.

57. Jill Neimark, "Shaman in Chicago: Religious Transcendence or Midlife Crisis?," *Psychology Today*, September 1, 1993, 46.

58. Neimark, "Shaman in Chicago," 50.

59. Neimark, "Shaman in Chicago," 70.

60. http://www.ifafoundation.org/library_show.php?tableID=46.

61. http://www.ifafoundation.org/library_show.php?tableID=46.

62. http://www.ifafoundation.org/library_show.php?tableID=46.

63. Philip John Neimark, *Way of the Orisa: Empowering Your Life Through the Ancient African Religion of Ifa* (San Francisco: HarperSanFrancisco, 1993), xiii.

64. Neimark, *Way of the Orisa*, xiii.

65. Matory, *Black Atlantic Religion*, 64.

66. Neimark, *Way of the Orisa*, xv.

67. Neimark, *Way of the Orisa*, xv–xvi.

68. Neimark, *Way of the Orisa*, xv–xvi.

69. "Kingdom of Oyotunji Yoruba Village Press Release," reprinted in Chief Dr. Adeleri Onisegun, *Onisegun Ile Orisa Obatala Newsletter* 2, no. 2 (1994): 5.

70. Personal notes from field notebook, August 1996.

71. Anonymous priest, personal interview, January 1998.

72. http://www.ifafoundation.org/library_show.php?tableID=46.

73. http://www.ifafoundation.org/library_show.php?tableID=46.

74. http://www.ifafoundation.org/library_show.php?tableID=46.

75. http://www.ifafoundation.org/library_show.php?tableID=46.

76. Davis, *American Voudou*, 165.

77. Arthur Hall, founder of Afro-American Dance Ensemble of Philadelphia, personal interview with the author, November 27, 1993, 18.

78. Anonymous priest, personal interview, August 1996.

79. Pemberton, postscript to *Orisa Devotion as World Religion*, 570.

80. OrishaNet, http://wworisanet.org (accessed July 18, 1997).

81. Isischei, *Religious Traditions of Africa*, 241.

82. Adefunmi, "Notes," 39.

83. Adefunmi, "Notes," 39.

84. Oba Oseijeman Efuntola Adelabu Adefunmi I, personal interviews with the author, August 1994, January 1995, August 1996, and August 1997.

85. Oba Oseijeman Efuntola Adelabu Adefunmi I, personal interviews with the author, August 1994, January 1995, August 1996, and August 1997.

86. Personal notes from field notebook, January 1996.

87. Baba Ifa Karade, *The Handbook of Yoruba Religious Concepts* (Cape Neddick, ME: Samuel Weiser, 1994), 74. Under the heading, "The Development of Self-Yoruba Philosophy," Karade outlines "Thirteen Guidelines for Yoruba Self-Development" that he argues were handed down by Yoruba ancestors in order to enhance what he calls "right living." The thirteen moral and ethical guidelines read as a Yoruba American "ten commandments" and are as follows: 1. There is to be no practice of wickedness. 2. There is to be no stealing. 3. There is to be no selfishness. 4. There is to be no covenant breaking nor falsehood. 5. There is to be no hypocrisy. 6. There are to be no acts of atrocity committed against one's neighbors. 7. There is to be honor and respect to the elders. 8. There is to be protection of the women. 9. There is to be truthfulness and uprighteousness. 10. There is to be kindness and generosity. 11. There is to be sensitivity in respect to person-to-person relationships. 12. There is to be chastity in respect to vows of mates. 13. There are to be hospitable directives.

88. Mason, *Orin Orisa*, 387.

89. Mason, *Orin Orisa*, 387.

90. Luisah Teish, *Jambalaya: The Natural Woman's Book of Personal Charms and Practical Rituals* (San Francisco: Harper & Row, 1985), 76.

91. Baba Ifa Karade, *Ojise: Messenger of the Yoruba Tradition* (York Beach: Samuel Weiser, 1996), ix.

92. Yewande, personal interview, August 23, 2006.

93. Olomo, *Core of Fire*, 28.

94. Olomo, *Core of Fire*, 28.

95. Olomo, *Core of Fire*, 28.

96. Kamari Maxine Clarke, "Ritual Change and the Changing Canon: Divinatory Legitimization of Yoruba Ancestral Roots in Oyotunji African Village," in *Orisa Devotion as World Religion: The Globalization of Yoruba Religious Culture*, ed. Jacob K. Olupona and Terry Rey (Madison: University of Wisconsin Press, 2008), 293.

97. Clarke, "Ritual Change and the Changing Canon," 293.

98. Brooks, "Eku Odun," 1.

99. Clarke, "Ritual Change and the Changing Canon," 298.

100. Baba Medahochi Kofi Omowale Zannu, personal interviews, August 7, 2006, and August 23, 2006.

101. Matory, "English Professors of Brazil," 97.

102. Karade, *Ojise*, 78–79.

103. Karade, *Ojise*, 78–79.

104. Karade, *Ojise*, 78–79; Curry, *Making the Gods in New York*, 8.

105. J. Lorand Matory, "Gendered Agendas: the Secrets Scholars Keep about Yoruba-Atlantic Religion," in *Dialogues of Dispersal: Gender, Sexuality, and African Diasporas*, ed. Sandra Gunning, Tera W. Hunter, and Michelle Mitchell (Malden, MA: Blackwell Publishing, 2004), 37–38.

106. Matory, "Gendered Agendas," 38.

107. Cros Sandoval, *Worldview, the Orichas, and Santería*, 334.

108. Cros Sandoval, *Worldview, the Orichas, and Santería*, 334.

109. Yewande, personal interview, August 23, 2006.

110. Olomo, *Core of Fire*, 165.

111. Olomo, *Core of Fire*, 157.

112. Olabiyi Babalola Yai, "Yoruba Religion and Globalization: Some Reflections," in *Orisa Devotion as World Religion: The Globalization of Yoruba Religious Culture*, edited by Jacob K. Olupona and Terry Rey (Madison: University of Wisconsin Press, 2008), 241.

113. Yai, "Yoruba Religion," 241.

114. Ayoka, telephone interview, March 2, 1998.

115. Love, "Odu Outcomes," 40.

116. Love, "Odu Outcomes," 40.

117. Baba IfaTunji, World Congress on Orisa Tradition and Culture (Port of Spain, Trinidad, August 15–22, 1999).

118. Tunji, World Congress on Orisa Tradition and Culture.

119. Tunji, World Congress on Orisa Tradition and Culture.

120. Eason, *Ifa*, 27–28.

121. Lionel F. Scott, *Beads of Glass, Beads of Stone: An Introduction to the Orisha & Apataki of the Yoruba Religion* (Brooklyn, NY: Athelia Henrietta Press, 1995), 10–11.

122. John Mason (public lecture, Swarthmore College, Swarthmore, PA, April 13, 1998).

123. Sandra Barnes, *Africa's Ogun: Old World and New*, 2nd exp. ed. (Bloomington: Indiana University Press, 1997), xvi.

124. John Mason, *Four New World Rituals* (New York: Yoruba Theological Archministry, 1985).

125. Babalosa John Mason, personal interview, December 11, 1997.

126. Babalosa John Mason, personal interview, December 11, 1997.

127. Babalosa John Mason, personal interview, December 11, 1997.

128. Oba Oseijeman Efuntola Adelabu Adefunmi I, personal interviews, August 1994, January 1995, August 1996, and August 1997.

129. Babalosa John Mason, personal interview, December 11, 1997.

130. Mason has contributed several works to the literary corpus of African American Yoruba studies. Some of these texts include *Four New World Yoruba Ritual Songs*; *Orin Orisa*; *Olokun: Owner of Rivers and Seas*; *Black Gods: Orisa Studies in the New World*, with Gary Edwards; and recently, *Osaiyan*. Note that despite the contributions both Adefunmi and Mason have made to African American Yoruba literature, they are not without their critics. Some African American practitioners find Adefunmi's nationalist discourse and conception of Oyotunji Village somewhat anachronistic. Yoruba American critics of John Mason's work cite his dependence on Cuban religious thought and his favoring Matanzas, Cuba, over Africa.

131. John Mason, "Yoruba-American Art: New Rivers to Explore," in *The Yoruba Art: New Theoretical Perspectives on African Arts*, ed. Rowland Abiodun, Henry J. Drewal, and John Pemberton III (Washington, DC: Smithsonian Institution Press, 1994), 244.

132. John Mason and Gary Edwards, *Black Gods: Orisa Studies in the New World* (Brooklyn: Yoruba Theological Archministry, 1985), iii.
133. Mason, *Orin Orisa*.
134. Mason, public lecture.
135. Babalosa John Mason, personal interview, December 11, 1997.
136. Babalosa John Mason, personal interview, December 11, 1997.
137. John Mason, public lecture.
138. John Mason, public lecture.
139. Oba Oseijeman Efuntola Adelabu Adefunmi I, personal interviews with the author, August 1994, January 1995, August 1996, and August 1997.
140. Adefunmi, "Notes," 40.
141. "Kingdom of Oyotunji Yoruba Village Press Release."
142. Adefunmi, *Olorisha*, 23.
143. Iya Omolewa Eniolorunopa, personal interview, July 2006.
144. Teish, *Jambalaya*, 175.
145. Teish, *Jambalaya*, 263.
146. Adefunmi, "Notes," 43.
147. Adefunmi, "Notes," 43.
148. Adefunmi, "Notes," 43.
149. Adefunmi, "Notes," 43.
150. Adefunmi, "Notes," 43.
151. Chief Akintobe, personal interview, August 1996.
152. Chief Dr. Adeleri Onisegun, ed., *Onisegun Ile Orisa Obatala Newsletter* 2, no. 2 (1994).
153. Hunt, *Oyotunji Village*, 38.
154. Mason and Edwards, *Black Gods*, 2.
155. Mason and Edwards, *Black Gods*, 2.
156. In September 1981, however, Jimmy A. Oparaji founded a religious organization called the Aquarian Church of the Angels in Imo State in Nigeria. From the sparse information known about the church, astrology is not its central focus, but instead, according to its leader, it espouses "a new concept of religion which is almost akin to the traditional worshipping in the ancient times." See Rosalind I. J. Hackett, "Revitalization in African Traditional Religion," in *African Traditional Religions in Contemporary Society*, ed. Jacob K. Oluponaf (New York: Paragon House, 1991), 138.
157. J. Lorand Matory, "Purity and Privilege in a Black Atlantic Nation: Yoruba, 1830–1950" (unpublished manuscript), 33; see also Matory, *Black Atlantic Religion*.
158. Abayomi Cole, "Astrological Geomancy in Africa," in *At the Back of the Black Man's Mind or Notes on the Kingly Office in West Africa*, ed. R. E. Dennett (London: Macmillan and Co., 1906), 269–71.
159. Abimbola and Miller, *Ifa Will Mend Our Broken World*, 116.
160. Donald J. Cosentino, "Repossession: Ogun in Folklore and Literature," in *Africa's Ogun: Old World and New*, ed. Sandra Barnes, 2nd exp. ed. (Bloomington: Indiana University Press, 1997), 304–5. Cosentino argues a similar phenomenon among Nigerian Yoruba as well. He cites the example of Obafemi Awolowo's intense

allegiance to Rosicrucianism and his pilgrimages to its headquarters in San Jose, California. He cites this as "an example of an analogous Yoruba attraction to cabalism."

161. Karade, *Path to Priesthood*, 69.

162. Karade, *Path to Priesthood*, 57.

163. Baba Medahochi Kofi Omowale Zannu, "The Memoirs of an Old Swamp Priest," http://singlelink.typepad.com/medahochi/old-swamp-priest.html.

164. Baba Medahochi Kofi Omowale Zannu, personal interviews, August 7, 2006, and August 23, 2006.

165. Sterling Stuckey, *Slave Culture: Nationalist Theory and the Foundations of Black America* (New York: Oxford University Press, 1987), 83–85.

166. Dianne Stewart, "The Image of Africa in Black Religious Thought and Activism" (Protestant University of Congo in Kinshasa, Democratic Republic of Congo, February13, 2007).

167. Evelyn Brooks Higginbotham, "African-American Women's History and the Metalanguage of Race," in *History and Theory: Feminist Research, Debates, Contestations*, ed. Barbara Laslett, Ruth-Ellen Boetcher Joeres, Mary Jo Maynes, Evelyn Brooks Higginbotham, and Jeanne Barker-Nunn (Chicago: University of Chicago Press, 1997), 321.

168. Zannu, "Memoirs," http://singlelink.typepad.com/medahochi/old-swamp-priest. html.

169. Olomo, *Core of Fire*, 153.

170. Zannu, "Memoirs," http://singlelink.typepad.com/medahochi/old-swamp-priest. html.

171. Zannu, "Memoirs," http://singlelink.typepad.com/medahochi/old-swamp-priest. html.

172. Baba Medahochi Kofi Omowale Zannu, personal interviews, August 7, 2006, and August 23, 2006.

173. Capone, *Les Yoruba du Nouveau Monde*, 228–32.

174. Karenga, *Odù Ifá*, iv–v.

175. Eason, *Ifa*, 154.

176. Oba Sekou Olayinka, personal interviews, August 2003 and September 2003.

177. Lear, "An Old African Religion," 24.

178. Oba Sekou Olayinka, personal interviews, August 2003 and September 2003.

179. http://www.sankofa.com.

180. http://www.egbesankofa.org/about/index.htm#mission.

181. Oba Sekou Olayinka, personal interviews, August 2003 and September 2003.

Conclusion

1. Carolyn M. Jones, "From Colonialism to Community: Religion and Culture in Charles H. Long's *Significations*," *Callaloo*, no. 36 (Summer 1988), 596.

2. Charles H. Long, "Passage and Prayer: The Origin of Religion in the Atlantic World," in *The Courage to Hope: From Black Suffering to Human Redemption*, edited by Quinton Hosford Dixie and Cornel West (Boston: Beacon Press, 1999), 13.

3. Long, "Passage and Prayer," 14.

4. Long, "Passage and Prayer," 15.

5. Long, "Passage and Prayer," 16.

6. Long, "Passage and Prayer," 17.

7. Long, "Passage and Prayer," 20.

8. Olupona, "Globalization and African Immigrant Religious Communities," 93; Perkinson, "Ogu's Iron or Jesus' Irony," 106.

9. Cornel West, "Race and Modernity," *The Cornel West Reader* (New York: Basic Civitas Books, 1999), 81–82.

10. Adeleke, *UnAfrican Americans*, 121.

11. Rosenthal, *Possession, Ecstasy, and Law*, 216.

12. Gordon, *Existentia Africana*, 8.

13. The general purpose of the World Conference, according to its convener, Marta Vega, director of the Caribbean Cultural Center in New York, "was to continue the process of establishing linkages and networks between people and organizations contributing to the accurate documentation and dissemination of the belief systems and world view of people of color."

14. "The World Conference on Orisa," 5.

15. Abimbola and Miller, *Ifa Will Mend Our Broken World*, 107 (emphasis in quote is mine).

16. *OrishaNet*, http://www.orishanet.org/ (accessed July 18, 1997).

17. Yai, "Yoruba Religion and Globalization," 246; Olupona, "Globalization and African Immigrant Religious Communities," 84.

18. *OrishaNet*, http://www.orishanet.org/.

19. Young, *Pan-African Theology*, 17.

20. Matory, "Gendered Agendas," 15.

21. "The World Conference on Orisa," 5; Kwenda, "Mthunzini (A Place in the Shade)," 78.

22. http://eleda.org/obaoriatecouncil/.

23. Vega, "Yoruba Philosophy," 199.

24. Omari, "Completing the Circle," 96.

25. "The World Conference on Orisa," 5.

26. Wale Ogunlola, "Africa Abroad: A Yoruba Village in America (I)," *West Africa*, January 26–February 1, 1998, 124.

27. Apter, "Que Faire?," 102.

28. Pemberton, postscript to *Orisa Devotion as World Religion*, 569.

29. Baba Medahochi Kofi Omowale Zannu, personal interviews with the author, August 7, 2006, and August 23, 2006.

30. Lefever, "When the Saints Go Riding In," 324.

31. Babalosa John Mason, personal interview with the author, December 11, 1997.

32. Gregory, "Santería in New York City," 162.

33. Iya Omolewa Eniolorunopa, personal interview with the author, July 2006.

34. Baba Medahochi Kofi Omowale Zannu, personal interviews with the author, August 7, 2006, and August 23, 2006.

35. Oba Sekou Olayinka, personal interviews with the author, August 2003 and September 2003.

36. http://www.egbesankofa.org.

37. Oba Sekou Olayinka, personal interviews with the author, August 2003 and September 2003.

38. Yewande, personal interview with the author, August 23, 2006.

39. John Mason, personal interview with the author, Yoruba Theological Archministry, Brooklyn, New York, December 1997.

40. John Mason, personal interview with the author, Yoruba Theological Archministry, Brooklyn, New York, December 1997.

41. John Mason, personal interview with the author, Yoruba Theological Archministry, Brooklyn, New York, December 1997.

42. John Mason, personal interview with the author, Yoruba Theological Archministry, Brooklyn, New York, December 1997.

43. John Mason, personal interview with the author, Yoruba Theological Archministry, Brooklyn, New York, December 1997.

44. John Mason, personal interview with the author, Yoruba Theological Archministry, Brooklyn, New York, December 1997.

45. Oba Sekou Olayinka, personal interviews with the author, August 2003 and September 2003.

46. Oba Adejuyibe Adefunmi II, personal interview with the author, September 19, 2008.

47. Oba Adejuyibe Adefunmi II, personal interview with the author, September 19, 2008.

48. Oba Adejuyibe Adefunmi II, personal interview with the author, September 19, 2008.

49. Oba Adejuyibe Adefunmi II, personal interview with the author, September 19, 2008.

50. Yewande, personal interview with the author, August 23, 2006.

51. Yewande, personal interview with the author, August 23, 2006.

52. Yewande, personal interview with the author, August 23, 2006.

53. Yai, "Yoruba Religion and Globalization," 245.

54. Yewande, personal interview with the author, August 23, 2006.

55. Yewande, personal interview with the author, August 23, 2006.

56. Afi-Odelia Scruggs, personal interview with the author, April 2007.

57. Afi-Odelia Scruggs, personal interview with the author, April 2007; Iya Omolewa Eniolorunopa, personal interview with the author, July 2006.

58. Anonymous priestess, personal interview with the author, June 2008.

59. Anonymous priestess, personal interview with the author, June 2008.

60. Eason, *Ifa*, xiii.

61. Brochure, Egbe Odu Ifa Sacred African Literary Society, founded 2000, Atlanta, GA, EgbeOduIfa@bellsouth.net.

62. Brochure, Egbe Odu Ifa Sacred African Literary Society.

63. Anonymous priestess, personal interview with the author, June 2008.

64. Anonymous priestess, personal interview with the author, June 2008.

65. Anonymous priestess, personal interview with the author, June 2008.

66. Randy P. Conner and David Hatfield Sparks, *Queering Creole Spiritual Traditions: Lesbian, Gay, Bisexual and Transgender Participation in African-Inspired Traditions in the Americas* (New York: Harrington Park Press, 2004), 155.

67. Conner and Sparks, *Queering Creole Spiritual Traditions*, 309.

68. Conner and Sparks, *Queering Creole Spiritual Traditions*, 309.

69. Conner and Sparks, *Queering Creole Spiritual Traditions*, 224.

70. Conner and Sparks, *Queering Creole Spiritual Traditions*, 199–200.

71. Randy P. Conner, *Blossom of Bone: Reclaiming the Connections Between Homoeroticism and the Sacred* (San Francisco: HarperSanFrancisco, 1993), 239.

72. Conner and Sparks, *Queering Creole Spiritual Traditions*, 99, 106, 127, 153, 155; Conner, *Blossom of Bone*, 239.

73. Conner and Sparks, *Queering Creole Spiritual Traditions*, 210.

74. Conner and Sparks, *Queering Creole Spiritual Traditions*, 211.

75. Conner and Sparks, *Queering Creole Spiritual Traditions*, 153–54, 119–20.

76. Alexander, *Pedagogies of Crossing*, 326.

77. Conner and Sparks, *Queering Creole Spiritual Traditions*, 89.

78. Conner and Sparks, *Queering Creole Spiritual Traditions*, 89–90.

79. Babalosa John Mason, personal interview with the author, December 11, 1997.

80. Abimbola and Miller, *Ifa Will Mend Our Broken World*, 28; Conner and Sparks, *Queering Creole Spiritual Traditions*, 138.

81. Conner and Sparks, *Queering Creole Spiritual Traditions*, 139–40.

82. Conner and Sparks, *Queering Creole Spiritual Traditions*, 173.

83. Conner and Sparks, *Queering Creole Spiritual Traditions*, 167.

84. Conner, *Blossom of Bone*, 260.

85. Conner and Sparks, *Queering Creole Spiritual Traditions*, 91, 100, 268; Conner, *Blossom of Bone*, 240.

86. Conner and Sparks, *Queering Creole Spiritual Traditions*, 140, 225–26.

87. Conner and Sparks, *Queering Creole Spiritual Traditions*, 158.

88. David Kinsley, *Ecology and Religion: Ecological Spirituality in Cross-Cultural Perspective* (Upper Saddle River, NJ: Prentice Hall, 1997), xiii, xxi.

89. Abimbola and Miller, *Ifa Will Mend Our Broken World*, 23.

90. Abimbola and Miller, *Ifa Will Mend Our Broken World*, 23; Cathie Pelchat, "Ecospirituality" (unpublished paper), 3.

91. Amanda D. Holmes, "Yoruba Religion and Ecology in Cuba," Forum on Religion and Ecology Newsletter, December 2008, http://fore.research.yale.edu/publications/newsletters/index.html.

92. http://www.amandala.org/index.php?option=com_content&view=article&id=47&Itemid=54.

93. Olomo, *Core of Fire*, 57.

94. Olomo, *Core of Fire*, 58.

95. Olomo, *Core of Fire*, 62, 66.

96. Olomo, *Core of Fire*, 64.

97. Olomo, *Core of Fire*, 64–65.

98. Dwight N. Hopkins, "Holistic Health and Healing: Environmental Racism and Ecological Justice," in *Faith, Health, and Healing in African American Life*, ed. Stephanie Y. Mitchem and Emilie M. Townes (London: Praeger, 2008), 26.

99. Hopkins, "Holistic Health and Healing," 26.

100. Julian Kunnie, "The Future of Our World: Indigenous Peoples, Indigenous Philosophies, and the Preservation of Mother Earth," in *Religion and Global Culture: New Terrain in the Study of Religion and the Work of Charles H. Long*, ed. Jennifer I. M. Reid (Lanham, MD: Lexington Books, 2003), 140.

101. Egbe Omo Obatala Inc., First International Orisha Conference (October 30–November 1, 1998).

102. Egbe Omo Obatala Inc., First International Orisha Conference.

103. Oba Sekou Olayinka, personal interviews with the author, August 2003 and September 2003.

104. Oba Sekou Olayinka, personal interviews with the author, August 2003 and September 2003.

105. Olomo, *Core of Fire*, 149.

106. Olomo, *Core of Fire*, 151.

107. Olomo, *Core of Fire*, 150.

108. Oba Sekou Olayinka, personal interviews with the author, August 2003 and September 2003.

109. Oba Sekou Olayinka, personal interviews with the author, August 2003 and September 2003.

110. Oba Sekou Olayinka, personal interviews with the author, August 2003 and September 2003.

111. Oba Sekou Olayinka, personal interviews with the author, August 2003 and September 2003.

112. Anonymous priest, personal interview with the author, July 2006.

113. John Mason, personal interview with the author, Yoruba Theological Archministry, Brooklyn, New York, December 1997.

114. Karade, *Path to Priesthood*, 30.

115. Yewande, personal interview with the author, August 23, 2006.

116. Yewande, personal interview with the author, August 23, 2006.

117. Capone, *Les Yoruba du Nouveau Monde*, 249.

118. Capone, *Les Yoruba du Nouveau Monde*, 249.

119. Yewande, personal interview with the author, August 23, 2006.

120. Iya Omolewa Eniolorunopa, personal interview with the author, July 2006.

121. Karade, *Path to Priesthood*, 31.

122. Oba Sekou Olayinka, personal interviews with the author, August 2003 and September 2003.

123. Iya Igberohinjade Oludoye, personal interview with the author, September 2008.

124. Yai, "Yoruba Religion and Globalization," 244.

125. Baba Medahochi Kofi Omowale Zannu, personal interviews with the author, August 7, 2006, and August 23, 2006.

126. Alexander, *Pedagogies of Crossing*, 328.

127. Alexander, *Pedagogies of Crossing*, 328.

128. Mark Ogunwale Keita Lomax, personal interview with the author, August 4, 2006.

129. Mark Ogunwale Keita Lomax, personal interview with the author, August 4, 2006.

130. Iya Omolewa Eniolorunopa, personal interview with the author, July 2006.

131. Iya Omolewa Eniolorunopa, personal interview with the author, July 2006.

132. Iya Omolewa Eniolorunopa, personal interview with the author, July 2006.

133. Love, "Odu Outcomes," 153.

134. Oluweri Egundyao Onisegun, personal interview with the author, March 26, 2009.

135. Oluweri Egundyao Onisegun, personal interview with the author, March 26, 2009.

136. Oluweri Egundyao Onisegun, personal interview with the author, March 26, 2009.

137. Oluweri Egundyao Onisegun, personal interview with the author, March 26, 2009.

138. Yewande, personal interview with the author, August 23, 2006.

139. Yewande, personal interview with the author, August 23, 2006.

140. Yewande, personal interview with the author, August 23, 2006.

141. Yewande, personal interview with the author, August 23, 2006.

142. Oba Adejuyibe Adefunmi II, personal interview with the author, September 19, 2008.

143. Oba Adejuyibe Adefunmi II, personal interview with the author, September 19, 2008.

144. Iya Omolewa Eniolorunopa, personal interview with the author, July 2006.

145. Michael D. McNally, *Objibwe Singers: Hymns, Grief, and a Native Culture in Motion* (New York: Oxford University Press, 2000), 5.

146. James Baldwin, *The Price of the Ticket: Collected Nonfiction 1948-1985* (New York: St. Martin's Press, 1985), xix.

147. Baldwin, *Price of the Ticket*, xix.

148. John Mason, personal interview with the author, Yoruba Theological Archministry, Brooklyn, New York, December 1997.

BIBLIOGRAPHY

Books

Abimbola, Kola. *Yoruba Culture: A Philosophical Account*. Birmingham, UK: Iroko Academic Publishers, 2006.

Abimbola, Wande, and Ivor Miller. *Ifa Will Mend Our Broken World: Thoughts on Yoruba Religion and Culture in Africa and the Diaspora*. Roxbury, MA: Aim Books, 1997.

Abiodun, Rowland, Henry Drewal, and John Pemberton III, eds. *The Yoruba Art: New Theoretical Perspectives on African Arts*. Washington, DC: Smithsonian Institution Press, 1994.

Adams, Charles. J., ed. *A Reader's Guide to the Great Religions*. 2nd ed. New York: Free Press, 1977.

Adaramola, Odufunade. *Rites of Passage: An Explanation of the Cycles and Stages of Human Growth and Development*. Sheldon, SC: Great Benin Books, 1991.

Adaramola, Odunfonda, I. "Obatala: The Yoruba God of Creation." Sheldon, SC: African Theological Archministry, n.d.

Adefunmi, Oba Oseijeman Adelabu. *An African Marriage*. New York: Great Benin Books, n.d.

———. *The African State*. New York: Great Benin Books, 1962.

———. *The Gods of Africa*. African Library Series. New York: Great Benin Books, 1960.

———. *Olorisha: A Guidebook into Yoruba Religion*. Sheldon, SC: Great Benin Books, 1982.

———. *Orisha: A First Glimpse of the African Religion of Brazil, Cuba, Haiti, Trinidad and now U.S.A.* New York: Great Benin Books, 1959.

———, ed. *Oshoun Festival*. Sheldon, SC: Great Benin Books, n.d.

———. *Oyotunji SHANGOFEST*. Sheldon, SC: African Theological Archministry, n.d.

———. *Tribal Origins of the African-Americans*. New York: Great Benin Books 1962.

Adeleke, Tunde. *UnAfrican Americans: Nineteenth-Century Black Nationalists and the Civilizing Mission*. Lexington: University Press of Kentucky, 1998.

Adepedgba, Cornelius O. "Associated Place-Names and Sacred Icons of Seven Yoruba Deities: Historicity in Yoruba Religious Tradition." In *Orisa Devotion as World Religion: The Globalization of Yoruba Religious Culture*, edited by Jacob K. Olupona and Terry Rey, 106–27. Madison: University of Wisconsin Press, 2008.

Alexander, M. Jacqui. *Pedagogies of Crossing: Meditations on Feminism, Sexual Politics, Memory, and the Sacred*. Durham, NC: Duke University Press, 2005.

Ali, Duse Mohammed. *In the Land of the Pharaohs: A Short History of Egypt*. London: Stanley Paul & Co., 1911.

Anderson, Benedict. *Imagined Communities: Reflections on the Origin and Spread of Nationalism*. New York: Verso, 1991.

Anderson, Victor. *Beyond Ontological Blackness: An Essay on African American Religious and Cultural Criticism*. New York: Continuum Publishing, 1995.

———. *Creative Exchange: A Constructive Theology of African American Religious Experience*. Minneapolis: Fortress Press, 2008.

Archer-Straw, Petrine. *Negrophilia: Avant-Garde Paris and Black Culture in the 1920s*. New York: Thames and Hudson, 2000.

Asante, Molefi Kete. *Afrocentricity*. Trenton, NJ: Africa World Press, 1988.

Ashcraft-Eason, Lillian, Darnise C. Martin, and Oyeronke Olademo, eds. *Women and New and Africana Religions*. Santa Barbara: ABC-CLIO, 2010.

Ayorinde, Christine. "Writing Out Africa: Racial Politics and the Cuban *regal de ocha*." In *The African Diaspora and the Study of Religion*, edited by Theodore Louis Trost, 151–66. New York: Palgrave MacMillan, 2007.

Baer, Hans A., and Merrill Singer. *African-American Religion in the Twentieth Century: Varieties of Protest and Accommodation*. Knoxville: University of Tennessee Press, 1992.

Bailey, Cornelia Walker. *God, Dr. Buzzard, and the Bolito Man: A Saltwater Geechee Talks about Life on Sapelo Island*. New York: First Anchor Books Edition, 2001.

Baldwin, James. *The Evidence of Things Not Seen*. New York: Henry Holt and Company, 1985.

———. *The Price of the Ticket: Collected Nonfiction 1948–1985*. New York: St. Martin's Press, 1985.

———. "White Man's Guilt." In *The Price of the Ticket: Collected Nonfiction 1948–1985*, 409–14. New York: St. Martin's Press, 1985.

Baraka, Amiri. *The Autobiography of LeRoi Jones*. Chicago: Lawrence Hill Books, 1984.

Barnes, Sandra. *Africa's Ogun: Old World and New*. 2nd exp. ed. Bloomington: Indiana University Press, 1997.

Bascom, William. *Ifa Divination: Communication between Gods and Men in West Africa*. Bloomington: Indiana University Press, 1991.

———. *Sixteen Cowries: Yoruba Divination from Africa to the New World*. Bloomington: Indiana University Press, 1993.

———. *The Yoruba of Southwestern Nigeria*. New York: Holt, Rinehart and Winston, 1937.

Berghahn, Marion. *Images of Africa in Black American Literature*. Totowa, NJ: Rowman and Littlefield, 1977.

Bracey, Jr., John H., August Meier, and Elliott Rudwick. *Black Nationalism in America*. Indianapolis, IN: Bobbs-Merrill Company, 1970.

Brandon, George. *Santeria from Africa to the New World: The Dead Sell Memories.* Bloomington: Indiana University Press, 1993.

Brown, Karen McCarthy. *Mama Lola: A Vodou Priestess in Brooklyn.* Berkeley: University of California Press, 2001.

———. "Writing about 'the Other,' Revisited." In *Personal Knowledge and Beyond: Reshaping the Ethnography of Religion,* edited by James V. Spickard, J. Shawn Landres, and Meredith B. McGuire, 127–33. New York: New York University Press, 2002.

Burdick, John. *Blessed Anastácia: Women, Race, and Popular Christianity in Brazil.* New York: Routledge, 1998.

Burkett, Randall. *Black Redemption: Churchmen Speak for the Garvey Movement.* Philadelphia: Temple University Press, 1978.

Butler, Kim D. "Africa in the Reinvention of Nineteenth-Century Afro-Bahian Identity." In *Rethinking the African Diaspora: The Making of a Black Atlantic World in the Bight of Benin and Brazil,* edited by Kristin Mann and Edna G. Bay, 135–54. London: Frank Cass, 2001.

———. *Freedoms Given, Freedoms Won: Afro-Brazilians in Post-Abolition São Paulo and Salvador.* New Brunswick, NJ: Rutgers University Press, 1998.

Butler, Jr., Lee H. *Liberating Our Dignity, Saving Our Souls: A New Theory of African American Identity Formation.* St. Louis, MO: Chalice Press, 2006.

Canizares, Raul. *Walking with the Night: The Afro-Cuban World of Santería.* Rochester, VT: Destiny Books, 1993.

Capone, Stefania. *Les Yoruba du Nouveau Monde: Religion, Ethnicité et Nationalism Noir aux États-Unis.* Paris: Éditions Karthala, 2005.

Cassirer, Ernst. *The Philosophy of the Enlightenment.* Princeton, NJ: Princeton University Press, 1959.

Castillo, Susan, and Ivy Schweitzer, eds. *A Companion to the Literatures of Colonial America.* Malden, MA: Blackwell Publishing, 2005.

Chireau, Yvonne P. *Black Magic: Religion and the African American Conjuring Tradition.* Berkeley: University of California Press, 2003.

———. "Natural and Supernatural: African American Hoodoo Narratives of Sickness and Healing." In *Faith, Health, and Healing in African American Life,* edited by Stephanie Y. Mitchem and Emilie M. Townes, 3–15. London: Praeger, 2008.

———, and Nathaniel Deutsch, eds. *Black Zion: African American Religious Encounters with Judaism.* New York: Oxford University Press, 2000.

Christian, Jr., William A. *Local Religion in Sixteenth-Century Spain.* Princeton, NJ: Princeton University Press, 1981.

Clapp, Stephen C. *A Reporter at Large: African Theological Arch-Ministry, Inc.* New York Public Library, Schomburg Collection, 1966.

Clark, Mary Ann. *Santería: Correcting the Myths and Uncovering the Realities of a Growing Religion.* Westport, CT: Praeger Publishers, 2007.

Clarke, John Henrik. *Marcus Garvey and the Vision of Africa.* New York: Vintage Books, 1974.

Clarke, Kamari Maxine. *Mapping Yoruba Networks: Power and Agency in the Making of Transnational Communities.* Durham, NC: Duke University Press, 2004.

———. "Ritual Change and the Changing Canon: Divinatory Legitimization of Yoruba Ancestral Roots in Oyotunji African Village." In *Orisa Devotion as World Religion: The Globalization of Yoruba Religious Culture*, edited by Jacob K. Olupona and Terry Rey, 286–319. Madison: University of Wisconsin Press, 2008.

Clegg III, Claude Andrew. *An Original Man*. New York: St. Martin's Press, 1997.

Cole, Abayomi. "Astrological Geomancy in Africa." In *At the Back of the Black Man's Mind or Notes on the Kingly Office in West Africa*, edited by R. E. Dennett, 269–70. London: Macmillan and Co., 1906.

Coleman, James S. *Nigeria: Background to Nationalism*. Berkeley: University of California Press, 1958.

Collins, Patricia Hill. "Black Nationalism and African American Ethnicity: The Case of Afrocentrism as Civil Religion." In *Ethnicity, Nationalism, and Minority Rights*, edited by Stephen May, Tariq Modood, and Judith Squires, 96–120. New York: Cambridge University Press, 2004.

Cone, James H. *Martin and Malcolm and America: A Dream or a Nightmare*. New York: Orbis Books, 1991.

———. *The Spirituals and the Blues*. New York: Orbis Books, 1971.

Conner, Randy P. *Blossom of Bone: Reclaiming the Connections between Homoeroticism and the Sacred*. San Francisco: HarperSanFrancisco, 1993.

———, and David Hatfield Sparks. *Queering Creole Spiritual Traditions: Lesbian, Gay, Bisexual and Transgender Participation in African-Inspired Traditions in the Americas*. New York: Harrington Park Press, 2004.

Cook, Carlos. "Speech on the 'Buy Black' Campaign." In *Modern Black Nationalism: From Marcus Garvey to Louis Farrakhan*, edited by William L. Van Deburg, 85–92. New York: New York University Press, 1997.

Cornelius, Janet. *Slave Missions and the Black Church in the Antebellum South*. Columbia: University of South Carolina Press, 1999.

Cosentino, Donald J. "Repossession: Ogun in Folklore and Literature." In *Africa's Ogun: Old World and New*, edited by Sandra Barnes, 290–314, 2nd exp. ed. Bloomington: Indiana University Press, 1997.

Crang, Mike, and Ian Cook. *Doing Ethnographies*. Los Angeles: SAGE Publications, 2007.

Creel, Margaret Washington. *A Peculiar People: Slave Religion and Community-Culture Among the Gullahs*. New York: New York University Press, 1989.

Cros Sandoval, Mercedes. "Afro-Cuban Religion in Perspective." In *Enigmatic Powers: Syncretism with African and Indigenous Peoples' Religions Among Latinos*, edited by Anthony Stevens-Arroyo and Andrés Pérez y Mena, 81–98. New York: Bildner Center for Western Hemisphere Studies, 1995.

———. *Worldview, the Orichas, and Santería: Africa to Cuba and Beyond*. Gainesville: University Press of Florida, 2006.

Cunnigen, Donald. "The Republic of New Africa in Mississippi." In *Black Power in the Belly of the Beast*, edited by Judson L. Jeffries, 93–115. Urbana: University of Illinois Press, 2006.

Curry, Mary Cuthrell. *Making the Gods in New York: The Yoruba Religion in the African American Community*. New York: Garland Publishers, 1997.

Davis, Rod. *American Voudou: Journey into a Hidden World.* Denton: University of North Texas Press, 1998.

Davis, Susan. *Parades and Power: Street Theatre in Nineteenth-Century Philadelphia.* Philadelphia: Temple University Press, 1986.

Dennett, R. E. *At the Back of the Black Man's Mind or Notes on the Kingly Office in West Africa.* London: Macmillan and Co., 1906.

Diouf, Sylviane A. *Dreams of Africa in Alabama: The Slave Ship Clotilda and the Story of the Last Africans Brought to America.* New York: Oxford University Press, 2007.

Dixie, Quinton Hosford, and Cornel West. *The Courage to Hope: From Black Suffering to Human Redemption.* Boston: Beacon Press, 1999.

Drewal, Henry John, and John Mason. *Beads, Body and Soul: Art and Light in the Yoruba Universe.* Los Angeles: UCLA Fowler Museum of Cultural History, 1998.

Dubois, W. E. B. *Black Folk Then and Now.* New York: Holt & Co., 1939.

———. *The Souls of Black Folk.* New York: Bantam Books, 1989.

Dunham, Katherine. *Dances of Haiti.* Los Angeles: Center for Afro-American Studies at UCLA, 1983.

Earl, Riggins R. *Dark Symbols, Obscure Signs: God, Self, and Community in the Slave Mind.* Knoxville: University of Tennessee Press, 2003.

Eason, Ikukomi Djisovi. "Historicizing Ifa Culture in Oyotunji African Village." In *Orisa Devotion as World Religion: The Globalization of Yoruba Religious Culture,* edited by Jacob K. Olupona and Terry Rey, 278–85. Madison: University of Wisconsin Press, 2008.

Eason, Louis Djisovi Ikukomi. *Ifa: The Yoruba God of Divination in Nigeria and the United States.* Trenton, NJ: Africa World Press, 2008.

Echeruo, Michael J. C. "An African Diaspora: The Ontological Project." In *The African Diaspora: African Origins and New World Identities,* edited by Isidore Okpewho, Carole Boyce Davies, and Ali A. Mazrui, 3–18. Bloomington: Indiana University Press, 1999.

Efunbolade, Yeyefini. "The Living Shrine: Life and Meaning in Oyotunji." In *Women and New and Africana Religions,* edited by Lillian Ashcraft-Eason, Darnise C. Martin, and Oyeronke Olademo. Santa Barbara: ABC-CLIO, 2010.

Ellis, George W. *Negro Culture in West Africa.* New York: Neale Publishing, 1914.

Eriksen, Thomas Hylland. *Ethnicity and Nationalism.* London: Pluto Press, 2002.

Ernest, John. *Liberation Historiography: African American Writers and the Challenge of History, 1794–1861.* Chapel Hill: University of North Carolina Press, 2004.

Essien-Udom, E. U. *Black Nationalism: A Search for an Identity in America.* Chicago: University of Chicago Press, 1971.

Evans, Curtis J. *The Burden of Black Religion.* New York: Oxford University Press, 2008.

Fardon, Richard, ed. *Counterworks: Managing the Diversity of Knowledge.* New York: Routledge, 1995.

Fauset, Arthur Huff. *Black Gods of the Metropolis: Negro Religious Cults in the Urban North.* Philadelphia: University of Pennsylvania Press, 1944, 1971.

Fleuckiger, Joyce. *In Amma's Healing Room: Gender and Vernacular Islam in South India.* Bloomington: Indiana University Press, 2006.

Fossett, Judith Jackson, and Jeffrey A. Tucker, eds. *Race Consciousness: African-American Studies for the New Century*. New York: New York University Press, 1997.

Franklin, John Hope, and Alfred A. Moss. *From Slavery to Freedom: A History of African Americans*. New York: McGraw-Hill, 1994.

Frobenius, Leo. *The Voice of Africa*. London: Hutchison and Co., 1913.

"From the Anti-Depression Program of the Republic of New Africa." In *Modern Black Nationalism from Marcus Garvey to Louis Farrakhan*, edited by William L. Van Deburg, 198–202. New York: New York University Press, 1997.

Garcia-Moreno, Laura, and Peter C. Pfeiffer, eds. *Text and Nation: Cross-Disciplinary Essays on Cultural and National Identities*. Columbia, SC: Camden House, 1996.

Geertz, Clifford. "As the Other Sees Us: On Reciprocity and the Mutual Reflection in the Study of Native American Religions." In *Personal Knowledge and Beyond: Reshaping the Ethnography of Religion*, edited by James V. Spickard, J. Shawn Landres, and Meredith B. McGuire, 225–36. New York: New York University Press, 2002.

———. *The Interpretation of Cultures*. New York: Basic Books, 1973.

Genovese, Eugene. *Roll, Jordan, Roll: The World the Slaves Made*. New York: Pantheon, 1974.

Gilroy, Paul. "Urban Social Movements, 'Race' and Community." In *Colonial Discourse and Post-Colonial Theory: A Reader*, edited by Patrick Williams and Laura Chrisman, 404–20. New York: Columbia University Press, 1994.

Glaude, Jr., Eddie S. *Exodus!: Religion, Race, and Nation in Early Nineteenth-Century Black America*. Chicago: University of Chicago Press, 2000.

———, ed. *Is It Nation Time?: Contemporary Essays on Black Power and Black Nationalism*. Chicago: University of Chicago Press, 2002.

Goldman, Marion S. "Voicing Spiritualities: Anchored Composites as an Approach to Understanding Religious Commitment." In *Personal Knowledge and Beyond: Reshaping the Ethnography of Religion*, edited by James V. Spickard, J. Shawn Landres, and Meredith B. McGuire, 146–61. New York: New York University Press, 2002.

Gordon, Dexter B. *Black Identity: Rhetoric, Ideology, and Nineteenth-Century Black Nationalism*. Carbondale: Southern Illinois University Press, 2003.

Gordon, Lewis R. *Existentia Africana: Understanding Africana Existential Thought*. New York: Routledge, 2000.

Gregory, Steven. *Santería in New York City: A Study in Cultural Resistance*. New York: Garland Publishing, 1999.

Guadeloupe, Francio. *Chanting Down the New Jerusalem: Calypso, Christianity, and Capitalism in the Caribbean*. Los Angeles: University of California Press, 2009.

Guillaumin, Colette. "Race and Nature: The System of Marks." In *Racism*, edited by Leonard Harris, 219–36. Amherst, MA: Humanity Books, 1999.

Gunning, Sandra, Tera W. Hunter, and Michelle Mitchell, eds. *Dialogues of Dispersal: Gender, Sexuality, and African Diasporas*. Malden, MA: Blackwell Publishing, 2004.

Gutmann, Amy. *Identity in Democracy*. Princeton, NJ: Princeton University Press, 2003.

Hackett, Rosalind I. J. "Revitalization in African Traditional Religion." In *African Traditional Religions in Contemporary Society*, edited by Jacob K. Olupona, 125–48. New York: Paragon House, 1991.

Hall, David, D. *A History of the Book in America*. Cambridge: Cambridge University Press, 2001.

———, ed. *Lived Religion in America: Toward a History of Practice*. Princeton, NJ: Princeton University Press, 1997.

———. *Ways of Writing: The Practice and Politics of Text-Making in Seventeenth-Century New England*. Philadelphia: University of Pennsylvania Press, 2008.

Hall, Raymond. *Black Separatism and Social Reality: Rhetoric and Reason*. New York: Pergamon, 1977.

Hall, Stuart. "Cultural Identity and Diaspora." In *Colonial Discourse and Post-Colonial Theory: A Reader*, edited by Patrick Williams and Laura Chrisman, 392–403. New York: Columbia University Press, 1994.

Hallpike, C. R. "Social Hair." In *Reader in Comparative Religion: An Anthropological Approach*, edited by William Lessa and Evon Z. Vogt, 99–104. New York: Harper and Row, 1972.

Hanchard, Michael George. *Orpheus and Power: The Movimento Negro of Rio de Janeiro and São Paulo, Brazil, 1945–1988*. Princeton, NJ: Princeton University Press, 1994.

Hardy, Clarence, III. *James Baldwin's God: Sex, Hope, and Crisis in Black Holiness Culture*. Knoxville: University of Tennessee Press, 2003.

Hart, William D. *Black Religion: Malcolm X, Julius Lester, and Jan Willis*. New York: Palgrave Macmillan, 2008.

Hayden, Dolores. *The Power of Place: Urban Landscapes as Public History*. Cambridge, MA: MIT Press, 1995.

Herskovits, Melville. *Dahomey: An Ancient West African Kingdom*. 2 vols. New York: J. J. Augustin, 1938.

Higginbotham, Evelyn Brooks. "African-American Women's History and the Meta-language of Race." In *History and Theory: Feminist Research, Debates, Contestations*, edited by Barbara Laslett, Ruth-Ellen Boetcher Joeres, Mary Jo Maynes, Evelyn Brooks Higginbotham, and Jeanne Barker-Nunn, 304–27. Chicago: University of Chicago Press, 1997.

———. "Religion, Politics, and Gender: The Leadership of Nannie Helen Burroughs." In *This Far by Faith: Readings in African-American Women's Religious Biography*, edited by Judith Weisenfeld, 140–57. New York: Routledge, 1996.

———. *Righteous Discontent: The Women's Movement in the Black Baptist Church, 1880–1920*. Cambridge, MA: Harvard University Press, 1993.

Hill, Robert A., ed. *The Marcus Garvey and Universal Negro Improvement Association Papers, Volume 1, 1826–August 1919*. Berkeley: University of California Press, 1983.

Hill, Ruth Edmonds. *The Black Women Oral History Project from the Arthur and Elizabeth Library on the History of Women in America, Radcliffe College*. London: Mechler, 1990.

Hine, Darlene Clark, and Jacqueline McLeod. *Crossing Boundaries: Comparative History of Black People in Diaspora*. Bloomington: Indiana University Press, 1999.

Ho, Karen, and Wende Elizabeth Marshall. "Criminality and Citizenship: Implicating the White Nation." In *Race Consciousness: African-American Studies for the New*

Century, edited by Judith Jackson Fossett and Jeffrey A. Tucker, 208–26. New York: New York University Press, 1997.

Holt, Thomas C. "Slavery and Freedom in the Atlantic World: Reflections on the Diasporan Framework." In *Crossing Boundaries: Comparative History of Black People in Diaspora*, edited by Darlene Clark Hine and Jacqueline McLeod, 33–44. Bloomington: Indiana University Press, 1999.

Hood, Robert E. *Begrimed and Black: Christian Traditions on Black and Blackness.* Minneapolis, MN: Fortress Press, 1994.

hooks, bell. "Postmodern Blackness." In *Colonial Discourse and Post-Colonial Theory: A Reader*, edited by Patrick Williams and Laura Chrisman, 421–27. New York: Columbia University Press, 1994.

Hopkins, Dwight N. "Holistic Health and Healing: Environmental Racism and Ecological Justice." In *Faith, Health, and Healing in African American Life*, edited by Stephanie Y. Mitchem and Emilie M. Townes, 16–32. London: Praeger, 2008.

Howard, George. *Gifts from Ile Ife: Africa's Impact on the Americas.* Philadelphia: Black History Museum Committee, 1982.

Hucks, Tracey E. "From Cuban Santeria to African Yoruba: Evolutions in African American Orisa History, 1959–1970." In *Orisa Devotion as World Religion: The Globalization of Yoruba Religious Culture*, edited by Jacob K. Olupona and Terry Rey, 337–54. Madison: University of Wisconsin Press, 2008.

———. "The Black Church, Invisible and Visible." *The Encyclopedia of American Cultural and Intellectual History*, edited by Mary Kupiec Clayton and Peter W. Williams, 227–34. New York: Scribner, 2001

Hulme, Peter. "Survival and Invention: Indigeneity in the Caribbean." In *Text and Nation : Cross-Disciplinary Essays on Cultural and National Identities*, edited by Laura García-Moreno and Peter C. Pfeiffer, 48–64. Columbia, SC: Camden House, 1996.

Hunt, Carl. *Oyotunji Village: The Yoruba Movement in America.* Washington, DC: University Press of America, 1979.

Hurston, Zora Neale. *Mules and Men.* Bloomington: Indiana University Press, 1963.

Idowu, E. Bolaji. *Olodumare: God in Yoruba Belief.* London: Longsman, 1962.

Ifekwunigwe, Jayne O. "Scattered Belongings: Reconfiguring the 'African' in the English-African Diaspora." In *New African Diasporas*, edited by Khalid Koser, 56–70. New York: Routledge, 2003.

Isichei, Elizabeth. *The Religious Traditions of Africa: A History.* Westport, CT: Praeger, 2004.

Jacobson, Matthew Frye. *Whiteness of a Different Color: European Immigrants and the Alchemy of Race.* Cambridge, MA: Harvard University Press, 1998.

James, Joy, and T. Sharpley-Whiting, eds. *The Black Feminist Reader.* Malden, MA: Blackwell Publishers, 2000.

Jeffries, Judson L., ed. *Black Power in the Belly of the Beast.* Urbana: University of Illinois Press, 2006.

Johnson, James Weldon. *Native Races and Cultures.* Charlottesville, VA: The Michie Company, 1927.

Johnson, Samuel. *History of the Yoruba.* London: Routledge, 1921.

Johnson, Sylvester A. *The Myth of Ham in Nineteenth-Century American Christianity: Race, Heathens, and the People of God.* New York: Palgrave MacMillan, 2004.

Jones-Jackson, Patricia. Let the Church Say "Amen": The Language of Religious Rituals in Coastal South Carolina. In *The Crucible of Carolina: Essays in the Development of Gullah Language and Culture,* edited by Michael Montgomery, 115–32. Athens: University of Georgia Press, 1994.

Jordan, Winthrop. *White Over Black: American Attitudes Towards the Negro, 1550–1812.* Chapel Hill: University of North Carolina Press, 1968.

Josipovici, Gabriel. *Text and Voice: Essays 1981–1991.* New York: St. Martin's Press, 1992.

Joyner, Charles. *Down by the Riverside: A South Carolina Slave Community.* Urbana: University of Illinois Press, 1984.

Karade, Baba Akinkugbe. *Path to Priesthood: The Making of an African Priest in an American World.* New York: Kanda Mukutu Books, 2001.

Karade, Baba Ifa. *Ojise: Messenger of the Yoruba Tradition.* York Beach: Samuel Weiser, 1996.

———. *The Handbook of Yoruba Religious Concepts.* Cape Neddick, ME: Samuel Weiser, 1994.

Karanga, Maulana. *Odù Ifá: The Ethical Teachings.* Los Angeles: University of Sankore Press, 1999.

Kedar, Benjamin Z., and R. J. Zwi Werblowsy, eds. *Sacred Space: Shrine, City, Land.* New York: New York University Press, 1998.

Keim, Curtis. *Mistaking Africa: Curiosities and Inventions of the American Mind.* Boulder, CO: Westview Press, 1999.

Koser, Khalid, ed. *New African Diasporas.* New York: Routledge, 2003.

Kinsley, David. *Ecology and Religion: Ecological Spirituality in Cross-Cultural Perspective.* Upper Saddle River, NJ: Prentice Hall, 1997.

Kunnie, Julian. "The Future of Our World: Indigenous Peoples, Indigenous Philosophies, and the Preservation of Mother Earth." In *Religion and Global Culture: New Terrain in the Study of Religion and the Work of Charles H. Long,* edited by Jennifer I. M. Reid, 125–44. Lanham, MD: Lexington Books, 2003.

Kwenda, Chirevo V. "Mthunzini (A Place in the Shade): Religion and the Heat of Globalization." In *Religion and Global Culture: New Terrain in the Study of Religion and the Work of Charles H. Long,* edited by Jennifer I. M. Reid, 67–82. Lanham, MD: Lexington Books, 2003.

Laslett, Barbara, Ruth-Ellen Boetcher Joeres, Mary Jo Maynes, Evelyn Brooks Higginbotham, and Jeanne Barker-Nunn, eds. *History and Theory: Feminist Research, Debates, Contestations.* Chicago: University of Chicago Press, 1997.

Lawal, Babatunde. "Art and Architecture, History of African." In *Encyclopedia of African History Volume 1 A–G,* edited by Kevin Shillington, 103–8. New York: Fitzboy Dearborn, 2005.

Leeming, David. *James Baldwin: A Biography.* New York: Knopf, 1994.

Lemelle, Sidney J., and Robin D. G. Kelly, eds. *Imagining Home: Class, Culture and Nationalism in the African Diaspora.* New York: Verso, 1994.

Lessa, William, and Evon Z. Vogt, eds. *Reader in Comparative Religion: An Anthropological Approach.* New York: Harper and Row, 1972.

Levine, Lawrence. *Black Culture and Black Conscious.* New York: Oxford University Press, 1977.

Levi-Strauss, Claude. Foreword to the French edition to *Dances of Haiti,* by Katherine Dunham, xv–xvii. Los Angeles: Center for Afro-American Studies at UCLA, 1983.

Levy, André, and Alex Weingrod, eds. *Homelands and Diasporas: Holy Lands and Other Places.* Stanford, CA: Stanford University Press, 2005.

Lippy, Charles H., ed. *Religion in South Carolina.* Columbia: University of South Carolina Press, 1993.

Livingstone, David. *Livingstone's Africa.* Philadelphia: Hubbard Brothers, 1872.

Locke, Alain. *The Negro in Art.* New York: Hacker Art Books, 1940, 1968.

Long, Charles H. "Bodies in Time and the Healing of Spaces: Religion, Temporalities, and Health." In *Faith, Health, and Healing in African American Life,* edited by Stephanie Y. Mitchem and Emilie M. Townes, 35–54. London: Praeger, 2008.

———. "The History of the History of Religions." In *A Reader's Guide to the Great Religions: Second Edition,* edited by Charles J. Adams, 467–75. New York: Free Press, 1977.

———. "Indigenous People, Materialities, and Religion: Outline for a New Orientation to Religious Meaning." In *Religion and Global Culture: New Terrain in the Study of Religion and the Work of Charles H. Long,* edited by Jennifer I. M. Reid, 167–80. Lanham, MD: Lexington Books, 2003.

———. "Passage and Prayer: The Origin of Religion in the Atlantic World." In *The Courage to Hope: From Black Suffering to Human Redemption,* edited by Quinton Hosford Dixie and Cornel West, 11–21. Boston: Beacon Press, 1999.

———. *Significations: Signs, Symbols, and Images in the Interpretation of Religion.* Philadelphia: Fortress Press, 1986.

Lorini, Alessandra. *Rituals of Race: American Public Culture and the Search for Racial Democracy.* Charlottesville: University of Virginia Press, 1999.

MacIntyre, Alasdair C. *After Virtue: A Study in Moral Theory.* Notre Dame, IN: University of Notre Dame Press, 1981.

———. *Three Rival Versions of Moral Enquiry: Encyclopaedia, Genealogy, and Tradition.* Notre Dame, IN: University of Notre Dame Press, 1990.

Mackenthun, Gesa. "The Transoceanic Emergence of American Postcolonial Identities." In *A Companion to the Literatures of Colonial America,* edited by Susan Castillo and Ivy Schweitzer, 336–52. Malden, MA: Blackwell Publishing, 2005.

Mann, Kristin, and Edna Bay, eds. *Rethinking the African Diaspora: The Making of a Black Atlantic World in the Bight of Benin and Brazil.* London: Frank Cass, 2001.

Manning, Patrick. *The African Diaspora: A History Through Culture.* New York: Columbia University Press, 2009.

Marable, Manning. *Race, Reform and Rebellion: The Second Reconstruction in Black America.* Jackson: University Press of Mississippi, 1984.

Markowitz, Fran. "Claiming the Pain, Making a Change: The African Hebrew Israelite Community's Alternative to the Black Diaspora." In *Homelands and Diasporas: Holy Lands and Other Places,* edited by André Levy and Alex Weingrod, 321–50. Stanford, CA: Stanford University Press, 2005.

Masferrer, Marianne, and Carmelo Mesa-Lago. "The Gradual Integration of the Black in Cuba: Under the Colony, the Republic, and the Revolution." In *Slavery and Race Relations in Latin America*, edited by Robert Brent Toplin, 348–84. Westport, CT: Greenwood Press, 1974.

Mason, John. *Four New World Rituals*. Brooklyn: Yoruba Theological Archministry, 1985.

———. *Olokun: Owner of Rivers and Seas*. Brooklyn: Yoruba Theological Archministry, 1996.

———. *Orin Orisa: Songs for Selected Heads*. Brooklyn: Yoruba Theological Archministry, 1992.

———. *Who's Knocking on My Floor?: Esu Arts in the Americas*. Brooklyn: Yoruba Theological Archministry, 2003.

———. "Yoruba-American Art: New Rivers to Explore." In *The Yoruba Art: New Theoretical Perspectives on African Arts*, edited by Rowland Abiodun, Henry J. Drewal, and John Pemberton III, 241–50. Washington, DC: Smithsonian Institution Press, 1994.

———, and Gary Edwards. *Black Gods: Orisa Studies in the New World*. Brooklyn: Yoruba Theological Archministry, 1985.

Mather, Cotton. *The Negro Christianized: An Essay to Excite and Assist the Good Work, the Instruction of Negro-Servants in Christianity*. Boston, 1706.

Matibag, Eugenio. *Afro-Cuban Experience: Cultural Reflections in Narrative*. Gainesville: University Press of Florida, 1996.

Matory, J. Lorand. *Black Atlantic Religion: Tradition, Transnationalism, and Matriarchy in the Afro-Brazilian Candomblé*. Princeton, NJ: Princeton University Press, 2005.

———. "Free to Be a Slave: Slavery as Metaphor in the Afro-Atlantic Religions." In *Africas of the Americas*, edited by Stephan Palmié, 225–40. Leiden, Netherlands: Brill, 2008.

———. "Gendered Agendas: the Secrets Scholars Keep about Yoruba-Atlantic Religion." In *Dialogues of Dispersal: Gender, Sexuality, and African Diasporas*, edited by Sandra Gunning, Tera W. Hunter, and Michelle Mitchell, 13–43. Malden, MA: Blackwell Publishing, 2004.

———. *Sex and the Empire That Is No More: Gender and the Politics of Metaphor in Oyo Yoruba Religion*. Minneapolis: University of Minnesota Press, 1994.

May, Stephen, Tariq Modood, and Judith Squires, eds. *Ethnicity, Nationalism, and Minority Rights*. New York: Cambridge University Press, 2004.

McCutcheon, Russell T. "Africa on Our Minds." In *The African Diaspora and the Study of Religion*, edited by Theodore Louis Trost, 229–38. New York: Palgrave MacMillan, 2007.

McFague, Sallie. *The Body of God: An Ecological Theology*. Minneapolis: Fortress Press, 1993.

McGarrity, Gayle, and Osvaldo Cárdenas. "Cuba." In *No Longer Invisible: Afro-Latin Americans Today*, edited by Minority Right Group, 77–108. London: Minority Rights Publications, 1995.

McGuire, Meredith. *Ritual Healing in Suburban America*. New Brunswick, NJ: Rutgers University Press, 1988.

McKever-Floyd, Preston L. "Masks of the Sacred: Religious Pluralism in South Carolina." In *Religion in South Carolina*, edited by Charles H. Lippy, 153–67. Columbia:
University of South Carolina Press, 1993.

McNally, Michael D. *Objibwe Singers: Hymns, Grief, and a Native Culture in Motion.*
New York: Oxford University Press, 2000.

Melton, J. Gordon, ed. *Encyclopedia of American Religions.* 3rd ed. Farmington Hills, MI:
Gale Research, 1989.

Metraux, Alfred. *Voodoo in Haiti.* New York: Schocken Books, 1972.

Miller, Timothy, ed. *America's Alternative Religions.* Albany: State University of New
York Press, 1995.

Minority Rights Group, eds. *No Longer Invisible: Afro-Latin Americans Today.* London:
Minority Rights Group, 1995.

Mitchem, Stephanie Y. "Healing Heart and Broken Bodies: An African American
Women's Spirituality of Healing." In *Faith, Health, and Healing in African
American Life*, edited by Stephanie Y. Mitchem and Emilie M. Townes, 181–92.
London: Praeger, 2008.

———, and Emilie M. Townes, eds. *Faith, Health, and Healing in African American Life.*
London: Praeger, 2008.

Montgomery, Michael, ed. *The Crucible of Carolina: Essays in the Development of Gullah
Language and Culture.* Athens: University of Georgia Press, 1994.

Moore, Carlos. "Afro-Cubans and the Communist Revolution." In *African Presence in
the Americas*, edited by Carlos Moore, Tanya Sanders, and Shawna Moore, 199–
240. Trenton, NJ: Africa World Press, 1995.

———. *Castro, the Blacks, and Africa.* Los Angeles: University of California Center for
Afro-American Studies, 1988.

———, Tanya Sanders, and Shawna Moore, eds. *African Presence in the Americas.*
Trenton, NJ: Africa World Press, 1995.

Morales, Beatriz. "Returning to the Source: Yoruba Religion in the South." In *Religion in
the Contemporary South: Diversity, Community, and Identity*, edited by O. Kendall
White Jr. and Daryl White, 124–32. Athens: University of Georgia Press, 1995.

Morrison, Toni. "Unspeakable Things Unspoken: The Afro-American Presence
in American Literature." In *The Black Feminist Reader*, edited Joy James and
T. Denean Sharpley-Whiting, 24–56. Malden, MA: Blackwell Publishers, 2000.

Moses, Wilson Jeremiah. *Classical Black Nationalism: From the American Revolution to
Marcus Garvey.* New York: New York University Press, 1996.

———. *The Golden Age of Black Nationalism, 1850–1925.* New York: Oxford University
Press, 1978.

Murakami, Tatsuo. "Asking the Question of the Origin of Religion in the Age of
Globalization." *Religion and Global Culture: New Terrain in the Study of Religion
and the Work of Charles H. Long*, edited by Jennifer I. M. Reid, 7–24. Lanham,
MD: Lexington Books, 2003.

Murphy, Joseph. "Santería and Vodou in the United States." In *America's Alternative
Religions*, edited by Timothy Miller, 291–96. Albany: State University of New York
Press, 1995.

Murphy, Larry, J. Gordon Melton, and Gary L. Ward. *Encyclopedia of African American
Religions.* New York: Garland Publishing, 1993.

Neimark, Philip John. *Way of the Orisa: Empowering Your Life Through the Ancient African Religion of Ifa*. San Francisco: HarperSanFrancisco, 1993.

Noel, James A. *Black Religion and the Imagination of Matter in the Atlantic World*. New York: Palgrave MacMillan, 2009.

Nyabongo, HRH Prince Akiki. *Africa Answers Back*. London: Routledge, 1936.

Obadele, Imari. "An Act to Stimulate Economic Growth in the United States and Compensate, in Part for the Grievous Wrongs of Slavery and the Unjust Enrichment which Accrued to the United States Therefrom." In *Modern Black Nationalism from Marcus Garvey to Louis Farrakhan*, edited by William L. Van Deburg, 334–41. New York: New York University Press, 1997.

Ogbar, Jeffrey O. G. *Black Power: Radical Politics and African American Identity*. Baltimore, MD: Johns Hopkins University Press, 2004.

Ojike, Mbonu. *My Africa*. New York: John Doubleday Company, 1946.

Okin, Susan Moller. *Justice, Gender, and the Family*. New York: Basic Books, 1989.

Okpewho, Isidore, Carole Boyce Davies, and Ali A. Mazrui. *African Diaspora: African Origins and New World Identities*. Bloomington: Indiana University Press, 1999.

Olaitan, Alagba. *Ancestor Veneration*. Sheldon, SC: African Theological Archministry, n.d.

Olasowo, HRG Iya Orite (Iyale Imole). "The Relationship Between Ifa and Osun." In *Oshoun Festival*, edited by Oseijeman Adelabu Adefunmi, 17. Sheldon, SC: African Theological Archministry, 1980.

Olasowo, Iya Orite (Iyale Imole). *Oshoun Festival*. Sheldon, SC: African Theological Archministry, 1980.

Olatunji, Babatunde. *The Beat of My Drum: An Autobiography*. Philadelphia: Temple University Press, 2005.

Olomo, Aina. *The Core of Fire: A Path to Yoruba Spiritual Activism*. New York: Athelia Henrietta Press, 2002.

Olupona, Jacob K. *African Traditional Religions in Contemporary Society*. New York: Paragon House, 1991.

———. "Globalization and African Immigrant Religious Communities." In *Religion and Global Culture: New Terrain in the Study of Religion and the Work of Charles H. Long*, edited by Jennifer I. M. Reid, 83–96. Lanham, MD: Lexington Books, 2003.

———. "Owner of the Day and Regulator of the Universe: Ifa Divination and Healing among the Yoruba of Southwestern Nigeria." In *Divination and Healing: Potent Vision*, edited by Michael Winkelman and Philip M. Peek, 103–20. Tucson: University of Arizona Press, 2004.

———, and Terry Rey, eds. *Orisa Devotion as World Religion: The Globalization of Yoruba Religious Culture*. Madison: University of Wisconsin Press, 2008.

Omari-Tunkara, Mikelle Smith. "Oyo Tunji: A Yoruba Community in the USA." In *African Folklore: An Encyclopedia*, edited by Philip M. Peek and Kwesi Yankah, 328–30. New York: Routledge, 2004.

Orizu, Prince A. A. Nwafo. *Without Bitterness*. New York: Creative Age Press, 1944.

Orsi, Robert Anthony. *The Madonna of 115th Street: Faith and Community in Italian Harlem, 1880–1950*. New Haven, CT: Yale University Press, 1985.

Padmore, George. *Africa and World Peace*. London: Secker and Warburg, 1937.

Palmié, Stephan, ed. *Africas of the Americas: Beyond the Search for Origins in the Study of Afro-Atlantic Religions*. Leiden, Netherlands: Brill, 2008.

———. "Against Syncretism, 'Africanizing' and 'Cubanizing' Discourses in North American Orisa Worship." In *Counterworks: Managing the Diversity of Knowledge*, edited by Richard Fardon, 73–104. New York: Routledge, 1995.

———. *Wizard and Scientists: Explorations in Afro-Cuban Modernity and Tradition*. Durham, NC: Duke University Press, 2002.

Parrinder, Geoffrey. *Religion in an African City*. London: Oxford University Press, 1953.

Peek, Philip M., and Kwesi Yankah, eds. *African Folklore: An Encyclopedia*. New York: Routledge, 2004.

Pemberton III, John. Postscript to *Orisa Devotion as World Religion: The Globalization of Yoruba Religious Culture*, edited by Jacob K. Olupona and Terry Rey, 559–72. Madison: University of Wisconsin Press, 2008.

Perez y Mena, Andres Isidoro. *Speaking with the Dead: Development of Afro-Latin Religion Among Puerto Ricans in the United States: A Study into the Interpenetration of Civilizations in the New World*. New York: AMS Press, 1991.

Perkinson, Jim. "Ogu's Iron or Jesus' Irony: Who's Zooming Who in Diasporic Possession Cult Activity." In *Religion and Global Culture: New Terrain in the Study of Religion and the Work of Charles H. Long*, edited by Jennifer I. M. Reid, 97–124. Lanham, MD: Lexington Books, 2003.

Piersen, William D. *Black Yankees: The Development of an Afro-American Subculture in Eighteenth-Century New England*. Amherst: University of Massachusetts Press, 1988.

Pinckney, Daryl. *Out There: Mavericks of Black Literature*. New York: Basic Civitas Books, 2002.

Pinn, Anthony, and Benjamin Valentin, eds. *The Ties that Bind: African American and Hispanic American/Latino/a Theologies in Dialogue*. New York: Continuum, 2001.

Raboteau, Albert. *Slave Religion: The "Invisible Institution" in the Antebellum South*. New York: Oxford University Press, 1978.

Read, William Winwood. *Savage Africa; being the narrative of a tour in equatorial, southwestern, and northwestern Africa; with notes on the habits of the gorilla; on the existence of unicorns and tailed men; on the slave trade; on the origin, character, and capabilities of the negro, and on the future civilization of western Africa*. New York: Harper, 1864.

Reid, Jennifer I. M., ed. *Religion and Global Culture: New Terrain in the Study of Religion and the Work of Charles H. Long*. Lanham, MD: Lexington Books, 2003.

Rhyne, Nancy. *Tales of the South Carolina Low Country*. Winston-Salem, SC: John F. Blair, 1982.

Robeson, Eslanda. *African Journey*. New York: John Day Company, 1945.

Rogers, J. A. *Sex and Race: Negro-Caucasian Mixing in All Ages and All Lands*. New York: H. M. Rogers, 1942–1967.

———. "The Suppression of Negro History, 1940." In *Modern Black Nationalism from Marcus Garvey to Louis Farrakhan*, edited by William L. Van Deburg, 65–72. New York: New York University Press, 1997.

Rosenthal, Judy. *Possession, Ecstasy, and Law in Ewe Voodoo*. Charlottesville: University Press of Virginia, 1998.

Scott, Lionel F. *Beads of Glass, Beads of Stone: An Introduction to the Orisha & Apataki of the Yoruba Religion*. Brooklyn, NY: Athelia Henrietta Press, 1995.

Sernett, Milton C. *Bound for the Promised Land: African American Religion and the Great Migration*. Durham, NC: Duke University Press, 1997.

Shavit, Yaacov. *History in Black: African-Americans in Search of an Ancient Past*. London: Frank Cass Publishers, 2001.

Shillington, Kevin, ed. *Encyclopedia of African History Volume 1 A–G*. New York: Fitzboy Dearborn, 2005.

Sinclair, Abiola. *The Harlem Cultural/Political Movements, 1960–1970: From Malcolm X to "Black is Beautiful"*. New York: Gumbs and Thomas Publishers, 1995.

Smith, Jonathan Z. *Imagining Religion: From Babylon to Jonestown*. Chicago: University of Chicago Press, 1982.

Snow, Loudell. *Walkin' Over Medicine*. Boulder, CO: Westview Press, 1993.

Sosa, Juan J. "La Santería: An Integrating, Mythological Worldview in a Disintegrating Society." In *Òrìṣà Devotion as World Religion: The Globalization of Yorùbá Religious Culture*, edited by Jacob K. Olupona and Terry Rey, 372–99. Madison: University of Wisconsin Press, 2008.

Speller, Julia. *Walkin' the Talk: Keepin' the Faith in Africentric Congregations*. Cleveland, OH: Pilgrim Press, 2005.

Spickard, James V. "On the Epistemology of Post-Colonial Ethnography." In *Personal Knowledge and Beyond: Reshaping the Ethnography of Religion*, edited by James V. Spickard, J. Shawn Landres, and Meredith B. McGuire, 237–52. New York: New York University Press, 2002.

———, J. Shawn Landres, and Meredith B. McGuire. *Personal Knowledge and Beyond: Reshaping the Ethnography of Religion*. New York: New York University Press, 2002.

Stanley, Henry M. *Through the dark continent or, The sources of the Nile around the great lakes of equatorial Africa and down the Livingstone River to the Atlantic Ocean*. New York: Harper & Brothers, 1878.

Stevens-Arroyo, Anthony, and Andrés Pérez y Mena, eds. *Enigmatic Powers: Syncretism with African and Indigenous Peoples' Religions Among Latinos*. New York: Bildner Center for Western Hemisphere Studies, 1995.

Stewart, Dianne M. "Response." In *The Ties that Bind: African American and Hispanic American/Latino/a Theologies in Dialogue*, edited by Anthony B. Pinn and Benjamin Valentin, 200–203. New York: Continuum, 2001.

———. *Three Eyes for the Journey: African Dimensions of the Jamaican Religious Experience*. New York: Oxford University Press, 2005.

Stout, Jeffrey. *Democracy and Tradition*. Princeton, NJ: Princeton University Press, 2004.

———. "Theses on Black Nationalism" In *Is It Nation Time?: Contemporary Essays on Black Power and Black Nationalism*, edited by Eddie S. Glaude Jr., 234–56. Chicago: University of Chicago Press, 2002.

Stuckey, Sterling. *Slave Culture: Nationalist Theory and the Foundations of Black America*. New York: Oxford University Press, 1987.

Taeuber, Irene B., and Conrad Taeuber. *People of the United States in the 20th Century*. Washington, DC: Government Printing Office, 1971.

Teish, Luisah. *Jambalaya: The Natural Woman's Book of Personal Charms and Practical Rituals.* San Francisco: Harper & Row, 1985.

Tete-Ansa, W. *Africa at Work.* New York, 1930.

Thomas, Hugh. *Cuba: The Pursuit of Freedom.* New York: Harper & Row, 1971.

Thompson, Robert Farris. "The Three Warriors: Atlantic Altars of Esu, Ogun and Osoosi." In *The Yoruba Artist: New Theoretical Perspectives on African Arts,* edited by Rowland Abiodun, Henry J. Drewal, and John Pemberton III, 225–40. Washington, DC: Smithsonian Institution Press, 1994.

Toplin, Robert Brent, ed. *Slavery and Race Relations in Latin America.* Westport, CT: Greenwood Press, 1974.

Trost, Theodore Louis, ed. *The African Diaspora and the Study of Religion.* New York: Palgrave MacMillan, 2007.

Tweed, Thomas A. "Between the Living and the Dead: Fieldwork, History, and the Interpreter's Position." In *Personal Knowledge and Beyond: Reshaping the Ethnography of Religion,* edited by James V. Spickard, J. Shawn Landres, and Meredith McGuire, 63–74. New York: New York University Press, 2002.

Van Deburg, William L., ed. *Modern Black Nationalism: From Marcus Garvey to Louis Farrakhan.* New York: New York University Press, 1997.

———. *New Day in Babylon: The Black Power Movement and American Culture 1965–1975.* Chicago: University of Chicago Press, 1992.

Vanzant, Iyanla. *Yesterday, I Cried: Celebrating the Lessons of Living and Loving.* New York: Vega, Simon & Schuster, 1998.

Vega, Marta Moreno. "The Dynamic Influence of Cubans, Puerto Ricans, and African Americans in the Growth of Ocha in New York City." In *Orisa Devotion as World Religion: The Globalization of Yoruba Religious Culture,* edited by Jacob K. Olupona and Terry Rey, 320–36. Madison: University of Wisconsin Press, 2008.

Washington, Joseph R. *Anti-Blackness in English Religion 1500–1800.* New York: E. Mellen Press, 1984.

Washington, Joseph R. *Black Sects and Cults.* Garden City, NY: Doubleday and Company, 1972.

Weisbord, Robert. *Ebony Kinship: Africa, Africans, and the Afro-American.* Westport, CT: Greenwood Press, 1973.

Weisenfeld, Judith. *This Far By Faith: Readings in African-American Women's Religious Biography.* New York: Routledge, 1996

West, Cornel. *The Cornel West Reader.* New York: Basic Civitas Books, 1999.

White, Jr., O. Kendall, and Daryl White, eds. *Religion in the Contemporary South: Diversity, Community, and Identity.* Athens: University of Georgia Press, 1995.

Williams, George Washington. *History of the Negro Race in America, 1619–1880.* New York: Arno Press and the New York Times, 1968.

Williams, Patrick, and Laura Chrisman, eds. *Colonial Discourse and Post-Colonial Theory: A Reader.* New York: Columbia University Press, 1994.

Wilmore, Gayraud. *Black Religion and Black Radicalism: An Interpretation of the Religious History of Afro-American People.* New York: Orbis Books, 1993.

Winkelman, Michael, and Philip M. Peek, eds. *Divination and Healing: Potent Vision.* Tucson: University of Arizona Press, 2004.

Winthrop, Jordan. *White Over Black: American Attitudes Towards the Negro, 1550–1812*. Chapel Hill: University of North Carolina Press, 1968.

Wirtz, Kristina. *Ritual, Discourse, and Community in Cuban Santería: Speaking of a Sacred World*. Gainesville: University Press of Florida, 2007.

Wolfson, Bernard J. "African American Jews: Dispelling Myths, Bridging the Divide." In *Black Zion: African American Religious Encounters with Judaism*, edited by Yvonne Chireau and Nathaniel Deutsch, 33–54. New York: Oxford University Press, 2000.

Wood, J. G. *The uncivilized races of men in all countries of the world; being a comprehensive account of their manners and customs, and of their physical, social, mental, moral and religious characteristics*. Hartford, CT: J. B. Burr and Company, 1871.

Woodson, Carter G. *The African Background*. New York: Negroes Universities Press, 1936.

Wyss, Hilary E. "Indigenous Literacies: New England and New Spain." In *A Companion to the Literatures of Colonial America*, edited by Susan Castillo and Ivy Schweitzer, 387–401. Malden, MA: Blackwell Publishing, 2005.

Yai, Olabiyi Babalola. "Yoruba Religion and Globalization: Some Reflections." In *Orisa Devotion as World Religion: The Globalization of Yoruba Religious Culture*, edited by Jacob K. Olupona and Terry Rey, 233–46. Madison: University of Wisconsin Press, 2008.

Young, Josiah U. *A Pan-African Theology: Providence and the Legacy of the Ancestors*. Trenton, NJ: Africa World Press, 1992.

Articles

Adams, Samuel Hopkins. "Dr. Bug, Dr. Buzzard, and the U.S.A." *True*, July 1949, 23–33, 69, 71.

Adefunmi, Oseijeman Adelabu. "Building a Community." *Caribe* (Fall/Winter 1981): 1–12.

———. "Notes on the Return of the Gods of Africa and the Rising of Oyotunji." *Sagala, A Journey of Art and Ideas* 2, no. 1 (December 1988): 38–43.

"African Affairs: An Africa Village in South Carolina." *Jet Magazine*, January 1974, 51–52.

African Times and Orient Review 4, no. 5 (May 1917) (advertisement).

Aguirre, Benigno E. "Differential Migration of Cuban Social Races: A Review and Interpretation of the Problem." *Latin American Research Review* 11, no. 1 (1976): 103–24.

Apter, Andrew. "*Que Faire?* Reconsidering Inventions of Africa." *Critical Inquiry* 19, no. 1 (Autumn 1992): 87–104.

Baraka, Imamu Amiri (LeRoi Jones). "The Pan-African Party and the Black Nation." *The Black Scholar* 2, no. 7 (March 1971): 24–32.

Brandon, George. "Hierarchy Without a Head: Observations on Changes in the Social Organization of Some Afroamerican Religions in the United States, 1959–1999 with Special Reference to Santeria." *Archives de sciences sociales des religions* 117 (Janvier–Mars 2002): 151–74.

Brown, David H. "Conjure/Doctors: An Exploration of a Black Discourse in America, Antebellum to 1940." *Folklore Forum* 23, nos. 1/2 (1990): 3–46.

Butler, Kim D. "Up from Slavery: Afro-Brazilian Activism in São Paul, 1888–1938." *The Americas* 49, no. 2 (October 1992): 179–206.

Carlisle, Dolly. "King or Con Man: The Controversial Ruler of Yoruba, S.C. is really just Walter from Detroit." *People*, October 12, 1981, 135–40.

Clark, Mary Ann. "¡No Hay Ningún Santo Aquí! (There Are No Saints Here!): Symbolic Language within Santería." *Journal of the American Academy of Religion* 69, no. 1 (March 2001): 21–41.

Cochran, Tracy. "Among the Believers: Converts to Santeria." *New York*, October 12, 1987, 33–34.

Coleman, Monica A. "The Womb Circle: A Womanist Practice of Multiple-Religious Belonging." *Practical Matters: A Transdisciplinary Multimedia Journal of Religious Practices and Practical Theology*, no. 4 (Spring 2011), 1–12.

"Cuban Refugees: The Preferred Minority." *Sepia*, June 6, 1970, 8–13.

Daniel, Yvonne. "The Potency of Dance: A Haitian Examination." *The Black Scholar* 11, no. 18 (November/December 1980): 61–73.

De La Torre, Miguel A. "Ochun: (N)Either the (M)Other of All Cubans (n)or the Bleached Virgin." *Journal of the American Academy of Religion* 69, no. 4 (December 2001): 837–61.

Delgado De Torres, Lena. "Reformulating Nationalism in the African Diaspora: The Aponte Rebellion of 1812." *The New Centennial Review* 3, no. 3 (Fall 2003): 27–46.

Denton, Nancy A., and Douglas S. Massey. "Racial Identity Among Caribbean Hispanics: The Effect of Double Minority Status on Residential Segregation." *American Sociological Review* 54, no. 5 (October 1989): 790–808.

"Discovery and Invention: Religions in Contact in the Americas." *Harvard University Center for the Study of World Religions* 1, no. 1 (Fall 1993): 3–5.

Dixon, Heriberto. "Cuban-American Counterpoint: Black Cubans in the United States." *Dialectical Anthropology* 13, no. 3 (1988): 227–39.

Dobbs, Cynthia. "Toni Morrison's Beloved: Bodies Returned, Modernism Revisited." *African American Review* 32, no. 4 (Winter 1998): 563–78.

Dubois, W. E. B. Review of *The Negro in Africa and America*, by Joseph Alexander Tillinghast. *Political Science Quarterly* 18 (December 1903): 695.

Eltis, David. "The Volume and Structure of the Transatlantic Slave Trade: A Reassessment." *William and Mary Quarterly* 58, no. 1 (2001): 17–46.

Friedland, Roger. "Religious Nationalism and the Problem of Collective Representation." *Annual Review of Sociology* 27 (August 2001): 125–52.

Gaut, Greg. "Can a Christian be a Nationalist? Vladimir Solov'ev's Critique of Nationalism." *Slavic Review* 57, no. 1 (Spring 1998): 77–94.

Gikandi, Simon. "Culture and Reasonableness." *Contemporary Literature* 34, no. 4 (Winter 1993): 777–82.

Gold, Roberta S. "The Blacks Jews of Harlem: Representation, Identity, and Race, 1920–1939." *American Quarterly* 55, no. 2 (June 2003): 179–225.

Goodman, George. "Harlem's Yorubas: A Search for Something to Believe In." *Look Magazine*, January 1969, 32–33.

Hall, David D. "Review Essay: What is the Place of 'Experience' in Religious History?" *Religion and American Culture* 13, no. 2 (Summer 2003): 241–50.

Harvard University Center for the Study of World Religions. *NEWS* 1, no. 1 (Fall 1993): 3–5, 7.

Hayward, Jr., Henry. "Toward a Religion of Revolution." *The Black Scholar* 2, no. 4 (December 1970): 27–31.

Higginbotham, Evelyn Brooks. "African-American Women's History and the Meta-language of Race." *Signs* 17, no. 2 (Winter 1992): 251–74.

Honebrink, Andrea. "Yoruba Renaissance: The Religious Teachings of a Great African Civilization Attract New Followers." *Utne Reader*, November/December 1993, 46–47.

Hucks, Tracey E. "Burning With a Flame in America: African American Women in African-Derived Traditions." *Journal of Feminist Studies in Religion* 17, no. 2 (Fall 2001): 89–106.

Johnston, Hank. "Religio-Nationalist Subcultures under the Communists: Comparisons from the Baltics, Transcaucasia and Ukraine." *International Studies in the Sociology of Religion* 54, no. 3 (Autumn 1993): 237–55.

Jones, Carolyn M. "From Colonialism to Community: Religion and Culture in Charles H. Long's *Significations*." *Callaloo*, no. 36 (Summer 1988): 582–96.

Jordan, Milton. "African Kingdom in South Carolina." *Sepia*, April 1975, 24–25.

Khan, Zillur R. "Islam and Bengali Nationalism." *Asian Survey* 25, no. 8 (August 1985): 834–51.

"Kingdom of Oyotunji Yoruba Village Press Release." Reprinted in Chief Dr. Adeleri Onisegun. *Onisegun Ile Orisa Obatala Newsletter* 2 (1994): 50.

Lear, Leonard. "An Old African Religion Makes a U.S. Comeback." *Sepia*, November 1976, 23–25.

Lefever, Harry G. "Leaving the United States: The Black Nationalist Themes of Orisha-Vodu." *Journal of Black Studies* 31, no. 2 (November 2000): 174–95.

———. "When the Saints Go Riding In: Santeria in Cuba and the United States." *Journal for the Scientific Study of Religion* 35, no. 3 (September 1996): 318–30.

Llorens, David. "Black Separatism in Perspective: Movement Reflects Failure in Integration." *Ebony*, September 1968, 88–95.

Long, Charles. "Perspectives for a Study of Afro-American Religion in the United States." *History of Religions* 11, no. 1 (August 1971): 54–66.

Matory, J. Lorand. "The English Professors of Brazil: On the Diaspora Roots of the Yoruba Nation." *Comparative Studies in Society and History* 41, no. 1 (January 1999): 72–103.

———. "Revisiting the African Diaspora." *American Anthropologist* 98, no. 1 (March 1996): 167–70.

McAlister, Melani. "One Black Allah: The Middle East in the Cultural Politics of African American Liberation, 1955–1970." *American Quarterly* 51, no. 3 (1999): 622–56.

Murphy, Joseph. "Afro-American Religion and Oracles: Santeria in Cuba." *Journal of the Interdenominational Theological Center* 8, no. 1 (Fall 1980): 83–88.

Nance, Susan. "Mystery of the Moorish Science Temple: Southern Blacks and American Alternative Spirituality in the 1920s Chicago." *Religion and American Culture* 12, no. 2 (Summer 2002): 123–66.

———. "Respectability and Representation: The Moorish Science Temple, Morocco, and Black Public Culture in 1920s Chicago." *American Quarterly* 54, no. 4 (December 2002): 623–59.

Neimark, Jill. "Shaman in Chicago: Religious Transcendence or Midlife Crisis?" *Psychology Today*, September 1, 1993, 46–50.

Obadele, Imari Abubkarai. "The Struggle of the Republic of New Africa." *The Black Scholar* 5 (June 1974): 32–41.

Ogunlola, Chief Wale. "A Yoruba Village in America (II)." *West Africa*, February 2–8, 1998, 64.

Ogunlola, Wale. "Africa Abroad: A Yoruba Village in America (I)." *West Africa*, January 26–February 1, 1998, 124.

Omari, Mikelle Smith. "Completing the Circle: Notes on African Art, Society, and Religion in Oyotunji, South Carolina." *African Arts Magazine*, July 1991, 66–75, 96.

Onyewu, Nicholas D. U. "An Approach to African Politics." *African Studies Review* 13, no. 1 (April 1970): 9–16.

Oommen, T. K. "Religious Nationalism and Democratic Polity: The Indian Case." *Sociology of Religion* 55, no .4 (Winter 1994): 455–72.

Painter, Nell Irvin. "Was Marie White? The Trajectory of a Question in the United States." *The Journal of Southern History* 74, no. 1 (February 2008): 3–30.

Porter, Brian. "The Catholic Nation: Religion, Identity, and the Narratives of Polish History." *The Slavic and East European Journal* 45, no. 2 (Summer 2001): 289–99.

Price, Richard and Sally. "Shadowboxing in the Mangrove." *Cultural Anthropology* 12, no. 1 (1997): 3–36.

Record, Wilson. "The Negro Intellectual and Negro Nationalism." *Social Forces* 33, no. 1 (October 1954): 1–18.

Rivera, Maritza Quiñones. "From Trigueñita to Afro-Puerto Rican: Intersections of the Racialized, Gendered, and Sexualized Body in Puerto Rico and the U.S. Mainland." *Meridians*, no. 1 (2006): 162–82.

Roberts, J. Deotis. "Afro-Arab Islam and the Black Revolution." *Journal of Black Religious Thought* 28, no. 2 (Autumn–Winter 1971): 95–111.

Smith, R. Drew. "Black Religious Nationalism and the Politics of Transcendence." *Journal of the American Academy of Religion* 66, no. 3 (Autumn 1998): 533–47.

Spillers, Hortense, Saidiya Hartman, Farah Jasmine Griffin, Shelly Eversley, and Jennifer L. Morgan. "'Whatcha Gonna Do?': Revisiting 'Mama's Baby, Pap's Maybe: An American Grammar Book': A Conversation with Hortense Spillers, Saidiya Hartman, Farah Jasmine Griffin, Shelly Eversley, & Jennifer L. Morgan." *Women's Studies Quarterly* 35, nos. 1/2 (Spring–Summer 2007): 299–309.

Taylor, Susan L. "Courage to Love with Cornel West." *Essence: The Men's Issue*, November 2005, 162–64.

Turner, James. "The Sociology of Black Nationalism." *The Black Scholar* 1, no. 2 (December 1969): 18–27.

Wakankar, Milind. "Body, Crowd, Identity: Genealogy of Hindu Nationalist Ascetics." *Social Text* 45 (Winter 1995): 45–73.

White, Shane. "'It Was a Proud Day': African Americans, Festivals, and Parades in the North, 1741–1834." *The Journal of American History* 81, no. 1 (June 1994): 13–50.

"The World Conference on Orisa, Ile-Ife, Nigeria, June 1–7, 1981: A Special Report." *Caribe* 5, no. 4 (Fall/Winter 1981): 1–14.

Dissertations and Theses

Abrams, Andrea. "Who I Am and Whose I Am: Race, Class, Gender and Nation in an Afrocentric Church." Ann Arbor, MI: UMI Dissertation Services, 2006.

Brooks, Christopher Antonio, BM, MM. "Eku Odun: A Yoruba Celebration." Master's thesis, University of Texas at Austin, 1984.

Cohn, Sandra. "Ethnic Identity in New York City." Master's thesis, New York University, 1973.

Cornelius, Steven Harry. "The Convergence of Power: An Investigation into the Music Liturgy of Santeria in New York City." Ann Arbor, MI: UMI Dissertation Service, 1989.

Curry, Mary Elaine. "Making the Gods: The Yoruba Religion in the Black Community." Ann Arbor, MI: UMI Dissertation Services, 1991.

Eason, Ikulomi Djisovi. "A Time of Destiny: Ifa Culture and Festivals in Ile-Ife, Nigeria and Oyotunji African Village in Sheldon, South Carolina." Ann Arbor, MI: UMI Dissertation Services, 1997.

Gregory, Steven. "Santería in New York City: A Study in Cultural Resistance." Ann Arbor, MI: UMI Dissertation Series, 1986.

Huntington, Velana Annemarie. "Bodies in Contexts: Holistic Ideals of Health, Healing, and Wellness in an American Orisa Community." PhD diss., University of Iowa, 2002.

Lessane, Patricia Williams. "Tell My Feet I've Made It Home: African-American Imaginings of Home and to Find the Orixas." PhD diss., University of Illinois at Chicago, 2005.

Love, Velma. "Odu Outcomes: Yoruba Scriptures in African American Constructions of Self and World." Ann Arbor, MI: UMI Dissertation Services, 2007.

Tucker, Tamelyn Norene. "Bringing the Church 'Back In' Black Megachurch and Community Development." Ann Arbor, MI: UMI Dissertation Services, 2002.

Vega, Marta Moreno. "Yoruba Philosophy: Multiple Levels of Transformation and Understanding." Ann Arbor, MI: UMI Dissertation Services, 1995.

Papers, Public Lectures, and Conferences

Abimbola, Oshunbemi. Public lecture. Religion 010, Swarthmore College, Swarthmore, PA, November 20, 1997.

Adefunmi, Oseijeman. "Keynote Address." Ifa Festival, Columbia University, New York, January 16, 1993.

Butler, Jr., Lee H. "Loving . . . Body and Soul Together." Chicago Theological Seminary Convocation, Chicago, IL, December 2004.

Clark, Adam. "Black Theology, Afrocentricity, and the Womanist Challenge." Black Theology Group, American Academy of Religion, Atlanta, GA, October 30, 2010.

Crosby, David. "Roots: African Dimensions of the History and Cultures of the Americas Through the Trans-Atlantic Slave Trade." NEH Summer Seminar for College Instructors, Virginia Foundation for the Humanities and Public Policy, Charlottesville, VA, June 8–July 10, 2009.

Egbe Omo Obatala Inc., First International Orisha Conference, New York, NY, October 30–November 1, 1998.

Flueckiger, Joyce. "Roundtable: Anthropology, Ethnography, and Theology." Ethnography and Theology: A Critical Roundtable Discussion, Emory University, Atlanta, GA, March 4–6, 2009.

Karade, Baba Ifa. Panel discussion. International Congress of Orisa Tradition and Culture, Trinidad, W.I., August 19, 1999.

Kinney, John. "State of Black Religion Lecture." Society for the Study of Black Religion, Washington, DC, March 28, 2009.

Lawal, Babatunde. NEH Roots 2009 Seminar Lecture. University of Virginia, Charlottesville, VA, June 19, 2009.

Masjeed, Debra Mubashshir. Lecture. Society for the Study of Black Religion, Washington, DC, March 26, 2009.

Mason, John. Public lecture. Religion 132, Swarthmore College, Swarthmore, PA, April 13, 1998.

Miller, Joseph, director. "Roots: African Dimensions of the History and Cultures of the Americas Through the Trans-Atlantic Slave Trade." NEH Summer Seminar for College Instructors, Virginia Foundation for the Humanities and Public Policy, Charlottesville, VA, June 8–July 10, 2009.

Oyelaran, Olasope O. "From Local to Global: Rethinking Yoruba Religious Traditions for the Next Millennium." Florida International University, December 9–12, 1999.

Pelchat, Cathie. "Ecospirituality." Unpublished paper.

Perkinson, James W. "The Ghost in the Global Machine: Categorical Whiteness as 'Religious' Violence." Religion, Social Conflict and Peace Group, American Academy of Religion, Montreal, Canada, October 31, 2010.

Stewart, Dianne. "The Image of Africa in Black Religious Thought and Activism." Protestant University of Congo in Kinshasa, Democratic Republic of Congo, February 13, 2007.

Tunji, Baba Ifa. World Congress on Orisa Tradition and Culture, Port of Spain, Trinidad, August 15–22, 1999.

Weaver, Oloosa Lloyd. "Notes on Orisa Worship in an Urban Setting: The New York Example." Paper presented at the International Conference on Orisa Tradition, Ile-Ife, Nigeria, July 1–6, 1986.

Visual Materials

Bahia, Africa in the Americas. Directed by Geovanni Brewer. Berkeley: University of California Extension Media Center, 1988. VHS.

Voices of the Gods. Directed by Alfred Santana. New York: Akuaba Productions, 1985. VHS.

Voodoo Rituals. New York: A&E Home Video, 2002. DVD.

Unpublished Materials

Egbe Odu Ifa Sacred African Literary Society, Brochure, Atlanta, GA, 2000. EgbeOduIfa@bellsouth.net.

Web Pages

Grattan, Wilbur. "Republic of New Africa Denounces Ron Everett (Karenga)." http://www.etext.org/Politics/MIM/bpp/bpp110569a_p7.htm.

Holmes, Amanda D. "Yoruba Religion and Ecology in Cuba." Forum on Religion and Ecology Newsletter, December 2008. http://fore.research.yale.edu/publications/newsletters/index.html.

http://eleda.org/obaoriatecouncil/

http://fore.research.yale.edu/publications/newsletters/index.html

http://www.amandala.org/index.php?option=com_content&view=article&id=47&Itemid=54

http://www.egbesankofa.org/about/index.htm#mission

http://www.ifafoundation.org/library_show.php?tablelID=46

http://www.oyotunjiafricanvillage.org/news.html

http://www.sankofa.com

http://www.virginiafoundation.org/roots/background.html

Lakesi, Iya L'Orisa Yeye Olashun OladeKoju. "Racism and Racists in Ifa Orisha Religion." OrishaNet, http://www.orishanet.org/.

"The Life and Times of J. A. Rogers 1880–1966," http://www.everygeneration.co.uk/profiles/jarogers.htm.

"Memoirs," http://singlelink.typepad.com/medahochi/old-swamp-priest.html.

Radical Information Project: "Contention in Space-Time—The Republic of New Africa, 1967–1974," http://www.cidcm.umd.edu/projects/rip/rightframe.htm.

Zannu, Baba Medahochi Kofi Omowale. "The Memoirs of an Old Swamp Priest," http://singlelink.typepad.com/medahochi/old-swamp-priest.html.

INDEX

Page numbers in italic type indicate illustrations.

Abimbola, Kola, 3, 329
Abimbola, Wande, 302, 313–14, 316–17, 319, 329, 331, 337; *Ifa*, oral teachings of, 240
Abrams, Andrea, 254, 266
Adaramola, Odunfonda, 211, 220
Adefunmi, Adejuyigbe II, 216–18, 220–22, *221*, 322–23
Adefunmi, Oseijeman Efuntola Adelabu, I, 3, 17, *112*; African Cultural Restoration Plan and, 136; African Library Series and, 125, *126*; *An African Marriage*, 136–38; *African State*, 135–36; Afro-American Day and, 76–77; on the ambiguities of his rule, 216–18; on ancestor worship, 289; on astrology, 299; on being Africans, 167; black nationalism and, 96; as Chief Priest of the Yoruba Temple and Chief of the Yoruba Nation of North America, 119; conflict with Order of Damballah Hwedo, 78; Cuban initiation of, 89–92, 366n7; Cubans versus African Americans, color and, 274; on divination and Christianity, 210–11; *Gods of Africa*, 128–32; on his vision for Oyotunji, 219–20; on independence of Ghana, 76; as king, 216; leading a parade in Harlem, *115*; on legacy of Oyotunji, 225; on Mama Keke, 106–7; meanings of, 75–76; New York bembes and, 118–19; in Nigeria, 223–24; on the nine souls of the Yoruba,

274–75; Oliana and, 78–80, 86, 366n7; *Orisha*, 125–28; Orisha-Vodu and, 127; Oshun Festival and, 119; on Oyotunji, 171–73; on Oyotunji as embodiment of dissent, 215; Oyotunji chiefs and, *224*; on Pancho Mora, 86, 149; performing Ifa divination, *204*; on the power of the "Work," 210–11; on racism, 277; religion of revolution and, 97; on Santería, 89; Santería and, 79; symbolic vocabulary and, 41–42; *Tribal Origins of the African Americans*, 133–35; visit to Nigeria and, 181–82; written works of, 122–25, 140–41; at Yoruba Temple, *148*; on Yoruba Temple initiations, 102. *See also* King, Walter Eugene
Adejoke, Yoruba (Ifa) and the Baptist Church, 235–41
Adeleke, Tunde, 45
Adeyemi, Oladepo, 89
Africa: Adefunmi and, 95; recovery of in the twenty-first century, 46–49; re-ownership of, 15, 351n55; as symbol, 47, 51, 58
Africa Town, 178
African American Cultural Foundation, 106
African American dialect in a Yoruba global culture, expression of, 334–39
African American women, future role of, 183–87, 323, 324–26
African Descendants Nationalist Independence Partition Party, 155
African diasporic religious traditions, 5–6

430

Olaitan, Chief (Alagba), *175*, 184, 211; on
   Oyotunji village, 195–96
Olatunji, Babatunde, 70, 115–16, 213, 273, 322;
   Drums of Passion and, 116; James Brown
   and, *116*; Ngoma Festival and, 117
Olayinka, Sekou, 308, 319–20, 334, 335–36,
   338
Oliana, Cristobal, *77, 78*, 78–80, 88, 91–92,
   94, 126
Olomo, Aina, 143, 187, 241, 291–92, 326,
   331–33, 335
Olupona, Jacob, 11, 207
Omari-Tunkara, Mikelle Smith, 170
Omolewa, Iya, 342
Onisegun, Oluweri Egundyao, 245–53,
   340; animal sacrifice and, 249–50; the
   Bible, Jesus, and Yoruba and, 251–52; Big
   Mama and, 245–46; initiation of, 246–47;
   "Transformative and Transcendental," 245
Onyewu, Nicholas D. U., 14
Ooni of Ife, 336
Order of Damballah Hwedo Ancestor
   Priests, 73–77, 106
organization of the study, 16–19
Orin Orisa (Mason), 273, 298
Orisa World Congress of 1997, 337
Orisha (Adefunmi), 125–28
Orisha-Vodu, 49, 88, 97, 115, 127–28
Orsi, Robert Anthony, 51, 111, 117, 371n104
Orunmila, story of, 226–27
Orunmlaism, 230, 231–32
Orunmlaism, the Basis of Jesuism (Beyioku),
   230–31
Osunbunmi, Majile Olafemi, 103, 163, 186
Otero, Juan, 83
Ottley, Roi, 77
Ovington, John, 30
Oyotunji African Village, 3, 18, 129; activism
   and, 322; Akinkonju and Egbebinrin
   societies and, 181; animal sacrifice and,
   208–9; arched entranceway to, *171*;
   community of, 173–74; cultural ethnic
   philosophy and, 222–23; daily life in,
   188–94; dancers and drummers perform,
   183; divination in, 207–8; Dr. Buzzard
   and, 202; economic sustainability and,
   190–92; education and, 182–83; Egungun
   Society and, 181; as experiment in the
   historical ontology of the present, 170;
   food stamps and, 191–92; future of,
   218–25; health care in, 189; influence
   and symbolic meaning of, 173; initiation
   of whites and, 281; insiders' narratives,
   194–95; land ownership in, 189; language

training and, 188–89; legacy of, 225; legal
   challenges, 190; Nigeria and, 223–24;
   Ogboni Society and, 180–81, 182; plural
   marriage in, 184–85; polity, infrastructure, and gender construction, 178–88;
   recycle receptacle, *332*; reparations and,
   379n80; residents and chieftains, *175*;
   Royal Yoruba Academy, 188; sense of
   spatial ownership and, 215; shifting articulations of, 170–71; shrine of Esu-Elegba
   in, *169*; sociology of religious knowledge
   and, 209; tourist brochure, *193*; website
   of, 193; welcome sign, *167*; women's
   movement in, 186; as Yorubaland, 169

Painter, Nell Irvin, 36–37
Palmié, Stephan, 4, 7, 13; on Africa as trope, 15
Payne, Daniel, 46
A Peculiar People (Creel), 198
Pemberton, John, III, 317
Pen and Palette Club, 69
Perkinson, James W., 265, 351n55
Pichardo, Ernesto, 149, 275–76, 315, 317–18,
   337
Piersen, William: *Black Yankees*, 113
Power in the Blood (Terrell), 250
Power of Place (Hayden), 145
Pozo, Chano, 85
Price, Richard and Sally, 231
Prosser, Thomas, 242
Psalms 68:31, 64–65
public events, importance of, 113–14
Purchas, Samuel: *Hakluyt Posthumus*, 30
purity and authenticity, 80
"Purity and Privilege in a Black Atlantic
   Nation" (Matory), 302

Quiñones, Marjorie Baynes, 104, 151

Raboteau, Albert, 229, 262; on conjure,
   107–8; *Slave Religion*, 5
Reade, William Winwood: *Savage Africa*, 57
Reid, Vernon, 14, 15
religion and the politics of race, 150–55
Religion of the Yoruba (Lucas), 180
religiosity, community's agency and, 3
religious identity, history and textuality and,
   10–14
religious nationalism, 42–46; power of,
   42–43; return to text and, 121
"Religious Nationalism and the Problem of
   Collective Representation" (Friedland),
   136–37
Religious Traditions of Africa (Isichei), 228